Mike Holt's Illustrated Guide to

UNDERSTANDING NEC® REQUIREMENTS FOR SOLAR PHOTOVOLTAIC SYSTEMS

Includes Related Code Changes and Analysis

Based on the 2017 NEC®

Mike Holt Enterprises
888.NEC.CODE (632.2633) • www.MikeHolt.com

NOTICE TO THE READER

The text and commentary in this book is the author's interpretation of the 2017 Edition of NFPA 70, the *National Electrical Code®*. It shall not be considered an endorsement of or the official position of the NFPA® or any of its committees, nor relied upon as a formal interpretation of the meaning or intent of any specific provision or provisions of the 2017 edition of NFPA 70, *National Electrical Code*.

The publisher does not warrant or guarantee any of the products described herein or perform any independent analysis in connection with any of the product information contained herein. The publisher does not assume, and expressly disclaims, any obligation to obtain and include information other than that provided to it by the manufacturer.

The reader is expressly warned to consider and adopt all safety precautions and applicable federal, state, and local laws and regulations. By following the instructions contained herein, the reader willingly assumes all risks in connection with such instructions.

Mike Holt Enterprises disclaims liability for any personal injury, property or other damages of any nature whatsoever, whether special, indirect, consequential or compensatory, directly or indirectly resulting from the use of this material. The reader is responsible for relying on his or her personal independent judgment in determining safety and appropriate actions in all circumstances.

The publisher makes no representation or warranties of any kind, including but not limited to, the warranties of fitness for particular purpose or merchantability, nor are any such representations implied with respect to the material set forth herein, and the publisher takes no responsibility with respect to such material. The publisher shall not be liable for any special, consequential, or exemplary damages resulting, in whole or part, from the reader's use of, or reliance upon, this material.

Mike Holt's Illustrated Guide to Understanding NEC® Requirements for Solar Photovoltaic Systems Based on the 2017 NEC®

First Printing: May 2017

Author: Mike Holt
Technical Illustrator: Mike Culbreath
Cover Design: Bryan Burch
Layout Design and Typesetting: Cathleen Kwas

COPYRIGHT © 2017 Charles Michael Holt
ISBN 978-0-9863534-4-4

Produced and Printed in the USA

All rights reserved. No part of this work covered by the copyright hereon may be reproduced or used in any form or by any means graphic, electronic, or mechanical, including photocopying, recording, taping, or information storage and retrieval systems without the written permission of the publisher. You can request permission to use material from this text by e-mailing Info@MikeHolt.com.

For more information, call 888.NEC.CODE (632.2633), or e-mail Info@MikeHolt.com.

NEC®, NFPA 70®, NFPA 70E® and National Electrical Code® are registered trademarks of the National Fire Protection Association.

This logo is a registered trademark of Mike Holt Enterprises, Inc.

If you are an instructor and would like to request an examination copy of this or other Mike Holt Publications:

Call: 888.NEC.CODE (632.2633) • Fax: 352.360.0983
E-mail: Info@MikeHolt.com • Visit: www.MikeHolt.com/Instructors

You can download a sample PDF of all our publications by visiting www.MikeHolt.com.

I dedicate this book to the
Lord Jesus Christ, *my mentor and teacher.*

Proverbs 16:3

We Care...

Since the day we started our business over 40 years ago, we have been working hard to produce products that get results, and to help individuals in their pursuit of learning more about this exciting industry. I have built my business on the idea that customers come first, and that everyone on my team will do everything they possibly can to take care of you. I want you to know that we value you, and are honored that you have chosen us to be your partner in electrical training.

I believe that you are the future of this industry and that it is you who will make the difference in years to come. My goal is to share with you everything that I know and to encourage you to pursue your education on a continuous basis. That not only will you learn theory, code, calculations or how to pass an exam, but that in the process you will become the expert in the field and the person who others know to trust.

We are dedicated to providing quality electrical training that will help you take your skills to the next level and we genuinely care about you. Thanks for choosing Mike Holt Enterprises for your electrical training needs.

God bless and much success,

Mike Holt

Exam Preparation | Continuing Education | Apprenticeship Products | In-House Training

"...as for me and my house, we will serve the Lord." [Joshua 24:15]

TABLE OF CONTENTS

About This Textbook xv

How to Use the *National Electrical Code* 1

Article 90—Introduction to the *National Electrical Code* 7
90.1 Purpose of the *NEC* 7
90.2 Scope of the *NEC* 9
90.3 *Code* Arrangement 11
90.4 Enforcement 12
90.5 Mandatory Requirements and Explanatory Material 14
90.6 Formal Interpretations 14
90.7 Examination of Equipment for Product Safety 14
90.9 Units of Measurement 15
Article 90 Practice Questions 16

CHAPTER 1—GENERAL RULES 19
Article 100—Definitions 21
Part I. General 21
100 Definitions 21

Article 110—Requirements for Electrical Installations 47
Part I. General Requirements 47
110.1 Scope 47
110.2 Approval of Conductors and Equipment 47
110.3 Examination, Identification, Installation, Use, and Product Listing (Certification) of Equipment 48
110.4 Voltages 48
110.5 Conductor Material 48
110.6 Conductor Sizes 49
110.7 Wiring Integrity 49
110.8 Suitable Wiring Methods 49
110.9 Interrupting Overcurrent Protection Rating 50
110.10 Equipment Short-Circuit Current Rating 51
110.11 Deteriorating Agents 51
110.12 Mechanical Execution of Work 53
110.13 Mounting and Cooling of Equipment 54

110.14 Conductor Termination and Splicing 54
110.15 High-Leg Conductor Identification 59
110.16 Arc-Flash Hazard Warning 60
110.21 Markings 61
110.22 Identification of Disconnecting Means 62
110.24 Available Fault Current 62
110.25 Lockable Disconnecting Means 63
Part II. 1,000V, Nominal, or Less 63
110.26 Spaces About Electrical Equipment 63
110.27 Guarding 71
110.28 Enclosure Types 72
Chapter 1 Practice Questions 73

CHAPTER 2—WIRING AND PROTECTION 79
Article 200—Use and Identification of Grounded [Neutral] Conductors 81
Part I. General 82
200.1 Scope 82
200.2 General 82
200.4 Neutral Conductor 82
200.6 Neutral Conductor Identification 83
200.7 Use of White or Gray Color 85
200.9 Terminal Identification 86
200.10 Identification of Terminals 86

Article 210—Branch Circuits 89
Part I. General Provisions 89
210.1 Scope 89
210.3 Other Articles 90
210.4 Multiwire Branch Circuits 90
210.5 Identification for Branch Circuits 93
210.7 Multiple Branch Circuits 94
Part II. Branch-Circuit Ratings 95
210.18 Branch-Circuit Rating 95
210.19 Conductor Sizing 95
210.20 Overcurrent Protection 98
210.21 Receptacle Rating 99

Table of Contents

210.22	Permissible Loads, Individual Branch Circuits	99
210.23	Permissible Loads, Multiple-Outlet Branch Circuits	100
210.25	Branch Circuits in Buildings with Multiple Occupancies	101

Article 215—Feeders 103
215.1	Scope	103
215.2	Minimum Rating	104
215.3	Overcurrent Protection Sizing	107
215.4	Feeders with Common Neutral Conductor	107
215.6	Equipment Grounding Conductor	107
215.10	Ground-Fault Protection of Equipment	108
215.12	Conductor Identification	108

Article 225—Outside Branch Circuits and Feeders 111

Part I. General 111
225.1	Scope	111
225.2	Other Articles	112
225.6	Minimum Size of Conductors	112
225.7	Luminaires Installed Outdoors	112
225.12	Open-Conductor Supports	113
225.15	Supports Over Buildings	113
225.16	Attachment	113
225.17	Masts as Supports	113
225.18	Clearance for Overhead Conductors	114
225.19	Clearances from Buildings	115
225.22	Raceways on Exterior Surfaces	116
225.26	Trees for Conductor Support	116
225.27	Raceway Seals	117
225.30	Number of Feeder Supplies	117
225.31	Disconnecting Means	117
225.32	Disconnect Location	117
225.33	Maximum Number of Disconnects	119
225.34	Grouping of Disconnects	119
225.35	Access to Occupants	119
225.36	Type of Disconnecting Means	119
225.37	Identification of Multiple Feeders	120
225.38	Disconnect Construction	120
225.39	Rating of Disconnecting Means	120

Article 230—Services 121

Part I. General 122
230.1	Scope	122
230.2	Number of Services	122
230.3	Not to Pass Through a Building	123
230.6	Conductors Considered Outside a Building	123
230.7	Service Conductors Separate from Other Conductors	124
230.8	Raceway Seals	125
230.9	Clearance from Building Openings	125
230.10	Vegetation as Support	125

Part II. Overhead Service Conductors 126
230.23	Overhead Service Conductor Size and Rating	126
230.24	Vertical Clearance for Overhead Service Conductors	127
230.26	Point of Attachment	128
230.27	Means of Attachment	128
230.28	Service Masts Used as Supports	128
230.29	Supports over Buildings	129

Part III. Underground Service Conductors 129
230.31	Underground Service Conductor Size and Rating	129
230.32	Protection Against Damage	130

Part IV. Service-Entrance Conductors 130
230.40	Number of Service-Entrance Conductor Sets	130
230.42	Size and Rating	131
230.43	Wiring Methods	132
230.46	Spliced Conductors	132
230.50	Protection Against Physical Damage	133
230.51	Cable Supports	134
230.53	Raceways to Drain	134
230.54	Overhead Service Locations	134
230.56	High-Leg Identification	134
230.66	Marking for Service Equipment	135

Part VI. Service Equipment—Disconnecting Means 136
230.70	Service Disconnect Requirements	136
230.71	Number of Disconnects	137
230.72	Grouping of Disconnects	138
230.76	Manual or Power Operated	138
230.77	Indicating	138
230.79	Rating of Disconnect	139
230.81	Connection to Terminals	139
230.82	Connected on Supply Side of the Service Disconnect	139

Part VII. Service Equipment Overcurrent Protection 141
230.90	Overload Protection	141
230.91	Location	142
230.95	Ground-Fault Protection of Equipment	142

Article 240—Overcurrent Protection 143

Part I. General 143
240.1	Scope	143
240.2	Definitions	144

240.3	Overcurrent Protection of Equipment	145	Part II. System Grounding and Bonding		177
240.4	Overcurrent Protection of Conductors	145	250.20	Systems Required to be Grounded	177
240.5	Overcurrent Protection of Flexible Cords and Fixture Wires	148	250.21	Ungrounded Systems	178
			250.24	Service Equipment—Grounding and Bonding	179
240.6	Standard Ampere Ratings	149	250.28	Main Bonding Jumper and System Bonding Jumper	183
240.10	Supplementary Overcurrent Protection	149	250.30	Separately Derived Systems—Grounding and Bonding	184
240.13	Ground-Fault Protection of Equipment	150			
240.15	Ungrounded Conductors	150	**Special Section 250.30**		
Part II. Location		151	**Separately Derived Systems**		190
240.21	Overcurrent Protection Location in Circuit	151	**Outdoor Installations**		190
240.24	Location of Overcurrent Protection Devices	156	**Indoor Installations**		191
Part III. Enclosures		158	250.32	Buildings Supplied by a Feeder	193
240.32	Damp or Wet Locations	158	250.34	Generators—Portable and Vehicle-Mounted	195
240.33	Vertical Position	158	250.35	Permanently Installed Generators	195
Part V. Plug Fuses, Fuseholders, and Adapters		159	250.36	High-Impedance Grounded Systems	196
240.50	General	159	**Part III. Grounding Electrode System and Grounding Electrode Conductor**		196
240.51	Edison-Base Fuses	159			
240.52	Edison-Base Fuseholders	159	250.50	Grounding Electrode System	196
240.53	Type S Fuses	159	250.52	Grounding Electrode Types	197
240.54	Type S Fuses, Adapters, and Fuseholders	159	250.53	Grounding Electrode Installation Requirements	200
Part VI. Cartridge Fuses and Fuseholders		160	**Measuring the Ground Resistance**		204
240.60	General	160	**Soil Resistivity**		205
240.61	Classification	161	250.54	Auxiliary Grounding Electrodes	205
Part VII. Circuit Breakers		161	250.58	Common Grounding Electrode	206
240.80	Method of Operation	161	250.60	Lightning Protection Electrode	206
240.81	Indicating	161	250.62	Grounding Electrode Conductor	207
240.82	Nontamperable	161	250.64	Grounding Electrode Conductor Installation	208
240.83	Markings	161	250.66	Sizing Grounding Electrode Conductor	212
240.85	Applications	162	250.68	Termination to the Grounding Electrode	213
240.87	Arc Energy Reduction	163	250.70	Grounding Electrode Conductor Termination Fittings	215
Article 250—Grounding and Bonding		165	**Part IV. Grounding Enclosure, Raceway, and Service Cable Connections**		216
Part I. General		165	250.80	Service Raceways and Enclosures	216
250.1	Scope	165	250.86	Other Enclosures	216
250.2	Definition	165	**Part V. Bonding**		216
250.4	Performance Requirements for Grounding and Bonding	166	250.90	General	216
			250.92	Bonding Equipment for Services	217
Earth Shells		170	250.94	Bonding Communications Systems	220
250.6	Objectionable Current	172	250.96	Bonding Other Enclosures	221
Objectionable Current		173	250.97	Bonding Metal Parts Containing 277V and 480V Circuits	222
Dangers of Objectionable Current		175			
250.8	Termination of Grounding and Bonding Conductors	176	250.98	Bonding Loosely Jointed Metal Raceways	223
250.10	Protection of Fittings	177	250.102	Grounded Conductor, Bonding Conductors, and Jumpers	223
250.12	Clean Surfaces	177			

Table of Contents

250.104	Bonding of Piping Systems and Exposed Structural Metal	225
250.106	Lightning Protection System	229

Part VI. Equipment Grounding and Equipment Grounding Conductors ... 230

250.110	Fixed Equipment Connected by Permanent Wiring Methods—General	230
250.112	Specific Equipment Fastened in Place or Connected by Permanent Wiring Methods	230
250.114	Cord-and-Plug-Connected Equipment	230
250.118	Types of Equipment Grounding Conductors	231
250.119	Identification of Equipment Grounding Conductors	235
250.120	Equipment Grounding Conductor Installation	236
250.121	Use of Equipment Grounding Conductors	237
250.122	Sizing Equipment Grounding Conductor	237

Part VII. Methods of Equipment Grounding ... 241

250.130	Equipment Grounding Conductor Connections	241
250.134	Equipment Connected by Permanent Wiring Methods	241
250.136	Equipment Considered Grounded	242
250.138	Cord-and-Plug-Connected	242
250.140	Ranges, Ovens, and Clothes Dryers	242
250.142	Use of Neutral Conductor for Equipment Grounding (Bonding)	243
250.146	Connecting Receptacle Grounding Terminal to Metal Enclosure	244
250.148	Continuity and Attachment of Equipment Grounding Conductors in Metal Boxes	247

Article 285—Surge Protective Devices (SPDs) ... 249

Part I. General ... 250

285.1	Scope	250
285.3	Uses Not Permitted	250
285.4	Number Required	250
285.6	Listing	250
285.7	Short-Circuit Current Rating	251

Part II. Installation ... 251

285.11	Location	251
285.12	Routing of Conductors	251
285.13	Type 4 and Other Component Type SPDs	251

Part III. Connecting Surge Protective Devices ... 251

285.23	Type 1 SPD—Line Side of Service Equipment	251
285.24	Type 2 SPD—Feeder Circuits	253
285.25	Type 3 SPDs—Branch Circuits	253

Chapter 2 Practice Questions ... 254

CHAPTER 3—WIRING METHODS AND MATERIALS ... 261

Article 300—General Requirements for Wiring Methods and Materials ... 265

Part I. General ... 265

300.1	Scope	265
300.3	Conductors	266
300.4	Protection Against Physical Damage	269
300.5	Underground Installations	272
300.6	Protection Against Corrosion and Deterioration	278
300.7	Raceways Exposed to Different Temperatures	279
300.8	Not Permitted in Raceways	280
300.9	Raceways in Wet Locations Above Grade	280
300.10	Electrical Continuity	280
300.11	Securing and Supporting	281
300.12	Mechanical Continuity	283
300.13	Splices and Pigtails	283
300.14	Length of Free Conductors	285
300.15	Boxes or Conduit Bodies	285
300.16	Raceway or Cable to Open or Concealed Wiring	288
300.17	Raceway Sizing	288
300.18	Inserting Conductors in Raceways	290
300.19	Supporting Conductors in Vertical Raceways	290
300.20	Induced Currents in Ferrous Metal Enclosures and Raceways	291
300.21	Spread of Fire or Products of Combustion	292
300.22	Wiring in Ducts and Plenum Spaces	293
300.23	Panels Designed to Allow Access	297

Article 310—Conductors for General Wiring ... 299

Part I. General ... 299

310.1	Scope	299

Part II. Installation ... 299

310.10	Uses Permitted	299
310.15	Conductor Ampacity	303

Part III. Construction Specifications ... 312

310.104	Conductor Construction and Application	312
310.106	Conductors	312
310.110	Conductor Identification	313

Article 312—Cabinets, Cutout Boxes, and Meter Socket Enclosures ... 315

Part I. Scope and Installation ... 315

312.1	Scope	315

312.2	Damp or Wet Locations	315	Part III. Construction Specifications		347
312.3	Installed in Walls	316	320.100	Construction	347
312.4	Repairing Gaps	316	320.108	Equipment Grounding Conductor	348
312.5	Enclosures	316			
312.6	Deflection of Conductors	318			
312.8	Overcurrent Protection Device Enclosures	318			

Article 314—Outlet, Device, Pull, and Junction Boxes; Conduit Bodies; and Handhole Enclosures ... 321

Part I. Scope and General ... 321
- 314.1 Scope ... 321
- 314.3 Nonmetallic Boxes ... 321
- 314.4 Metal Boxes ... 322

Part II. Installation ... 322
- 314.15 Damp or Wet Locations ... 322
- 314.16 Number of Conductors in Boxes and Conduit Bodies ... 323
- 314.17 Conductors That Enter Boxes or Conduit Bodies ... 328
- 314.20 Flush-Mounted Box Installations ... 329
- 314.21 Repairing Noncombustible Surfaces ... 330
- 314.22 Surface Extensions ... 330
- 314.23 Support of Boxes and Conduit Bodies ... 330
- 314.25 Covers and Canopies ... 333
- 314.27 Outlet Box ... 334
- 314.28 Sizing Conductors 4 AWG and Larger ... 336
- 314.29 Wiring to be Accessible ... 339
- 314.30 Handhole Enclosures ... 340

Article 320—Armored Cable (Type AC) ... 343

Part I. General ... 343
- 320.1 Scope ... 343
- 320.2 Definition ... 343
- 320.6 Listing Requirements ... 344

Part II. Installation ... 344
- 320.10 Uses Permitted ... 344
- 320.12 Uses Not Permitted ... 344
- 320.15 Exposed Work ... 344
- 320.17 Through or Parallel to Framing Members ... 344
- 320.23 In Accessible Attics or Roof Spaces ... 345
- 320.24 Bends ... 345
- 320.30 Securing and Supporting ... 345
- 320.40 Boxes and Fittings ... 346
- 320.80 Conductor Ampacity ... 347

Article 330—Metal-Clad Cable (Type MC) ... 349

Part I. General ... 349
- 330.1 Scope ... 349
- 330.2 Definition ... 349
- 330.6 Listing Requirements ... 349

Part II. Installation ... 350
- 330.10 Uses Permitted ... 350
- 330.12 Uses Not Permitted ... 351
- 330.15 Exposed Work ... 351
- 330.17 Through or Parallel to Framing Members ... 351
- 330.23 In Accessible Attics or Roof Spaces ... 352
- 330.24 Bends ... 352
- 330.30 Securing and Supporting ... 352
- 330.80 Conductor Ampacities ... 354

Part III. Construction Specifications ... 354
- 330.108 Equipment Grounding Conductor ... 354

Article 334—Nonmetallic-Sheathed Cable (Types NM and NMC) ... 357

Part I. General ... 357
- 334.1 Scope ... 357
- 334.2 Definition ... 357
- 334.6 Listing Requirements ... 358

Part II. Installation ... 358
- 334.10 Uses Permitted ... 358
- 334.12 Uses Not Permitted ... 359
- 334.15 Exposed Work ... 360
- 334.17 Through or Parallel to Framing Members ... 361
- 334.23 Attics and Roof Spaces ... 362
- 334.24 Bends ... 362
- 334.30 Securing and Supporting ... 362
- 334.40 Boxes and Fittings ... 363
- 334.80 Conductor Ampacity ... 364

Part III. Construction Specifications ... 365
- 334.100 Construction ... 365
- 334.104 Conductors ... 365
- 334.108 Equipment Grounding Conductor ... 365
- 334.112 Insulation ... 365

Table of Contents

Article 336—Power and Control Tray Cable (Type TC) 367
Part I. General 367
- 336.1 Scope 367
- 336.2 Definition 367
- 336.6 Listing Requirements 367

Part II. Installation 367
- 336.10 Uses Permitted 367
- 336.12 Uses Not Permitted 368
- 336.24 Bending Radius 368
- 336.80 Ampacity 368

Article 338—Service-Entrance Cable (Types SE and USE) 369
Part I. General 369
- 338.1 Scope 369
- 338.2 Definitions 369
- 338.6 Listing Requirements 370

Part II. Installation 370
- 338.10 Uses Permitted 370
- 338.12 Uses Not Permitted 371
- 338.24 Bends 371

Article 340—Underground Feeder and Branch-Circuit Cable (Type UF) 373
Part I. General 373
- 340.1 Scope 373
- 340.2 Definition 373

Part II. Installation 374
- 340.10 Uses Permitted 374
- 340.12 Uses Not Permitted 374
- 340.24 Bends 374
- 340.80 Ampacity 374

Part III. Construction Specifications 374
- 340.112 Insulation 374

Article 342—Intermediate Metal Conduit (Type IMC) 375
Part I. General 375
- 342.1 Scope 375
- 342.2 Definition 375
- 342.6 Listing Requirements 376

Part II. Installation 376
- 342.10 Uses Permitted 376
- 342.14 Dissimilar Metals 376
- 342.20 Trade Size 376
- 342.22 Number of Conductors 376
- 342.24 Bends 377
- 342.26 Number of Bends (360°) 377
- 342.28 Reaming 377
- 342.30 Securing and Supporting 377
- 342.42 Couplings and Connectors 379
- 342.46 Bushings 379

Article 344—Rigid Metal Conduit (Type RMC) 381
Part I. General 381
- 344.1 Scope 381
- 344.2 Definition 381
- 344.6 Listing Requirements 382

Part II. Installation 382
- 344.10 Uses Permitted 382
- 344.14 Dissimilar Metals 382
- 344.20 Trade Size 382
- 344.22 Number of Conductors 383
- 344.24 Bends 383
- 344.26 Number of Bends (360°) 383
- 344.28 Reaming 383
- 344.30 Securing and Supporting 384
- 344.42 Couplings and Connectors 385
- 344.46 Bushings 386

Article 348—Flexible Metal Conduit (Type FMC) 387
Part I. General 387
- 348.1 Scope 387
- 348.2 Definition 387
- 348.6 Listing Requirements 387

Part II. Installation 387
- 348.10 Uses Permitted 387
- 348.12 Uses Not Permitted 388
- 348.20 Trade Size 388
- 348.22 Number of Conductors 388
- 348.24 Bends 389
- 348.26 Number of Bends (360°) 389
- 348.28 Trimming 389
- 348.30 Securing and Supporting 389
- 348.42 Fittings 390
- 348.60 Grounding and Bonding 390

Article 350—Liquidtight Flexible Metal Conduit (Type LFMC) ... 393

Part I. General ... 393
- 350.1 Scope ... 393
- 350.2 Definition ... 393
- 350.6 Listing Requirements ... 394

Part II. Installation ... 394
- 350.10 Uses Permitted ... 394
- 350.12 Uses Not Permitted ... 394
- 350.20 Trade Size ... 394
- 350.22 Number of Conductors ... 395
- 350.24 Bends ... 395
- 350.26 Number of Bends (360°) ... 395
- 350.28 Trimming ... 395
- 350.30 Securing and Supporting ... 395
- 350.42 Fittings ... 396
- 350.60 Grounding and Bonding ... 396

Article 352—Rigid Polyvinyl Chloride Conduit (Type PVC) ... 399

Part I. General ... 399
- 352.1 Scope ... 399
- 352.2 Definition ... 399

Part II. Installation ... 400
- 352.10 Uses Permitted ... 400
- 352.12 Uses Not Permitted ... 401
- 352.20 Trade Size ... 401
- 352.22 Number of Conductors ... 401
- 352.24 Bends ... 402
- 352.26 Number of Bends (360°) ... 402
- 352.28 Trimming ... 402
- 352.30 Securing and Supporting ... 402
- 352.44 Expansion Fittings ... 403
- 352.46 Bushings ... 404
- 352.48 Joints ... 405
- 352.60 Equipment Grounding Conductor ... 405

Article 356—Liquidtight Flexible Nonmetallic Conduit (Type LFNC) ... 407

Part I. General ... 407
- 356.1 Scope ... 407
- 356.2 Definition ... 407
- 356.6 Listing Requirements ... 407

Part II. Installation ... 408
- 356.10 Uses Permitted ... 408
- 356.12 Uses Not Permitted ... 408
- 356.20 Trade Size ... 408
- 356.22 Number of Conductors ... 408
- 356.24 Bends ... 409
- 356.26 Number of Bends (360°) ... 409
- 356.30 Securing and Supporting ... 409
- 356.42 Fittings ... 410
- 356.60 Equipment Grounding Conductor ... 410

Article 358—Electrical Metallic Tubing (Type EMT) ... 411

Part I. General ... 411
- 358.1 Scope ... 411
- 358.2 Definition ... 411
- 358.6 Listing Requirements ... 411

Part II. Installation ... 411
- 358.10 Uses Permitted ... 411
- 358.12 Uses Not Permitted ... 412
- 358.20 Trade Size ... 412
- 358.22 Number of Conductors ... 412
- 358.24 Bends ... 413
- 358.26 Number of Bends (360°) ... 413
- 358.28 Reaming and Threading ... 413
- 358.30 Securing and Supporting ... 414
- 358.42 Couplings and Connectors ... 414
- 358.60 Grounding ... 415

Article 362—Electrical Nonmetallic Tubing (Type ENT) ... 417

Part I. General ... 417
- 362.1 Scope ... 417
- 362.2 Definition ... 417

Part II. Installation ... 418
- 362.10 Uses Permitted ... 418
- 362.12 Uses Not Permitted ... 419
- 362.20 Trade Sizes ... 420
- 362.22 Number of Conductors ... 420
- 362.24 Bends ... 420
- 362.26 Number of Bends (360°) ... 420
- 362.28 Trimming ... 420
- 362.30 Securing and Supporting ... 420
- 362.46 Bushings ... 421
- 362.48 Joints ... 421
- 362.60 Equipment Grounding Conductor ... 422

Table of Contents

Article 376—Metal Wireways ... 423
Part I. General ... 423
- 376.1 Scope ... 423
- 376.2 Definition ... 423

Part II. Installation ... 424
- 376.10 Uses Permitted ... 424
- 376.12 Uses Not Permitted ... 424
- 376.20 Conductors Connected in Parallel ... 424
- 376.21 Conductors—Maximum Size ... 424
- 376.22 Number of Conductors and Ampacity ... 424
- 376.23 Wireway Sizing ... 425
- 376.30 Supports ... 425
- 376.56 Splices, Taps, and Power Distribution Blocks ... 425

Part III. Construction Specifications ... 426
- 376.100 Construction ... 426

Article 392—Cable Trays ... 427
Part I. General ... 427
- 392.1 Scope ... 427
- 392.2 Definition ... 427

Part II. Installation ... 428
- 392.10 Uses Permitted ... 428
- 392.12 Uses Not Permitted ... 429
- 392.18 Cable Tray Installations ... 429
- 392.20 Cable and Conductor Installation ... 430
- 392.22 Number of Conductors or Cables ... 430
- 392.30 Securing and Supporting ... 430
- 392.46 Bushed Raceway ... 430
- 392.56 Cable Splices ... 430
- 392.60 Equipment Grounding Conductor ... 431

Chapter 3 Practice Questions ... 433

CHAPTER 4—EQUIPMENT FOR GENERAL USE ... 439

Article 400—Flexible Cords and Flexible Cables ... 441
Part I. General ... 441
- 400.1 Scope ... 441
- 400.3 Suitability ... 441
- 400.4 Types of Flexible Cords and Flexible Cables ... 442
- 400.5 Ampacity of Flexible Cords and Flexible Cables ... 442
- 400.10 Uses Permitted ... 442
- 400.12 Uses Not Permitted ... 443
- 400.14 Pull at Joints and Terminals ... 445
- 400.17 Protection from Damage ... 445
- 400.23 Equipment Grounding Conductor Identification ... 445

Article 404—Switches ... 447
Part I. Installation ... 447
- 404.1 Scope ... 447
- 404.2 Switch Connections ... 447
- 404.3 Switch Enclosures ... 450
- 404.4 Damp or Wet Locations ... 450
- 404.6 Position of Knife Switches ... 451
- 404.7 Indicating ... 451
- 404.8 Accessibility and Grouping ... 451
- 404.9 Switch Faceplates ... 453
- 404.10 Mounting Snap Switches ... 454
- 404.11 Circuit Breakers Used as Switches ... 455
- 404.12 Grounding of Enclosures ... 455
- 404.14 Rating and Use of Snap Switches ... 455

Part II. Construction Specifications ... 456
- 404.20 Switch Marking ... 456
- 404.22 Electronic Lighting Switches ... 457

Article 408—Switchboards, Switchgear, and Panelboards ... 459
Part I. General ... 459
- 408.1 Scope ... 459
- 408.3 Arrangement of Busbars and Conductors ... 459
- 408.4 Field Identification ... 461
- 408.5 Clearance for Conductors Entering Bus Enclosures ... 462
- 408.7 Unused Openings ... 462

Part III. Panelboards ... 462
- 408.36 Protection of Panelboards ... 462
- 408.37 Panelboards in Damp or Wet Locations ... 463
- 408.40 Equipment Grounding Conductor ... 464
- 408.41 Neutral Conductor Terminations ... 464

Part IV. Construction Specifications ... 465
- 408.54 Maximum Number of Overcurrent Protection Devices ... 465

Article 445—Generators ... 467
- 445.1 Scope ... 467
- 445.12 Overcurrent Protection ... 467
- 445.13 Ampacity of Conductors ... 468
- 445.18 Disconnecting Means and Shutdown of Prime Mover ... 468

Article 450—Transformers 471
Part I. General 471
450.1 Scope 471
450.3 Overcurrent Protection 471
450.9 Ventilation 472
450.10 Grounding and Bonding 472
450.11 Marking 473
450.13 Transformer Accessibility 473
450.14 Disconnecting Means 474

Article 480—Storage Batteries 475
480.1 Scope 475
480.2 Definitions 475
480.3 Listing Requirement 476
480.4 Battery and Cell Terminations 476
480.5 Wiring and Equipment Supplied from Batteries 476
480.7 Battery Disconnect 477
480.9 Battery Support Systems 477

Chapter 4 Practice Questions 478

CHAPTER 6—SPECIAL EQUIPMENT 485
Article 690—Solar Photovoltaic (PV) Systems 487
Part I. General 487
690.1 Scope 487
690.2 Definitions 488
690.4 General Requirements 493
690.6 Alternating-Current Modules 494
Part II. Circuit Requirements 494
690.7 Maximum Voltage 494
690.8 Circuit Current and Conductor Sizing 498
690.9 Overcurrent Protection 504
690.10 Stand-Alone Systems 506
690.11 Arc-Fault Circuit Protection (Direct Current) 507
690.12 Rapid Shutdown of PV Systems on Buildings 507
Part III. Disconnecting Means 508
690.13 PV System Disconnecting Means 508
690.15 PV Equipment Isolating/Disconnecting 509
Part IV. Wiring Methods 511
690.31 Wiring Methods 511
690.32 Component Interconnections 515
690.33 Connectors 515
690.34 Access to Boxes 515

Part V. Grounding and Bonding 516
690.41 System Grounding 516
690.42 Point of Grounding Connection 516
690.43 Equipment Grounding and Bonding 516
690.45 Size of Equipment Grounding Conductors 517
690.46 Array Equipment Grounding Conductors 518
690.47 Grounding Electrode System 518
Part VI. Marking 519
690.53 Power Source Label 519
690.54 Interactive System Point of Interconnection 520
690.55 PV Systems Connected to Energy Storage Systems 520
690.56 Identification of Power Sources 521
Part VII. Connection to Other Power Sources 522
690.59 Connection to Other Power Sources 522
Part VIII. Energy Storage Systems 522
690.71 Energy Storage, General 522
690.72 Self-Regulated PV Charge Control 522

Article 691—Large-Scale Photovoltaic (PV) Electric Power Production Facility 523
691.1 Scope 523
691.2 Definitions 523
691.4 Special Requirements for Large-Scale PV Electric Supply Stations 524
691.5 Equipment Approval 524
691.6 Engineered Design 524
691.7 Conformance of Construction to Engineered Design 524
691.7 Direct-Current Operating Voltage 524
691.9 Disconnection of Photovoltaic Equipment 524
691.10 Arc-Fault Mitigation 525
691.11 Fence Grounding 525

Chapter 6 Practice Questions 527

CHAPTER 7—SPECIAL CONDITIONS 535
Article 705—Interconnected Electric Power Production Sources 537
Part I. General 537
705.1 Scope 537
705.2 Definitions 537
705.6 Equipment Approval 538
705.8 System Installation 538
705.10 Directory 538
705.12 Point of Connection 538

Table of Contents

705.31	Location of Overcurrent Protection	544
705.40	Loss of Utility Power	544

Part II. Interactive Inverters 544

705.100 Voltage Unbalanced (Imbalanced) Interconnections 544

Article 710—Stand-Alone Systems 547

710.1	Scope	547
710.6	Equipment Approval	547
710.15	General	548

Chapter 7 Practice Questions 549

Final Exam A 551

Final Exam B 560

Appendix A—Analysis of 2017 *NEC* Changes Relating to Solar Photovolatic Systems 569

Index 577

About the Author 585

About the Illustrator 586

About the Mike Holt Team 587

ABOUT THIS TEXTBOOK

Mike Holt's Illustrated Guide to Understanding NEC® Requirements for Solar Photovoltaic Systems, Based on the 2017 NEC®

This textbook covers the *National Electrical Code®* requirements as they relate to Solar Photovoltaic (PV) systems. The *NEC®* rules that govern PV systems are very comprehensive and complicated, and as a result, could easily be misinterpreted. The intent of this textbook is to help you better understand how the *NEC* safety requirements should be applied to all solar photovoltaic systems. Changes to the text in the *NEC* are indicated throughout the textbook by underlining in the chapter color; for additional explanation on those changes in Chapter 6, we've added an Appendix, which contains the analysis of the rules for Articles 690 and 691 that changed for the 2017 *NEC*.

This textbook is easy to use because of Mike's practical and informative writing style. Just like all of Mike Holt's textbooks, this one is built around hundreds of full-color illustrations that show the safety requirements of the *National Electrical Code* in practical use, helping you visualize *Code* rules as they're applied to electrical installations. This illustrated textbook also contains cautions regarding possible conflicts or confusing *NEC* requirements, tips on proper electrical installations, and warnings of dangers related to improper electrical installations.

Sometimes a requirement seems confusing and it might be hard to understand its actual application. When this occurs, this textbook will point the situation out in an upfront and straightforward manner. We apologize in advance if that ever seems disrespectful, but our intention is to help the industry understand the current *NEC* as best as possible, point out areas that need refinement, and encourage *Code* users to be a part of the change process that creates a better *NEC* for the future.

Keeping up with requirements of the *Code* should be the goal of everyone involved in electrical safety—whether you're a solar installer, contractor, inspector, engineer, or instructor. This textbook is the perfect tool to help you do that.

The Scope of This Textbook

This textbook, *Mike Holt's Illustrated Guide to Understanding NEC Requirements for Solar Photovoltaic Systems, Based on the 2017 NEC*, covers the important NEC rules that apply to Solar PV systems. The scope of the textbook covers the general requirements contained in Articles 90 through 480, that every solar installer should know, as well as the specific rules relating to Solar PV systems, Articles 690, 691, 705, and 710.

This program is based on solidly grounded alternating-current systems, 1,000V or less, using 90°C insulated copper conductors sized to 60°C rated terminals for 100A and less rated circuits, and 75°C rated terminals for over 100A rated circuits, unless indicated otherwise.

How to Use This Textbook

This textbook is to be used along with the *NEC* and not as a replacement for it. Be sure to have a copy of the 2017 *National Electrical Code* handy. You'll notice that we've paraphrased a great deal of the wording, and some of the article and section titles appear different from the text in the actual *Code* book. We believe doing so makes it easier to understand the content of the rule, so keep this in mind when comparing this textbook to the actual *NEC*.

Always compare what's being explained in this textbook to what the *Code* book says. Get with others who are knowledgeable about the *NEC* to discuss any topics that you find difficult to understand, or join our free Code Forum www.MikeHolt.com/Forum to post your question.

This textbook follows the *Code* format, but it doesn't cover every change or requirement. For example, it doesn't include every article, section, subsection, exception, or Informational Note. So don't be concerned if you see that the textbook contains Exception 1 and Exception 3, but not Exception 2.

Cross-References. *NEC* cross-references to other related *Code* requirements are included to help you develop a better understanding of how the *NEC* rules relate to one another. These cross-references

About This Textbook

are indicated by *Code* section numbers in brackets, an example of which is "[90.4]."

Informational Notes. Informational Notes contained in the *NEC* will be identified in this textbook as "Note."

Exceptions. Exceptions contained in this textbook will be identified as "Ex" and not spelled out.

As you read through this textbook, allow yourself sufficient time to review the text along with the outstanding graphics and examples, to give yourself the opportunity for a deeper understanding of the *Code*, especially as it relates to Solar PV systems.

Technical Questions

As you progress through this textbook, you might find that you don't understand every explanation, example, calculation, or comment. Don't become frustrated, and don't get down on yourself. Remember, this is the *National Electrical Code*, and sometimes the best attempt to explain a concept isn't enough to make it perfectly clear. If you're still confused, visit www.MikeHolt.com/forum, and post your question on our free *Code* Forum. The forum is a moderated community of electrical professionals.

Book Corrections

We're committed to providing the finest product with the fewest errors, and take great care to ensure our books are correct. But we're realistic and know that errors might be found after printing. The last thing we want is for you to have problems finding, communicating, or accessing this information, so we list any corrections on our website.

If you believe there's an error of any kind (typographical, grammatical, technical, etc.) in this book or in the Answer Key, and it's not listed on the website, send an e-mail and be sure to include the book title, page number, and any other pertinent information.

To check for known errors, visit www.MikeHolt.com/corrections.

To report an error, e-mail corrections@MikeHolt.com.

Key Features of Mike Holt Textbooks

The layout and design of Mike Holt textbooks incorporate special features and icons designed to help you navigate easily through the material, and enhance your understanding.

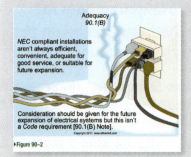

Code Rule Headers

The *Code* rule being taught is identified with a chapter color bar and white text.

Full-Color, Detailed Educational Graphics

Industry-leading graphics help you visualize the sometimes complex language of the *Code*, and illustrate the rule in real-world application(s). This is a great aid to reinforce learning.

Author's Comments

The author provides additional information to clarify the rule, and help you understand the background and context of the information.

Danger, Caution, and Warning Icons

These icons highlight areas of concern.

 Caution—Possible damage to property or equipment.

 Warning—Severe property damage or personal injury.

 Danger—Severe injury or death.

About This Textbook

Examples

Practical application questions and examples are contained in framed yellow boxes. These support the rules and help you understand how to do the calculations. If you see an ellipsis (• • •) at the bottom of the example, it is continued on the following page.

Underlined *Code* Changes

All changes to the text in the *Code* for the 2017 *NEC* are identified by underlining in the chapter color.

Additional Background Information Boxes

Where the author believes that information unrelated to the specific rule will help you understand the concept being taught, he includes these topics, easily identified in boxes outlined in the chapter color.

Formulas

$P = I \times E$

Formulas are easily identifiable in green text on a gray bar.

Modular Color Coded Page Layout

Chapters are color coded and modular to make it easy to navigate through each section of the textbook.

QR Codes

A few **QR Codes** are found throughout the textbook, and can be scanned with a smartphone app to take you to a sample video clip to watch Mike and the DVD panel discuss this topic.

Code Rule Icons

A *Code* Rule icon signifies whether the rule is new, deleted, edited, reduced, clarified, expanded, reorganized, or moved.

 Clarified—A change that clarifies the requirements of a rule that wasn't clear in the previous *Code* cycle.

 Edited—An editorial revision that doesn't change the requirement; but it gives us the opportunity to review the rule.

 Expanded—A change where a previous requirement(s) was expanded to cover additional applications.

 New—A new requirement which could be an entirely new section, subsection, exception, table, and/or Informational Note.

 Reduced—A change that's reduced the requirements from the previous edition of the *NEC*.

 Relocated—This identifies a rule that was relocated from one section of the *Code* to another without a change in the requirement(s).

 Reorganized—A change made to place the existing requirements in a more logical order or list.

About This Textbook

Additional Products to Help You Learn

Understanding 2017 NEC Requirements for Solar Photovoltaic Systems DVDs

One of the best ways to get the most out of this textbook is to use it in conjunction with the corresponding DVDs. Mike Holt's DVDs provide a 360° view of each topic with specialized commentary from Mike and his panel of industry experts. These DVDs are ideal for auditory and visual learners.

To order your copy of the DVDs at a discounted price, call our office at 888.632.2633.

Understanding the NEC Complete Training Library

Do you want a comprehensive understanding of the *Code*? Then you need Mike's Understanding the *NEC* Complete Training Library. This program takes you step-by-step through the *NEC* in *Code* order, with detailed illustrations, great practice questions, and in-depth DVD analysis. This library is perfect for engineers, electricians, contractors, and electrical inspectors. The library includes:

- **Understanding the National Electrical Code, Volume 1** textbook
- **Understanding the National Electrical Code, Volume 2** textbook
- **NEC Exam Practice Questions** workbook
- *General Requirements* DVD
- *Bonding and Grounding* DVDs (3)
- *Wiring and Protection* DVD
- *Wiring Methods and Materials* DVDs (2)
- *Equipment for General Use* DVD
- *Special Occupancies and Special Equipment* DVDs (3)
- *Limited Energy and Communications Systems* DVD

To order, visit www.MikeHolt.com/Code.

Theory DVD Training Program

Understanding electrical theory is critical for anyone who works with electricity. This textbook teaches the fundamentals that you need in order to understand and comply with *NEC* rules that govern installations—starting from basic scientific principles, to electrical formulas, to practical applications of electricity. This library includes:

- **Basic Electrical Theory** textbook
- *Electrical Fundamentals and Basic Electricity* DVD
- *Electrical Circuits, Systems, and Protection* DVD
- *Alternating Current, Motors, Generators, and Transformers* DVD

To order, visit www.MikeHolt.com/Theory.

2017 *Code* Book and Tabs

The ideal way to use your *Code* book is to tab it for quick reference—Mike's best-selling tabs make organizing the *NEC* easy. If you're using your *Code* book for an exam, please confirm with your testing authority that a tabbed *Code* book is allowed into the exam room.

To order your *Code* book and tabs visit www.MikeHolt.com/Code, or call 1.888.NEC.CODE (632.2633).

HOW TO USE THE *NATIONAL ELECTRICAL CODE*

The original *NEC* document was developed in 1897 as a result of the united efforts of various insurance, electrical, architectural, and other allied interests. The National Fire Protection Association (NFPA) has sponsored the *National Electrical Code* since 1911.

The purpose of the *Code* is the practical safeguarding of persons and property from hazards arising from the use of electricity. It isn't intended as a design specification or an instruction manual for untrained persons. It is, in fact, a standard that contains the minimum requirements for electrical installations. Learning to understand and use the *Code* is critical to you working safely, whether you're training to become an electrician, or are already an electrician, electrical contractor, inspector, engineer, designer, or instructor.

The *NEC* was written for those who understand electrical terms, theory, safety procedures, and electrical trade practices. Learning to use the *Code* is a lengthy process and can be frustrating if you don't approach it the right way. First of all, you'll need to understand electrical theory and if you don't have theory as a background when you get into the *NEC*, you're going to be struggling—so take one step back if you need to, and learn electrical theory. You must also understand the concepts and terms, and know grammar and punctuation in order to understand the complex structure of the rules and their intended purpose(s). Our goal for the next few pages is to give you some guidelines and suggestions on using your *Code* book to help you understand what you're trying to accomplish, and how to get there.

Language Considerations for the *NEC*

Terms and Concepts

The *NEC* contains many technical terms, so it's crucial for *Code* users to understand their meanings and applications. If you don't understand a term used in a rule, it will be impossible to properly apply the *NEC* requirement. Article 100 defines the terms that are used in two or more *Code* articles; for example, the term "Dwelling Unit" is found in many articles. If you don't know the *NEC* definition for a "dwelling unit" you can't properly identify the *Code* requirements for it.

Many articles have terms unique to that specific article, and the definitions of those terms are only applicable to that given article. These definitions are usually found in the beginning of the article. For example, Section 250.2 contains the definitions of terms that only apply to Article 250—Grounding and Bonding.

Small Words, Grammar, and Punctuation

It's not only the technical words that require close attention since simple words can make a big difference to the application of a rule. Was there a comma; was it "or," "and," "other than," "greater than," or "smaller than"? The word "or" can imply alternate choices for wiring methods. A word like "or" gives us choices while the word "and" can mean an additional requirement must be met.

An example of these words being used in the *NEC* is found in 110.26(C)(2), where it says equipment containing overcurrent, switching, "or" control devices that are 1,200A or more "and" over 6 ft wide that require a means of egress at each end of the working space. In this section, the word "or" clarifies that equipment containing any of the three types of devices listed must follow this rule. The word "and" clarifies that 110.26(C)(2) only applies if the equipment is both 1,200A or more and over 6 ft wide.

How to Use the *National Electrical Code*

Grammar and punctuation play an important role in establishing the meaning of a rule. The location of a comma can dramatically change the requirement of a rule such as in 250.28(A), where it says a main bonding jumper must be a wire, bus, screw, or similar suitable conductor. If the comma between "bus" and "screw" was removed, only a "bus screw" could be used. That comma makes a big change in the requirements of the rule.

Slang Terms or Technical Jargon

Trade-related professionals in different areas of the country often use local "slang" terms that aren't shared by all. This can make it difficult to communicate if it isn't clear what the meaning of those slang terms are. Use the proper terms by finding out what their definitions and applications are before you use them. For example, the term "pigtail" is often used to describe the short piece of conductor used to connect a device to a splice, but a "pigtail" is also a term used for a rubberized light socket with pre-terminated conductors. Although the term is the same, the meaning is very different and could cause confusion.

NEC Style and Layout

It's important to understand the structure and writing style of the *Code* if you want to use it effectively. The *National Electrical Code* is organized using eleven major components.

1. Table of Contents
2. Chapters—Chapters 1 through 9 (major categories)
3. Articles—Chapter subdivisions that cover specific subjects
4. Parts—Divisions used to organize article subject matter
5. Sections—Divisions used to further organize article subject matter
6. Tables and Figures—Represent the mandatory requirements of a rule
7. Exceptions—Alternatives to the main *Code* rule
8. Informational Notes—explanatory material for a specific rule (not a requirement)
9. Tables—Applicable as referenced in the *NEC*
10. Annexes—Additional explanatory information such as tables and references (not a requirement)
11. Index

1. Table of Contents. The Table of Contents displays the layout of the chapters, articles, and parts as well as the page numbers. It's an excellent resource and should be referred to periodically to observe the interrelationship of the various *NEC* components. When attempting to locate the rules for a particular situation, knowledgeable *Code* users often go first to the Table of Contents to quickly find the specific *NEC* rule that applies.

2. Chapters. There are nine chapters, each of which is divided into articles. The articles fall into one of four groupings: General Requirements (Chapters 1 through 4), Specific Requirements (Chapters 5 through 7), Communications Systems (Chapter 8), and Tables (Chapter 9).

- Chapter 1—General
- Chapter 2—Wiring and Protection
- Chapter 3—Wiring Methods and Materials
- Chapter 4—Equipment for General Use
- Chapter 5—Special Occupancies
- Chapter 6—Special Equipment
- Chapter 7—Special Conditions
- Chapter 8—Communications Systems (Telephone, Data, Satellite, Cable TV, and Broadband)
- Chapter 9—Tables–Conductor and Raceway Specifications

3. Articles. The *NEC* contains approximately 140 articles, each of which covers a specific subject. It begins with Article 90, the introduction to the *Code*, and contains the purpose of the *NEC*, what's covered and what isn't covered, along with how the *Code* is arranged. It also gives information on enforcement and how mandatory and permissive rules are written and how explanatory material is included. Article 90 also includes information on formal interpretations, examination of equipment for safety, wiring planning, and information about formatting units of measurement. Here are some other examples of articles you'll find in the *NEC*:

- Article 110—Requirements for Electrical Installations
- Article 250—Grounding and Bonding
- Article 300—General Requirements for Wiring Methods and Materials
- Article 430—Motors and Motor Controllers
- Article 500—Hazardous (Classified) Locations
- Article 680—Swimming Pools, Fountains, and Similar Installations
- Article 725—Remote-Control, Signaling, and Power-Limited Circuits
- Article 800—Communications Circuits

4. Parts. Larger articles are subdivided into parts. Because the parts of a *Code* article aren't included in the section numbers, we have a tendency to forget what "part" an *NEC* rule is relating to. For example, Table 110.34(A) contains working space clearances for electrical equipment. If we aren't careful, we might think this table applies to all electrical installations, but Table 110.34(A) is located in Part III, which only contains requirements for "Over 1,000 Volts, Nominal" installations. The rules for working clearances for electrical equipment for systems 1,000V, nominal, or less are contained in Table 110.26(A)(1), which is located in Part II—1,000 Volts, Nominal, or Less.

5. Sections. Each *NEC* rule is called a "*Code* Section." A *Code* section may be broken down into subsections by letters in parentheses like (A), numbers in parentheses like (1), and lowercase letters like (a), (b), and so on, to further break the rule down to the second and third level. For example, the rule requiring all receptacles in a dwelling unit bathroom to be GFCI protected is contained in Section 210.8(A)(1) which is located in Chapter 2, Article 210, Section 8, Subsection (A), Sub-subsection (1).

Many in the industry incorrectly use the term "Article" when referring to a *Code* section. For example, they say "Article 210.8," when they should say "Section 210.8." Section numbers in this textbook are shown without the word "Section," unless they begin a sentence. For example, Section 210.8(A) is shown as simply 210.8(A).

6. Tables and Figures. Many *NEC* requirements are contained within tables, which are lists of *Code* rules placed in a systematic arrangement. The titles of the tables are extremely important; you must read them carefully in order to understand the contents, applications and limitations of each table. Many times notes are provided in or below a table; be sure to read them as well since they're also part of the requirement. For example, Note 1 for Table 300.5 explains how to measure the cover when burying cables and raceways, and Note 5 explains what to do if solid rock is encountered.

7. Exceptions. Exceptions are *Code* requirements or permissions that provide an alternative method to a specific rule. There are two types of exceptions—mandatory and permissive. When a rule has several exceptions, those exceptions with mandatory requirements are listed before the permissive exceptions.

Mandatory Exceptions. A mandatory exception uses the words "shall" or "shall not." The word "shall" in an exception means that if you're using the exception, you're required to do it in a particular way. The phrase "shall not" means it isn't permitted.

Permissive Exceptions. A permissive exception uses words such as "shall be permitted," which means it's acceptable (but not mandatory) to do it in this way.

8. Informational Notes. An Informational Note contains explanatory material intended to clarify a rule or give assistance, but it isn't a *Code* requirement.

9. Tables. Chapter 9 consists of tables applicable as referenced in the *NEC*. The tables are used to calculate raceway sizing, conductor fill, the radius of raceway bends, and conductor voltage drop.

10. Annexes. Annexes aren't a part of the *NEC* requirements, and are included in the *Code* for informational purposes only.

> Annex A. Product Safety Standards
> Annex B. Application Information for Ampacity Calculation
> Annex C. Raceway Fill Tables for Conductors and Fixture Wires of the Same Size
> Annex D. Examples
> Annex E. Types of Construction
> Annex F. Critical Operations Power Systems (COPS)
> Annex G. Supervisory Control and Data Acquisition (SCADA)
> Annex H. Administration and Enforcement
> Annex I. Recommended Tightening Torques
> Annex J. ADA Standards for Accessible Design

11. Index. The Index at the back of the *Code* book is helpful in locating a specific rule.

Author's Comment:

- Changes in the 2017 *Code* book are indicated as follows:
    - Changed rules are identified by shading the text that was changed since the previous edition.
    - New rules aren't shaded like a change, instead they have a shaded "N" in the margin to the left of the section number.
    - Relocated rules are treated like new rules with a shaded "N" in the left margin by the section number.
    - Deleted rules are indicated by a bullet symbol "•" located in the left margin where the rule was in the previous edition.

How to Locate a Specific Requirement

How to go about finding what you're looking for in the *Code* book depends, to some degree, on your experience with the *NEC*. Experts typically know the requirements so well that they just go to the correct rule. Very experienced people might only need the Table of Contents to locate the requirement they're looking for. On the other hand, average users should use all of the tools at their disposal, including the Table of Contents, the Index, and the search feature on electronic versions of the *Code* book.

Let's work through a simple example: What *NEC* rule specifies the maximum number of disconnects permitted for a service?

How to Use the *National Electrical Code*

Table of Contents. If you're an experienced *Code* user, you might use the Table of Contents. You'll know Article 230 applies to "Services," and because this article is so large, it's divided up into multiple parts (actually eight parts). With this knowledge, you can quickly go to the Table of Contents and see it lists the Service Equipment Disconnecting Means requirements in Part VI.

> **Author's Comment:**
> - The number 70 precedes all page numbers because the *NEC* is NFPA Standard Number 70.

Index. If you use the Index, which lists subjects in alphabetical order, to look up the term "service disconnect," you'll see there's no listing. If you try "disconnecting means," then "services," you'll find that the Index indicates the rule is located in Article 230, Part VI. Because the *NEC* doesn't give a page number in the Index, you'll need to use the Table of Contents to find it, or flip through the *Code* book to Article 230, then continue to flip through pages until you find Part VI.

Many people complain that the *NEC* only confuses them by taking them in circles. Once you gain experience in using the *Code* and deepen your understanding of words, terms, principles, and practices, you'll find the *NEC* much easier to understand and use than you originally thought.

Customizing Your *Code* Book

One way to increase your comfort level with the *Code* book is to customize it to meet your needs. You can do this by highlighting and underlining important *NEC* requirements. Preprinted adhesive tabs are also an excellent aid to quickly find important articles and sections that are regularly referenced. Be aware that if you're using your *Code* book to prepare to take an exam, some exam centers don't allow markings of any type. Visit www.MikeHolt.com/tabs for more information.

Highlighting. As you read through textbooks or find answers to your questions, be sure you highlight those requirements in the *NEC* that are the most important or relevant to you. Use one color, like yellow, for general interest and a different one for important requirements you want to find quickly. Be sure to highlight terms in the Index and the Table of Contents as you use them.

Underlining. Underline or circle key words and phrases in the *Code* with a red or blue pen (not a lead pencil) using a short ruler or other straightedge to keep lines straight and neat. This is a very handy way to make important requirements stand out. A short ruler or other straightedge also comes in handy for locating the correct information in a table.

Different Interpretations

Industry professionals often enjoy the challenge of discussing the *NEC* requirements. This discussion is important to the process of better understanding the *Code* requirements and application(s). If you decide you're going to participate in one of these discussions, don't spout out what you think without having the actual *NEC* book in your hand. The professional way of discussing a *Code* requirement is by referring to a specific section, rather than talking in vague generalities. This will help everyone involved clearly understand the point and become better educated.

Become Involved in the *NEC* Process

The actual process of changing the *Code* takes about two years and involves hundreds of individuals making an effort to have the *NEC* as current and accurate as possible. As you study and learn how to use it, you'll find it very interesting, enjoy it more, and realize that you can also be a part of the process. Rather than sitting back and just reading it and learning it, you can participate by making proposals and being a part of its development. For the 2017 *Code*, there were 4,000 public inputs and 1,500 comments. Hundreds of updates and five new articles were added to keep the *NEC* up to date with new technologies, and pave the way to a safer and more efficient electrical future.

Let's review how this process works:

STEP 1—Public Input Stage

Public Input. The revision cycle begins with the acceptance of Public Input (PI): the public notice asking for anyone interested to submit input on an existing standard or a committee-approved new draft standard. Following the closing date, the Committee conducts a First Draft Meeting to respond to all public inputs.

First Draft Meeting. At the First Draft (FD) Meeting, the Technical Committee considers and provides a response to all Public Input. The Technical Committee may use the input to develop First Revisions to the standard. The First Draft documents consist of the initial meeting consensus of the committee by simple majority. However, the final position of the Technical Committee must be established by a ballot which follows.

Committee Ballot on First Draft. The First Draft developed at the First Draft Meeting is balloted: to appear in the First Draft, a revision must be approved by at least two-thirds of the Technical Committee.

How to Use the *National Electrical Code*

First Draft Report Posted. First revisions which pass ballot are ultimately compiled and published as the First Draft Report on the document's NFPA web page. This report serves as documentation for the Input Stage and is published for review and comment. The public may review the First Draft Report to determine whether to submit Public Comments on the First Draft.

STEP 2—Public Comment Stage

Public Comment. Once the First Draft Report becomes available, there's a public comment period during which anyone can submit a Public Comment on the First Draft. After the Public Comment closing date, the Technical Committee conducts/holds their Second Draft Meeting.

Second Draft Meeting. After the Public Comment closing date, if Public Comments are received or the committee has additional proposed revisions, a Second Draft Meeting is held. At the Second Draft Meeting, the Technical Committee reviews the First Draft and may make additional revisions to the draft Standard. All Public Comments are considered, and the Technical Committee provides an action and response to each Public Comment. These actions result in the Second Draft.

Committee Ballot on Second Draft. The Second Revisions developed at the Second Draft Meeting are balloted. To appear in the Second Draft, a revision must be approved by at least two-thirds of the Technical Committee.

Second Draft Report Posted. Second Revisions which pass ballot are ultimately compiled and published as the Second Draft Report on the document's NFPA website. This report serves as documentation of the Comment Stage and is published for public review.

Once published, the public can review the Second Draft Report to decide whether to submit a Notice of Intent to Make a Motion (NITMAM) for further consideration.

STEP 3—NFPA Technical Meeting (Tech Session)

Following completion of the Public Input and Public Comment stages, there's further opportunity for debate and discussion of issues through the NFPA Technical Meeting that takes place at the NFPA Conference & Expo®. These motions are attempts to change the resulting final Standard from the committee's recommendations published as the Second Draft.

STEP 4—Council Appeals and Issuance of Standard

Issuance of Standards. When the Standards Council convenes to issue an NFPA standard, it also hears any related appeals. Appeals are an important part of assuring that all NFPA rules have been followed and that due process and fairness have continued throughout the standards development process. The Standards Council considers appeals based on the written record and by conducting live hearings during which all interested parties can participate. Appeals are decided on the entire record of the process, as well as all submissions and statements presented.

After deciding all appeals related to a standard, the Standards Council, if appropriate, proceeds to issue the Standard as an official NFPA Standard. The decision of the Standards Council is final subject only to limited review by the NFPA Board of Directors. The new NFPA standard becomes effective twenty days following the Standards Council's action of issuance.

> **Author's Comment:**
> - Proposals and comments can be submitted online at the NFPA website at www.nfpa.org/doc# (for NFPA 70, go to www.nfpa.org/70 for example). From the homepage, look for "Codes & Standards," then find "How the Process Works." If you'd like to see something changed in the *Code*, you're encouraged to participate in the process.

Notes

ARTICLE 90
INTRODUCTION TO THE *NATIONAL ELECTRICAL CODE*

Introduction to Article 90—Introduction to the *National Electrical Code*

Many *NEC* violations and misunderstandings wouldn't occur if people doing the work simply understood Article 90. For example, many people see *Code* requirements as performance standards. In fact, the *NEC* requirements are bare minimums for safety. This is exactly the stance electrical inspectors, insurance companies, and courts take when making a decision regarding electrical design or installation.

Article 90 opens by saying the *NEC* isn't intended as a design specification or instruction manual. The *National Electrical Code* has one purpose only, and that's the "practical safeguarding of persons and property from hazards arising from the use of electricity." The necessity of carefully studying the *NEC* rules can't be overemphasized, and the role of textbooks such as this one are to help in that undertaking. Understanding where to find the rules in the *Code* that apply to the installation is invaluable. Rules in several different articles often apply to even a simple installation.

Article 90 then describes the scope and arrangement of the *NEC*. The balance of this article provides the reader with information essential to understanding the *Code* rules.

Typically, electrical work requires you to understand the first four chapters of the *NEC* which apply generally, plus have a working knowledge of the Chapter 9 tables. That understanding begins with Article 90. Chapters 5, 6, and 7 make up a large portion of the *Code*, but they apply to special occupancies, special equipment, or other special conditions. They build on, modify, or amend the rules in the first four chapters. Chapter 8 contains the requirements for communications systems, such as twisted pair conductors for telephone and data systems, satellite receivers, antenna systems, and coaxial cable wiring. Communications systems (twisted wire, antennas, and coaxial cable) aren't subject to the general requirements of Chapters 1 through 4, or the special requirements of Chapters 5 through 7, unless there's a specific reference in Chapter 8 to a rule in Chapters 1 through 7.

90.1 Purpose of the *NEC*

(A) Practical Safeguarding. The purpose of the *NEC* is to ensure that electrical systems are installed in a manner that protects people and property by minimizing the risks associated with the use of electricity. It isn't a design specification standard or instruction manual for the untrained and unqualified. ▶Figure 90–1

Author's Comment:

- The *Code* is intended to be used by those skilled and knowledgeable in electrical theory, electrical systems, construction, and the installation and operation of electrical equipment.

(B) Adequacy. The *Code* contains requirements considered necessary for a safe electrical installation. If an electrical system is installed in compliance with the *NEC*, it will be essentially free from electrical hazards. The *Code* is a safety standard, not a design guide.

90.1 | Introduction to the National Electrical Code

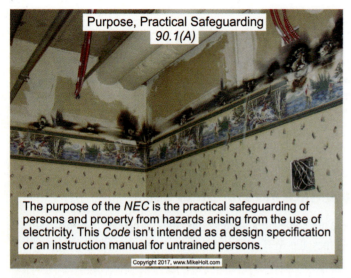

▶Figure 90–1

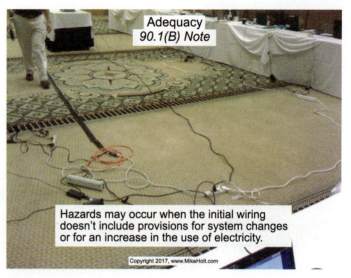

▶Figure 90–3

NEC requirements aren't intended to ensure the electrical installation will be efficient, convenient, adequate for good service, or suitable for future expansion. Specific items of concern, such as electrical energy management, maintenance, and power quality issues aren't within the scope of the *Code*. ▶Figure 90–2

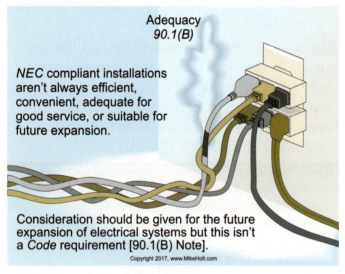

▶Figure 90–2

Note: Hazards in electrical systems often occur because circuits are overloaded or not properly installed in accordance with the *NEC*. These often occur if the initial wiring didn't provide reasonable provisions for system changes or for the increase in the use of electricity. ▶Figure 90–3

Author's Comment:

- See the definition of "Overload" in Article 100.
- The *NEC* doesn't require electrical systems to be designed or installed to accommodate future loads. However, the electrical designer (typically an electrical engineer) is concerned with not only ensuring electrical safety (*Code* compliance), but also with ensuring the system meets the customers' needs, both of today and in the near future. To satisfy customers' needs, electrical systems are often designed and installed above the minimum requirements contained in the *NEC*. But just remember, if you're taking an exam, licensing exams are based on your understanding of the minimum *Code* requirements.

(C) Relation to International Standards. The requirements of the *NEC* address the fundamental safety principles contained in the International Electrotechnical Commission (IEC) Standard, including protection against electric shock, adverse thermal effects, overcurrent, fault currents, and overvoltage. ▶Figure 90–4

Author's Comment:

- The *NEC* is used in Chile, Ecuador, Peru, and the Philippines. It's also the *Electrical Code* for Colombia, Costa Rica, Mexico, Panama, Puerto Rico, and Venezuela. Because of these adoptions, it's available in Spanish from the National Fire Protection Association, 617.770.3000, or www.NFPA.org.

Introduction to the *National Electrical Code* | 90.2

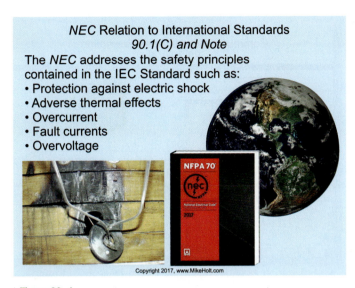

▶Figure 90–4

90.2 Scope of the *NEC*

(A) What Is Covered by the *NEC*. The *NEC* contains requirements necessary for the proper installation and removal of electrical conductors, equipment, cables, and raceways for power, signaling, fire alarm, optical cable, and communications systems (twisted wire, antennas, and coaxial cable) for: ▶Figure 90–5

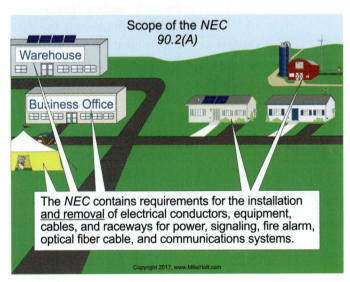

▶Figure 90–5

Author's Comment:

- The *NEC* contains the following requirements on the removal of equipment and cables; temporary wiring 590.3 and abandoned cables for Audio [640.6(B)], Signaling [725.25], Fire Alarm [760.25], Optical Fiber [770.25], Twisted Pair [800.25], and Coaxial [820.25].

(1) Public and private premises, including buildings, mobile homes, recreational vehicles, and floating buildings. ▶Figure 90–6

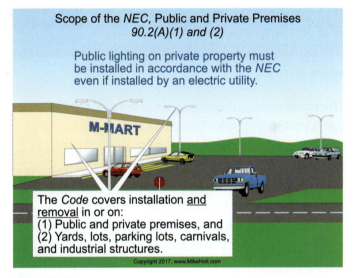

▶Figure 90–6

(2) Yards, lots, parking lots, carnivals, and industrial substations.

(3) Conductors and equipment connected to the electric utility supply.

(4) Installations used by an electric utility, such as office buildings, warehouses, garages, machine shops, recreational buildings, and other electric utility buildings that aren't an integral part of a utility's generating plant, substation, or control center. ▶Figure 90–7

(B) What Isn't Covered by the *NEC*. The *NEC* doesn't apply to the installation of electrical or communications systems (twisted wire, antennas, and coaxial cable) for:

(1) Transportation Vehicles. The *NEC* doesn't apply to installations in cars, trucks, boats, ships and watercraft, planes, or electric trains.

(2) Mining Equipment. The *NEC* doesn't apply to installations underground in mines and self-propelled mobile surface mining machinery and its attendant electrical trailing cables.

90.2 | Introduction to the National Electrical Code

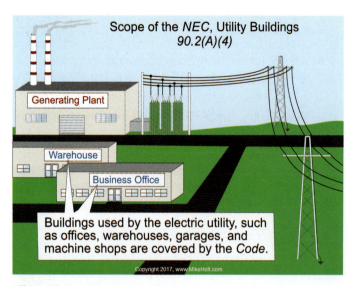
▶Figure 90–7

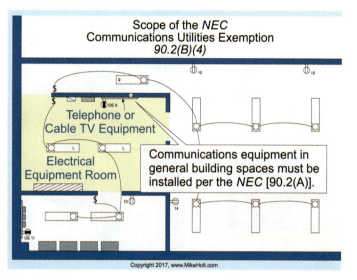
▶Figure 90–9

(3) Railways. The *NEC* doesn't apply to railway power, signaling, energy storage, and communications wiring.

(4) Communications Utilities. If the installation is under the exclusive control of the communications utility, the installation requirements of the *NEC* don't apply to the communications (telephone) or network-powered broadband utility equipment located in building spaces used exclusively for these purposes, or located outdoors if the installation is under the exclusive control of the communications utility. ▶Figure 90–8 and ▶Figure 90–9

(5) Electric Utilities. The *NEC* doesn't apply to electrical installations under the exclusive control of an electric utility, where such installations:

a. Consist of electric utility installed service drops or service laterals under their exclusive control. ▶Figure 90–10

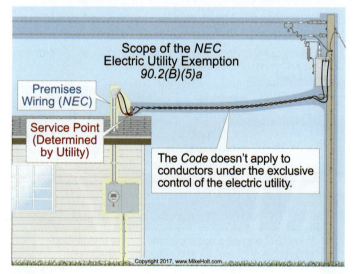
▶Figure 90–10

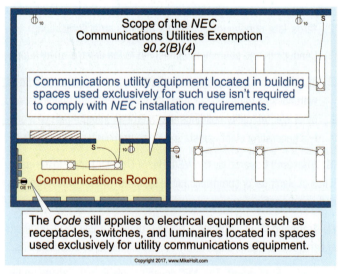
▶Figure 90–8

b. Are on property owned or leased by the electric utility for the purpose of generation, transformation, transmission, energy storage, distribution, or metering of electric energy. ▶Figure 90–11

Introduction to the *National Electrical Code* | 90.3

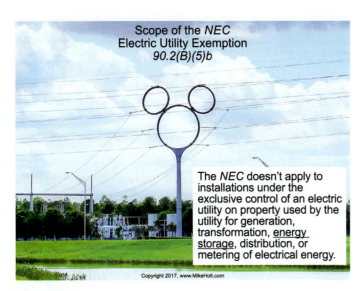
▶Figure 90–11

Author's Comment:

- Luminaires located in legally established easements, or rights-of-way, such as at poles supporting transmission or distribution lines, are exempt from the *NEC*. However, if the electric utility provides site and public lighting on private property, then the installation must comply with the *Code* [90.2(A)(4)].

c. Are located on legally established easements or rights-of-way. ▶Figure 90–12

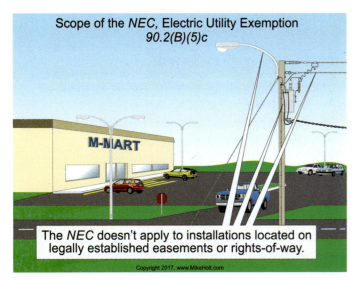
▶Figure 90–12

d. Are located by other written agreements either designated by or recognized by public service commissions, electric utility commissions, or other regulatory agencies having jurisdiction for such installations; limited to installations for the purpose of communications, metering, generation, control, transformation, transmission, energy storage, or distribution of electric energy where legally established easements or rights-of-way can't be obtained. These installations are limited to federal lands, Native American reservations through the U.S. Department of the Interior Bureau of Indian Affairs, military bases, lands controlled by port authorities and state agencies and departments, and lands owned by railroads.

Note to 90.2(B)(4) and (5): Utilities include entities that install, operate, and maintain communications systems (twisted wire, antennas, and coaxial cable) or electric supply (generation, transmission, or distribution systems) and are designated or recognized by governmental law or regulation by public service/utility commissions. Utilities may be subject to compliance with codes and standards covering their regulated activities as adopted under governmental law or regulation.

90.3 *Code* Arrangement

General Requirements. The *Code* is divided into an introduction and nine chapters followed by informational annexes. Chapters 1, 2, 3, and 4 are general conditions. ▶Figure 90–13

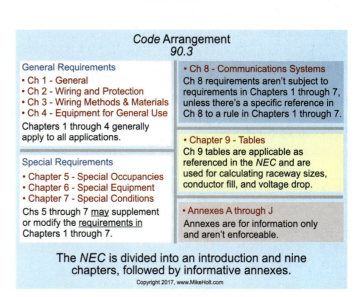
▶Figure 90–13

90.4 | Introduction to the *National Electrical Code*

Author's Comment:

- These first four chapters may be thought of as the foundation for the rest of the *Code*.

Special Requirements. The requirements contained in Chapters 5, 6, and 7 apply to special occupancies, special equipment, or other special conditions, which may supplement or modify the requirements contained in Chapters 1 through 7, but not Chapter 8.

Communications Systems. Chapter 8 contains the requirements for communications systems (twisted wire, antennas, and coaxial cable) which aren't subject to the general requirements of Chapters 1 through 4, or the special requirements of Chapters 5 through 7, unless there's a specific reference in Chapter 8 to a rule in Chapters 1 through 7.

Author's Comment:

- An example of how Chapter 8 works is in the rules for working space about equipment. The typical 3-ft working space isn't required in front of communications equipment, because Table 110.26(A)(1) isn't referenced in Chapter 8.

Tables. Chapter 9 consists of tables applicable as referenced in the *NEC*. The tables are used to calculate raceway sizing, conductor fill, the radius of raceway bends, and conductor voltage drop.

Annexes. Annexes aren't part of the *Code*, but are included for informational purposes. There are ten annexes:

- Annex A. Product Safety Standards
- Annex B. Application Information for Ampacity Calculation
- Annex C. Raceway Fill Tables for Conductors and Fixture Wires of the Same Size
- Annex D. Examples
- Annex E. Types of Construction
- Annex F. Critical Operations Power Systems (COPS)
- Annex G. Supervisory Control and Data Acquisition (SCADA)
- Annex H. Administration and Enforcement
- Annex I. Recommended Tightening Torques
- Annex J. ADA Standards for Accessible Design

90.4 Enforcement

The *Code* is intended to be suitable for enforcement by governmental bodies that exercise legal jurisdiction over electrical installations for power, lighting, signaling circuits, and communications systems, such as: ▶Figure 90–14

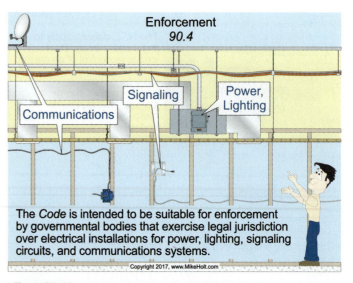

▶Figure 90–14

Signaling circuits which include:

- Article 725 Class 1, Class 2, and Class 3 Remote-Control, Signaling, and Power-Limited Circuits
- Article 760 Fire Alarm Systems
- Article 770 Optical Fiber Cables and Raceways

Communications systems which include:

- Article 810 Radio and Television Equipment (satellite dish and antenna)
- Article 820 Community Antenna Television and Radio Distribution Systems (coaxial cable)

Author's Comment:

- The installation requirements for signaling circuits and communications circuits are covered in Mike Holt's *Understanding the National Electrical Code, Volume 2* textbook.

The enforcement of the *NEC* is the responsibility of the authority having jurisdiction (AHJ), who is responsible for interpreting requirements, approving equipment and materials, waiving *Code* requirements, and ensuring equipment is installed in accordance with listing instructions.

Introduction to the *National Electrical Code* | 90.4

Author's Comment:

- See the definition of "Authority Having Jurisdiction" in Article 100.

Interpretation of the Requirements. The authority having jurisdiction is responsible for interpreting the *NEC*.

Author's Comment:

- The AHJ's decisions must be based on a specific *Code* requirement. If an installation is rejected, the authority having jurisdiction is legally responsible for informing the installer of the specific *NEC* rule that was violated. ▶Figure 90–15

▶Figure 90–15

Author's Comment:

- The art of getting along with the authority having jurisdiction consists of doing good work and knowing what the *Code* actually says (as opposed to what you only think it says). It's also useful to know how to choose your battles when the inevitable disagreement does occur.

Approval of Equipment and Materials. Only the authority having jurisdiction has authority to approve the installation of equipment and materials. Typically, the authority having jurisdiction will approve equipment listed by a product testing organization, such as Underwriters Laboratories, Inc. (UL). The *NEC* doesn't require all equipment to be listed, but many state and local AHJs do. See 90.7, 110.2, 110.3, and the definitions for "Approved," "Identified," "Labeled," and "Listed" in Article 100. ▶Figure 90–16

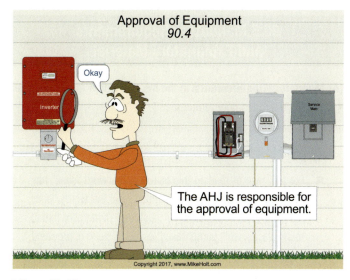

▶Figure 90–16

Author's Comment:

- According to the *NEC*, the authority having jurisdiction determines the approval of equipment. This means he or she can reject an installation of listed equipment and can approve the use of unlisted equipment. Given our highly litigious society, approval of unlisted equipment is becoming increasingly difficult to obtain.

Approval of Alternate Means. By special permission, the authority having jurisdiction may approve alternate methods where it's assured equivalent safety can be achieved and maintained.

Author's Comment:

- Special permission is defined in Article 100 as the written consent of the authority having jurisdiction.

Waiver of New Product Requirements. If the current *NEC* requires products that aren't yet available at the time the *Code* is adopted, the authority having jurisdiction can allow products that were acceptable in the previous *Code* to continue to be used.

Author's Comment:

- Sometimes it takes years before testing laboratories establish product standards for new *NEC* requirements, and then it takes time before manufacturers can design, manufacture, and distribute those products to the marketplace.

90.5 Mandatory Requirements and Explanatory Material

(A) Mandatory Requirements. In the *NEC* the words "shall" or "shall not," indicate a mandatory requirement.

Author's Comment:

- For the ease of reading this textbook, the word "shall" has been replaced with the word "must," and the words "shall not" have been replaced with "must not." Remember that in many places, we'll paraphrase the *Code* instead of providing exact quotes, to make it easier to read and understand.

(B) Permissive Requirements. When the *Code* uses "shall be permitted" it means the identified actions are permitted but not required, and the authority having jurisdiction isn't permitted to restrict an installation from being completed in that manner. A permissive rule is often an exception to the general requirement.

Author's Comment:

- For ease of reading, the phrase "shall be permitted," as used in the *Code*, has been replaced in this textbook with the phrase "is permitted" or "are permitted."

(C) Explanatory Material. References to other standards or sections of the *NEC*, or information related to a *Code* rule, are included in the form of Informational Notes. Such notes are for information only and aren't enforceable as requirements of the *NEC*.

For example, Informational Note 4 in 210.19(A)(1) recommends that the voltage drop of a circuit not exceed 3 percent. This isn't a requirement; it's just a recommendation.

Author's Comment:

- For convenience and ease of reading in this textbook, Informational Notes will simply be identified as "Note."
- Informational Notes aren't enforceable, but Table Notes are. This textbook will call notes found in a table "Table Notes."

(D) Informative Annexes. Nonmandatory information annexes contained in the back of the *Code* book are for information only and aren't enforceable as requirements of the *NEC*.

90.6 Formal Interpretations

To promote uniformity of interpretation and application of the provisions of the *NEC*, formal interpretation procedures have been established and are found in the NFPA Regulations Governing Committee Projects.

Author's Comment:

- This is rarely done because it's a very time-consuming process, and formal interpretations from the NFPA aren't binding on the authority having jurisdiction.

90.7 Examination of Equipment for Product Safety

Product evaluation for safety is typically performed by a nationally recognized testing laboratory that's approved by the authority having jurisdiction. The suitability of equipment use is determined by the application of product safety listing standards that are compatible with the *NEC*.

Author's Comment:

- See Article 100 for the definition of "Approved."

Except to detect alterations or damage, listed factory-installed internal wiring and construction of equipment need not be inspected at the time of installation [300.1(B)]. ▶Figure 90–17

▶Figure 90–17

Note 1: See 110.3 on the required use of listed products.

Note 2: "Listed" is defined in Article 100.

Note 3: Annex A contains a list of product safety standards that comply with the *NEC*.

90.9 Units of Measurement

(B) Dual Systems of Units. Both the metric and inch-pound measurement systems are shown in the *NEC*, with the metric units appearing first and the inch-pound system immediately following in parentheses.

Author's Comment:

- This is the standard practice in all NFPA standards, even though the U.S. construction industry uses inch-pound units of measurement. You'll need to be cautious when using the tables in the *Code* because the additional units can make the tables more complex and more difficult to read.

(D) Compliance. Installing electrical systems in accordance with the metric system or the inch-pound system is considered to comply with the *Code*.

Author's Comment:

- Since the use of either the metric or the inch-pound system of measurement constitutes compliance with the *NEC*, this textbook uses only inch-pound units.

ARTICLE 90 PRACTICE QUESTIONS

Please use the 2017 *Code* book to answer the following questions.

Article 90. Introduction to the *National Electrical Code*

1. The *NEC* is _____.
   (a) intended to be a design manual
   (b) meant to be used as an instruction guide for untrained persons
   (c) for the practical safeguarding of persons and property
   (d) published by the Bureau of Standards

2. The *Code* isn't intended as a design specification standard or instruction manual for untrained persons.
   (a) True
   (b) False

3. Compliance with the provisions of the *NEC* will result in _____.
   (a) good electrical service
   (b) an efficient electrical system
   (c) an electrical system essentially free from hazard
   (d) all of these

4. The *Code* contains provisions considered necessary for safety, which will not necessarily result in _____.
   (a) efficient use
   (b) convenience
   (c) good service or future expansion of electrical use
   (d) all of these

5. Hazards often occur because of _____.
   (a) overloading of wiring systems by methods or usage not in conformity with the *NEC*
   (b) initial wiring not providing for increases in the use of electricity
   (c) a and b
   (d) none of these

6. Which of the following systems shall be installed and removed in accordance with the *NEC* requirements?
   (a) Signaling conductors, equipment, and raceways.
   (b) Communications conductors, equipment, and raceways.
   (c) Electrical conductors, equipment, and raceways.
   (d) all of these

7. The *NEC* applies to the installation of _____.
   (a) electrical conductors and equipment within or on public and private buildings
   (b) outside conductors and equipment on the premises
   (c) optical fiber cables and raceways
   (d) all of these

8. This *Code* covers the installation of _____ for public and private premises, including buildings, structures, mobile homes, recreational vehicles, and floating buildings.
   (a) optical fiber cables
   (b) electrical equipment
   (c) raceways
   (d) all of these

9. The *NEC* does not cover electrical installations in ships, watercraft, railway rolling stock, aircraft, or automotive vehicles.

    (a) True
    (b) False

10. The *Code* covers underground mine installations and self-propelled mobile surface mining machinery and its attendant electrical trailing cable.

    (a) True
    (b) False

11. Installations of communications equipment that are under the exclusive control of communications utilities, and located outdoors or in building spaces used exclusively for such installations _____ covered by the *NEC*.

    (a) are
    (b) are sometimes
    (c) are not
    (d) may be

12. Electric utilities may include entities that install, operate, and maintain _____.

    (a) communications systems (telephone, CATV, Internet, satellite, or data services)
    (b) electric supply systems (generation, transmission, or distribution systems)
    (c) local area network wiring on the premises
    (d) a or b

13. Utilities may be subject to compliance with codes and standards covering their regulated activities as adopted under governmental law or regulation.

    (a) True
    (b) False

14. The *NEC* does not apply to electric utility-owned wiring and equipment _____.

    (a) installed by an electrical contractor
    (b) installed on public property
    (c) consisting of service drops or service laterals
    (d) in a utility office building

15. Utilities may include entities that are designated or recognized by governmental law or regulation by public service/utility commissions.

    (a) True
    (b) False

16. Chapters 1 through 4 of the *NEC* apply _____.

    (a) generally to all electrical installations
    (b) only to special occupancies and conditions
    (c) only to special equipment and material
    (d) all of these

17. Chapters 5, 6, and 7 apply to special occupancies, special equipment, or other special conditions and may supplement or modify the requirements in Chapters 1 through 7.

    (a) True
    (b) False

18. Communications wiring such as telephone, antenna, and CATV wiring within a building shall not be required to comply with the installation requirements of Chapters 1 through 7, except where specifically referenced in Chapter 8.

    (a) True
    (b) False

19. Installations shall comply with the material located in the *NEC* Annexes because they are part of the requirements of the *Code*.

    (a) True
    (b) False

20. The authority having jurisdiction shall not be allowed to enforce any requirements of Chapter 7 (Special Conditions) or Chapter 8 (Communications Systems).

    (a) True
    (b) False

21. The _____ has the responsibility for deciding on the approval of equipment and materials.

    (a) manufacturer
    (b) authority having jurisdiction
    (c) testing agency
    (d) none of these

Article 90 | Practice Questions

22. By special permission, the authority having jurisdiction may waive specific requirements in this *Code* where it is assured that equivalent objectives can be achieved by establishing and maintaining effective safety.

    (a) True
    (b) False

23. The authority having jurisdiction has the responsibility for _____.

    (a) making interpretations of rules
    (b) deciding upon the approval of equipment and materials
    (c) waiving specific requirements in the *Code* and permitting alternate methods and material if safety is maintained
    (d) all of these

24. If the *NEC* requires new products that are not yet available at the time a new edition is adopted, the _____ may permit the use of the products that comply with the most recent previous edition of the *Code* adopted by that jurisdiction.

    (a) electrical engineer
    (b) master electrician
    (c) authority having jurisdiction
    (d) permit holder

25. In the *NEC*, the word(s) "_____" indicate a mandatory requirement.

    (a) shall
    (b) shall not
    (c) shall be permitted
    (d) a or b

26. When the *Code* uses "_____," it means the identified actions are allowed but not required, and they may be options or alternative methods.

    (a) shall
    (b) shall not
    (c) shall be permitted
    (d) a or b

27. Explanatory material, such as references to other standards, references to related sections of the *NEC*, or information related to a *Code* rule, are included in the form of Informational Notes.

    (a) True
    (b) False

28. Nonmandatory Informative Annexes contained in the back of the *Code* book are _____.

    (a) for information only
    (b) not enforceable as a requirement of the *Code*
    (c) enforceable as a requirement of the *Code*
    (d) a and b

29. Factory-installed _____ wiring of listed equipment need not be inspected at the time of installation of the equipment, except to detect alterations or damage.

    (a) external
    (b) associated
    (c) internal
    (d) all of these

30. Compliance with either the SI or the inch-pound unit of measurement system shall be permitted.

    (a) True
    (b) False

CHAPTER 1

GENERAL RULES

Introduction to Chapter 1—General Rules

Before you can make sense of the *Code*, you must become familiar with a few basic rules, concepts, definitions, and requirements. As you study the *NEC*, you'll see that these are the foundation for a proper understanding of the *Code*.

Chapter 1 consists of two topics. Article 100 provides definitions so people can understand one another when trying to communicate about *Code*-related matters and Article 110 provides the general requirements needed to correctly apply the rest of the *NEC*.

Time spent learning this general material is a great investment. After understanding Chapter 1, some of the *Code* requirements that seem confusing to other people will become increasingly clear to you. The requirements will begin to make sense because you'll have the foundation from which to understand and apply them. When you read the *NEC* requirements in later chapters, you'll understand the principles upon which many of them are based, and not be surprised at all. You'll read them and feel like you already know them.

- **Article 100—Definitions.** Part I of Article 100 contains the definitions of terms used throughout the *Code* for systems that operate at 1,000V, nominal, or less. The definitions of terms in Part II apply to systems that operate at over 1,000V, nominal.

    Definitions of standard terms, such as volt, voltage drop, ampere, impedance, and resistance, aren't listed in Article 100. If the *NEC* doesn't define a term, then a dictionary suitable to the authority having jurisdiction should be consulted. A building code glossary might provide better definitions than a dictionary found at your home or school.

    Definitions located at the beginning of an article apply only to that specific article. For example, the definition of a "Pool" is contained in 680.2, because this term applies only to the requirements contained in Article 680—Swimming Pools, Fountains, and Similar Installations. As soon as a defined term is used in two or more articles, its definition should be included in Article 100.

- **Article 110—Requirements for Electrical Installations.** This article contains general requirements for electrical installations for the following:
    - Part I. General
    - Part II. 1,000V, Nominal, or Less

Notes

ARTICLE 100 DEFINITIONS

Introduction to Article 100—Definitions

Have you ever had a conversation with someone, only to discover that what you said and what he or she heard were completely different? This often happens when people in a conversation have different definitions for the words being used, and that's why the definitions of key terms are located right at the beginning of the *NEC* (Article 100), or at the beginning of each article. If we can all agree on important definitions, then we speak the same language and avoid misunderstandings. Because the *Code* exists to protect people and property, it's very important to know the definitions presented in Article 100.

Here are a few tips for learning the many definitions in the *NEC*:

- **Break the task down.** Study a few words at a time, rather than trying to learn them all at one sitting.
- **Review the graphics in the textbook.** These will help you see how terms are applied.
- **Relate the definitions to your work.** As you read a word, think about how it applies to the work you're doing. This will provide a natural reinforcement to the learning process.

Part I. General

100 Definitions

Scope. This article contains definitions essential to the application of this *Code*; it doesn't include general terms or technical terms from other codes and standards. In general, only those terms that are used in two or more articles are defined in Article 100.

Accessible (as it applies to wiring methods). Not permanently closed in by the building structure or finish and capable of being removed or exposed without damaging the building structure or finish. ▶Figure 100–1

Accessible, Readily (Readily Accessible). Capable of being reached quickly for operation, renewal or inspections without requiring those to whom ready access is requisite to take actions such as the use tools (other than keys), to climb over or under, remove obstacles, or resort to portable ladders, and so forth. ▶Figure 100–2

Note: Use of keys is a common practice under controlled or supervised conditions.

▶Figure 100–1

Adjustable Speed Drive. A piece of equipment that provides a way to adjust the speed of an electric motor.

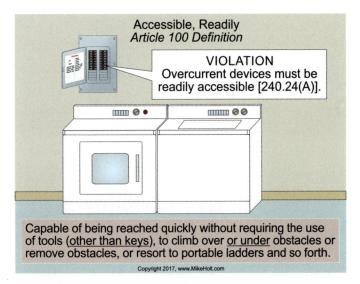

▶Figure 100–2

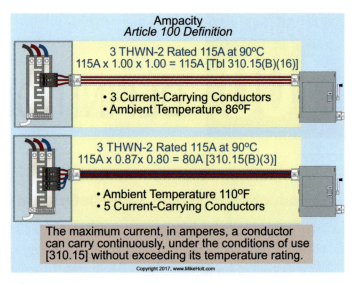

▶Figure 100–3

Author's Comment:

- Adjustable-speed drives are often referred to as "variable-speed drives" or "variable-frequency drives (VFDs)."

Note: A variable frequency drive is one type of electronic adjustable speed drive that controls the speed of an alternating-current motor by changing the frequency and voltage of the motor's power supply.

Ampacity. The maximum current, in amperes, a conductor can carry continuously, under the conditions of use without exceeding its temperature rating.

Author's Comment:

- See 310.10 and 310.15 for details and examples. ▶Figure 100–3

Approved. Acceptable to the authority having jurisdiction, usually the electrical inspector. ▶Figure 100–4

Author's Comment:

- Product listing doesn't mean the product is approved, but it can be a basis for approval. See 90.4, 90.7, 110.2, and the definitions in this article for "Authority Having Jurisdiction," "Identified," "Labeled," and "Listed."

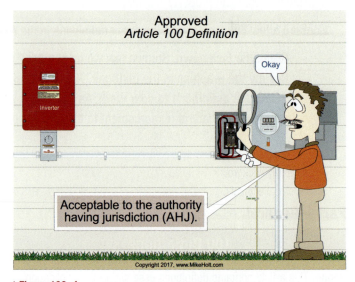

▶Figure 100–4

Attachment Plug (Plug Cap), (Plug) [Article 406]. A wiring device at the end of a flexible cord intended to be inserted into a receptacle in order to make an electrical connection. ▶Figure 100–5

Authority Having Jurisdiction (AHJ). The organization, office, or individual responsible for approving equipment, materials, an installation, or a procedure. See 90.4 and 90.7 for more information.

Note: The authority having jurisdiction may be a federal, state, or local government department or an individual, such as a fire chief, fire marshal, chief of a fire prevention bureau or labor department or health department, a building official or electrical inspector, or others having statutory authority. In some circumstances, the property owner or his/her agent assumes the role, and at government installations, the commanding officer, or departmental official may be the authority having jurisdiction.

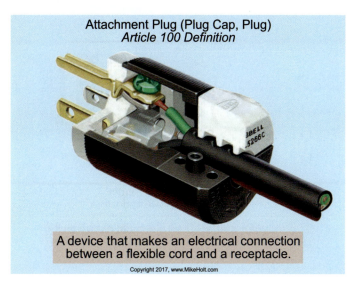
▶Figure 100–5

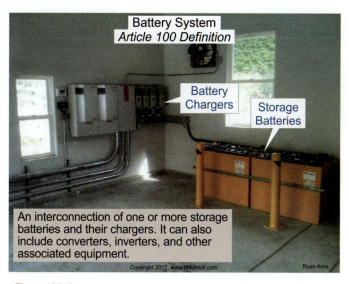
▶Figure 100–6

Author's Comment:

- Typically, the authority having jurisdiction is the electrical inspector who has legal statutory authority. In the absence of federal, state, or local regulations, the operator of the facility or his or her agent, such as an architect or engineer of the facility, can assume the role.

- Some believe the authority having jurisdiction should have a strong background in the electrical field, such as having studied electrical engineering or having obtained an electrical contractor's license, and in a few states this is a legal requirement. Memberships, certifications, and active participation in electrical organizations, such as the International Association of Electrical Inspectors (IAEI), speak to an individual's qualifications. Visit www.IAEI.org for more information about that organization.

Automatic. Functioning without the necessity of human intervention.

Battery System. An interconnection of one or more storage batteries and their chargers. It can also include converters, inverters, and other associated equipment. ▶Figure 100–6

Bonded (Bonding). Connected to establish electrical continuity and conductivity. ▶Figure 100–7

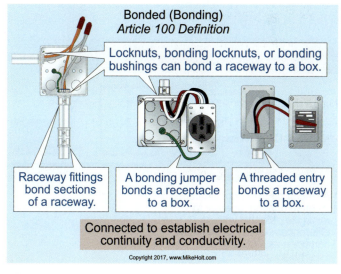
▶Figure 100–7

Author's Comment:

- The purpose of bonding is to connect two or more conductive objects together to ensure the electrical continuity of the ground-fault current path, provide the capacity and ability to conduct safely any fault current likely to be imposed, and to minimize voltage between conductive components. ▶Figure 100–8 and ▶Figure 100–9

100 | Definitions

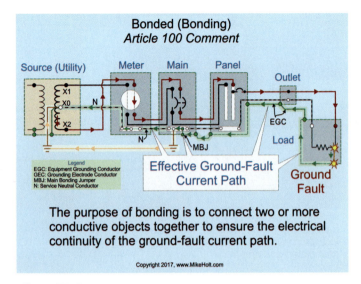
▶Figure 100–8

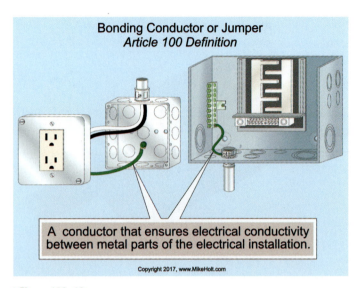
▶Figure 100–10

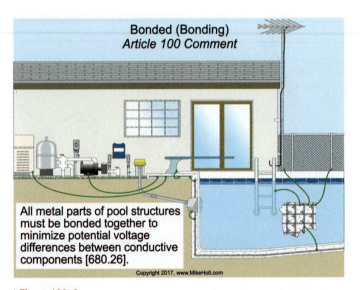
▶Figure 100–9

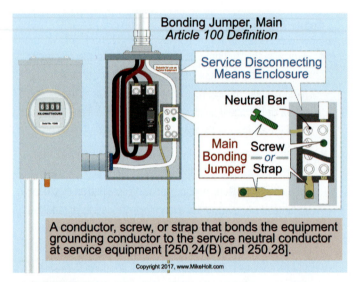
▶Figure 100–11

Bonding Conductor or Jumper. A conductor that ensures electrical conductivity between metal parts of the electrical installation. ▶Figure 100–10

Bonding Jumper, Main. A conductor, screw, or strap that connects the circuit equipment grounding conductor to the neutral conductor at service equipment in accordance with 250.24(B) [250.24(A)(4), 250.28, and 408.3(C)]. ▶Figure 100–11

Bonding Jumper, System. The connection between the neutral conductor and the supply-side bonding jumper or equipment grounding conductor, or both, at a separately derived system transformer or separately derived system generator. ▶Figure 100–12 and ▶Figure 100–13

Branch Circuit [Article 210]. The conductors between the final overcurrent protection device and the receptacle outlets, lighting outlets, or other outlets as defined in this article. ▶Figure 100–14

Definitions | 100

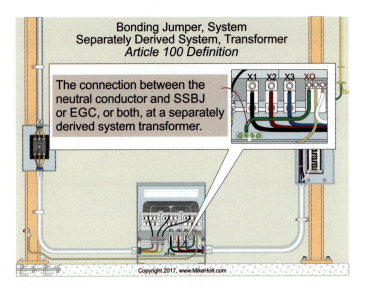
▶Figure 100–12

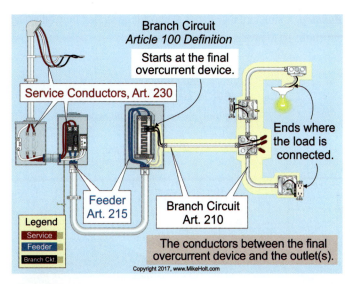
▶Figure 100–14

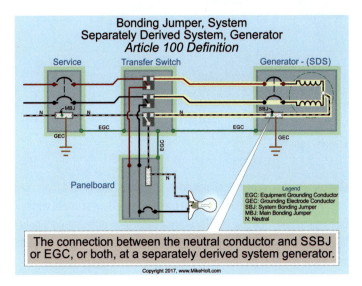
▶Figure 100–13

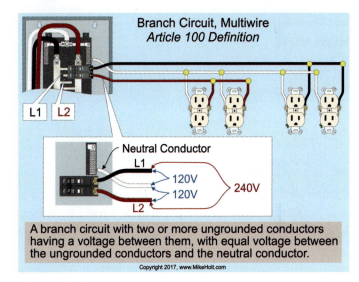
▶Figure 100–15

Branch Circuit, Individual. A branch circuit that only supplies one load.

Branch Circuit, Multiwire. A branch circuit that consists of two or more ungrounded circuit conductors with a common neutral conductor. There must be a voltage between the ungrounded conductors and an equal difference of voltage from each ungrounded conductor to the common neutral conductor. ▶Figure 100–15

Author's Comment:

- Multiwire branch circuits offer the advantage of fewer conductors within a raceway, smaller raceway sizing, and a reduction of material and labor costs. In addition, multiwire branch circuits can reduce circuit voltage drop by as much as 50 percent. However, because of the dangers associated with multiwire branch circuits, the *NEC* contains additional requirements to ensure a safe installation. See 210.4, 300.13(B), and 408.41 in this textbook for details.

100 | Definitions

Building. A structure that stands alone or is separated from adjoining structures by fire walls. ▶Figure 100–16

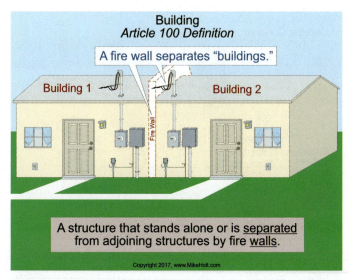

▶Figure 100–16

Author's Comment:

- A cable routing assembly is typically a "U" shaped trough, with or without covers, designed to hold cables, and it isn't a raceway.

Cabinet [Article 312]. An enclosure for either surface mounting or flush mounting provided with a frame in which a door can be hung. ▶Figure 100–17

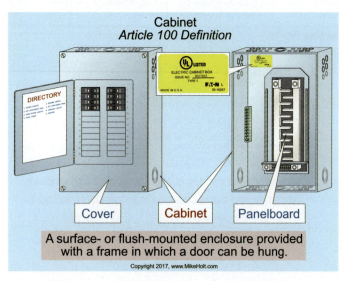

▶Figure 100–17

Author's Comment:

- Cabinets are used to enclose panelboards. See the definition of "Panelboard" in this article.

Charge Controller. Equipment that controls dc voltage or dc current, or both, and is used to charge a battery or other energy storage device. ▶Figure 100–18

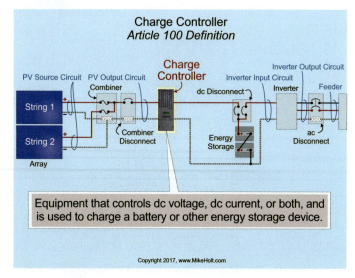

▶Figure 100–18

Circuit Breaker. A device designed to be opened and closed manually, and which opens automatically on a predetermined overcurrent without damage to itself. Circuit breakers are available in different configurations, such as inverse time, adjustable trip (electronically controlled), and instantaneous trip/motor-circuit protectors. ▶Figure 100–19

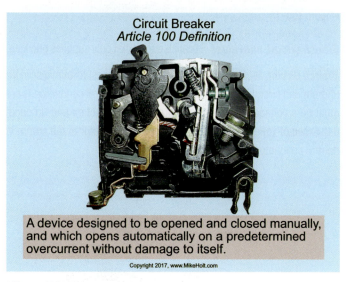

▶Figure 100–19

Circuit Breaker, Inverse Time. Inverse time breakers operate on the principle that as the current increases, the time it takes for the devices to open decreases. This type of breaker provides overcurrent protection (overload, short circuit, and ground fault). This is the most common type of circuit breaker that you'll buy over-the-counter.

Circuit Breaker, Adjustable Trip. Adjustable trip breakers permit the thermal trip setting to be adjusted. The adjustment is often necessary to coordinate the operation of the circuit breakers with other overcurrent protection devices.

Author's Comment:

- Coordination means that the devices with the lowest ratings, closest to the fault, operate and isolate the fault and minimize disruption so the rest of the system can remain energized and functional. This sounds simple, but large systems (especially emergency systems) may require an expensive engineering study. If you're responsible for bidding a project, be aware of this requirement.

Circuit Breaker, Instantaneous Trip. Instantaneous trip breakers operate on the principle of electromagnetism only and are used for motors. Sometimes these devices are called motor-circuit protectors. This type of overcurrent protection device doesn't provide overload protection. It only provides short-circuit and ground-fault protection; overload protection must be provided separately.

Author's Comment:

- Instantaneous trip circuit breakers have no intentional time delay and are sensitive to current inrush, and to vibration and shock. Consequently, they shouldn't be used where these factors are known to exist.

Clothes Closet. A nonhabitable room or space intended primarily for the storage of garments and apparel. ▶Figure 100–20

Author's Comment:

- The definition of "Clothes Closet" provides clarification in the application of overcurrent protection devices [240.24(D)] and luminaires [410.16] in clothes closets.

Concealed. Rendered inaccessible by the structure or finish of the building.

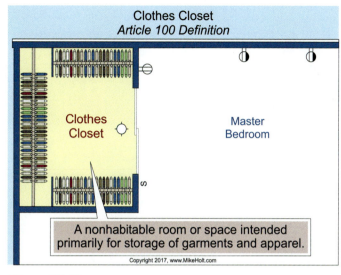

▶Figure 100–20

Note: Conductors in a concealed raceway are considered concealed, even though they may be made accessible by withdrawing them from the raceway.
▶Figure 100–21

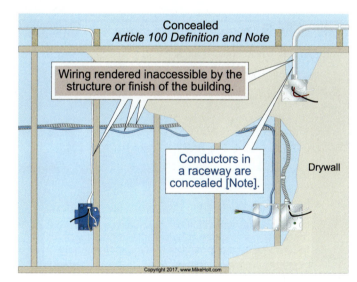

▶Figure 100–21

Author's Comment:

- Wiring behind panels designed to allow access, such as removable ceiling tile, is considered exposed.

Conduit Body. A fitting that's installed in a conduit or tubing system and provides access to conductors through a removable cover. ▶Figure 100–22

100 | Definitions

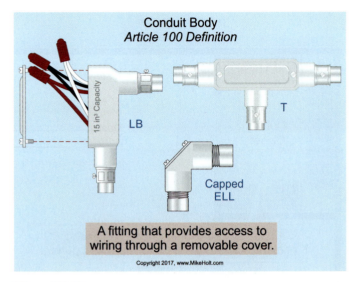
▶Figure 100–22

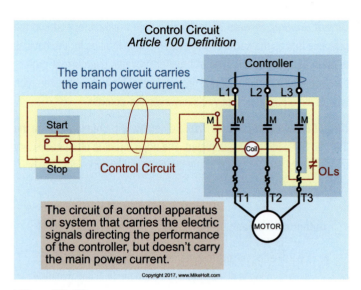
▶Figure 100–24

Connector, Pressure (Solderless). A device that establishes a conductive connection between conductors or between a conductor and a terminal by the means of mechanical pressure. ▶Figure 100–23

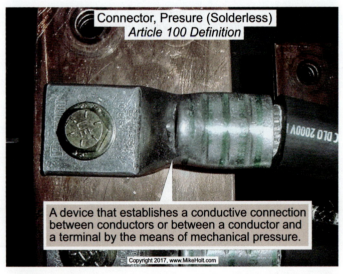
▶Figure 100–23

Continuous Load. A load where the maximum current is expected to exist for 3 hours or more continuously, such as store or parking lot lighting.

Control Circuit. The circuit of a control apparatus or system that carries the electric signals directing the performance of the controller but doesn't carry the main power current. ▶Figure 100–24

Device. A component of an electrical installation, other than a conductor, intended to carry or control electric energy as its principal function. ▶Figure 100–25

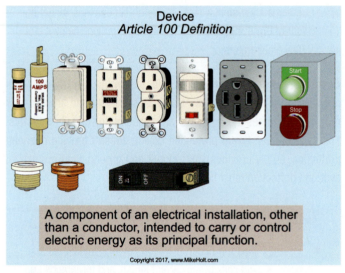
▶Figure 100–25

Author's Comment:

- Devices include receptacles, switches, illuminated switches, circuit breakers, fuses, time clocks, controllers, and so forth, but not locknuts or other mechanical fittings. A device may consume very small amounts of energy, such as an illuminated switch, but still be classified as a device based on its principal function.

Disconnecting Means. A device that opens all of the ungrounded circuit conductors from their power source. This includes devices such as switches, attachment plugs and receptacles, and circuit breakers. ▶Figure 100–26

Definitions | 100

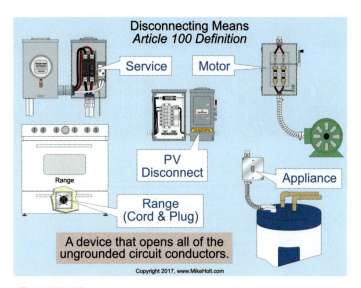

▶Figure 100–26

Dwelling Unit. A space that provides independent living facilities, with space for eating, living, and sleeping; as well as permanent facilities for cooking and sanitation. ▶Figure 100–27

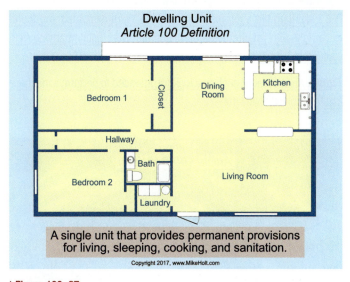

▶Figure 100–27

Effective Ground-Fault Current Path. An intentionally constructed low-impedance conductive path designed to carry fault current from the point of a ground fault to the source for the purpose of opening the circuit overcurrent protective device. ▶Figure 100–28

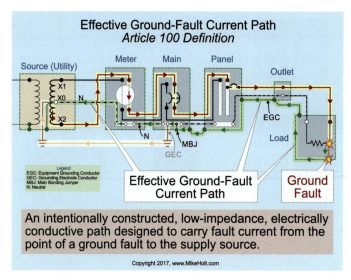

▶Figure 100–28

Author's Comment:

- In the preceding Figure, "EGC" represents the equipment grounding conductor [250.118], "MBJ" represents the main bonding jumper, "N" represents the service neutral conductor (grounded service conductor), and "GEC" represents the grounding electrode conductor.
- The current path shown between the supply source grounding electrode and the grounding electrode at the service main shows that some current will flow through the earth but the earth isn't part of the effective ground-fault current path.
- The effective ground-fault current path is intended to help remove dangerous voltage from a ground fault by opening the circuit overcurrent protection device.

Enclosed. Surrounded by a case, housing, fence, or wall(s) that prevents accidental contact with energized parts.

Energized. Electrically connected to a source of voltage.

Equipment. A general term including fittings, devices, appliances, luminaires, machinery, and the like as part of, or in connection with, an electrical installation. ▶Figure 100–29

Exposed (as applied to live parts). Capable of being accidentally touched or approached to an unsafe distance.

Note: This term applies to parts that aren't suitably guarded, isolated, or insulated for the condition.

100 | Definitions

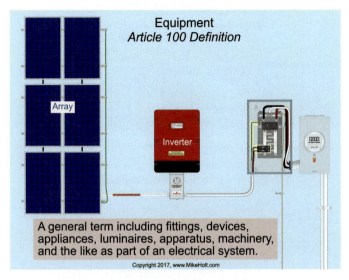
▶Figure 100–29

Exposed (as applied to wiring methods). On or attached to the surface of a building, or behind panels designed to allow access. ▶Figure 100–30

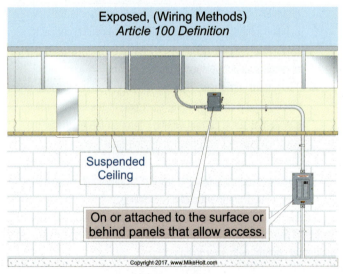
▶Figure 100–30

Feeder [Article 215]. The conductors between the service equipment, a separately derived system, or other power supply and the final branch-circuit overcurrent protection device. ▶Figure 100–31

Author's Comment:

- An "other power source" includes a solar PV system or conductors from a generator.

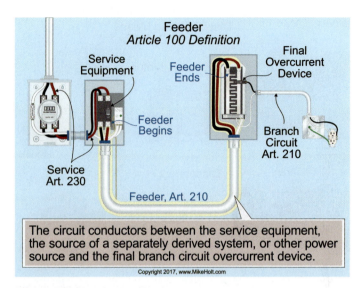
▶Figure 100–31

Field Evaluation Body (FEB). An organization or part of an organization that performs field evaluations of electrical or other equipment.

Field Labeled (as applied to evaluated products). Equipment or materials which have a label, symbol, or other identifying mark of an FEB indicating the equipment or materials were evaluated and found to comply with requirements as described in an accompanying field evaluation report.

Fitting. An accessory, such as a locknut, intended to perform a mechanical function. ▶Figure 100–32

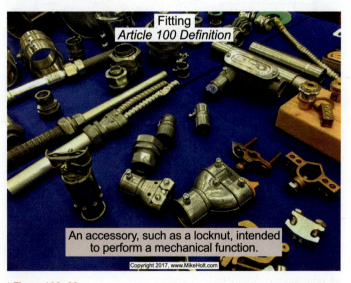
▶Figure 100–32

Definitions | 100

Ground. The earth. ▶Figure 100–33

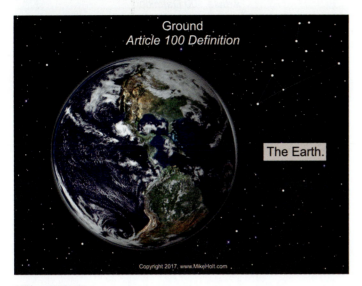

▶Figure 100–33

Ground Fault. An unintentional electrical connection between an ungrounded conductor and the metal parts of enclosures, raceways, or equipment. ▶Figure 100–34

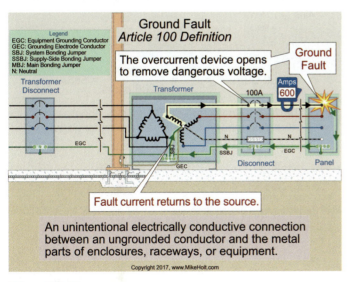

▶Figure 100–34

Ground-Fault Protection of Equipment. A system intended to provide protection of equipment from damaging ground-fault currents by opening all ungrounded conductors of the faulted circuit. This protection is provided at current levels less than those required to protect conductors from damage through the operation of a supply circuit overcurrent device [215.10, 230.95, and 240.13].

Author's Comment:

- This type of protective device isn't intended to protect people and trips at a higher level than required for "Class A" GFCIs. This type of device is typically referred to as ground-fault protection for equipment, or GFPE, but should never be called a GFCI.

Grounded (Grounding). Connected to ground or to a conductive body that extends the ground connection. ▶Figure 100–35

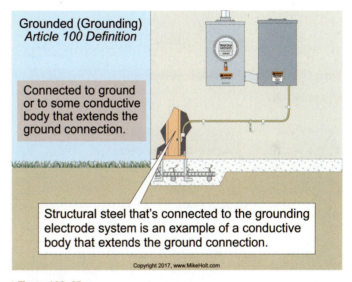

▶Figure 100–35

Author's Comment:

- An example of a "body that extends the ground (earth) connection" is the termination to structural steel that's connected to the earth either directly or by the termination to another grounding electrode in accordance with 250.52.

Grounded System, Solidly. A power-supply system connected to ground (earth) without inserting any resistor or impedance device between the system and ground. ▶Figure 100–36

Grounded Conductor [Article 200]. The system or circuit conductor that's intentionally grounded (connected to the earth). ▶Figure 100–37

Grounding Conductor, Equipment (EGC). The conductive path(s) that provides a ground-fault current path and connects metal parts of equipment to the system neutral conductor, to the grounding electrode conductor, or both [250.110 through 250.126]. ▶Figure 100–38

Note 1: The circuit equipment grounding conductor also performs bonding.

100 | Definitions

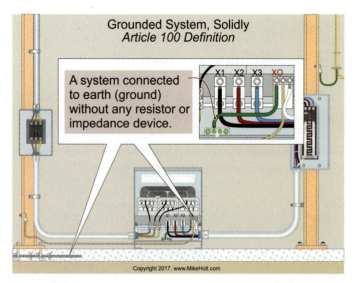
▶Figure 100–36

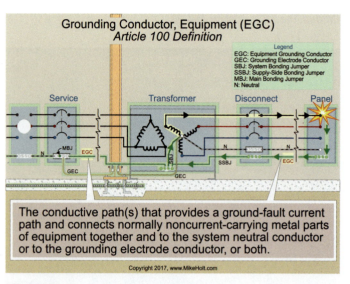
▶Figure 100–38

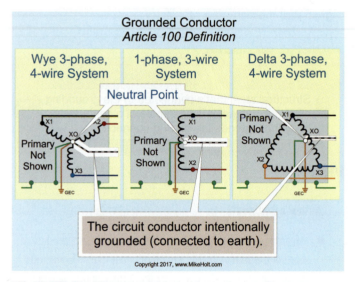
▶Figure 100–37

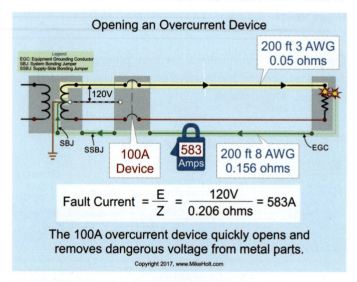
▶Figure 100–39

Author's Comment:

- To quickly remove dangerous touch voltage on metal parts from a ground fault, the equipment grounding conductor must be connected to the system neutral conductor at the source, and have low enough impedance so fault current will quickly rise to a level that will open the circuit's overcurrent protection device [250.2 and 250.4(A)(3)]. ▶Figure 100–39

Note 2: An equipment grounding conductor can be any one or a combination of the types listed in 250.118. ▶Figure 100–40

Definitions | 100

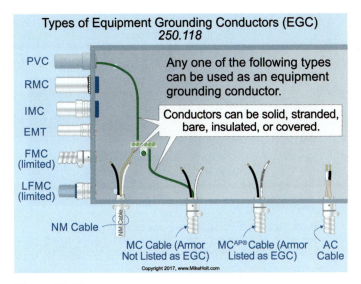
▶Figure 100–40

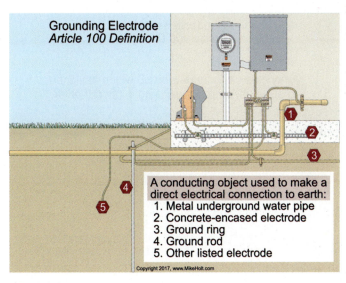
▶Figure 100–41

Author's Comment:

- Equipment grounding conductors include:
    ♦ A bare or insulated conductor
    ♦ Rigid Metal Conduit
    ♦ Intermediate Metal Conduit
    ♦ Electrical Metallic Tubing
    ♦ Listed Flexible Metal Conduit as limited by 250.118(5)
    ♦ Listed Liquidtight Flexible Metal Conduit as limited by 250.118(6)
    ♦ Armored Cable
    ♦ The copper metal sheath of Mineral-Insulated Cable
    ♦ Metal-Clad Cable as limited by 250.118(10)
    ♦ Metal cable trays as limited by 250.118(11) and 392.60
    ♦ Electrically continuous metal raceways listed for grounding
    ♦ Surface Metal Raceways listed for grounding

Grounding Electrode. A conducting object used to make a direct electrical connection to the earth [250.50 through 250.70]. ▶Figure 100–41

Grounding Electrode Conductor (GEC). The conductor used to connect the system neutral conductor or the equipment to the grounding electrode system. ▶Figure 100–42

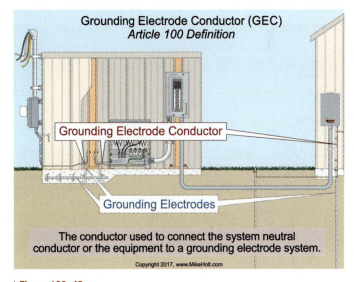
▶Figure 100–42

Handhole Enclosure. An enclosure for underground system use sized to allow personnel to reach into it for the purpose of installing or maintaining equipment or wiring. It may have an open or closed bottom. ▶Figure 100–43

Author's Comment:

- See 314.30 for the installation requirements for handhole enclosures.

100 | Definitions

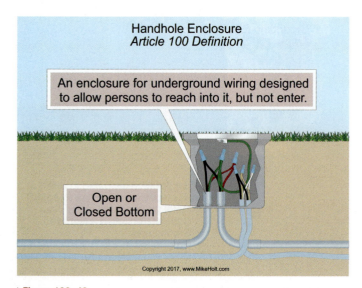

▶Figure 100–43

▶Figure 100–45

Hybrid System. A system comprised of multiple electric power sources, such as photovoltaic, wind, micro-hydro generators, engine-driven generators, and others, but not the electric utility power system. ▶Figure 100–44

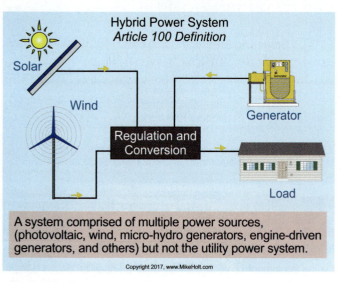

▶Figure 100–44

Identified Equipment. Recognized as suitable for a specific purpose, function, or environment by listing, labeling, or other means approved by the authority having jurisdiction. ▶Figure 100–45

Author's Comment:

- See 90.4, 90.7, 110.3(A)(1), and the definitions for "Approved," "Labeled," and "Listed" in this article.

In Sight From (Within Sight). Visible and not more than 50 ft away from the equipment. ▶Figure 100–46

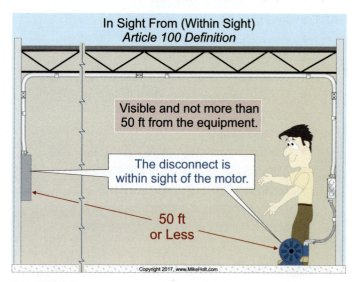

▶Figure 100–46

Interactive Inverter. An inverter is used in parallel with an electric utility to supply common loads. ▶Figure 100–47

Interrupting Rating. The highest short-circuit current at rated voltage the device is identified to interrupt under standard test conditions.

Author's Comment:

- For more information, see 110.9 in this textbook.

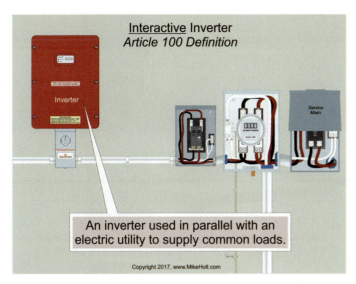

▶Figure 100–47

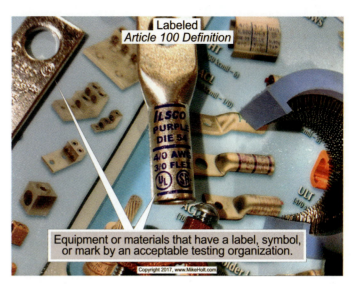

▶Figure 100–49

Intersystem Bonding Termination. A device that provides a means to connect intersystem bonding conductors for communications systems (twisted wire, antennas, and coaxial cable) to the grounding electrode system, in accordance with 250.94. ▶Figure 100–48

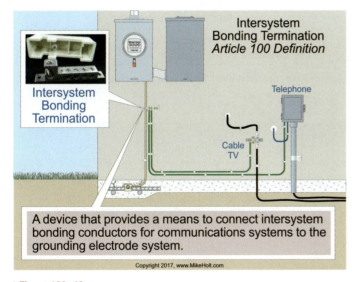

▶Figure 100–48

Isolated. Not readily accessible to persons unless special means for access are used.

Labeled. Equipment or materials that have a label, symbol, or other identifying mark in the form of a sticker, decal, printed label, or with the identifying mark molded or stamped into the product by a testing laboratory acceptable to the authority having jurisdiction. ▶Figure 100–49

Author's Comment:

- Labeling and listing of equipment typically provides the basis for equipment approval by the authority having jurisdiction [90.4, 90.7, 110.2, and 110.3].

Listed. Equipment or materials included in a list published by a testing laboratory acceptable to the authority having jurisdiction. The listing organization must periodically inspect the production of listed equipment or material to ensure the equipment or material meets appropriate designated standards and is suitable for a specified purpose.

Author's Comment:

- The *NEC* doesn't require all electrical equipment to be listed, but some *Code* requirements do specifically require product listing. Organizations such as OSHA increasingly require that listed equipment be used when such equipment is available [90.7, 110.2, and 110.3].

Location, Damp. Locations protected from weather and not subject to saturation with water or other liquids.

Note: This includes locations partially protected under canopies, marquees, roofed open porches, and interior locations subject to moderate degrees of moisture, such as some basements, barns, and cold-storage warehouses. ▶Figure 100–50

Location, Dry. An area not normally subjected to dampness or wetness, but which may temporarily be subjected to dampness or wetness, such as a building under construction.

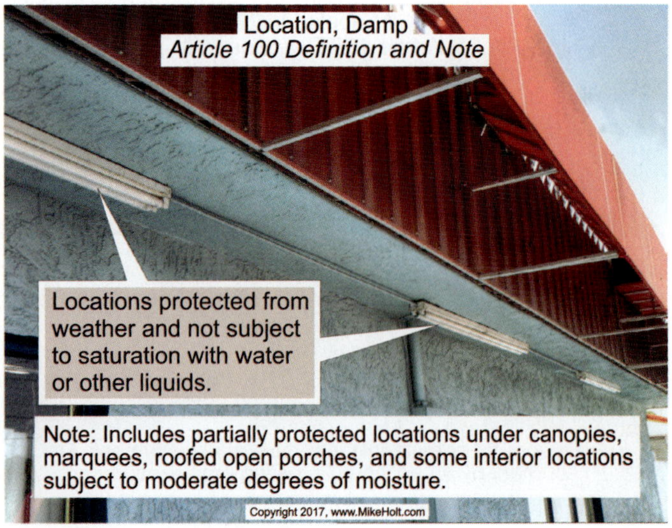

100 | Definitions

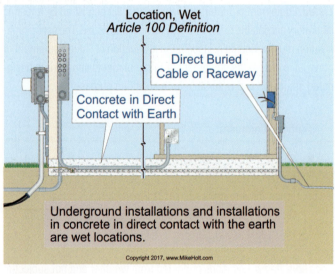
▶Figure 100–50

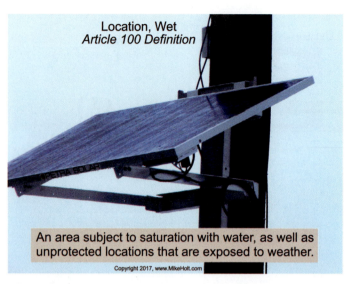
▶Figure 100–52

Location, Wet. An installation underground, in concrete slabs in direct contact with the earth, as well as locations subject to saturation with water, and unprotected locations exposed to weather. ▶Figure 100–51 and ▶Figure 100–52

Neutral Conductor. The conductor connected to the neutral point of a system that's intended to carry current under normal conditions. ▶Figure 100–53

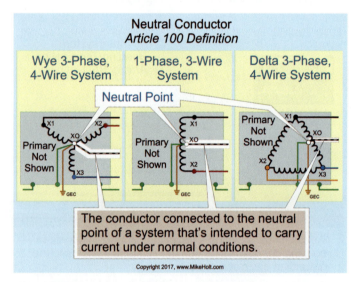
▶Figure 100–51

▶Figure 100–53

Author's Comment:

- The interior of a raceway installed in wet locations is considered a wet location, and the conductors used must be suitable for wet locations [300.5(B) and 300.9].

Author's Comment:

- The neutral conductor of a solidly grounded system is required to be grounded (connected to the earth), therefore this conductor is also called a "grounded conductor."

Neutral Point. The common point of a 4-wire, three-phase, wye-connected system; the midpoint of a 3-wire, single-phase system; or the midpoint of the single-phase portion of a three-phase, delta-connected system. ▶Figure 100–54

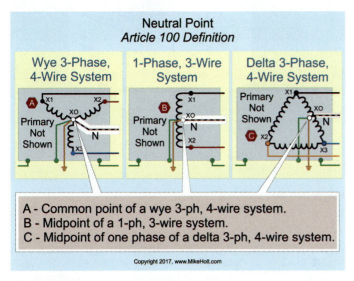

▶Figure 100–54

Nonautomatic. Requiring human intervention to perform a function.

Outlet. A point in the wiring system where electric current is taken to supply a load (utilization equipment). This includes receptacle outlets and lighting outlets, as well as outlets for ceiling paddle fans and smoke alarms. ▶Figure 100–55

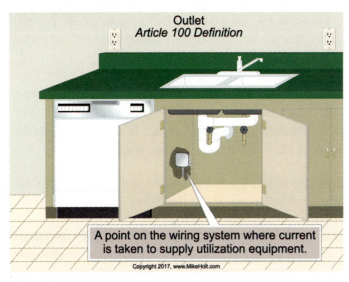

▶Figure 100–55

Overcurrent. Current, in amperes, greater than the rated current of the equipment or conductors resulting from an overload, short circuit, or ground fault. ▶Figure 100–56

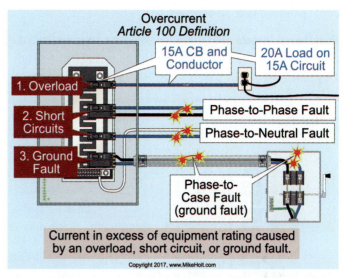

▶Figure 100–56

Overcurrent Protective Device, Supplementary. A device intended to provide limited overcurrent protection for specific applications and utilization equipment, such as luminaires and appliances. This limited overcurrent protection is in addition to the required overcurrent protection provided in the branch circuit by the branch-circuit overcurrent protection device. ▶Figure 100–57

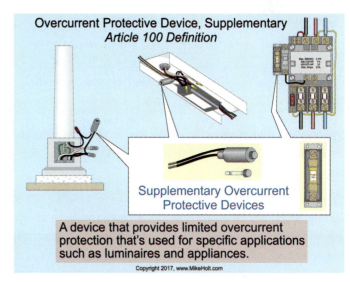

▶Figure 100–57

100 | Definitions

Overload. The operation of equipment above its current rating, or current in excess of conductor ampacity. When an overload condition persists for a sufficient length of time, it can result in equipment failure or in a fire from damaging or dangerous overheating. A fault, such as a short circuit or ground fault, isn't an overload.

Panelboard [Article 408]. A distribution point containing overcurrent protection devices and designed to be installed in a cabinet.
▶ Figure 100–58

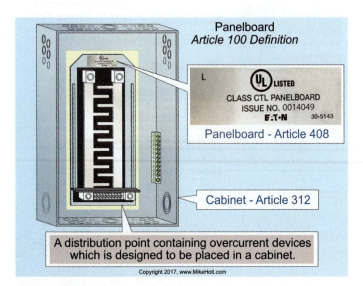

▶ Figure 100–58

Author's Comment:

- See the definition of "Cabinet" in this article.
- The slang term in the electrical field for a panelboard is "the guts." This is the interior of the panelboard assembly and is covered by Article 408, while the cabinet is covered by Article 312.

Photovoltaic (PV) System. The combination of all components and subsystems that convert solar energy into electric energy for utilization loads. ▶ Figure 100–59

Premises Wiring. The interior and exterior wiring, including power, lighting, control, and signal circuits, and all associated hardware, fittings, and wiring devices. This includes both permanently and temporarily installed wiring from the service point to the outlets, or where there's no service point, wiring from and including the electric power source, such as a generator, transformer, or PV system to the outlets. ▶ Figure 100–60

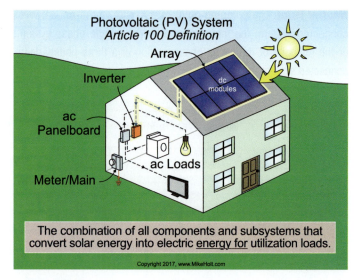

▶ Figure 100–59

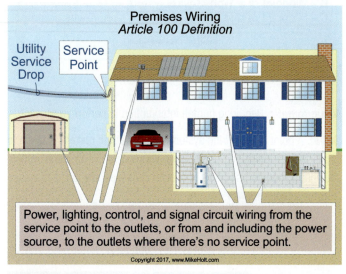

▶ Figure 100–60

Premises wiring doesn't include the internal wiring of electrical equipment and appliances, such as luminaires, dishwashers, water heaters, motors, controllers, motor control centers, air-conditioning equipment, and so on [90.7 and 300.1(B)]. ▶ Figure 100–61

Note: Electric power sources include, but aren't limited to, interconnected or stand-alone batteries, PV systems, other distributed generation systems, or generators.

Qualified Person. A person who has the skill and knowledge related to the construction and operation of electrical equipment and its installation. This person must have received safety training to recognize and avoid the hazards involved with electrical systems. ▶ Figure 100–62

Definitions | 100

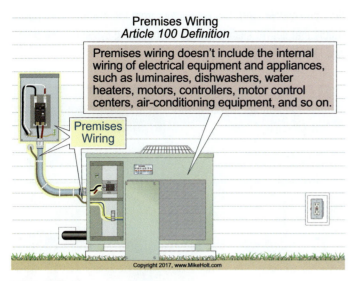

▶Figure 100–61

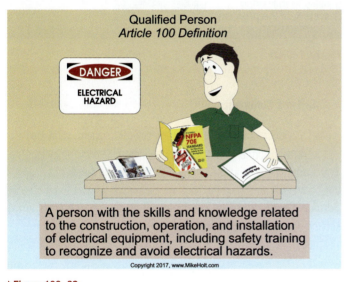

▶Figure 100–62

Note: NFPA 70E, *Standard for Electrical Safety in the Workplace*, provides information on safety training requirements expected of a "qualified person."

Author's Comment:

- Examples of this safety training include, but aren't limited to, training in the use of special precautionary techniques, personal protective equipment (PPE), insulating and shielding materials, and in the use of insulated tools and test equipment when working on or near exposed conductors or circuit parts that can become energized.

- In many parts of the United States, electricians, electrical contractors, electrical inspectors, and electrical engineers must complete from 6 to 24 hours of *NEC* review each year as a requirement to maintain licensing. This in itself doesn't make one qualified to deal with the specific hazards involved with electrical systems.

Raceway. An enclosed channel designed for the installation of conductors, cables, or busbars.

Author's Comment:

- A cable tray system isn't a raceway; it's a support system for cables and raceways [392.2].

Rainproof. Constructed, protected, or treated to prevent rain from interfering with the successful operation of the apparatus under specified test conditions.

Raintight. A raintight enclosure is constructed or protected so that exposure to a beating rain won't result in the entrance of water under specified test conditions.

Separately Derived System. An electrical source, other than a service, having no direct connection(s) to circuit conductors of any other electrical source other than those established by grounding and bonding connections. ▶Figure 100–63 and ▶Figure 100–64

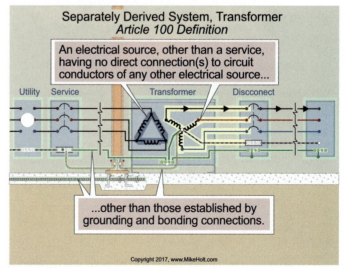

▶Figure 100–63

100 | Definitions

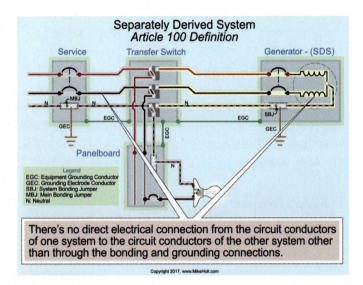

▶Figure 100–64

Author's Comment:

- An alternate alternating-current power source such as an on-site generator isn't a separately derived system if the neutral conductor is solidly interconnected to a service-supplied system neutral conductor. An example is a generator provided with a transfer switch that includes a neutral conductor that's not switched. ▶Figure 100–65

- Separately derived systems are actually much more complicated than the above definition suggests, and understanding them requires additional study. For more information, see 250.30.

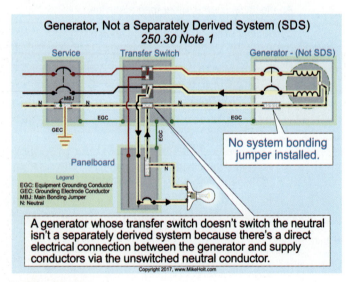

▶Figure 100–65

Service [Article 230]. The conductors from the electric utility power supply that deliver electric energy to the wiring system of the premises. ▶Figure 100–66

▶Figure 100–66

Author's Comment:

- Conductors from a UPS system, solar PV system, generator, or transformer aren't service conductors. See the definitions of "Feeder" and "Service Conductors" in this article.

Service Conductors. The conductors from the service point to the service disconnect. ▶Figure 100–67

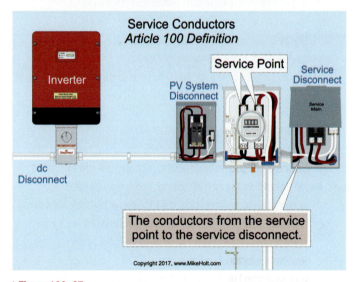

▶Figure 100–67

Author's Comment:

- These conductors fall within the requirements of Article 230, since they're owned by the customer.

Service Conductors, Overhead. Overhead conductors between the service point and the first point of connection to the service-entrance conductors at the building. ▶Figure 100–68

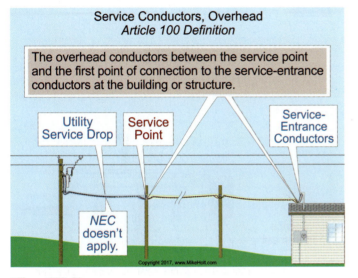

▶Figure 100–68

Author's Comment:

- Service conductors fall within the requirements of Article 230, since they aren't under the exclusive control of the electric utility.

- Service conductors can include overhead service conductors, overhead service entrance-conductors, and underground service conductors. Service conductors don't include service lateral conductors, which fall within the scope of the electric utility, not the *NEC*.

Service Conductors, Underground. Underground conductors between the service point and the first point of connection to the service-entrance conductors in a terminal box, meter, or other enclosure, inside or outside the building wall. ▶Figure 100–69

Author's Comment:

- Service conductors fall within the requirements of Article 230, since they aren't under the exclusive control of the electric utility.

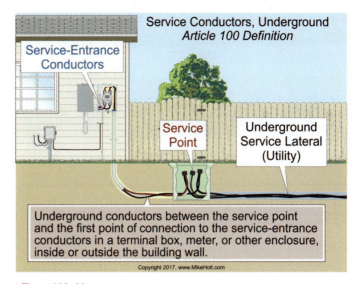

▶Figure 100–69

Note: Where there's no terminal box, meter, or other enclosure, the point of connection is the point of entrance of the service conductors into the building.

Service Drop. Overhead conductors between the electric utility supply and the service point. ▶Figure 100–70

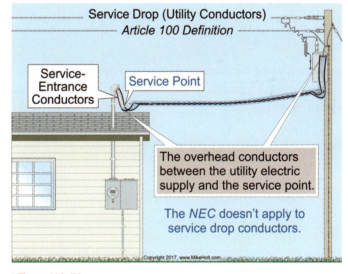

▶Figure 100–70

Author's Comment:

- Service drop conductors don't fall within the requirements of Article 230, since they're under the exclusive control of the electric utility.

100 | Definitions

Service-Entrance Conductors, Overhead System. The conductors between the terminals of service equipment and service drop or overhead service conductors. ▶Figure 100–71

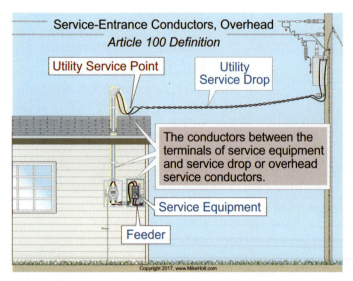

▶Figure 100–71

Author's Comment:

- Overhead service-entrance conductors fall within the requirements of Article 230, since they aren't under the exclusive control of the electric utility.

Service-Entrance Conductors, Underground System. The conductors between the terminals of service equipment and underground service conductors.

Author's Comment:

- Underground service-entrance conductors fall within the requirements of Article 230, since they aren't under the exclusive control of the electric utility.

Service Equipment [Article 230]. Disconnects such as circuit breaker(s) or switch(es) connected to the load end of service conductors, intended to control and cut off the service supply to the buildings or structure. ▶Figure 100–72

Author's Comment:

- It's important to know where a service begins and where it ends in order to properly apply the *NEC* requirements. Sometimes the service ends before the metering equipment. ▶Figure 100–73

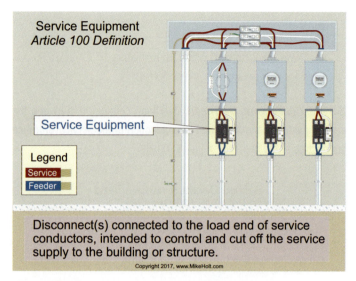

▶Figure 100–72

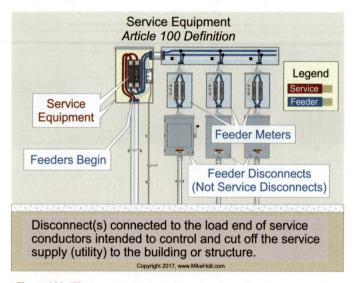

▶Figure 100–73

- Service equipment is often referred to as the "service disconnect" or "service disconnecting means."

Service Lateral. Underground electric utility conductors from the electric utility supply to the service point. ▶Figure 100–74

Author's Comment:

- These conductors don't fall within the requirements of Article 230, since they're under the exclusive control of the electric utility.

Service Point [Article 230]. The point where the electric utility conductors make contact with premises wiring. ▶Figure 100–75

Definitions | 100

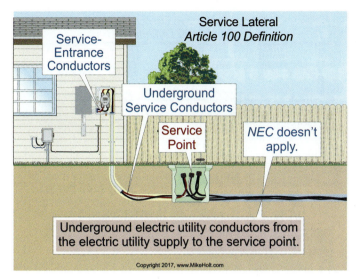
▶Figure 100–74

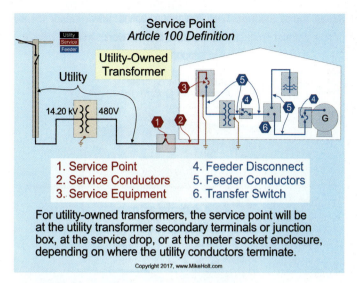
▶Figure 100–76

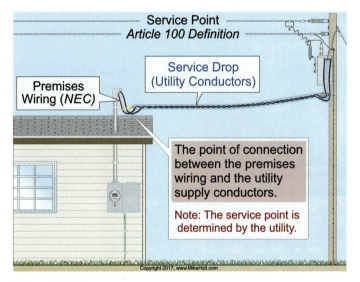
▶Figure 100–75

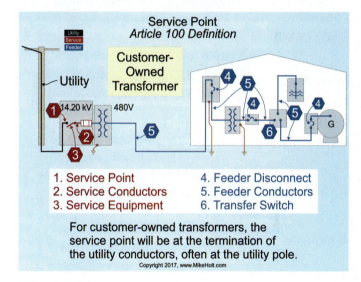
▶Figure 100–77

Note: The service point is the point where the serving electric utility ends and the premises wiring begins.

Author's Comment:

- For utility-owned transformers, the service point will be at the electric utility transformer secondary terminals, at the service drop, or the meter socket enclosure, depending on where the electric utility conductors terminate. ▶Figure 100–76
- For customer-owned transformers, the service point will be at the termination of the electric utility conductors, often at the electric utility pole. ▶Figure 100–77

Short-Circuit Current Rating. The prospective symmetrical fault current at a nominal voltage to which electrical equipment can be connected without sustaining damage exceeding defined acceptance criteria.

Special Permission. Written consent from the authority having jurisdiction.

Author's Comment:

- See the definition of "Authority Having Jurisdiction."

100 | Definitions

Stand-Alone System. A system that supplies power independently of an electrical production and distribution network. ▶Figure 100–78

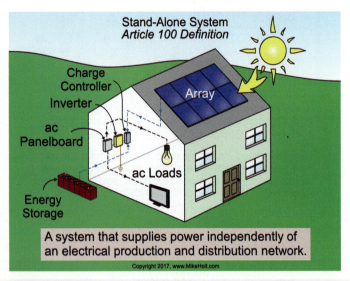
▶Figure 100–78

Structure. That which is built or constructed, other than equipment. ▶Figure 100–79

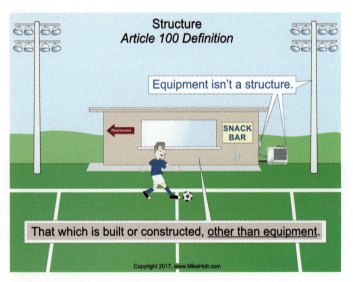
▶Figure 100–79

Surge Protective Device (SPD) [Article 285]. A protective device intended to limit transient voltages by diverting or limiting surge current and preventing the continued flow of current while remaining capable of repeating these functions. ▶Figure 100–80

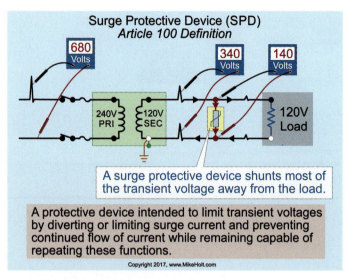
▶Figure 100–80

Type 1. A permanently connected surge protective device listed for installation at or ahead of service equipment. ▶Figure 100–81

▶Figure 100–81

Type 2. A permanently connected surge protective device listed for installation on the load side of the service disconnect. ▶Figure 100–82

Type 3. A surge protective device listed for installation on branch circuits. ▶Figure 100–83

Definitions | 100

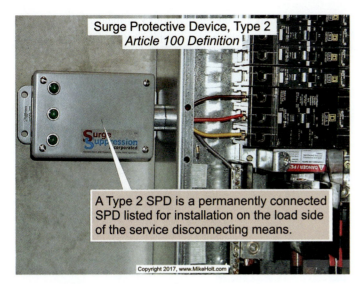

▶Figure 100–82

▶Figure 100–83

Author's Comment:

- Type 3 surge protective devices can be installed anywhere on the load side of branch-circuit overcurrent protection up to the equipment served, provided there's a minimum of 30 ft of conductor length between the connection and the service or separately derived system [285.25].

Type 4. A component surge protective device; this includes those installed in receptacles and relocatable power taps (plug strips).

Note: For further information, see UL 1449, *Standard for Surge Protective Devices.*

Ungrounded System. An electrical power system that's not connected to the ground (earth) or a conductive body that extends the ground (earth) connection. ▶Figure 100–84

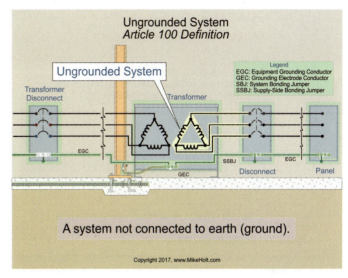

▶Figure 100–84

Utilization Equipment. Equipment that utilizes electricity for electronic, electromechanical, chemical, heating, lighting, or similar purposes.

Voltage (of a circuit). The greatest effective root-mean-square (RMS) difference of voltage between any two conductors of the circuit. ▶Figure 100–85

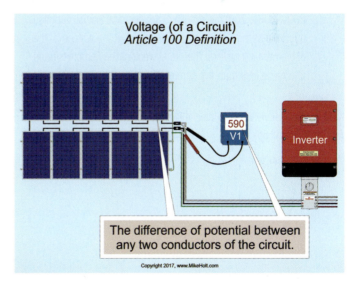

▶Figure 100–85

Mike Holt Enterprises • www.MikeHolt.com • 888.NEC.CODE (632.2633)

100 | Definitions

Voltage, Nominal. A value assigned for conveniently designating voltage classes, such as 120/240V, 120/208V, or 277/480V [220.5(A)].
▶Figure 100–86

Voltage to Ground. The greatest difference of voltage (RMS) between an ungrounded conductor and the neutral point of the circuit that's grounded. ▶Figure 100–87

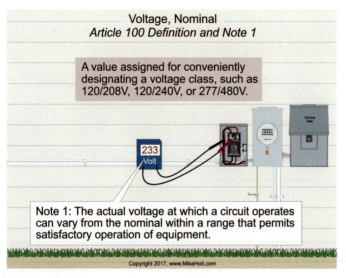

▶Figure 100–86

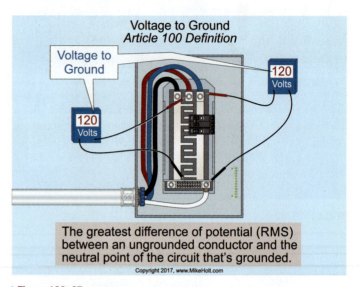

▶Figure 100–87

Note 1: The actual voltage at which a circuit operates can vary from the nominal within a range that permits satisfactory operation of equipment.

Author's Comment:

- Common voltage ratings of electrical equipment are 115V, 200V, 208V, 230V, and 460V. The electrical power supplied might be at the 240V, nominal voltage, but the voltage at the equipment will be less. Therefore, electrical equipment is rated at a value less than the nominal system voltage.

Note 3: Some battery units are rated 48V dc nominal, even if they have a charging float voltage up to 58V dc.

Watertight. Constructed so that moisture won't enter the enclosure under specific test conditions.

Weatherproof. Constructed or protected so that exposure to the weather won't interfere with successful operation.

ARTICLE 110 — REQUIREMENTS FOR ELECTRICAL INSTALLATIONS

Introduction to Article 110—Requirements for Electrical Installations

Article 110 sets the stage for how you'll implement the rest of the *NEC*. This article contains a few of the most important and yet neglected parts of the *Code*. For example:

- How should conductors be terminated?
- What kinds of warnings, markings, and identification does a given installation require?
- What's the right working clearance for a given installation?
- What do the temperature limitations at terminals mean?
- What are the *NEC* requirements for dealing with flash protection?

It's critical that you master Article 110; as you read this article, you're building your foundation for correctly applying the *NEC*. In fact, this article itself is a foundation for much of the *Code*. The purpose for the *National Electrical Code* is to provide a safe installation, but Article 110 is perhaps focused a little more on providing an installation that's safe for the installer and maintenance electrician, so time spent in this article is time well spent.

Part I. General Requirements

110.1 Scope

Article 110 covers the general requirements for the examination and approval, installation and use, access to and spaces about electrical equipment; as well as general requirements for enclosures intended for personnel entry (manholes, vaults, and tunnels).

Note: See Annex J for information regarding ADA accessibility design.

Author's Comment:

- Requirements for people with disabilities include things like mounting heights for switches and receptacles, and requirements for the distance that objects such as wall sconces protrude from a wall.

110.2 Approval of Conductors and Equipment

The authority having jurisdiction must approve all electrical conductors and equipment. ▶Figure 110–1

Author's Comment:

- For a better understanding of product approval, review 90.4, 90.7, 110.3, and the definitions for "Approved," "Identified," "Labeled," and "Listed" in Article 100.

110.3 | Requirements for Electrical Installations

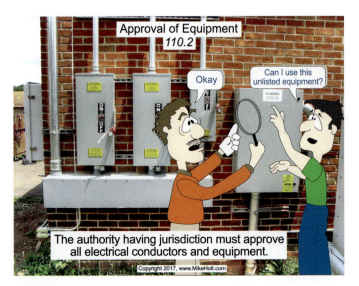

▶Figure 110–1

110.3 Examination, Identification, Installation, Use, and Product Listing (Certification) of Equipment

(A) Guidelines for Approval. The authority having jurisdiction must approve equipment. In doing so, consideration must be given to the following:

(1) Suitability for installation and use in accordance with the *NEC*

Note 1: Equipment may be new, reconditioned, refurbished, or remanufactured.

Note 2: Suitability of equipment use may be identified by a description marked on, or provided with, a product to identify the suitability of the product for a specific purpose, environment, or application. Special conditions of use or other limitations may be marked on the equipment, in the product instructions, or appropriate listing and labeling information. Suitability of equipment may be evidenced by listing or labeling.

(2) Mechanical strength and durability

(3) Wire-bending and connection space

(4) Electrical insulation

(5) Heating effects under all conditions of use

(6) Arcing effects

(7) Classification by type, size, voltage, current capacity, and specific use

(8) Other factors contributing to the practical safeguarding of persons using or in contact with the equipment

(B) Installation and Use. Equipment must be installed and used in accordance with any instructions included in the listing or labeling requirements. ▶Figure 110–2

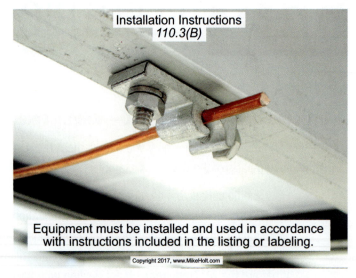

▶Figure 110–2

(C) Product Listing (Certification). Product certification (testing, evaluation, and listing) must be performed by a recognized qualified testing laboratory in accordance with standards that achieve effective safety to comply with the *NEC*.

Note: OSHA recognizes qualified electrical testing laboratories that provide product certification that meets OSHA electrical standards.

110.4 Voltages

The voltage rating of electrical equipment isn't permitted to be less than the nominal voltage of a circuit to which it's connected. ▶Figure 110–3

110.5 Conductor Material

Conductors are to be copper or aluminum unless otherwise provided in this *Code*; and when the conductor material isn't specified in a rule, the sizes given in the *NEC* are based on a copper conductor. ▶Figure 110–4

Requirements for Electrical Installations | 110.8

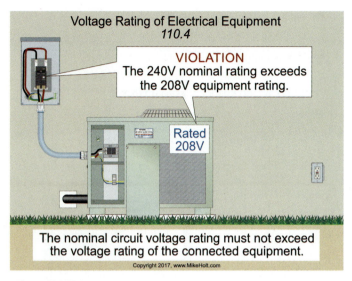

▶Figure 110–3

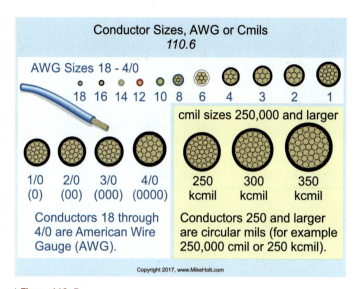

▶Figure 110–5

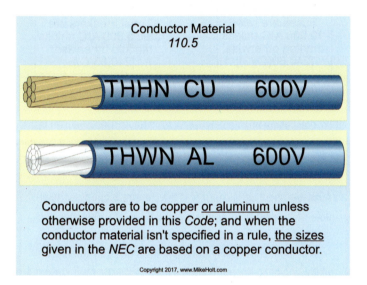

▶Figure 110–4

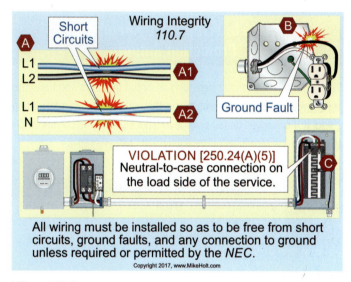

▶Figure 110–6

110.6 Conductor Sizes

Conductor sizes are expressed in American Wire Gage (AWG), typically from 18 AWG up to 4/0 AWG. Conductor sizes larger than 4/0 AWG are expressed in kcmil (thousand circular mils). ▶Figure 110–5

110.7 Wiring Integrity

Completed installations must be free from short circuits, ground faults, or any connections to ground unless required or permitted by the *Code*. ▶Figure 110–6

110.8 Suitable Wiring Methods

Only wiring methods recognized as suitable are included in the *NEC*, and they must be installed in accordance with the *Code*. ▶Figure 110–7

Author's Comment:

- See Chapter 3 for power and lighting wiring methods; Chapter 7 for signaling, remote-control, and power-limited circuits; and Chapter 8 for communications circuits.

110.9 | Requirements for Electrical Installations

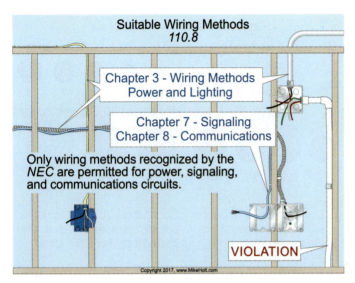

▶Figure 110–7

- Ampere Interrupting Rating (AIR) is also described as "Ampere Interrupting Capacity" (AIC) by many in the industry.
- Unless marked otherwise, the ampere interrupting rating for circuit breakers is 5,000A [240.83(C)], and for fuses it's 10,000A [240.60(C)(3)]. ▶Figure 110–9

110.9 Interrupting Overcurrent Protection Rating

Overcurrent protection devices such as circuit breakers and fuses are intended to interrupt the circuit, and they must have an interrupting rating at the nominal circuit voltage <u>at least equal to</u> the current available at the line terminals of the equipment. ▶Figure 110–8

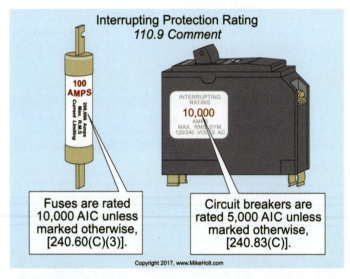

▶Figure 110–9

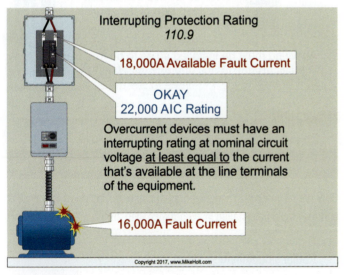

▶Figure 110–8

Author's Comment:

- See the definition of "Interrupting Rating" in Article 100.

Available Short-Circuit Current

Available short-circuit current is the current, in amperes, available at a given point in the electrical system. This available short-circuit current is first determined at the secondary terminals of the electric utility transformer, as given by the electric utility engineer. Thereafter, the available short-circuit current is calculated at the terminals of service equipment, then at branch-circuit panelboards and other equipment. The available short-circuit current is different at each point of the electrical system. It's highest at the electric utility transformer and lowest at the branch-circuit load.

The available short-circuit current depends on the impedance of the circuit. The greater the circuit impedance (utility transformer and the additive impedances of the circuit conductors), the lower the available short-circuit current. ▶Figure 110–10

The factors that affect the available short-circuit current at the electric utility transformer include the system voltage, the transformer kVA rating, and the circuit impedance (expressed in a percentage on the equipment nameplate). Properties that have

Requirements for Electrical Installations | 110.11

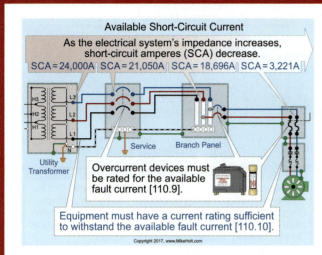
▶Figure 110–10

an impact on the impedance of the circuit include the conductor material (copper versus aluminum), conductor size, conductor length, and motor-operated equipment supplied by the circuit.

⚡ **DANGER:** Extremely high values of current flow (caused by short circuits or ground faults) produce tremendously destructive thermal and magnetic forces. An overcurrent protection device not rated to interrupt the current at the available fault values at its listed voltage rating can explode while attempting to open the circuit overcurrent protection device from a short circuit or ground fault, which can cause serious injury or death, as well as property damage.
▶Figure 110–11

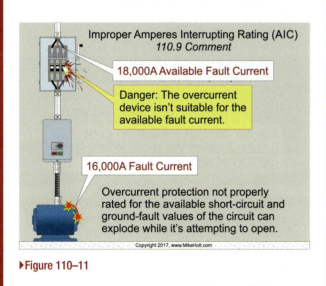
▶Figure 110–11

110.10 Equipment Short-Circuit Current Rating

Electrical equipment must have a short-circuit current rating that permits the circuit protective device to open from a short circuit or ground fault without extensive damage to the electrical equipment of the circuit. This fault is assumed to be either between two or more of the circuit conductors or between any circuit conductor and the equipment grounding conductor(s) permitted in 250.118. Listed equipment applied in accordance with their listing is considered to have met the requirements of this section. ▶Figure 110–12

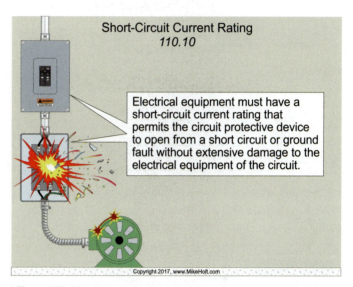
▶Figure 110–12

Author's Comment:

- For example, a motor controller must have a sufficient short-circuit rating for the available fault current. If the fault current exceeds the controller's short-circuit current rating it can explode, endangering persons and property. ▶Figure 110–13

110.11 Deteriorating Agents

Electrical equipment and conductors must be suitable for the environment and conditions of use. Consideration must also be given to the presence of corrosive gases, fumes, vapors, liquids, or other substances that can have a deteriorating effect on the conductors or equipment.
▶Figure 110–14

110.11 | Requirements for Electrical Installations

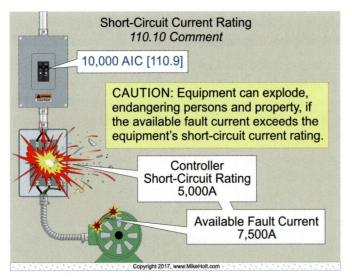
▶Figure 110–13

▶Figure 110–15

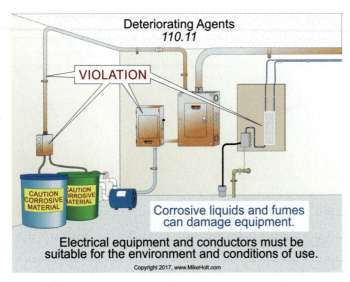
▶Figure 110–14

Equipment not identified for outdoor use and equipment identified only for indoor use must be protected against damage from the weather during construction.

Note 3: See Table 110.28 for NEMA enclosure-type designations.

Note 4: See the *International Building Code (IBC)* and the *International Residential Code (IRC)* for minimum flood provisions. ▶Figure 110–16

▶Figure 110–16

Author's Comment:

- Conductors aren't permitted to be exposed to ultraviolet rays from the sun unless identified for the purpose [310.10(D)].

Note 1: Raceways, cable trays, cablebus, cable armor, boxes, cable sheathing, cabinets, elbows, couplings, fittings, supports, and support hardware must be of materials that are suitable for the environment in which they're to be installed, in accordance with 300.6. ▶Figure 110–15

Note 2: Some cleaning and lubricating compounds contain chemicals that can cause deterioration of the plastic used for insulating and structural applications in equipment.

110.12 Mechanical Execution of Work

Electrical equipment must be installed in a neat and workmanlike manner. ▶Figure 110–17

▶Figure 110–17

(A) Unused Openings. Unused openings, other than those intended for the operation of equipment or for mounting purposes, or those that are part of the design for listed products, must be closed by fittings that provide protection substantially equivalent to the wall of the equipment. ▶Figure 110–18

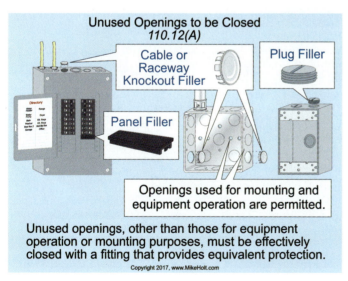

▶Figure 110–18

Note: Accepted industry practices are described in ANSI/NECA 1, *Standard for Good Workmanship in Electrical Construction.*

Author's Comment:

- The National Electrical Contractors Association (NECA) created a series of National Electrical Installation Standards (NEIS)® that established the industry's first quality guidelines for electrical installations. These standards define a benchmark or baseline of quality and workmanship for installing electrical products and systems. They explain what installing electrical products and systems in a "neat and workmanlike manner" means. For more information about these standards, visit www.NECA-NEIS.org.

(B) Integrity of Electrical Equipment. Internal parts of electrical equipment aren't permitted to be damaged or contaminated by foreign material, such as paint, plaster, cleaners, and so forth. ▶Figure 110–19

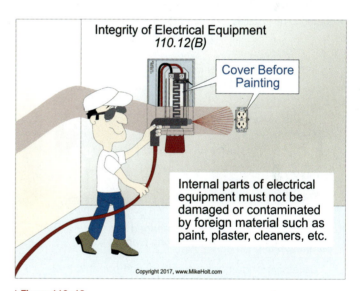

▶Figure 110–19

Author's Comment:

- Precautions must be taken to provide protection from contamination of the internal parts of panelboards and receptacles during building construction. Make sure that electrical equipment is properly masked and protected before painting or other phases of the project that can cause damage take place.
▶Figure 110–20

110.13 | Requirements for Electrical Installations

▶Figure 110–20

Electrical equipment containing damaged parts, such as broken, bent, cut, or deteriorated by corrosion, chemical action, or overheating aren't permitted to be installed. ▶Figure 110–21

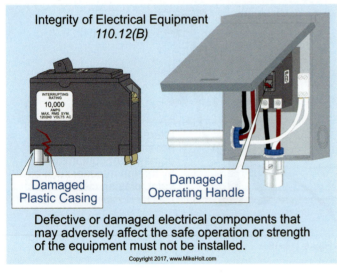

▶Figure 110–21

Author's Comment:

- Damaged parts include cracked insulators, arc shields not in place, overheated fuse clips, and damaged or missing switch handles or circuit-breaker handles.

110.13 Mounting and Cooling of Equipment

(A) Mounting. Electrical equipment must be firmly secured to the surface on which it's mounted. ▶Figure 110–22

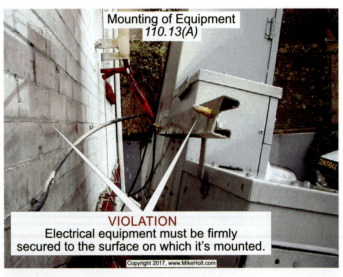

▶Figure 110–22

110.14 Conductor Termination and Splicing

Conductor terminal and splicing devices must be identified for the conductor material and they must be properly installed and used. ▶Figure 110–23

▶Figure 110–23

Requirements for Electrical Installations | 110.14

Author's Comment:

- Switches and receptacles marked "CO/ALR" are designed to ensure a good connection through the use of a larger contact area and compatible materials. The terminal screws are plated with the element called "Indium." Indium is an extremely soft metal that forms a gas-sealed connection with the aluminum conductor.

Connectors and terminals for conductors more finely stranded than Class B and Class C, as shown in Table 10 of Chapter 9, must be identified for the use of finely stranded conductors. ▶Figure 110–24

▶Figure 110–24

Author's Comment:

- According to UL Standard 486 A-B, a terminal/lug/connector must be listed and marked for use with other than Class B stranded conductors. With no marking or factory literature/instructions to the contrary, terminals may only be used with Class B stranded conductors.

- See the definition of "Identified" in Article 100.

- Conductor terminations must comply with the manufacturer's instructions as required by 110.3(B). For example, if the instructions for the device state "Suitable for 18-12 AWG Stranded," then only stranded conductors can be used with the terminating device. If the instructions state "Suitable for 18-12 AWG Solid," then only solid conductors are permitted, and if the instructions state "Suitable for 18-12 AWG," then either solid or stranded conductors can be used with the terminating device.

Copper and Aluminum Mixed. Copper and aluminum conductors must not make contact with each other in a device unless the device is listed and identified for this purpose. ▶Figure 110–25

▶Figure 110–25

Author's Comment:

- Few terminations are listed for the mixing of aluminum and copper conductors, but if they are, that will be marked on the product package or terminal device. The reason copper and aluminum shouldn't be in contact with each other is because corrosion develops between the two different metals due to galvanic action, resulting in increased contact resistance at the splicing device. This increased resistance can cause the splice to overheat and cause a fire.

(A) Terminations. Conductor terminals must ensure a good connection without damaging the conductors.

Terminals for more than one conductor and terminals used for aluminum conductors must be identified for this purpose, either within the equipment instructions or on the terminal itself. ▶Figure 110–26

110.14 | Requirements for Electrical Installations

▶Figure 110–26

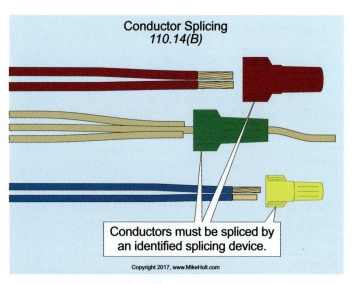
▶Figure 110–28

Author's Comment:

- Split-bolt connectors are commonly listed for only two conductors, although some are listed for three conductors. However, it's a common industry practice to terminate as many conductors as possible within a split-bolt connector, even though this violates the *NEC*. ▶Figure 110–27

Author's Comment:

- Conductors aren't required to be twisted together prior to the installation of a twist-on wire connector, unless specifically required in the installation instructions. ▶Figure 110–29

- Unused circuit conductors aren't required to be removed. However, to prevent an electrical hazard, the free ends of the conductors must be insulated to prevent the exposed end of the conductor from touching energized parts. This requirement can be met by the use of an insulated twist-on or push-on wire connector. ▶Figure 110–30

- See the definition of "Energized" in Article 100.

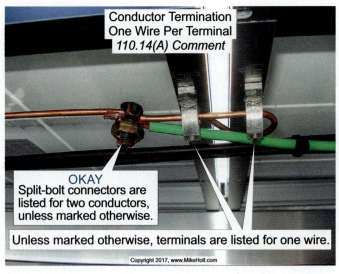
▶Figure 110–27

(B) Conductor Splices. Conductors must be spliced by a splicing device identified for the purpose or by exothermic welding. ▶Figure 110–28

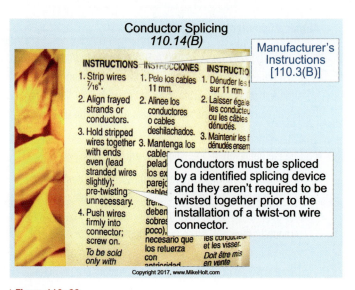
▶Figure 110–29

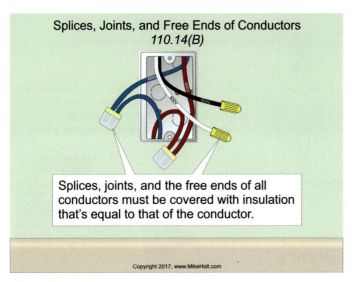

▶Figure 110–30

Underground Splices, Single Conductors. Single direct burial conductors of types UF or USE can be spliced underground without a junction box, but the conductors must be spliced with a device listed for direct burial [300.5(E) and 300.15(G)]. ▶Figure 110–31

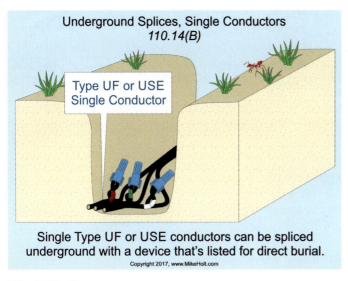

▶Figure 110–31

Underground Splices, Multiconductor Cable. Multiconductor UF or USE cable can have the individual conductors spliced underground without a junction box as long as a listed splice kit that encapsulates the conductors as well as the cable jacket is used.

(C) Temperature Limitations (Conductor Size). Conductors are to be sized using their ampacity from the insulation temperature rating column of Table 310.15(B)(16) that corresponds to the lowest temperature rating of any terminal, device, or conductor of the circuit.

Conductors with insulation temperature ratings higher than the termination's temperature rating can be used for ampacity adjustment, correction, or both. ▶Figure 110–32

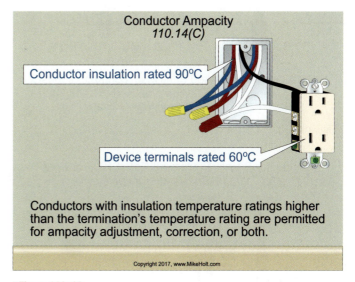

▶Figure 110–32

(1) Equipment Temperature Rating Provisions. Unless the equipment is listed and marked otherwise, conductor sizing for equipment terminations must be based on Table 310.15(B)(16) in accordance with (a) or (b):

(a) Equipment Rated 100A or Less.

(1) Conductors must be sized using the 60°C temperature column of Table 310.15(B)(16). ▶Figure 110–33

(3) Conductors terminating on terminals rated 75°C are to be sized in accordance with the ampacities listed in the 75°C temperature column of Table 310.15(B)(16). ▶Figure 110–34

(4) For motors marked with design letters B, C, or D, conductors having an insulation rating of 75°C or higher can be used, provided the ampacity of such conductors doesn't exceed the 75°C ampacity. ▶Figure 110–35

110.14 | Requirements for Electrical Installations

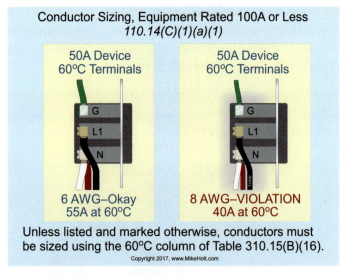

▶Figure 110–33

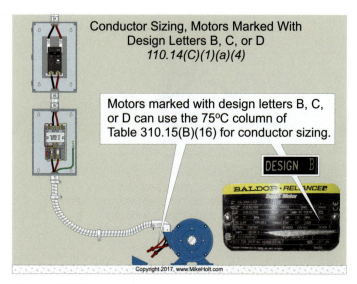

▶Figure 110–35

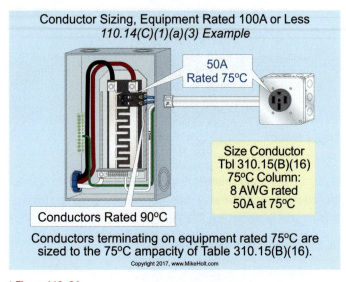

▶Figure 110–34

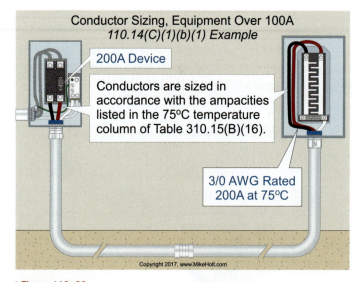

▶Figure 110–36

Note: Equipment markings or listing information may restrict the sizing and temperature ratings of connected conductors.

(b) Equipment Rated Over 100A.

(1) Conductors with an insulation temperature rating of 75°C must be sized to the 75°C temperature column of Table 310.15(B)(16).
▶Figure 110–36

(2) Conductors with an insulation temperature rating of 90°C can be sized to the 75°C column of Table 310.15(B)(16).

(2) Separate Connector Provisions. Conductors can be sized to the 90°C column of Table 310.15(B)(16) if the conductors and pressure connectors are rated at least 90°C. ▶Figure 110–37

(D) Torque. Where tightening torque values are indicated on equipment or installation instructions, a calibrated torque tool must be used to achieve the indicated torque value, unless the equipment manufacturer provides an alternative method of achieving the required torque.
▶Figure 110–38

Requirements for Electrical Installations | 110.15

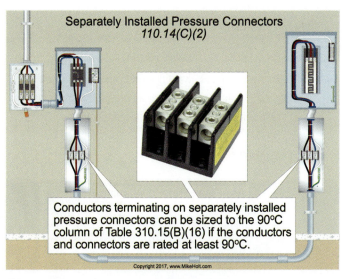

▶Figure 110–37

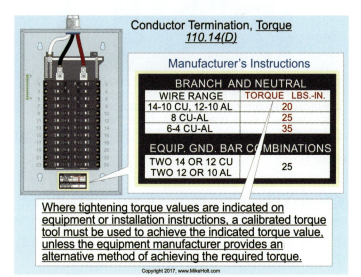

▶Figure 110–38

110.15 High-Leg Conductor Identification

On a 4-wire, delta-connected, three-phase system, where the midpoint of one phase winding of the secondary is grounded (a high-leg system), the conductor with 208V to ground must be durably and permanently marked by an outer finish orange in color, or other effective means. Such identification must be placed at each point on the system where a connection is made if the neutral conductor is present [230.56]. ▶Figure 110–39

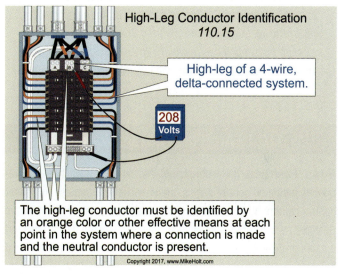

▶Figure 110–39

Author's Comment:

- The high-leg conductor is also called the "wild leg," "stinger leg," or "bastard leg."

- Other important *NEC* rules relating to the high leg are as follows:
    ♦ **Panelboards.** Since 1975, panelboards supplied by a 4-wire, delta-connected, three-phase system must have the high-leg conductor terminate to the "B" phase of a panelboard [408.3(E)]. Section 408.3(F)(1) requires panelboards to be field-marked with "Caution Phase B Has 208V to Ground."
    ♦ **Disconnects.** The *NEC* doesn't specify the termination location for the high-leg conductor in switch equipment (Switches—Article 404), but the generally accepted practice is to terminate this conductor to the "B" phase.
    ♦ **Utility Meter Equipment.** The ANSI standard for meter equipment requires the high-leg conductor (208V to neutral) to terminate on the "C" (right) phase of the meter socket enclosure. This is because the demand meter needs 120V, and it obtains that voltage from the "B" phase.

Author's Comment:

- Conductors must terminate in devices that have been properly tightened in accordance with the manufacturer's torque specifications included with equipment instructions. Failure to torque terminals properly can result in excessive heating of terminals or splicing devices due to a loose connection. A loose connection can also lead to arcing which increases the heating effect and may also lead to a short circuit or ground fault. Any of these can result in a fire or other failure, including an arc-flash event. In addition, this is a violation of 110.3(B), which requires all equipment to be installed in accordance with listing or labeling instructions.

110.16 | Requirements for Electrical Installations

- Also hope the electric utility lineman isn't color blind and doesn't inadvertently cross the "orange" high-leg conductor (208V) with the red (120V) service conductor at the weatherhead. It's happened before…

⚠️ **WARNING:** When replacing equipment in existing facilities that contain a high-leg conductor, care must be taken to ensure the high-leg conductor is replaced in its original location. Prior to 1975, the high-leg conductor was required to terminate on the "C" phase of panelboards and switchboards. Failure to re-terminate the high leg in accordance with the existing installation can result in 120V circuits being inadvertently connected to the 208V high leg, with disastrous results.

110.16 Arc-Flash Hazard Warning

(A) Arc-Flash Hazard Warning Label. Switchboards, switchgear, panelboards, industrial control panels, meter socket enclosures, and motor control centers in other than dwelling units must be marked to warn qualified persons of the danger associated with an arc flash from short circuits or ground faults. The arc-flash hazard warning marking must be permanently affixed, have sufficient durability to withstand the environment involved [110.21(B)], and be clearly visible to qualified persons before they examine, adjust, service, or perform maintenance on the equipment. ▶Figure 110–40

Author's Comment:

- See the definition of "Qualified Person" in Article 100.
- This rule is intended to warn qualified persons who work on energized electrical systems that an arc-flash hazard exists so they'll select proper personal protective equipment (PPE) in accordance with industry accepted safe work practice standards. ▶Figure 110–41

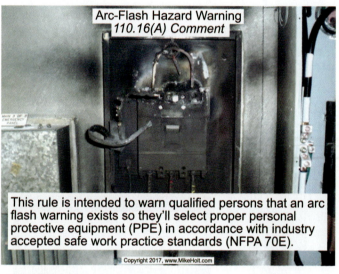

▶Figure 110–41

(B) Service Equipment Available Fault Current Label. Service equipment rated 1,200A or more must have a field or factory installed label containing the following details and have sufficient durability to withstand the environment: ▶Figure 110–42

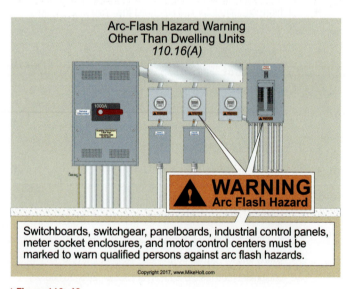

▶Figure 110–40

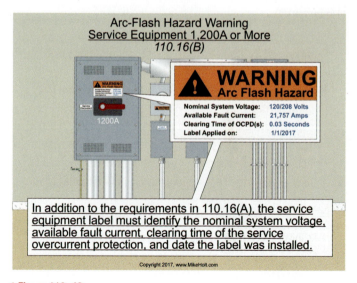

▶Figure 110–42

(1) Nominal system voltage

(2) Available fault current at the service overcurrent protection device

(3) Clearing time of the service overcurrent protection device based on the available fault current at the service equipment

(4) Date the service equipment available fault current label was installed

Ex: Service equipment labeling isn't required if an arc-flash label in accordance with NFPA 70E, Standard for Electrical Safety in the Workplace [see Note 3] is applied. ▶Figure 110–43

▶Figure 110–43

Note 1: NFPA 70E, Standard for Electrical Safety in the Workplace, provides guidance in determining the severity of potential exposure, planning safe work practices, arc-flash labeling, and selecting personal protective equipment. ▶Figure 110–44

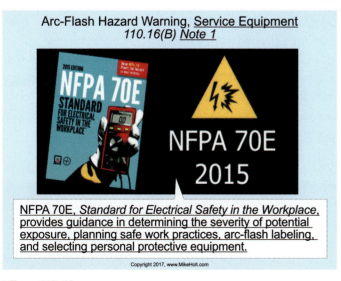

▶Figure 110–44

Note No. 3: NFPA 70E, Standard for Electrical Safety in the Workplace provides specific criteria for developing arc-flash labels, such as nominal system voltage, incident energy levels, arc-flash boundaries, and selecting personal protective equipment.

110.21 Markings

(A) Equipment Markings.

(1) General. The manufacturer's name, trademark, or other descriptive marking must be placed on all electrical equipment and, where required by the *Code*, markings such as voltage, current, wattage, or other ratings must be provided. Marking must have sufficient durability to withstand the environment involved.

(2) Reconditioned Equipment. Reconditioned equipment must be marked with the name, trademark, or other descriptive marking by the organization responsible for reconditioning the electrical equipment, along with the date of the reconditioning.

Reconditioned equipment must be identified as "reconditioned" and approval of the reconditioned equipment isn't based solely on the equipment's original listing.

Ex: Reconditioning markings aren't required in industrial occupancies, where conditions of maintenance and supervision ensure that only qualified persons service the equipment.

Note: Normal servicing of equipment isn't considered to be reconditioning equipment.

(B) Field-Applied Hazard Markings. Where caution, warning, or danger signs or labels are required, the labels must meet the following:

(1) The markings must warn of the hazards using effective words, colors, symbols, or a combination of words, colors, and symbols. ▶Figure 110–45

Note: ANSI Z535.4, *Product Safety Signs and Labels*, provides guidelines for the design and durability of signs and labels.

(2) The label can't be handwritten, and it must be permanently affixed to the equipment. ▶Figure 110–46

Ex to (2): Labels that contain information that's likely to change can be handwritten, if it's legible.

Author's Comment:

- A permanently affixed sign includes a sticker, but not a piece of paper taped to the equipment.

110.22 | Requirements for Electrical Installations

▶Figure 110–45

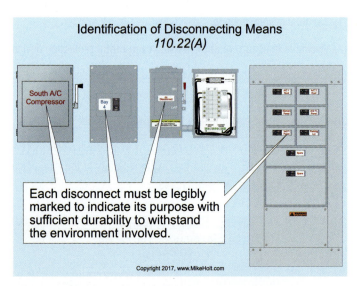
▶Figure 110–47

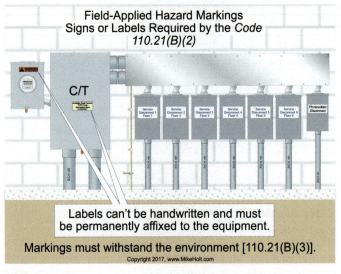
▶Figure 110–46

(3) The marking must be of sufficient durability to withstand the environment involved.

110.22 Identification of Disconnecting Means

(A) General. Each disconnect must be legibly marked to indicate its purpose unless located and arranged so the purpose is evident. The marking must be of sufficient durability to withstand the environment involved. ▶Figure 110–47

(C) Tested Series Combination Systems. Tested series-rated installations must be legibly field-marked in accordance with 240.86(B) with a readily visible permanently affixed caution label having sufficient durability to withstand the environment involved and comply with 110.21(B) to indicate that the equipment has been applied with a series combination rating:

CAUTION—SERIES COMBINATION SYSTEM RATED _____ AMPERES. IDENTIFIED REPLACEMENT COMPONENTS REQUIRED

110.24 Available Fault Current

(A) Field Marking. Service equipment, in other than dwelling units, must be field marked with the maximum available fault current, the date the fault current calculation was performed, and be of sufficient durability to withstand the environment involved. The available fault current calculation for the service equipment label must be documented and be available to those who are authorized to design, install, inspect, maintain, or operate the system. ▶Figure 110–48

Note: The fault current markings required by this section are to ensure compliance with 110.9 and 110.10. They're not intended to be used for arc-flash analysis. Arc-flash hazard information is available in NFPA 70E, *Standard for Electrical Safety in the Workplace*. ▶Figure 110–49

Requirements for Electrical Installations | 110.26

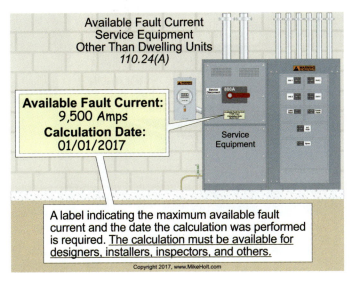

▶Figure 110–48

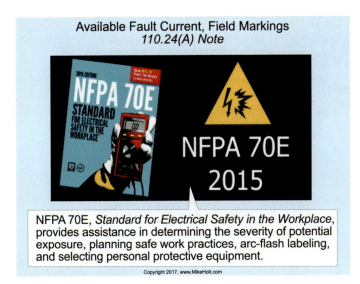

▶Figure 110–49

(B) Modifications. When modifications to the electrical installation affect the maximum available fault current at the service, the maximum available fault current must be recalculated to ensure the service equipment ratings are sufficient for the maximum available fault current at the line terminals of the equipment. The required field marking(s) in 110.24(A) must be adjusted to reflect the new level of maximum available fault current.

Ex: Field markings aren't required for industrial installations where conditions of maintenance and supervision ensure that only qualified persons service the equipment.

110.25 Lockable Disconnecting Means

If the *Code* requires a disconnect to be lockable in the open position, the provisions for locking must remain in place whether the lock is installed or not. ▶Figure 110–50

▶Figure 110–50

Part II. 1,000V, Nominal, or Less

110.26 Spaces About Electrical Equipment

For the purpose of safe operation and maintenance of equipment, access and working space must be provided about all electrical equipment. ▶Figure 110–51

▶Figure 110–51

110.26 | Requirements for Electrical Installations

(A) Working Space. Equipment that may need examination, adjustment, servicing, or maintenance while energized must have working space provided in accordance with 110.26(A)(1), (2), (3), and (4):

> **Author's Comment:**
> - The phrase "while energized" is the root of many debates. As always, check with the AHJ to see what equipment he or she believes needs a clear working space.

Note: NFPA 70E, *Standard for Electrical Safety in the Workplace*, provides guidance in determining the severity of potential exposure, planning safe work practices, arc-flash labeling, and selecting personal protective equipment.

(1) Depth of Working Space. The working space, which is measured from the enclosure front, isn't permitted to be less than the distances contained in Table 110.26(A)(1). ▶Figure 110–52

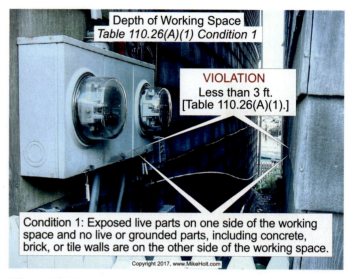

▶Figure 110–53

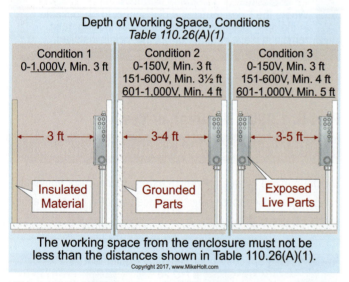

▶Figure 110–52

▶Figure 110–54

| Table 110.26(A)(1) Working Space ||||
Voltage–to–Ground	Condition 1	Condition 2	Condition 3
0–150V	3 ft	3 ft	3 ft
151–600V	3 ft	3½ ft	4 ft
601–1,000V	3 ft	4 ft	5 ft

▶Figure 110–53, ▶Figure 110–54, and ▶Figure 110–55

(a) Rear and Sides. Working space isn't required for the back or sides of assemblies where all connections and all renewable or adjustable parts are accessible from the front. ▶Figure 110–56

(b) Low Voltage. If special permission is granted in accordance with 90.4, working space for equipment that operates at not more than 30V ac or 60V dc can be less than the distance in Table 110.26(A)(1). ▶Figure 110–57

> **Author's Comment:**
> - See the definition of "Special Permission" in Article 100.

Requirements for Electrical Installations | 110.26

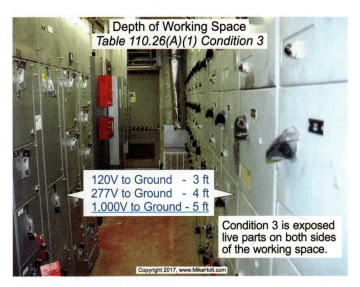
▶Figure 110–55

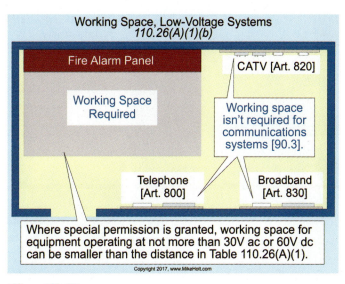
▶Figure 110–57

▶Figure 110–56

(c) Existing Buildings. If electrical equipment is being replaced, Condition 2 working space is permitted between dead-front switchboards, switchgear, panelboards, or motor control centers located across the aisle from each other where conditions of maintenance and supervision ensure that written procedures have been adopted to prohibit equipment on both sides of the aisle from being open at the same time, and only authorized, qualified persons will service the installation.

Author's Comment:

- The working space requirements of 110.26 don't apply to equipment included in Chapter 8—Communications Circuits [90.3].

(2) Width of Working Space. The width of the working space must be a minimum of 30 in., but in no case less than the width of the equipment. ▶Figure 110–58 and ▶Figure 110–59

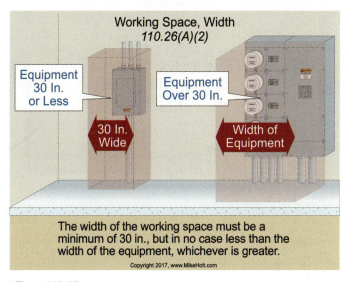
▶Figure 110–58

Author's Comment:

- The width of the working space can be measured from left-to-right, from right-to-left, or simply centered on the equipment, and can overlap the working space for other electrical equipment. ▶Figure 110–60

110.26 | Requirements for Electrical Installations

▶Figure 110–59

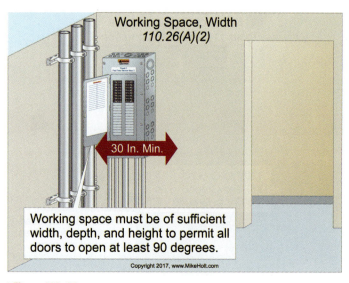
▶Figure 110–61

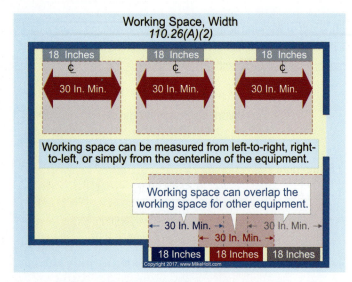
▶Figure 110–60

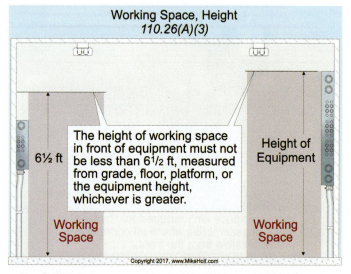
▶Figure 110–62

The working space must be of sufficient width, depth, and height to permit all equipment doors to open 90 degrees. ▶Figure 110–61

(3) Height of Working Space (Headroom). The height of the working space in front of equipment isn't permitted to be less than 6½ ft, measured from the grade, floor, platform, or the equipment height, whichever is greater. ▶Figure 110–62

Equipment such as raceways, cables, wireways, cabinets, panels, and so on, can be located above or below electrical equipment, but must not extend more than 6 in. into the equipment's working space. ▶Figure 110–63

Ex 1: The minimum headroom requirement doesn't apply to service equipment or panelboards rated 200A or less located in an existing dwelling unit.

Author's Comment:

■ See the definition of "Dwelling Unit" in Article 100.

Ex 2: Meters are permitted to extend beyond the other equipment.

Ex 3: For battery systems, see 480.10(D) for top clearance requirements.

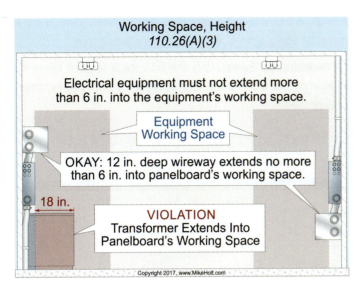

▶Figure 110–63

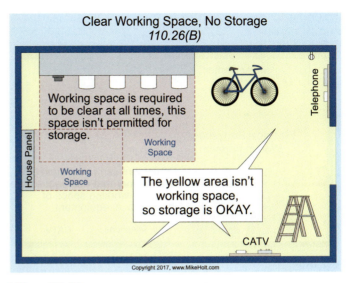

▶Figure 110–64

(4) Limited Access. Where equipment is likely to require examination, adjustment, servicing, or maintenance while energized is located in a space with limited access, all of the following conditions apply:

(a)(1) Above Suspended Ceiling. Equipment installed above a suspended ceiling must have an access opening not smaller than 22 in. × 22 in.

(a)(2) Crawl Space. Equipment installed in a crawl space must have an accessible opening not smaller than 22 in. × 30 in.

(b) The width of the working space must be a minimum of 30 in., but in no case less than the width of the equipment.

(c) The working space must permit equipment doors to open 90 degrees.

(d) The working space in front of the equipment must comply with the depth requirements of Table 110.26(A)(1), and horizontal ceiling structural members are permitted in this space.

(B) Clear Working Space. The working space required by this section must be clear at all times; therefore, this space isn't permitted for storage. ▶Figure 110–64

When normally enclosed live parts are exposed for inspection or servicing, the working space, if in a passageway or open space, must be suitably guarded.

Author's Comment:

- When working in a passageway, the working space should be guarded from occupants using it. When working on electrical equipment in a passageway one must be mindful of a fire alarm evacuation with numerous occupants congregated and moving through the area.

CAUTION: *It's very dangerous to service energized parts in the first place, and it's unacceptable to be subjected to additional dangers by working around bicycles, boxes, crates, appliances, and other impediments.*

Author's Comment:

- Signaling and communications equipment aren't permitted to be installed in a manner that encroaches on the working space of the electrical equipment. ▶Figure 110–65

(C) Entrance to and Egress from Working Space.

(1) Minimum Required. At least one entrance of sufficient area must provide access to and egress from the working space.

110.26 | Requirements for Electrical Installations

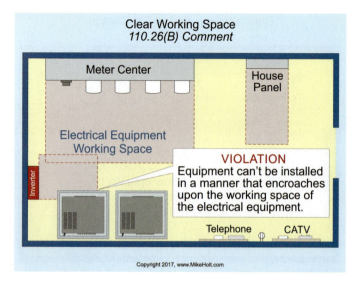
▶Figure 110–65

Author's Comment:

- Check to see what the authority having jurisdiction considers "Sufficient Area." Building codes contain minimum dimensions for doors and openings for personnel travel.

(2) Large Equipment. An entrance to and egress from each end of the working space of electrical equipment rated 1,200A or more that's over 6 ft wide is required. The opening must be a minimum of 24 in. wide and 6½ ft high. ▶Figure 110–66

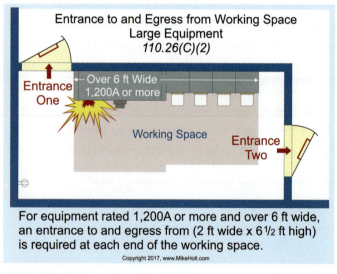
▶Figure 110–66

A single entrance to and egress from the required working space is permitted where either of the following conditions is met:

(a) Unobstructed Egress. Only one entrance is required where the location permits a continuous and unobstructed way of egress travel.
▶Figure 110–67

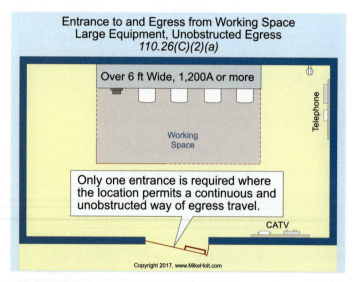
▶Figure 110–67

(b) Double Workspace. Only one entrance is required where the required working space depth is doubled, and the equipment is located so the edge of the entrance is no closer than the required working space distance. ▶Figure 110–68

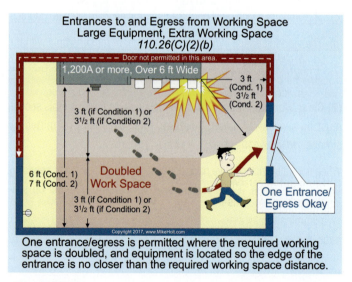
▶Figure 110–68

(3) Personnel Doors. If equipment with overcurrent or switching devices rated 800A or more is installed, personnel door(s) for entrance to and egress from the working space located less than 25 ft from the nearest edge of the working space must have the door(s) open in the direction of egress and be equipped with listed panic hardware. ▶Figure 110–69

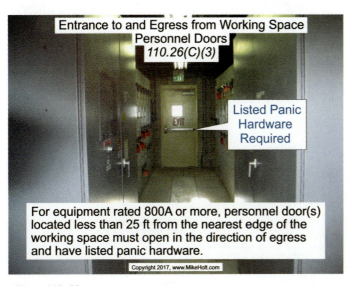

▶Figure 110–69

Author's Comment:

- History has shown that electricians who suffer burns on their hands in electrical arc-flash or arc-blast events often can't open doors equipped with knobs that must be turned.

- Since this requirement is in the *NEC*, the electrical contractor is responsible for ensuring that panic hardware is installed where required. Some are offended at being held liable for nonelectrical responsibilities, but this rule is designed to save the lives of electricians. For this and other reasons, many construction professionals routinely hold "pre-construction" or "pre-con" meetings to review potential opportunities for miscommunication—before the work begins.

(D) Illumination. Service equipment, switchboards, switchgear, and panelboards, as well as motor control centers located indoors must have illumination located indoors controlled by manual means; automatic control without manual control isn't permitted. ▶Figure 110–70

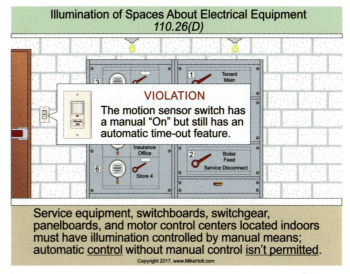

▶Figure 110–70

Author's Comment:

- The *Code* doesn't provide the minimum foot-candles required to provide proper illumination. Proper illumination of electrical equipment rooms is essential for the safety of those qualified to work on such equipment.

(E) Dedicated Equipment Space. Switchboards, switchgear, panelboards, and motor control centers must have dedicated equipment space and be protected from damage as follows:

(1) Indoors.

(a) Dedicated Electrical Space. The footprint space (width and depth of the equipment) extending from the floor to a height of 6 ft above the equipment or to the structural ceiling, whichever is lower, must be dedicated for the electrical installation. ▶Figure 110–71

No piping, ducts, or other equipment foreign to the electrical installation can be installed in this dedicated footprint space. ▶Figure 110–72

Ex: Suspended ceilings with removable panels can be within the dedicated footprint space [110.26(E)(1)(d)].

Author's Comment:

- Electrical raceways and cables not associated with the dedicated space can be within the dedicated space. These aren't considered "equipment foreign to the electrical installation."
▶Figure 110–73

110.26 | Requirements for Electrical Installations

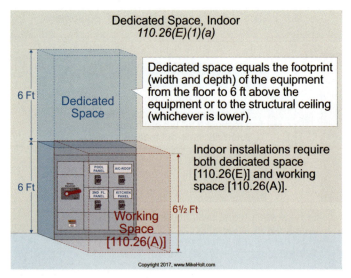
▶Figure 110–71

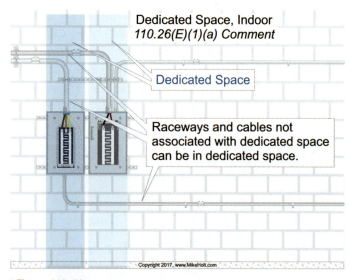
▶Figure 110–73

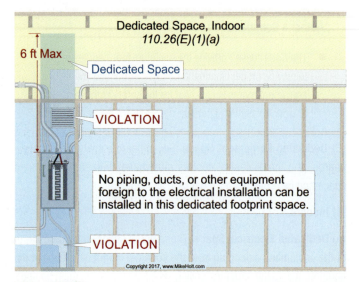
▶Figure 110–72

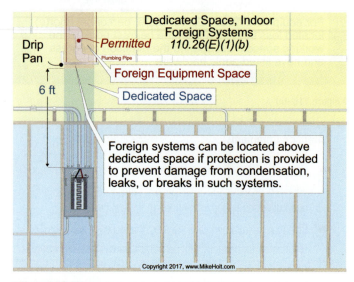
▶Figure 110–74

(b) Foreign Systems. Foreign systems can be located above the dedicated space if protection is installed to prevent damage to the electrical equipment from condensation, leaks, or breaks in the foreign systems. Such protection can be as simple as a drip-pan. ▶Figure 110–74

(c) Sprinkler Protection. Sprinkler protection piping isn't permitted in the dedicated space, but the *NEC* doesn't prohibit sprinklers from spraying water on electrical equipment.

(d) Suspended Ceilings. A dropped, suspended, or similar ceiling isn't considered a structural ceiling. ▶Figure 110–75

(2) Outdoor. Outdoor installations must comply with the following:

(a) Installation Requirements. Switchboards, switchgear, panelboards, and motor control centers installed outdoors must be:

(1) Installed in <u>identified</u> enclosures

(2) Protected from accidental contact by unauthorized personnel, or by vehicular traffic ▶Figure 110–76

(3) Protected by accidental spillage or leakage from piping systems

(b) Work Space. Switchboards, switchgear, panelboards, and motor control centers installed outdoors must have sufficient <u>working space</u> clearance in accordance with 110.26(A). No architectural appurtenance or other equipment is permitted in the work space.

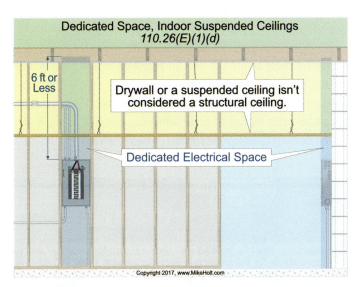

▶Figure 110–75

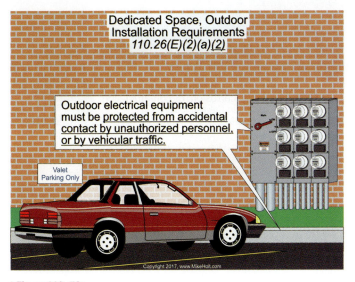

▶Figure 110–76

(c) Dedicated Equipment Space Outdoor. The footprint space (width and depth of the equipment) extending from grade to a height of 6 ft above the equipment must be dedicated for the electrical installation. No piping, ducts, or other equipment foreign to the electrical installation can be installed in this dedicated footprint space.

Author's Comment:

- See the definition of "Accessible (as applied to equipment)" in Article 100.

(F) Locked Electrical Equipment Rooms or Enclosures. Electrical equipment rooms or enclosures containing electrical apparatus controlled by a lock(s) are considered accessible to qualified persons. ▶Figure 110–77

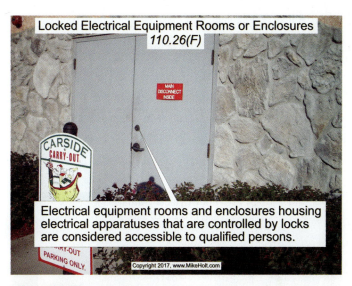

▶Figure 110–77

110.27 Guarding

(A) Guarding Live Parts. Live parts of electrical equipment operating at 50V to 1,000V between ungrounded conductors must be guarded against accidental contact. This can be done by:

(1) Locating them in a separate room, vault, or enclosure.

(2) Guarding with a permanent partition or screen. ▶Figure 110–78

▶Figure 110–78

(3) Locating them on a balcony or platform to exclude unqualified persons.

(4) Elevating them above the floor or working surface, in accordance with the following:

(a) 8 ft for 50V through 300V between ungrounded conductors.

(b) 8 ft for 301V through 600V between ungrounded conductors.

(c) 8 ft 7 in. for 601V through 1,000V between ungrounded conductors.

(B) Prevent Physical Damage. Electrical equipment must not be installed where subject to physical damage, unless enclosures or guards are arranged and they're of sufficient strength to prevent damage. ▶Figure 110–79

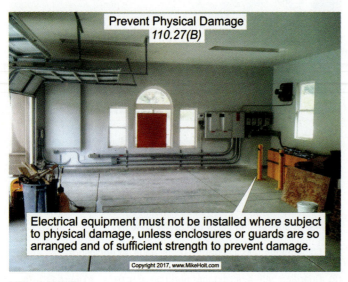

▶Figure 110–79

(C) Warning Signs. Entrances to rooms and other guarded locations containing exposed live parts must be marked with conspicuous signs forbidding unqualified persons from entering.

110.28 Enclosure Types

Enclosures must be marked with an enclosure-type number and be suitable for the location in accordance with Table 110.28. The enclosures aren't intended to protect against condensation, icing, corrosion, or contamination that might occur within the enclosure or that enters via the raceway or unsealed openings. ▶Figure 110–80

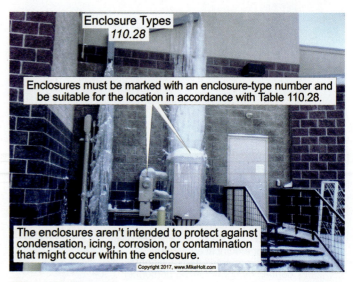

▶Figure 110–80

Note: Raintight enclosures include Types 3, 3S, 3SX, 3X, 4, 4X, 6, and 6P; rainproof enclosures are Types 3R, and 3RX; watertight enclosures are Types 4, 4X, 6, and 6P; driptight enclosures are Types 2, 5, 12, 12K, and 13; and dusttight enclosures are Types 3, 3S, 3SX, 3X, 5, 12, 12K, and 13.

CHAPTER 1 PRACTICE QUESTIONS

Please use the 2017 *Code* book to answer the following questions.

Article 100. Definitions

1. "_____" means acceptable to the authority having jurisdiction.

    (a) Identified
    (b) Listed
    (c) Approved
    (d) Labeled

2. According to the *Code*, "automatic" is performing a function without the necessity of _____.

    (a) protection from damage
    (b) human intervention
    (c) mechanical linkage
    (d) all of these

3. The circuit conductors between the final overcurrent device protecting the circuit and the outlet(s) are known as "_____ conductors."

    (a) feeder
    (b) branch-circuit
    (c) home run
    (d) none of these

4. A circuit breaker is a device designed to _____ the circuit automatically on a predetermined overcurrent without damage to itself when properly applied within its rating.

    (a) energize
    (b) reset
    (c) connect
    (d) open

5. Conductive optical fiber cables contain noncurrent-carrying conductive members such as metallic _____.

    (a) strength members
    (b) vapor barriers
    (c) armor or sheath
    (d) any of these

6. A separate portion of a raceway system that provides access through a removable cover(s) to the interior of the system defines the term "_____."

    (a) junction box
    (b) accessible raceway
    (c) conduit body
    (d) cutout box

7. A unit of an electrical system, other than a conductor, that carries or controls electric energy as its principal function is a(n) "_____."

    (a) raceway
    (b) fitting
    (c) device
    (d) enclosure

8. An effective ground-fault current path is an intentionally constructed, low-impedance electrically conductive path designed and intended to carry current during a ground-fault condition from the point of a ground fault on a wiring system to _____.

    (a) ground
    (b) earth
    (c) the electrical supply source
    (d) none of these

Chapter 1 | Practice Questions

9. As used in the *NEC*, equipment includes ____.

    (a) fittings
    (b) appliances
    (c) machinery
    (d) all of these

10. As applied to wiring methods, "on or attached to the surface, or behind access panels designed to allow access" is known as ____.

    (a) open
    (b) uncovered
    (c) exposed
    (d) bare

11. The *NEC* defines a "____" as all circuit conductors between the service equipment, the source of a separately derived system, or other power supply source, and the final branch-circuit overcurrent device.

    (a) service
    (b) feeder
    (c) branch circuit
    (d) all of these

12. Equipment or materials to which has been attached a(n) ____ of an FEB indicating the equipment or materials were evaluated and found to comply with requirements as described in an accompanying field evaluation report is known as "field labeled (as applied to evaluated products)."

    (a) symbol
    (b) label
    (c) other identifying mark
    (d) any of these

13. A Class A GFCI protection device is designed to trip when the current to ground is ____ or higher.

    (a) 4 mA
    (b) 5 mA
    (c) 6 mA
    (d) 7 mA

14. "Within sight from" means visible and not more than ____ ft distant from the equipment.

    (a) 10
    (b) 20
    (c) 25
    (d) 50

15. A device that provides a means to connect intersystem bonding conductors for ____ systems to the grounding electrode system is an "intersystem bonding termination."

    (a) limited-energy
    (b) low-voltage
    (c) communications
    (d) power and lighting

16. Equipment or materials to which a label, symbol, or other identifying mark of a product evaluation organization that is acceptable to the authority having jurisdiction has been attached is known as "____."

    (a) listed
    (b) labeled
    (c) approved
    (d) identified

17. A "neutral conductor" is the conductor connected to the ____ of a system, which is intended to carry current under normal conditions.

    (a) grounding electrode
    (b) neutral point
    (c) intersystem bonding termination
    (d) none of these

18. "Nonautomatic" is defined as requiring ____ to perform a function.

    (a) protection from damage
    (b) human intervention
    (c) mechanical linkage
    (d) all of these

19. Nonconductive optical fiber cable contains no metallic members and no other ____ materials.

    (a) electrically conductive
    (b) inductive
    (c) synthetic
    (d) insulating

20. Any current in excess of the rated current of equipment or the ampacity of a conductor is called "____."

    (a) trip current
    (b) fault current
    (c) overcurrent
    (d) a short circuit

21. A "____" is the total components and subsystem that, in combination, converts solar energy into electric energy for connection to a utilization load.

    (a) photovoltaic system
    (b) solar array
    (c) a and b
    (d) none of these

22. The *NEC* defines a(n) "____" as one who has skills and knowledge related to the construction and operation of the electrical equipment and installations and has received safety training to recognize and avoid the hazards involved.

    (a) inspector
    (b) master electrician
    (c) journeyman electrician
    (d) qualified person

23. A "raceway" is an enclosed channel designed expressly for the holding of wires, cables, or busbars, with additional functions as permitted in the *Code*.

    (a) True
    (b) False

24. Service conductors originate at the service point and terminate at the service disconnecting means.

    (a) True
    (b) False

25. "Overhead service conductors" are the conductors between the ____ and the first point of connection to the service-entrance conductors at the building or other structure.

    (a) service disconnect
    (b) service point
    (c) grounding electrode
    (d) equipment grounding conductor

26. "Underground service conductors" are the underground conductors between the service point and the first point of connection to the service-entrance conductors in a terminal box, meter, or other enclosure, ____ the building wall.

    (a) inside
    (b) outside
    (c) above
    (d) a or b

27. "Overhead system service-entrance conductors" are the service conductors between the terminals of the ____ and a point where they are joined by a tap or splice to the service drop or overhead service conductors.

    (a) service equipment
    (b) service point
    (c) grounding electrode
    (d) equipment grounding conductor

28. "Underground system service-entrance conductors" are the service conductors between the terminals of the ____ and the point of connection to the service lateral or underground service conductors.

    (a) service equipment
    (b) service point
    (c) grounding electrode
    (d) equipment grounding conductor

29. The prospective symmetrical fault current at a nominal voltage to which an apparatus or system is able to be connected without sustaining damage exceeding defined acceptance criteria is known as the "____."

    (a) short-circuit current rating
    (b) arc-flash rating
    (c) overcurrent rating
    (d) available fault current

30. A "signaling circuit" is any electrical circuit that energizes signaling equipment.

    (a) True
    (b) False

31. A "stand-alone system" supplies power independently of an electrical production and distribution network.

    (a) True
    (b) False

32. "Utilization equipment" is equipment that utilizes electricity for _____ purposes.

    (a) electromechanical
    (b) heating
    (c) lighting
    (d) any of these

33. The "voltage of a circuit" is defined by the *Code* as the _____ root-mean-square (effective) difference of potential between any two conductors of the circuit concerned.

    (a) lowest
    (b) greatest
    (c) average
    (d) nominal

Article 110. Requirements for Electrical Installations

34. When protecting equipment against damage from the weather during construction, minimum _____ provisions provided in NFPA 5000 Building Construction and Safety *Code*, the International Building *Code* (IBC), and the International Residential *Code* for One- and Two-Family Dwellings (IRC) can be referenced for additional information.

    (a) safety
    (b) flood
    (c) weather
    (d) none of these

35. The *NEC* requires that electrical equipment be _____.

    (a) installed in a neat and workmanlike manner
    (b) installed under the supervision of a licensed person
    (c) completed before being inspected
    (d) all of these

36. Unused openings other than those intended for the operation of equipment, intended for mounting purposes, or permitted as part of the design for listed equipment shall be _____.

    (a) filled with cable clamps or connectors only
    (b) taped over with electrical tape
    (c) repaired only by welding or brazing in a metal slug
    (d) closed to afford protection substantially equivalent to the wall of the equipment

37. Soldered splices shall first be spliced or joined so as to be mechanically and electrically secure without solder and then be soldered.

    (a) True
    (b) False

38. Separately installed pressure connectors shall be used with conductors at the _____ not exceeding the ampacity at the listed and identified temperature rating of the connector.

    (a) voltages
    (b) temperatures
    (c) listings
    (d) ampacities

39. Where a tightening torque is indicated as a numeric value on equipment or in installation instructions provided by the manufacturer, a(n) _____ torque tool shall be used to achieve the indicated torque value, unless the equipment manufacturer has provided installation instructions for an alternative method of achieving the required torque.

    (a) calibrated
    (b) identified
    (c) adjustable
    (d) listed

40. The *NEC* requires tested series-rated installations of circuit breakers or fuses to be legibly marked in the field to indicate the equipment has been applied with a series combination rating.

    (a) True
    (b) False

41. Access and _____ shall be provided and maintained about all electrical equipment to permit ready and safe operation and maintenance of such equipment.

    (a) ventilation
    (b) cleanliness
    (c) circulation
    (d) working space

42. NFPA 70E, Standard for Electrical Safety in the Workplace, provides guidance for working space about electrical equipment, such as determining severity of potential exposure, planning safe work practices, arc-flash labeling, and selecting personal protective equipment.

    (a) True
    (b) False

43. The minimum working space on a circuit for equipment operating at 120 volts-to-ground, with exposed live parts on one side and no live or grounded parts on the other side of the working space, is _____ ft.

    (a) 1
    (b) 3
    (c) 4
    (d) 6

44. The required working space for access to live parts of equipment operating at 300 volts-to-ground, where there are exposed live parts on both sides of the workspace is _____ ft.

    (a) 3
    (b) 3½
    (c) 4
    (d) 4½

45. Where equipment operating at 1,000 volts, nominal, or less to ground and likely to require examination, adjustment, servicing, or maintenance while energized is required by installation instructions or function to be located in a space with limited access, and where equipment is installed above a lay-in ceiling, there shall be an opening not smaller than _____.

    (a) 6 in. x 6 in.
    (b) 12 in. x 12 in.
    (c) 22 in. x 22 in.
    (d) 22 in. x 30 in.

46. Working space shall not be used for _____.

    (a) storage
    (b) raceways
    (c) lighting
    (d) accessibility

47. The minimum height of dedicated equipment space for motor control centers installed indoors is _____ ft above the enclosure, or to the structural ceiling, whichever is lower.

    (a) 3
    (b) 5
    (c) 6
    (d) 6½

48. For indoor installations, piping, ducts, leak protection apparatus, or other equipment foreign to the electrical installation shall not be installed in the dedicated space above a panelboard or switchboard.

    (a) True
    (b) False

49. The dedicated equipment space for electrical equipment that is required for panelboards installed indoors is measured from the floor to a height of _____ ft above the equipment, or to the structural ceiling, whichever is lower.

    (a) 3
    (b) 6
    (c) 12
    (d) 30

50. All switchboards, switchgear, panelboards, and motor control centers shall be located in dedicated spaces and protected from damage, and outdoor installations shall be _____.

    (a) installed in identified enclosures
    (b) protected from accidental contact by unauthorized personnel or by vehicular traffic
    (c) protected from accidental spillage or leakage from piping systems
    (d) all of these

Notes

CHAPTER 2

WIRING AND PROTECTION

Introduction to Chapter 2—Wiring and Protection

Chapter 2 provides general rules for wiring and for the overcurrent protection of conductors. The rules in this chapter apply to all electrical installations covered by the *NEC*—except as modified in Chapters 5, 6, and 7 [90.3].

Communications systems (twisted wire, antennas, and coaxial cable) (Chapter 8 systems) aren't subject to the general requirements of Chapters 1 through 4, or the special requirements of Chapters 5 through 7, unless there's a specific reference in Chapter 8 to a rule in Chapters 1 through 7 [90.3].

As you go through Chapter 2, remember its purpose. It's primarily concerned with correctly sizing and protecting circuits. Every article in this chapter deals with a different aspect of this purpose. This differs from the purpose of Chapter 3, which is to correctly install the conductors that make up those circuits.

Chapter 1 introduced you to the *NEC* and provided a solid foundation for understanding the *Code*. Chapter 2 (Wiring and Protection) and Chapter 3 (Wiring Methods and Materials) continue building the foundation for applying the *NEC*. Chapter 4 applies the preceding chapters to general equipment. It's beneficial to learn the first four chapters of the *Code* in a sequential manner because each of the first four chapters builds on the one before it. Once you've become familiar with the first four chapters, you can learn the next four in any order you wish.

- **Article 200—Use and Identification of Grounded [Neutral] Conductors.** This article contains the requirements for the use and identification of the grounded conductor and its terminals.

    Author's Comment:

    - Throughout this textbook, we'll use the term "neutral" when referring to the grounded conductor when the application isn't related to PV systems or corner-grounded delta-connected systems.

- **Article 210—Branch Circuits.** Article 210 contains the requirements for branch circuits, such as conductor sizing, identification, and GFCI protection, as well as receptacle and lighting outlet requirements.

- **Article 215—Feeders.** This article covers the requirements for the installation and ampacity of feeders.

Chapter 2 | Wiring and Protection

- **Article 220—Branch-Circuit, Feeder, and Service Calculations.** Article 220 provides the requirements for calculating the minimum size for branch circuits, feeders, and services. This article also aids in determining related factors such as the number of receptacles on a circuit in nondwelling installations, and the minimum number of branch circuits required.

- **Article 225—Outside Branch Circuits and Feeders.** This article covers the installation requirements for equipment, including branch circuits and feeders located outside (overhead and underground) that run on or between buildings, poles, and other structures on the premises.

- **Article 230—Services.** Article 230 covers the installation requirements for service conductors and equipment. It's very important to know where the service begins and ends when applying Article 230.

  Author's Comment:

  - Conductors from a battery, uninterruptible power supply, solar PV system, generator, or transformer aren't service conductors; they're feeder conductors.

- **Article 240—Overcurrent Protection.** This article provides the requirements for overcurrent protection and overcurrent protection devices. Overcurrent protection for conductors and equipment is provided to open the circuit if the current reaches a value that will cause an excessive or dangerous temperature on the conductors or conductor insulation.

- **Article 250—Grounding and Bonding.** Article 250 covers the grounding requirements for providing a path to the earth to reduce overvoltage from lightning, and the bonding requirements for a low-impedance fault current path necessary to facilitate the operation of overcurrent protection devices in the event of a ground fault.

- **Article 285—Surge Protective Devices (SPDs).** This article covers the general, installation, and connection requirements for surge protective devices (SPDs) permanently installed on both the line side and load side of service equipment.

ARTICLE 200
USE AND IDENTIFICATION OF GROUNDED [NEUTRAL] CONDUCTORS

Introduction to Article 200—Use and Identification of Grounded [Neutral] Conductors

This article contains the requirements for the identification of the grounded [neutral] conductor and its terminals. Article 100 contains definitions for both "Grounded Conductor" and "Neutral Conductor." In some cases, both terms apply to the same conductor. ▶Figure 200–1 and ▶Figure 200–2

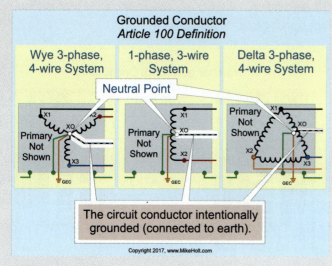

▶Figure 200–1

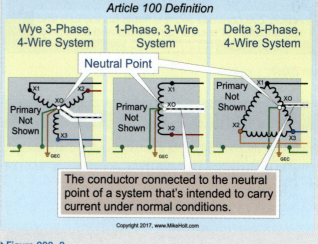

▶Figure 200–2

Author's Comment:

- Throughout this textbook, we'll use the term "neutral" when referring to the grounded conductor when the application isn't related to PV systems or corner-grounded delta-connected systems.

200.1 | Use and Identification of Grounded [Neutral] Conductors

Part I. General

200.1 Scope

Article 200 contains requirements for the use and identification of grounded [neutral] conductors and terminals. ▶Figure 200–3

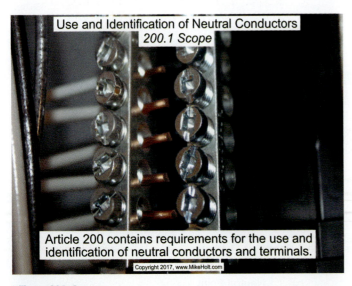

▶Figure 200–3

200.2 General

(B) Continuity. The continuity of the grounded [neutral] conductor isn't permitted to be dependent on metal enclosures, raceways, or cable armor. ▶Figure 200–4

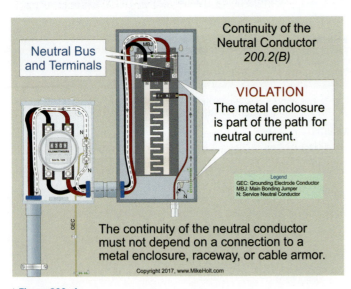

▶Figure 200–4

Author's Comment:

- This requirement prohibits the practice of terminating the grounded [neutral] conductor on the enclosure of a panel or other equipment, rather than on the neutral terminal bar. This ensures the metal panelboard, raceway, or cable armor doesn't carry neutral current. Some panelboards have two terminal bars, one on either side of the panelboard with a strap connecting the terminal bars together. Caution must be taken to terminate the neutral conductor to the neutral terminal, not to the equipment grounding conductor terminal.

200.4 Neutral Conductor

Neutral conductors must comply with (A) and (B).

(A) Installation. A single neutral conductor can't be used for more than one branch circuit. ▶Figure 200–5

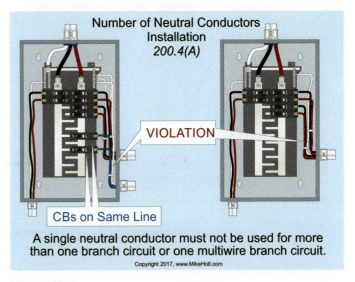

▶Figure 200–5

(B) Grouping. The ungrounded and neutral conductors of multiple branch circuits must be identified or grouped together by cable ties or similar means in every enclosure. ▶Figure 200–6 and ▶Figure 200–7

Ex 1: Grouping isn't required where the circuit conductors are contained in a single raceway or cable unique to that circuit and makes the grouping obvious.

Ex 2: Grouping isn't required if the conductors pass through a box or conduit body without any splices or terminations, or if the conductors don't have a loop as described in 314.16(B)(1).

Use and Identification of Grounded [Neutral] Conductors | 200.6

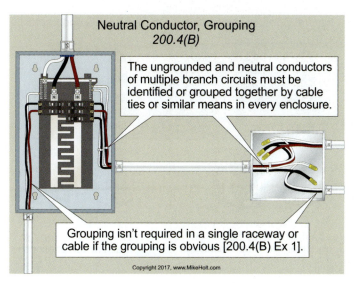

▶Figure 200–6

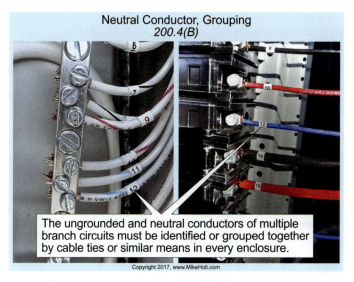

▶Figure 200–7

Author's Comment:

■ Grouping all associated conductors of a multiwire branch circuit together by cable ties or other means within the point of origination makes it easier to visually identify the conductors of the multiwire branch circuit. The grouping will assist in making sure the correct neutral is used at junction points and in connecting multiwire branch-circuit conductors to circuit breakers correctly, particularly where twin breakers are used. If proper diligence isn't exercised when making these connections, two circuit conductors can be accidentally connected to the same phase or line.

■ Individual current carrying circuit conductors will create magnetic fields. Grouping the associated conductors of a circuit together will reduce the size and strength of these fields.

CAUTION: If the ungrounded conductors of a multiwire circuit aren't terminated to different phases or lines, the currents on the neutral conductor won't cancel, which can cause an overload on the neutral conductor. ▶Figure 200–8

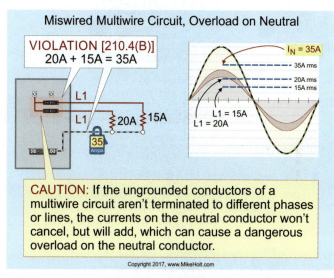

▶Figure 200–8

200.6 Neutral Conductor Identification

(A) Size 6 AWG or Smaller. Neutral conductors 6 AWG and smaller must be identified by any of the following means: ▶Figure 200–9

(1) A continuous white outer finish.

(2) A continuous gray outer finish.

(3) Three continuous white or gray stripes along its entire length on other than green insulation.

(4) Wires that have their outer covering finished to show a white or gray color but have colored tracer threads in the braid identifying the source of manufacture are considered to meet the provisions of this section.

200.6 | Use and Identification of Grounded [Neutral] Conductors

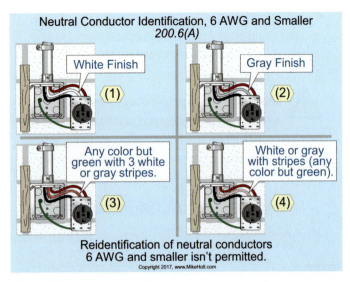

▶Figure 200–9

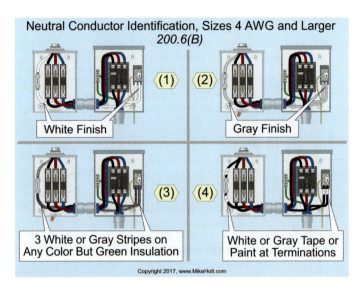

▶Figure 200–11

Author's Comment:

- The use of white tape, paint, or other methods of identification aren't permitted for neutral conductors 6 AWG and smaller.
  ▶Figure 200–10

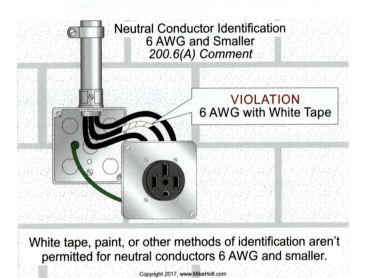

▶Figure 200–10

(6) A single-conductor, sunlight-resistant, outdoor-rated cable used as the grounded conductor in PV power systems as permitted by 690.31(B) can be identified by distinctive white marking at all terminations.

(B) Size 4 AWG or Larger. Neutral conductors 4 AWG or larger must be identified by any of the following means: ▶Figure 200–11

(1) A continuous white outer finish along its entire length.

(2) A continuous gray outer finish along its entire length.

(3) Three continuous white or gray stripes along its length.

(4) White or gray tape or markings at the terminations.

(D) Neutral Conductors of Different Systems. If neutral conductors of different voltage systems are installed in the same raceway, cable, or enclosure, each system neutral conductor must be identified by:

(1) A continuous white or gray outer finish along its entire length.
  ▶Figure 200–12

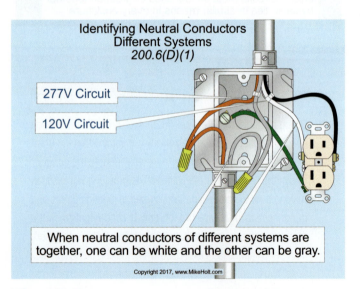

▶Figure 200–12

Use and Identification of Grounded [Neutral] Conductors | 200.7

(2) The neutral conductor of the other system must have a different outer covering of continuous white or gray outer finish along its entire length or an outer covering of white or gray with a readily distinguishable color stripe (other than green) along its entire length. ▶Figure 200–13

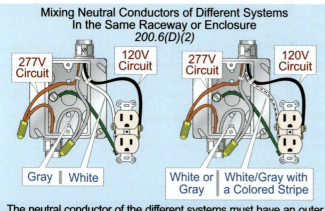

▶Figure 200–13

(3) Other identification allowed by 200.6(A) or (B) that will distinguish the neutral conductor from other systems. ▶Figure 200–14

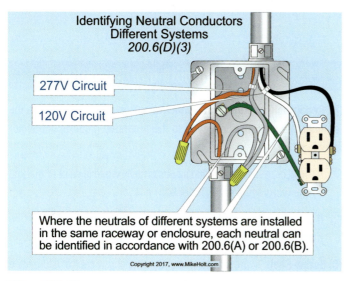

▶Figure 200–14

200.7 Use of White or Gray Color

(A) General. Only the grounded circuit conductor is permitted to use the following, unless otherwise permitted in 200.7(B) and (C):

(1) A conductor with continuous white or gray covering

(2) A conductor with three continuous white or gray stripes on other than green insulation

(3) A marking of white or gray color at the termination

(C) Circuits of 50V or More. A conductor with white or gray insulation can only be used for the ungrounded conductor as follows:

(1) Cable Assembly. The white or gray conductor within a cable can be used for the ungrounded conductor, if permanently reidentified by marking tape, painting, or other effective means at each location where the conductor is visible to indicate its use as an ungrounded conductor. Identification must encircle the insulation and must be a color other than white, gray, or green. ▶Figure 200–15

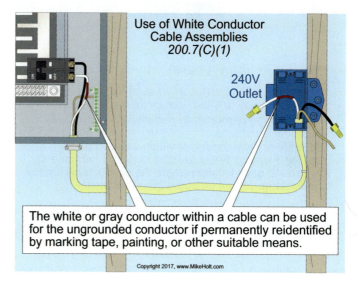

▶Figure 200–15

The white or gray conductor within a cable can be used to supply power to single-pole, 3-way, and 4-way switch loops, as well as travelers for 3-way and 4-way switching if permanently reidentified at each location where the conductor is visible to indicate its use as an ungrounded conductor. ▶Figure 200–16 and ▶Figure 200–17

(2) Flexible Cord. The white or gray conductor within a flexible cord can be used for the ungrounded conductor for connecting an appliance or equipment as permitted by 400.10.

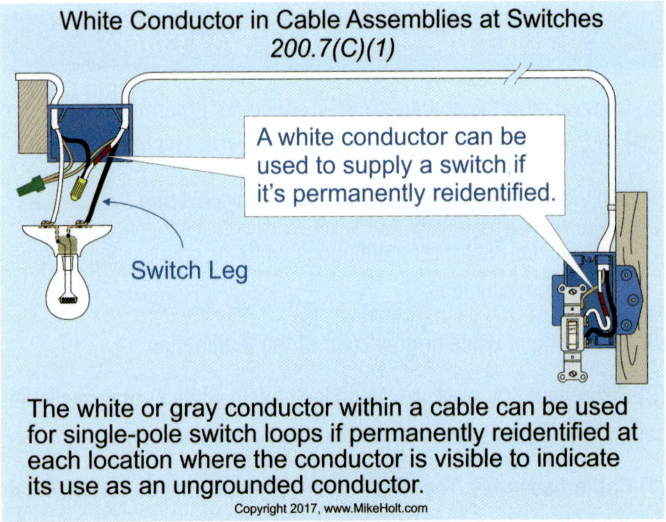

200.9 | Use and Identification of Grounded [Neutral] Conductors

▶Figure 200–16

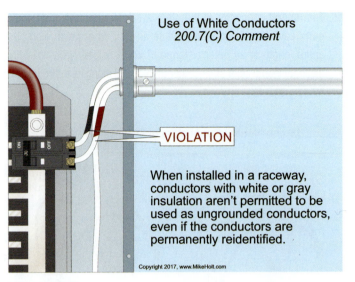

▶Figure 200–18

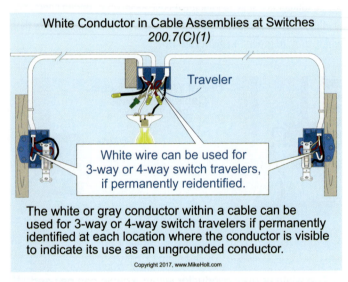

▶Figure 200–17

Note: Care should be taken when working on existing systems because a gray insulated conductor may have been used in the past as an ungrounded conductor.

Author's Comment:

- The *NEC* doesn't permit the use of white or gray conductor insulation for ungrounded conductors within a raceway, even if the conductors are permanently reidentified. ▶Figure 200–18

200.9 Terminal Identification

The terminal for the grounded [neutral] conductor must be colored white (silver). The terminal for the ungrounded conductor must be a color readily distinguishable from white (brass or copper).

Author's Comment:

- Terminals for the circuit equipment grounding conductor must be green [250.126 and 406.10(B)].

200.10 Identification of Terminals

(B) Receptacles, Plugs, and Connectors. Receptacles must have the terminal intended for connection to the grounded [neutral] conductor identified by:

(1) A metal or metal coating that's substantially white in color or marked by the word white or the letter W.

(2) If the terminal isn't visible, the conductor entrance hole must be marked with the word white or the letter W.

(C) Screw Shell. To prevent electric shock, the screw shell of a luminaire or lampholder must be connected to the grounded [neutral] conductor [410.90]. ▶Figure 200–19

Use and Identification of Grounded [Neutral] Conductors | 200.10

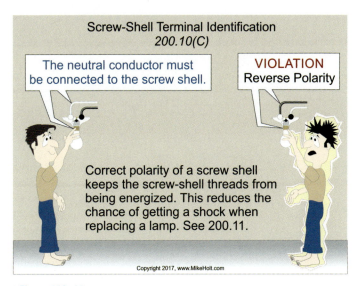

▶Figure 200–19

Author's Comment:

- See the definition of "Luminaire" in Article 100.

Notes

ARTICLE 210
BRANCH CIRCUITS

Introduction to Article 210—Branch Circuits

This article contains the requirements for branch circuits, such as conductor sizing and identification, GFCI protection, and receptacle and lighting outlet requirements. It consists of three parts:

- Part I. General Provisions
- Part II. Branch-Circuit Ratings
- Part III. Required Outlets

Table 210.3 of this article identifies specific-purpose branch circuits. The provisions for branch circuits that supply equipment listed in Table 210.3 amend or supplement the provisions given in Article 210 for branch circuits, so it's important to be aware of the contents of this table.

Mastering the branch-circuit requirements in Article 210 will give you a jump-start toward completing installations that are free of *Code* violations.

Part I. General Provisions

210.1 Scope

Article 210 provides the general requirements for branch circuits such as, conductor sizing, overcurrent protection, identification, GFCI and AFCI protection, as well as receptacle outlets and lighting outlet requirements.

> **Author's Comment:**
>
> - Article 100 defines a "Branch Circuit" as the conductors between the final overcurrent protection device and the receptacle outlets, lighting outlets, or other outlets. ▶Figure 210–1

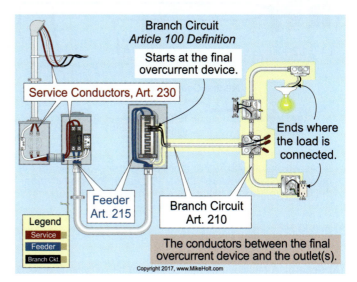

▶Figure 210–1

210.3 | Branch Circuits

210.3 Other Articles

Table 210.3 lists references for specific equipment and applications not located in Chapters 5, 6, and 7.

- Air-Conditioning and Refrigeration, 440.6, 440.31, and 440.32
- Central Heating Equipment, 422.12
- Electric Space-Heating Equipment, 424.3(B)
- Motors, 430.22

210.4 Multiwire Branch Circuits

Author's Comment:

- A multiwire branch circuit consists of two or more ungrounded circuit conductors with a common neutral conductor. There must be a difference of voltage between the ungrounded conductors and an equal difference of voltage from each ungrounded conductor to the common neutral conductor. ▶Figure 210–2

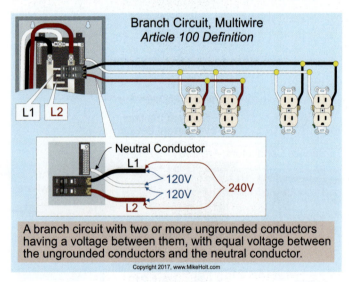

▶Figure 210–2

(A) General. A multiwire branch circuit can be considered a single circuit or a multiple circuit. To prevent inductive heating and to reduce conductor impedance for fault currents, all conductors of a multiwire branch circuit must originate from the same panelboard. ▶Figure 210–3

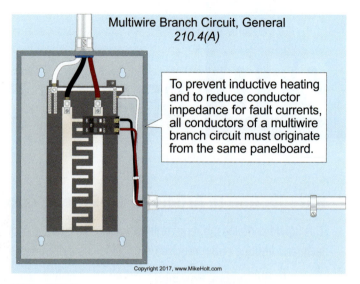

▶Figure 210–3

Author's Comment:

- For more information on the inductive heating of metal parts, see 300.3(B), 300.5(I), and 300.20.

Note 2: See 300.13(B) for the requirements relating to the continuity of the neutral conductor on multiwire branch circuits.

▶ **Hazard of Open Neutral**

Example: A 3-wire, single-phase, 120/240V multiwire circuit supplies a 1,200W, 120V hair dryer and a 600W, 120V television.
▶Figure 210–4

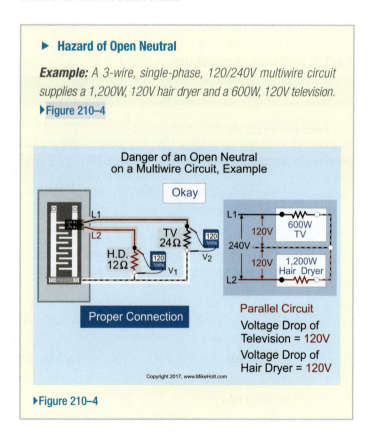

▶Figure 210–4

If the neutral conductor of the multiwire circuit is interrupted, it will cause the 120V television to operate at 160V and consume 1,067W of power (instead of 600W) for only a few seconds before it burns up. ▶Figure 210–5

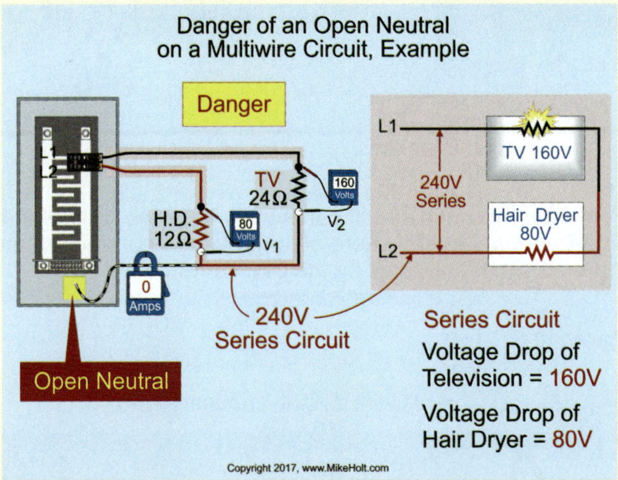

▶Figure 210–5

Solution:

Step 1: Determine the resistance of each appliance:

$R = E^2/P$

R of the hair dryer = $120V^2/1,200W$

R of the hair dryer = 12 ohms

R of the television = $120V^2/600W$

R of the television = 24 ohms

Step 2: Determine the current of the circuit:

$I = E/R$

E = 240V

R = 36 ohms (12 ohms + 24 ohms)

I = 240V/36 ohms

I = 6.70A

Step 3: Determine the operating voltage for each appliance:

$E = I \times R$

I = 6.70A

R = 12 ohms for hair dryer and 24 ohms for TV

Voltage of hair dryer = 6.70A × 12 ohms

Voltage of hair dryer = 80V

Voltage of television = 6.70A × 24 ohms

Voltage of television = 160V

WARNING: *Failure to terminate the ungrounded conductors to separate phases can cause the neutral conductor to become overloaded, and the insulation can be damaged or destroyed by excessive heat. Conductor overheating is known to decrease the service life of insulating materials, which creates the potential for arcing faults in hidden locations, and can ultimately lead to fires. It isn't known just how long conductor insulation lasts, but heat does decrease its life span.*

(B) Disconnect. Each multiwire branch circuit must have a means to simultaneously disconnect all ungrounded conductors at the point where the branch circuit originates. ▶Figure 210–6

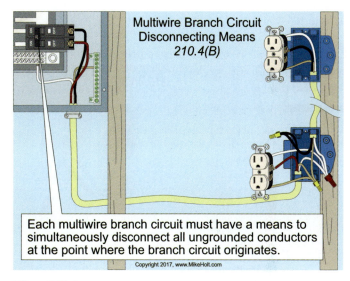

▶Figure 210–6

Note: Individual single-pole circuit breakers with handle ties identified for the purpose can be used for this application [240.15(B)(1)]. ▶Figure 210–7

CAUTION: *This rule is intended to prevent people from working on energized circuits they thought were disconnected.*

(C) Line-to-Neutral Loads. Multiwire branch circuits must supply only line-to-neutral loads.

Ex 1: A multiwire branch circuit can supply an individual piece of line-to-line utilization equipment, such as a range or dryer. ▶Figure 210–8

210.4 | Branch Circuits

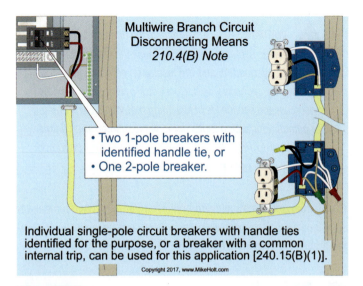

▶Figure 210–7

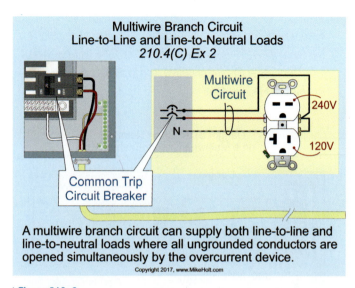

▶Figure 210–9

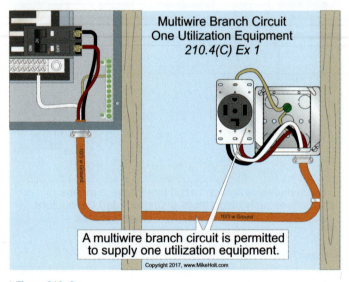

▶Figure 210–8

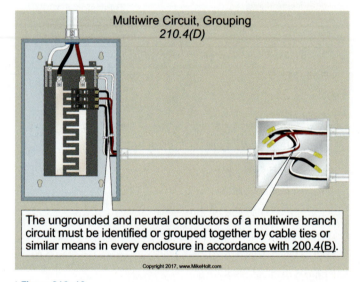

▶Figure 210–10

Ex 2: A multiwire branch circuit can supply both line-to-line and line-to-neutral loads if the circuit is protected by a device such as a multipole circuit breaker with a common internal trip that opens all ungrounded conductors of the multiwire branch circuit simultaneously under a fault condition. ▶Figure 210–9

(D) Grouping. Ungrounded and neutral conductors of a multiwire branch circuit must be identified or grouped together by cable ties or similar means in every enclosure in accordance with 200.4(B). ▶Figure 210–10

Author's Comment:

- Grouping isn't required where the circuit conductors are contained in a single raceway or cable unique to that circuit and makes the grouping obvious [200.4(B) Ex 1].

- Grouping isn't required if the conductors pass through a box or conduit body without any splices or terminations, or if the conductors don't have a loop as described in 314.16(B)(1) [200.4(B) Ex 2].

- Grouping all associated conductors of a multiwire branch circuit together by cable ties or other means within the point of origination makes it easier to visually identify the conductors of the multiwire branch circuit. The grouping will assist in making sure the correct neutral is used at junction points and in connecting multiwire branch-circuit conductors to circuit breakers correctly, particularly where twin breakers are used. If proper diligence isn't exercised when making these connections, two circuit conductors can be accidentally connected to the same phase or line.

⚠ **CAUTION:** If the ungrounded conductors of a multiwire circuit aren't terminated to different phases or lines, the currents on the neutral conductor won't cancel, which can cause an overload on the neutral conductor. ▶Figure 210–11

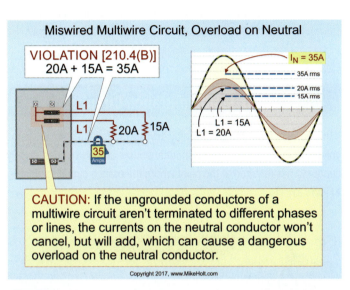

▶Figure 210–11

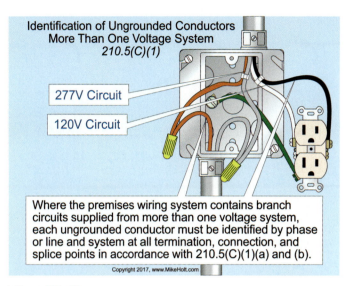

▶Figure 210–12

210.5 Identification for Branch Circuits

(A) Neutral Conductor. The neutral conductor of a branch circuit must be identified in accordance with 200.6.

(B) Equipment Grounding Conductor. Equipment grounding conductors can be bare, covered, or insulated. Insulated equipment grounding conductors size 6 AWG and smaller must have a continuous outer finish either green or green with one or more yellow stripes [250.119].

On equipment grounding conductors 4 AWG and larger, insulation can be permanently reidentified with green marking at the time of installation at every point where the conductor is accessible [250.119(A)].

(C) Identification of Ungrounded Conductors. Ungrounded circuit conductors must be identified as follows:

(1) More Than One Voltage System. Where the premises wiring system has branch circuits supplied from more than one nominal voltage system, each ungrounded conductor must be identified by phase and system at all termination, connection, and splice points as follows: ▶Figure 210–12

(a) Means of Identification. Identification can be by color coding, marking tape, tagging, or other means approved by the authority having jurisdiction. ▶Figure 210–13

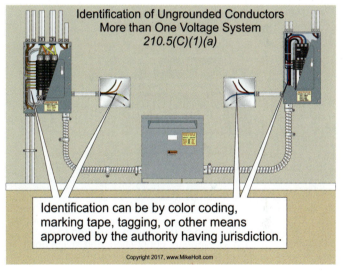

▶Figure 210–13

(b) Posting of Branch Circuit Identification. The method of identification must be readily available or permanently posted at each branch-circuit panelboard, not be handwritten, and be of sufficient durability to withstand the environment involved. ▶Figure 210–14

Ex: Where a different voltage system is added to an existing installation, branch circuit identification is required for the new voltage system. Existing unidentified systems aren't required to be identified at each termination, connection, and splice point in compliance with 210.5(C)(1)(a) and (b). Each voltage system distribution equipment must have a label with the words "other unidentified systems exist on the premises." ▶Figure 210–15

210.7 | Branch Circuits

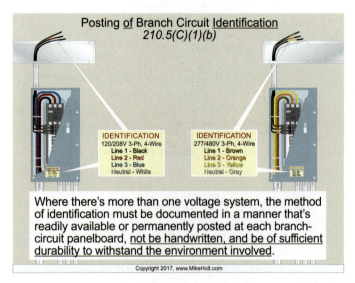
▶Figure 210–14

- Although the *NEC* doesn't require a specific color code for ungrounded conductors, electricians often use the following color system for power and lighting conductor identification:
  - 120/240V, single-phase—black, red, and white
  - 120/208V, three-phase—black, red, blue, and white
  - 120/240V, three-phase—black, orange, blue, and white
  - 277/480V, three-phase—brown, orange, yellow, and gray; or, brown, purple, yellow, and gray

210.7 Multiple Branch Circuits

If two or more branch circuits supply devices or equipment on the same yoke, a means to disconnect simultaneously all ungrounded supply conductors is required at the point where the branch circuit originates.
▶Figure 210–16

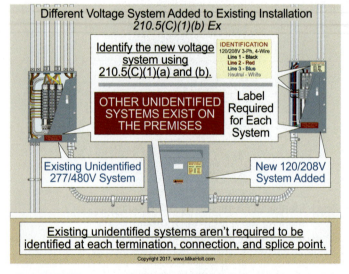
▶Figure 210–15

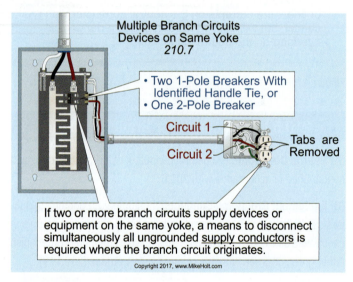
▶Figure 210–16

Author's Comment:

- When a premises has more than one voltage system supplying branch circuits, the ungrounded conductors must be identified by phase and system. This can be done by permanently posting an identification legend that describes the method used, such as color-coded marking tape or color-coded insulation.

- Conductors with insulation that's green or green with one or more yellow stripes can't be used for an ungrounded or neutral conductor [250.119].

Author's Comment:

- A yoke, also called a strap, is the metal mounting structure for such items as receptacles, switches, switches with pilot lights, and switch-receptacles to name a few. ▶Figure 210–17 and ▶Figure 210–18

- Individual single-pole circuit breakers with handle ties identified for the purpose, or a circuit breaker with a common internal trip, can be used for this application [240.15(B)(1)].

Branch Circuits | 210.19

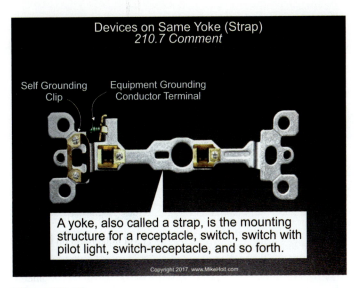
▶Figure 210–17

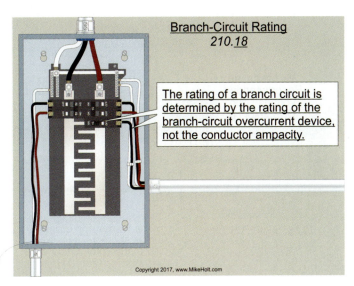
▶Figure 210–19

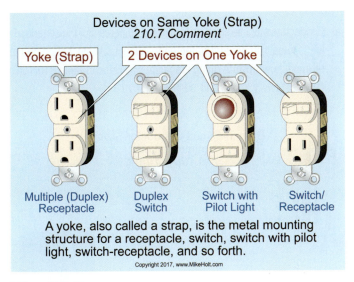
▶Figure 210–18

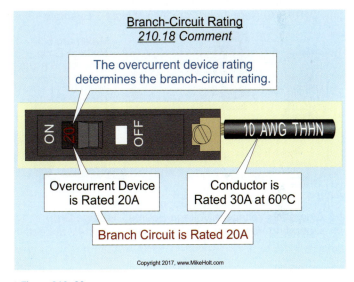
▶Figure 210–20

Part II. Branch-Circuit Ratings

210.18 Branch-Circuit Rating

The rating of a branch circuit is determined by the rating of the branch-circuit overcurrent protection device, not the conductor ampacity.
▶Figure 210–19

Author's Comment:

- For example, the branch-circuit rating of 10 THHN, rated 30A at 60°C, protected by a 20A circuit breaker is 20A.
  ▶Figure 210–20

210.19 Conductor Sizing

(A) Branch Circuits.

Note 4: To provide reasonable efficiency of operation of electrical equipment, branch-circuit conductors should be sized to prevent a voltage drop not to exceed 3 percent. In addition, the maximum total voltage drop on both feeders and branch circuits shouldn't exceed 5 percent [215.2(A)(1)]. ▶Figure 210–21 and ▶Figure 210–22

210.19 | Branch Circuits

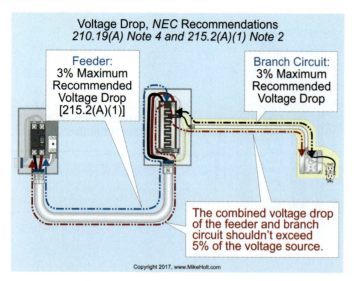

▶Figure 210–21

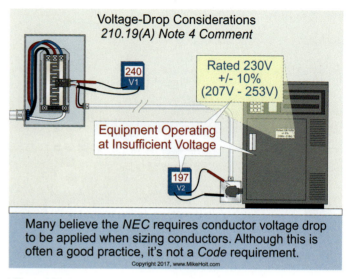

▶Figure 210–23

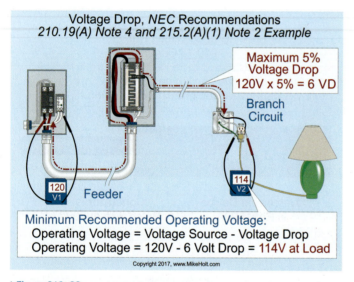

▶Figure 210–22

Author's Comment:

- Many believe the *NEC* requires conductor voltage drop, as per Note 4 to be applied when sizing conductors. Although this is often a good practice, it's not a *Code* requirement because Notes are only advisory statements [90.5(C)]. ▶Figure 210–23
- The *NEC* doesn't consider voltage drop to be a safety issue, except for fire pumps [695.7].

(1) General. Branch-circuit conductors must have an ampacity of not less than the maximum load to be served. The conductor must be the larger of (a) or (b).

(a) Conductors must be sized no less than 125 percent of the continuous loads, plus 100 percent of the noncontinuous loads, based on the terminal temperature rating ampacities as listed in Table 310.15(B)(16). ▶Figure 210–24 and ▶Figure 210–25

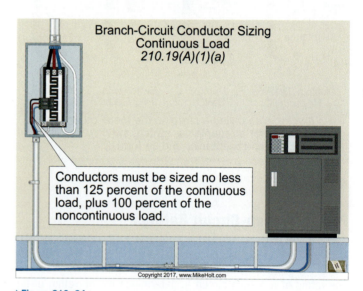

▶Figure 210–24

(b) Conductors must be sized to the maximum load to be served after the application of any adjustment or correction factors. ▶Figure 210–26

Ex 1: If the assembly and the overcurrent protection device are both listed for operation at 100 percent of their rating, the conductors can be sized at 100 percent of the continuous load.

Branch Circuits | 210.19

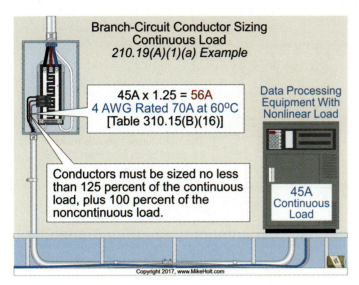

▶Figure 210–25

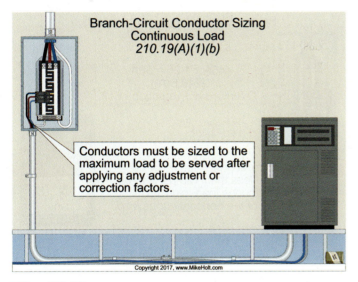

▶Figure 210–26

Author's Comment:

- Equipment suitable for 100 percent continuous loading is rarely available in ratings under 400A.
- See the definition of "Continuous Load" in Article 100.
- See 210.20 for the sizing requirements for the branch-circuit overcurrent protection device for continuous and noncontinuous loads.

Example: What size branch-circuit conductors are required for a 4-wire circuit of a 45A nonlinear continuous load, if the equipment terminals are rated 75ºC? ▶Figure 210–27

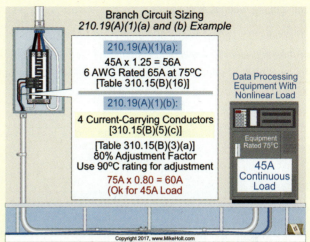

▶Figure 210–27

Answer: 6 AWG rated 75A at 90ºC. Since the load is 45A continuous, the conductors must be sized to have an ampacity of not less than 56A (45A × 1.25). According to the 75ºC column of Table 310.15(B)(16), a 6 AWG conductor is suitable, because it has an ampere rating of 65A at 75ºC. This satisfies the portion of the calculation discussed in 210.19(A)(1)(a).

For 210.19(A)(1)(b), we need to address ambient temperature and conductor bundling.

Because the neutral in this example is considered a current-carrying conductor [310.15(B)(5)(c)], there are four current-carrying conductors. Table 310.15(B)(3)(a) requires an adjustment factor of 80% for this example.

6 AWG rated 75A at 90ºC × 0.80 = 60A after adjustment factors which is adequate for the 45A load.

If we had selected an 8 AWG conductor rated 55A at 90ºC, based on the 45A load, it would be too small for the load after applying the adjustment factor (55A × 0.80 = 44A).

(2) Branch Circuits Supplying More than One Receptacle. Branch circuits that supply more than one receptacle must have an ampacity not less than the rating of the circuit overcurrent protection device [210.18].

210.20 | Branch Circuits

(3) Household Ranges and Cooking Appliances. Branch-circuit conductors that supply household ranges, wall-mounted ovens, or counter-mounted cooking units must have an ampacity not less than the rating of the branch circuit, and not less than the maximum load to be served. For ranges of 8¾ kW or more rating, the minimum branch-circuit ampere rating is 40A.

Ex 1: Conductors tapped from a 50A branch circuit for electric ranges, wall-mounted electric ovens, and counter-mounted electric cooking units must have an ampacity not less than 20A, and must have sufficient ampacity for the load to be served. ▶Figure 210–28

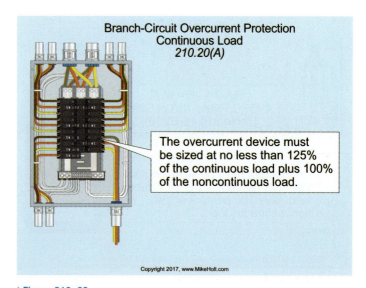

▶Figure 210–29

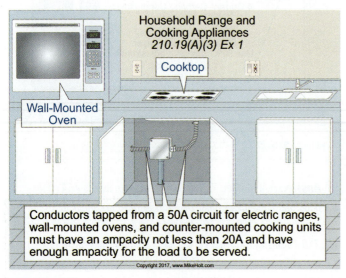

▶Figure 210–28

210.20 Overcurrent Protection

(A) Continuous and Noncontinuous Loads. Branch-circuit overcurrent protection devices must have a rating of not less than 125 percent of the continuous loads, plus 100 percent of the noncontinuous loads. ▶Figure 210–29 and ▶Figure 210–30

Author's Comment:

- See 210.19(A)(1) for branch-circuit conductor sizing requirements.

Ex: If the assembly and the overcurrent protection devices are both listed for operation at 100 percent of their rating, the branch-circuit overcurrent protection device can be sized at 100 percent of the continuous load.

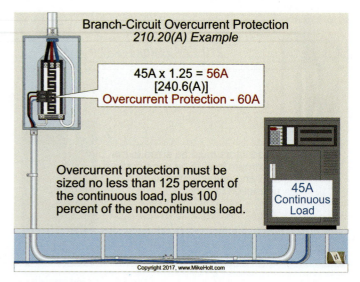

▶Figure 210–30

Author's Comment:

- Equipment suitable for 100 percent continuous loading is rarely available in ratings under 400A.

(B) Conductor Protection. Branch-circuit conductors must be protected against overcurrent in accordance with 240.4.

(C) Equipment Protection. Branch-circuit equipment must be protected in accordance with 240.3.

210.21 Receptacle Rating

(A) Lampholder Ratings. Lampholders connected to a branch circuit rated over 20A must be of the heavy-duty type.

Author's Comment:

- Fluorescent lampholders aren't rated heavy duty, so fluorescent luminaires aren't permitted to be installed on circuits rated over 20A.

(B) Receptacle Ratings and Loadings.

(1) Single Receptacles. A single receptacle on an individual branch circuit must have an ampacity not less than the rating of the overcurrent protection device. ▶Figure 210–31

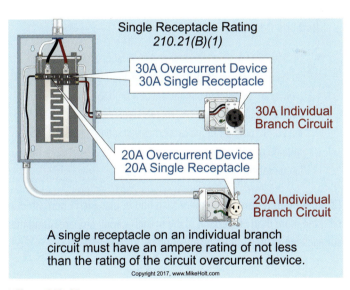

▶Figure 210–31

Note: A single receptacle has only one contact device on its yoke [Article 100]; this means a duplex receptacle is considered to be two receptacles.

(2) Multiple Receptacle Loading. If connected to a branch circuit that supplies two or more receptacles, the total cord-and-plug-connected load must not exceed 80 percent of the receptacle rating.

Author's Comment:

- A duplex receptacle has two contact devices on the same yoke [Article 100]. This means that one duplex receptacle on a branch circuit makes it a branch circuit with multiple receptacles.

(3) Multiple Receptacle Rating. If connected to a branch circuit that supplies two or more receptacles, the receptacles must have an ampere rating in accordance with the values listed in Table 210.21(B)(3). ▶Figure 210–32

▶Figure 210–32

Table 210.21(B)(3) Receptacle Ratings	
Circuit Rating	Receptacle Rating
15A	15A
20A	15A or 20A
30A	30A
40A	40A or 50A
50A	50A

210.22 Permissible Loads, Individual Branch Circuits

An individual branch circuit can supply any load that doesn't exceed the ampere rating of the branch circuit. ▶Figure 210–33

210.23 | Branch Circuits

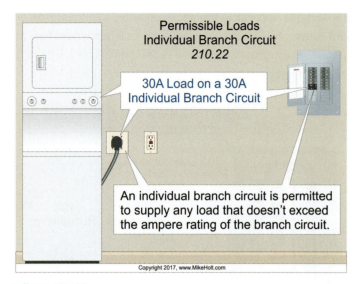

▶Figure 210–33

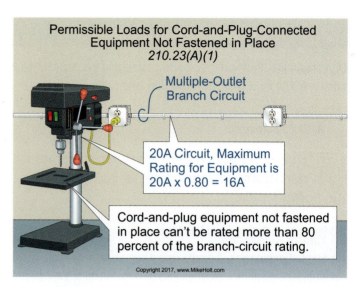

▶Figure 210–35

210.23 Permissible Loads, Multiple-Outlet Branch Circuits

(A) 15A and 20A Circuit. A 15A or 20A branch circuit can supply lighting, equipment, or any combination of both. ▶Figure 210–34

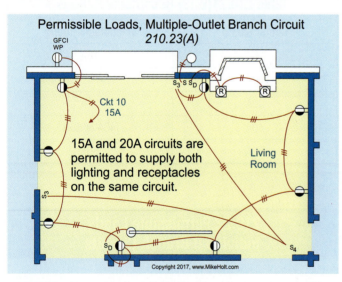

▶Figure 210–34

(1) Cord-and-Plug-Connected Equipment Not Fastened in Place. Cord-and-plug-connected equipment not fastened in place, such as a drill press or table saw, must not have an ampere rating more than 80 percent of the branch-circuit rating. ▶Figure 210–35

Author's Comment:

- UL and other testing laboratories list portable equipment (such as hair dryers) up to 100 percent of the circuit rating. The *NEC* is an installation standard, not a product standard, so it can't prohibit this practice. There's really no way to limit the load to 80 percent of the branch-circuit rating if testing laboratories permit equipment to be listed for 100 percent of the circuit rating.

(2) Fixed Equipment. Equipment fastened in place isn't permitted to be rated more than 50 percent of the branch-circuit ampere rating that supplies luminaires, receptacles, or both. ▶Figure 210–36

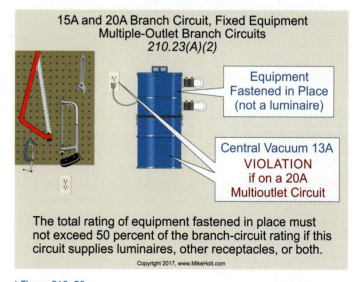

▶Figure 210–36

210.25 Branch Circuits in Buildings with Multiple Occupancies

(A) Dwelling Unit Branch Circuits. Dwelling unit branch circuits are only permitted to supply loads within or associated with the dwelling unit.

(B) Common Area Branch Circuits. Branch circuits installed for public or common areas of a multi-occupancy building aren't permitted to originate from equipment that supplies an individual dwelling unit or tenant space.

> **Author's Comment:**
> - This rule prohibits common area branch circuits from being supplied from an individual dwelling unit or tenant space to prevent common area circuits from being turned off by tenants or by the electric utility due to nonpayment of electric bills.

Notes

ARTICLE 215 FEEDERS

Introduction to Article 215—Feeders

Article 215 covers the rules for the installation and ampacity of feeders. The requirements for feeders have some similarities to those for branch circuits, but in some ways, feeders bear a resemblance to service conductors. It's important to understand the distinct differences between these three types of circuits in order to correctly apply the *Code* requirements.

Feeders are the conductors between the service equipment, the separately derived system, or other supply source, and the final branch-circuit overcurrent protection device. Conductors past the final overcurrent protection device protecting the circuit and the outlet are branch-circuit conductors and fall within the scope of Article 210 [Article 100 Definitions].

Service conductors are the conductors from the service point to the service disconnect. [Article 100 Definition]. If there's no serving utility, and the electrical power is derived from a generator or other on-site electric power source, then the conductors from the supply source are defined as feeders and there are no service conductors.

It's easy to be confused between feeder, branch circuit, and service conductors, so it's important to evaluate each installation carefully using the Article 100 Definitions to be sure the correct *NEC* rules are followed.

215.1 Scope

Article 215 covers the installation, conductor sizing, and overcurrent protection requirements for feeder conductors.

Author's Comment:

- Article 100 defines feeders as the conductors between service equipment, a separately derived system, or other power supply, and the final branch-circuit overcurrent protection device. ▶Figure 215–1 and ▶Figure 215–2

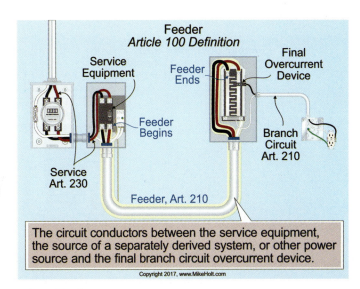

▶Figure 215–1

215.2 | Feeders

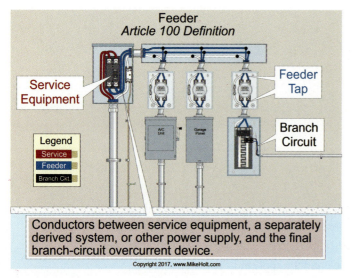

▶Figure 215–2

215.2 Minimum Rating

(A) Feeder Conductor Size.

(1) General. Feeder conductors must be sized to carry the larger of (a) or (b):

(a) The feeder conductor must have an ampacity before ampacity correction and adjustment of not less than 125 percent of the continuous load, plus 100 percent of the noncontinuous load, based on the terminal temperature rating ampacities as listed in Table 310.15(B)(16) [110.14(C)(1)]. ▶Figure 215–3

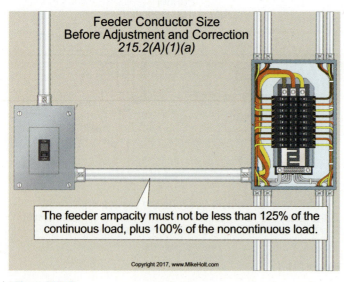

▶Figure 215–3

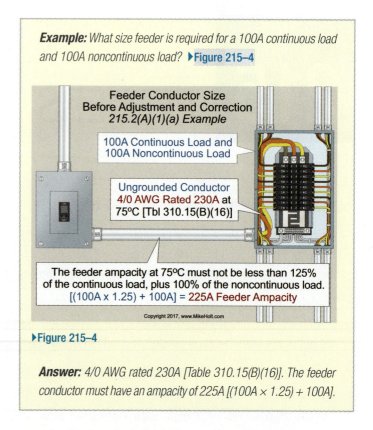

▶Figure 215–4

Answer: 4/0 AWG rated 230A [Table 310.15(B)(16)]. The feeder conductor must have an ampacity of 225A [(100A × 1.25) + 100A].

Ex 1: If the assembly and the overcurrent protection device are both listed for operation at 100 percent of their rating, the conductors can be sized at 100 percent of the continuous and noncontinuous load.

Author's Comment:

- Equipment suitable for 100 percent continuous loading is rarely available in ratings under 400A.

Ex 2: A section of feeder conductors that terminates in a junction box at both ends to 90°C terminals in accordance with 110.14(C)(2) are permitted to have an ampacity of not less than 100 percent of the continuous and 100 percent of the noncontinuous load based on the 90°C column of Table 310.15(B)(16) for 90°C conductor insulation. The 100 percent at 90°C feeder conductors aren't permitted to extend into the supply or the load terminations to the feeder circuit. ▶Figure 215–5

Author's Comment:

- **Equipment Terminals Rated 75°C.** Feeder circuits must be sized to 125% of the continuous load [215.2(A)(1)(a)] for circuits over 100A. The conductors must be sized to the 75°C ampacity listed on Table 310.15(B)(16) [110.14(C)(1)(b)]. Circuits rated not over 800A can have overcurrent protection

Feeders | 215.2

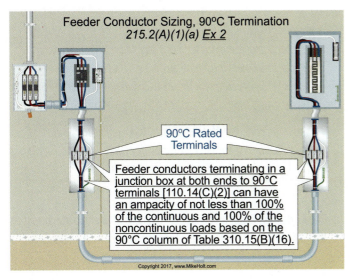

▶Figure 215–5

Answer: *Feeder 500 kcmil, rated 380A at 75°C, neutral 3 AWG, rated 100A at 75°C, and equipment grounding conductor of 3 AWG. The feeder conductor must have an ampacity of at least 375A (125 percent of the 300A continuous load) [215.2(A)(1)(a)]; 500 kcmil, rated 380A at 75°C in accordance with Table 310.15(B)(16) is suitable [110.14(C)(1)(b)]. The 500 kcmil conductor, rated 375A at 75°C is permitted to be protected by a 400A protection device [240.4(B)].*

The neutral conductor must be sized to carry 50A continuously, which can be 6 AWG, rated 50A [100 Ampacity, 110.14(C)(1)(b), 215.2(A), and 220.61], but it can't be smaller than 3 AWG based on the 400A overcurrent protection device size in accordance with Table 250.122.

Author's Comment:

- **Equipment Terminals Rated 90°C.** Feeder circuits can be sized to 100% of the continuous load based [215.2(A)(1)(a) Ex 1] according to the 90°C ampacity listed on Table 310.15(B)(16) [110.14(C)(2)]. Circuits rated not over 800A can have overcurrent protection sized in accordance with 240.4(B), and for circuits rated over 800A feeder, overcurrent must be in accordance with 240.4(C). The neural conductor is sized to 100% of the continuous load [215.2(A)(1) Ex 3] to the 75°C ampacity listed on Table 310.15(B)(16) [110.14(C)(1)(b)], based on the maximum unbalanced load in accordance with 220.61, and not smaller than required by 250.122 for equipment grounding conductor.

sized in accordance with 240.4(B), and for circuits rated over 800A, overcurrent must be in accordance with 240.4(C). The neural conductor is sized to 100 percent of the continuous load [215.2(A)(1) Ex 3] to the 75°C ampacity listed on Table 310.15(B)(16) [110.14(C)(1)(b)], based on the maximum unbalanced load in accordance with 220.61, and not smaller than required by 250.122 for equipment grounding conductor.

▶ **75°C Equipment Terminals**

Example: *What size feeder conductors are required for a 300A continuous load, having a neutral load of 50A?* ▶Figure 215–6

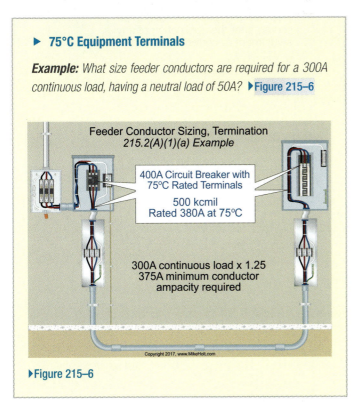

▶Figure 215–6

▶ **90°C Equipment Terminals**

Example: *What size feeder conductor is required for a 300A continuous load?* ▶Figure 215–7

Answer: *Feeder 400 kcmil, rated 380A at 90°C, neutral 3 AWG, rated 100A at 75°C, and equipment grounding conductor of 3 AWG. The feeder conductor must have an ampacity of at least 300A (100 percent of the 300A continuous load) [215.2(A)(1)(a) Ex 1]; 400 kcmil, rated 380A at 90°C in accordance with Table 310.15(B)(16) is suitable [110.14(C)(1)(b)]. The 400 kcmil conductor, rated 380A at 90°C is permitted to be protected by a 400A protection device [240.4(B)].*

The neutral conductor must be sized to carry 50A continuously, which can be 6 AWG, rated 50A [100 Ampacity, 110.14(C)(1)(b), 215.2(A), and 220.61], but it can't be smaller than 3 AWG based on the 400A overcurrent protection device size in accordance with Table 250.122.

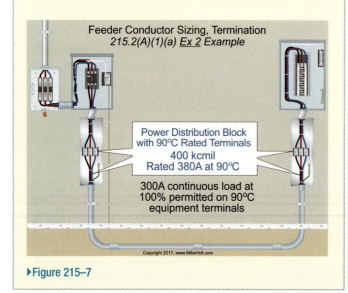

▸Figure 215–7

Ex 3: Neutral conductors must have an ampacity of not less than 100 percent of the continuous and noncontinuous loads.

Example: What size feeder conductors are required for a 200A continuous load if the terminals are rated 75°C? ▸Figure 215–8

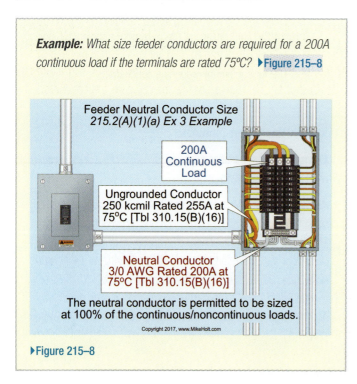

▸Figure 215–8

Answer: 250 kcmil AWG ungrounded conductors and a 3/0 AWG neutral conductor are required. Since the load is 200A continuous, the feeder conductors must have an ampacity of not less than 250A (200A × 1.25). According to the 75°C column of Table 310.15(B)(16) [110.14(C)(1)(b)], 250 kcmil has an ampacity of 255A.

The neutral conductor is sized to the 200A continuous load (100 percent). According to the 75°C column of Table 310.15(B)(16) [110.14(C)(1)(b)], 3/0 has an ampacity of 200A.

(b) The feeder conductor must have an ampacity after ampacity correction and adjustment of not less than the load to be served. ▸Figure 215–9

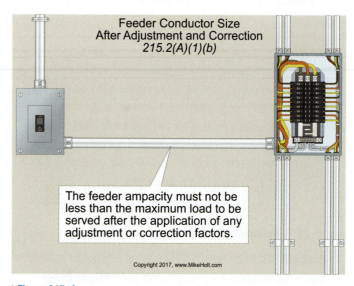

▸Figure 215–9

Author's Comment:

- See 215.3 for the feeder overcurrent protection device sizing requirements for continuous and noncontinuous loads.

Note 2: To provide reasonable efficiency of operation of electrical equipment, feeder conductors should be sized to prevent a voltage drop not to exceed 3 percent. In addition, the maximum total voltage drop on both feeders and branch circuits shouldn't exceed 5 percent.

Note 3: See 210.19(A), Note 4, for voltage drop for branch circuits.

(2) Neutral Conductor Size. The feeder neutral conductor must be sized to carry the maximum unbalanced load in accordance with 220.61, and isn't permitted to be smaller than listed in 250.122, based on the rating of the feeder overcurrent protection device.

> **Example:** What size neutral conductor is required for a feeder consisting of 250 kcmil ungrounded conductors and one neutral conductor protected by a 250A overcurrent protection device, where the unbalanced load is only 50A, with 75°C terminals?
> ▶ Figure 215–10
>
>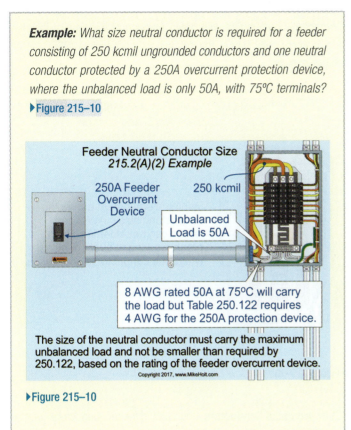
>
> ▶ Figure 215–10
>
> **Answer:** A 4 AWG neutral conductor is required [Table 250.122]. Table 310.15(B)(16) and 220.61 permit an 8 AWG neutral conductor rated 50A at 75°C to carry the 50A unbalanced load, but the neutral conductor isn't permitted to be smaller than 4 AWG, as listed in Table 250.122, based on the 250A overcurrent protection device.

215.3 Overcurrent Protection Sizing

Feeder overcurrent protection devices must have a rating of not less than 125 percent of the continuous loads, plus 100 percent of the noncontinuous loads. ▶ Figure 215–11

Author's Comment:

- See 215.2(A)(1) for feeder conductor sizing requirements.

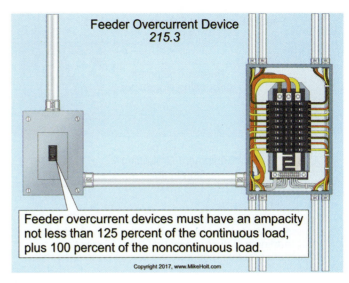

▶ Figure 215–11

Ex: If the assembly and the overcurrent protection device are both listed for operation at 100 percent of their rating, the overcurrent protection device can be sized at 100 percent of the continuous load.

Author's Comment:

- Equipment suitable for 100 percent continuous loading is rarely available in ratings under 400A.

215.4 Feeders with Common Neutral Conductor

(A) Feeders with Common Neutral. Up to three sets of 3-wire feeders or two sets of 4-wire feeders can use the same neutral conductor.

Author's Comment:

- The neutral conductor must be sized to carry the total unbalanced load for all feeders as determined in Article 220, see 220.61.

215.6 Equipment Grounding Conductor

Feeder circuits must include or provide an equipment grounding conductor of a type listed in 250.118, and it must terminate in a manner so that branch-circuit equipment grounding conductors can be connected to it, and installed in accordance with 250.134. ▶ Figure 215–12

215.10 | Feeders

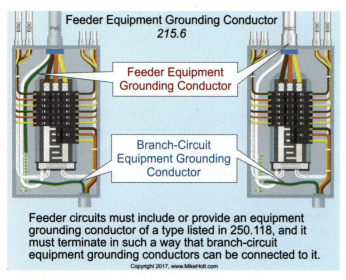

▶Figure 215–12

215.10 Ground-Fault Protection of Equipment

Each feeder disconnecting means rated 1,000A or more supplied by a 4-wire, three-phase, 277/480V wye-connected system must be provided with ground-fault protection of equipment in accordance with 230.95 and 240.13.

Author's Comment:

- See the definition of "Ground-Fault Protection of Equipment" in Article 100.

Ex 2. Equipment ground-fault protection isn't required if ground-fault protection of equipment is provided on the supply side of the feeder and on the load side of the transformer supplying the feeder.

Author's Comment:

- Ground-fault protection of equipment isn't permitted for fire pumps [695.6(G)], and it's not required for emergency systems [700.31] or legally required standby systems [701.26].

215.12 Conductor Identification

(A) Neutral Conductor. An insulated feeder neutral conductor must be identified in accordance with 200.6.

(B) Equipment Grounding Conductor. Equipment grounding conductors can be bare, and individually covered or insulated equipment grounding conductors sized 6 AWG and smaller must have a continuous outer finish either green or green with one or more yellow stripes [250.119].

Insulated equipment grounding conductors 4 AWG and larger can be permanently reidentified with green marking at the time of installation at every point where the conductor is accessible [250.119(A)].
▶Figure 215–13

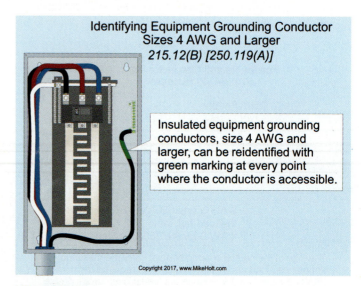

▶Figure 215–13

(C) Ungrounded Conductors. Ungrounded feeder conductors must be identified in accordance with (1) or (2).

(1) Multiple Voltage Systems. If the premises wiring system contains feeders supplied from more than one voltage system, each ungrounded conductor, at all termination, connection, and splice points, must be identified by phase or line and system, in accordance with (a) and (b).

(a) Identification Method. Identification can be by color coding, marking tape, tagging, or other means approved by the authority having jurisdiction. ▶Figure 215–14

(b) Posting of Identification Method. Such identification must be documented in a manner that's readily available, or it must be permanently posted at each panelboard. ▶Figure 215–15

Feeders | 215.12

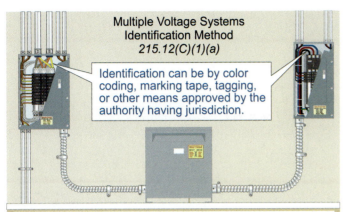

▶Figure 215–14

▶Figure 215–15

Author's Comment:

- Although the *NEC* doesn't require a specific color code for ungrounded conductors, electricians often use the following color system for power and lighting conductor identification:
    - ♦ 120/240V, single-phase—black, red, and white
    - ♦ 120/208V, three-phase—black, red, blue, and white
    - ♦ 120/240V, three-phase—black, orange, blue, and white
    - ♦ 277/480V, three-phase—brown, orange, yellow, and gray; or, brown, purple, yellow, and gray ▶Figure 215–16

Conductor Identification
210.5, 215.12, 310.110 Comment

Although the *NEC* doesn't require a specific color code for ungrounded conductors, electricians often use the following color system for power and lighting conductor identification:
- 120/240V, single-phase–black, red, and white
- 120/208V, three-phase–black, red, blue, and white
- 120/240V, three-phase–black, orange, blue, and white
- 277/480V, three-phase–brown, orange, yellow, and gray; or, brown, purple, yellow, and gray

▶Figure 215–16

Notes

ARTICLE 225
OUTSIDE BRANCH CIRCUITS AND FEEDERS

Introduction to Article 225—Outside Branch Circuits and Feeders

This article covers the installation requirements for equipment, including-branch circuit and feeder conductors (overhead and underground), located outdoors on or between buildings, poles, and other structures on the premises. Conductors installed outdoors can serve many purposes such as area lighting, power for outdoor equipment, or providing power to a separate building or structure. It's important to remember that the power supply for buildings isn't always a service conductor, but in many cases may be feeders or branch-circuit conductors originating in another building. Be careful not to assume that the conductors supplying power to a building are service conductors until you've identified where the service point is [Article 100] and reviewed the Article 100 Definitions for feeders, branch circuits, and service conductors. If they're service conductors, use Article 230. For outside branch-circuit and feeder conductors, whatever they feed, use this article.

Table 225.3 shows other articles that may furnish additional requirements, then Part I of Article 225 goes on to address installation methods intended to provide a secure installation of outside conductors while providing sufficient conductor size, support, attachment means, and maintaining safe clearances.

Part II of this article limits the number of supplies (branch circuits or feeders) permitted to a building or structure and provides rules regarding disconnects for them. These rules include the disconnect rating, construction characteristics, labeling, and where to locate the disconnect and the grouping of multiple disconnects.

Outside branch circuits and feeders over 1,000V are the focus of Part III of Article 225.

Part I. General

225.1 Scope

Article 225 contains the installation requirements for outside branch circuits and feeders installed on or between buildings, structures, or poles. ▶Figure 225–1

Author's Comment:

- Review the following definitions in Article 100:
    - "Branch Circuit"
    - "Building"
    - "Feeder"
    - "Structure"

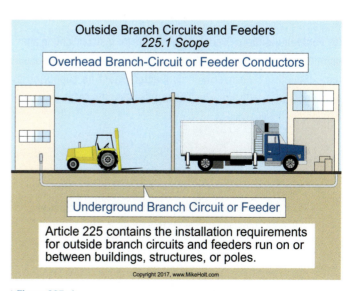

▶Figure 225–1

225.2 Other Articles

Other articles containing important requirements include:

- Branch Circuits, Article 210
- Class 1, Class 2, and Class 3 Remote-Control, Signaling, and Power-Limited Circuits, Article 725
- Communications Circuits, Article 800
- Community Antenna Television and Radio Distribution Systems, Article 820
- Conductors for General Wiring, Article 310
- Electric Signs and Outline Lighting, Article 600
- Feeders, Article 215
- Floating Buildings, Article 553
- Grounding and Bonding, Article 250
- Marinas, Boatyards, and Commercial and Noncommercial Docking Facilities, Article 555
- Radio and Television Equipment, Article 810
- Services, Article 230
- Solar PV Systems, Article 690
- Swimming Pools, Fountains, and Similar Installations, Article 680

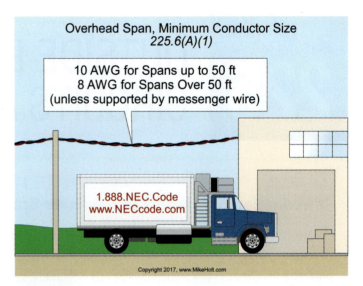

▶Figure 225–2

225.6 Minimum Size of Conductors

(A) Overhead Spans.

(1) Conductor Size. Conductors 10 AWG and larger are permitted for overhead spans up to 50 ft long. For spans over 50 ft in length, the minimum size conductor is 8 AWG, unless supported by a messenger wire. ▶Figure 225–2

(B) Festoon Lighting. Overhead conductors for festoon lighting aren't permitted to be smaller than 12 AWG, unless messenger wires support the conductors. The overhead conductors must be supported by messenger wire, with strain insulators, whenever the spans exceed 40 ft in length. ▶Figure 225–3

Author's Comment:

- Festoon lighting is a string of outdoor lights suspended between two points [Article 100]. It's commonly used at carnivals, circuses, fairs, and Christmas tree lots [525.20(C)].

▶Figure 225–3

225.7 Luminaires Installed Outdoors

(C) 277V to Ground Circuits. 277V and 480V branch circuits are permitted to supply luminaires for lighting outdoor areas of industrial establishments, office buildings, schools, stores, and other commercial or public buildings. ▶Figure 225–4

Author's Comment:

- See 210.6(C) for the types of luminaires permitted on 277V or 480V branch circuits.

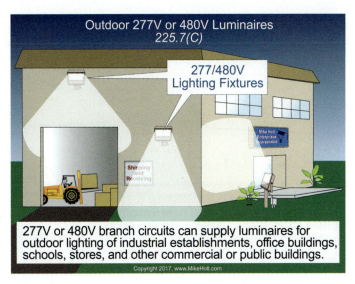
▶Figure 225–4

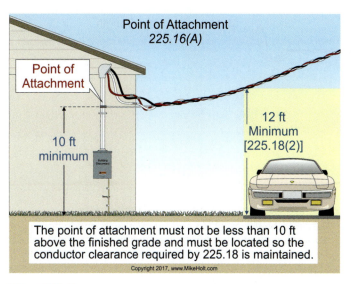
▶Figure 225–5

225.12 Open-Conductor Supports

Open conductors must be supported on knobs, racks, brackets, or strain insulators that are made of glass, porcelain, or other approved materials.

225.15 Supports Over Buildings

Conductor spans over a building must be securely supported by substantial structures. If practicable, such supports must be independent of the building [230.29].

225.16 Attachment

(A) Point of Attachment. The point of attachment for overhead conductors isn't permitted to be less than 10 ft above the finished grade, and it must be located so the minimum conductor clearance required by 225.18 can be maintained. ▶Figure 225–5

CAUTION: Conductors might need to have the point of attachment raised so the overhead conductors will comply with the clearances from building openings and other building areas required by 225.19.

(B) Means of Attachment to Buildings. Open conductors must be attached to fittings identified for use with conductors, or to noncombustible, nonabsorbent insulators securely attached to the building or other structure.

Author's Comment:

- The point of attachment of the overhead conductor spans to a building or other structure must provide the minimum clearances as specified in 225.18 and 225.19. In no case can this point of attachment be less than 10 ft above the finished grade.

225.17 Masts as Supports

Masts for the support of overhead conductors must be installed as follows:

Author's Comment:

- Aerial cables and antennas for radio and TV equipment aren't permitted to be attached to the feeder or branch-circuit mast [810.12]. In addition, 800.133(B) prohibits communications cables from being attached to raceways, including a mast for power conductors.

(A) Strength. The mast must have adequate mechanical strength, braces, or guy wires to safely withstand the strain caused by the conductors. ▶Figure 225–6

(B) Attachment. Overhead conductors can't be attached to a mast where the conductor attachment is located between a weatherhead and a coupling located above the last point of securement to the building or structure, or where the coupling is located above the roof or structure. ▶Figure 225–7

225.18 | Outside Branch Circuits and Feeders

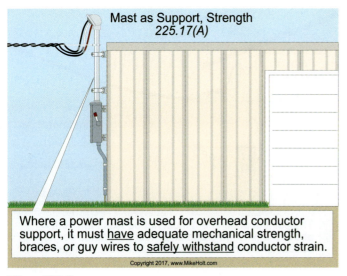

▶Figure 225–6

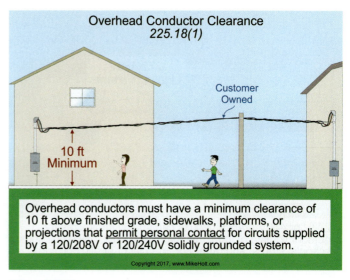

▶Figure 225–8

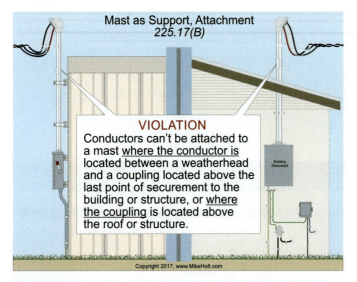

▶Figure 225–7

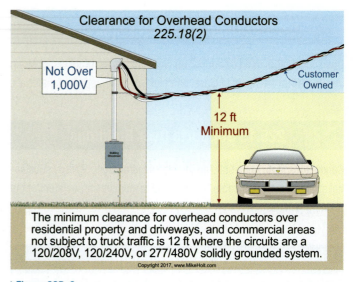

▶Figure 225–9

225.18 Clearance for Overhead Conductors

Overhead conductor spans must maintain vertical clearances of:

(1) 10 ft above finished grade, sidewalks, platforms, or projections that permit personal contact for circuits supplied by a 120/208V or 120/240V solidly grounded system. ▶Figure 225–8

(2) 12 ft above residential property and driveways, and commercial areas not subject to truck traffic for circuits supplied by a 120/208V, 120/240V, or 277V/480V solidly grounded system. ▶Figure 225–9

(3) 15 ft above residential property and driveways, and commercial areas not subject to truck traffic for circuits supplied by a system having a voltage exceeding 300V to ground.

(4) 18 ft over public streets, alleys, roads, parking areas subject to truck traffic, driveways on other than residential property, and other areas traversed by vehicles (such as those used for cultivation, grazing, forestry, and orchards). ▶Figure 225–10

(5) 24½ ft over track rails of railroads.

Outside Branch Circuits and Feeders | 225.19

▶Figure 225–10

Author's Comment:

■ Overhead conductors located above pools, outdoor spas, outdoor hot tubs, diving structures, observation stands, towers, or platforms must be installed in accordance with the clearance requirements in 680.9.

225.19 Clearances from Buildings

(A) Above Roofs. Overhead conductors must maintain a vertical clearance of 8 ft 6 in. above the surface of a roof and must be maintained for a distance of at least 3 ft from the edge of the roof. ▶Figure 225–11

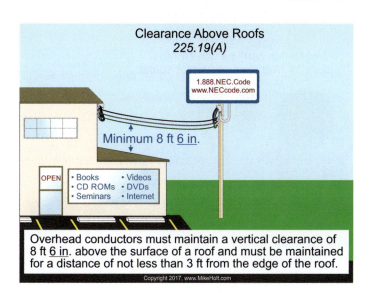

▶Figure 225–11

Ex 2: The overhead conductor clearances from the roof can be reduced to 3 ft if the slope of the roof meets or exceeds 4 in. of vertical rise for every 12 in. of horizontal run.

Ex 3: For 120/208V or 120/240V circuits, the conductor clearance over the roof overhang can be reduced to 18 in., if no more than 6 ft of conductor passes over no more than 4 ft of roof. ▶Figure 225–12

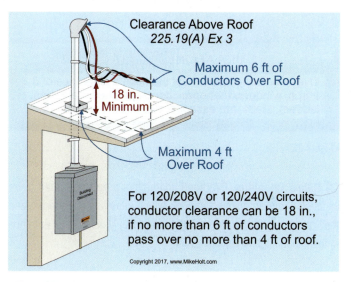

▶Figure 225–12

Ex 4: The 3-ft clearance from the roof edge doesn't apply when the point of attachment is on the side of the building below the roof.

(B) From Other Structures. Overhead conductors must maintain a clearance of at least 3 ft from signs, chimneys, radio and television antennas, tanks, and other nonbuilding or nonbridge structures.

(D) Final Span Clearance.

(1) Clearance from Windows. Overhead conductors must maintain a clearance of 3 ft from windows that open, doors, porches, balconies, ladders, stairs, fire escapes, or similar locations. ▶Figure 225–13

Ex: Overhead conductors installed above a window aren't required to maintain the 3-ft distance from the window.

(2) Vertical Clearance. Overhead conductors must maintain a vertical clearance of at least 10 ft above platforms, projections, or surfaces that permit personal contact in accordance with 225.18. This vertical clearance must be maintained for 3 ft, measured horizontally from the platforms, projections, or surfaces from which they might be reached.

225.22 | Outside Branch Circuits and Feeders

▶Figure 225–13

▶Figure 225–15

(3) Below Openings. Overhead conductors aren't permitted to be installed under an opening through which materials might pass, and they're not permitted to be installed where they'll obstruct an entrance to these openings. ▶Figure 225–14

Author's Comment:

- A "Wet Location" is an area subject to saturation with water and unprotected locations exposed to weather [Article 100].

225.26 Trees for Conductor Support

Trees or other vegetation aren't permitted to be used for the support of overhead conductor spans. ▶Figure 225–16

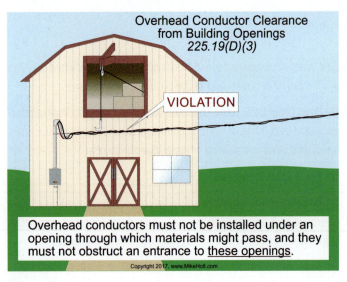

▶Figure 225–14

225.22 Raceways on Exterior Surfaces

Raceways on exterior surfaces must be arranged to drain and be listed or approved for use in wet locations. ▶Figure 225–15

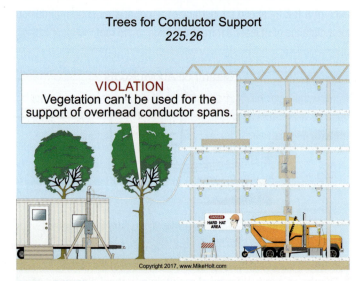

▶Figure 225–16

Author's Comment:

- Overhead conductor spans for services [230.10] and temporary wiring [590.4(J)] aren't permitted to be supported by vegetation.

225.27 Raceway Seals

Raceways (used or unused) entering buildings from outside must be sealed with a sealant identified for use with the conductor or cable insulation. ▶Figure 225–17

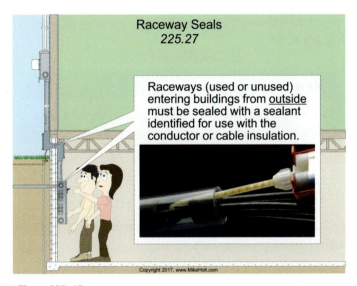

▶Figure 225–17

225.30 Number of Feeder Supplies

If more than one building or other structure is on the same property, each building must be served by no more than one feeder or single or multiwire branch circuit, except for the following conditions:

Author's Comment:

- Article 100 defines a "Structure" as, "That which is built or constructed, other than equipment."

(A) Special Conditions. Additional supplies are permitted for:

(1) Fire pumps

(2) Emergency systems

(3) Legally required standby systems

(4) Optional standby systems

(5) Parallel power production systems

(6) Systems designed for connection to multiple sources of supply for the purpose of enhanced reliability

(7) Electric vehicle charging systems listed, labeled, and identified for more than a single branch circuit or feeder

Author's Comment:

- To minimize the possibility of simultaneous interruption, the disconnecting means for the fire pump or standby power must be located remotely away from the normal power disconnecting means [225.34(B)].

(B) Special Occupancies. By special permission, additional supplies are permitted for:

(1) Multiple-occupancy buildings where there's no available space for supply equipment accessible to all occupants, or

(2) A building so large that two or more supplies are necessary.

(C) Capacity Requirements. Additional supplies are permitted for a building where the capacity requirements exceed 2,000A.

(D) Different Characteristics. Additional supplies are permitted for different voltages, frequencies, or uses, such as control of outside lighting from multiple locations.

(E) Documented Switching Procedures. Additional supplies are permitted where documented safe switching procedures are established and maintained for disconnection.

225.31 Disconnecting Means

A disconnect is required for all conductors that enter a building. ▶Figure 225–18

225.32 Disconnect Location

The disconnect for a building must be installed at a readily accessible location either outside or inside nearest the point of entrance of the conductors. ▶Figure 225–19

225.32 | Outside Branch Circuits and Feeders

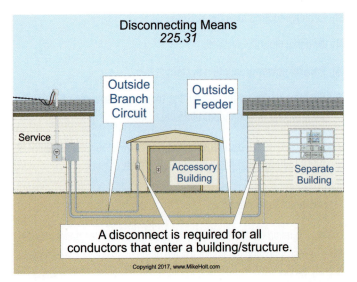

▶Figure 225–18

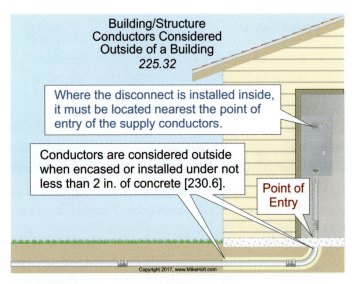

▶Figure 225–20

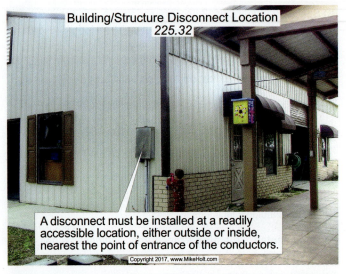

▶Figure 225–19

Supply conductors are considered outside of a building or other structure where they're encased or installed under not less than 2 in. of concrete or brick [230.6]. ▶Figure 225–20

Ex 1: If documented safe switching procedures are established and maintained, the building disconnect can be located elsewhere on the premises, if monitored by qualified persons.

Author's Comment:

- A "Qualified Person" is one who has skills and knowledge related to the construction and operation of the electrical equipment and installation, and has received safety training to recognize and avoid the hazards involved with electrical systems [Article 100].

Ex 3: A disconnecting means isn't required within sight of poles that support luminaires. ▶Figure 225–21

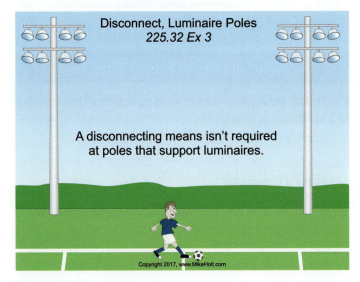

▶Figure 225–21

Author's Comment:

- According to Article 100, "Within Sight" means that it's visible and not more than 50 ft from one to the other.

Ex 4: The disconnecting means for a sign must be controlled by an externally operable switch or circuit breaker that opens all ungrounded conductors to the sign. The sign disconnect must be within sight of the sign, or the disconnect must be capable of being locked in the open position [600.6(A)]. ▶Figure 225–22

▶Figure 225–22

225.33 Maximum Number of Disconnects

(A) General. The building disconnecting means can consist of no more than six switches or six circuit breakers in a single enclosure, or separate enclosures for each supply grouped in one location as permitted by 225.30. ▶Figure 225–23

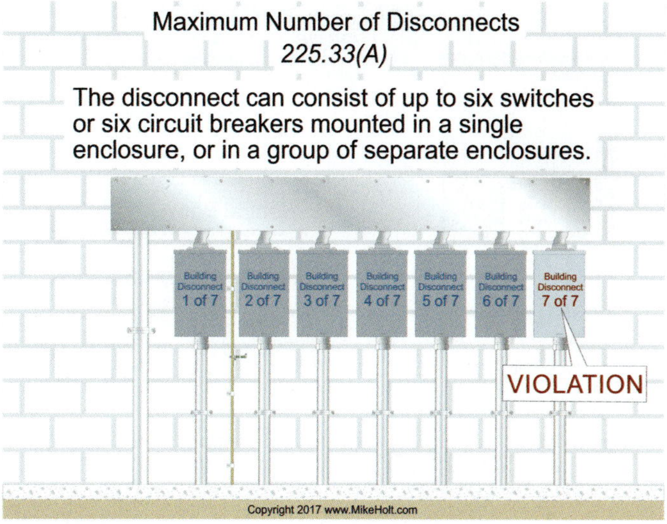

225.34 Grouping of Disconnects

(A) General. The building disconnecting means must be grouped in one location, and must be marked to indicate the loads they serve [110.22].

(B) Additional Disconnects. To minimize the possibility of accidental interruption of the critical power systems, the disconnecting means for a fire pump or for standby power must be located remotely away from the normal power disconnect.

▶Figure 225–23

225.35 Access to Occupants

In a multiple-occupancy building, each occupant must have access to the disconnecting means for their occupancy.

Ex: The occupants' disconnecting means can be accessible only to building management if electrical maintenance under continuous supervision is provided by the building management.

225.36 Type of Disconnecting Means

The building disconnecting means can be comprised of a circuit breaker, molded case switch, general-use switch, snap switch, or other approved means. If an existing building uses the neutral conductor for the bonding of metal parts as permitted by 250.32(B) Ex, the disconnect must be listed for use as service equipment. ▶Figure 225–24

Author's Comment:

- "Suitable for use as service equipment" means, among other things, that the service disconnect is supplied with a main bonding jumper so a neutral-to-case connection can be made, as required in 250.24(C) and 250.142(A).

225.37 | Outside Branch Circuits and Feeders

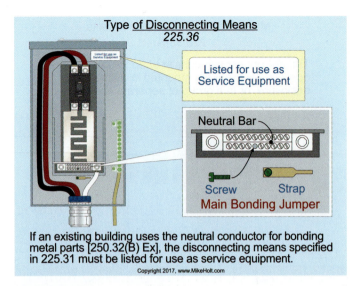

▶Figure 225–24

225.37 Identification of Multiple Feeders

If a building is fed by more than one supply, a permanent plaque or directory must be installed at each feeder disconnect location denoting all other feeders or branch circuits that supply that building, and the area served by each.

225.38 Disconnect Construction

(A) Manual or Power-Operated Circuit Breakers. The building disconnect can consist of either a manual switch or a power-operated switch or circuit breaker capable of being operated manually.

> **Author's Comment:**
> - A shunt-trip pushbutton can be used to open a power-operated circuit breaker. The circuit breaker is the disconnect, not the pushbutton.

(D) Indicating. The disconnecting means for a building supplied by a feeder must plainly indicate whether it's in the open or closed position.

225.39 Rating of Disconnecting Means

A single disconnect for a building must have an ampere rating not less than the calculated load as determined by Article 220. If the disconnecting means consists of more than one switch or circuit breaker, the combined ratings of the circuit breakers aren't permitted to be less than the calculated load as determined by Article 220. In addition, the disconnect isn't permitted to be rated lower than:

(A) One-Circuit Installation. For installations consisting of a single branch circuit, the disconnect must have a rating of not less than 15A.

(B) Two-Circuit Installation. For installations consisting of two 2-wire branch circuits, the feeder disconnect must have a rating of not less than 30A.

(C) One-Family Dwelling. For a one-family dwelling, the feeder disconnect must have a rating of not less than 100A, 3-wire.

(D) Other Installations. For all other installations, the feeder or branch-circuit disconnect must have a rating of not less than 60A.

ARTICLE 230 SERVICES

Introduction to Article 230—Services

This article covers the installation requirements for service conductors and service equipment. The requirements for service conductors differ from those for other conductors. For one thing, service conductors for one building can't pass through the interior of another building or structure [230.3], and you apply different rules depending on whether a service conductor is inside or outside a building. When are they "outside" as opposed to "inside"? The answer may seem obvious, but 230.6 should be consulted before making this decision.

Let's review the following definitions in Article 100 to understand when the requirements of Article 230 apply:

- **Service Point.** The point of connection between the serving electric utility and the premises wiring.
- **Service Conductors.** The conductors from the service point to the service disconnecting means. Service-entrance conductors can either be overhead or underground.
- **Service Equipment.** The necessary equipment, usually consisting of circuit breakers or switches and fuses and their accessories, connected to the load end of service conductors at a building or other structure, and intended to constitute the main control and cutoff of the electrical supply. Service equipment doesn't include individual meter socket enclosures [230.66].

After reviewing these definitions, you should understand that service conductors originate at the serving electric utility (service point) and terminate on the line side of the service disconnect. Conductors and equipment on the load side of service equipment are considered feeder conductors or branch circuits, and must be installed in accordance with Articles 210 and 215. They must also comply with Article 225 if they're outside branch circuits and feeders, such as the supply to a building. Feeder conductors include: ▶Figure 230–1 and ▶Figure 230–2

- Secondary conductors from customer-owned transformers,
- Conductors from generators, UPS systems, or PV systems, and
- Conductors to remote buildings

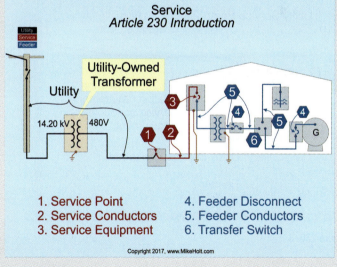

▶Figure 230–1

230.1 | Services

Article 230 consists of seven parts:

- Part I. General
- Part II. Overhead Service Conductors
- Part III. Underground Service Conductors
- Part IV. Service-Entrance Conductors
- Part V. Service Equipment
- Part VI. Disconnecting Means
- Part VIII. Overcurrent Protection

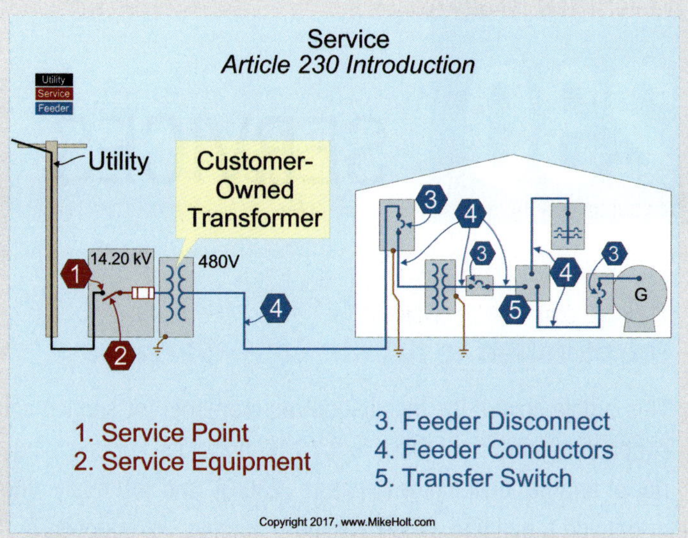

▶Figure 230–2

Part I. General

230.1 Scope

Article 230 covers the installation requirements for service conductors and service equipment. ▶Figure 230–3

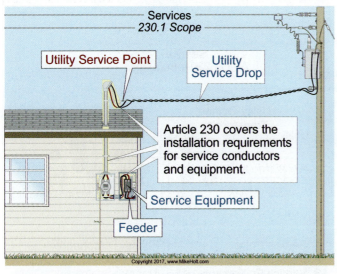

▶Figure 230–3

230.2 Number of Services

A building can only be served by one service drop or service lateral, except as permitted by (A) through (D). ▶Figure 230–4

▶Figure 230–4

For the purposes of 230.40, Ex. 2, underground sets of conductors, 1/0 AWG and larger, running to the same location and connected together at their supply end, but not connected together at their load end, are considered to be supplying one service.

(A) Special Conditions. Additional services are permitted for the following:

(1) Fire pumps

(2) Emergency systems

(3) Legally required standby systems

Author's Comment:

- A separate service for emergency and legally required systems is permitted only when approved by the authority having jurisdiction [700.12(D) and 701.11(D)].

(4) Optional standby power

(5) Parallel power production systems

(6) Systems designed for connection to multiple sources of supply to enhance reliability

Author's Comment:

- To minimize the possibility of simultaneous interruption, the disconnecting means for the fire pump, emergency system, or standby power system must be located remotely away from the normal power disconnecting means [230.72(B)].

(B) Special Occupancies. By special permission, additional services are permitted for:

(1) Multiple-occupancy buildings where there's no available space for supply equipment accessible to all occupants, or

(2) A building or other structure so large that two or more supplies are necessary.

(C) Capacity Requirements. Additional services are permitted:

(1) If the capacity requirements exceed 2,000A, or

(2) If the load requirements of a single-phase installation exceed the electric utility's power capacity, or

(3) By special permission.

Author's Comment:

- Special permission is defined in Article 100 as "the written consent of the authority having jurisdiction."

(D) Different Characteristics. Additional services are permitted for different voltages, frequencies, or phases, or for different uses, such as for different electricity rate schedules.

(E) Identification of Multiple Services. If a building is supplied by more than one service, or a combination of feeders and services, a permanent plaque or directory must be installed at each service and feeder disconnecting means location to denote all other services and feeders supplying that building, and the area served by each. ▶Figure 230–5

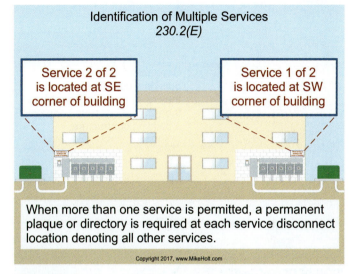

▶Figure 230–5

230.3 Not to Pass Through a Building

Service conductors must not pass through the interior of another building or other structure.

230.6 Conductors Considered Outside a Building

Conductors are considered outside of a building when they're installed:

(1) Under not less than 2 in. of concrete beneath a building. ▶Figure 230–6

(2) Within a building within a raceway encased in not less than 2 in. of concrete or brick.

(3) In a vault that meets the construction requirements of Article 450, Part III.

(4) In a raceway not less than 18 in. below a building.

(5) Within rigid or intermediate metal conduit that passes directly through an eave but not a wall of a building. ▶Figure 230–7

230.7 | Services

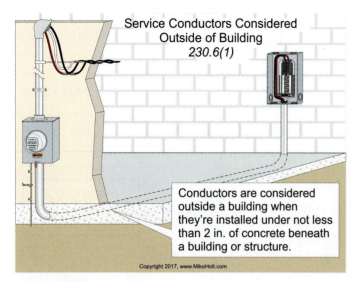
▶Figure 230–6

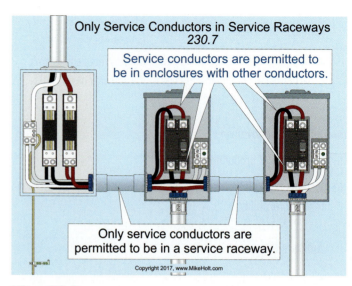
▶Figure 230–8

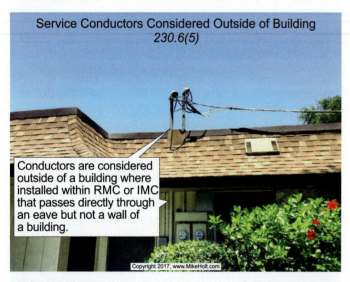
▶Figure 230–7

230.7 Service Conductors Separate from Other Conductors

Feeder and branch-circuit conductors aren't permitted to be installed in a service raceway containing service conductors. ▶Figure 230–8

Ex 1: Grounding electrode conductors or supply-side bonding jumpers are permitted in a service raceway with service conductors.

Ex 2: Conductors used for load management with overcurrent protection are permitted in service raceways with service conductors.

WARNING: *Overcurrent protection for the feeder or branch-circuit conductors can be bypassed or a fault can occur if service conductors are mixed with feeder or branch-circuit conductors in the same raceway and a fault occurs between the service and feeder or branch-circuit conductors.*
▶Figure 230–9

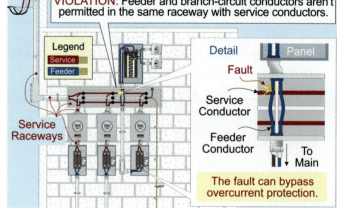
▶Figure 230–9

Author's Comment:

- This rule doesn't prohibit the mixing of service, feeder, and branch-circuit conductors in the same service equipment enclosure.

- This requirement may be the root of the misconception that "line" and "load" conductors aren't permitted to be installed in the same raceway. It's true that service conductors aren't permitted to be installed in the same raceway with feeder or branch-circuit conductors, but line and load conductors for feeders and branch circuits can be in the same raceway or enclosure. ▶Figure 230–10

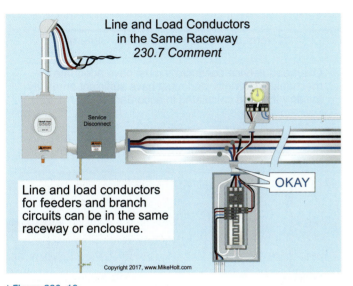

▶Figure 230–10

230.8 Raceway Seals

Underground raceways (used or unused) entering buildings must be sealed or plugged to prevent moisture from contacting energized live parts [225.27 and 300.5(G)]. ▶Figure 230–11

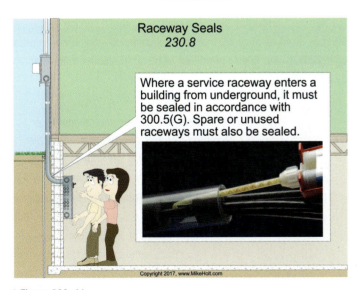

▶Figure 230–11

230.9 Clearance from Building Openings

(A) Clearance. Overhead service conductors must maintain a clearance of 3 ft from windows that open, doors, porches, balconies, ladders, stairs, fire escapes, or similar locations. ▶Figure 230–12

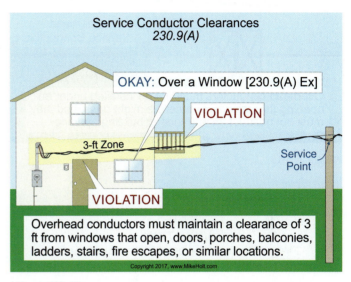

▶Figure 230–12

Ex: Overhead conductors installed above a window aren't required to maintain the 3-ft distance.

(B) Vertical Clearance. Overhead service conductors within 3 ft measured horizontally of platforms, projections, or surfaces that will permit personal contact, must have a vertical clearance of not less than 10 ft above the platforms, projections, or surfaces in accordance with 230.24(B).

(C) Below Openings. Service conductors aren't permitted to be installed under an opening through which materials might pass, and they're not permitted to be installed where they'll obstruct entrance to building openings. ▶Figure 230–13

230.10 Vegetation as Support

Trees or other vegetation aren't permitted to be used for the support of overhead service conductor spans or service equipment. ▶Figure 230–14

230.23 | Services

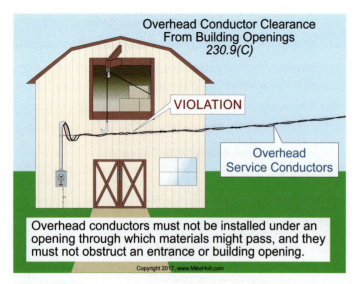

▶Figure 230–13

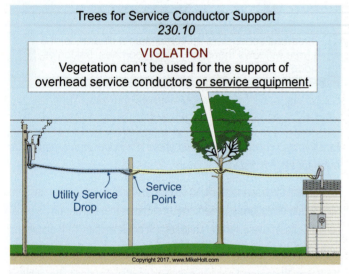

▶Figure 230–14

Author's Comment:

- Service-drop conductors installed by the electric utility must comply with the *National Electrical Safety Code* (NESC), not the *National Electrical Code* [90.2(B)(5)]. Overhead service conductors that aren't under the exclusive control of the electric utility must be installed in accordance with the *NEC*.

Part II. Overhead Service Conductors

230.23 Overhead Service Conductor Size and Rating

(A) General. Overhead service conductors must have adequate mechanical strength, and they must have sufficient ampacity to carry the load as calculated in accordance with Article 220. ▶Figure 230–15

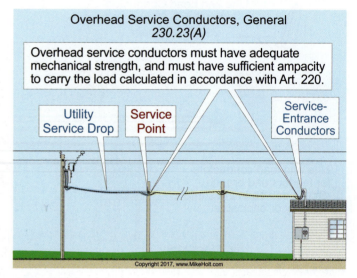

▶Figure 230–15

(B) Ungrounded Conductor Size. Overhead service conductors aren't permitted to be smaller than 8 AWG copper or 6 AWG aluminum.

Ex: Overhead service conductors can be as small as 12 AWG for limited-load installations.

(C) Neutral Conductor Size. The neutral overhead service conductor must be sized to carry the maximum unbalanced load, in accordance with 220.61, and it isn't permitted to be sized smaller than required by 250.24(C).

⚠️ **WARNING:** *In all cases, the service neutral conductor size isn't permitted to be smaller than required by 250.24(C) to ensure that it has sufficiently low impedance and current-carrying capacity to safely carry fault current in order to facilitate the operation of the overcurrent protection device.*

Example: What size neutral conductor is required for a structure with a 400A service supplied with 500 kcmil conductors if the maximum line-to-neutral load is no more than 100A?

Answer: 1/0 AWG. According to Table 310.15(B)(16), 3 AWG rated 100A at 75°C [110.14(C)(1)] is sufficient to carry 100A of neutral current. However, the service neutral conductor must be sized not smaller than 1/0 AWG, in accordance with Table 250.102(C)(1), based on the area of the service conductor [250.24(C)].

230.24 Vertical Clearance for Overhead Service Conductors

Overhead service conductor spans must maintain vertical clearances as follows:

(A) Above Roofs. A minimum of 8 ft above the surface of a roof for a minimum distance of 3 ft in all directions from the edge of the roof.

Ex 2: If the slope of the roof exceeds 4 in. of vertical rise for every 12 in. of horizontal run, 120/208V or 120/240V overhead service conductor clearances can be reduced to 3 ft over the roof.

Ex 3: If no more than 6 ft of conductors pass over no more than 4 ft of roof, 120/208V or 120/240V overhead service conductor clearances over the roof overhang can be reduced to 18 in. ▶Figure 230–16

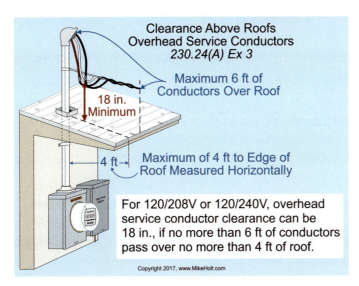

▶Figure 230–16

Ex 4: The 3-ft vertical clearance for overhead service conductors that extends from the roof doesn't apply when the point of attachment is on the side of the building below the roof.

Ex 5: If the voltage between conductors doesn't exceed 300V and the roof area is guarded or isolated, a reduction in clearance to 3 ft is permitted.

(B) Vertical Clearance for Overhead Service Conductors. Overhead service conductor spans must maintain the following vertical clearances: ▶Figure 230–17

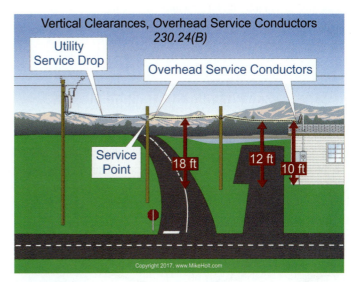

▶Figure 230–17

(1) 10 ft above finished grade, sidewalks, platforms, or projections that permit personal contact for circuits supplied by a 120/208V or 120/240V solidly grounded system.

(2) 12 ft above residential property and driveways, and commercial areas not subject to truck traffic for circuits supplied by a 120/208V, 120/240V, or 277V/480V solidly grounded system.

(3) 15 ft above residential property and driveways, and commercial areas not subject to truck traffic for circuits supplied by a system having a voltage exceeding 300V to ground.

(4) 18 ft over public streets, alleys, roads, parking areas subject to truck traffic, driveways on other than residential property, and other areas traversed by vehicles, such as those used for cultivation, grazing, forestry, and orchards.

230.26 | Services

Author's Comment:

- Department of Transportation (DOT) type rights-of-ways in rural areas are often used by slow-moving and tall farming machinery to avoid impeding road traffic.

(5) 24 ft 6 in. over tracks of railroads.

(D) Swimming Pools. Overhead service conductors that aren't under the exclusive control of the electric utility located above pools, outdoor spas, outdoor hot tubs, diving structures, observation stands, towers, or platforms must be installed in accordance with the clearance requirements contained in 680.9.

230.26 Point of Attachment

The point of attachment for overhead service conductors isn't permitted to be less than 10 ft above the finished grade, and it must be located so the minimum service conductor clearances required by 230.9 and 230.24 can be maintained. ▶Figure 230–18

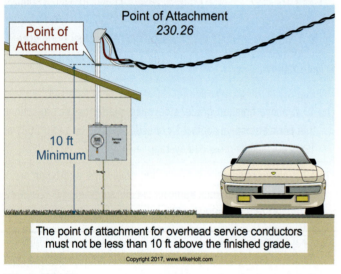

▶Figure 230–18

CAUTION: The point of attachment for conductors might need to be raised so the overhead service conductors will comply with the clearances from building openings required by 230.9 and from other areas as required by 230.24.

230.27 Means of Attachment

Multiconductor cables used for overhead service conductors must be attached to buildings or other structures by fittings identified for use with service conductors.

Open conductors must be attached to fittings identified for use with service conductors or to noncombustible, nonabsorbent insulators securely attached to the building or other structure.

230.28 Service Masts Used as Supports

Masts used for the support of overhead service conductors or service drops must be installed in accordance with (A) and (B). Only these conductors can be attached to the mast. ▶Figure 230–19

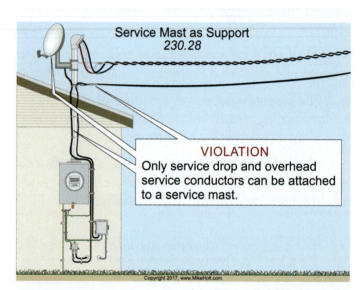

▶Figure 230–19

(A) Strength. If a mast is used for overhead conductor support, it must have adequate mechanical strength, braces, or guy wires to withstand the strain caused by the conductors. Conduit hubs must be identified for use with a mast. ▶Figure 230–20 and ▶Figure 230–21

(B) Attachment. Conductors can't be attached to a mast between a weatherhead or end of the conduit and a coupling if the coupling is above the last conduit support, or if the coupling is above the building or structure. ▶Figure 230–22

▶Figure 230–20

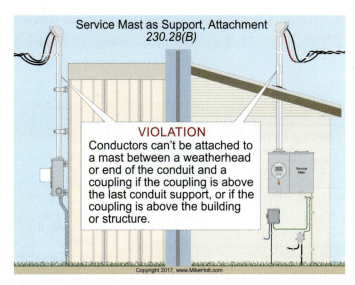

▶Figure 230–22

▶Figure 230–21

Author's Comment:

- Some local codes require a minimum trade size 2 rigid metal conduit to be used for the service mast. In addition, many electric utilities contain specific requirements for the installation of the service mast.

230.29 Supports over Buildings

Service conductors over a roof must be securely supported by substantial structures. Where the support structure is metal, it must be bonded to the grounded overhead service conductor with a supply-side bonding conductor, sized in accordance with 250.102(C)(1), based on the size of the ungrounded service conductors. Where practicable, overhead service conductor support must be independent of the building.

Author's Comment:

- This rule doesn't apply to utility overhead service-drop conductors, which are beyond the scope of the *NEC* [90.2(B)(5)].

Part III. Underground Service Conductors

230.31 Underground Service Conductor Size and Rating

Author's Comment:

- Underground service conductors installed by the electric utility must comply with the *National Electrical Safety Code* (NESC), not the *National Electrical Code* [90.2(B)(5)]. Underground conductors that aren't under the exclusive control of the electric utility must be installed in accordance with the *NEC*.

230.32 | Services

(A) General. Underground service conductors must have sufficient ampacity to carry the load as calculated in accordance with Article 220. ▶Figure 230–23

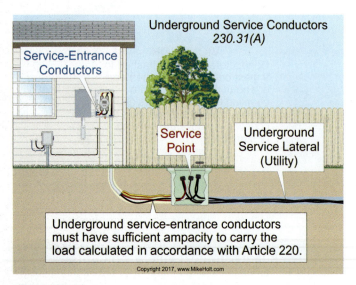

▶Figure 230–23

(B) Ungrounded Conductor Size. Underground service conductors aren't permitted to be smaller than 8 AWG copper or 6 AWG aluminum.

Ex: Underground service conductors can be as small as 12 AWG for limited-load installations.

(C) Neutral Conductor Size. The neutral conductor must be sized to carry the maximum unbalanced load in accordance with 220.61, and isn't permitted to be sized smaller than required by 250.24(C).

Author's Comment:

- 250.24(C) requires the service neutral conductor to be sized no smaller than Table 250.102(C)(1).

230.32 Protection Against Damage

Underground service conductors must be installed in accordance with 300.5, and have minimum cover in accordance with Table 300.5. ▶Figure 230–24

▶Figure 230–24

Part IV. Service-Entrance Conductors

230.40 Number of Service-Entrance Conductor Sets

Each service drop, service lateral, or set of underground or overhead service conductors can only supply one set of service-entrance conductors.

Ex 2: Service conductors can supply two to six service disconnecting means as permitted in 230.71(A).

Author's Comment:

- Underground sets of conductors, 1/0 AWG and larger, running to the same location and connected at their supply end, but not connected at their load end, are considered to supply one service [230.2].

Ex 3: A one-family dwelling unit and its accessory structure(s) can have one set of service conductors run to each structure.

Ex 4: Two-family dwellings, multifamily dwellings, and multiple-occupancy buildings are permitted to have one set of service conductors to supply branch circuits for public or common areas.

Ex 5: One set of service-entrance conductors connected to the supply side of the normal service disconnect can supply standby power systems, fire pump equipment, fire, and sprinkler alarms [230.82(5)], as well as Solar PV systems. ▶Figure 230–25

Services | 230.42

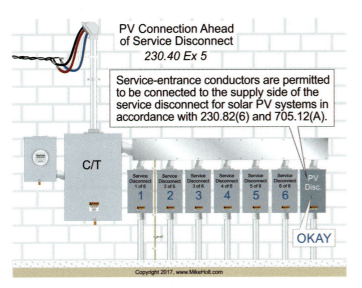

▶Figure 230–25

230.42 Size and Rating

(A) General. Service-entrance conductors must be sized to carry not less than the largest of the following:

(1) Before Ampacity Adjustment and Correction. Service-entrance conductors must be sized to carry not less than 100 percent of the noncontinuous load(s), plus 125 percent of the continuous load(s).
▶Figure 230–26

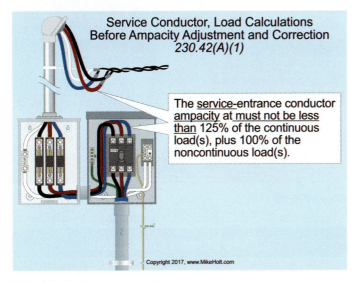

▶Figure 230–26

Example: What size service-entrance conductors are required for a 200A continuous three-phase load, where the four conductors are considered current carrying? ▶Figure 230–27

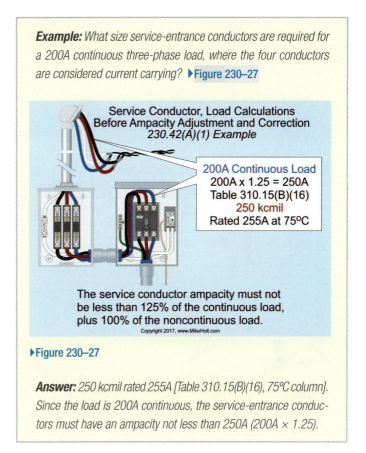

▶Figure 230–27

Answer: 250 kcmil rated 255A [Table 310.15(B)(16), 75°C column]. Since the load is 200A continuous, the service-entrance conductors must have an ampacity not less than 250A (200A × 1.25).

(2) After Ampacity Adjustment and Correction. Service-entrance conductors must be sized to carry not less than 100 percent of the noncontinuous load plus 100 percent of the continuous load, after the application of conductor ampacity adjustment [310.15(B)(3)(a)] and ampacity correction [310.15(B)(2)(a)]. ▶Figure 230–28

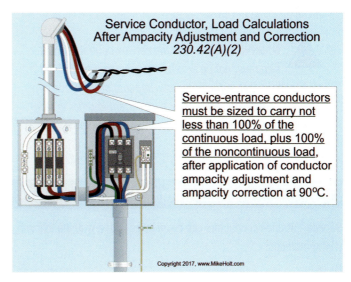

▶Figure 230–28

Example: *What size service-entrance conductors are required for a 200A continuous three-phase load, where the four conductors are considered current carrying?* ▶Figure 230–29

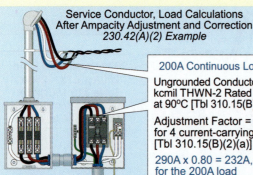

▶Figure 230–29

Answer: *250 kcmil. Since the load is 200A continuous, the service-entrance conductors must have an ampacity not less than 200A after conductor adjustment of 80 percent [310.15(B)(3)(a)]. According to the 90ºC column of Table 310.15(B)(16), 250 kcmil conductors have an ampere rating of 290A before adjustment and 232A (255A × 0.80) after adjustment.*

(C) Neutral Conductor Size. The service neutral conductor must be sized to carry the maximum unbalanced load in accordance with 220.61, and isn't permitted to be sized smaller than required by 250.24(C).

⚠ **WARNING:** *In all cases the service neutral conductor size must not be smaller than required by 250.24(C) to ensure it has sufficiently low impedance and current-carrying capacity to safely carry fault current in order to facilitate the operation of the overcurrent protection device.*

230.43 Wiring Methods

Service-entrance conductors can be installed with any of the following wiring methods:

(1) Open wiring on insulators

(3) Rigid metal conduit

(4) Intermediate metal conduit

(5) Electrical metallic tubing

(6) Electrical nonmetallic tubing (ENT)

(7) Service-entrance cables

(8) Wireways

(9) Busways

(11) PVC conduit

(13) Type MC cable

(15) Flexible metal conduit (FMC) or liquidtight flexible metal conduit (LFMC) in lengths not longer than 6 ft

(16) Liquidtight flexible nonmetallic conduit (LFNC) ▶Figure 230–30

(17) High-density polyethylene conduit (HDPE)

(18) Nonmetallic underground conduit with conductors (NUCC)

(19) Reinforced thermosetting resin conduit (RTRC)

▶Figure 230–30

230.46 Spliced Conductors

Service-entrance conductors can be spliced or tapped in accordance with 110.14, 300.5(E), 300.13, and 300.15. ▶Figure 230–31

Services | 230.50

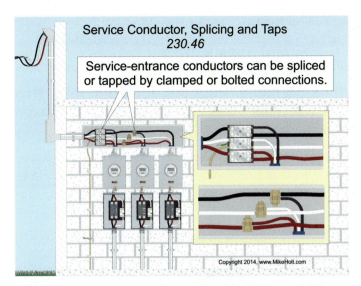

▶Figure 230–31

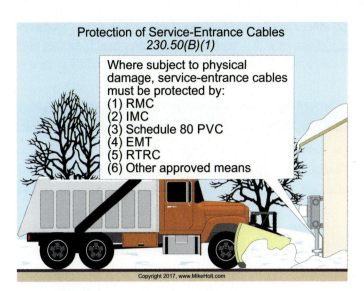

▶Figure 230–33

230.50 Protection Against Physical Damage

(A) Underground Service-Entrance Conductors. Underground service-entrance conductors must be protected against physical damage in accordance with 300.5. ▶Figure 230–32

Author's Comment:

- If the authority having jurisdiction determines the raceway isn't subject to physical damage, Schedule 40 PVC conduit can be used. ▶Figure 230–34

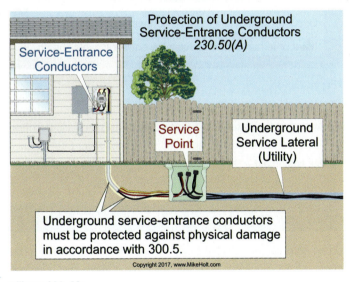

▶Figure 230–32

(B) Service-Entrance Cables Subject to Physical Damage.

(1) Service-Entrance Cables. Service-entrance cables that are subject to physical damage must be protected by any of the following: ▶Figure 230–33

(1) Rigid metal conduit

(2) Intermediate metal conduit

(3) Schedule 80 PVC conduit

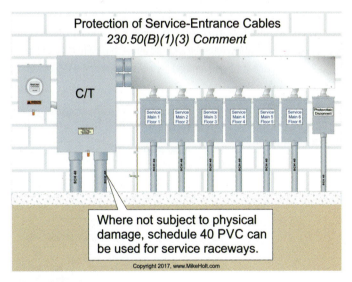

▶Figure 230–34

(4) Electrical metallic tubing

(5) Reinforced thermosetting resin conduit (RTRC)

(6) Other means approved by the authority having jurisdiction

Mike Holt Enterprises • www.MikeHolt.com • 888.NEC.CODE (632.2633) 133

230.51 | Services

(2) Other Than Service-Entrance Cable. Individual open conductors and cables, other than service-entrance cables, aren't permitted to be installed within 10 ft of grade level or where exposed to physical damage.

230.51 Cable Supports

(A) Service-Entrance Cable Supports. Service-entrance cable must be supported within 1 ft of the weatherhead, raceway connections or enclosure, and at intervals not exceeding 30 in.

230.53 Raceways to Drain

Raceways on exterior surfaces of buildings or other structures must be arranged to drain, and be listed or approved for use in wet locations.

230.54 Overhead Service Locations

(A) Service Head. Raceways for overhead service drops or overhead service conductors must have a weatherhead listed for wet locations.

(B) Service-Entrance Cable. Service-entrance cables must be equipped with a weatherhead listed for wet locations.

(C) Above the Point of Attachment. Service heads on raceways or service-entrance cables must be located above the point of attachment [230.26] for service-drop or overhead service conductors. ▶Figure 230–35

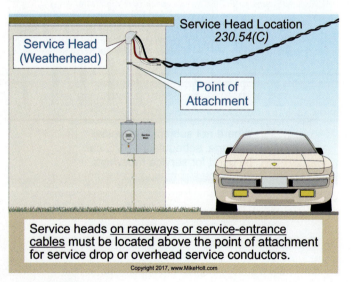

▶Figure 230–35

Ex: If it's impractical to locate the service head above the point of attachment, it must be located within 2 ft of the point of attachment.

(D) Secured. Service-entrance cables must be held securely in place.

(E) Opposite Polarity Through Separately Bushed Holes. Service heads must provide a bushed opening, and ungrounded conductors must be in separate openings.

(F) Drip Loops. Drip loop conductors must be connected to the service-drop or overhead service conductors below the service head or termination of the service-entrance cable sheath. ▶Figure 230–36

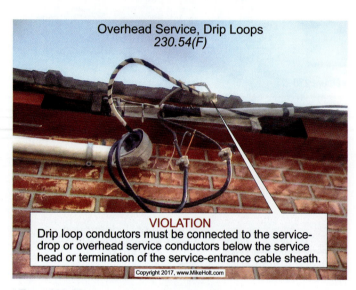

▶Figure 230–36

(G) Arranged So Water Won't Enter. Service-entrance and overhead service conductors must be arranged to prevent water from entering service equipment.

230.56 High-Leg Identification

On a 4-wire, delta-connected, three-phase system, where the midpoint of one phase winding is grounded (high-leg system), the conductor with the higher phase voltage-to-ground (208V) must be durably and permanently marked by an outer finish that's orange in color, or by other effective means. Such identification must be placed at each point on the system where a connection is made if the neutral conductor is present [110.15]. ▶Figure 230–37

Services | 230.66

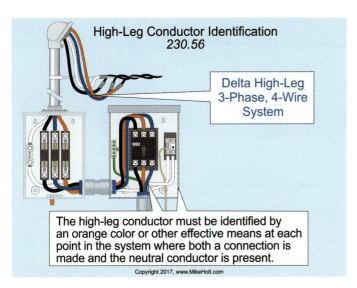
▶Figure 230–37

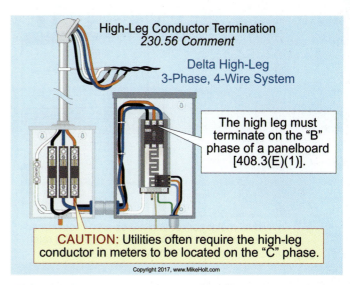
▶Figure 230–38

Author's Comment:

- The high-leg conductor is also called the "wild leg," "stinger leg," or "bastard leg."
- Since 1975, panelboards supplied by a 4-wire, delta-connected, three-phase system must have the high-leg conductor (208V) terminate to the "B" (center) phase of a panel board [408.3(E)].
- The ANSI standard for meter equipment requires the high-leg conductor (208V to neutral) to terminate on the "C" (right) phase of the meter socket enclosure. This is because the demand meter needs 120V and it gets this from the "B" phase. Hopefully, the electric utility lineman isn't colorblind and doesn't inadvertently cross the "orange" high-leg conductor (208V) with the red (120V) service conductor at the weatherhead. It's happened before… ▶Figure 230–38

230.66 Marking for Service Equipment

The service disconnect must be listed or field labeled as service equipment. ▶Figure 230–39

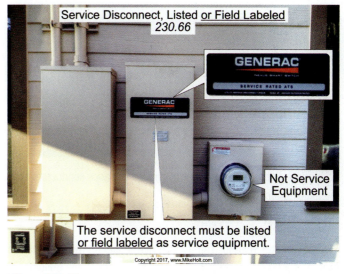
▶Figure 230–39

Author's Comment:

- "Listed or field labeled for use as service equipment" means, among other things, that the service disconnect is supplied with a main bonding jumper so a neutral-to-case connection can be made, as required in 250.24(C) and 250.142(A).

Individual meter socket enclosures aren't considered service equipment, but they must be listed and rated for the voltage and ampacity of the service. ▶Figure 230–40

230.70 | Services

▶Figure 230–40

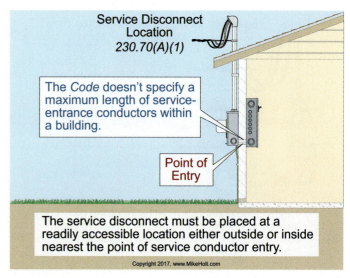

▶Figure 230–41

Ex: Meter socket enclosures supplied by and under the exclusive control of an electric utility aren't required to be listed.

Part VI. Service Equipment— Disconnecting Means

230.70 Service Disconnect Requirements

The service disconnect must open all service-entrance conductors from the building premises wiring.

(A) Location.

(1) Readily Accessible. The service disconnecting means must be placed at a readily accessible location either outside the building, or inside nearest the point of service conductor entry. ▶Figure 230–41

> ⚠ **WARNING:** Because service-entrance conductors don't have short-circuit or ground-fault protection, they must be limited in length when installed inside a building. Some local jurisdictions have a specific requirement as to the maximum length permitted within a building.

(2) Bathrooms. The service disconnect isn't permitted to be installed in a bathroom. ▶Figure 230–42

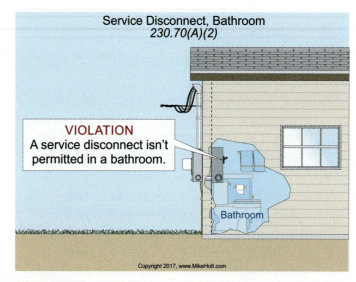

▶Figure 230–42

(3) Remote Control. If a remote-control device (such as a pushbutton for a shunt-trip breaker) is used to actuate the service disconnect, the service disconnect must be located at a readily accessible location either outside the building, or nearest the point of entrance of the service conductors as required by 230.70(A)(1). ▶Figure 230–43

> **Author's Comment:**
> - See the definition of "Remote Control" in Article 100.
> - The service disconnect must consist of a manually operated switch, a power-operated switch, or a circuit breaker that's also capable of being operated manually [230.76].

Services | 230.71

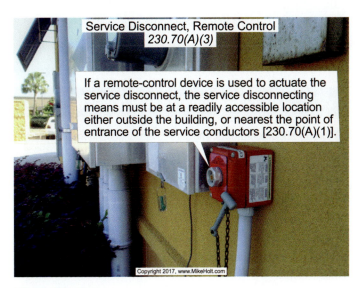

▶Figure 230–43

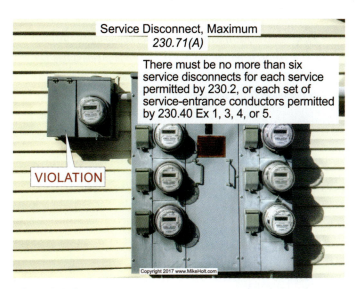

▶Figure 230–45

(B) Disconnect Identification. Each service disconnecting means must be permanently marked to identify it as part of the service disconnecting means. ▶Figure 230–44

Author's Comment:

- A PV disconnect(s) connected to the supply side of service equipment isn't a service disconnect and shouldn't be counted when you're determining the number of service disconnects [230.82(6)]. ▶Figure 230–46

▶Figure 230–44

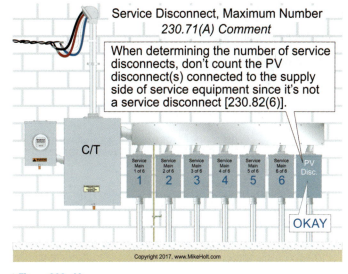

▶Figure 230–46

(C) Suitable for Use. Each service disconnect must be suitable for the prevailing conditions.

230.71 Number of Disconnects

(A) Maximum. There must be no more than six service disconnects for each service permitted by 230.2, or each set of service-entrance conductors permitted by 230.40 Ex 1, 3, 4, or 5. ▶Figure 230–45

The service disconnecting means can consist of up to six switches or six circuit breakers mounted in a single enclosure, in a group of separate enclosures, or in or on a switchboard, or in switchgear.

137

230.72 | Services

CAUTION: The rule is six disconnecting means for each service, not for each building. If the building has two services, then there can be a total of 12 service disconnects (six disconnects per service). ▶Figure 230–47

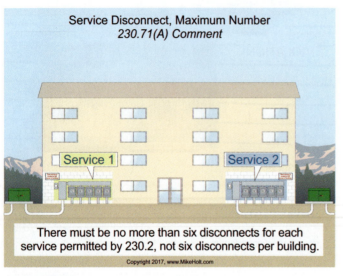

▶Figure 230–47

Disconnecting means used only for the following aren't considered a service disconnect:

(1) Power monitoring equipment

(2) Surge protective device(s) ▶Figure 230–48

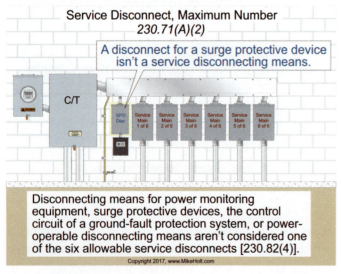

▶Figure 230–48

(3) Control circuit of the ground-fault protection system

(4) Power-operable service disconnect

230.72 Grouping of Disconnects

(A) Two to Six Disconnects. The service disconnecting means for each service must be grouped.

(B) Additional Service Disconnecting Means. To minimize the possibility of simultaneous interruption of power, the disconnecting means for fire pumps [Article 695], emergency systems [Article 700], legally required standby [Article 701], or optional standby [Article 702] systems must be located remote from the one to six service disconnects for normal service.

Author's Comment:

- Because emergency systems are just as important as fire pumps and standby systems, they need to have the same safety precautions to prevent unintended interruption of the supply of electricity.

(C) Access to Occupants. In a multiple-occupancy building, each occupant must have access to their service disconnect.

Ex: In multiple-occupancy buildings where electrical maintenance is provided by continuous building management, the service disconnecting means can be accessible only to building management personnel.

230.76 Manual or Power Operated

The service disconnect can consist of:

(1) A manually operable switch or circuit breaker equipped with a handle or other suitable operating means.

(2) A power-operated switch or circuit breaker, provided it can be opened by hand in the event of a power supply failure. ▶Figure 230–49

230.77 Indicating

The service disconnect must indicate whether it's in the off (open) or on (closed) position.

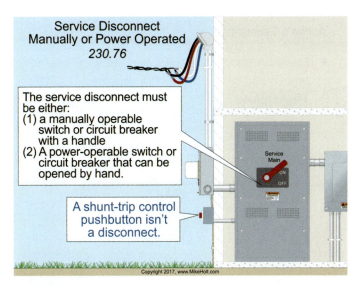

▶Figure 230–49

230.79 Rating of Disconnect

The service disconnect for a building must have an ampere rating of not less than the calculated load according to Article 220, and in no case less than:

(A) One-Circuit Installation. For installations consisting of a single branch circuit, the disconnect must have a rating not less than 15A.

(B) Two-Circuit Installation. For installations consisting of two 2-wire branch circuits, the disconnect must have a rating not less than 30A.

(C) One-Family Dwelling. For a one-family dwelling, the disconnect must have a rating not less than 100A, 3-wire.

(D) Other Installations. For all other installations, the disconnect must have a rating not less than 60A.

Author's Comment:

- A shunt-trip button doesn't qualify as a service disconnecting means because it doesn't meet any of the above requirements.

230.81 Connection to Terminals

The service conductors must be connected to the service disconnect by pressure connectors, clamps, or other means approved by the authority having jurisdiction. Connections aren't permitted to be made using solder.

230.82 Connected on Supply Side of the Service Disconnect

Electrical equipment isn't permitted to be connected to the supply side of the service disconnect enclosure, except for: ▶Figure 230–50

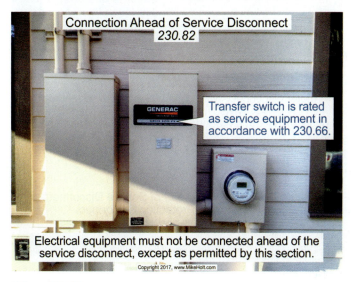

▶Figure 230–50

(2) Meter sockets can be connected to the supply side of the service disconnect enclosure.

(3) Meter disconnect switches are permitted to be connected to the supply side of the service disconnect, and they must be legibly field marked on the exterior in a manner suitable for the environment as follows: ▶Figure 230–51

METER DISCONNECT
NOT SERVICE EQUIPMENT

Author's Comment:

- Some electric utilities require a disconnect switch ahead of the meter enclosure for 277/480V services for the purpose of enhancing safety for electric utility personnel when they install or remove a meter socket.

(4) Type 1 surge protective devices can be connected to the supply side of the service disconnect enclosure. ▶Figure 230–52

230.82 | Services

▶Figure 230–51

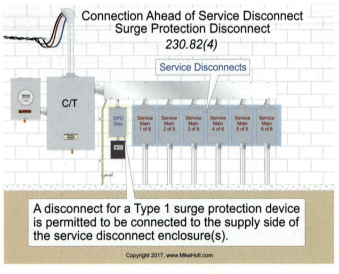

▶Figure 230–52

Author's Comment:

- A Type 1 surge protective device is listed to be permanently connected on the line side of service equipment [285.23].

(5) Taps used to supply legally required and optional standby power systems, fire pump equipment, fire and sprinkler alarms, and load (energy) management devices can be connected to the supply side of the service disconnect enclosure.

Author's Comment:

- Emergency standby power isn't permitted to be supplied by a connection ahead of service equipment [700.12]. ▶Figure 230–53

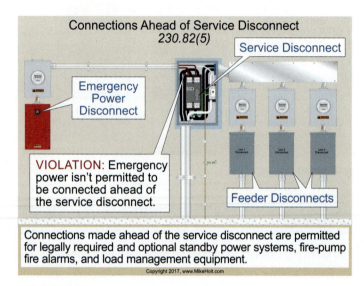

▶Figure 230–53

(6) Solar PV systems, wind electric systems, energy storage systems, or interconnected electric power production sources can be connected to the supply side of the service disconnect enclosure in accordance with 705.12(A). ▶Figure 230–54

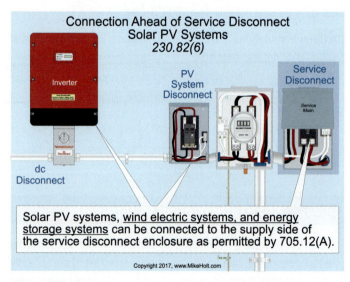

▶Figure 230–54

Services | 230.90

Author's Comment:

- Transfer switches for generators aren't permitted ahead of the service disconnecting means unless they're rated as the service disconnect in accordance with 230.66.

Part VII. Service Equipment Overcurrent Protection

230.90 Overload Protection

Each ungrounded service conductor must have overload protection [240.21(D)]. ▶Figure 230–55

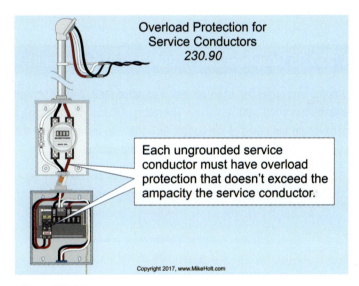

▶Figure 230–55

Author's Comment:

- The *NEC* doesn't require service conductors to be provided with short-circuit or ground-fault protection, but the feeder overcurrent protection device provides overload protection for the service conductors.

(A) Overcurrent Protection Device Rating. The rating of the overcurrent protection device isn't permitted to be more than the ampacity of the conductors.

Ex 2: If the ampacity of the ungrounded conductors doesn't correspond with the standard rating of overcurrent protection devices as listed in 240.6(A), the next higher overcurrent protection device can be used, if it doesn't exceed 800A [240.4(B)]. ▶Figure 230–56

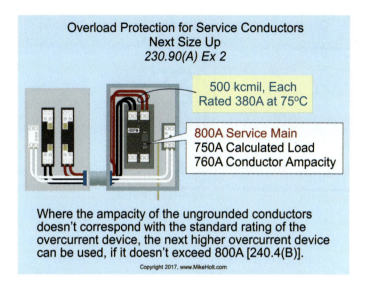

▶Figure 230–56

Ex 3: The combined ratings of two to six service disconnecting means can exceed the ampacity of the service conductors provided the calculated load, in accordance with Article 220, doesn't exceed the ampacity of the service conductors. ▶Figure 230–57

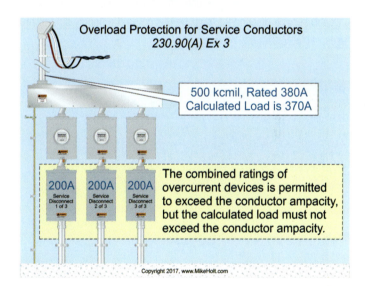

▶Figure 230–57

Ex 5: Overload protection for 3-wire, single-phase, 120/240V dwelling unit service conductors can be in accordance with 310.15(B)(7). ▶Figure 230–58

Mike Holt Enterprises • www.MikeHolt.com • 888.NEC.CODE (632.2633) 141

230.91 | Services

▶Figure 230–58

▶Figure 230–59

230.91 Location

Where circuit breakers are used for service overcurrent protection, they must be integral with or located immediately adjacent to the service disconnect. Where fuses are used for service overcurrent protection, the service disconnect must be placed on the supply side of the fuses. ▶Figure 230–59

230.95 Ground-Fault Protection of Equipment

Ground-fault protection of equipment is required for 277/480V service disconnects rated 1,000A or more. The rating of the service disconnect is based on the rating of the largest fuse that can be installed or the circuit breaker's highest continuous current trip setting.

ARTICLE 240 — OVERCURRENT PROTECTION

Introduction to Article 240—Overcurrent Protection

This article provides the requirements for selecting and installing overcurrent protection devices. Overcurrent exists when current exceeds the rating of equipment or the ampacity of a conductor due to an overload, short circuit, or ground fault [Article 100].

- **Overload.** An overload is a condition where equipment or conductors carry current exceeding their current rating [Article 100]. A fault, such as a short circuit or ground fault, isn't an overload. An example of an overload is plugging two 12.50A (1,500W) hair dryers into a 20A branch circuit.

- **Short Circuit.** A short circuit is the unintentional electrical connection between any two normally current-carrying conductors of an electrical circuit, either line-to-line or line-to-neutral.

- **Ground Fault.** A ground fault is an unintentional, electrically conducting connection between an ungrounded conductor of an electrical circuit and the normally noncurrent-carrying conductors, metal enclosures, metal raceways, metallic equipment, or the earth [Article 100]. During the period of a ground fault, dangerous voltages will be present on metal parts until the circuit overcurrent protection device opens.

Overcurrent protection devices protect conductors and equipment. Selecting the proper overcurrent protection for a specific circuit can become more complicated than it sounds. The general rule for overcurrent protection is that conductors must be protected in accordance with their ampacities at the point where they receive their supply [240.4 and 240.21]. There are many special cases that deviate from this basic rule, such as the overcurrent protection limitations for small conductors [240.4(D)] and the rules for specific conductor applications found in other articles, as listed in Table 240.4(G). There are also a number of rules allowing tap conductors in specific situations [240.21(B)]. Article 240 even has limits on where overcurrent protection devices are allowed to be located [240.24].

An overcurrent protection device must be capable of opening a circuit when an overcurrent situation occurs, and must also have an interrupting rating sufficient to avoid damage in fault conditions [110.9]. Carefully study this article to be sure you provide sufficient overcurrent protection in the correct location.

Part I. General

240.1 Scope

Article 240 covers the general requirements for overcurrent protection and the installation requirements of overcurrent protection devices.
▶Figure 240–1

Author's Comment:

- Overcurrent is a condition where the current exceeds the rating of equipment or ampacity of a conductor due to overload, short circuit, or ground fault [Article 100]. ▶Figure 240–2

240.2 | Overcurrent Protection

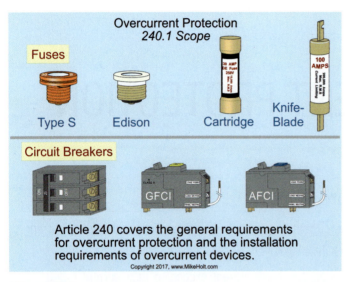

▶Figure 240–1

240.2 Definitions

Current-Limiting Overcurrent Protection Device. An overcurrent protection device (typically a fast-acting fuse) that reduces the fault current to a magnitude substantially less than that obtainable in the same circuit if the current-limiting device wasn't used. See 240.40 and 240.60(B). ▶Figure 240–3

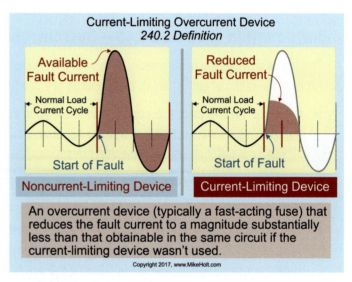

▶Figure 240–3

Author's Comment:

- A current-limiting fuse is a type of fuse designed for operations related to short circuits only. When a fuse operates in its current-limiting range, it will begin to melt in less than a quarter of a cycle, and it will open a bolted short circuit in less than half a cycle. This type of fuse limits the instantaneous peak let-through current to a value substantially less than what will occur in the same circuit if the fuse is replaced with a solid conductor of equal impedance. If the available short-circuit current exceeds the equipment/conductor short-circuit current rating, then the thermal and magnetic forces can cause the equipment circuit conductors, as well as the circuit equipment grounding conductors, to vaporize. The only solutions to the problem of excessive available fault current are to:

  ♦ Install equipment with a higher short-circuit rating, or
  ♦ Protect the components of the circuit by a current-limiting overcurrent protection device such as a fast-clearing fuse, which can reduce the let-through energy.

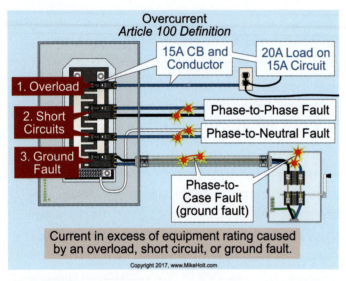

▶Figure 240–2

Note: An overcurrent protection device protects the circuit by opening the device when the current reaches a value that will cause excessive or dangerous temperature rise (overheating) in conductors. Overcurrent protection devices must have an interrupting rating sufficient for the maximum possible fault current available on the line-side terminals of the equipment [110.9]. Electrical equipment must have a short-circuit current rating that permits the circuit's overcurrent protection device to clear short circuits or ground faults without extensive damage to the circuit's electrical components [110.10].

- A breaker or a fuse does limit current, but it may not be listed as a current-limiting device. A thermal-magnetic circuit breaker typically clears fault current in less than three to five cycles when subjected to a short circuit or ground fault of 20 times its rating. A standard fuse will clear the same fault in less than one cycle and a current-limiting fuse in less than half of a cycle.

Tap Conductors. A conductor, other than a service conductor, that has overcurrent protection rated more than the ampacity of a conductor. See 240.21(A) and 240.21(B) for details. ▶Figure 240–4

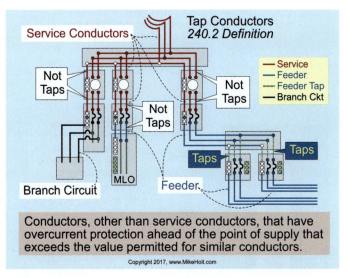

▶Figure 240–4

240.3 Overcurrent Protection of Equipment

The following equipment and their conductors are protected against overcurrent in accordance with the article that covers the type of equipment:

Table 240.3—Other Articles		
Equipment	Article	Section
Air-Conditioning and Refrigeration Equipment	440	440.22
Appliances	422	All
Audio Circuits	640	640.9
Branch Circuits	210	210.20
Class 1, 2, and 3 Circuits	725	All
Feeder Conductors	215	215.3
Flexible Cords	240	240.5(B)(1)
Fire Alarms	760	All
Fire Pumps	695	All
Fixed Electric Space-Heating Equipment	424	424.3(B)
Fixture Wire	240	240.5(B)(2)
Panelboards	408	408.36
Service Conductors	230	230.90(A)
Transformers	450	450.3

240.4 Overcurrent Protection of Conductors

Except as permitted by (A) through (G), conductors must be protected against overcurrent in accordance with their ampacity after ampacity correction and adjustment as specified in 310.15. ▶Figure 240–5

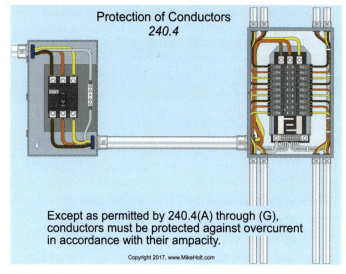

▶Figure 240–5

(A) Power Loss Hazard. Conductor overload protection isn't required, but short-circuit overcurrent protection is required where the interruption of the circuit will create a hazard; such as in a material-handling electromagnet circuit or fire pump circuit.

(B) Overcurrent Protection Devices Rated 800A or Less. The next higher standard rating of overcurrent protection device listed in 240.6 (above the ampacity of the ungrounded conductors being protected) is permitted, provided all of the following conditions are met:

240.4 | Overcurrent Protection

(1) The conductors aren't part of a branch circuit supplying more than one receptacle for cord-and-plug-connected loads.

(2) The ampacity of a conductor, after the application of ambient temperature correction [310.15(B)(2)(a)], conductor bundling adjustment [310.15(B)(3)(a)], or both, doesn't correspond with the standard rating of a fuse or circuit breaker in 240.6(A).

(3) The overcurrent protection device rating doesn't exceed 800A.
▶Figure 240–6

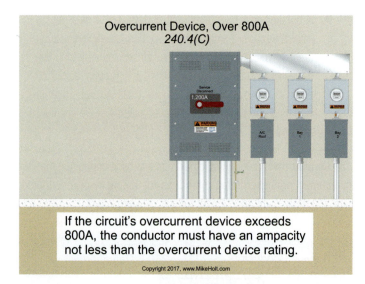

▶Figure 240–7

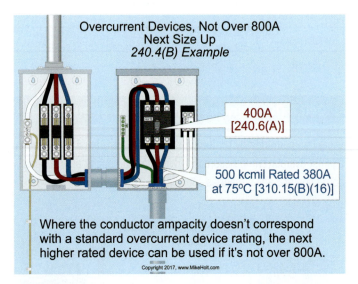

▶Figure 240–6

Author's Comment:

- This "next size up" rule doesn't apply to feeder tap conductors [240.21(B)] or transformer secondary conductors [240.21(C)].

(C) Overcurrent Protection Devices Rated Over 800A. If the circuit's overcurrent protection device exceeds 800A, the conductor ampacity, after the application of ambient temperature correction [310.15(B)(2)(a)], conductor bundling adjustment [310.15(B)(3)(a)], or both, must have a rating of not less than the rating of the overcurrent protection device defined in 240.6. ▶Figure 240–7

(D) Small Conductors. Unless specifically permitted in 240.4(E) or (G), overcurrent protection must not exceed the following: ▶Figure 240–8

(1) 18 AWG Copper—7A

(2) 16 AWG Copper—10A

(3) 14 AWG Copper—15A

(4) 12 AWG Aluminum/Copper-Clad Aluminum—15A

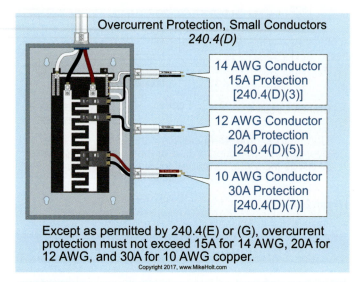

▶Figure 240–8

(5) 12 AWG Copper—20A

(6) 10 AWG Aluminum/Copper-Clad Aluminum—25A

(7) 10 AWG Copper—30A

(E) Tap Conductors. Tap conductors must be protected against overcurrent as follows:

(1) Household Ranges, Cooking Appliances and Other Loads, 210.19(A)(3) and (4)

(2) Fixture Wire, 240.5(B)(2)

(3) Location in Circuit, 240.21

(4) Reduction in Ampacity Size of Busway, 368.17(B)

(5) Feeder or Branch Circuits (busway taps), 368.17(C)

(6) Single Motor Taps, 430.53(D)

(F) Transformer Secondary Conductors. The primary overcurrent protection device sized in accordance with 450.3(B) is considered suitable to protect the secondary conductors of a 2-wire (single voltage) system, provided the primary overcurrent protection device doesn't exceed the value determined by multiplying the secondary conductor ampacity by the secondary-to-primary transformer voltage ratio.

Example: What's the minimum secondary conductor size required for a 2-wire, 480V to 120V transformer rated 1.50 kVA with 60°C terminals? ▶Figure 240–9

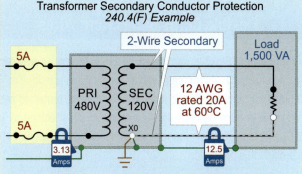

▶Figure 240–9

Solution:

Primary Current = VA/E

VA = 1,500 VA

E = 480V

Primary Current = 1,500 VA/480V
Primary Current = 3.13A

Primary overcurrent protection [450.3(B)] = 3.13A × 1.67
Primary overcurrent protection = 5.22A or 5A Fuse

Secondary conductor must have an ampacity no less than five times the primary protection ampere rating.
Secondary Conductor Ampacity = Primary Protection Ampacity × (Primary Voltage/Secondary Voltage)

Secondary Conductor Ampacity = 5A × 480V/120V
Secondary Conductor Ampacity = 5A × 4 times
Secondary Conductor Ampacity = 20A

Answer: 12 AWG rated 20A at 60°C [Table 310.15(B)(16)].

(G) Overcurrent Protection for Specific Applications. Overcurrent protection for specific equipment and conductors must comply with the requirements referenced in Table 240.4(G).

Air-Conditioning and Refrigeration [Article 440]. Air-conditioning and refrigeration equipment, and their circuit conductors, must be protected against overcurrent in accordance with 440.22.

Author's Comment:

■ Typically, the branch-circuit ampacity and overcurrent protection size is marked on the equipment nameplate [440.4(A)].

Air-Conditioning Example: What size branch-circuit overcurrent protection device is required for an air conditioner when the nameplate indicates the minimum circuit ampacity is 23A, with maximum overcurrent protection of 40A? ▶Figure 240–10

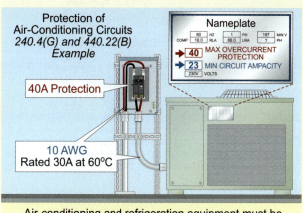

▶Figure 240–10

Answer: 10 AWG, 40A protection

240.5 | Overcurrent Protection

Author's Comment:

- Air-conditioning and refrigeration nameplate values are calculated by the manufacturer according to the following:
  - Branch-Circuit Conductor Size [440.32]
    18A × 1.25 = 22.50A, 10 AWG rated 30A at 60°C
  - Branch-Circuit Overcurrent Protection Size [440.22(A)]
    18A × 2.25 = 40.50A, 40A maximum overcurrent protection size [240.6(A)]
  - Motors [Article 430]. Motor circuit conductors must be protected against short circuits and ground faults in accordance with 430.52 and 430.62 [430.51].

If the nameplate calls for fuses, then fuses must be used to comply with the manufacturer's instructions [110.3(B)].

Motor Example: What size branch-circuit conductor and overcurrent protection device (circuit breaker) is required for a 7½ hp, 230V, three-phase motor with 60°C terminals? ▶Figure 240–11

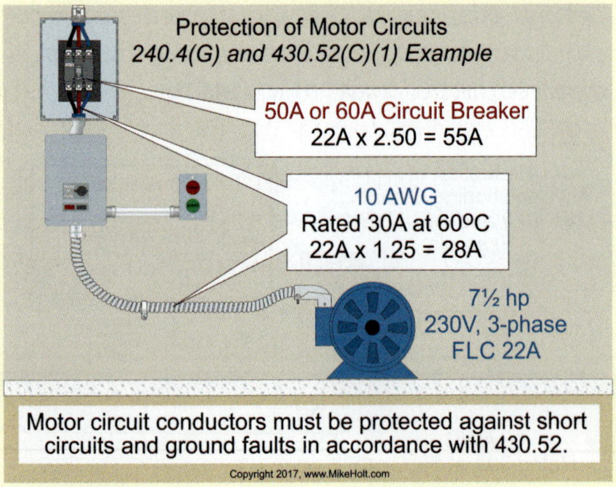

Protection of Motor Circuits
240.4(G) and 430.52(C)(1) Example

50A or 60A Circuit Breaker
22A × 2.50 = 55A

10 AWG
Rated 30A at 60°C
22A × 1.25 = 28A

7½ hp
230V, 3-phase
FLC 22A

Motor circuit conductors must be protected against short circuits and ground faults in accordance with 430.52.

Copyright 2017, www.MikeHolt.com

▶Figure 240–11

Solution:

Step 1: Determine the branch-circuit conductor size [Table 310.15(B)(16), 430.22, and Table 430.250]:

FLC = 22A [Table 430.250]
22A × 1.25 = 28A

Step 2: Determine the branch-circuit overcurrent protection size [240.6(A), 430.52(C)(1) Ex 1, and Table 430.250].

Inverse Time Breaker: 22A × 2.50 = 55A

Answer: 10 AWG rated 30A at 60°C branch-circuit conductor with a 60A (next size up) overcurrent protection device.

Motor Control [Article 430]. Motor control circuit conductors must be sized and protected in accordance with 430.72.

Remote-Control, Signaling, and Power-Limited Circuits [Article 725]. Remote-control, signaling, and power-limited circuit conductors must be protected against overcurrent in accordance with 725.43.

240.5 Overcurrent Protection of Flexible Cords and Fixture Wires

(A) Ampacities. Flexible cord must be protected by an overcurrent protection device in accordance with its ampacity as specified in Table 400.5(A)(1) or Table 400.5(A)(2). Fixture wires must be protected against overcurrent in accordance with their ampacity as specified in Table 402.5. Supplementary overcurrent protection, as discussed in 240.10, can provide this protection.

(B) Branch-Circuit Overcurrent Protection.

(1) Cords for Listed Appliances or Luminaires. If flexible cord is used with a specific listed appliance or luminaire, the conductors are considered protected against overcurrent when used within the appliance or luminaire listing requirements. ▶Figure 240–12

Author's Comment:

- The *NEC* only applies to premises wiring, not to the supply cords of listed appliances and luminaires.

(2) Fixture Wire. Fixture wires can be tapped to the following circuits:

(1) 20A–18 AWG, up to 50 ft of run length
(2) 20A–16 AWG, up to 100 ft of run length
(3) 20A–14 AWG and larger

(3) Extension Cord Sets. Flexible cord used in listed extension cord sets is considered protected against overcurrent when used within the extension cord's listing requirements. ▶Figure 240–13

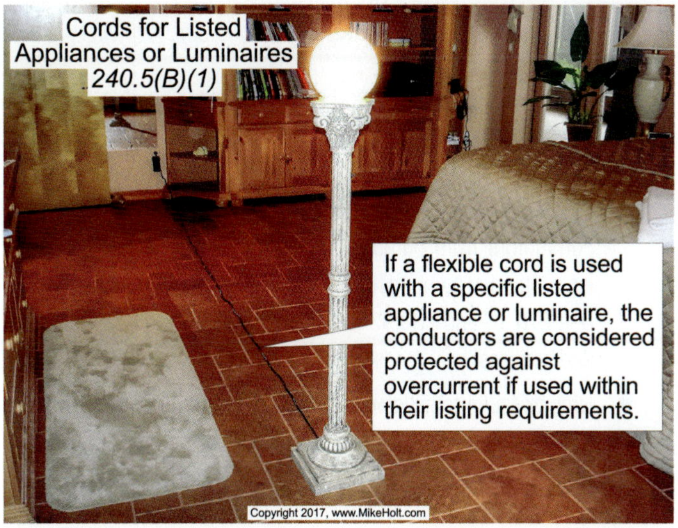

Overcurrent Protection | 240.10

▶Figure 240–12

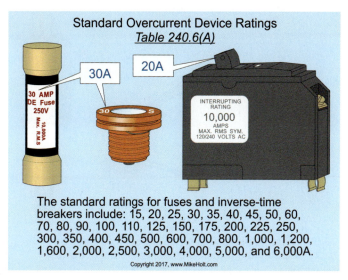
▶Figure 240–14

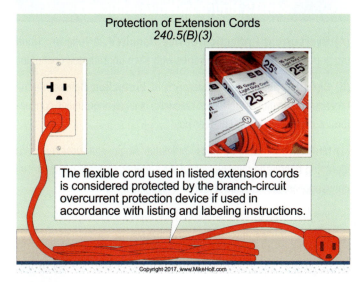
▶Figure 240–13

240.6 Standard Ampere Ratings

(A) Fuses and Fixed-Trip Circuit Breakers. The standard ratings in amperes for fuses and inverse time breakers are shown in Table 240.6(A). The use of fuses and inverse time circuit breakers with nonstandard ampere ratings are permitted. ▶Figure 240–14

Additional standard ampere ratings for fuses include 1, 3, 6, 10, and 601.

Author's Comment:

- Fuses rated less than 15A are sometimes required for the overcurrent protection of fractional horsepower motor circuits [430.52], motor control circuits [430.72], small transformers [450.3(B)], and remote-control circuit conductors [725.43].

(B) Adjustable Circuit Breakers. The ampere rating of an adjustable circuit breaker is equal to its maximum long-time pickup current setting.

(C) Restricted Access, Adjustable-Trip Circuit Breakers. The ampere rating of adjustable-trip circuit breakers that have restricted access to the adjusting means is equal to their adjusted long-time pickup current settings.

240.10 Supplementary Overcurrent Protection

Supplementary overcurrent protection devices aren't permitted to be used as the required branch-circuit overcurrent protection device.
▶Figure 240–15

A supplementary overcurrent protection device isn't required to be readily accessible [240.24(A)(2)].

240.13 | Overcurrent Protection

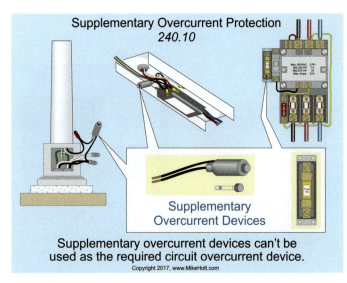

▶Figure 240–15

Author's Comment:

- Article 100 defines a "Supplementary Overcurrent Protection Device" as a device intended to provide limited overcurrent protection for specific applications and utilization equipment. This limited overcurrent protection is in addition to the overcurrent protection provided in the required branch circuit by the branch-circuit overcurrent protection device.

240.13 Ground-Fault Protection of Equipment

Service disconnects and feeder circuits rated 1,000A or more, supplied from a 4-wire, three-phase, 277/480V wye-connected system must be protected against ground faults in accordance with 230.95 [215.10 and 230.95].

The requirement for ground-fault protection of equipment doesn't apply to:

(1) Continuous industrial processes where a nonorderly shutdown will introduce additional or increased hazards.

(2) Installations where ground-fault protection of equipment is already provided.

(3) Fire pumps [695.6(H)].

Author's Comment:

- Article 100 defines "Ground-Fault Protection of Equipment" as a system intended to provide overcurrent protection of equipment from ground faults by opening the overcurrent protection device at current levels less than those required to protect conductors from damage. This type of protective system isn't intended to protect people, only connected equipment. See 215.10 and 230.95 for similar requirements for feeders and services.

- Ground-fault protection of equipment isn't required for emergency power systems [700.26] or legally required standby power systems [701.17].

240.15 Ungrounded Conductors

(A) Overcurrent Protection Device Required. A fuse or circuit breaker must be connected in series with each ungrounded conductor.

(B) Circuit Breaker as an Overcurrent Protection Device. Circuit breakers must automatically (and manually) open all ungrounded conductors of the circuit, except as follows:

(1) Multiwire Branch Circuits. Individual single-pole breakers with identified handle ties are permitted for a multiwire branch circuit that only supplies line-to-neutral loads. ▶Figure 240–16

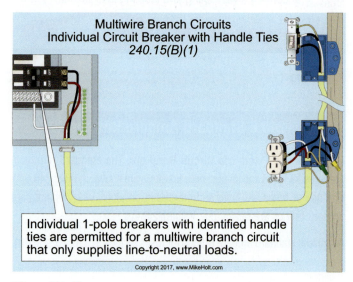

▶Figure 240–16

Overcurrent Protection | 240.21

Author's Comment:

- According to Article 100, "Identified" means recognized as suitable for a specific purpose, function, or environment by listing, labeling, or other means approved by the authority having jurisdiction. This means handle ties made from nails, screws, wires, or other nonconforming materials aren't suitable. ▶Figure 240–17

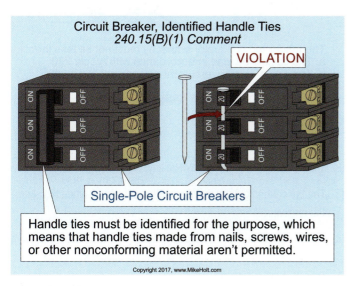

▶Figure 240–17

(2) Single-Phase, Line-to-Line Loads. Individual single-pole circuit breakers rated 120/240V with handle ties identified for the purpose are permitted on each ungrounded conductor of a branch circuit that supplies single-phase, line-to-line loads. ▶Figure 240–18

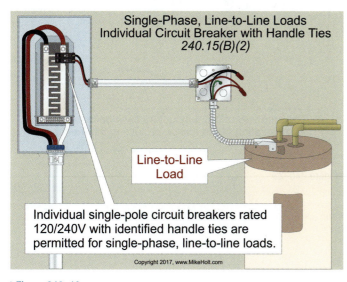

▶Figure 240–18

(3) Three-Phase, Line-to-Line Loads. Individual single-pole breakers rated 120/240V with handle ties identified for the purpose are permitted on each ungrounded conductor of a branch circuit that serves three-phase, line-to-line loads on systems not exceeding 120V to ground. ▶Figure 240–19

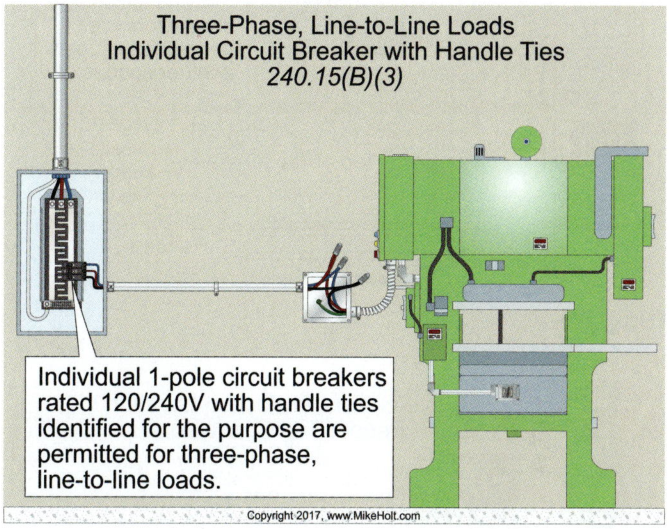

▶Figure 240–19

Part II. Location

240.21 Overcurrent Protection Location in Circuit

Except as permitted by (A) through (H), overcurrent protection devices must be placed at the point where the branch-circuit or feeder conductors receive their power. Taps and transformer secondary conductors aren't permitted to supply another conductor (tapping a tap isn't permitted). ▶Figure 240–20

(A) Branch-Circuit Taps. Branch-circuit taps are permitted in accordance with 210.19.

(B) Feeder Taps. Conductors can be tapped to a feeder as specified in 240.21(B)(1) through (B)(5). The "next size up overcurrent protection rule" of 240.4(B) isn't permitted for tap conductors. ▶Figure 240–21

240.21 | Overcurrent Protection

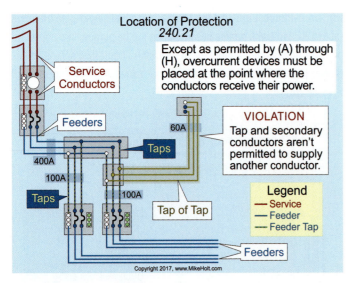

▶Figure 240–20

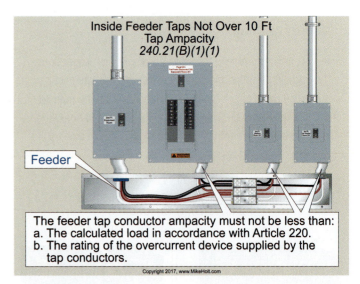

▶Figure 240–22

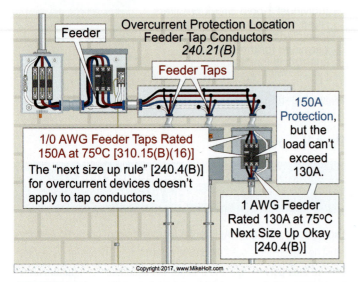

▶Figure 240–21

(2) The tap conductors must not extend beyond the equipment they supply.

(3) The tap conductors are installed within a raceway when they leave the enclosure.

(4) The tap conductors must have an ampacity not less than 10 percent of the rating of the overcurrent protection device that protects the feeder. ▶Figure 240–23

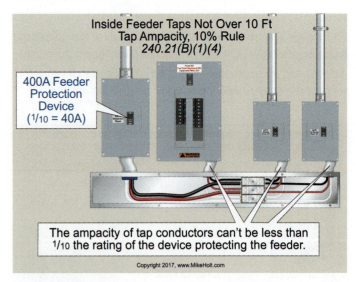

▶Figure 240–23

Note: See 408.36 for the overcurrent protection requirements for panelboards.

(1) 10-Foot Feeder Tap. Feeder tap conductors up to 10 ft long are permitted without overcurrent protection at the tap location if the tap conductors comply with the following:

(1) The tap conductors must have an ampacity less than: ▶Figure 240–22

   a. The calculated load in accordance with Article 220, and

   b. The rating of the overcurrent protection device termination or equipment containing overcurrent protection devices supplied by the tap conductors.

Ex: Listed equipment, such as a surge protection device, can have their conductors sized in accordance with the manufacturer's instructions.

Overcurrent Protection | 240.21

▶ 10-Foot Tap Rule

Example: A 400A breaker protects a set of 500 kcmil feeder conductors. There are three taps fed from the 500 kcmil feeder that supply disconnects with 200A, 150A, and 30A overcurrent protection devices. What are the minimum size conductors for these taps? ▶Figure 240–24

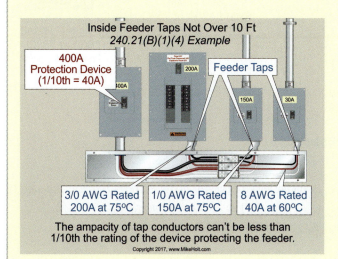

▶Figure 240–24

Answer:

- **200A Disconnect Tap:** 3/0 AWG is rated 200A at 75°C, and is greater than 10 percent of the rating of the overcurrent protection device (400A).

- **150A Disconnect Tap:** 1/0 AWG is rated 150A at 75°C, and is greater than 10 percent of the rating of the overcurrent protection device (400A).

- **30A Disconnect Tap:** 8 AWG rated 40A at 60°C. The tap conductors from the 400A feeder to the 30A overcurrent protection device can't be less than 40A (10 percent of the rating of the 400A feeder overcurrent protection device).

(2) 25-Foot Feeder Tap. Feeder tap conductors up to 25 ft long are permitted without overcurrent protection at the tap location if the tap conductors comply with the following: ▶Figure 240–25 and ▶Figure 240–26

(1) The ampacity of the tap conductors aren't permitted to be less than one-third the rating of the overcurrent protection device that protects the feeder.

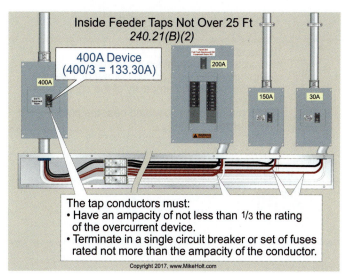

▶Figure 240–25

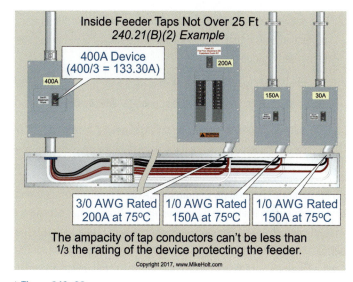

▶Figure 240–26

(2) The tap conductors terminate in an overcurrent protection device rated no more than the tap conductor ampacity in accordance with 310.15 [Table 310.15(B)(16)].

(5) Outside Feeder Taps of Unlimited Length. Outside feeder tap conductors can be of unlimited length, without overcurrent protection at the point they receive their supply, if they comply with all of the following: ▶Figure 240–27

(1) The outside feeder tap conductors are protected from physical damage within a raceway or manner approved by the authority having jurisdiction.

240.21 | Overcurrent Protection

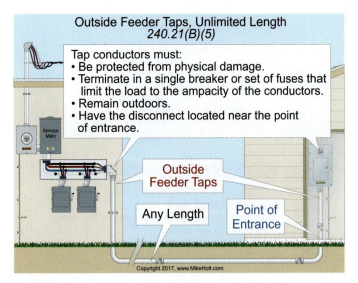

▶Figure 240–27

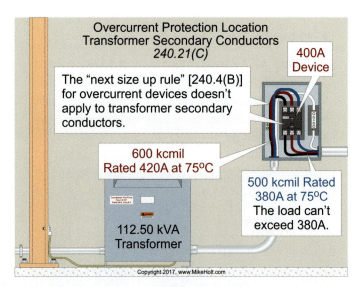

▶Figure 240–28

(2) The outside feeder tap conductors terminate at a single overcurrent protection device that limits the load to the ampacity of the outside feeder tap conductors.

(3) The terminating overcurrent protection device for the outside feeder tap conductors is part of the building feeder disconnect.

(4) The building feeder disconnecting means is readily accessible, either outside the building, or nearest the point of entrance of the outside feeder tap conductors.

(C) Transformer Secondary Conductors. A set of conductors supplying single or separate loads can be connected to a transformer secondary without overcurrent protection in accordance with (1) through (6). The permission of the "next size up" overcurrent protection rule when the conductor ampacity doesn't correspond with the standard size overcurrent protection device of 240.4(B) doesn't apply to transformer secondary conductors. ▶Figure 240–28

(1) Overcurrent Protection by Primary Overcurrent Protection Device. The primary overcurrent protection device sized in accordance with 450.3(B) is considered suitable to protect the secondary conductors of a 2-wire (single-voltage) system, provided the primary overcurrent protection device doesn't exceed the value determined by multiplying the secondary conductor ampacity by the secondary-to-primary transformer voltage ratio.

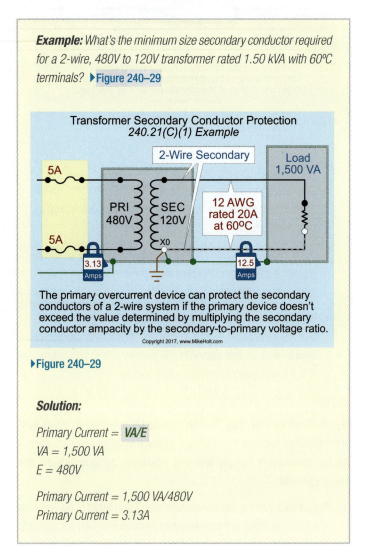

▶Figure 240–29

Solution:

Primary Current = VA/E

VA = 1,500 VA

E = 480V

Primary Current = 1,500 VA/480V

Primary Current = 3.13A

Overcurrent Protection | 240.21

Primary Overcurrent Protection [450.3(B)] = 3.13A × 1.67
Primary Overcurrent Protection [450.3(B)] = 5.22A or 5A Fuse

Secondary Current = 1,500 VA/120V
Secondary Current = 12.50A

Secondary Conductor = 12 AWG, rated 20A at 60ºC, [Table 310.15(B)(16)]

The 5A primary overcurrent protection device can be used to protect 12 AWG secondary conductors because it doesn't exceed the value determined by multiplying the secondary conductor ampacity by the secondary-to-primary transformer voltage ratio.

Overcurrent Protection Device = 20A × (120V/480V)
Overcurrent Protection Device = 20A × ¼ (25%)
Overcurrent Protection Device = 5A fuse

Answer: *12 AWG*

(2) 10-Foot Secondary Conductors. Secondary conductors can be run up to 10 ft without overcurrent protection if installed as follows:

(1) The secondary conductor must have an ampacity not less than: ▶Figure 240–30

(4) Outside Secondary Conductors of Unlimited Length. Secondary conductors located <u>outside</u> a building or structure can be of unlimited length, without overcurrent protection at the point they receive their supply, if they're installed as follows: ▶Figure 240–31

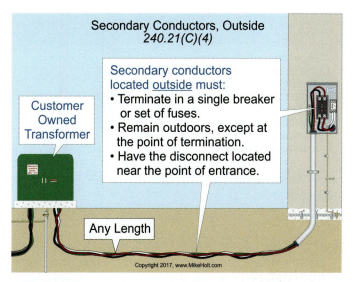

▶Figure 240–31

(1) The conductors are protected from physical damage within a raceway or manner approved by the authority having jurisdiction.

(2) The conductors terminate at a single overcurrent protection device that limits the load to the ampacity of the outside secondary conductors.

(3) The terminating overcurrent protection device for the outside secondary conductors is part of the building feeder disconnect.

(4) The building feeder disconnecting means is readily accessible, either outside the building, or nearest the point of entrance of the outside secondary conductors.

(5) Secondary Conductors from a Feeder Tapped Transformer. Transformer secondary conductors must be installed in accordance with 240.21(B)(3).

(6) 25-Foot Secondary Conductor. Secondary conductors can be run up to 25 ft without overcurrent protection if they comply with all of the following: ▶Figure 240–32

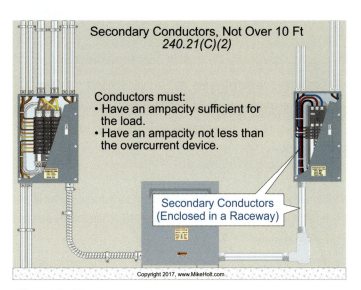

▶Figure 240–30

a. The calculated load in accordance with Article 220, and

b. The rating of the overcurrent protection device termination or equipment containing overcurrent protection devices supplied by the tap conductors.

240.24 | Overcurrent Protection

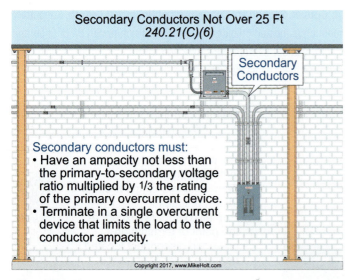
▶Figure 240–32

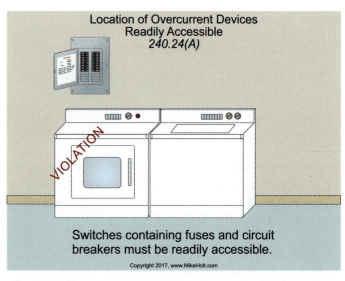
▶Figure 240–33

(1) The secondary conductors must have an ampacity that's not less than the value of the primary-to-secondary voltage ratio multiplied by one-third of the rating of the overcurrent protection device protecting the primary of the transformer.

(2) Secondary conductors terminate in a single overcurrent protection device that limits the load to the secondary conductor ampacity.

(D) Service Conductors. Service conductors must be protected against overload in accordance with 230.90 and 91.

(H) Battery Conductors. Overcurrent protection is installed as close as practicable to the storage battery terminals.

240.24 Location of Overcurrent Protection Devices

(A) Readily Accessible. Circuit breakers and switches containing fuses must be readily accessible and installed so the center of the grip of the operating handle of the circuit breaker or switch, when in its highest position, isn't more than 6 ft 7 in. above the floor or working platform, except for: ▶Figure 240–33 and ▶Figure 240–34

(1) Busways, as provided in 368.17(C).

(2) Supplementary overcurrent protection devices [240.10]. ▶Figure 240–35

(3) For overcurrent protection devices, as described in 225.40 and 230.92.

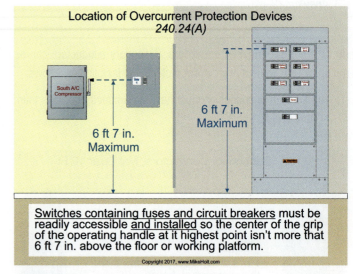
▶Figure 240–34

(4) Circuit breakers and switches containing fuses are permitted above 6 ft 7 in. where located next to equipment if accessible by portable means [404.8(A) Ex 2]. ▶Figure 240–36

Ex. The use of a tool is permitted to access overcurrent protection devices located within listed industrial control panels or similar enclosures.

(C) Not Exposed to Physical Damage. Overcurrent protection devices aren't permitted to be exposed to physical damage. ▶Figure 240–37

Overcurrent Protection | 240.24

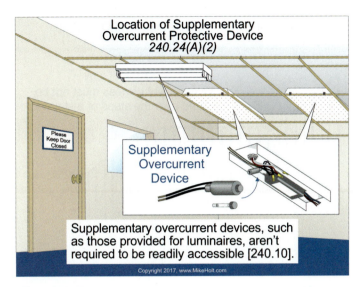

▶Figure 240–35

▶Figure 240–37

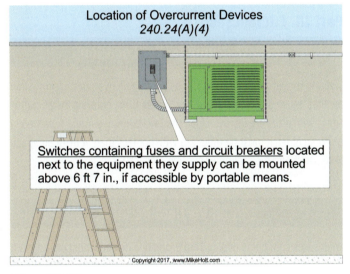

▶Figure 240–36

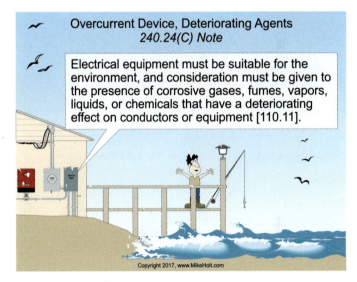

▶Figure 240–38

Note: Electrical equipment must be suitable for the environment, and consideration must be given to the presence of corrosive gases, fumes, vapors, liquids, or chemicals that have a deteriorating effect on conductors or equipment [110.11]. ▶Figure 240–38

(D) Not in Vicinity of Easily Ignitible Material. Overcurrent protection devices aren't permitted to be located near easily ignitible material, such as in clothes closets. ▶Figure 240–39

(E) Not in Bathrooms. Overcurrent protection devices aren't permitted to be located in the bathrooms of dwelling units, dormitories, or guest rooms or guest suites of hotels or motels. ▶Figure 240–40

Author's Comment:

- The service disconnect switch isn't permitted to be located in a bathroom, even in commercial or industrial facilities [230.70(A)(2)].

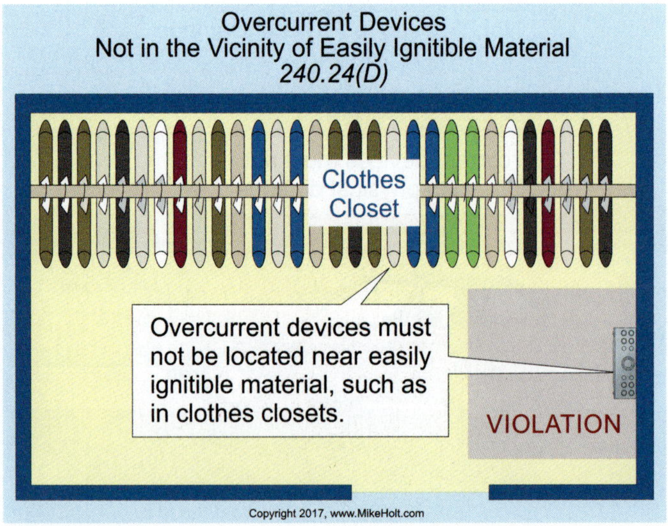

240.32 | Overcurrent Protection

▶Figure 240–39

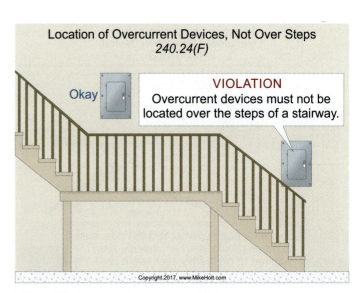
▶Figure 240–41

▶Figure 240–40

(F) Over Steps. Overcurrent protection devices aren't permitted to be located over the steps of a stairway. ▶Figure 240–41

Author's Comment:

- Clearly, it's difficult for electricians to safely work on electrical equipment that's located on uneven surfaces such as over stairways.

Part III. Enclosures

240.32 Damp or Wet Locations

In damp or wet locations, enclosures containing overcurrent protection devices must prevent moisture or water from entering or accumulating within the enclosure. When the enclosure is surface mounted in a wet location, it must be mounted with not less than ¼ in. of air space between it and the mounting surface. See 312.2.

240.33 Vertical Position

Enclosures containing overcurrent protection devices must be mounted in a vertical position unless this isn't practical. Circuit-breaker enclosures can be mounted horizontally if the circuit breaker is installed in accordance with 240.81. ▶Figure 240–42

Author's Comment:

- Section 240.81 specifies that where circuit-breaker handles are operated vertically, the "up" position of the handle must be in the "on" position. So, in effect, an enclosure that contains one row of circuit breakers can be mounted horizontally, but an enclosure that contains a panelboard with multiple circuit breakers on opposite sides of each other must be mounted vertically.

Overcurrent Protection | 240.54

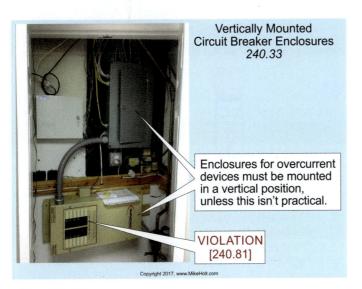

▶Figure 240–42

▶Figure 240–43

Part V. Plug Fuses, Fuseholders, and Adapters

240.50 General

(A) Maximum Voltage. Plug fuses are permitted to be used only when:

(1) The circuit voltage doesn't exceed 125V between conductors.

(2) The circuits are supplied by a system with a line-to-neutral voltage not exceeding 150V.

(C) Hexagon Configuration. Plug fuses of 15A or lower rating must be identified by a hexagonal configuration of the window, cap, or other prominent part.

240.51 Edison-Base Fuses

(A) Classification. Edison-base fuses are classified to operate at not more than 125V and have an ampere rating of not more than 30A. ▶Figure 240–43

(B) Replacement Only. Edison-base fuses are permitted only for replacement in an existing installation if there's no evidence of tampering or overfusing. ▶Figure 240–44

240.52 Edison-Base Fuseholders

Edison-base fuseholders must be used only if they're made to accept Type S fuses by the use of adapters.

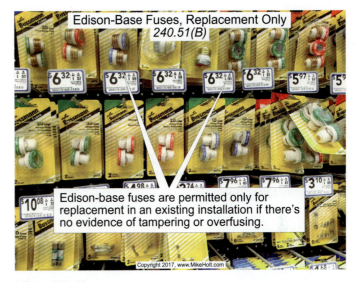

▶Figure 240–44

240.53 Type S Fuses

(A) Classification. Type S fuses operate at not more than 125V and have ampere ratings of 15A, 20A, and 30A. ▶Figure 240–45

(B) Not Interchangeable. Type S fuses are made so different ampere ratings aren't interchangeable.

240.54 Type S Fuses, Adapters, and Fuseholders

(A) Type S Adapters. Type S adapters are designed to fit Edison-base fuseholders.

240.60 | Overcurrent Protection

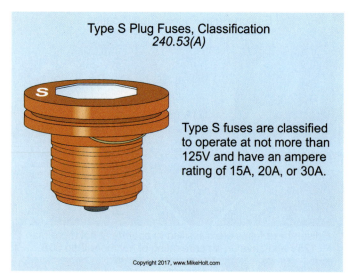
▶Figure 240–45

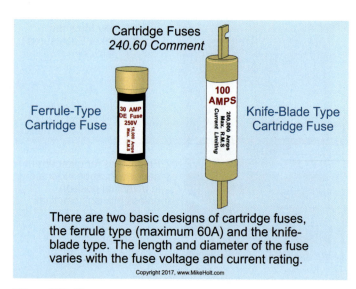
▶Figure 240–46

(B) Prevent Edison-Base Fuses. Type S fuseholders and adapters are designed for Type S fuses only.

(C) Nonremovable Adapters. Type S adapters are designed so they can't be removed once installed.

(D) Nontamperable. Type S fuses, fuseholders, and adapters must be designed so that tampering or shunting would be difficult.

(E) Interchangeability. Dimensions of Type S fuses, fuseholders, and adapters must be standardized to permit interchangeability regardless of the manufacturer.

Part VI. Cartridge Fuses and Fuseholders

240.60 General

Author's Comment:

- There are two basic designs of cartridge fuses, the ferrule type with a maximum rating of 60A and the knife-blade type rated over 60A. The fuse length and diameter varies with the voltage and current rating. ▶Figure 240–46

(A) Maximum Voltage—300V Type. Cartridge fuses and fuseholders of the 300V type can only be used for:

- Circuits not exceeding 300V between conductors.
- Circuits not exceeding 300V from any ungrounded conductor to the neutral point.

(B) Noninterchangeable Fuseholders. Fuseholders must be designed to make it difficult to interchange fuses of any given class for different voltages and current ratings.

Fuseholders for current-limiting fuses must be designed so only current-limiting fuses can be inserted.

Author's Comment:

- A current-limiting fuse is a fast-clearing overcurrent protection device that reduces the fault current to a magnitude substantially lower than that obtainable in the same circuit if the current-limiting device isn't used [240.2].

(C) Marking. Cartridge fuses have an interrupting rating of 10,000A, unless marked otherwise. They must be marked with:

(1) Ampere rating

(2) Voltage rating

(3) Interrupting rating if not 10,000A

(4) Current limiting if applicable

(5) Name or trademark of manufacturer

⚠️ **WARNING:** Fuses must have an interrupting rating sufficient for the short-circuit current available at the line terminals of the equipment. Using a fuse with an inadequate interrupting current rating can cause equipment to be destroyed from a line-to-line or ground fault, and result in death or serious injury. See 110.9 for more details. ▶Figure 240–47

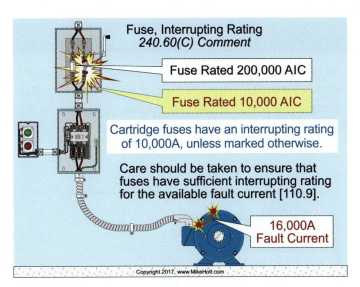
▶Figure 240–47

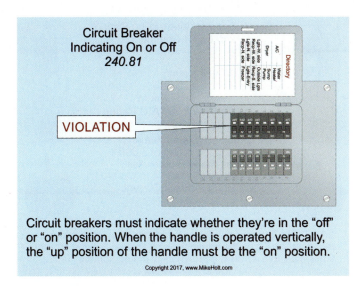
▶Figure 240–48

240.61 Classification

Cartridge fuses and fuseholders are classified according to their voltage and amperage ranges. Fuses rated 1,000V, nominal, or less are permitted for voltages at or below their ratings.

Part VII. Circuit Breakers

240.80 Method of Operation

Circuit breakers must be capable of being opened and closed by hand.

240.81 Indicating

Circuit breakers must clearly indicate whether they're in the open "off" or closed "on" position. When the handle of a circuit breaker is operated vertically, the "up" position of the handle must be the "on" position. See 240.33 and 404.6(C). ▶Figure 240–48

240.82 Nontamperable

A circuit breaker must be designed so that any alteration of its trip point (calibration) or the time required for its operation requires dismantling of the device or breaking of a seal for other than intended adjustments.

240.83 Markings

(A) Durable and Visible. Circuit breakers must be marked with their ampere rating in a manner that's durable and visible after installation. Such marking can be made visible by removal of a trim or cover.

(C) Interrupting Rating. Circuit breakers have an interrupting rating of 5,000A unless marked otherwise.

⚠ **WARNING:** *Take care to ensure the circuit breaker has an interrupting rating sufficient for the short-circuit current available at the line terminals of the equipment. Using a circuit breaker with an inadequate interrupting current rating can cause equipment to be destroyed from a line-to-line or ground fault, and result in death or serious injury. See 110.9 for more details.* ▶Figure 240–49

(D) Used as Switches. Circuit breakers used to switch 120V or 277V fluorescent lighting circuits must be listed and marked "SWD" or "HID." Circuit breakers used to switch high-intensity discharge lighting circuits must be listed and marked "HID." ▶Figure 240–50

Author's Comment:

■ This rule applies only when the circuit breaker is used as the switch. If a general-use snap switch or contactor is used to control the lighting, this rule doesn't apply.

240.85 | Overcurrent Protection

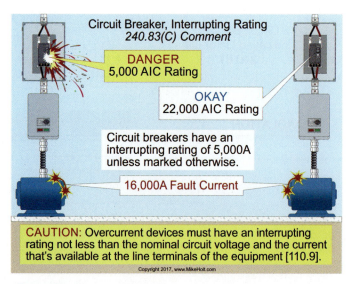

▶Figure 240–49

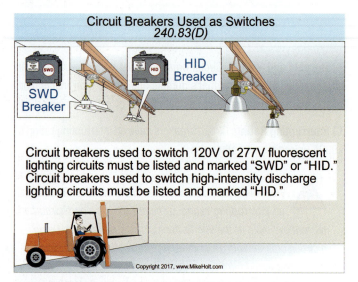

▶Figure 240–50

- UL 489, *Standard for Molded Case Circuit Breakers*, permits "HID" breakers to be rated up to 50A, whereas an "SWD" breaker can only be rated up to 20A. The tests for "HID" breakers include an endurance test at 75 percent power factor, whereas "SWD" breakers are endurance-tested at 100 percent power factor. The contacts and the spring of an "HID" breaker are of a heavier-duty material to dissipate the increased heat caused by the increased current flow in the circuit, because the "HID" luminaire takes a minute or two to ignite the lamp.

(E) Voltage Markings. Circuit breakers must be marked with a voltage rating that corresponds with their interrupting rating. See 240.85.

240.85 Applications

Straight Voltage Rating. A circuit breaker with a straight voltage rating, such as 240V or 480V, is permitted on a circuit if the nominal voltage between any two conductors (line-to-neutral or line-to-line) doesn't exceed the circuit breaker's voltage rating. ▶Figure 240–51 and ▶Figure 240–52

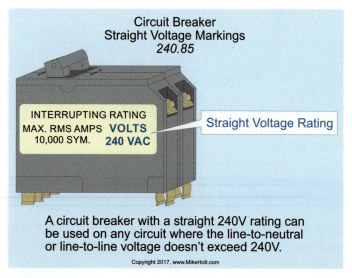

▶Figure 240–51

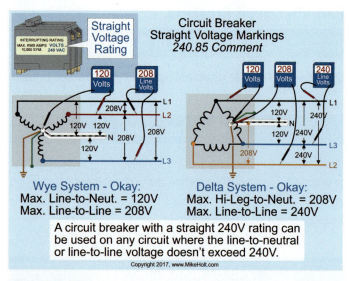

▶Figure 240–52

Slash Voltage Rating. A circuit breaker with a slash rating, such as 120/240V or 277/480V, is permitted on a solidly grounded system if the nominal voltage of any one conductor to ground doesn't exceed the lower of the two values, and the nominal voltage between any two conductors doesn't exceed the higher value. ▶Figure 240–53

Overcurrent Protection | 240.87

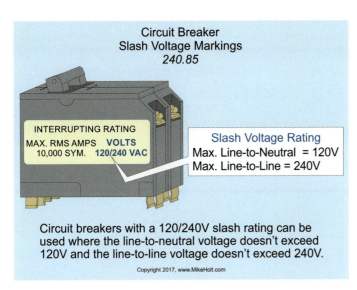

▶Figure 240–53

CAUTION: *A 120/240V slash circuit breaker isn't permitted to be used on the high leg of a solidly grounded 4-wire, three-phase, 120/240V delta-connected system because the line-to-ground voltage of the high leg is 208V, which exceeds the 120V line-to-ground voltage rating of the breaker.* ▶Figure 240–54

Note: When installing circuit breakers on corner-grounded delta systems, consideration needs to be given to the circuit breakers' individual pole-interrupting capability.

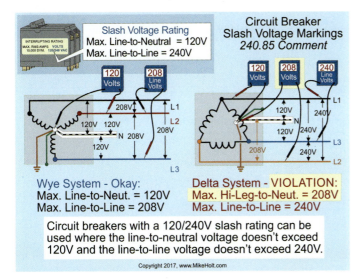

▶Figure 240–54

240.87 Arc Energy Reduction

Arc Energy Reduction. Where the highest continuous current trip setting for which the overcurrent protection device in a circuit breaker is rated or can be adjusted to 1,200A or higher, 240.87(A) and (B) apply.

(A) Documentation. Documentation must be available to those authorized to design, install, operate, or inspect the installation as to the location of the arc energy reduction circuit breaker(s).

(B) Method to Reduce Clearing Time. One of the following means must be used so as to reduce the overcurrent clearing times, resulting in reduced arc energy:

(1) Zone-selective interlocking

(2) Differential relaying

(3) Energy-reducing maintenance switching with local status indicator

(4) Energy-reducing active arc flash mitigation system

(5) An instantaneous trip setting that's less than the available arcing current

(6) An instantaneous override that's less than the available arcing current

(7) An approved equivalent means

Note 1: An energy-reducing maintenance switch [240.87(B)(3)] allows a worker to set a circuit breaker trip unit to "no intentional delay" to reduce the clearing time while the worker is working within an arc-flash boundary as defined in NFPA 70E, *Standard for Electrical Safety in the Workplace,* and then to set the trip unit back to a normal setting after the potentially hazardous work is complete.

Note 2: An energy-reducing active arc flash mitigation system [240.87(B)(4)] helps in reducing arcing duration in the electrical distribution system. No change in the circuit breaker or the settings of other devices is required during maintenance when a worker is working within an arc-flash boundary as defined in NFPA 70E, *Standard for Electrical Safety in the Workplace.*

Note 3: An instantaneous trip [240.87(B)(5)] is a function that causes a circuit breaker to trip with no intentional delay when currents exceed the instantaneous trip setting or current level. If arcing currents are above the instantaneous trip level, the circuit breaker will trip in the minimum possible time.

Note 4: IEEE 1584, *IEEE Guide for Performing Arc Flash Hazard Calculations,* is one of the available methods that provides guidance in determining arcing current.

Notes

ARTICLE 250 GROUNDING AND BONDING

Introduction to Article 250—Grounding and Bonding

No other article can match Article 250 for misapplication, violation, and misinterpretation. Terminology used in this article has been a source for much confusion, but that's improved during the last few *NEC* revisions. It's very important to understand the difference between grounding and bonding in order to correctly apply the provisions of Article 250. Pay careful attention to the definitions that apply to grounding and bonding both here and in Article 100 as you begin the study of this important article. Article 250 covers the grounding requirements for providing a path to the earth to reduce overvoltage from lightning, and the bonding requirements for a low-impedance fault current path back to the source of the electrical supply to facilitate the operation of overcurrent protection devices in the event of a ground fault.

Over the past several *Code* cycles, this article was extensively revised to organize it better and make it easier to understand and implement. It's arranged in a logical manner, so it's a good idea to just read through Article 250 to get a big picture view—after you review the definitions. Next, study the article closely so you understand the details. The illustrations will help you understand the key points.

Part I. General

250.1 Scope

Article 250 contains the following grounding and bonding requirements:

(1) What systems and equipment are required to be grounded.

(3) Location of grounding connections.

(4) Types of electrodes and sizes of grounding and bonding conductors.

(5) Methods of grounding and bonding.

250.2 Definition

Bonding Jumper, Supply-Side. The conductor on the supply side of the service or separately derived system overcurrent protection device that ensures electrical conductivity between metal parts and the grounded conductor. ▶Figure 250–1, ▶Figure 250–2, and ▶Figure 250–3

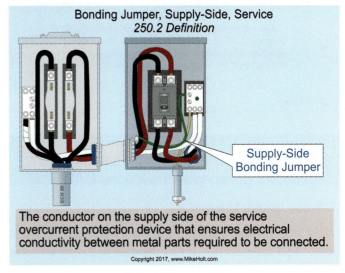

▶Figure 250–1

250.4 | Grounding and Bonding

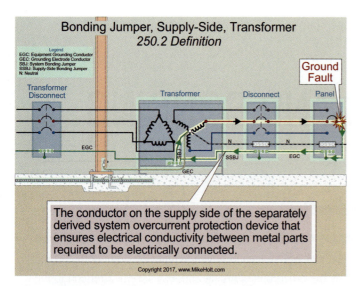
▶Figure 250–2

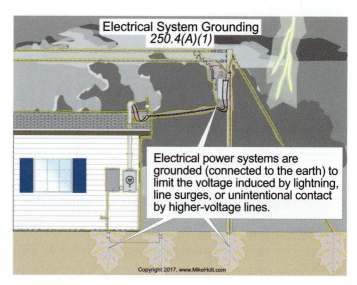
▶Figure 250–4

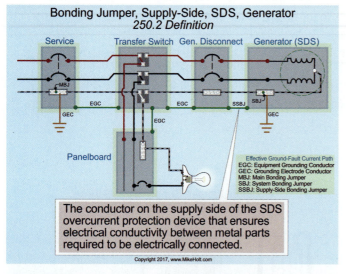
▶Figure 250–3

250.4 Performance Requirements for Grounding and Bonding

(A) Solidly Grounded Systems.

(1) Electrical System Grounding. Electrical power systems are grounded (connected to the earth) to limit the voltage induced by lightning, line surges, or unintentional contact by higher-voltage lines. ▶Figure 250–4

Author's Comment:

- System grounding helps reduce fires in buildings as well as voltage stress on electrical insulation, thereby ensuring longer insulation life for motors, transformers, and other system components. ▶Figure 250–5

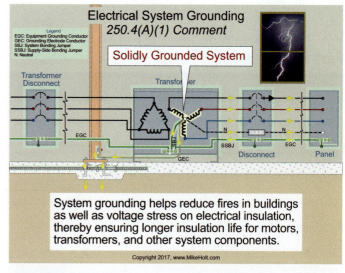
▶Figure 250–5

Note 1: To limit imposed voltage, the grounding electrode conductors shouldn't be any longer than necessary and unnecessary bends and loops should be avoided. ▶Figure 250–6

Grounding and Bonding | 250.4

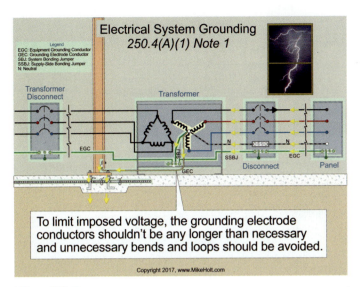
▶Figure 250–6

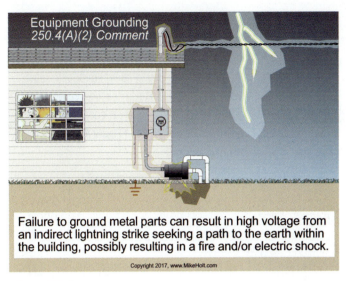
▶Figure 250–8

Note 2: See NFPA 780, *Standard for the Installation of Lightning Protection Systems* for grounding and bonding of lightning protection systems.

(2) Equipment Grounding. Metal parts of electrical equipment are grounded to reduce arcing within the buildings/structures from induced voltage from indirect lightning strikes. ▶Figure 250–7

Author's Comment:

- Grounding metal parts helps drain off static electricity charges before flashover potential is reached. Static grounding is often used in areas where the discharge (arcing) of the voltage buildup (static) can cause dangerous or undesirable conditions [500.4 Note 3].

(3) Equipment Bonding. Metal parts of electrical raceways, cables, enclosures, and equipment must be connected to the supply source via an effective ground-fault current path. ▶Figure 250–9

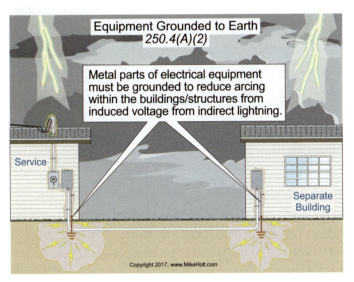
▶Figure 250–7

⚡ **DANGER:** Failure to ground metal parts to earth can result in induced voltage on metal parts from an indirect lightning strike seeking a path to the earth within the building—possibly resulting in a fire and/or electric shock from a side flash. ▶Figure 250–8

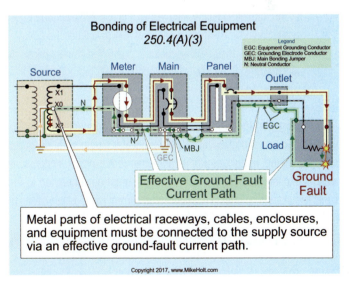
▶Figure 250–9

250.4 | Grounding and Bonding

Author's Comment:

- To quickly remove dangerous voltage on metal parts from a ground fault, the effective ground-fault current path must have sufficiently low impedance to the source so fault current will quickly rise to a level that will open the branch-circuit overcurrent protection device. ▶Figure 250–10

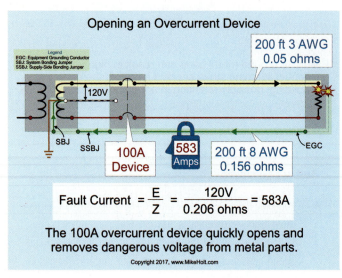

▶Figure 250–10

- The time it takes for an overcurrent protection device to open is dependent on the magnitude of the fault current. A higher fault current value will result in a shorter clearing time for the overcurrent protection device. For example, a 20A overcurrent protection device with an overload of 40A (two times the 20A rating) takes 25 to 150 seconds to open. The same device at 100A (five times the 20A rating) trips in 5 to 20 seconds. ▶Figure 250–11

(4) Bonding Conductive Materials. Electrically conductive materials likely to become energized, such as metal water piping systems, metal sprinkler piping, metal gas piping, and other metal-piping systems, as well as exposed structural steel members, must be connected to the supply source via an effective ground-fault current path. ▶Figure 250–12

Author's Comment:

- The phrase "likely to become energized" is subject to interpretation by the authority having jurisdiction.

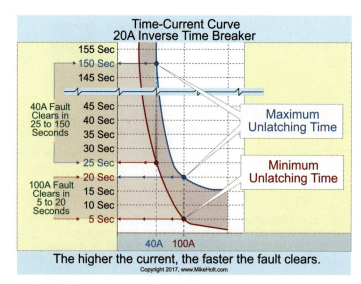

▶Figure 250–11

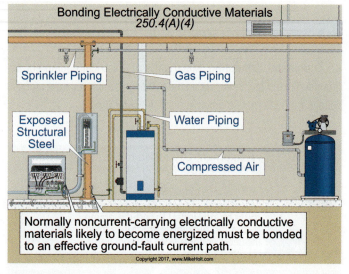

▶Figure 250–12

(5) Effective Ground-Fault Current Path. Metal parts of electrical raceways, cables, enclosures, or equipment must be bonded together and to the supply source in a manner that creates a low-impedance path for ground-fault current that facilitates the operation of the circuit overcurrent protection device. ▶Figure 250–13

Author's Comment:

- To ensure a low-impedance ground-fault current path, all circuit conductors must be grouped together in the same raceway, cable, or trench [300.3(B), 300.5(I), and 300.20(A)]. ▶Figure 250–14

Grounding and Bonding | 250.4

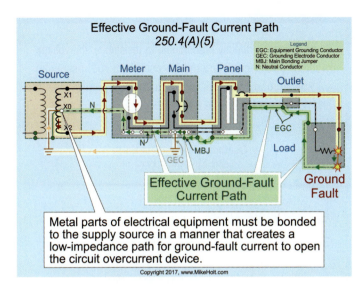

▶Figure 250–13

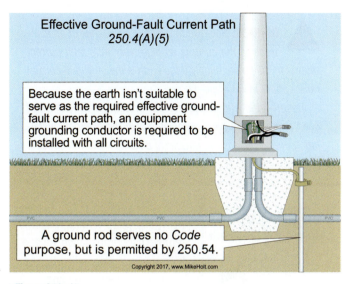

▶Figure 250–15

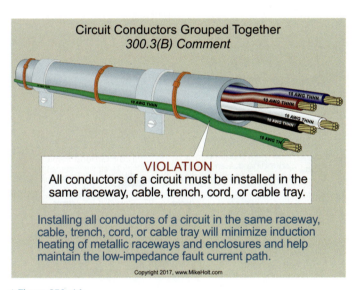

▶Figure 250–14

Because the earth isn't a low impedance path for fault current, it isn't suitable to serve as the required effective ground-fault current path, therefore an equipment grounding conductor of a type recognized in 250.118 is required to be installed with all circuits. ▶Figure 250–15

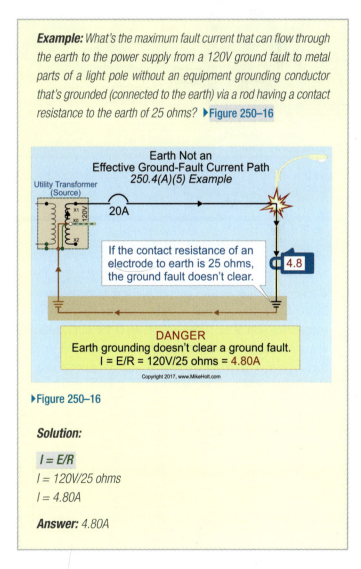

▶Figure 250–16

Solution:

$I = E/R$

$I = 120V/25 \text{ ohms}$

$I = 4.80A$

Answer: 4.80A

250.4 | Grounding and Bonding

DANGER: Because the contact resistance of an electrode to the earth is so high, very little fault current returns to the power supply if the earth is the only fault current return path. ▶Figure 250–17

Result—the circuit overcurrent protection device won't open and all metal parts associated with the electrical installation, metal piping, and structural building steel will become and remain energized.

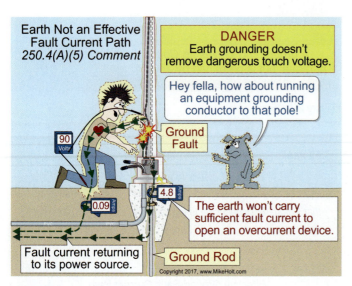

▶Figure 250–17

Earth Shells

According to ANSI/IEEE 142, *Recommended Practice for Grounding of Industrial and Commercial Power Systems* (Green Book) [4.1.1], the resistance of the soil outward from a rod is equal to the sum of the series resistances of the earth shells. The shell nearest the rod has the highest resistance and each successive shell has progressively larger areas and progressively lower resistances. Don't be concerned if you don't understand this statement; just review the table below.

Distance from Rod	Soil Contact Resistance
1 ft (Shell 1)	68% of total contact resistance
3 ft (Shells 1 and 2)	75% of total contact resistance
5 ft (Shells 1, 2, and 3)	86% of total contact resistance

Since voltage is directly proportional to resistance, the voltage gradient of the earth around an energized rod, assuming a 120V ground fault, will be as follows: ▶Figure 250–18 and ▶Figure 250–19

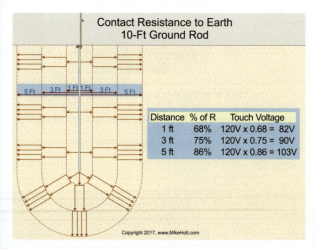

▶Figure 250–18

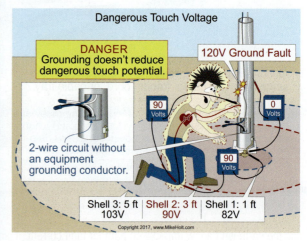

▶Figure 250–19

Distance from Rod	Soil Contact Resistance	Voltage Gradient
1 ft (Shell 1)	68%	82V
3 ft (Shells 1 and 2)	75%	90V
5 ft (Shells 1, 2, and 3)	86%	103V

(B) Ungrounded Systems.

> **Author's Comment:**
>
> - Ungrounded systems are those systems with no connection to the ground or to a conductive body that extends the ground connection [Article 100]. ▶Figure 250–20

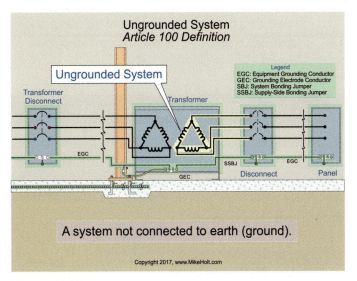

▶Figure 250–20

(1) Equipment Grounding. Metal parts of electrical equipment are grounded (connected to the earth) to reduce induced voltage on metal parts from lightning so as to prevent fires from an arc within the buildings. ▶Figure 250–21

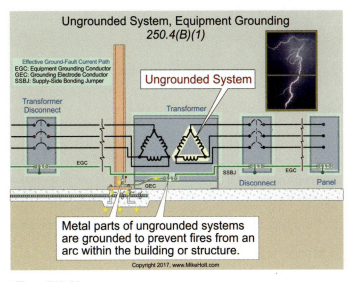

▶Figure 250–21

Note 2: See NFPA 780, *Standard for the Installation of Lightning Protection Systems* for grounding and bonding of lightning protection systems.

> **Author's Comment:**
>
> - Grounding metal parts helps drain off static electricity charges before an electric arc takes place (flashover potential). Static grounding is often used in areas where the discharge (arcing) of the voltage buildup (static) can cause dangerous or undesirable conditions [500.4 Note 3].

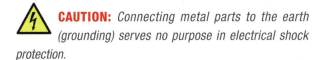

CAUTION: *Connecting metal parts to the earth (grounding) serves no purpose in electrical shock protection.*

(2) Equipment Bonding. Metal parts of electrical raceways, cables, enclosures, or equipment must be bonded together in a manner that creates a low-impedance path for ground-fault current to facilitate the operation of the circuit overcurrent protection device. ▶Figure 250–22

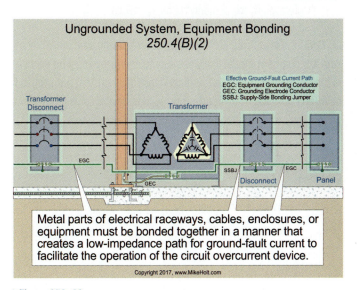

▶Figure 250–22

The fault current path must be capable of safely carrying the maximum ground-fault current likely to be imposed on it from any point on the wiring system should a ground fault occur to the electrical supply source.

(3) Bonding Conductive Materials. Conductive materials such as metal water piping systems, metal sprinkler piping, metal gas piping, and other metal-piping systems, as well as exposed structural steel members likely to become energized must be bonded together in a manner that creates a low-impedance fault current path that's capable of carrying the maximum fault current likely to be imposed on it. ▶Figure 250–23

250.6 | Grounding and Bonding

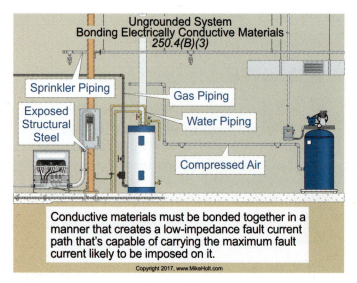

▶Figure 250–23

Author's Comment:

- The phrase "likely to become energized" is subject to interpretation by the authority having jurisdiction.

(4) Fault Current Path. Electrical equipment, wiring, and other electrically conductive material likely to become energized must be installed in a manner that creates a low-impedance fault current path to facilitate the operation of overcurrent protection devices should a second ground fault from a different phase occur. ▶Figure 250–24

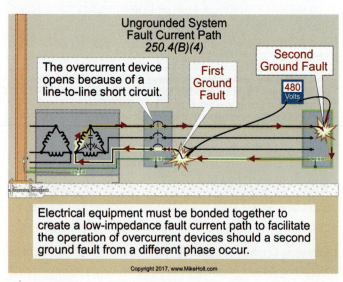

▶Figure 250–24

Author's Comment:

- A single ground fault can't be cleared on an ungrounded system because there's no low-impedance fault current path to the electric power source. The first ground fault simply grounds the system and initiates the ground detector. However, a second ground fault on a different phase results in a line-to-line short circuit between the two ground faults. The conductive path, between the ground faults, provides the low-impedance fault current path necessary so the overcurrent protection device will open.

250.6 Objectionable Current

(A) Preventing Objectionable Current. To prevent a fire, electric shock, or improper operation of circuit overcurrent protection devices or electronic equipment, electrical systems and equipment must be installed in a manner that prevents objectionable neutral current from flowing on metal parts. ▶Figure 250–25

▶Figure 250–25

(B) Stopping Objectionable Current. If the use of multiple grounding connections results in objectionable current and the requirements of 250.4(A)(5) or (B)(4) are met, <u>one or more of the following alterations are permitted</u>:

(1) Discontinue one or more but not all of such grounding connections.

(2) Change the locations of the grounding connections.

(3) Interrupt the continuity of the conductor or conductive path causing the objectionable current.

(4) Take other suitable remedial and approved action.

(C) Temporary Currents Not Classified as Objectionable Currents. Temporary currents from abnormal conditions, such as ground faults, aren't to be classified as objectionable current. ▶Figure 250–26

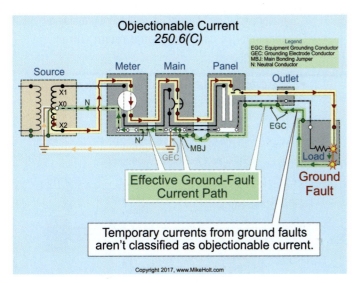

▶Figure 250–26

Objectionable Current

Objectionable neutral current occurs because of improper neutral-to-case connections or wiring errors that violate 250.142(B).

Improper Neutral-to-Case Connection [250.142]

Panelboards. Objectionable neutral current will flow on metal parts and the equipment grounding conductor when the neutral conductor is connected to the metal case of a panelboard on the load side of service equipment. ▶Figure 250–27

Separately Derived Systems. Objectionable neutral current will flow on metal parts if the neutral conductor is connected to the circuit equipment grounding conductor on the load side of the system bonding jumper for a separately derived system. ▶Figure 250–28

Generator. Objectionable neutral current will flow on metal parts and the equipment grounding conductor if a generator is connected to a transfer switch with a solidly connected neutral and a neutral-to-case connection is made at the generator. ▶Figure 250–29

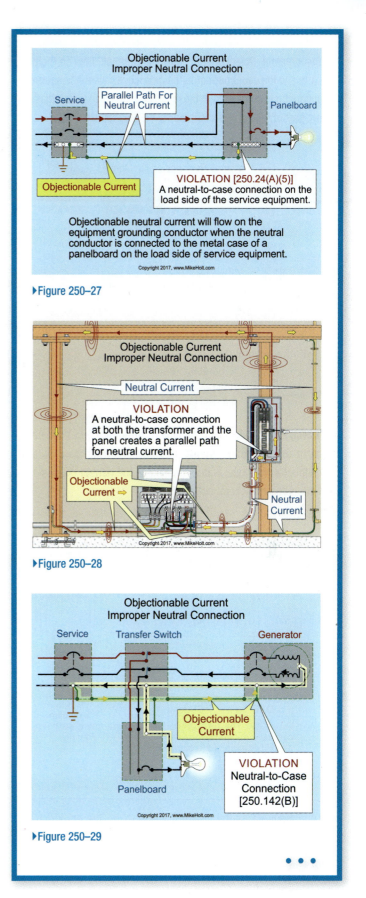

▶Figure 250–27

▶Figure 250–28

▶Figure 250–29

250.6 | Grounding and Bonding

Disconnects. Objectionable neutral current will flow on metal parts and the equipment grounding conductor when the neutral conductor is connected to the metal case of a disconnect that's not part of the service equipment. ▶Figure 250–30

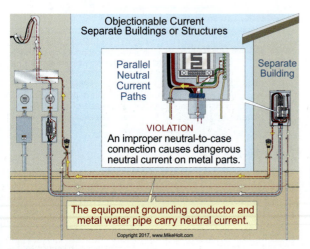

▶Figure 250–30

Wiring Errors. Objectionable neutral current will flow on metal parts and equipment grounding conductors when the neutral conductor from one system is used as the neutral conductor for a different system. ▶Figure 250–31

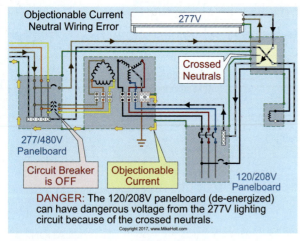

▶Figure 250–31

Objectionable neutral current will flow on the equipment grounding conductor when the circuit equipment grounding conductor is used as a neutral conductor such as where:

- A 230V time-clock motor is replaced with a 115V time-clock motor, and the circuit equipment grounding conductor is used for neutral return current.

- A 115V water filter is wired to a 240V well-pump motor circuit, and the circuit equipment grounding conductor is used for neutral return current. ▶Figure 250–32

- The circuit equipment grounding conductor is used for neutral return current. ▶Figure 250–33

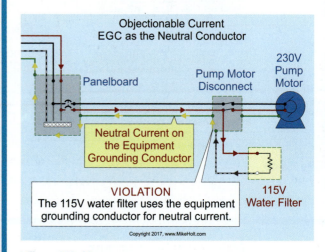

▶Figure 250–32

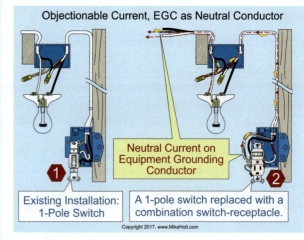

▶Figure 250–33

Grounding and Bonding | 250.6

Dangers of Objectionable Current

Objectionable neutral current on metal parts can cause electric shock, fires, and improper operation of electronic equipment and overcurrent protection devices such as GFPs, GFCIs, and AFCIs.

Shock Hazard. When objectionable neutral current flows on metal parts or the equipment grounding conductor, electric shock and even death can occur from the elevated voltage on those metal parts. ▶Figure 250–34 and ▶Figure 250–35

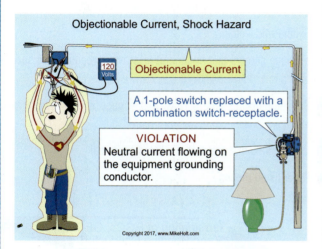

▶Figure 250–34

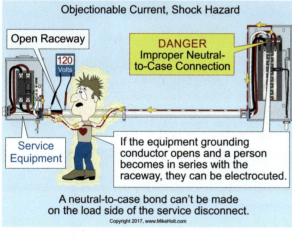

▶Figure 250–35

Fire Hazard. When objectionable neutral current flows on metal parts, a fire can ignite adjacent combustible material. Heat is generated whenever current flows, particularly over high-resistance parts. In addition, arcing at loose connections is especially dangerous in areas containing easily ignitible and explosive gases, vapors, or dust. ▶Figure 250–36

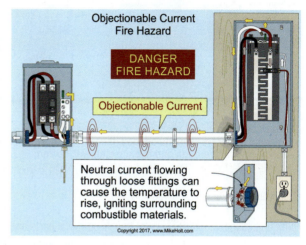

▶Figure 250–36

Improper Operation of Electronic Equipment. Objectionable neutral current flowing on metal parts of electrical equipment and building parts can cause electromagnetic fields which negatively affect the performance of electronic devices, particularly medical equipment. ▶Figure 250–37

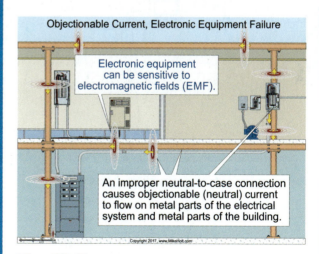

▶Figure 250–37

For more information, visit www.MikeHolt.com, click on the "Technical" link, and then on "Power Quality."

When a solidly grounded system is properly bonded, the voltage of all metal parts to the earth and to each other will be zero. ▶Figure 250–38

250.8 | Grounding and Bonding

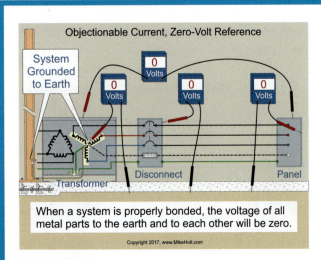

▶Figure 250–38

When objectionable neutral current travels on metal parts and equipment grounding conductors because of the improper bonding of the neutral to metal parts, a difference of voltage will exist between all metal parts. This situation can cause some electronic equipment to operate improperly. ▶Figure 250–39

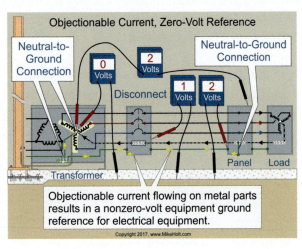

▶Figure 250–39

Operation of Overcurrent Protection Devices. When objectionable neutral current travels on metal parts, tripping of electronic overcurrent protection devices equipped with ground-fault protection can occur because some neutral current flows on the circuit equipment grounding conductor instead of the neutral conductor.

250.8 Termination of Grounding and Bonding Conductors

(A) Permitted Methods. Equipment grounding conductors, grounding electrode conductors, and bonding jumpers must terminate in one or more of the following methods:

(1) Listed pressure connectors

(2) Terminal bars

(3) Pressure connectors listed for grounding and bonding

(4) Exothermic welding

(5) Machine screws that engage at least two threads or are secured with a nut, ▶Figure 250–40

(6) Self-tapping machine screws that engage at least two threads ▶Figure 250–41

(7) Connections that are part of a listed assembly

(8) Other listed means

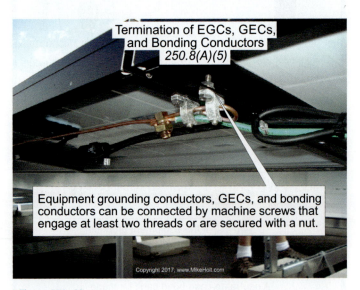

▶Figure 250–40

Grounding and Bonding | 250.20

▶Figure 250–41

(B) Methods Not Permitted. Connection devices or fittings that depend solely on solder aren't allowed.

250.10 Protection of Fittings

Where subject to physical damage, grounding and bonding fittings must be protected by enclosing the fittings in metal, wood, or an equivalent protective covering. ▶Figure 250–42

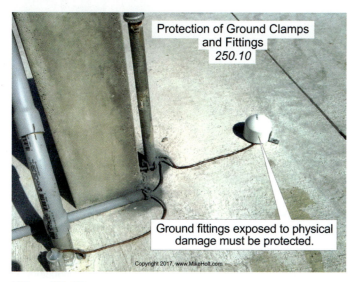

▶Figure 250–42

250.12 Clean Surfaces

Nonconductive coatings, such as paint, must be removed to ensure good electrical continuity, or the termination fittings must be designed so as to make such removal unnecessary [250.53(A) and 250.96(A)].

Author's Comment:

- Tarnish on copper water pipe needn't be removed before making a termination.

Part II. System Grounding and Bonding

250.20 Systems Required to be Grounded

(A) Systems Below 50V. Systems operating below 50V aren't required to be grounded or bonded in accordance with 250.30 unless the transformer's primary supply is from: ▶Figure 250–43

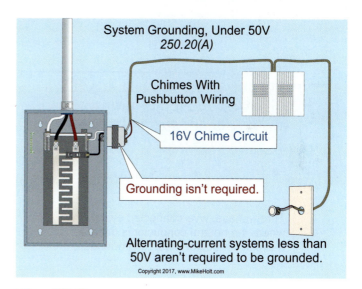

▶Figure 250–43

(1) A 277V or 480V system.

(2) An ungrounded system.

(B) Systems 50V to 1,000V. The following systems must be grounded (connected to the earth):

(1) Single-phase systems where the neutral conductor is used as a circuit conductor. ▶Figure 250–44

250.21 | Grounding and Bonding

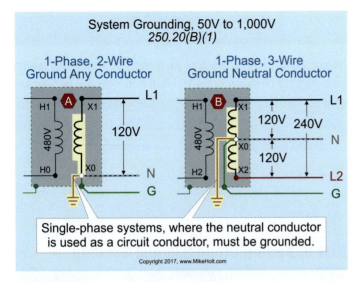

▶Figure 250–44

(2) Three-phase, wye-connected systems where the neutral conductor is used as a circuit conductor. ▶Figure 250–45

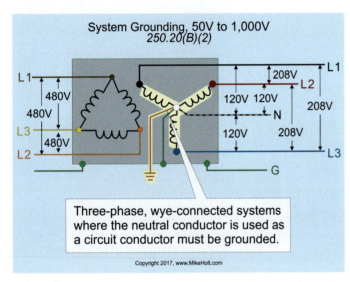

▶Figure 250–45

(3) Three-phase, high-leg delta-connected systems where the neutral conductor is used as a circuit conductor. ▶Figure 250–46

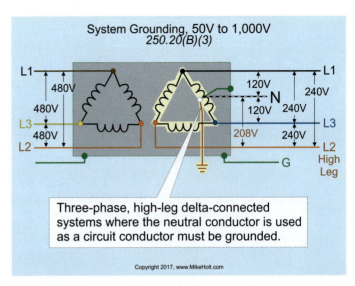

▶Figure 250–46

250.21 Ungrounded Systems

(B) Ground Detectors. Ungrounded systems must have ground detectors installed as close as practicable to where the system receives its supply. ▶Figure 250–47

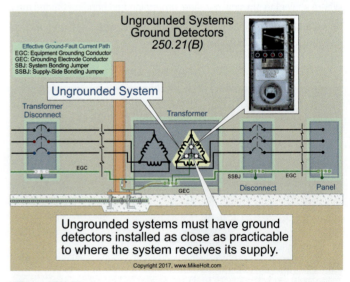

▶Figure 250–47

(C) Marking. Ungrounded systems must be legibly marked "Caution Ungrounded System Operating—_____ Volts Between Conductors" at the source or first disconnect of the system, with sufficient durability to withstand the environment involved. ▶Figure 250–48

Grounding and Bonding | 250.24

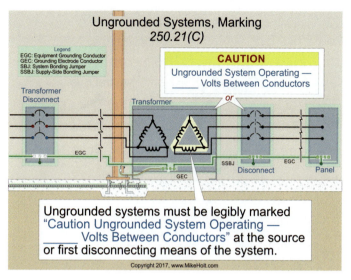

▶Figure 250–48

250.24 Service Equipment— Grounding and Bonding

(A) Grounded System. Service equipment supplied from a grounded system must have the grounding electrode conductor terminate in accordance with (1) through (5).

(1) Grounding Location. A grounding electrode conductor must connect the service neutral conductor to the grounding electrode at any accessible location, from the load end of the overhead service conductors, service drop, underground service conductors, or service lateral, up to and including the service disconnect. ▶Figure 250–49

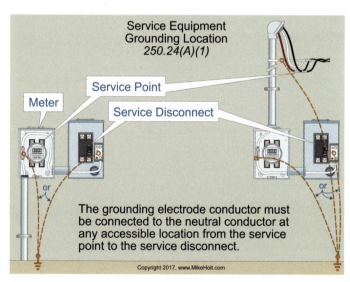

▶Figure 250–49

Author's Comment:

- Some inspectors require the service neutral conductor to be grounded (connected to the earth) from the meter socket enclosure, while other inspectors insist that it be grounded (connected to the earth) only from the service disconnect. Grounding at either location complies with this rule.

(4) Grounding Termination. When the service neutral conductor is connected to the service disconnect [250.24(B)] by a wire or busbar [250.28], the grounding electrode conductor can terminate to either the neutral terminal or the equipment grounding terminal within the service disconnect.

(5) Neutral-to-Case Connection. A neutral-to-case connection isn't permitted on the load side of service equipment, except as permitted by 250.142(B). ▶Figure 250–50

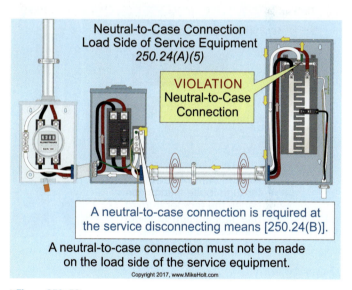

▶Figure 250–50

Author's Comment:

- If a neutral-to-case connection is made on the load side of service equipment, dangerous objectionable neutral current will flow on conductive metal parts of electrical equipment [250.6(A)]. Objectionable neutral current on metal parts of electrical equipment can cause electric shock and even death from ventricular fibrillation, as well as a fire. ▶Figure 250–51 and ▶Figure 250–52

250.24 | Grounding and Bonding

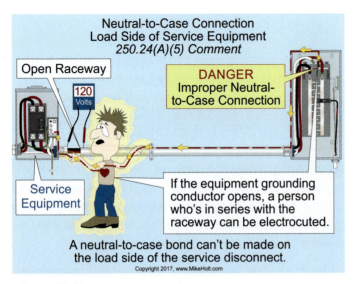

▶Figure 250–51

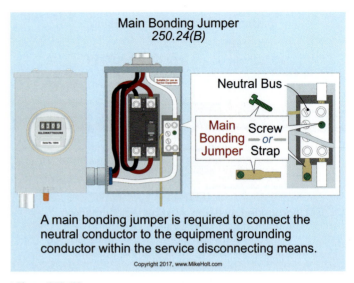

▶Figure 250–53

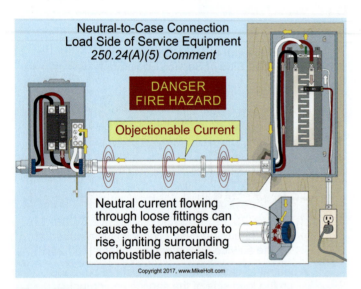

▶Figure 250–52

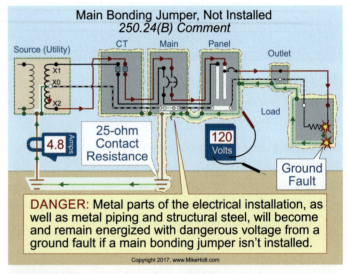

▶Figure 250–54

(B) Main Bonding Jumper. A main bonding jumper [250.28] is required to connect the neutral conductor to the equipment grounding conductor within the service disconnect. ▶Figure 250–53 and ▶Figure 250–54

(C) Neutral Conductor Brought to Service Equipment. A service neutral conductor must be run from the electric utility power supply with the ungrounded conductors and terminate to the service disconnect neutral terminal. A main bonding jumper [250.24(B)] must be installed between the service neutral terminal and the service disconnect enclosure [250.28]. ▶Figure 250–55 and ▶Figure 250–56

Author's Comment:

- The service neutral conductor provides the effective ground-fault current path to the power supply to ensure that dangerous voltage from a ground fault will be quickly removed by opening the overcurrent protection device [250.4(A)(3) and 250.4(A)(5)]. ▶Figure 250–57

Grounding and Bonding | 250.24

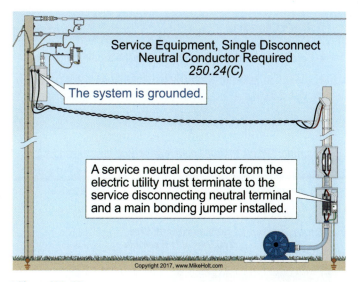
▶Figure 250–55

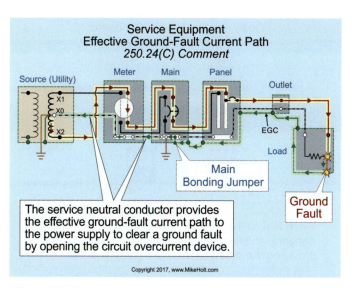
▶Figure 250–57

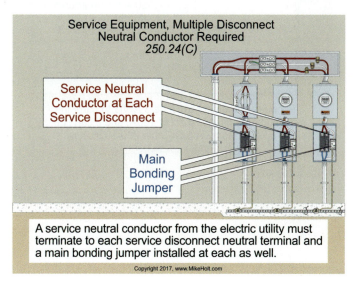
▶Figure 250–56

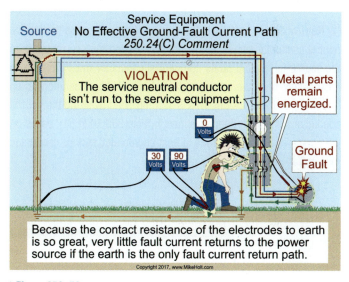
▶Figure 250–58

DANGER: *Dangerous voltage from a ground fault won't be removed from metal parts, metal piping, and structural steel if the service disconnect enclosure isn't connected to the service neutral conductor. This is because the contact resistance of a grounding electrode to the earth is so great that insufficient fault current returns to the power supply if the earth is the only fault current return path to open the circuit overcurrent protection device.* ▶Figure 250–58

Author's Comment:

- If the neutral conductor is opened, dangerous voltage will be present on metal parts under normal conditions, providing the potential for electric shock. If the earth's ground resistance is 25 ohms and the load's resistance is 25 ohms, the voltage drop across each of these resistors will be half of the voltage source. Since the neutral is connected to the service disconnect, all metal parts will be elevated to 60V above the earth's voltage for a 120/240V system. ▶Figure 250–59

250.24 | Grounding and Bonding

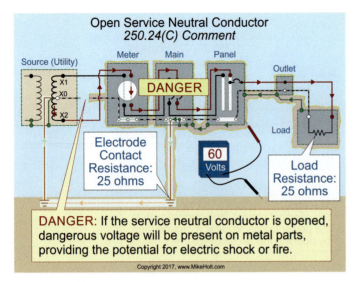

▶Figure 250–59

(1) Neutral Sizing for Single Raceway or Cable. Because the service neutral conductor serves as the effective ground-fault current path to the source for ground faults, the neutral conductor must be sized so it can safely carry the maximum fault current likely to be imposed on it [110.10 and 250.4(A)(5)]. This is accomplished by sizing the neutral conductor not smaller than specified in Table 250.102(C)(1), based on the cross-sectional area of the largest ungrounded service conductor.

▶Figure 250–60

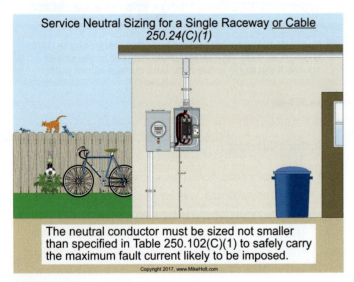

▶Figure 250–60

Author's Comment:

- In addition, the neutral conductors must have the capacity to carry the maximum unbalanced neutral current in accordance with 220.61.

Example: What's the minimum size service neutral conductor required where the ungrounded service conductors are 350 kcmil and the maximum unbalanced load is 100A? ▶Figure 250–61

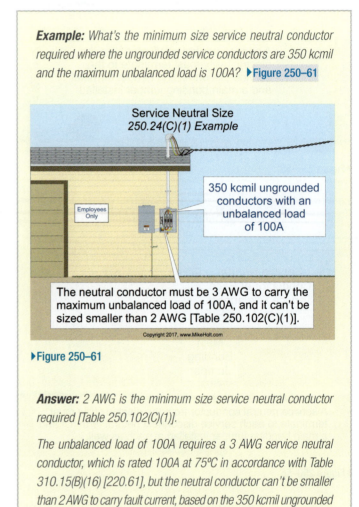

▶Figure 250–61

Answer: 2 AWG is the minimum size service neutral conductor required [Table 250.102(C)(1)].

The unbalanced load of 100A requires a 3 AWG service neutral conductor, which is rated 100A at 75°C in accordance with Table 310.15(B)(16) [220.61], but the neutral conductor can't be smaller than 2 AWG to carry fault current, based on the 350 kcmil ungrounded conductors in accordance with Table 250.102(C)(1).

(2) Neutral Sizing for Parallel Conductors in Two or More Raceways or Cables. If service conductors are paralleled in two or more raceways or cables, a neutral conductor must be installed in each of the parallel raceways or cables. The size of the neutral conductor in each raceway or cable isn't permitted to be smaller than specified in Table 250.102(C)(1), based on the cross-sectional area of the largest ungrounded service conductor in each raceway or cable. In no case can the neutral conductor in each parallel set be sized smaller than 1/0 AWG [310.10(H)(1)].

Grounding and Bonding | 250.28

Author's Comment:

- In addition, the neutral conductors must have the capacity to carry the maximum unbalanced neutral current in accordance with 220.61.

Example: What's the minimum size service neutral conductor required for each of two raceways, where the ungrounded service conductors in each of the raceways are 350 kcmil and the maximum unbalanced load is 100A? ▶Figure 250–62

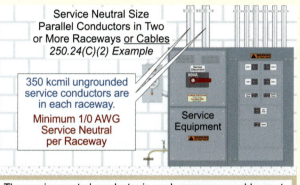

▶Figure 250–62

Answer: The minimum size service neutral conductor required is 1/0 AWG per raceway [Table 250.102(C)(1) and 310.10(H)].

The unbalanced load of 50A in each raceway requires an 8 AWG service neutral conductor, which is rated 50A at 75ºC in accordance with Table 310.15(B)(16) [220.61]. Also, Table 250.102(C)(1) requires a minimum of 2 AWG in each raceway, however, 1/0 AWG is the smallest conductor permitted to be paralleled [310.10(H) and Table 310.15(B)(16)].

(D) Grounding Electrode Conductor. A grounding electrode conductor, sized in accordance with 250.66 based on the area of the ungrounded service conductor, must connect the neutral conductor and metal parts of service equipment enclosures to a grounding electrode in accordance with Part III of Article 250.

Example: What's the minimum size grounding electrode conductor for a 400A service where the ungrounded service conductors are sized at 500 kcmil? ▶Figure 250–63

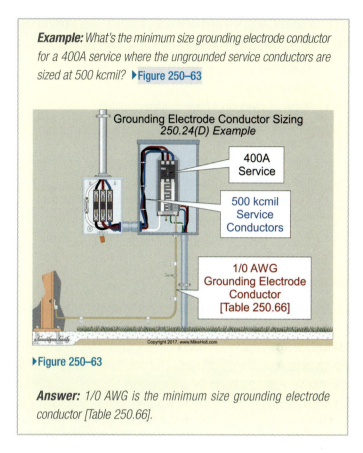

▶Figure 250–63

Answer: 1/0 AWG is the minimum size grounding electrode conductor [Table 250.66].

Author's Comment:

- If the grounding electrode conductor or bonding jumper connects to one or more ground rods [250.52(A)(5)] and doesn't connect to any another type of electrode, the grounding electrode conductor isn't required to be larger than 6 AWG copper.

- If the grounding electrode conductor or bonding jumper is connected to one or more concrete-encased electrodes [250.52(A)(3)] and doesn't connect to another type of electrode that requires a larger size conductor, the grounding electrode conductor isn't required to be larger than 4 AWG copper.

250.28 Main Bonding Jumper and System Bonding Jumper

Main and system bonding jumpers must be installed as follows:

(A) Material. The bonding jumper can be a wire, bus, or screw.

(B) Construction. If the bonding jumper is a screw, it must be identified with a green finish visible with the screw installed.

250.30 | Grounding and Bonding

(C) Attachment. Main and system bonding jumpers must terminate by any of the following means in accordance with 250.8(A):

- Listed pressure connectors
- Terminal bars
- Pressure connectors listed as grounding and bonding equipment
- Exothermic welding
- Machine screw-type fasteners that engage not less than two threads or are secured with a nut
- Thread-forming machine screws that engage not less than two threads in the enclosure
- Connections that are part of a listed assembly
- Other listed means

(D) Size.

(1) Main and system bonding jumpers must be sized not smaller than the sizes shown in Table 250.102(C)(1). ▶Figure 250–64

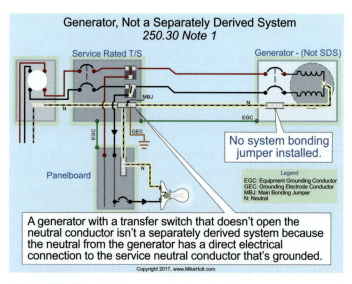

▶Figure 250–65

Author's Comment:

- According to Article 100, a separately derived system is a wiring system whose power is derived from a source, other than the electric utility, where there's no direct electrical connection to the supply conductors of another system, other than through grounding and bonding connections.

- Transformers are separately derived when the primary conductors have no direct electrical connection from circuit conductors of one system to circuit conductors of another system, other than connections through grounding and bonding connections. ▶Figure 250–66

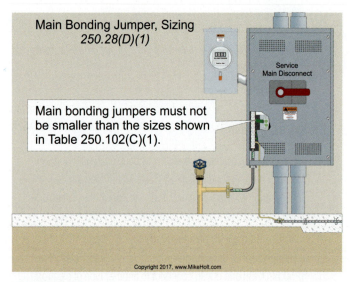

▶Figure 250–64

250.30 Separately Derived Systems—Grounding and Bonding

Note 1: An alternate alternating-current power source such as an on-site generator isn't a separately derived system if the neutral conductor is solidly interconnected to a service-supplied system neutral conductor. An example is a generator provided with a transfer switch that includes a neutral conductor that's not switched.

▶Figure 250–65

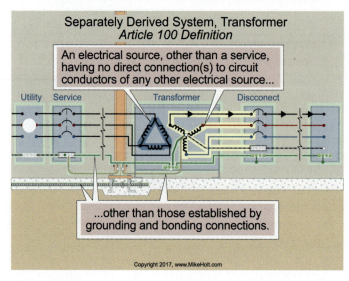

▶Figure 250–66

- A generator having transfer equipment that switches the neutral conductor, or one that has no neutral conductor at all, is a separately derived system and must be grounded and bonded in accordance with 250.30(A). ▶Figure 250–67

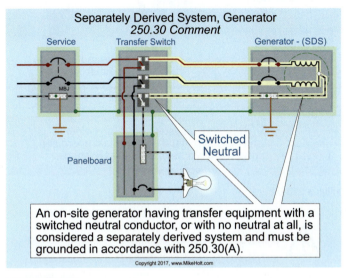

▶Figure 250–67

Note 2: For nonseparately derived systems, see 445.13 for the minimum size neutral conductors necessary to carry fault current. ▶Figure 250–68

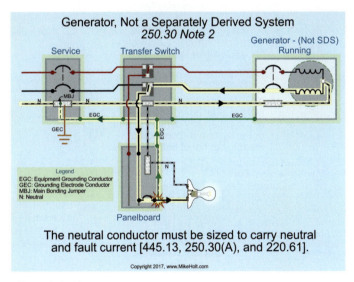

▶Figure 250–68

(A) Grounded Systems. Separately derived systems must be grounded and bonded in accordance with (A)(1) through (A)(8). A neutral-to-case connection isn't permitted to be made on the load side of the system bonding jumper, except as permitted by 250.142(B).

(1) System Bonding Jumper. A system bonding jumper must be installed at the same location where the grounding electrode conductor terminates to the neutral terminal of the separately derived system; either at the separately derived system or the system disconnect, but not at both locations [250.30(A)(5)]. ▶Figure 250–69

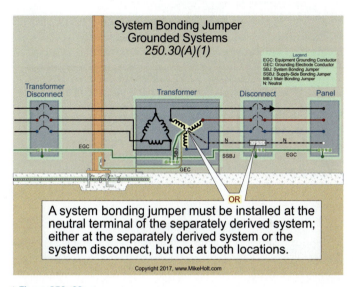

▶Figure 250–69

If the separately derived source is located outside the building or structure supplied, a system bonding jumper must be installed at the grounding electrode connection in accordance with 250.30(C).

Ex. 2: If a building or structure is supplied by a feeder from an outdoor separately derived system, a system bonding jumper at both the source and the first disconnect is permitted. The grounded conductor isn't permitted to be smaller than the size specified for the system bonding jumper, but it's not required to be larger than the ungrounded conductor(s).

(a) System Bonding Jumper at Source. Where the system bonding jumper is installed at the source of the separately derived system, the system bonding jumper must connect the neutral conductor of the derived system to the metal enclosure of the derived system. ▶Figure 250–70

(b) System Bonding Jumper at Disconnect. Where the system bonding jumper is installed at the first disconnect of a separately derived system, the system bonding jumper must connect the neutral conductor of the derived system to the metal disconnect enclosure. ▶Figure 250–71

250.30 | Grounding and Bonding

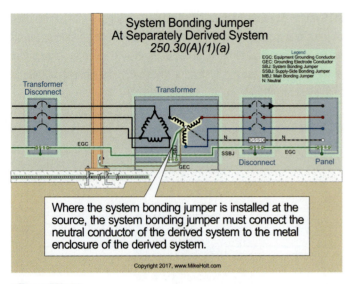

▶Figure 250–70

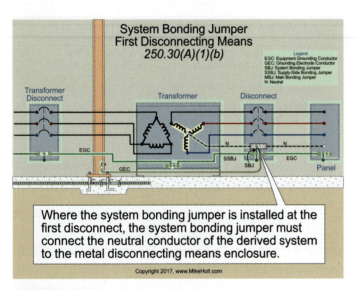

▶Figure 250–71

Author's Comment:

- A system bonding jumper is a conductor, screw, or strap that bonds the metal parts of a separately derived system to the system neutral point [Article 100 Bonding Jumper, System], and it's sized to Table 250.102(C)(1) in accordance with 250.28(D).

DANGER: During a ground fault, metal parts of electrical equipment, as well as metal piping and structural steel, will become and remain energized providing the potential for electric shock and fire if the system bonding jumper isn't installed. ▶Figure 250–72

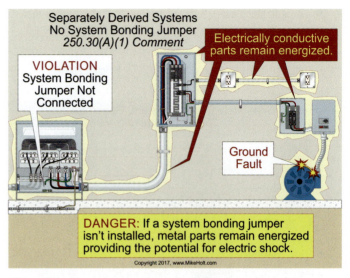

▶Figure 250–72

CAUTION: Dangerous objectionable neutral current will flow on conductive metal parts of electrical equipment as well as metal piping and structural steel, in violation of 250.6(A), if more than one system bonding jumper is installed, or if it's not located where the grounding electrode conductor terminates to the neutral conductor. ▶Figure 250–73

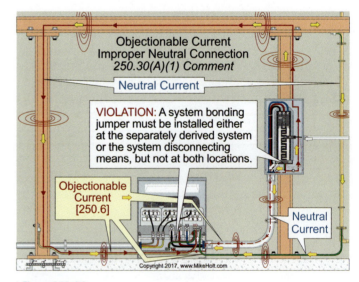

▶Figure 250–73

(2) Supply-Side Bonding Jumper to Disconnect. A supply-side bonding jumper (nonflexible metal raceway or wire) must be run from the derived system to the derived system disconnect.

(a) If the supply-side bonding jumper is of the wire type, it must be sized in accordance with Table 250.102(C)(1), based on the area of the largest ungrounded derived system conductor in the raceway or cable.

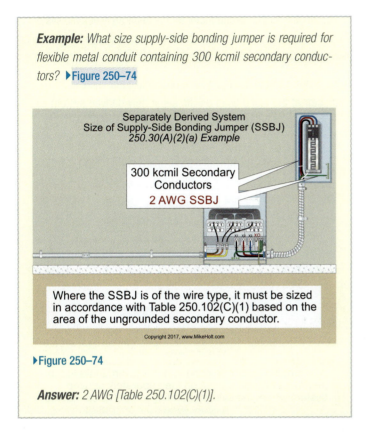

Example: What size supply-side bonding jumper is required for flexible metal conduit containing 300 kcmil secondary conductors? ▶Figure 250–74

▶Figure 250–74

Answer: 2 AWG [Table 250.102(C)(1)].

(3) Neutral Conductor Size, System Bonding Jumper at Derived System Disconnect. If the system bonding jumper is installed at the disconnect instead of at the source, the following requirements apply:

(a) Sizing for Single Raceway. The neutral conductor must be routed with the ungrounded conductors of the derived system to the disconnect and be sized not smaller than specified in Table 250.102(C)(1), based on the area of the ungrounded conductor of the derived system. ▶Figure 250–75

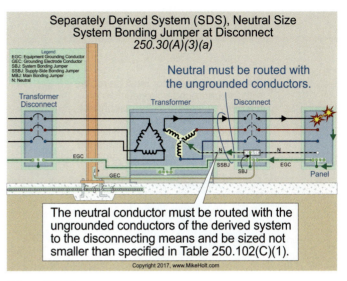

▶Figure 250–75

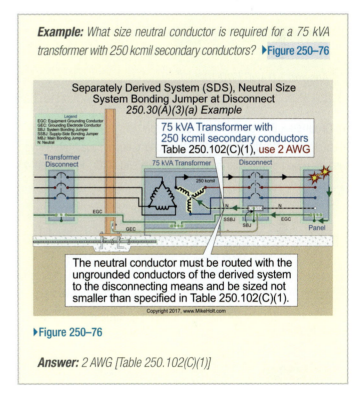

Example: What size neutral conductor is required for a 75 kVA transformer with 250 kcmil secondary conductors? ▶Figure 250–76

▶Figure 250–76

Answer: 2 AWG [Table 250.102(C)(1)]

(b) Parallel Conductors in Two or More Raceways. If the conductors from the derived system are installed in parallel in two or more raceways, the neutral conductor of the derived system in each raceway or cable must be sized not smaller than specified in Table 250.102(C)(1), based on the area of the largest ungrounded conductor of the derived system in the raceway or cable. In no case is the neutral conductor of the derived system permitted to be smaller than 1/0 AWG [310.10(H)]. ▶Figure 250–77

250.30 | Grounding and Bonding

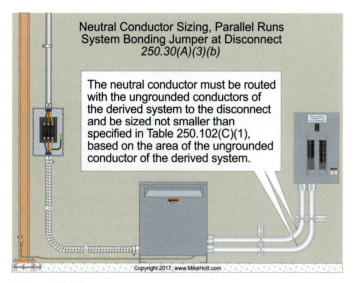

▶Figure 250–77

Example: What size neutral conductor is required for a 112.50 kVA transformer with two sets of 3/0 AWG secondary conductors?

Answer: 1/0 AWG [310.10(H)(1)]

(4) Grounding Electrode. Indoor separately derived systems must use the building or structure grounding electrode; outdoor separately derived systems must be grounded in accordance with 250.30(C). ▶Figure 250–78

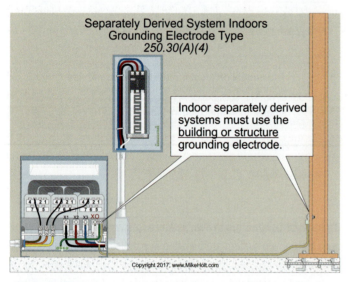

▶Figure 250–78

Note 1: Interior metal water piping in the area served by separately derived systems must be bonded to the separately derived system in accordance with 250.104(D).

Note 2: See 250.50 and 250.58 for requirements for bonding all electrodes together if located at the same building or structure.

(5) Grounding Electrode Conductor, Single Separately Derived System. The grounding electrode conductor for the separately derived system is sized in accordance with 250.66 and it must terminate to the grounding electrode in accordance with 250.30(A)(4).

The grounding electrode conductor is required to terminate to the neutral conductor at the same point on the separately derived system where the system bonding jumper is connected. ▶Figure 250–79

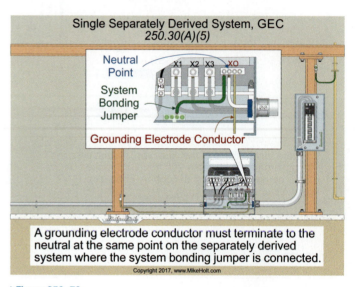

▶Figure 250–79

Author's Comment:

- System grounding helps reduce fires in buildings as well as voltage stress on electrical insulation, thereby ensuring longer insulation life for motors, transformers, and other system components. ▶Figure 250–80

- To prevent objectionable neutral current from flowing [250.6] onto metal parts, the grounding electrode conductor must originate at the same point on the separately derived system where the system bonding jumper is connected [250.30(A)(1)].

Ex 1: If the system bonding jumper [250.30(A)(1)] is a wire or busbar, the grounding electrode conductor is permitted to terminate to the equipment grounding terminal, bar, or bus. ▶Figure 250–81

Ex 3: Separately derived systems rated 1 kVA or less aren't required to be grounded (connected to the earth).

Grounding and Bonding | 250.30

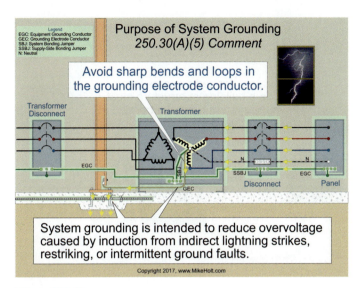

▶Figure 250–80

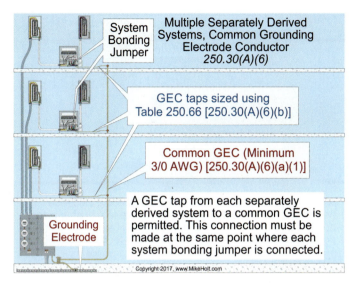

▶Figure 250–82

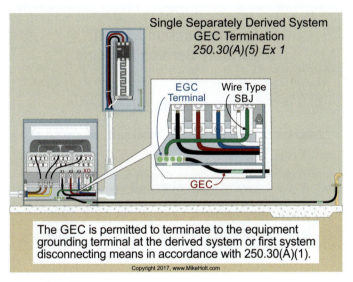

▶Figure 250–81

(6) Grounding Electrode Conductor, Multiple Separately Derived Systems. Where there are multiple separately derived systems, a grounding electrode conductor tap from each separately derived system to a common grounding electrode conductor is permitted. This connection is to be made at the same point on the separately derived system where the system bonding jumper is connected [250.30(A)(1)]. ▶Figure 250–82

Ex 1: If the system bonding jumper is a wire or busbar, the grounding electrode conductor tap can terminate to either the neutral terminal or the equipment grounding terminal, bar, or bus in accordance with 250.30(A)(1).

Ex 2: Separately derived systems rated 1 kVA or less aren't required to be grounded (connected to the earth).

(a) Common Grounding Electrode Conductor. The common grounding electrode conductor can be any of the following:

(1) A conductor not smaller than 3/0 AWG copper or 250 kcmil aluminum.

(2) Interior metal water pipe located not more than 5 ft from the point of entrance to the building [250.68(C)(1)].

(3) The metal frame of the building or structure that complies with 250.68(C)(2) or is connected to the grounding electrode system by a conductor not smaller than 3/0 AWG copper or 250 kcmil aluminum.

(b) Tap Conductor Size. Grounding electrode conductor taps must be sized in accordance with Table 250.66, based on the area of the largest ungrounded conductor of the given derived system.

(c) Connections. Tap connections to the common grounding electrode conductor must be made at an accessible location by any of the following methods:

(1) A connector listed as grounding and bonding equipment.

(2) Listed connections to aluminum or copper busbars not less than ¼ in. thick × 2 in. wide, and of sufficient length to accommodate the terminations necessary for the installation. ▶Figure 250–83

(3) Exothermic welding.

Grounding electrode conductor taps must be connected to the common grounding electrode conductor so the common grounding electrode conductor isn't spliced.

250.30 | Grounding and Bonding

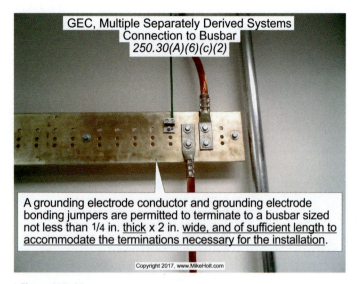

▶Figure 250–83

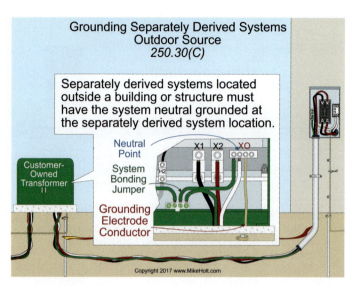

▶Figure 250–84

(7) Installation. The grounding electrode conductor must comply with the following:

- Be of copper where within 18 in. of the surface of the earth [250.64(A)].
- Be securely fastened to the surface on which it's carried [250.64(B)].
- Be adequately protected if exposed to physical damage [250.64(B)].
- Metal enclosures enclosing a grounding electrode conductor must be made electrically continuous from the point of attachment to cabinets or equipment to the grounding electrode [250.64(E)].

(8) Structural Steel and Metal Piping. To ensure dangerous voltage on metal parts from a ground fault is removed quickly, structural steel and metal piping in the area served by a separately derived system must be connected to the neutral conductor at the separately derived system in accordance with 250.104(D).

(C) Outdoor Source. Separately derived systems located outside the building must have the grounding electrode connection made at the separately derived system location. ▶Figure 250–84

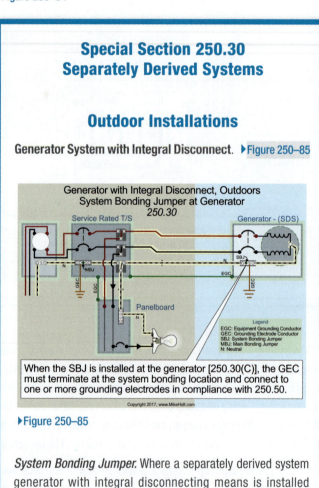

▶Figure 250–85

System Bonding Jumper. Where a separately derived system generator with integral disconnecting means is installed outdoors, a system bonding jumper sized in accordance with Table 250.102(C)(1), is required to be installed at the generator neutral terminal [250.30(A)(1)(a)].

Grounding Electrode Conductor. A grounding electrode conductor, sized in accordance with 250.66, must be run from the generator neutral terminal to one or more grounding electrodes in compliance with 250.50 in accordance with 250.30(C) [250.30(A)(4)].

Where the system bonding jumper is a wire or busbar, the grounding electrode conductor can originate at the generator equipment grounding terminal, bar, or bus [250.30(A)(5) Ex].

Transformer Outdoors. ▶Figure 250–86

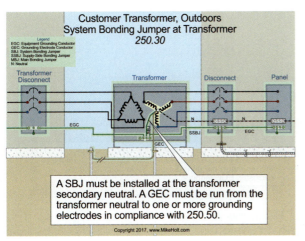

▶Figure 250–86

System Bonding Jumper. Where a separately derived system transformer is installed outdoors, a system bonding jumper sized in accordance with Table 250.102(C)(1), is required to be installed at the transformer secondary neutral [250.30(A)(1)].

Grounding Electrode Conductor. A grounding electrode conductor, sized in accordance with 250.66, must be run from the transformer neutral terminal to one or more grounding electrodes in compliance with 250.50 in accordance with 250.30(C) [250.30(A)(4)].

Where the system bonding jumper is a wire or busbar, the grounding electrode conductor can originate at the generator equipment grounding terminal, bar, or bus [250.30(A)(5) Ex].

Supply-Side Bonding Jumper. A supply-side bonding jumper must be run from the transformer equipment grounding conductor terminal to the secondary disconnect enclosure equipment grounding conductor terminal.

Where the supply-side bonding jumper is of the wire type, it must be sized in accordance with Table 250.102(C)(1), based on the area of the secondary conductor [250.30(A)(2)].

Example: What size system bonding jumper is required to be installed at a 75 kVA transformer having 250 kcmil secondary conductors? ▶Figure 250–87

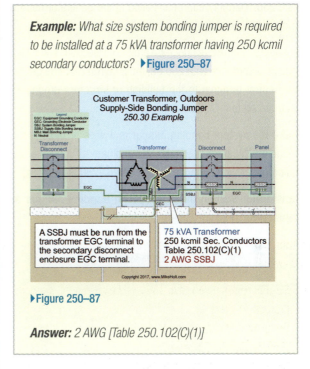

▶Figure 250–87

Answer: 2 AWG [Table 250.102(C)(1)]

Indoor Installations

Generator System Indoor with Integral Disconnect.
▶Figure 250–88

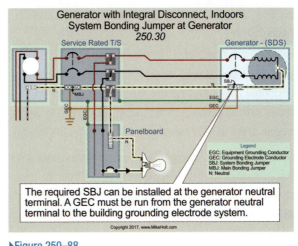

▶Figure 250–88

250.30 | Grounding and Bonding

System Bonding Jumper. Where a separately derived system generator with an integral disconnect is installed indoors, the required system bonding jumper, sized in accordance with Table 250.102(C)(1), can be installed at the generator neutral terminal [250.30(A)(1)(a)].

Grounding Electrode Conductor. A grounding electrode conductor, sized in accordance with 250.66, must be run from the generator neutral terminal to the building or structure grounding electrode system [250.30(A)(4)].

Where the system bonding jumper is a wire or busbar, the grounding electrode conductor can originate at the generator equipment grounding terminal, bar, or bus [250.30(A)(5) Ex].

Transformer System Indoors, System Bonding Jumper at Transformer. ▶Figure 250–89

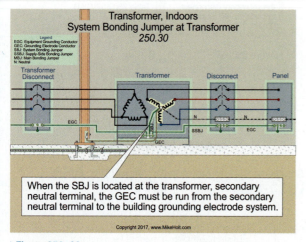

▶Figure 250–89

System Bonding Jumper. Where a separately derived system transformer is installed indoors, the required system bonding jumper, sized in accordance with Table 250.102(C)(1), can be installed at the transformer neutral terminal [250.30(A)(1)(a)].

Grounding Electrode Conductor. A grounding electrode conductor, sized in accordance with 250.66, must be run from the transformer neutral terminal to the building or structure grounding electrode system [250.30(A)(4)].

Where the system bonding jumper is a wire or busbar, the grounding electrode conductor can originate at the generator equipment grounding terminal, bar, or bus [250.30(A)(5) Ex].

Supply-Side Bonding Jumper. A supply-side bonding jumper, sized in accordance with Table 250.102(C)(1), must be run from the transformer equipment grounding conductor terminal to the secondary disconnect enclosure equipment grounding conductor terminal [250.30(A)(2)].

Example: What size SSBJ is required between a 75 kVA transformer with 250 kcmil secondary conductors in a single raceway to the first disconnect? ▶Figure 250–90

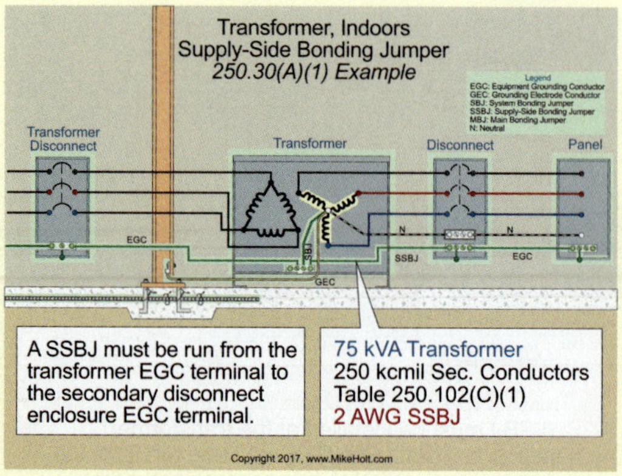

▶Figure 250–90

Answer: 2 AWG, based on 250 kcmil conductor [Table 250.102(C)(1)]

Transformer Indoors, System Bonding Jumper at Secondary Disconnect. ▶Figure 250–91

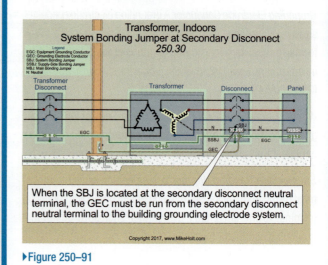

▶Figure 250–91

System Bonding Jumper. Where a separately derived system transformer is installed indoors, the required system bonding jumper, sized in accordance with Table 250.102(C)(1), can be installed at the transformer secondary disconnect [250.30(A)(1)(b)].

Grounding Electrode Conductor. A grounding electrode conductor, sized in accordance with 250.66, must be run from the transformer neutral terminal to the building or structure grounding electrode system [250.30(A)(4)].

Where the system bonding jumper is a wire or busbar, the grounding electrode conductor can originate at the generator equipment grounding terminal, bar, or bus [250.30(A)(5) Ex].

Supply-Side Bonding Jumper. A supply-side bonding jumper, sized in accordance with Table 250.102(C)(1), must be run from the transformer equipment grounding conductor terminal to the secondary disconnect enclosure equipment grounding conductor terminal [250.30(A)(2)].

> **Example:** What size SSBJ is required between a 112.6 kVA transformer paralleled in two raceways with 250 kcmil secondary conductors to the first disconnect?
>
> **Answer:** 1/0 AWG [Table 250.102(C)(1)]. The area of 3/0 AWG is 167,800 circular mills × 2 conductors equals 335,600 circular mills [Chapter 9, Table 8 and Table 250.102(C)(1)].

Neutral Conductor. When the system bonding jumper is installed at a secondary disconnect, a secondary neutral conductor in each raceway, sized no smaller than specified in Table 250.102(C)(1), must be run from the transformer secondary to the secondary disconnect enclosure.

> **Example:** What size neutral conductor is required for a 112.50 kVA transformer paralleled in two raceways with 3/0 AWG secondary conductors in each raceway?
>
> **Answer:** 1/0 AWG [310.10(H)(1)]

> **Author's Comment:**
> - When the system bonding jumper is installed at the secondary disconnect, the secondary neutral conductor will serve as part of the effective ground-fault current path.

250.32 Buildings Supplied by a Feeder

(A) Equipment Grounding Electrode. Building feeder disconnects must be connected to a grounding electrode system for the purpose of reducing induced voltages on the metal parts from nearby lightning strikes [250.4(A)(1)]. ▶Figure 250–92

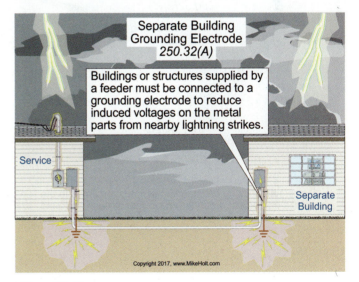

▶Figure 250–92

Ex: A grounding electrode isn't required for a building disconnect supplied by a branch circuit. ▶Figure 250–93

(B) Equipment Grounding Conductor.

(1) Building Supplied by a Feeder. To quickly clear a ground fault and remove dangerous voltage from metal parts, the building disconnect must be connected to the circuit equipment grounding conductor, of the type(s) described in 250.118. ▶Figure 250–94

250.32 | Grounding and Bonding

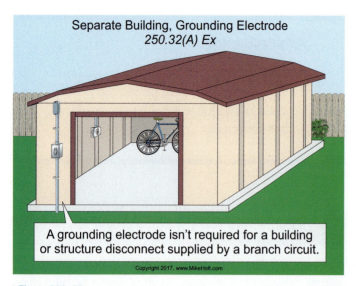
▶Figure 250–93

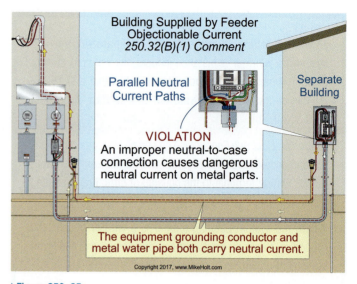
▶Figure 250–95

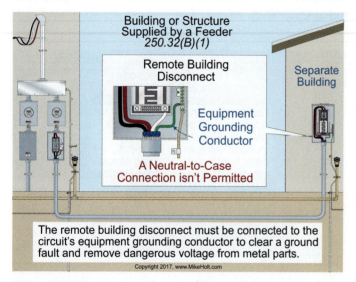
▶Figure 250–94

Where the supply circuit equipment grounding conductor is of the wire type, it must be sized in accordance with 250.122, based on the rating of the overcurrent protection device.

⚡ **CAUTION:** To prevent dangerous objectionable neutral current from flowing on metal parts [250.6(A)], the supply circuit neutral conductor isn't permitted to be connected to the remote building disconnect [250.142(B)]. ▶Figure 250–95

Ex 1: The neutral conductor can serve as the ground-fault return path for the building disconnect for existing installations where there are no continuous metallic paths between buildings and structures, ground-fault protection of equipment isn't installed on the supply side of the circuit, and the neutral conductor is sized no smaller than the larger of:

(1) The maximum unbalanced neutral load in accordance with 220.61.

(2) The minimum equipment grounding conductor size in accordance with 250.122.

(E) Grounding Electrode Conductor Size. The grounding electrode conductor must terminate to the equipment grounding terminal of the disconnect (not the neutral terminal), and it must be sized in accordance with 250.66, based on the conductor area of the ungrounded feeder conductor.

Example: What size grounding electrode conductor is required for a building disconnect supplied with a 3/0 AWG feeder? ▶Figure 250–96

Answer: A 4 AWG grounding electrode conductor is required [Table 250.66].

Grounding and Bonding | 250.35

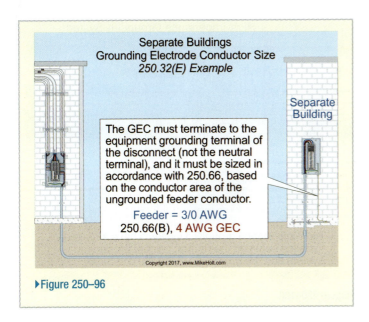
▶Figure 250–96

▶Figure 250–97

Author's Comment:

- If the grounding electrode conductor is connected to a rod(s), the portion of the conductor that connects only to the rod(s) isn't required to be larger than 6 AWG copper [250.66(A)]. If the grounding electrode conductor is connected to a concrete-encased electrode(s), the portion of the conductor that connects only to the concrete-encased electrode(s) isn't required to be larger than 4 AWG copper [250.66(B)].

250.34 Generators—Portable and Vehicle-Mounted

(A) Portable Generators. A portable generator isn't required to be grounded (connected to the earth) if all of the following apply:

(1) The generator only supplies equipment or receptacles mounted on the generator ▶Figure 250–97

(2) The metal parts of the generator and the receptacle grounding terminal are connected to the generator frame.

(B) Vehicle-Mounted Generators. A vehicle-mounted generator isn't required to be grounded (connected to the earth) if all of the following apply:

(1) The generator frame is bonded to the vehicle frame

(2) The generator only supplies equipment or receptacles mounted on the vehicle or generator ▶Figure 250–98

▶Figure 250–98

(3) The metal parts of the generator and the receptacle grounding terminal are connected to the generator frame.

250.35 Permanently Installed Generators

(A) Separately Derived System Generators. If the generator is installed as a separately derived system, the system must be grounded and bonded in accordance with the requirements contained in 250.30.

250.36 High-Impedance Grounded Systems

High-impedance grounded systems are only permitted for three-phase systems up to 1000V, where all of the following conditions are met:
▶Figure 250–99

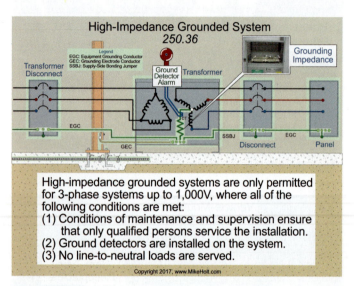
▶Figure 250–99

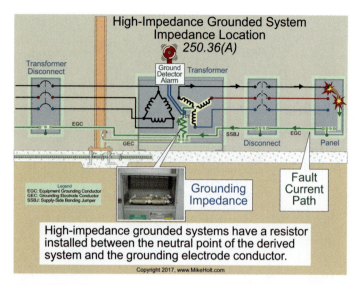
▶Figure 250–100

(1) Conditions of maintenance and supervision ensure that only qualified persons service the installation.

(2) Ground detectors are installed on the system [250.21(B)].

(3) Line-to-neutral loads aren't served.

> **Author's Comment:**
> ■ High-impedance grounded systems are generally referred to as "high-resistance grounded systems" in the industry.

(A) Grounding Impedance Location. To limit fault current to a very low value, high-impedance grounded systems must have a resistor installed between the neutral point of the derived system and the grounding electrode conductor. ▶Figure 250–100

Note: For more information on this topic see IEEE 142—Recommended Practice for Grounding of Industrial and Commercial Power Systems (Green Book).

Part III. Grounding Electrode System and Grounding Electrode Conductor

250.50 Grounding Electrode System

Any grounding electrodes described in 250.52(A)(1) through (A)(7) that are present at a building must be bonded together to form the grounding electrode system. ▶Figure 250–101

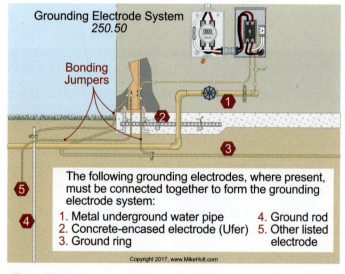
▶Figure 250–101

Ex: Concrete-encased electrodes aren't required for existing buildings where the conductive steel reinforcing bars aren't accessible without chipping up the concrete. ▶Figure 250–102

Grounding and Bonding | 250.52

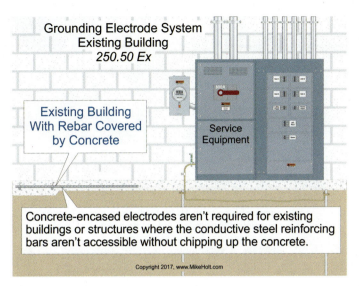

▶Figure 250–102

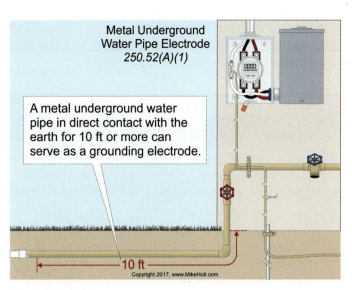

▶Figure 250–104

Author's Comment:

- When a concrete-encased electrode is used at a building that doesn't have an underground metal water pipe electrode, no additional electrode is required. ▶Figure 250–103

Author's Comment:

- Controversy about using metal underground water piping as a grounding electrode has existed since the early 1900s. The water industry believes that neutral current flowing on water piping corrodes the metal. For more information, contact the American Water Works Association about their report—*Effects of Electrical Grounding on Pipe Integrity and Shock Hazard*, Catalog No. 90702, 1.800.926.7337. ▶Figure 250–105

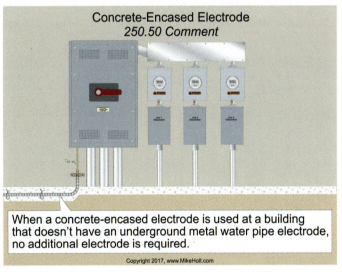

▶Figure 250–103

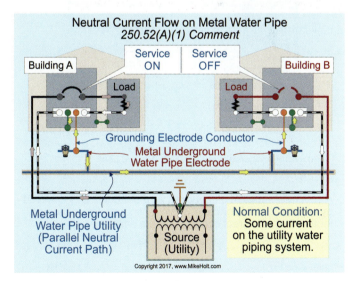

▶Figure 250–105

250.52 Grounding Electrode Types

(A) Electrodes Permitted for Grounding.

(1) Underground Metal Water Pipe Electrode. Underground metal water pipe in direct contact with the earth for 10 ft or more can serve as a grounding electrode. ▶Figure 250–104

250.52 | Grounding and Bonding

(2) Metal In-Ground Support Structure(s). Metal in-ground support structure(s) in direct contact with the earth vertically for 10 ft or more can serve as a grounding electrode. ▶Figure 250–106

▶Figure 250–106

Note: Metal in-ground support structures include, but aren't limited to, pilings, casings, and other structural metal.

(3) Concrete-Encased Electrode. ▶Figure 250–107

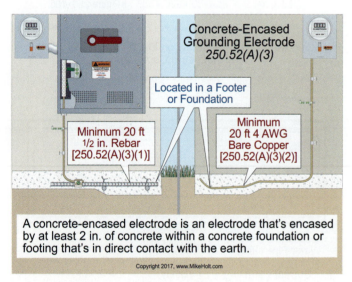

▶Figure 250–107

(1) One or more electrically conductive steel reinforcing bars of not less than ½ in. in diameter, mechanically connected together by steel tie wires, or other effective means to create a 20 ft or greater length can serve as a grounding electrode. ▶Figure 250–108

▶Figure 250–108

(2) Bare copper conductor not smaller than 4 AWG of 20 ft or greater length.

The reinforcing bars or bare copper conductor must be encased by at least 2 in. of concrete located horizontally within a concrete footing or vertically within a concrete foundation that's in direct contact with the earth can serve as a grounding electrode.

Where multiple concrete-encased electrodes are present at a building, only one is required to serve as a grounding electrode. ▶Figure 250–109

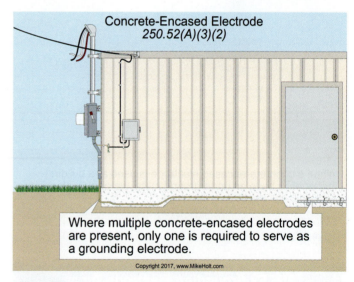

▶Figure 250–109

Note: Concrete separated from the earth because of insulation, vapor barriers, or similar items isn't considered to be in direct contact with the earth. ▶Figure 250–110

Grounding and Bonding | 250.52

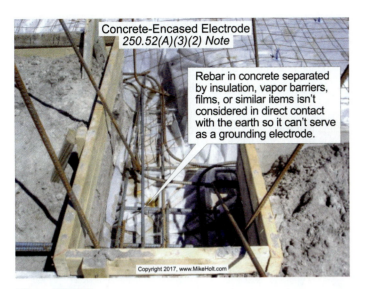
▶Figure 250–110

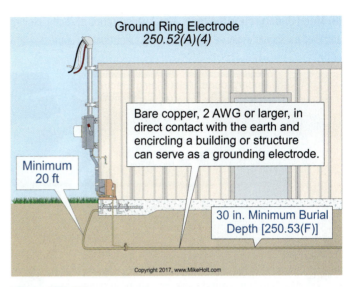
▶Figure 250–111

Author's Comment:

- The grounding electrode conductor to a concrete-encased grounding electrode isn't required to be larger than 4 AWG copper [250.66(B)].

- The concrete-encased grounding electrode is also called a "Ufer Ground," named after a consultant working for the U.S. Army during World War II. The technique Mr. Ufer came up with was necessary because the site needing grounding had no underground water table and little rainfall. The desert site was a series of bomb storage vaults in the area of Flagstaff, Arizona. This type of grounding electrode generally offers the lowest ground resistance for the cost.

(4) Ground Ring Electrode. A ground ring consisting of at least 20 ft of bare copper conductor not smaller than 2 AWG buried in the earth encircling a building, can serve as a grounding electrode. ▶Figure 250–111

(5) Rod Electrode. Rod electrodes must have at less 8 ft in length in contact with the earth [250.53(G)].

(b) Rod-type electrodes must have a diameter of at least ⅝ in., unless listed. ▶Figure 250–112

Author's Comment:

- The grounding electrode conductor, if it's the sole connection to the rod(s), isn't required to be larger than 6 AWG copper [250.66(A)].

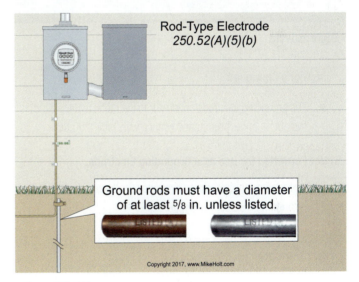
▶Figure 250–112

- The diameter of a rod has an insignificant effect on the contact resistance of a rod(s) to the earth. However, larger diameter rods (¾ in. and 1 in.) are sometimes installed where mechanical strength is desired, or to compensate for the loss of the electrode's metal due to corrosion.

(6) Listed Electrode. Other listed grounding electrodes can serve as a grounding electrode.

(7) Plate Electrode. Bare or electrically conductive coated iron or steel plate with not less than ¼ in. of thickness, or a solid uncoated copper metal plate not less than 0.06 in. of thickness, with an exposed surface area of not less than 2 sq ft can serve as a grounding electrode.

250.53 | Grounding and Bonding

(8) Metal Underground Systems. Metal underground systems, piping, and well casings can serve as a grounding electrode. ▶Figure 250–113

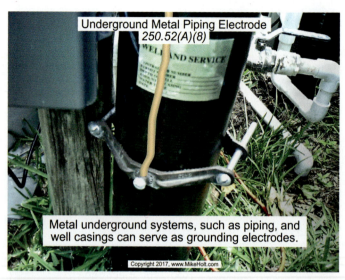

▶Figure 250–113

Author's Comment:

- The grounding electrode conductor to the metal underground system must be sized in accordance with Table 250.66.

(B) Not Permitted for Use as a Grounding Electrode.

(1) Underground metal gas-piping systems aren't permitted to be used as a grounding electrode. ▶Figure 250–114

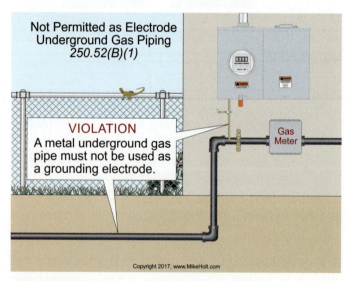

▶Figure 250–114

(2) Aluminum isn't permitted to be used as a grounding electrode.

(3) Swimming pool reinforcing steel for equipotential bonding in accordance with 680.26(B)(1) and 680.26(B)(2) isn't permitted to be used as a grounding electrode. ▶Figure 250–115

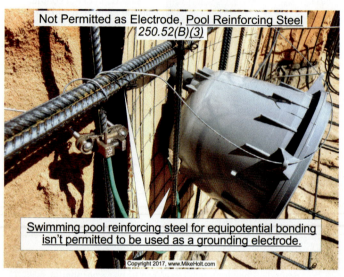

▶Figure 250–115

250.53 Grounding Electrode Installation Requirements

(A) Rod Electrodes.

(1) Below Permanent Moisture Level. If practicable, pipe electrodes must be embedded below the permanent moisture level and be free from nonconductive coatings such as paint or enamel.

(2) Supplemental Electrode. A rod electrode must be supplemented by an additional electrode that's bonded to: ▶Figure 250–116

(1) Another rod electrode

(2) The grounding electrode conductor

(3) The service neutral conductor

(4) A nonflexible metal service raceway

(5) The service disconnect

Ex: A single rod electrode having a contact resistance to the earth of 25 ohms or less isn't required to have a supplemental electrode.
▶Figure 250–117

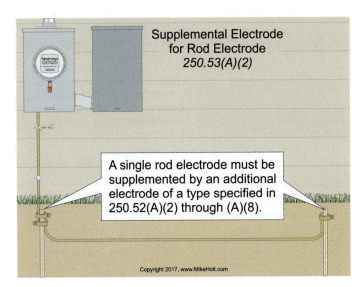

▶Figure 250–116

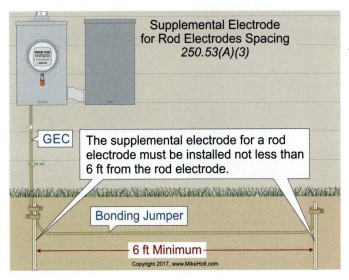

▶Figure 250–118

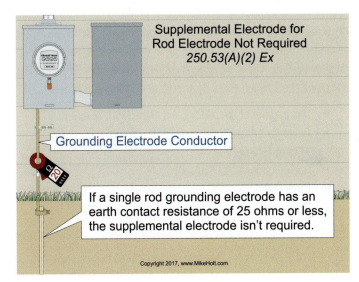

▶Figure 250–117

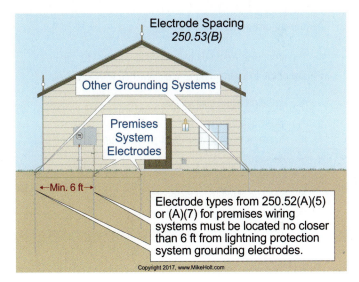

▶Figure 250–119

(3) Spacing. The supplemental electrode for a rod electrode must be installed not less than 6 ft from the rod electrode. ▶Figure 250–118

(B) Electrode Spacing. Electrodes for premises systems must be located no closer than 6 ft from lightning protection system grounding electrodes. Two or more grounding electrodes that are bonded together are considered a single grounding electrode system. ▶Figure 250–119

(C) Grounding Electrode Bonding Jumper. Grounding electrode bonding jumpers must be copper when within 18 in. of the earth [250.64(A)], be securely fastened to the surface, and be protected from physical damage [250.64(B)]. The bonding jumper to each electrode must be sized in accordance with 250.66. ▶Figure 250–120

250.53 | Grounding and Bonding

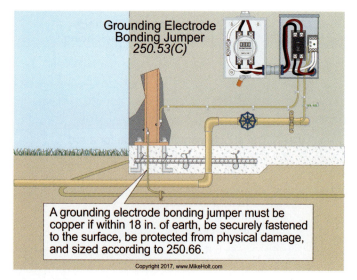

▶Figure 250–120

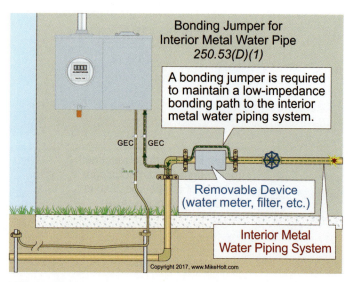

▶Figure 250–121

Author's Comment:

- The grounding electrode bonding jumpers must terminate by any of the following means in accordance with 250.8(A):
  - Listed pressure connectors
  - Terminal bars
  - Pressure connectors listed as grounding and bonding equipment
  - Exothermic welding
  - Machine screw-type fasteners that engage not less than two threads or are secured with a nut
  - Thread-forming machine screws that engage not less than two threads in the enclosure
  - Connections that are part of a listed assembly
  - Other listed means

When the termination is encased in concrete or buried, the termination fittings must be listed for this purpose [250.70].

(D) Underground Metal Water Pipe Electrode.

(1) Interior Metal Water Piping. The bonding connection for the interior metal water piping system, as required by 250.104(A), isn't permitted to be dependent on water meters, filtering devices, or similar equipment likely to be disconnected for repairs or replacement. When necessary, a bonding jumper must be installed around insulated joints and equipment likely to be disconnected for repairs or replacement. ▶Figure 250–121

(2) Underground Metal Water Pipe Supplemental Electrode. When an underground metal water pipe grounding electrode is present, it must be used as part of the grounding electrode system [250.52(A)(1)], and it must be supplemented by any of the following electrodes:

- Metal frame of the building electrode [250.52(A)(2)]
- Concrete-encased electrode [250.52(A)(3)]
  ▶Figure 250–122
- Rod electrode [250.52(A)(5)]
- Other listed electrode [250.52(A)(6)]
- Metal underground piping electrode [250.52(A)(8)]

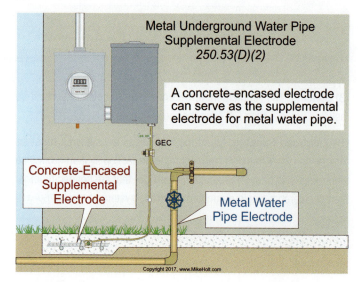

▶Figure 250–122

The supplemental grounding electrode conductor must terminate to any of the following: ▶Figure 250–123

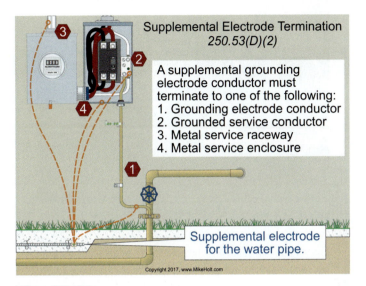

▶Figure 250–123

(1) Grounding electrode conductor

(2) Service neutral conductor

(3) Metal service raceway

(4) Service equipment enclosure

Ex: The supplemental electrode can be bonded to interior metal water piping located not more than 5 ft from the point of entrance to the building [250.68(C)(1)].

(E) Supplemental Rod Electrode. The grounding electrode conductor to a rod(s) that serves as a supplemental electrode isn't required to be larger than 6 AWG copper.

(F) Ground Ring. A bare 2 AWG or larger copper conductor installed not less than 30 in. below the surface of the earth encircling the building [250.52(A)(4)]. ▶Figure 250–124

(G) Rod Electrodes. Rod electrodes must be installed so that not less than 8 ft of length is in contact with the soil. If rock bottom is encountered, the rod must be driven at an angle not to exceed 45 degrees from vertical. If rock bottom is encountered at an angle up to 45 degrees from vertical, the rod can be buried in a minimum 30 in. below the surface of the earth. ▶Figure 250–125

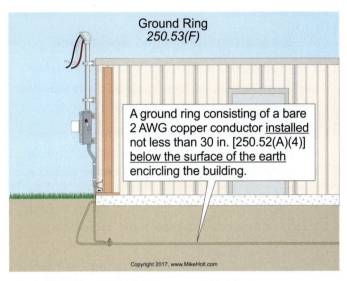

▶Figure 250–124

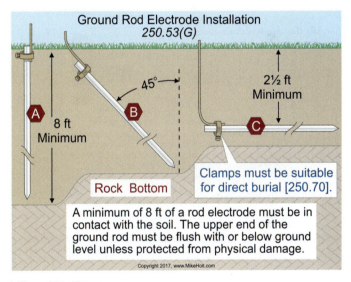

▶Figure 250–125

The upper end of the rod must be flush with or underground unless the grounding electrode conductor attachment is protected against physical damage as specified in 250.10.

Author's Comment:

- When the grounding electrode attachment fitting is located underground, it must be listed for direct soil burial [250.68(A) Ex 1 and 250.70].

Measuring the Ground Resistance

A ground resistance clamp meter, or a three-point fall-of-potential ground resistance meter, can be used to measure the contact resistance of a grounding electrode to the earth.

Ground Clamp Meter. The ground resistance clamp meter measures the contact resistance of the grounding electrode system to the earth by injecting a high-frequency signal via the service neutral conductor to the electric utility grounding connection, and then measuring the strength of the return signal through the earth to the grounding electrode being measured. ▶Figure 250–126

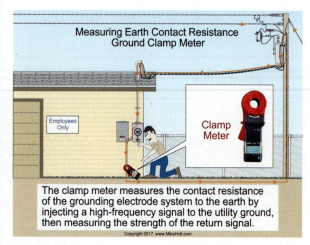

▶Figure 250–126

Fall-of-Potential Ground Resistance Meter. The three-point fall-of-potential ground resistance meter determines the contact resistance of a single grounding electrode to the earth by using Ohm's Law: $R=E/I$. ▶Figure 250–127

This meter divides the voltage difference between the electrode to be measured and a driven voltage test stake (P) by the current flowing between the electrode to be measured and a driven current test stake (C). The test stakes are typically made of ¼ in. diameter steel rods, 24 in. long, driven two-thirds of their length into the earth.

The distance and alignment between the voltage and current test stakes, and the electrode, is extremely important to the validity of the earth contact resistance measurements. For an 8-ft rod, the accepted practice is to space the current test stake (C) 80 ft from the electrode to be measured.

▶Figure 250–127

The voltage test stake (P) is positioned in a straight line between the electrode to be measured and the current test stake (C). The voltage test stake should be located at approximately 62 percent of the distance the current test stake is located from the electrode. Since the current test stake (C) for an 8-ft rod is located 80 ft from the grounding electrode, the voltage test stake (P) will be about 50 ft from the electrode to be measured.

Example: *If the voltage between the rod and the voltage test stake (P) is 3V and the current between the rod and the current test stake (C) is 0.20A, what will be the earth contact resistance of the electrode to the earth?* ▶Figure 250–128

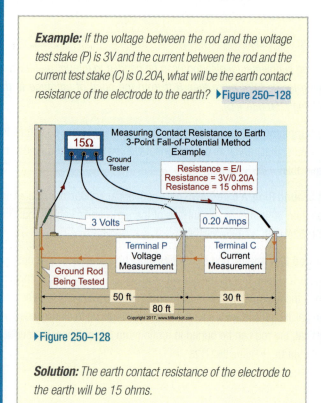

▶Figure 250–128

Solution: *The earth contact resistance of the electrode to the earth will be 15 ohms.*

Resistance = Voltage/Current
E (Voltage) = 3V
I (Current) = 0.20A

R = E/I
Resistance = 3V/0.20A
Resistance = 15 ohms

Answer: 15 ohms

Author's Comment:

- The three-point fall-of-potential meter should only be used to measure the contact resistance of one electrode to the earth at a time, and this electrode must be independent and not connected to any part of the electrical system. The contact resistance of two electrodes bonded together must not be measured until they've been separated. The contact resistance of two separate electrodes to the earth can be thought of as two resistors in parallel, if they're outside each other's sphere of influence.

250.54 Auxiliary Grounding Electrodes

Auxiliary electrodes are permitted, but they have no *Code* requirements since they serve no purpose related to electrical safety addressed by the *NEC*. ▶Figure 250–129

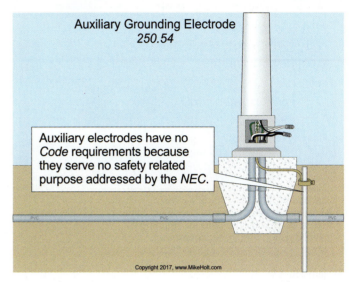

▶Figure 250–129

If an auxiliary electrode is installed, it's not required to be bonded to the building grounding electrode system, required to have the grounding conductor sized to 250.66, or comply with the 25-ohm requirement of 250.53(A)(2) Ex. ▶Figure 250–130

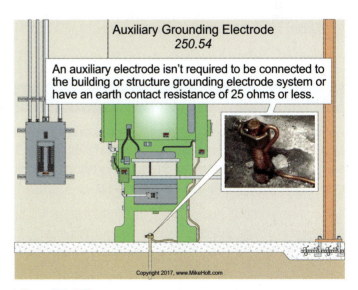

▶Figure 250–130

Soil Resistivity

The earth's ground resistance is directly impacted by soil resistivity, which varies throughout the world. Soil resistivity is influenced by electrolytes, which consist of moisture, minerals, and dissolved salts. Because soil resistivity changes with moisture content, the resistance of any grounding system varies with the seasons of the year. Since moisture is stable at greater distances below the surface of the earth, grounding systems are generally more effective if the grounding electrode can reach the water table. In addition, placing the grounding electrode below the frost line helps to ensure less deviation in the system's contact resistance to the earth year round.

The contact resistance to the earth can be lowered by chemically treating the earth around the grounding electrodes with electrolytes designed for this purpose.

250.58 | Grounding and Bonding

CAUTION: An auxiliary electrode typically serves no useful purpose, and in some cases it may actually cause equipment failures by providing a path for lightning to travel through electronic equipment. ▶Figure 250–131

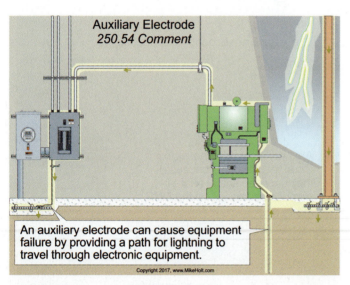

▶Figure 250–131

DANGER: Because the contact resistance of an electrode to the earth is so great, very little fault current returns to the power supply if the earth is the only fault current return path. Result—the circuit overcurrent protection device won't open and clear the ground fault, and all metal parts associated with the electrical installation, metal piping, and structural building steel will become and remain energized.

250.58 Common Grounding Electrode

Where an ac system is connected to a grounding electrode in or at a building or structure, the same grounding electrode must be used. If separate services, feeders, or branch circuits supply a building, the same grounding electrode must be used. ▶Figure 250–132

Two or more grounding electrodes that are bonded together will be considered as a single grounding electrode system in this sense.

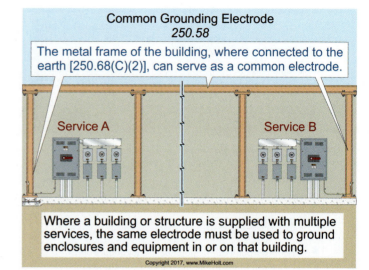

▶Figure 250–132

Author's Comment:

- Metal parts of the electrical installation are grounded (connected to the earth) to reduce induced voltage on the metal parts from lightning so as to prevent fires from a surface arc within the building/structure. Grounding electrical equipment doesn't serve the purpose of providing a low-impedance fault current path to open the circuit overcurrent device in the event of a ground fault.

CAUTION: Potentially dangerous objectionable neutral current flows on the metal parts when multiple service disconnecting means are connected to the same electrode. This is because neutral current from each service can return to the utility via the common grounding electrode and its conductors. This is especially a problem if a service neutral conductor is opened. ▶Figure 250–133

250.60 Lightning Protection Electrode

The lightning protection electrode isn't permitted to be used for the building or structure grounding electrode system required for service equipment [250.24] and remote building feeder disconnecting means [250.32(A)]. ▶Figure 250–134

Grounding and Bonding | 250.62

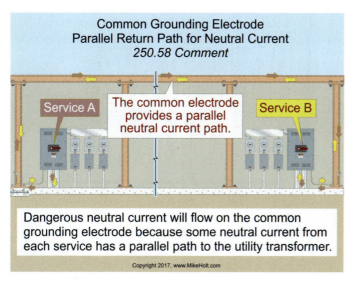
▶Figure 250–133

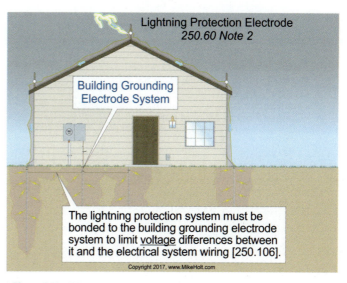
▶Figure 250–135

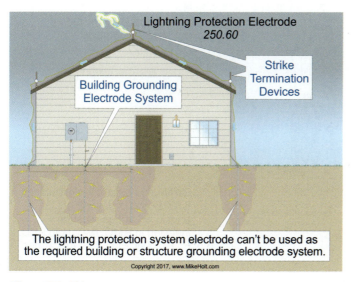
▶Figure 250–134

▶Figure 250–136

Note 1: See 250.106 for the bonding requirements of the lightning protection system to the building or structure grounding electrode system.

Note 2: If a lightning protection system is installed, the lightning protection system must be bonded to the building grounding electrode system so as to limit voltage differences between it and the electrical system wiring. ▶Figure 250–135

Author's Comment:

- A lightning protection system installed in accordance with NFPA 780 is intended to protect the structure from lighting damage. ▶Figure 250–136

250.62 Grounding Electrode Conductor

Grounding electrode conductors of the wire type must be solid or stranded, insulated or bare, and must be copper if within 18 in. of the earth [250.64(A)]. ▶Figure 250–137

250.64 | Grounding and Bonding

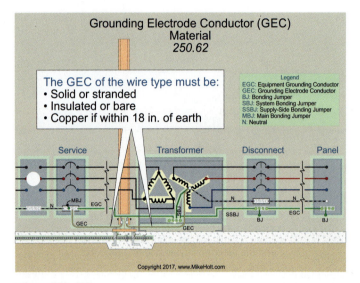

▶Figure 250–137

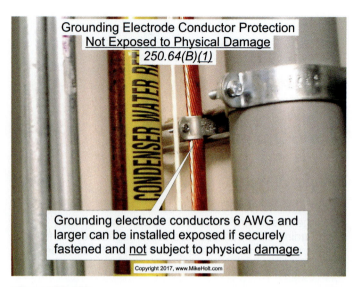

▶Figure 250–138

250.64 Grounding Electrode Conductor Installation

Grounding electrode conductors must be installed as specified in (A) through (F).

(A) Aluminum Conductors. Bare or covered aluminum grounding electrode conductors aren't permitted to be in contact with masonry, the earth, or subject to corrosive conditions. Where used outside, aluminum grounding electrode conductors aren't permitted within 18 in. of the earth.

(B) Conductor Protection. Where exposed, a grounding electrode conductor or its enclosure must be securely fastened to the surface on which it's carried.

(1) Not Exposed to Physical Damage. Grounding electrode conductors 6 AWG and larger can be installed exposed along the surface of the building if securely fastened and not exposed to physical damage. ▶Figure 250–138

(2) Exposed to Physical Damage. Grounding electrode conductors 6 AWG and larger subject to physical damage must be installed in rigid metal conduit, intermediate metal conduit, rigid polyvinyl chloride conduit, Type XW reinforced thermosetting resin conduit (RTRC-XW), electrical metallic tubing, or cable armor. ▶Figure 250–139

(3) Smaller than 6 AWG. Grounding electrode conductors sized 8 AWG must be protected by installing them in rigid metal conduit, intermediate metal conduit, PVC conduit, electrical metallic tubing, Type XW reinforced thermosetting resin conduit (RTRC-XW), or cable armor.

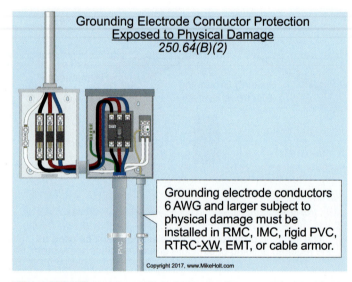

▶Figure 250–139

Author's Comment:

- A ferrous metal raceway containing a grounding electrode conductor must be made electrically continuous by bonding each end of the raceway to the grounding electrode conductor [250.64(E)], so it's best to use nonmetallic conduit.

(4) In Contact with the Earth. Grounding electrode conductors and bonding jumpers in contact with the earth aren't required to comply with the cover requirements of 300.5, but must be protected if subject to physical damage. ▶Figure 250–140

Grounding and Bonding | 250.64

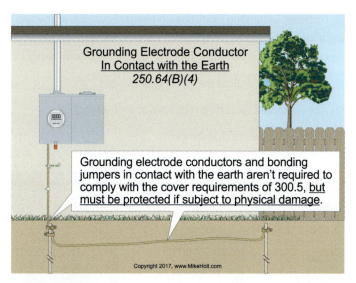

▶Figure 250–140

Author's Comment:

- Grounding and bonding fittings must be protected from physical damage by enclosing the fittings in metal, wood, or an equivalent protective covering [250.10].

(C) Continuous. Grounding electrode conductor(s) must be installed without a splice or joint except by: ▶Figure 250–141

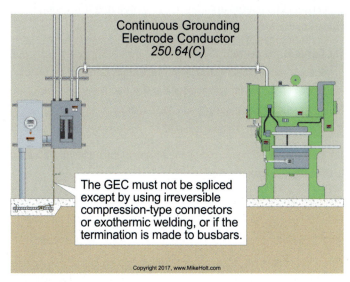

▶Figure 250–141

(1) Irreversible compression-type connectors or exothermic welding.
(2) Busbars connected together.

(3) Bolted, riveted, or welded connections of structural metal frames of buildings.
(4) Threaded, welded, brazed, soldered, or bolted-flange connections of metal water piping.

(D) Grounding Electrode Conductor for Multiple Building or Structure Disconnects. If a building or structure contains two or more building disconnects in separate enclosures, the grounding electrode connections must be made in any of the following methods:

(1) Common Grounding Electrode Conductor and Taps. A grounding electrode conductor tap must extend to the inside of each disconnect enclosure.

The common grounding electrode conductor must be sized in accordance with 250.66, based on the sum of the circular mil area of the largest ungrounded conductor supplying the equipment. ▶Figure 250–142

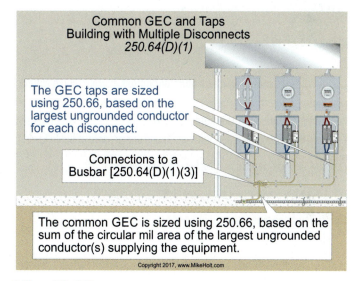

▶Figure 250–142

A grounding electrode conductor must extend from each disconnect, sized no smaller than specified in Table 250.66, based on the area of the largest ungrounded conductor for each disconnect.

The grounding electrode tap conductors must be connected to the common grounding electrode conductor, without splicing the common grounding electrode conductor, by any of the following methods:

(1) Exothermic welding.
(2) Connectors listed as grounding and bonding equipment.

250.64 | Grounding and Bonding

(3) Connections to a busbar of sufficient length and not less than ¼ in. thick × 2 in. wide that's securely fastened and installed in an accessible location. ▶Figure 250–143

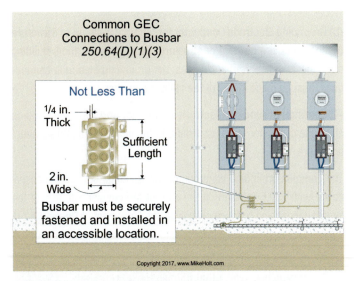

▶Figure 250–143

(2) Individual Grounding Electrode Conductors. A grounding electrode conductor, sized in accordance with 250.66 based on the ungrounded conductor(s) supplying the individual disconnect, must be connected between the grounding electrode system and one or more of the following:

(1) The service neutral conductor ▶Figure 250–144

(2) The equipment grounding conductor of the feeder circuit

(3) The supply-side bonding jumper

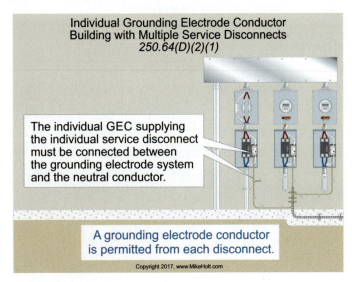

▶Figure 250–144

(3) Common Grounding Electrode Conductor Location. A grounding electrode conductor can be connected from an accessible enclosure on the supply side of the disconnect to one or more of the following locations:

(1) The service neutral conductor ▶Figure 250–145

(2) The equipment grounding conductor of the feeder circuit

(3) The supply-side bonding jumper

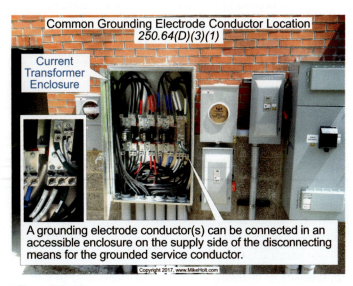

▶Figure 250–145

(E) Ferrous Enclosures and Raceways Containing Grounding Electrode Conductor.

(1) General. To prevent inductive choking of grounding electrode conductors, metal steel raceways and enclosures containing grounding electrode conductors must have each end of the raceway or enclosure bonded to the grounding electrode conductor so as to create an electrically parallel path. ▶Figure 250–146

(2) Methods. Bonding must be done by one of the methods discussed in 250.92(B)(2) through (B)(4).

(3) Size. Bonding jumpers must be the same size or larger than the required size of the grounding electrode conductor in the raceway or other enclosure.

Author's Comment:

- Nonferrous metal raceways, such as aluminum rigid metal conduit, enclosing the grounding electrode conductor aren't required to meet the "bonding each end of the raceway to the grounding electrode conductor" provisions of this section.

Grounding and Bonding | 250.64

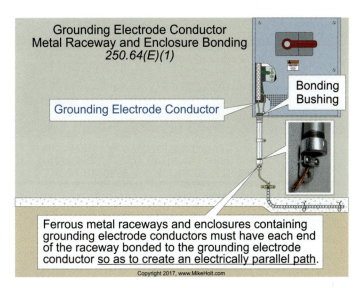
▶Figure 250–146

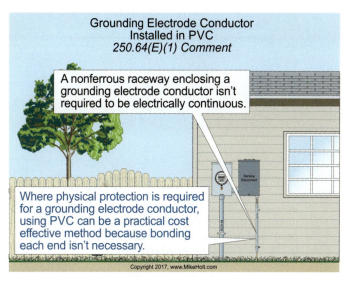
▶Figure 250–147

CAUTION: *The effectiveness of a grounding electrode is significantly reduced if a ferrous metal raceway containing a grounding electrode conductor isn't bonded to the ferrous metal raceway at both ends. This is because a single conductor carrying high-frequency induced lightning current in a ferrous raceway causes the raceway to act as an inductor, which severely limits (chokes) the current flow through the grounding electrode conductor. ANSI/IEEE 142—Recommended Practice for Grounding of Industrial and Commercial Power Systems (Green Book) states: "An inductive choke can reduce the current flow by 97 percent."*

Author's Comment:

- To save a lot of time and effort, install the grounding electrode conductor exposed if it's not subject to physical damage [250.64(B)], or enclose it in nonmetallic conduit suitable for the application [352.10(F)]. ▶Figure 250–147

(F) Termination to Grounding Electrode.

(1) Single Grounding Electrode Conductor. A single grounding electrode conductor can terminate to any grounding electrode of the grounding electrode system. ▶Figure 250–148

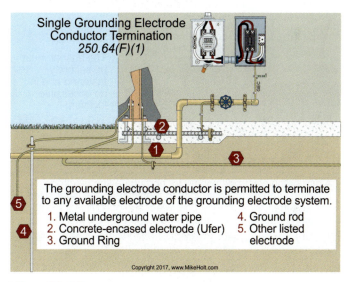
▶Figure 250–148

(2) Multiple Grounding Electrode Conductors. When multiple grounding electrode conductors are installed [250.64(D)(2)], each grounding electrode conductor can terminate to any grounding electrode of the grounding electrode system. ▶Figure 250–149

(3) Termination to Busbar. Grounding electrode conductors and grounding electrode bonding jumpers are permitted to terminate to a busbar not less than ¼ in. thick × 2 in. wide, and of sufficient length to accommodate the terminations necessary for the installation. The busbar must be securely fastened and be installed an accessible location. ▶Figure 250–150

250.66 | Grounding and Bonding

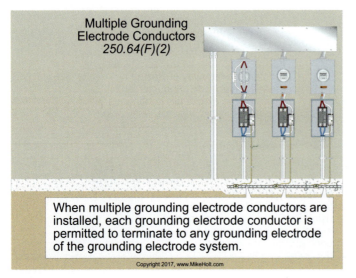

▶Figure 250–149

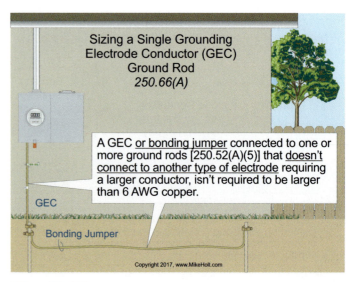

▶Figure 250–151

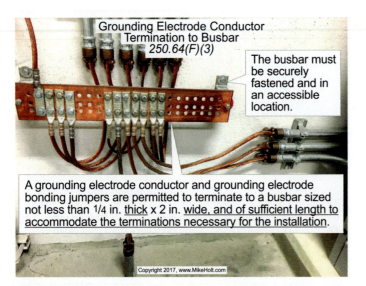

▶Figure 250–150

(B) Concrete-Encased Grounding Electrode. If the grounding electrode conductor or bonding jumper is connected to one or more concrete-encased electrodes [250.52(A)(3)] and doesn't connect to another type of electrode that requires a larger size conductor, the grounding electrode conductor isn't required to be larger than 4 AWG copper. ▶Figure 250–152

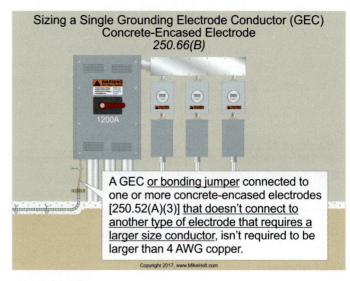

▶Figure 250–152

250.66 Sizing Grounding Electrode Conductor

Except as permitted in (A) through (C), the grounding electrode conductor must be sized in accordance with Table 250.66.

(A) Rod. If the grounding electrode conductor or bonding jumper connects to one or more ground rods [250.52(A)(5)] and doesn't connect to another type of electrode that requires a larger conductor, the grounding electrode conductor isn't required to be larger than 6 AWG copper. ▶Figure 250–151

Table 250.66 Sizing Grounding Electrode Conductor

Conductor or Area of Parallel Conductors	Copper Grounding Electrode Conductor
12 through 2 AWG	8 AWG
1 or 1/0 AWG	6 AWG
2/0 or 3/0 AWG	4 AWG
Over 3/0 through 350 kcmil	2 AWG
Over 350 through 600 kcmil	1/0 AWG
Over 600 through 1,100 kcmil	2/0 AWG
Over 1,100 kcmil	3/0 AWG

250.68 Termination to the Grounding Electrode

(A) Accessibility. The mechanical elements used to terminate a grounding electrode conductor or bonding jumper to a grounding electrode must be accessible. ▶Figure 250–153

▶Figure 250–153

Ex 1: The termination isn't required to be accessible if the termination to the electrode is encased in concrete or buried in the earth. ▶Figure 250–154

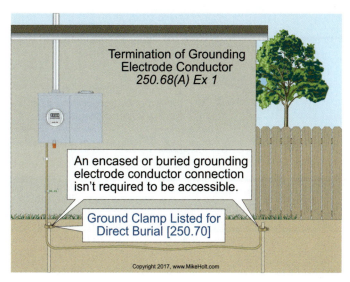

▶Figure 250–154

Author's Comment:

- If the grounding electrode attachment fitting is encased in concrete or buried in the earth, it must be listed for direct soil burial or concrete encasement [250.70].

Ex 2: Exothermic or irreversible compression connections, together with the mechanical means used to attach to fireproofed structural metal, aren't required to be accessible.

(B) Integrity of Underground Metal Water Pipe Electrode. A bonding jumper must be installed around insulated joints and equipment likely to be disconnected for repairs or replacement for an underground metal water piping system used as a grounding electrode. The bonding jumper must be of sufficient length to allow the removal of such equipment while retaining the integrity of the grounding path. ▶Figure 250–155

(C) Grounding Electrode Conductor Connections. Grounding electrode conductors and bonding jumpers are permitted to terminate and use the following to extend the connection to another electrode(s):

(1) Interior metal water piping that's electrically continuous with a metal underground water pipe electrode and is located not more than 5 ft from the point of entrance to the building can be used to extend the connection to electrodes. Interior metal water piping located more than 5 ft from the point of entrance to the building isn't permitted to be used as a conductor to interconnect electrodes of the grounding electrode system. ▶Figure 250–156

250.68 | Grounding and Bonding

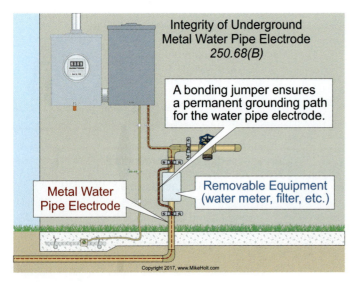

▶Figure 250–155

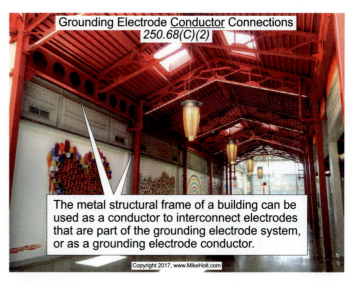

▶Figure 250–157

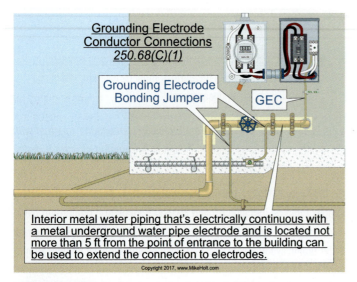

▶Figure 250–156

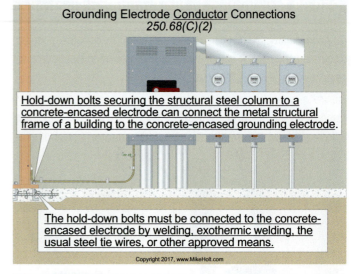

▶Figure 250–158

(2) The metal structural frame of a building can be used as a conductor to interconnect electrodes that are part of the grounding electrode system, or as a grounding electrode conductor. Hold-down bolts securing the structural steel column to a concrete-encased electrode [250.52(A)(3)] can connect the metal structural frame of a building to the concrete-encased grounding electrode. The hold-down bolts must be connected to the concrete-encased electrode by welding, exothermic welding, the usual steel tie wires, or other approved means. ▶Figure 250–157 and ▶Figure 250–158

(3) A rebar-type concrete-encased electrode [250.52(A)(3)] with an additional rebar section to an accessible location above the concrete, where not in contact with the earth or subject to corrosion, can be used for the connection of the grounding electrode conductors and bonding jumpers. ▶Figure 250–159

Grounding and Bonding | 250.70

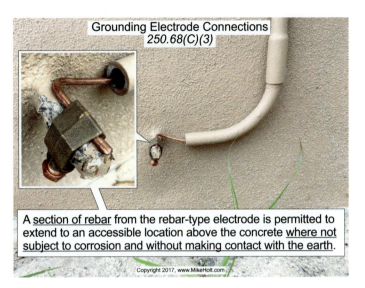

▶Figure 250–159

250.70 Grounding Electrode Conductor Termination Fittings

The grounding electrode conductor must terminate to the grounding electrode by exothermic welding, listed lugs, listed pressure connectors, listed clamps, or other listed means. In addition, fittings terminating to a grounding electrode must be listed for the materials of the grounding electrode and the grounding electrode conductor. ▶Figure 250–160

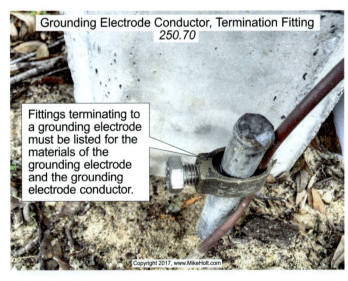

▶Figure 250–160

When the termination to a grounding electrode is buried in the earth or encased in concrete, the termination fitting must be listed for direct soil burial or concrete encasement. ▶Figure 250–161

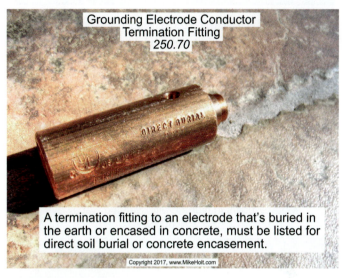

▶Figure 250–161

No more than one conductor can terminate on a single clamp or fitting unless the clamp or fitting is listed for multiple connections. ▶Figure 250–162

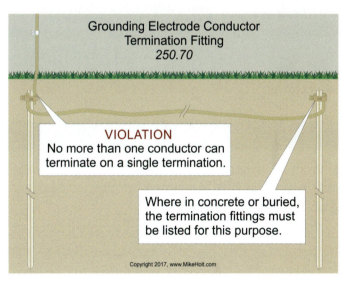

▶Figure 250–162

Mike Holt Enterprises • www.MikeHolt.com • 888.NEC.CODE (632.2633)   215

Part IV. Grounding Enclosure, Raceway, and Service Cable Connections

250.80 Service Raceways and Enclosures

Metal enclosures and raceways containing service conductors must be bonded to the neutral conductor at service equipment if the electrical system is grounded, or to the grounding electrode conductor for electrical systems that aren't grounded.

Ex: Metal components installed in a run of an underground nonmetallic raceway having a minimum cover of 18 in. isn't required to be bonded to the service neutral, supply-side bonding jumper, or grounding electrode conductor. ▶Figure 250–163

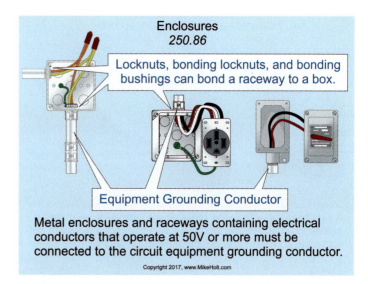

▶Figure 250–164

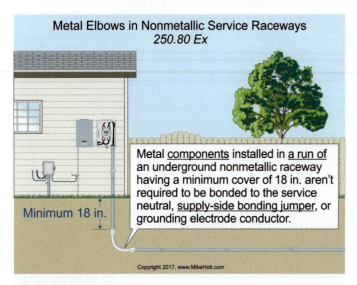

▶Figure 250–163

250.86 Other Enclosures

Metal raceways and enclosures containing electrical conductors operating at 50V or more [250.20(A)] must be connected to the circuit equipment grounding conductor. ▶Figure 250–164

Ex 2: Short sections of metal raceways used for the support or physical protection of cables aren't required to be connected to the circuit equipment grounding conductor. ▶Figure 250–165

Ex 3: Metal components aren't required to be connected to the circuit equipment grounding conductor or supply-side bonding jumper where either of the following conditions exist:

(1) The metal components are installed in a run of an underground nonmetallic raceway and isolated from possible contact by a minimum cover of 18 in. to any part of the metal components. ▶Figure 250–166

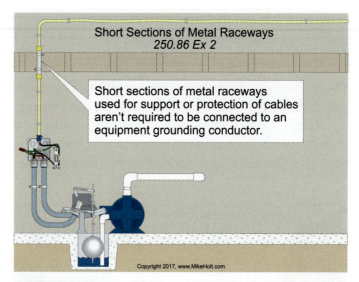

▶Figure 250–165

(2) The metal components are part of an installation of nonmetallic raceway(s) and are isolated from possible contact to any part of the metal components by being enclosed in not less than 2 in. of concrete.

Part V. Bonding

250.90 General

Bonding must be provided to ensure electrical continuity and the capacity to conduct safely any fault current likely to be imposed.

Grounding and Bonding | 250.92

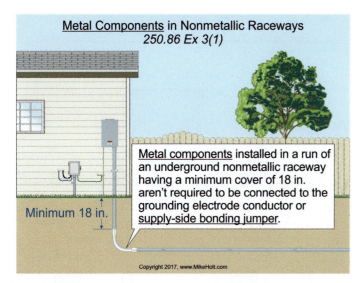

▶Figure 250–166

250.92 Bonding Equipment for Services

(A) Bonding Requirements for Equipment for Services. The metal parts of equipment indicated below must be bonded together in accordance with 250.92(B). ▶Figure 250–167

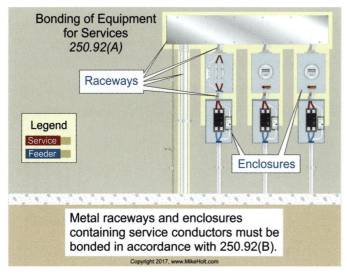

▶Figure 250–167

(1) Metal raceways containing service conductors.
(2) Metal enclosures containing service conductors.

Author's Comment:

- Metal raceways or metal enclosures containing feeder and branch-circuit conductors must be connected to the circuit equipment grounding conductor in accordance with 250.86.
  ▶Figure 250–168

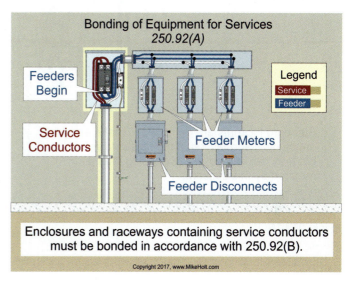

▶Figure 250–168

(B) Methods of Bonding. Bonding jumpers around reducing washers or oversized, concentric, or eccentric knockouts are required. ▶Figure 250–169

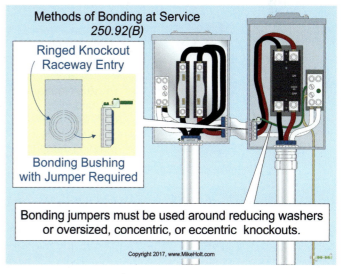

▶Figure 250–169

250.92 | Grounding and Bonding

Standard locknuts are permitted to make a mechanical connection to the raceway(s), but they can't serve as the bonding means required by this section. ▶Figure 250–170

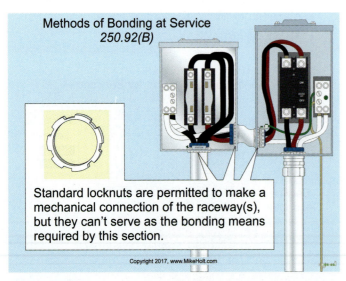

▶Figure 250–170

Electrical continuity at service equipment, service raceways, and service conductor enclosures must be ensured by any of the following methods:

(1) Bonding the metal parts to the service neutral conductor. ▶Figure 250–171

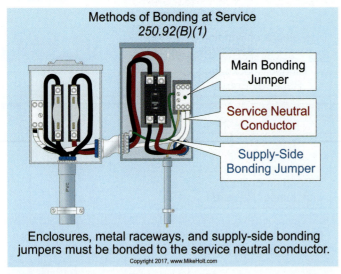

▶Figure 250–171

Author's Comment:

- A main bonding jumper is required to bond the service disconnect to the service neutral conductor [250.24(B) and 250.28].

- At service equipment, the service neutral conductor provides the effective ground-fault current path to the power supply [250.24(C)]; therefore, a supply-side bonding jumper (SSBJ) isn't required to be installed within PVC conduit containing service-entrance conductors [250.142(A)(1) and 352.60 Ex 2]. ▶Figure 250–172

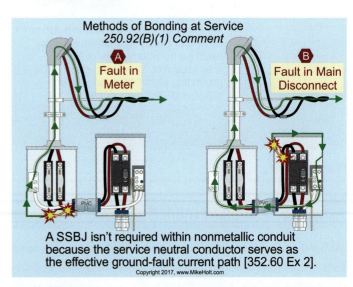

▶Figure 250–172

(2) Terminating metal raceways to metal enclosures by threaded hubs on enclosures if made up wrenchtight. ▶Figure 250–173

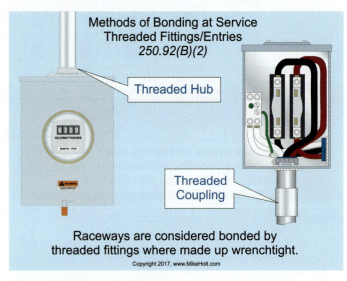

▶Figure 250–173

(3) Terminating metal raceways to metal enclosures by threadless fittings if made up tight. ▶Figure 250–174

Grounding and Bonding | 250.92

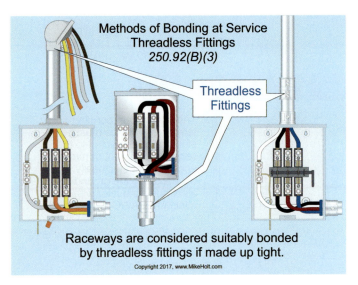

▶Figure 250–174

(4) Other listed devices, such as bonding-type locknuts, bushings, wedges, or bushings with bonding jumpers.

Author's Comment:

- A listed bonding wedge or bushing with a bonding jumper to the service neutral conductor is required when a metal raceway containing service conductors terminates to a ringed knockout. ▶Figure 250–175

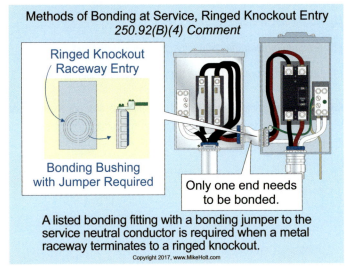

▶Figure 250–175

- The bonding jumper used for this purpose must be sized in accordance with Table 250.102(C)(1), based on the area of the largest ungrounded service conductors within the raceway [250.102(C)].

- A bonding-type locknut can be used for a metal raceway containing service conductors that terminates to an enclosure without a ringed knockout. ▶Figure 250–176

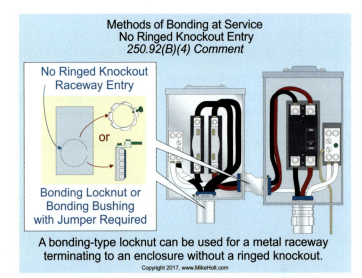

▶Figure 250–176

- A bonding locknut differs from a standard locknut in that it contains a bonding screw with a sharp point that drives into the metal enclosure to ensure a solid connection.
- Bonding one end of a service raceway to the service neutral provides the necessary low-impedance fault current path to the source. ▶Figure 250–177

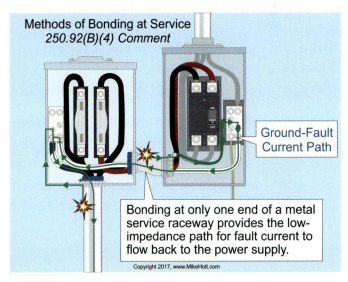

▶Figure 250–177

Note: The use of an intersystem bonding termination device can assist in reducing electrical noise on communications systems.

250.94 | Grounding and Bonding

250.94 Bonding Communications Systems

Where communications systems (twisted wire, antennas, and coaxial cable) are likely to be used in a building or structure, communications system bonding terminations must be provided in accordance with (A) or (B) at service equipment or building disconnects supplied by a feeder.

(A) Intersystem Bonding Termination Device. Where an intersystem bonding termination device is required, it must meet the following requirements:

(1) Be accessible for connection and inspection. ▶Figure 250–178

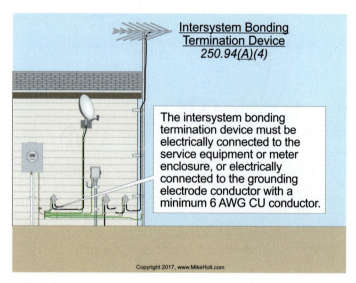

▶Figure 250–179

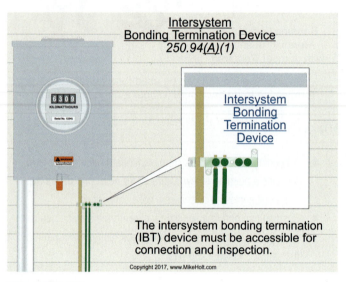

▶Figure 250–178

(2) Have a capacity for connection of at least three intersystem bonding conductors.

(3) Installed so that it doesn't interfere with opening any enclosure.

(4) Be securely mounted and electrically connected to the service equipment or meter enclosure, or grounding electrode conductor with a minimum 6 AWG copper conductor. ▶Figure 250–179

(5) Be securely mounted and electrically connected to the building's disconnect, or grounding electrode conductor with a minimum 6 AWG copper conductor.

(6) The terminals are listed as grounding and bonding equipment.

Author's Comment:

■ According to Article 100, an intersystem bonding termination is a device that provides a means to connect communications systems (twisted wire, antennas, and coaxial cable) bonding conductors to the building grounding electrode system.

Ex: At existing buildings, an external accessible means for bonding communications systems (twisted wire, antennas, and coaxial cable) together can be by the use of a:

(1) Nonflexible metallic raceway,

(2) Grounding electrode conductor, or

(3) Connection approved by the authority having jurisdiction.

Note 2: Communications systems (twisted wire, antennas, and coaxial cable) must be bonded to the intersystem bonding termination in accordance with the following requirements: ▶Figure 250–180

- Antennas/Satellite Dishes, 810.15 and 810.21
- Coaxial Circuits, 820.100
- Telephone Circuits, 800.100

Author's Comment:

■ External communications systems (twisted wire, antennas, and coaxial cable) must be connected to the intersystem bonding termination to minimize the damage to them from induced voltage differences between the systems from a lightning event. ▶Figure 250–181

Grounding and Bonding | 250.96

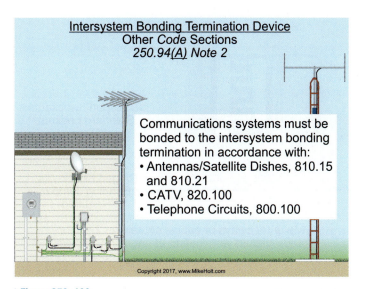
▶Figure 250–180

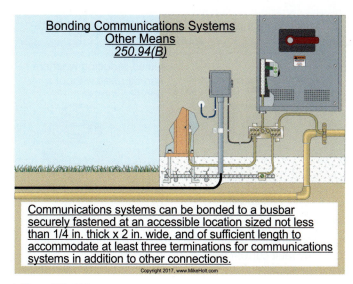
▶Figure 250–182

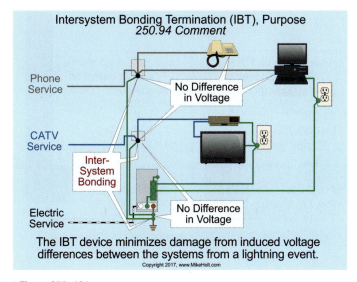
▶Figure 250–181

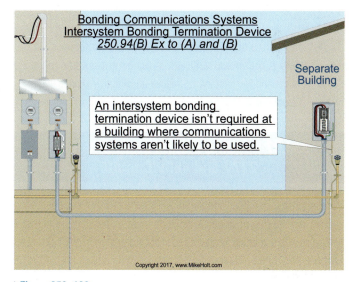
▶Figure 250–183

(B) Other Means. A busbar securely fastened at an accessible location sized not less than ¼ in. thick × 2 in. wide, and of sufficient length to accommodate at least three terminations for communications systems in addition to other connections. ▶Figure 250–182

Ex to (A) and (B): An intersystem bonding termination device isn't required where communications systems (twisted wire, antennas, and coaxial cable) aren't likely to be used. ▶Figure 250–183

250.96 Bonding Other Enclosures

(A) Maintaining Effective Ground-Fault Current Path. Metal parts intended to serve as equipment grounding conductors, including raceways, cables, equipment, and enclosures, must be bonded together to ensure they have the capacity to conduct safely any fault current likely to be imposed on them [110.10, 250.4(A)(5), and Note to Table 250.122]. ▶Figure 250–184

Nonconductive coatings such as paint, lacquer, and enamel on equipment must be removed to ensure an effective ground-fault current path, or the termination fittings must be designed so as to make such removal unnecessary [250.12].

250.97 | Grounding and Bonding

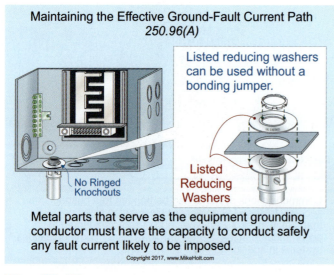

▸Figure 250–184

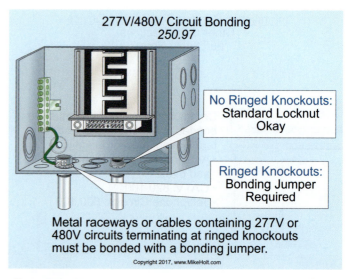

▸Figure 250–185

Author's Comment:

- The practice of driving a locknut tight with a screwdriver and pliers is considered sufficient in removing paint and other nonconductive finishes to ensure an effective ground-fault current path.

250.97 Bonding Metal Parts Containing 277V and 480V Circuits

Metal raceways or cables containing 277V and/or 480V feeder or branch circuits terminating at ringed knockouts must be bonded to the metal enclosure with a bonding jumper sized in accordance with 250.122, based on the rating of the circuit overcurrent protection device [250.102(D)].
▸Figure 250–185

Author's Comment:

- Bonding jumpers for raceways and cables containing 277V or 480V circuits are required at ringed knockout terminations to ensure the ground-fault current path has the capacity to safely conduct the maximum ground-fault current likely to be imposed [110.10, 250.4(A)(5), and 250.96(A)].

- Ringed knockouts aren't listed to withstand the heat generated by a 277V ground fault, which generates five times as much heat as a 120V ground fault. ▸Figure 250–186

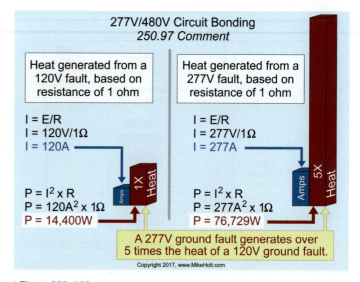

▸Figure 250–186

Ex: A bonding jumper isn't required where ringed knockouts aren't encountered, knockouts are totally punched out, or if the box is listed to provide a reliable bonding connection. ▸Figure 250–187

Grounding and Bonding | 250.102

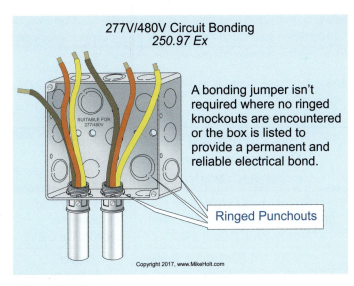

▶Figure 250–187

250.98 Bonding Loosely Jointed Metal Raceways

Expansion fittings and telescoping sections of metal raceways must be made electrically continuous by equipment bonding jumpers.
▶Figure 250–188

▶Figure 250–188

250.102 Grounded Conductor, Bonding Conductors, and Jumpers

(A) Material. Equipment bonding jumpers can be of copper, aluminum, or other corrosion-resistant material.

(B) Termination. Equipment bonding jumpers must terminate by any of the following means in accordance with 250.8(A):

- Listed pressure connectors
- Terminal bars
- Pressure connectors listed as grounding and bonding equipment
- Exothermic welding
- Machine screw-type fasteners that engage not less than two threads or are secured with a nut
- Thread-forming machine screws that engage not less than two threads in the enclosure
- Connections that are part of a listed assembly
- Other listed means

(C) Supply-Side Bonding Jumper Sizing.

(1) Single Raceway or Cable Installations. The supply-side bonding jumper is sized in accordance with Table 250.102(C)(1), based on the largest ungrounded conductor within the raceway or cable.
▶Figure 250–189

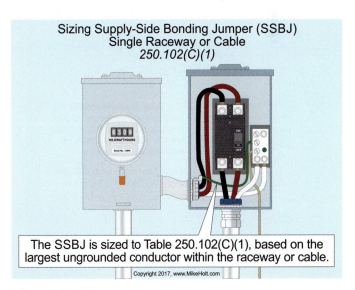

▶Figure 250–189

250.102 | Grounding and Bonding

(2) Parallel Conductor Installations in Two or More Raceways or Cables. If the ungrounded supply conductors are paralleled in two or more raceways or cables, the size of the supply-side bonding jumper for each raceway or cable is sized in accordance with Table 250.102(C)(1), based on the size of the largest ungrounded conductors in each raceway or cable. ▶Figure 250–190

Note 1: The term "supply conductors" includes ungrounded conductors that don't have overcurrent protection on their supply side and terminate at service equipment or the first disconnect of a separately derived system.

Note 2: See Chapter 9, Table 8, for the circular mil area of conductors 18 AWG through 4/0 AWG.

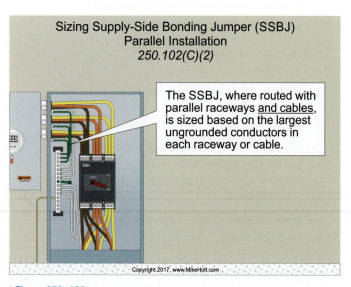

▶Figure 250–190

Table 250.102(C)(1) Grounded Conductor, Main Bonding Jumper, System Bonding Jumper, and Supply-Side Bonding Jumper

Size of Largest Ungrounded Conductor Per Raceway or Equivalent Area for Parallel Conductors		Size of Bonding Jumper or Grounded Conductor
Copper	Aluminum or Copper-Clad Aluminum	Copper-Aluminum
2 or smaller	1/0 or smaller	8—6
1 or 1/0	2/0 or 3/0	6—4
2/0 or 3/0	Over 3/0 250 kcmil	4—2
Over 3/0 through 350 kcmil	Over 250 through 500 kcmil	2—1/0
Over 350 through 600 kcmil	Over 500 through 900 kcmil	1/0—3/0

(D) Load-Side Bonding Jumper Sizing. Bonding jumpers on the load side of feeder and branch-circuit overcurrent protection devices are sized in accordance with 250.122, based on the rating of the circuit overcurrent protection device. ▶Figure 250–192

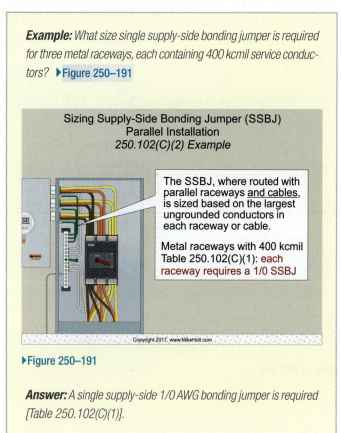

Example: What size single supply-side bonding jumper is required for three metal raceways, each containing 400 kcmil service conductors? ▶Figure 250–191

▶Figure 250–191

Answer: A single supply-side 1/0 AWG bonding jumper is required [Table 250.102(C)(1)].

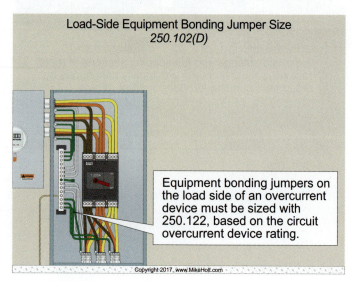

▶Figure 250–192

Grounding and Bonding | 250.104

Example: What size equipment bonding jumper is required for each metal raceway where the circuit conductors are protected by a 1,200A overcurrent protection device? ▶Figure 250–193

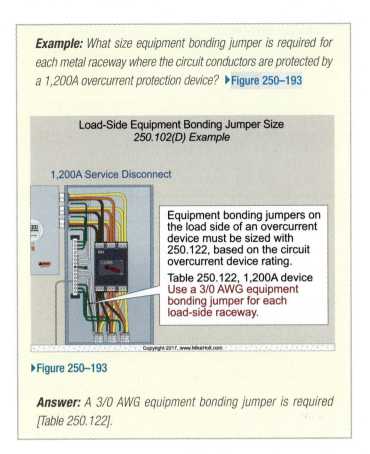

▶Figure 250–193

Answer: A 3/0 AWG equipment bonding jumper is required [Table 250.122].

If a single bonding jumper is used to bond two or more raceways, it must be sized in accordance with 250.122, based on the rating of the largest circuit overcurrent protection device. ▶Figure 250–194

▶Figure 250–194

(E) Installation of Bonding Jumpers.

(1) Inside Raceway. Bonding jumpers installed inside a raceway must be identified in accordance with 250.119 and must terminate to the enclosure in accordance with 250.148.

(2) Outside Raceway. Bonding jumpers installed outside a raceway must be routed with the raceway and can't exceed 6 ft in length.
▶Figure 250–195

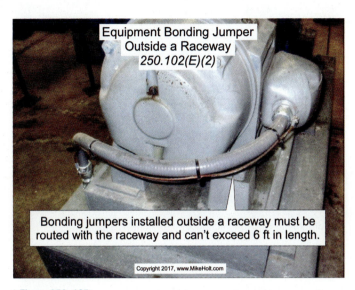

▶Figure 250–195

250.104 Bonding of Piping Systems and Exposed Structural Metal

Author's Comment:

- To remove dangerous voltage on metal parts from a ground fault, electrically conductive metal water piping systems, metal sprinkler piping, metal gas piping, as well as exposed structural metal members likely to become energized, must be connected to an effective ground-fault current path [250.4(A)(4)].

(A) Metal Water Piping System. Metal water piping systems that are interconnected to form a mechanically and electrically continuous system must be bonded in accordance with 250.104(A)(1), (A)(2), or (A)(3).

(1) Buildings Supplied by a Service. The metal water piping system, including the metal sprinkler water piping system, of a building supplied with service conductors must be bonded to any of the following:
▶Figure 250–196

250.104 | Grounding and Bonding

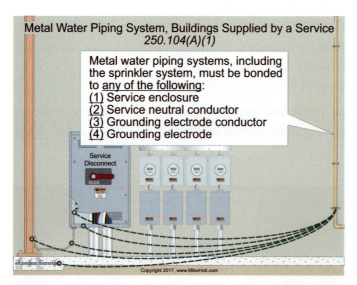

▶Figure 250–196

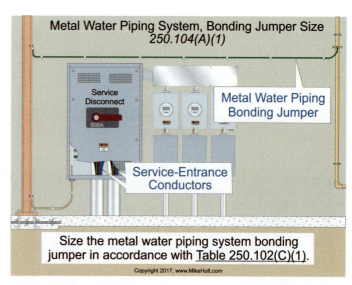

▶Figure 250–197

(1) Service equipment enclosure,

(2) Neutral at service equipment,

(3) Grounding electrode conductor if of sufficient size, or

(4) One of the grounding electrodes of the grounding electrode system if the grounding electrode conductor or bonding jumper to the electrode is of sufficient size.

The bonding jumper must be copper where within 18 in. of the surface of earth [250.64(A)], must be adequately protected if exposed to physical damage [250.64(B)], and all points of attachment must be accessible. A ferrous metal raceway containing a grounding electrode conductor must be made electrically continuous by bonding each end of the raceway to the grounding electrode conductor [250.64(E)], so it's best to use nonmetallic conduit.

The metal water piping system bonding jumper must be sized in accordance with Table 250.102(C)(1), based on the cross-sectional area of the ungrounded service conductors. ▶Figure 250–197

Example: What size bonding jumper is required for a metal water piping system, if the 300 kcmil service conductors are paralleled in two raceways? ▶Figure 250–198

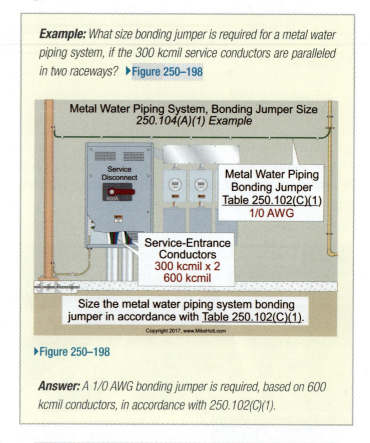

▶Figure 250–198

Answer: A 1/0 AWG bonding jumper is required, based on 600 kcmil conductors, in accordance with 250.102(C)(1).

Author's Comment:

- If hot and cold metal water pipes are electrically connected, only one bonding jumper is required, either to the cold or hot water pipe. Bonding isn't required for isolated sections of metal water piping connected to a nonmetallic water piping system. ▶Figure 250–199

Grounding and Bonding | 250.104

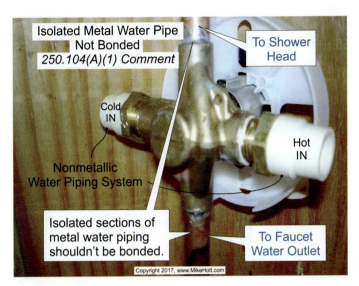

▶Figure 250–199

(a) The equipment grounding terminal of the building disconnect enclosure,

(b) The feeder equipment grounding conductor, or

(c) One of the building grounding electrodes of the grounding electrode system if the grounding electrode or bonding jumper to the electrode is of sufficient size.

The bonding jumper is sized to Table 250.102(C)(1), based on the cross-sectional area of the feeder conductor.

(B) Other Metal-Piping Systems. Metal-piping systems in or attached to a building that are likely to become energized must be bonded to one of the following:

(1) Equipment grounding conductor for the circuit that's likely to energize the piping system ▶Figure 250–201

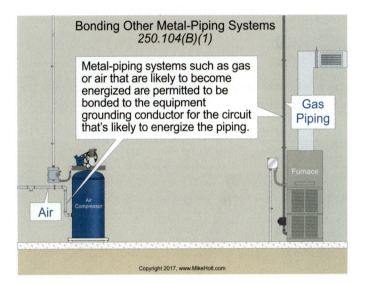

▶Figure 250–201

(2) Multiple Occupancy Building. When a metal water piping system in an individual occupancy is metallically isolated from other occupancies, the metal water piping system for that occupancy can be bonded to the equipment grounding terminal of the occupancy's switchgear, switchboard, or panelboard. The bonding jumper must be sized based on the rating of the circuit overcurrent protection device sized in accordance with 250.122 [250.102(D)]. ▶Figure 250–200

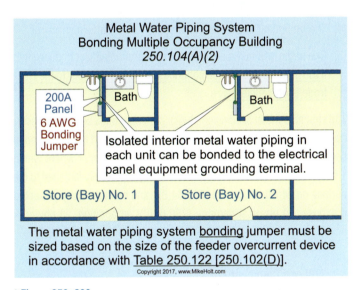

▶Figure 250–200

(3) Buildings Supplied by a Feeder. The metal water piping system of a building supplied by a feeder must be bonded to one of the following:

(2) Service equipment enclosure

(3) Neutral conductor at the service equipment

(4) Grounding electrode conductor, if of sufficient size

(5) One of the grounding electrodes of the grounding electrode system if the grounding electrode conductor or bonding jumper to the electrode is of sufficient size

The bonding jumper is sized to Table 250.122, based on the cross-sectional area of the feeder conductor, and equipment grounding conductors are sized to Table 250.122 using the rating of the circuit that's likely to energize the piping system(s). The points of attachment of the bonding jumper(s) must be accessible.

250.104 | Grounding and Bonding

Note 1: Bonding all piping and metal air ducts within the premises will provide additional safety. ▶Figure 250–202

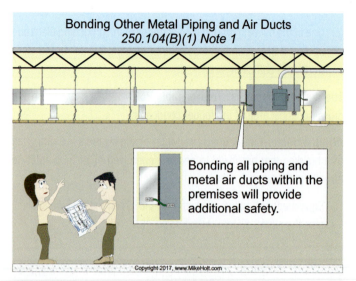

▶Figure 250–202

Note 2: The *National Fuel Gas Code*, NFPA 54, Section 7.13 contains further information about bonding gas piping. ▶Figure 250–203

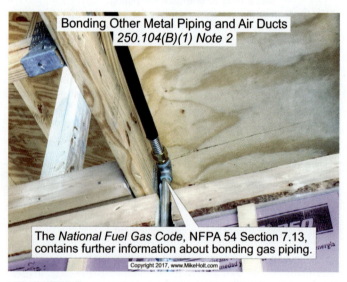

▶Figure 250–203

Author's Comment:

- Informational Notes in the *NEC* are for information purposes only and aren't enforceable as a requirement of the *Code* [90.5(C)].

(C) Structural Metal. Exposed structural metal that's interconnected to form a metal building frame and is likely to become energized must be bonded to any of the following: ▶Figure 250–204

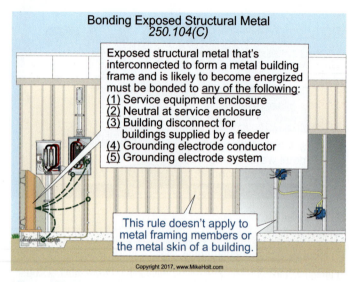

▶Figure 250–204

(1) The service equipment enclosure,

(2) The neutral at the service equipment,

(3) The building disconnect enclosure for buildings supplied by a feeder,

(4) The grounding electrode conductor where of sufficient size, or

(5) One of the grounding electrodes of the grounding electrode system if the grounding electrode conductor or bonding jumper to the electrode is of sufficient size.

The structural metal bonding conductor or jumper must be sized in accordance with Table 250.102(C)(1), based on the area of the ungrounded supply conductors. The bonding jumper must be copper where within 18 in. of the surface of the earth [250.64(A)], be securely fastened to the surface on which it's carried [250.64(B)], and be adequately protected if exposed to physical damage [250.64(B)]. In addition, all points of attachment must be accessible, except as permitted in 250.68(A) Ex.

Author's Comment:

- This rule doesn't require the bonding of sheet metal framing members (studs) or the metal skin of a wood-frame building.

(D) Separately Derived Systems. Metal water piping systems and structural metal that's interconnected to form a building frame must be bonded to the separately derived system in accordance with 250.104(D)(1) through (D)(3).

(1) Metal Water Pipe. If metal water piping systems exists in the area served by a separately derived system, it must be bonded to the neutral point of the separately derived system where the grounding electrode conductor is connected. ▶Figure 250–205

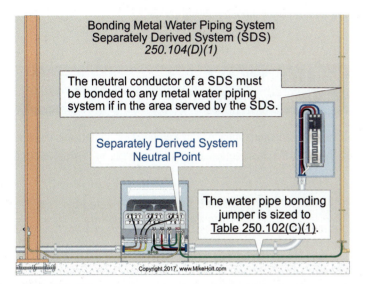

▶Figure 250–205

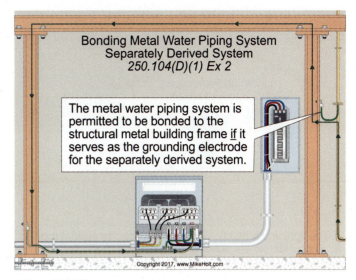

▶Figure 250–206

The bonding jumper must be sized in accordance with Table 250.102(C)(1), based on the area of the ungrounded conductor of the derived system.

Ex 2: The metal water piping system can be bonded to the structural metal building frame if it serves as the grounding electrode [250.52(A)(1)] for the separately derived system. ▶Figure 250–206

(2) Structural Metal. Exposed structural metal that's interconnected to form the building frame located in the area served by a separately derived system must be bonded to the neutral conductor where the grounding electrode conductor is connected at the separately derived system.

The bonding jumper must be sized in accordance with Table 250.102(C)(1), based on the largest ungrounded conductor of the separately derived system.

Ex 1: Bonding to the separately derived system isn't required if the metal serves as the grounding electrode [250.52(A)(2)] for the separately derived system.

(3) Common Grounding Electrode Conductor. If a common grounding electrode conductor is installed for multiple separately derived systems as permitted by 250.30(A)(6), and exposed structural metal that's interconnected to form the building frame or interior metal piping exists in the area served by the separately derived system, the metal piping and the structural metal member can be bonded to the common grounding electrode conductor in the area served by the separately derived system.

Ex: A separate bonding jumper from each derived system to metal water piping and to structural metal members isn't required if the metal water piping and the structural metal members in the area served by the separately derived system are bonded to the common grounding electrode conductor.

250.106 Lightning Protection System

When a lightning protection system is installed in accordance with NFPA 780, the lightning protection electrode system must be bonded to the building grounding electrode system. ▶Figure 250–207

Note 1: See NFPA 780—*Standard for the Installation of Lightning Protection Systems*, which contains detailed information on grounding, bonding, and side-flash distance from lightning protection systems.

Note 2: To minimize the likelihood of arcing between metal parts because of induced voltage, metal raceways, enclosures, and other metal parts of electrical equipment may require bonding or spacing from the lightning protection conductors in accordance with NFPA 780—*Standard for the Installation of Lightning Protection Systems.* ▶Figure 250–208

250.110 | Grounding and Bonding

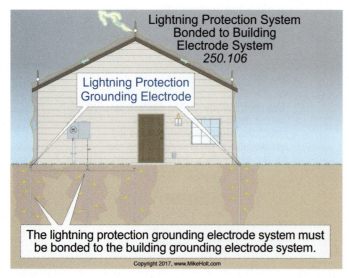

▶Figure 250–207

(2) Located in a wet or damp location

(3) In electrical contact with metal

(4) In a hazardous (classified) location [Articles 500 through 517]

(5) Supplied by a wiring method that provides an equipment grounding conductor

(6) Supplied by a 277V or 480V circuit

Ex 3: Listed double-insulated equipment isn't required to be connected to the circuit equipment grounding conductor.

250.112 Specific Equipment Fastened in Place or Connected by Permanent Wiring Methods

To remove dangerous voltage from a ground fault, metal parts must be connected to the circuit equipment grounding conductor. ▶Figure 250–209

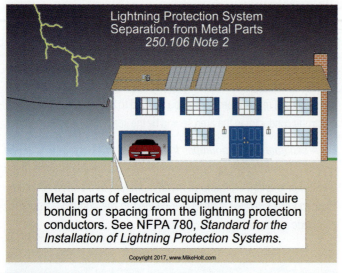

▶Figure 250–208

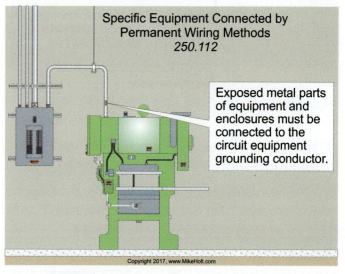

▶Figure 250–209

Part VI. Equipment Grounding and Equipment Grounding Conductors

250.110 Fixed Equipment Connected by Permanent Wiring Methods—General

Exposed metal parts of fixed equipment likely to become energized must be connected to the circuit equipment grounding conductor where the equipment is:

(1) Within 8 ft vertically or 5 ft horizontally from the surface of the earth or a grounded metal object

(I) Low-Voltage Circuits. Equipment supplied by circuits operating at less than 50V isn't required to be connected to the circuit equipment grounding conductor. ▶Figure 250–210

250.114 Cord-and-Plug-Connected Equipment

To remove dangerous voltage from a ground fault, metal parts must be connected to the circuit equipment grounding conductor. ▶Figure 250–211

Grounding and Bonding | 250.118

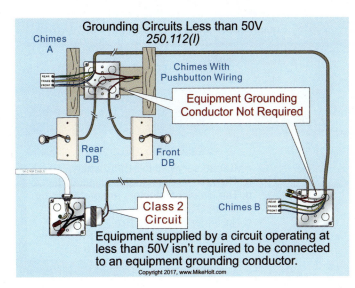
▶Figure 250–210

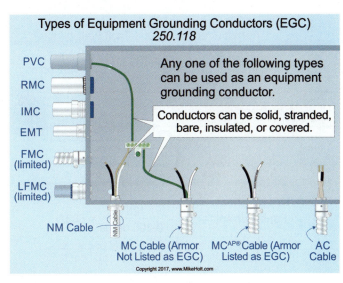
▶Figure 250–212

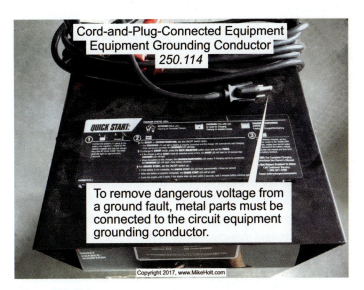
▶Figure 250–211

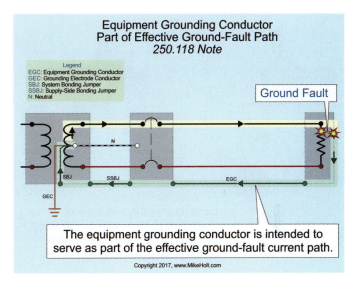
▶Figure 250–213

Ex: Listed double-insulated equipment isn't required to be connected to the circuit equipment grounding conductor.

250.118 Types of Equipment Grounding Conductors

An equipment grounding conductor can be any one or a combination of the following: ▶Figure 250–212

Note: The equipment grounding conductor is intended to serve as part of the effective ground-fault current path. See 250.2. ▶Figure 250–213

Author's Comment:

- The effective ground-fault path is an intentionally constructed low-impedance conductive path designed to carry fault current from the point of a ground fault on a wiring system to the electrical supply source. Its purpose is to quickly remove dangerous voltage from a ground fault by opening the circuit overcurrent protection device [250.2]. ▶Figure 250–214

(1) An equipment grounding conductor of the wire type can be a bare or insulated copper or aluminum conductor. ▶Figure 250–215

250.118 | Grounding and Bonding

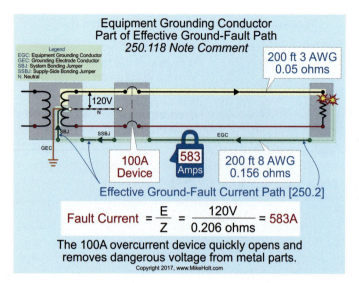

▶Figure 250–214

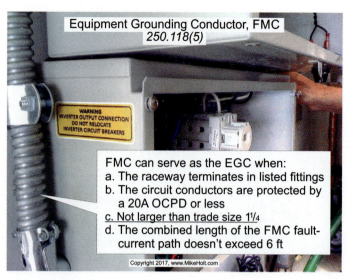

▶Figure 250–216

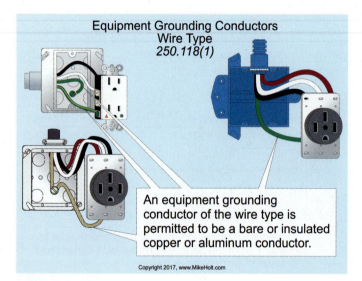

▶Figure 250–215

(2) Rigid metal conduit can serve as an equipment grounding conductor.

(3) Intermediate metal conduit can serve as an equipment grounding conductor.

(4) Electrical metallic tubing can serve as an equipment grounding conductor.

(5) Listed flexible metal conduit (FMC) can serve as an equipment grounding conductor where: ▶Figure 250–216

   a. The raceway terminates in listed fittings.

   b. The circuit conductors are protected by an overcurrent protection device rated 20A or less.

   c. The size of the flexible metal conduit doesn't exceed trade size 1¼.

   d. The combined length of the flexible conduit in the same ground-fault current path doesn't exceed 6 ft.

   e. If flexibility is required to minimize the transmission of vibration from equipment or to provide flexibility for equipment that requires movement after installation, an equipment grounding conductor of the wire type must be installed with the circuit conductors in accordance with 250.102(E), and it must be sized in accordance with 250.122, based on the rating of the circuit overcurrent protection device. ▶Figure 250–217

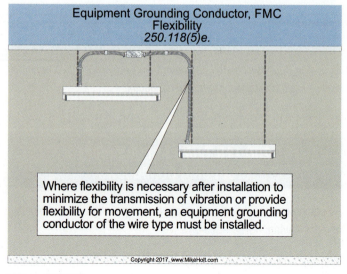

▶Figure 250–217

(6) Listed liquidtight flexible metal conduit (LFMC) can serve as an equipment grounding conductor where: ▶Figure 250–218

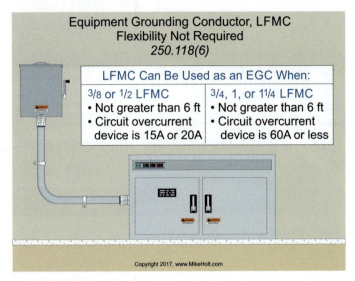

▶Figure 250–218

a. The raceway terminates in listed fittings.

b. For ⅜ in. through ½ in., the circuit conductors are protected by an overcurrent protection device rated 20A or less.

c. For ¾ in. through 1¼ in., the circuit conductors are protected by an overcurrent protection device rated 60A or less.

d. The combined length of the flexible conduit in the same ground-fault current path doesn't exceed 6 ft.

e. If flexibility is required to minimize the transmission of vibration from equipment or to provide flexibility for equipment that requires movement after installation, an equipment grounding conductor of the wire type must be installed with the circuit conductors in accordance with 250.102(E), and it must be sized in accordance with 250.122, based on the rating of the circuit overcurrent protection device.

(8) The sheath of Type AC cable containing an aluminum bonding strip can serve as an equipment grounding conductor. ▶Figure 250–219

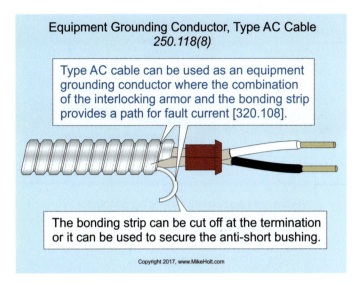

▶Figure 250–219

Author's Comment:

- The internal aluminum bonding strip isn't an equipment grounding conductor, but it allows the interlocked armor to serve as an equipment grounding conductor because it reduces the impedance of the armored spirals to ensure that a ground fault will be cleared. It's the aluminum bonding strip in combination with the cable armor that creates the circuit equipment grounding conductor. Once the bonding strip exits the cable, it can be cut off because it no longer serves any purpose.

- The effective ground-fault current path must be maintained by the use of fittings specifically listed for Type AC cable [320.40]. See 300.12, 300.15, and 320.100.

(9) The copper sheath of Type MI cable can serve as an equipment grounding conductor.

(10) Type MC cable

a. The interlock type cable that contains an insulated or uninsulated equipment grounding conductor in accordance with 250.118(1) can serve as an equipment grounding conductor. ▶Figure 250–220

b. The combined metallic sheath and uninsulated equipment grounding/bonding conductor of interlocked metal that's listed and identified as an equipment grounding conductor can serve as an equipment grounding conductor. ▶Figure 250–221

250.118 | Grounding and Bonding

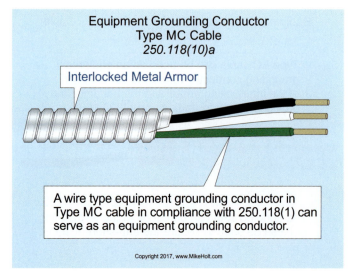

▶Figure 250–220

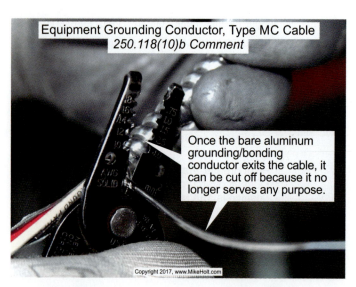

▶Figure 250–222

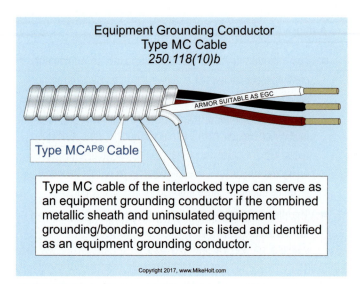

▶Figure 250–221

Author's Comment:

- Once the bare aluminum grounding/bonding conductor exits the cable, it can be cut off because it no longer serves any purpose. The effective ground-fault current path must be maintained by the use of fittings specifically listed for Type MC$^{AP®}$ cable [330.40]. See 300.12, 300.15, and 330.100.
  ▶Figure 250–222

c. The metallic sheath of the smooth or corrugated tube-type MC cable that's listed and identified as an equipment grounding conductor can serve as an equipment grounding conductor.

(11) Metal cable trays can serve as an equipment grounding conductor if continuous maintenance and supervision ensure only qualified persons will service the cable tray, with cable tray and fittings identified for grounding and the cable tray, fittings [392.10], and raceways are bonded together using bolted mechanical connectors or bonding jumpers sized and installed in accordance with 250.102 [392.60]. ▶Figure 250–223

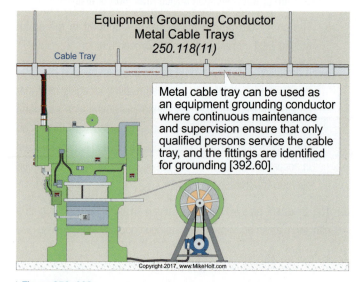

▶Figure 250–223

(13) Listed electrically continuous metal raceways, such as metal wireways [Article 376] or strut-type channel raceways [384.60] can serve as an equipment grounding conductor. ▶Figure 250–224

Grounding and Bonding | 250.119

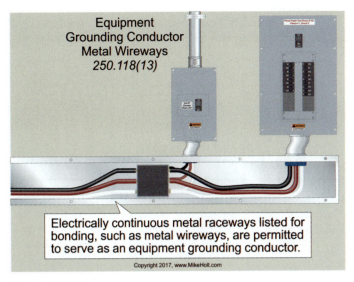

▶Figure 250–224

(14) Surface metal raceways listed for grounding [Article 386] can serve as an equipment grounding conductor.

250.119 Identification of Equipment Grounding Conductors

Unless required to be insulated, equipment grounding conductors can be bare or covered. Insulated equipment grounding conductors 6 AWG and smaller must have a continuous outer finish that's either green or green with one or more yellow stripes. ▶Figure 250–225

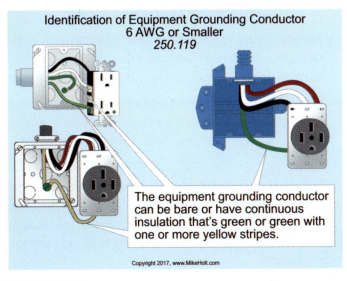

▶Figure 250–225

Conductors with insulation that's green, or green with one or more yellow stripes, aren't permitted be used for an ungrounded or neutral conductor. ▶Figure 250–226

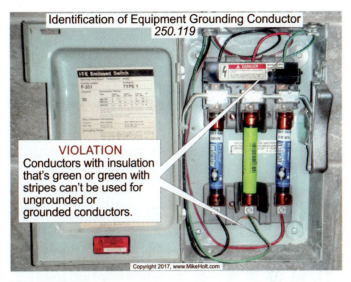

▶Figure 250–226

Author's Comment:

- The *NEC* neither requires nor prohibits the use of the color green for the identification of grounding electrode conductors. ▶Figure 250–227

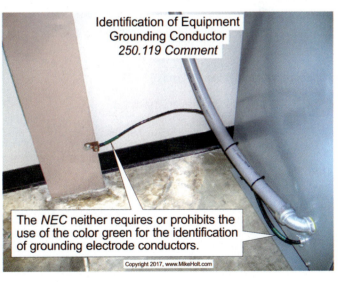

▶Figure 250–227

250.120 | Grounding and Bonding

Ex 3: Conductors with green insulation can be used as ungrounded signal conductors for traffic signal control and traffic signal indicating heads. The circuit must still include an equipment grounding conductor, and if it's of the wire type it must be bare or green with one or more yellow stripes.

(A) Conductors 4 AWG and Larger.

(1) Identified if Accessible. Insulated equipment grounding conductors 4 AWG and larger can be permanently reidentified at the time of installation at every point where the conductor is accessible. ▶Figure 250–228

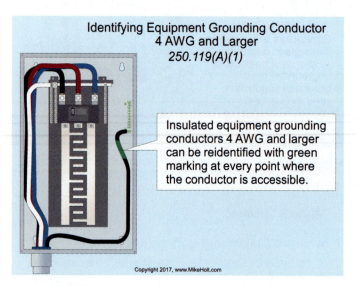

▶Figure 250–228

Ex: Identification of equipment grounding conductors 4 AWG and larger in conduit bodies isn't required.

(2) Identification Method. ▶Figure 250–229

    a. Removing the insulation at termination

    b. Coloring the insulation green at termination

    c. Marking the insulation at termination with green tape or green adhesive labels

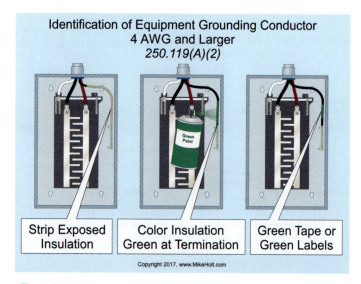

▶Figure 250–229

250.120 Equipment Grounding Conductor Installation

An equipment grounding conductor must be installed as follows:

(A) Raceway, Cable Trays, Cable Armor, Cablebus, or Cable Sheaths. If it consists of a raceway, cable tray, cable armor, cablebus framework, or cable sheath, fittings for joints and terminations must be made tight using suitable tools.

(B) Aluminum Conductors. Aluminum equipment grounding conductors must comply with the following:

(1) Bare or covered aluminum equipment grounding conductors are not permitted to be in contact with masonry or earth.

(2) Aluminum equipment grounding conductors within 18 in. of the earth are permitted to terminate within listed enclosures identified for outdoor use.

(3) Aluminum equipment grounding conductors located outdoors must be insulated when within 18 in. of the earth. The terminal must be listed as a sealed wire-connector system for grounding and bonding equipment.

(C) Equipment Grounding Conductors Smaller Than 6 AWG. If not routed with circuit conductors as permitted in 250.130(C) and 250.134(B) Ex 2, equipment grounding conductors smaller than 6 AWG must be installed within a raceway or cable if subject to physical damage. ▶Figure 250–230

Grounding and Bonding | 250.122

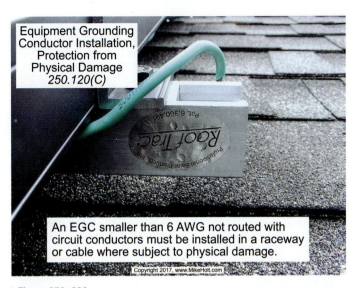

▶Figure 250–230

250.121 Use of Equipment Grounding Conductors

An equipment grounding conductor isn't permitted to be used as a grounding electrode conductor. ▶Figure 250–231

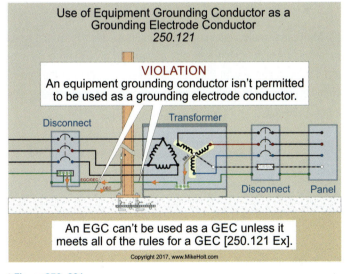

▶Figure 250–231

Ex: Equipment grounding conductors of the wire type can be used as a grounding electrode conductor provided they meet all of the rules for both.

250.122 Sizing Equipment Grounding Conductor

(A) General. Equipment grounding conductors of the wire type must be sized not smaller than shown in Table 250.122, based on the rating of the circuit overcurrent protection device; however, the circuit equipment grounding conductor isn't required to be larger than the circuit conductors. ▶Figure 250–232 and ▶Figure 250–233

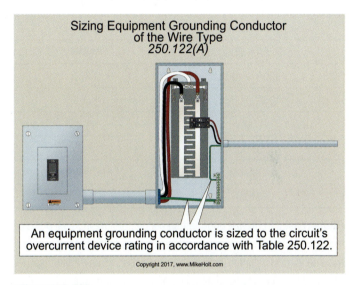

▶Figure 250–232

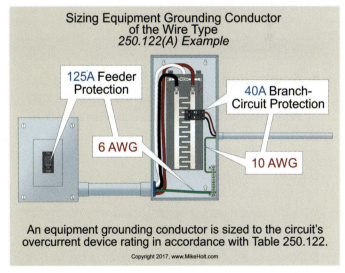

▶Figure 250–233

250.122 | Grounding and Bonding

Table 250.122 Sizing Equipment Grounding Conductor

Overcurrent Protection Device Rating	Copper Conductor
15A	14 AWG
20A	12 AWG
25A—60A	10 AWG
70A—100A	8 AWG
110A—200A	6 AWG
225A—300A	4 AWG
350A—400A	3 AWG
450A—500A	2 AWG
600A	1 AWG
700A—800A	1/0 AWG
1,000A	2/0 AWG
1,200A	3/0 AWG

(B) Increased in Size. If ungrounded conductors are increased in size for any reason from the minimum size that has sufficient ampacity for the intended installation before the application of any adjustment or correction factor(s), wire-type equipment grounding conductors must be at least proportionately increased in size according to the circular mil area of the ungrounded conductors.

Author's Comment:

- Ungrounded conductors are sometimes increased in size to accommodate conductor voltage drop, harmonic current heating, short-circuit rating, or simply for future capacity.

Example: If the ungrounded conductors for a 40A circuit (with 75°C terminals) are increased in size from 8 AWG to 6 AWG due to voltage drop, the circuit equipment grounding conductor must be increased in size from 10 AWG to what size? ▶Figure 250–234

Solution: The circuit equipment grounding conductor must be increased to size 8 AWG.

Conductor Size = 10,380 Cmil × 1.59
Conductor Size = 16,504 Cmil

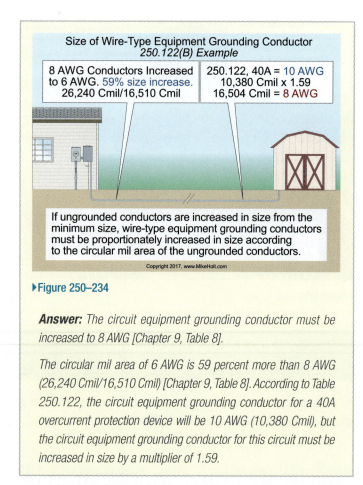

▶Figure 250–234

Answer: The circuit equipment grounding conductor must be increased to 8 AWG [Chapter 9, Table 8].

The circular mil area of 6 AWG is 59 percent more than 8 AWG (26,240 Cmil/16,510 Cmil) [Chapter 9, Table 8]. According to Table 250.122, the circuit equipment grounding conductor for a 40A overcurrent protection device will be 10 AWG (10,380 Cmil), but the circuit equipment grounding conductor for this circuit must be increased in size by a multiplier of 1.59.

(C) Multiple Circuits. When multiple circuits are installed in the same raceway, cable, or cable tray, one equipment grounding conductor sized in accordance with 250.122, based on the rating of the largest circuit overcurrent protection device is sufficient. ▶Figure 250–235 and ▶Figure 250–236

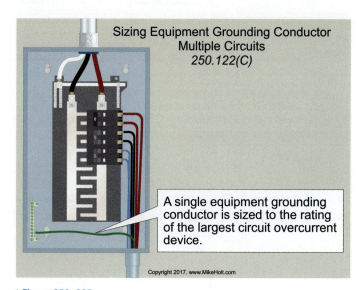

▶Figure 250–235

Grounding and Bonding | 250.122

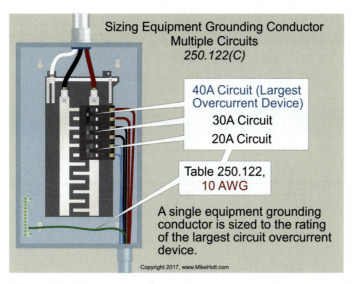

▶Figure 250–236

(D) Motor Branch Circuits.

(1) General. The equipment grounding conductor of the wire type must be sized in accordance with Table 250.122, based on the rating of the motor circuit branch-circuit short-circuit and ground-fault overcurrent protection device, but this conductor isn't required to be larger than the circuit conductors [250.122(A)]. ▶Figure 250–237

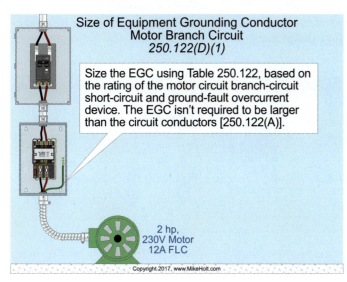

▶Figure 250–237

Example: What size equipment grounding conductor of the wire type is required for a 14 AWG motor branch circuit [430.22], protected with a 2-pole, 30A circuit breaker in accordance with 430.22 and 430.52(C)(1)? ▶Figure 250–238

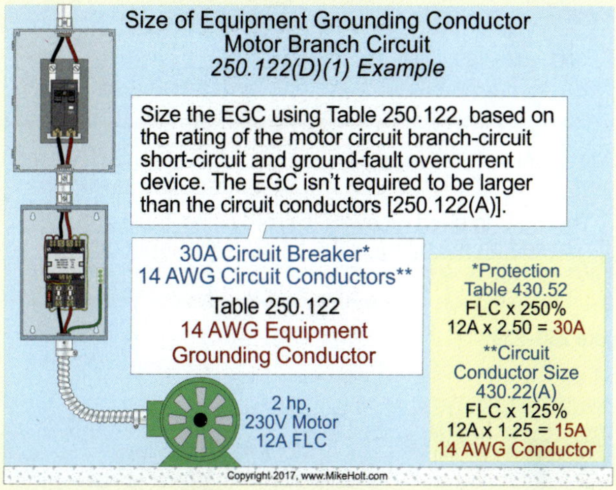

▶Figure 250–238

Answer: The equipment grounding conductor isn't required to be larger than the 14 AWG motor branch circuit conductors [250.122(D)(1) and 250.122(A)].

(F) Parallel Runs. If circuit conductors are installed in parallel as permitted by 310.10(H), an equipment grounding conductor must be installed for each parallel conductor set in accordance with the following:

(1) Raceways or Cable Trays.

(a) Parallel Feeder Runs in a Single Raceway or Cable Tray. The single wire-type equipment grounding conductor is required in each raceway or cable tray. It must be sized in accordance with Table 250.122, based on the rating of the circuit overcurrent protection device.

(b) Parallel Feeder Runs in Multiple Raceways. The equipment grounding conductor in each parallel run raceway must be sized in accordance with Table 250.122, based on the rating of the feeder overcurrent protection device. ▶Figure 250–239 and ▶Figure 250–240

(2) Parallel Feeder Runs Using Multiconductor Cables.

(a) Multiconductor cables used in parallel must have the equipment grounding conductors of all cables electrically paralleled with each other.

250.122 | Grounding and Bonding

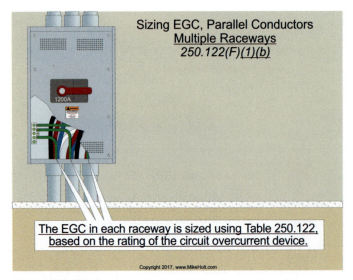

▶Figure 250–239

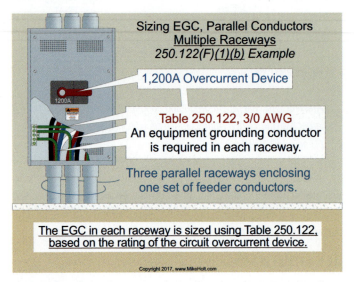

▶Figure 250–240

(b) Parallel multiconductor cables in a single raceway or cable tray are permitted to have a single equipment grounding conductor connected to the equipment grounding conductors within the multiconductor cables. This single equipment grounding conductor must be sized in accordance with 250.122, based on the rating of the feeder overcurrent protection device.

(c) Equipment grounding conductors installed in cable trays must comply with 392.10(B)(1)(c).

(d) Parallel multiconductor cables not installed in a raceway or cable tray must have an equipment grounding conductor of the wire type in each cable sized in accordance with 250.122, based on the rating of the circuit overcurrent protection device. ▶Figure 250–241

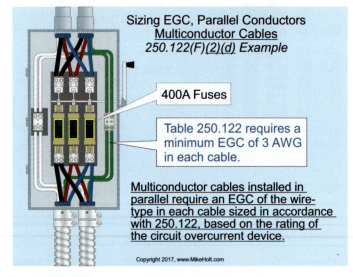

▶Figure 250–241

(G) Feeder Tap Conductors. Equipment grounding conductors for feeder taps must be sized in accordance with Table 250.122, based on the ampere rating of the overcurrent protection device ahead of the feeder, but in no case is it required to be larger than the feeder tap conductors. ▶Figure 250–242

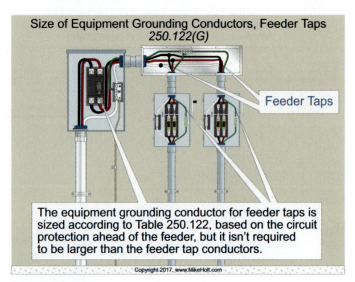

▶Figure 250–242

Part VII. Methods of Equipment Grounding

250.130 Equipment Grounding Conductor Connections

(C) Nongrounding Receptacle Replacement or Branch-Circuit Extension. If a grounding-type receptacle is installed or a branch circuit extension is made from an outlet box that doesn't contain an equipment grounding conductor, the grounding contacts of a grounding-type receptacle must be connected to any of the following: ▶Figure 250–243 and ▶Figure 250–244

(1) The grounding electrode system [250.50]

(2) The grounding electrode conductor

(3) The panelboard equipment grounding terminal

(4) An equipment grounding conductor that's part of a different circuit, if both circuits originate from the same panel

(5) The service neutral conductor

Note: A grounding-type receptacle can replace a nongrounding-type receptacle, without having the grounding terminal connected to an equipment grounding conductor, if the receptacle is GFCI protected and marked in accordance with 406.4(D)(2).

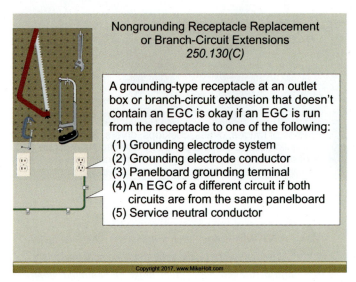

▶Figure 250–243

250.134 Equipment Connected by Permanent Wiring Methods

Except as permitted for services or separately derived systems [250.142(A)], metal parts of equipment, raceways, and enclosures must be connected to an equipment grounding conductor by any of the following methods:

(A) Equipment Grounding Conductor Types. By connecting to one of the equipment grounding conductors identified in 250.118.

(B) With Circuit Conductors. If an equipment grounding conductor of the wire type is installed, it must be in the same raceway, cable tray, trench, cable, or flexible cord with the circuit conductors in accordance with 300.3(B). ▶Figure 250–245

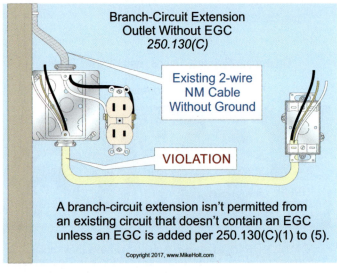

▶Figure 250–244

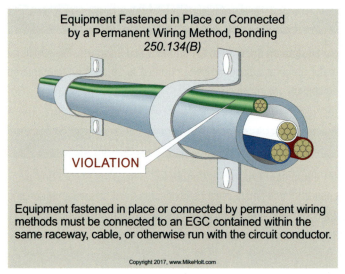

▶Figure 250–245

250.136 | Grounding and Bonding

Author's Comment:

- Conductors of a circuit must be installed in the same raceway, cable, trench, cord, or cable tray to minimize induction heating of ferrous metal raceways and enclosures, and to maintain a low-impedance ground-fault current path [250.4(A)(3)].

Ex 1: As provided in 250.130(C), the equipment grounding conductor is permitted to be run separately from the circuit conductors.

Ex 2: For dc circuits, the equipment grounding conductor is permitted to be run separately from the circuit conductors. ▶Figure 250–246

▶Figure 250–246

250.136 Equipment Considered Grounded

(A) Equipment Secured to Grounded Metal Supports. The structural metal frame of a building isn't permitted to be used as the required equipment grounding conductor.

250.138 Cord-and-Plug-Connected

(A) Equipment Grounding Conductor. Metal parts of cord-and-plug-connected equipment must be connected to an equipment grounding conductor that terminates to a grounding-type attachment plug.

250.140 Ranges, Ovens, and Clothes Dryers

The frames of electric ranges, wall-mounted ovens, counter-mounted cooking units, clothes dryers, and outlet boxes that are part of the circuit for these appliances must be connected to the equipment grounding conductor [250.134(A)]. ▶Figure 250–247

▶Figure 250–247

⚡ **CAUTION:** Ranges, dryers, and ovens have their metal cases connected to the neutral conductor at the factory. This neutral-to-case connection must be removed when these appliances are installed in new construction, and a 4-wire flexible cord and receptacle must be used [250.142(B)]. ▶Figure 250–248

▶Figure 250–248

Ex: For existing installations if an equipment grounding conductor isn't present in the outlet box, the frames of electric ranges, wall-mounted ovens, counter-mounted cooking units, clothes dryers, and outlet boxes that are part of the circuit for these appliances may be connected to the neutral conductor. ▶Figure 250–249

▶Figure 250–249

250.142 Use of Neutral Conductor for Equipment Grounding (Bonding)

(A) Supply-Side Equipment.

(1) Service Equipment. The neutral conductor can be used as the circuit equipment grounding conductor on the supply side or within the enclosure of the service disconnecting means in accordance with 250.24(B). ▶Figure 250–250

(B) Load-Side Equipment. The neutral conductor isn't permitted to serve as an equipment grounding conductor on the load side of service equipment except as permitted for separately derived system transformers and generators in accordance with 250.30(A)(1). ▶Figure 250–251

Ex 1: In existing installations, the frames of ranges, wall-mounted ovens, counter-mounted cooking units, and clothes dryers can be connected to the neutral conductor in accordance with 250.140 Ex.

Ex 2: The neutral conductor can be connected to meter socket enclosures on the load side of the service disconnecting means if: ▶Figure 250–252

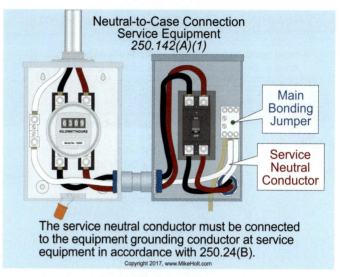

▶Figure 250–250

▶Figure 250–251

(1) Ground-fault protection isn't provided on service equipment,

(2) Meter socket enclosures are immediately adjacent to the service disconnect, and

(3) The neutral conductor is sized in accordance with 250.122, based on the ampere rating of the occupancy's feeder overcurrent protection device.

250.146 | Grounding and Bonding

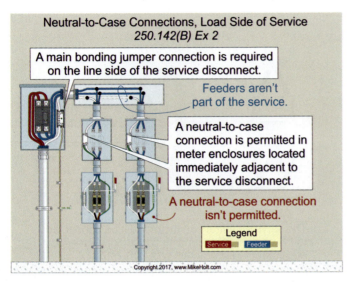

▶Figure 250–252

250.146 Connecting Receptacle Grounding Terminal to Metal Enclosure

Except as permitted for (A) through (D), an equipment bonding jumper sized in accordance with 250.122, based on the rating of the circuit overcurrent protection device, must connect the grounding terminal of a receptacle to a metal box. ▶Figure 250–253

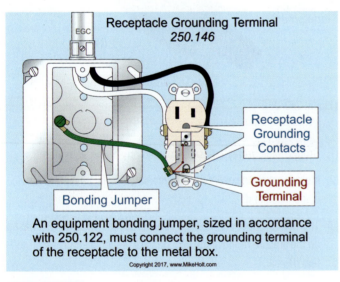

▶Figure 250–253

Author's Comment:

- The *NEC* doesn't restrict the position of the receptacle grounding terminal; it can be up, down, or sideways. *Code* proposals to specify the mounting position of receptacles have always been rejected. ▶Figure 250–254

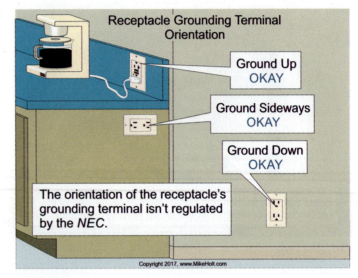

▶Figure 250–254

(A) Surface-Mounted Box. An equipment bonding jumper from a receptacle to a metal box that's surface mounted isn't required if there's direct metal-to-metal contact between the device yoke and the metal box. To ensure a suitable bonding path between the device yoke and a metal box, at least one of the insulating retaining washers on the yoke screw must be removed. ▶Figure 250–255

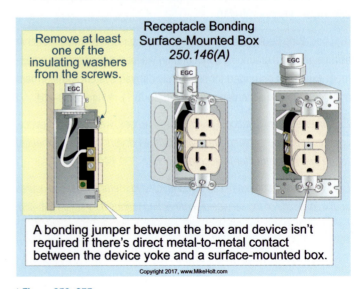

▶Figure 250–255

An equipment bonding jumper isn't required for receptacles attached to listed exposed work covers when the receptacle is attached to the cover with at least two fasteners that have a thread locking or screw or nut locking means, and the cover mounting holes are located on a flat non-raised portion of the cover. ▶Figure 250–256

(C) Floor Boxes. Listed floor boxes are designed to establish the bonding path between the device yoke and a metal box.

(D) Isolated Ground Receptacles. The grounding terminal of an isolated ground receptacle must be connected to an insulated equipment grounding conductor run with the circuit conductors. ▶Figure 250–258

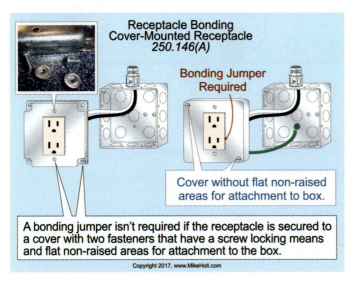

▶Figure 250–256

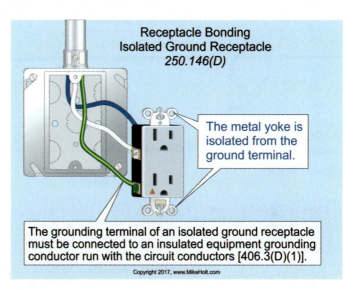

▶Figure 250–258

(B) Self-Grounding Receptacles. Receptacle yokes listed as self-grounding are designed to establish the equipment bonding between the device yoke and a metal box via the metal mounting screws. ▶Figure 250–257

The circuit equipment grounding conductor can pass through panelboards [408.40 Ex], boxes, wireways, or other enclosures without a connection to the enclosure [250.148 Ex].

> **Author's Comment:**
>
> ■ Type AC Cable—Type AC cable containing an insulated equipment grounding conductor of the wire type can be used to supply receptacles having insulated grounding terminals because the metal armor of the cable is listed as an equipment grounding conductor [250.118(8)]. ▶Figure 250–259
>
> ■ The armor assembly of interlocked Type MC^AP® cable with a 10 AWG bare aluminum grounding/bonding conductor running just below the metal armor is listed to serve as an equipment grounding conductor in accordance with 250.118(10)(b). ▶Figure 250–260

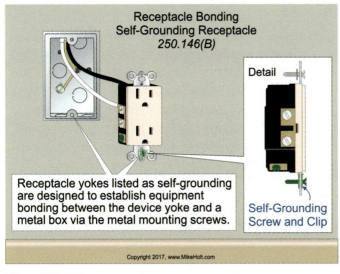

▶Figure 250–257

250.146 | Grounding and Bonding

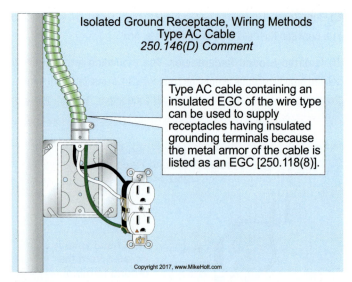
▶Figure 250–259

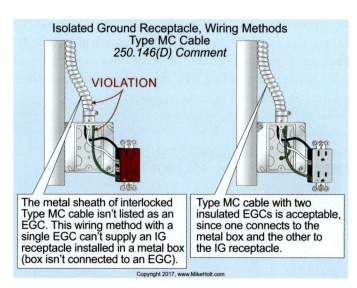
▶Figure 250–261

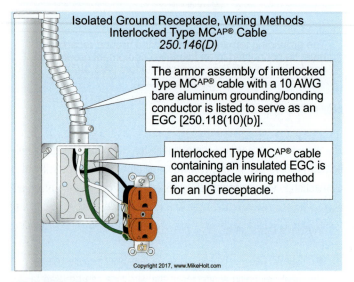
▶Figure 250–260

⚠ **CAUTION:** Type MC Cable. The metal armor sheath of interlocked Type MC cable containing an insulated equipment grounding conductor isn't listed as an equipment grounding conductor. Therefore, this wiring method with a single equipment grounding conductor can't supply an isolated ground receptacle installed in a metal box (because the box isn't connected to an equipment grounding conductor). However, Type MC cable with two insulated equipment grounding conductors is acceptable, since one equipment grounding conductor connects to the metal box and the other to the isolated ground receptacle. ▶Figure 250–261

Author's Comment:

- When should an isolated ground receptacle be installed and how should the isolated ground system be designed? These questions are design issues and must not be answered based on the *NEC* alone [90.1(A)]. In most cases, using isolated ground receptacles is a waste of money. For example, IEEE 1100—*Powering and Grounding Electronic Equipment (Emerald Book)* states, "The results from the use of the isolated ground method range from no observable effects, the desired effects, or worse noise conditions than when standard equipment bonding configurations are used to serve electronic load equipment [8.5.3.2]."

- In reality, few electrical installations truly require an isolated ground system. For those systems that can benefit from an isolated ground system, engineering opinions differ as to what's a proper design. Making matters worse—of those properly designed, few are correctly installed and even fewer are properly maintained. For more information on how to properly ground electronic equipment, go to: www.MikeHolt.com, click on the "Technical" link, and then visit the "Power Quality" page.

Grounding and Bonding | 250.148

250.148 Continuity and Attachment of Equipment Grounding Conductors in Metal Boxes

If circuit conductors are spliced or terminated on equipment within a box, all equipment grounding conductor associated with any of the spliced or terminated circuits must be connected together or to the metal box in accordance (A) through (E). ▶Figure 250–262

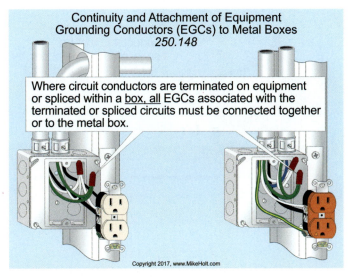

▶Figure 250–262

Ex: The circuit equipment grounding conductor for an isolated ground receptacle installed in accordance with 250.146(D) isn't required to terminate to a metal box. ▶Figure 250–263

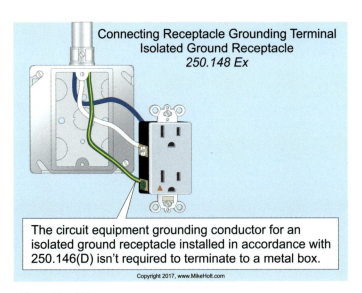

▶Figure 250–263

(A) Splicing. Equipment grounding conductors must be spliced together with a device identified for the purpose [110.14(B)]. ▶Figure 250–264

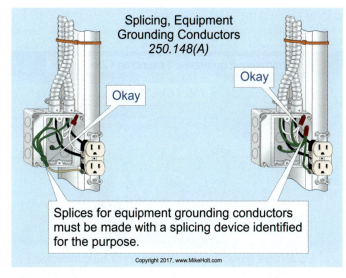

▶Figure 250–264

Author's Comment:

- Wire connectors of any color can be used with equipment grounding conductor splices, but green wire connectors can only be used with equipment grounding conductors since they're only tested for that application.

(B) Grounding Continuity. Equipment grounding conductors must terminate in a manner such that the disconnection or the removal of a receptacle, luminaire, or other device won't interrupt the grounding continuity. ▶Figure 250–265

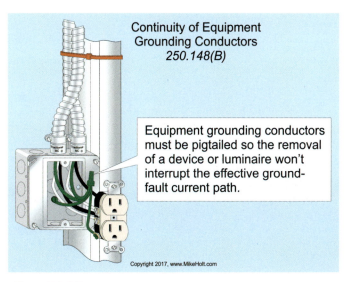

▶Figure 250–265

250.148 | Grounding and Bonding

(C) Metal Boxes. Terminating equipment grounding conductors within metal boxes must be with a grounding screw that's not used for any other purpose, a fitting listed for grounding, or a listed grounding device such as a ground clip. ▶Figure 250–266

Author's Comment:

- Equipment grounding conductors aren't permitted to terminate to a screw that secures a plaster ring. ▶Figure 250–267

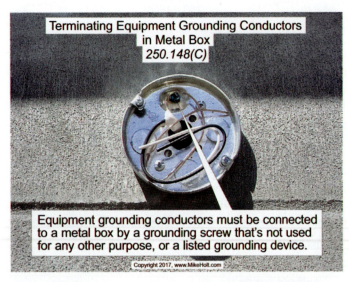

▶Figure 250–266

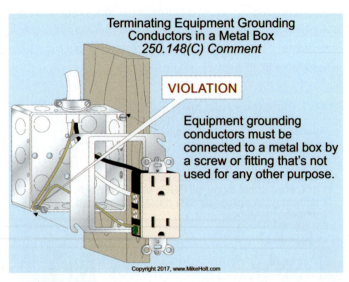

▶Figure 250–267

ARTICLE 285 — SURGE PROTECTIVE DEVICES (SPDs)

Introduction to Article 285—Surge Protective Devices (SPDs)

This article covers the general requirements, installation requirements, and connection requirements for surge protective devices (SPDs) rated 1kV or less that are permanently installed on premises wiring systems. The *NEC* doesn't require surge protective devices to be installed, but if they are, they must comply with this article.

Surge protective devices are designed to reduce transient voltages present on premises power distribution wiring and load-side equipment, particularly electronic equipment such as computers, telecommunications equipment, security systems, and electronic appliances.

These transient voltages can originate from several sources, including anything from lightning to laser printers. The best line of defense for all types of electronic equipment may be the installation of surge protective devices at the electrical service and source of power, as well as at the location of the utilization equipment. ▶Figure 285–1 and ▶Figure 285–2

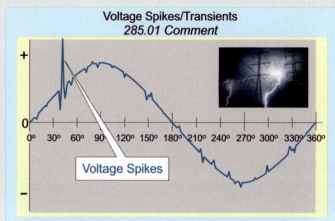

▶Figure 285–1

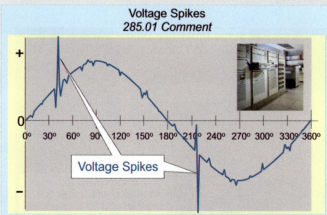

▶Figure 285–2

285.1 | Surge Protective Devices (SPDs)

The intent of a surge protection device is to limit transient voltages by diverting or limiting surge current and preventing continued flow of current while remaining capable of repeating these functions [Article 100]. ▶Figure 285–3

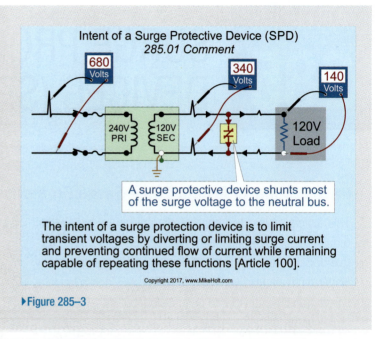

▶Figure 285–3

Part I. General

285.1 Scope

This article covers the installation and connection requirements for permanently installed surge protective devices not over 1,000V. ▶Figure 285–4

Note: Surge arresters rated 1,000V and less are known as Type 1 surge protective devices.

▶Figure 285–4

285.3 Uses Not Permitted

A surge protective device isn't permitted to be used in:

(1) Circuits that exceed 1,000V.

(2) Ungrounded systems, impedance grounded systems, or corner-grounded delta systems, unless listed specifically for use on these systems.

(3) If the voltage rating of the surge protective device is less than the maximum continuous phase-to-ground voltage available at the point of connection.

285.4 Number Required

If used, the surge protective device must be connected to each ungrounded conductor of the circuit. ▶Figure 285–5

285.6 Listing

Surge protective devices must be listed.

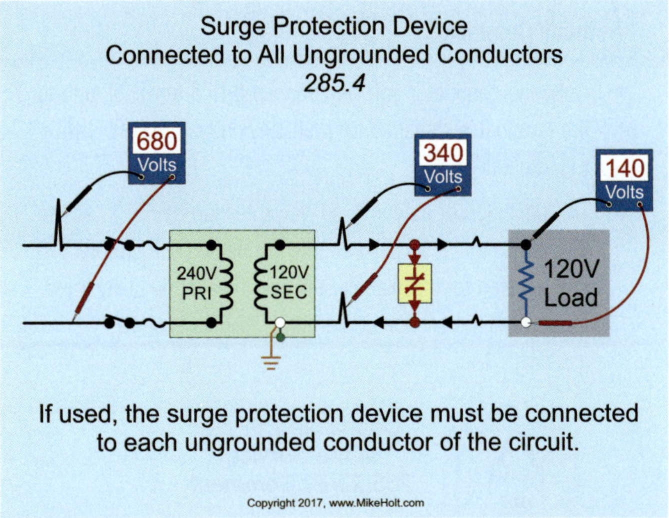

Surge Protective Devices (SPDs) | 285.23

▶Figure 285–5

Author's Comment:

- According to UL 1449, *Standard for Surge Protective Devices*, these units are intended to limit the maximum amplitude of transient voltage surges on power lines to specified values. They aren't intended to function as lightning arresters. The adequacy of the voltage suppression level to protect connected equipment from voltage surges hasn't been evaluated.

285.7 Short-Circuit Current Rating

Surge protective devices must be marked with short-circuit current rating, and they aren't permitted to be installed if the available fault current exceeds that rating. This short-circuit current marking requirement doesn't apply to receptacles containing surge protective device protection.

⚡ **WARNING:** *Surge protective devices of the series type are susceptible to failure at high fault currents. A hazardous condition is present if the surge protective device short-circuit current rating is less than the available fault current.*

Part II. Installation

285.11 Location

Surge protective devices can be located indoors or outdoors and be made inaccessible to unqualified persons, unless listed for installation in accessible locations.

285.12 Routing of Conductors

Surge protective device conductors aren't permitted to be any longer than necessary, and unnecessary bends must be avoided. ▶Figure 285–6

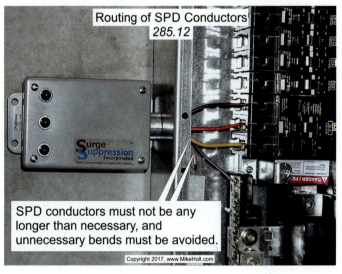

▶Figure 285–6

285.13 Type 4 and Other Component Type SPDs

Type 4 component assemblies and other component type SPDs can only be installed by the manufacturer.

Part III. Connecting Surge Protective Devices

285.23 Type 1 SPD—Line Side of Service Equipment

(A) Installation. Type 1 surge protective devices can be connected as follows:

(1) Supply side of service equipment [230.82(4)]. ▶Figure 285–7

(2) Load side of service equipment in accordance with 285.24.

285.23 | Surge Protective Devices (SPDs)

▶Figure 285–7

(2) Load side of service equipment in accordance with 285.24.

(B) Grounding. Type 1 surge protective devices located at service equipment must be connected to any of the following: ▶Figure 285–8

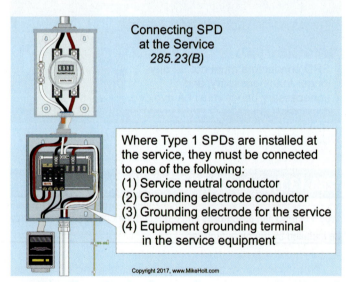

▶Figure 285–8

(1) Service neutral conductor,

(2) Grounding electrode conductor,

(3) Grounding electrode for the service, or

(4) Equipment grounding terminal in the service equipment.

Author's Comment:

- Only one conductor can be connected to a terminal, unless the terminal is identified for multiple conductors [110.14(A)]. ▶Figure 285–9

- The definition of a Type 1 surge protection device in Article 100 states that it's a permanently connected surge protective device listed for installation between the electric utility transformer and the service equipment. ▶Figure 285–10

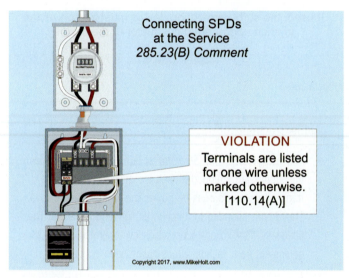

▶Figure 285–9

▶Figure 285–10

285.24 Type 2 SPD—Feeder Circuits

(A) Service Equipment. Type 2 surge protective devices can be connected to the load side of service equipment. ▶Figure 285–11

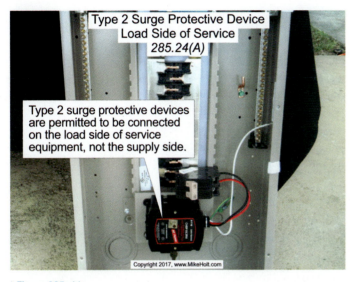

▶Figure 285–11

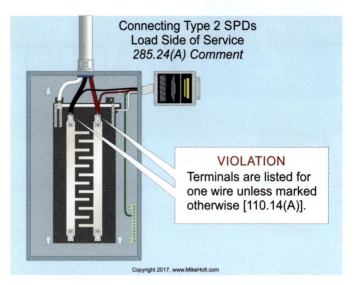

▶Figure 285–12

Author's Comment:

- Only one conductor can be connected to a terminal, unless the terminal is identified for multiple conductors [110.14(A)]. ▶Figure 285–12

- The definition of a Type 2 surge protection device in Article 100 states that it's a permanently connected surge protective device listed for installation on the load side of the service disconnect.

(B) Feeder-Supplied Buildings. Type 2 surge protective devices can be connected anywhere on the load side of the building overcurrent protection device.

(C) Separately Derived Systems. Type 2 surge protective devices can be connected anywhere on the premises wiring of the separately derived system.

285.25 Type 3 SPDs—Branch Circuits

Type 3 surge protective devices can be installed on the load side of a branch-circuit overcurrent protection device. If included in the manufacturer's instructions, the Type 3 SPD connection must be a minimum 30 ft of conductor distance from the service or separately derived system disconnect.

Author's Comment:

- The definition of a Type 3 surge protection device in Article 100 states it's a surge protective device listed for installation on branch circuits. ▶Figure 285–13

▶Figure 285–13

CHAPTER 2: PRACTICE QUESTIONS

Please use the 2017 *Code* book to answer the following questions.

Article 200. Use and Identification of Grounded [Neutral] Conductors

1. Where grounded conductors of different systems are installed in the same raceway, cable, or enclosure, each neutral conductor shall be identified to distinguish the systems by _____.

   (a) a continuous white or gray outer finish for one system
   (b) a neutral conductor with a different continuous white or gray outer finish or white or gray with a stripe for one system
   (c) other identification allowed by 200.6(A) or (B) that distinguishes each system from other systems
   (d) any of these

2. Receptacles shall have the terminal intended for connection to the grounded conductor identified by a metal or metal coating that is substantially _____ in color.

   (a) green
   (b) white
   (c) gray
   (d) b or c

Article 210. Branch Circuits

3. When connected to a branch circuit supplying two or more 15A receptacles, each receptacle shall not supply a total cord-and-plug-connected load in excess of _____.

   (a) 12A
   (b) 16A
   (c) 20A
   (d) 24A

4. The total rating of utilization equipment fastened in place, other than luminaires, shall not exceed _____ percent of the branch-circuit ampere rating where lighting units and cord-and-plug-connected utilization equipment not fastened in place are supplied.

   (a) 50
   (b) 75
   (c) 100
   (d) 125

Article 215. Feeders

5. Feeder grounded conductors shall be permitted to be sized at _____ percent of the continuous and noncontinuous load where a portion of the feeder is connected at both its supply and load ends to separately installed pressure connections.

   (a) 80
   (b) 100
   (c) 125
   (d) 150

6. When a feeder supplies _____ in which equipment grounding conductors are required, the feeder shall include or provide an equipment grounding conductor.

   (a) an equipment disconnecting means
   (b) electrical systems
   (c) branch circuits
   (d) electric-discharge lighting equipment

Article 225. Outside Branch Circuits and Feeders

7. Overhead feeder conductors shall have a minimum vertical clearance of _____ ft over residential property and driveways, as well as those commercial areas not subject to truck traffic, where the voltage does not exceed 300 volts-to-ground.

   (a) 10
   (b) 12
   (c) 15
   (d) 18

8. If a set of 120/240V overhead feeder conductors terminates at a through-the-roof raceway or approved support, with not more than 6 ft of these conductors, 4 ft horizontally, passing over the roof overhang, the minimum clearance above the roof for these conductors is not less than _____.

   (a) 12 in.
   (b) 18 in.
   (c) 2 ft
   (d) 5 ft

9. The vertical clearance of final spans of overhead conductors above or within _____ ft measured horizontally of platforms, projections, or surfaces that will permit personal contact shall be maintained in accordance with 225.18.

   (a) 3
   (b) 6
   (c) 8
   (d) 10

10. Outside wiring shall not be installed beneath openings through which materials may be moved, and shall not be installed where they will obstruct entrance to these buildings' openings.

    (a) True
    (b) False

11. A building or structure shall be supplied by a maximum of _____ feeder(s) or branch circuit(s), unless specifically permitted otherwise.

    (a) one
    (b) two
    (c) three
    (d) four

12. A building disconnecting means that supplies only limited loads of a single branch circuit shall have a rating of not less than _____.

    (a) 15A
    (b) 20A
    (c) 25A
    (d) 30A

13. For installations consisting of not more than two 2-wire branch circuits, the building disconnecting means shall have a rating of not less than _____.

    (a) 15A
    (b) 20A
    (c) 25A
    (d) 30A

Article 230. Services

14. Service conductors installed in overhead masts on the outside surface of the building traveling through the eave, but not the wall, of that building are considered to be outside of the building.

    (a) True
    (b) False

15. Service conductors installed as unjacketed multiconductor cable shall have a minimum clearance of _____ ft from windows that are designed to be opened, doors, porches, balconies, ladders, stairs, fire escapes, or similar locations.

    (a) 3
    (b) 4
    (c) 6
    (d) 10

Chapter 2 | Practice Questions

16. Service-drop conductors shall have ____.
    (a) sufficient ampacity to carry the load
    (b) adequate mechanical strength
    (c) a or b
    (d) a and b

17. Where conduits are used as service masts, hubs shall be ____ for use with service-entrance equipment.
    (a) identified
    (b) approved
    (c) of a heavy-duty type
    (d) listed

18. Underground service conductors that supply power to limited loads of a single branch circuit shall not be smaller than ____.
    (a) 14 AWG copper
    (b) 14 AWG aluminum
    (c) 12 AWG copper
    (d) 12 AWG aluminum

19. Two-family dwellings, multifamily dwellings, and multiple occupancy buildings shall be permitted to have one set of service-entrance conductors to supply branch circuits for public or common areas.
    (a) True
    (b) False

20. Wiring methods permitted for service-entrance conductors include ____.
    (a) rigid metal conduit
    (b) electrical metallic tubing
    (c) PVC conduit
    (d) all of these

21. Cable trays used to support service-entrance conductors shall contain only service-entrance conductors ____.
    (a) unless a solid fixed barrier of a material compatible with the cable tray separates the service-entrance conductors from other conductors
    (b) under 300V
    (c) in industrial locations
    (d) over 600V

22. There shall be no more than ____ disconnects installed for each service or for each set of service-entrance conductors as permitted in 230.2 and 230.40.
    (a) two
    (b) four
    (c) six
    (d) eight

Article 240. Overcurrent Protection

23. Ground-fault protection of equipment shall be provided for solidly grounded wye electrical systems of more than 150 volts-to-ground, but not exceeding 1,000V phase-to-phase for each individual device used as a building or structure main disconnecting means rated ____ or more, unless specifically exempted.
    (a) 1,000A
    (b) 1,500A
    (c) 2,000A
    (d) 2,500A

24. ____ shall not be located over the steps of a stairway.
    (a) Disconnect switches
    (b) Overcurrent devices
    (c) Knife switches
    (d) Transformers

25. Fuses shall be marked with their ____.
    (a) ampere and voltage rating
    (b) interrupting rating where other than 10,000A
    (c) name or trademark of the manufacturer
    (d) all of these

26. Circuit breakers used to switch 120V and 277V fluorescent lighting circuits shall be listed and marked ____.
    (a) UL
    (b) SWD or HID
    (c) Amps
    (d) VA

27. A circuit breaker with a _____ voltage rating, such as 240V or 480V, can be used where the nominal voltage between any two conductors does not exceed the circuit breaker voltage rating.

    (a) straight
    (b) slash
    (c) high
    (d) low

Article 250. Grounding and Bonding

28. NFPA 780, Standard for the Installation of Lightning Protection Systems provides information on the installation of _____ for lightning protection systems [250.4(A)(1)].

    (a) grounding
    (b) bonding
    (c) a and b
    (d) none of these

29. For grounded systems, normally noncurrent-carrying conductive materials enclosing electrical conductors or equipment shall be connected to earth so as to limit the voltage-to-ground on these materials.

    (a) True
    (b) False

30. For grounded systems, electrical equipment and electrically conductive material likely to become energized, shall be installed in a manner that creates a low-impedance circuit capable of safely carrying the maximum ground-fault current likely to be imposed on it from where a ground fault may occur to the _____.

    (a) ground
    (b) earth
    (c) electrical supply source
    (d) none of these

31. The grounding of electrical systems, circuit conductors, surge arresters, surge-protective devices, and conductive normally noncurrent-carrying metal parts of equipment shall be installed and arranged in a manner that will prevent objectionable current.

    (a) True
    (b) False

32. The grounded conductor of an alternating-current system operating at 1,000V or less shall be routed with the ungrounded conductors and connected to each disconnecting means grounded conductor terminal or bus, which is then connected to the service disconnecting means enclosure via a(n) _____ that is installed between the service neutral conductor and the service disconnecting means enclosure.

    (a) equipment bonding conductor
    (b) main bonding jumper
    (c) grounding electrode
    (d) intersystem bonding terminal

33. The common grounding electrode conductor installed for multiple separately derived systems shall not be smaller than _____ AWG copper when using a wire-type conductor.

    (a) 1/0
    (b) 2/0
    (c) 3/0
    (d) 4/0

34. A grounding electrode at a separate building or structure shall be required where one multiwire branch circuit serves the building or structure.

    (a) True
    (b) False

35. The frame of a portable generator shall not be required to be connected to a(n) _____ if the generator only supplies equipment mounted on the generator, cord-and-plug connected equipment using receptacles mounted on the generator, or both.

    (a) grounding electrode
    (b) grounded conductor
    (c) ungrounded conductor
    (d) equipment grounding conductor

36. When a permanently installed generator _____, the requirements of 250.30 shall apply.

    (a) is a separately derived system
    (b) is not a separately derived system
    (c) supplies only cord-and-plug-connected loads
    (d) none of these

Chapter 2 | Practice Questions

37. Grounding electrodes of bare or electrically conductive coated iron or steel plates shall be at least _____ in. thick.

    (a) ⅛
    (b) ¼
    (c) ½
    (d) ⅛

38. _____ shall not be used as grounding electrodes.

    (a) Metal underground gas piping systems
    (b) Aluminum
    (c) Metal well casings
    (d) a and b

39. Where a metal underground water pipe is used as a grounding electrode, the continuity of the grounding path or the bonding connection to interior piping shall not rely on _____ and similar equipment.

    (a) bonding jumpers
    (b) water meters or filtering devices
    (c) grounding clamps
    (d) all of these

40. Grounding electrode conductors and grounding electrode bonding jumpers in contact with _____ shall not be required to comply with 300.5, but shall be buried or otherwise protected if subject to physical damage.

    (a) water
    (b) the earth
    (c) metal
    (d) all of these

41. Ferrous metal raceways and enclosures for grounding electrode conductors shall be bonded at each end of the raceway or enclosure to the grounding electrode or grounding electrode conductor to create a(n) _____ parallel path.

    (a) mechanically
    (b) electrically
    (c) physically
    (d) none of these

42. If the grounding electrode conductor or bonding jumper connected to a single or multiple rod, pipe, or plate electrode(s), or any combination thereof, as described in 250.52(A)(5) or (A)(7), does not extend on to other types of electrodes that require a larger size conductor, the grounding electrode conductor shall not be required to be larger than _____ AWG copper wire.

    (a) 10
    (b) 8
    (c) 6
    (d) 4

43. The metal structural frame of a building shall be permitted to be used as a conductor to interconnect electrodes that are part of the grounding electrode system, or as a grounding electrode conductor. Hold-down bolts securing the structural steel column that are connected to a concrete-encased electrode that complies with 250.52(A)(3) and is located in the support footing or foundation shall be permitted to connect the metal structural frame of a building or structure to the concrete-encased grounding electrode.

    (a) True
    (b) False

44. A means external to enclosures for connecting intersystem _____ conductors shall be provided at the service equipment or metering equipment enclosure and disconnecting means of buildings or structures supplied by a feeder.

    (a) bonding
    (b) ungrounded
    (c) secondary
    (d) a and b

45. Metal water piping system(s) shall be bonded to the _____, or to one or more grounding electrodes used, if the grounding electrode conductor or bonding jumper to the grounding electrode is of sufficient size.

    (a) grounded conductor at the service
    (b) service equipment enclosure
    (c) grounding electrode conductor if of sufficient size
    (d) any of these

46. Which of the following appliances installed in residential occupancies need not be connected to an equipment grounding conductor?

    (a) A toaster.
    (b) An aquarium.
    (c) A dishwasher.
    (d) A refrigerator.

47. The receptacle grounding terminal of an isolated ground receptacle shall be connected to a(n) _____ equipment grounding conductor run with the circuit conductors.

    (a) insulated
    (b) covered
    (c) bare
    (d) solid

Article 285. Surge Protective Devices (SPDs)

48. Surge protective devices shall be marked with a short-circuit current rating and shall not be installed where the available fault current is in excess of that rating.

    (a) True
    (b) False

49. Surge protective devices shall only be located outdoors.

    (a) True
    (b) False

50. The conductors used to connect the surge protective device to the line or bus and to ground shall not be any longer than _____ and shall avoid unnecessary bends.

    (a) 6 in.
    (b) 12 in.
    (c) 18 in.
    (d) necessary

Notes

CHAPTER 3
WIRING METHODS AND MATERIALS

Chapter 3—Wiring Methods and Materials

Chapter 3 covers wiring methods and materials, and provides some very specific installation requirements for conductors, cables, boxes, raceways, and fittings. This chapter includes detailed information about the installation and restrictions involved with wiring methods.

It may be because of those details that many people incorrectly apply the rules from this chapter. Be sure to pay careful attention to the details, and be sure you make your installation comply with the rules in the *NEC*, not just completing it in the manner you may have been taught or because "it's always been done that way." This is especially true when it comes to applying the Tables.

Violations of the rules for wiring methods found in Chapter 3 can result in problems with power quality and can lead to fire, shock, and other hazards.

The type of wiring method you'll use depends on several factors; job specifications, *Code* requirements, the environment, need, and cost are among them.

Chapter 3 begins with rules that are common to most wiring methods [Article 300]. It then covers conductors [Article 310] and enclosures [Articles 312 and 314]. The articles that follow become more specific and deal more in-depth with individual wiring methods such as specific types of cables [Articles 320 through 340] and various raceways [Articles 342 through 390]. The chapter winds up with Article 392, a support system, and the final articles [Articles 394 through 398] for open wiring.

Notice as you read through the various wiring methods that the *Code* attempts to use similar subsection numbering for similar topics from one article to the next, using the same digits after the decimal point in the section number for the same topic. This makes it easier to locate specific requirements in a particular article. For example, the rules for securing and supporting can be found in the section that ends with ".30" of each article. In addition to this, you'll find a "uses permitted" and "uses not permitted" section in nearly every article.

Wiring Method Articles

- **Article 300—General Requirements for Wiring Methods and Materials.** Article 300 contains the general requirements for all wiring methods included in the *NEC*, except for signaling and communications systems (twisted wire, antennas, and coaxial cable), which are covered in Chapters 7 and 8.

Chapter 3 | Wiring Methods and Materials

- **Article 310—Conductors for General Wiring.** This article contains the general requirements for conductors, such as insulation markings, ampacity ratings, and conductor use. Article 310 doesn't apply to conductors that are part of flexible cords, fixture wires, or conductors that are an integral part of equipment [90.6 and 300.1(B)].

- **Article 312—Cabinets, Cutout Boxes, and Meter Socket Enclosures.** Article 312 covers the installation and construction specifications for cabinets, cutout boxes, and meter socket enclosures.

- **Article 314—Outlet, Device, Pull, and Junction Boxes; Conduit Bodies; Fittings; and Handhole Enclosures.** Installation requirements for outlet boxes, pull and junction boxes, as well as conduit bodies, and handhole enclosures are contained in this article.

Cable Articles

Articles 320 through 340 address specific types of cables. If you take the time to become familiar with the various types of cables, you'll:

- Understand what's available for doing the work.
- Recognize cable types that have special *NEC* requirements.
- Avoid buying cable that you can't install due to *Code* requirements you can't meet with that particular wiring method.

Here's a brief overview of each one:

- **Article 320—Armored Cable (Type AC).** Armored cable is an assembly of insulated conductors, 14 AWG through 1 AWG, individually wrapped with waxed paper. The conductors are contained within a flexible spiral metal (steel or aluminum) sheath that interlocks at the edges. Armored cable looks like flexible metal conduit. Many electricians call this metal cable "BX®."

- **Article 330—Metal-Clad Cable (Type MC).** Metal-clad cable encloses insulated conductors in a metal sheath of either corrugated or smooth copper or aluminum tubing, or spiral interlocked steel or aluminum. The physical characteristics of Type MC cable make it a versatile wiring method permitted in almost any location and for almost any application. The most commonly used Type MC cable is the interlocking kind, which looks similar to armored cable or flexible metal conduit.

- **Article 334—Nonmetallic-Sheathed Cable (Type NM).** Nonmetallic-sheathed cable encloses two, three, or four insulated conductors, 14 AWG through 2 AWG, within a nonmetallic outer jacket. Because this cable is nonmetallic, it contains a separate equipment grounding conductor. Nonmetallic-sheathed cable is a common wiring method used for residential and commercial branch circuits. Many electricians call this plastic-sheathed cable "Romex®."

- **Article 336—Power and Control Tray Cable (Type TC).** Power and control tray cable is flexible, inexpensive, and easily installed. It provides very limited physical protection for the conductors, so the installation restrictions are strict. Its low cost and relative ease of installation make it a common wiring method for industrial applications.

- **Article 338—Service-Entrance Cable (Types SE and USE).** Service-entrance cable can be a single-conductor or a multi-conductor assembly within an overall nonmetallic covering. This cable is used primarily for services not over 1,000V, but is also permitted for feeders and branch circuits.

- **Article 340—Underground Feeder and Branch-Circuit Cable (Type UF).** Underground feeder cable is a moisture-, fungus-, and corrosion-resistant cable suitable for direct burial in the earth, and it comes in sizes 14 AWG through 4/0 AWG [340.104]. Multiconductor UF cable is covered in molded plastic that surrounds the insulated conductors.

Raceway Articles

Articles 342 through 390 address specific types of raceways. Refer to Article 100 for the definition of a raceway. If you take the time to become familiar with the various types of raceways, you'll:

- Understand what's available for doing the work.
- Recognize raceway types that have special *Code* requirements.
- Avoid buying a raceway that you can't install due to *NEC* requirements you can't meet with that particular wiring method.

Here's a brief overview of each one:

- **Article 342—Intermediate Metal Conduit (Type IMC).** Intermediate metal conduit is a circular metal raceway with the same outside diameter as rigid metal conduit. The wall thickness of intermediate metal conduit is less than that of rigid metal conduit, so it has a greater interior cross-sectional area for holding conductors. Intermediate metal conduit is lighter and less expensive than rigid metal conduit, but it's permitted in all the same locations as rigid metal conduit. Intermediate metal conduit also uses a different steel alloy, which makes it stronger than rigid metal conduit, even though the walls are thinner.

- **Article 344—Rigid Metal Conduit (Type RMC).** Rigid metal conduit is similar to intermediate metal conduit, except the wall thickness is greater, so it has a smaller interior cross-sectional area. Rigid metal conduit is heavier than intermediate metal conduit and it's permitted to be installed in any location, just like intermediate metal conduit.

- **Article 348—Flexible Metal Conduit (Type FMC).** Flexible metal conduit is a raceway of circular cross section made of a helically wound, interlocked metal strip of either steel or aluminum. It's commonly called "Greenfield" or "Flex."

- **Article 350—Liquidtight Flexible Metal Conduit (Type LFMC).** Liquidtight flexible metal conduit is a raceway of circular cross section with an outer liquidtight, nonmetallic, sunlight-resistant jacket over an inner flexible metal core, with associated couplings, connectors, and fittings. It's listed for the installation of electrical conductors. Liquidtight flexible metal conduit is commonly called "Sealtite®" or simply "liquidtight." Liquidtight flexible metal conduit is of similar construction to flexible metal conduit, but it has an outer thermoplastic covering.

- **Article 352—Rigid Polyvinyl Chloride Conduit (Type PVC).** Rigid polyvinyl chloride conduit is a nonmetallic raceway of circular cross section with integral or associated couplings, connectors, and fittings. It's listed for the installation of electrical conductors.

- **Article 356—Liquidtight Flexible Nonmetallic Conduit (Type LFNC).** Liquidtight flexible nonmetallic conduit is a raceway of circular cross section with an outer liquidtight, nonmetallic, sunlight-resistant jacket over an inner flexible core, with associated couplings, connectors, and fittings.

- **Article 358—Electrical Metallic Tubing (EMT).** Electrical metallic tubing is a nonthreaded thinwall raceway of circular cross section designed for the physical protection and routing of conductors and cables. Compared to rigid metal conduit and intermediate metal conduit, electrical metallic tubing is relatively easy to bend, cut, and ream. EMT isn't threaded, so all connectors and couplings are of the threadless type. It's available in a range of colors, such as red and blue.

- **Article 362—Electrical Nonmetallic Tubing (ENT).** Electrical nonmetallic tubing is a pliable, corrugated, circular raceway made of PVC. It's often called "Smurf Pipe" or "Smurf Tube," because it was available only in blue when it came out at the time the children's cartoon characters "The Smurfs" were popular. It's now available in multiple colors such as red and yellow as well as blue.

- **Article 376—Metal Wireways.** A metal wireway is a sheet metal trough with hinged or removable covers for housing and protecting electrical conductors and cable, in which conductors are placed after the wireway has been installed as a complete system.

- **Article 380—Multioutlet Assemblies.** A multioutlet assembly is a surface, flush, or freestanding raceway designed to hold conductors and receptacles. It's assembled in the field or at the factory.

- **Article 386—Surface Metal Raceways.** A surface metal raceway is a metal raceway intended to be mounted to the surface with associated accessories, in which conductors are placed after the raceway has been installed as a complete system.

Cable Tray

- **Article 392—Cable Trays.** A cable tray system is a unit or assembly of units or sections with associated fittings that form a structural system used to securely fasten or support cables and raceways. A cable tray isn't a raceway; it's a support system for raceways, cables, and enclosures.

ARTICLE 300 — GENERAL REQUIREMENTS FOR WIRING METHODS AND MATERIALS

Introduction to Article 300—General Requirements for Wiring Methods and Materials

Article 300 contains the general requirements for all wiring methods included in the *NEC*. However, it doesn't apply to communications systems (twisted wire, antennas, and coaxial cable), which are covered in Chapter 8, except when Article 300 is specifically referenced in Chapter 8.

This article is primarily concerned with how to install, route, splice, protect, and secure conductors and raceways. How well you conform to the requirements of Article 300 will generally be evident in the finished work, because many of the requirements tend to determine the appearance of the installation. Because of this, it's often easy to spot Article 300 problems if you're looking for *Code* violations. For example, you can easily see when someone runs an equipment grounding conductor outside a raceway instead of grouping all conductors of a circuit together, as required by 300.3(B).

A good understanding of Article 300 will start you on the path to correctly installing the wiring methods included in Chapter 3. Be sure to carefully consider the accompanying illustrations, and refer to the definitions in Article 100 as needed.

Part I. General

300.1 Scope

(A) Wiring Installations. Article 300 contains the general requirements for wiring methods and materials for power and lighting. ▶Figure 300–1

▶Figure 300–1

Author's Comment:

- The requirements contained in Article 300 don't apply to the wiring methods for Class 2 and 3 circuits, fire alarm circuits, and communications systems (twisted wire, antennas, and coaxial cable), except where there's a specific reference in Chapters 7 or 8 to a rule in Article 300.
    ◆ Class 2 and 3 Remote Control and Signaling, 725.3
    ◆ Communications Cables and Raceways, 800.133(A)(2)
    ◆ Coaxial Circuits, 820.3
    ◆ Fire Alarm Circuits, 760.3

300.3 | General Requirements for Wiring Methods and Materials

(B) Integral Parts of Equipment. The requirements contained in Article 300 don't apply to the internal parts of electrical equipment. ▶Figure 300–2

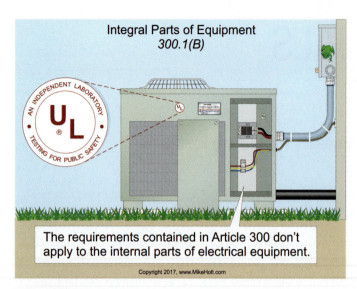

▶Figure 300–2

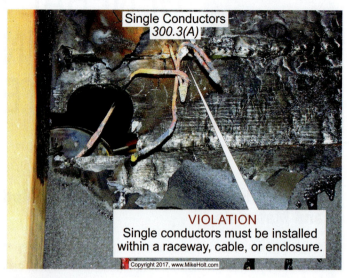

▶Figure 300–3

(C) Trade Sizes. Designators for raceway trade sizes are given in Table 300.1(C).

Author's Comment:

- Industry practice is to describe raceways using inch sizes, such as ½ in., 2 in., and so on; however, the proper reference is to use "Trade Size ½," or "Trade Size 2." In this textbook we use the term "Trade Size."

300.3 Conductors

(A) Conductors. Single conductors must be installed within a Chapter 3 wiring method, such as a raceway, cable, or enclosure. ▶Figure 300–3

Ex: Overhead conductors can be installed in accordance with 225.6.

(B) Circuit Conductors Grouped Together. Conductors of a circuit and, where used, the neutral and equipment grounding and bonding conductors must be installed in the same raceway, cable, trench, cord, or cable tray, except as permitted by (1) through (4).

(1) Paralleled Installations. Conductors installed in parallel in accordance with 310.10(H) must have all circuit conductors within the same raceway, cable tray, trench, or cable. ▶Figure 300–4

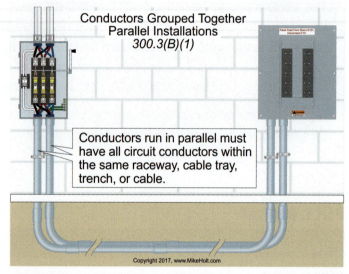

▶Figure 300–4

Author's Comment:

- To minimize induction heating of ferrous metal raceways and ferrous metal enclosures for alternating-current circuits, and to maintain an effective ground-fault current path, all conductors of a circuit must be installed in the same raceway, cable, trench, cord, or cable tray. See 250.102(E), 300.3(B), 300.5(I), 300.20(A), and 392.8(D). ▶Figure 300–5 and ▶Figure 300–6

General Requirements for Wiring Methods and Materials | 300.3

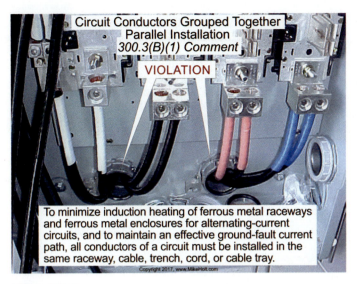
▶Figure 300–5

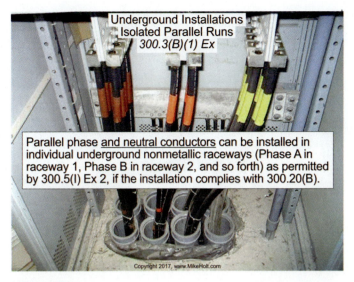
▶Figure 300–7

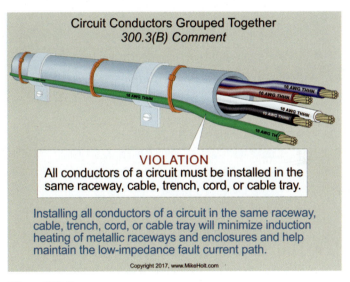
▶Figure 300–6

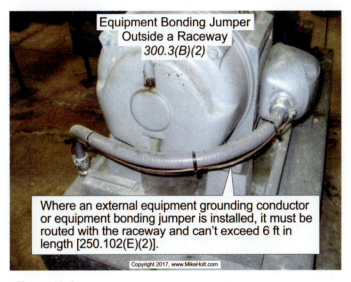
▶Figure 300–8

Ex: Parallel phase and neutral conductors can be installed in individual underground nonmetallic raceways (Phase A in raceway 1, Phase B in raceway 2, and so forth) as permitted by 300.5(I) Ex 2, if the installation complies with 300.20(B). ▶Figure 300–7

(2) Outside a Raceway or an Enclosure. Equipment grounding jumpers can be located outside of a flexible raceway if the bonding jumper is installed in accordance with 250.102(E)(2). ▶Figure 300–8

For dc circuits, the equipment grounding conductor can be run separately from the circuit conductors in accordance with 250.134(B) Ex 2. ▶Figure 300–9

(3) Nonferrous Wiring Methods. Circuit conductors can be installed in different raceways (Phase A in raceway 1, Phase B in raceway 2, and so on) if, in order to reduce or eliminate inductive heating, the raceway is nonmetallic or nonmagnetic and the installation complies with 300.20(B). See 300.3(B)(1) and 300.5(I) Ex 2.

300.3 | General Requirements for Wiring Methods and Materials

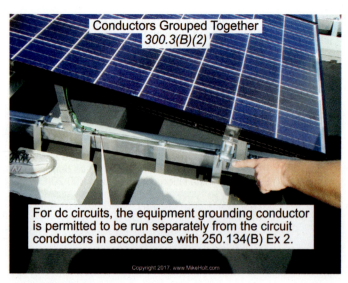

▶Figure 300–9

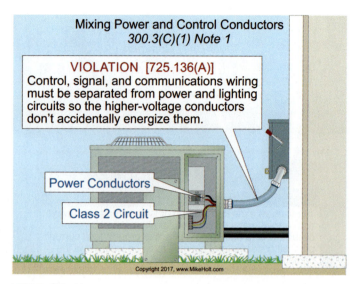

▶Figure 300–11

(C) Conductors of Different Systems.

(1) Mixing. Power conductors of alternating-current and direct-current systems rated 1,000V or less can occupy the same raceway, cable, or enclosure if all conductors have an insulation voltage rating not less than the maximum circuit voltage. ▶Figure 300–10

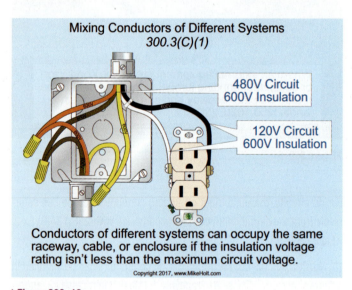

▶Figure 300–10

Note 1: See 725.136(A) for Class 2 and Class 3 circuit conductors. ▶Figure 300–11

Author's Comment:

- Control, signal, and communications wiring must be separated from power and lighting circuits so the higher-voltage conductors don't accidentally energize the control, signal, or communications wiring:

  ◆ Class 1 control circuits, 725.48
  ◆ Class 2 and Class 3 Control Circuits, 725.136(A)
  ◆ Communications Circuits, 800.133(A)(1)(c)
  ◆ Coaxial Cable, 820.133(A)
  ◆ Fire Alarm Circuits, 760.136(A)
  ◆ Sound Circuits, 640.9(C)

- Class 1 circuit conductors can be installed with associated power conductors [725.48(B)(1)] if all conductors have an insulation voltage rating not less than the maximum circuit voltage [300.3(C)(1)].

- A Class 2 circuit that's been reclassified as a Class 1 circuit [725.130(A) Ex 2] can be installed with associated power conductors [725.48(B)(1)] if all conductors have an insulation voltage rating not less than the maximum circuit voltage [300.3(C)(1)]. ▶Figure 300–12

General Requirements for Wiring Methods and Materials | 300.4

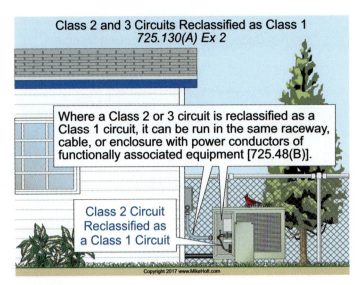

▶Figure 300–12

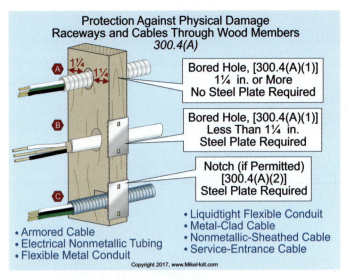

▶Figure 300–13

300.4 Protection Against Physical Damage

Where subject to physical damage, conductors, raceways, and cables must be protected in accordance with (A) through (H).

Note: Minor superficial damage to a raceway, cable armor, or cable insulation doesn't necessarily violate the integrity of either the contained conductors or the conductors' insulation.

(A) Cables and Raceways Through Wood Members. When the following wiring methods are installed through wood members, they must comply with (1) and (2). ▶Figure 300–13

- Armored Cable, Article 320
- Electrical Nonmetallic Tubing, Article 362
- Flexible Metal Conduit, Article 348
- Liquidtight Flexible Metal Conduit, Article 350
- Liquidtight Flexible Nonmetallic Conduit, Article 356
- Metal-Clad Cable, Article 330
- Nonmetallic-Sheathed Cable, Article 334
- Service-Entrance Cable, Article 338
- Underground Feeder and Branch-Circuit Cable, Article 340

(1) Holes in Wood Members. Holes through wood framing members for the above cables or raceways must be not less than 1¼ in. from the edge of the wood member. If the edge of a drilled hole in a wood framing member is less than 1¼ in. from the edge, a ¹⁄₁₆ in. thick steel plate of sufficient length and width must be installed to protect the wiring method from screws and nails. ▶Figure 300–14

▶Figure 300–14

Ex 1: A steel plate isn't required to protect rigid metal conduit, intermediate metal conduit, PVC conduit, or electrical metallic tubing.

(2) Notches in Wood Members. If notching of wood framing members for cables and raceways are permitted by the building code, a ¹⁄₁₆ in. thick steel plate of sufficient length and width must be installed to protect the wiring method laid in these wood notches from screws and nails.

CAUTION: When drilling or notching wood members, be sure to check with the building inspector to ensure you don't damage or weaken the structure and violate the building code.

300.4 | General Requirements for Wiring Methods and Materials

Ex 1: A steel plate isn't required to protect rigid metal conduit, intermediate metal conduit, PVC conduit, or electrical metallic tubing.

Ex 2: A listed and marked steel plate less than 1/16 in. thick that provides equal or better protection against nail or screw penetration is permitted.
▶ Figure 300–15

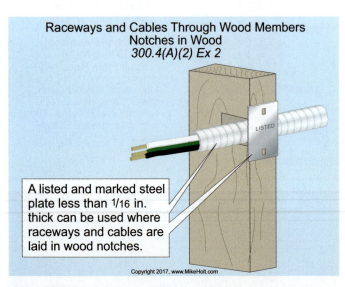

▶ Figure 300–15

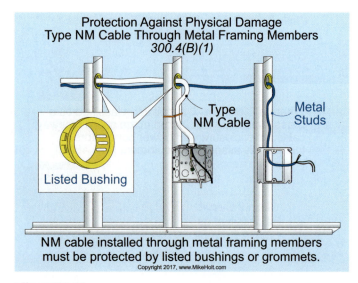

▶ Figure 300–16

▶ Figure 300–17

(B) Nonmetallic-Sheathed Cable and Electrical Nonmetallic Tubing Through Metal Framing Members.

(1) Nonmetallic-Sheathed Cable (NM). If Type NM cables pass through factory or field openings in metal framing members, the cable must be protected by listed bushings or listed grommets that cover all metal edges. The protection fitting must be securely fastened in the opening before the installation of the cable. ▶ Figure 300–16

(2) Type NM Cable and Electrical Nonmetallic Tubing. If nails or screws are likely to penetrate Type NM cable or electrical nonmetallic tubing, a steel sleeve, steel plate, or steel clip not less than 1/16 in. in thickness must be installed to protect the cable or tubing.

Ex: A listed and marked steel plate less than 1/16 in. thick that provides equal or better protection against nail or screw penetration is permitted.

(C) Behind Suspended Ceilings. Wiring methods, such as boxes, enclosures, cables, or raceways, installed behind panels designed to allow access must be supported in accordance with its applicable article.
▶ Figure 300–17

Author's Comment:

- Similar support requirements are contained in Chapters 6, 7, and 8 as follows:
  ◆ Audio Cable, 640.6(B)
  ◆ Communications (twisted pair) Cable, 800.21
  ◆ Control and Signaling Cable, 725.21 and 725.24
  ◆ Coaxial Cable, 820.21 and 820.24
  ◆ Optical Fiber Cable, 770.21 and 770.24

General Requirements for Wiring Methods and Materials | 300.4

(D) Cables and Raceways Parallel to Framing Members and Furring Strips. Cables or raceways run parallel to framing members or furring strips must be protected if they're likely to be penetrated by nails or screws, by installing the wiring method so it isn't less than 1¼ in. from the nearest edge of the framing member or furring strip. If the edge of the framing member or furring strip is less than 1¼ in. away, a 1/16 in. thick steel plate of sufficient length and width must be installed to protect the wiring method from screws and nails. ▶Figure 300–18

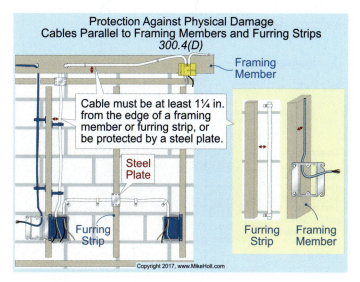

▶Figure 300–18

Author's Comment:

- This rule doesn't apply to control, signaling, and communications cables, but similar requirements are contained in Chapters 6, 7, and 8 as follows:
    ◆ Communications Cable, 800.24
    ◆ Control and Signaling Cable, 725.24
    ◆ Coaxial Cable, 820.24
    ◆ Optical Fiber Cable, 770.24
    ◆ Fire Alarm Cable, 760.24
    ◆ Audio Cable, 640.6(B)

Ex 1: Protection isn't required for rigid metal conduit, intermediate metal conduit, PVC conduit, or electrical metallic tubing.

Ex 2: For concealed work in finished buildings, or finished panels for prefabricated buildings if such supporting is impracticable, the cables can be fished between access points.

Ex 3: A listed and marked steel plate less than 1/16 in. thick that provides equal or better protection against nail or screw penetration is permitted.

(E) Wiring Under Roof Decking. Where subject to physical damage, cables, raceways, and enclosures under metal-corrugated sheet roof decking aren't permitted to be located within 1½ in. of the roof decking, measured from the lowest surface of the roof decking to the top of the cable, raceway, or box. ▶Figure 300–19

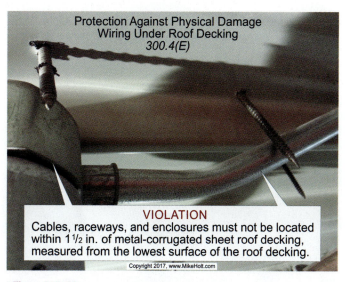

▶Figure 300–19

In addition, cables, raceways, and enclosures aren't permitted in concealed locations of metal-corrugated sheet decking type roofing.

Author's Comment:

- This requirement also applies to luminaires installed in or under roof decking [410.10(F)].

Note: Roof decking material will be installed or replaced after the initial raceway or cabling which may be penetrated by the screws or other mechanical devices designed to provide "hold down" strength of the waterproof membrane or roof insulating material.

Ex: Spacing from roof decking doesn't apply to rigid metal conduit and intermediate metal conduit.

(F) Cables and Raceways Installed in Grooves. Cables and raceways installed in a groove must be protected by a 1/16 in. thick steel plate or sleeve, or by 1¼ in. of free space.

300.5 | General Requirements for Wiring Methods and Materials

Author's Comment:

- An example is Type NM cable installed in a groove cut into the Styrofoam-type insulation building block structure and then covered with wallboard.

Ex 1: Protection isn't required if the cable is installed in rigid metal conduit, intermediate metal conduit, PVC conduit, or electrical metallic tubing.

Ex 2: A listed and marked steel plate less than 1/16 in. thick that provides equal or better protection against nail or screw penetration is permitted.

(G) Insulating Fittings. If raceways contain insulated circuit conductors 4 AWG and larger that enter an enclosure, the conductors must be protected from abrasion during and after installation by a fitting identified to provide a smooth, rounded insulating surface, such as an insulating bushing. ▶Figure 300–20

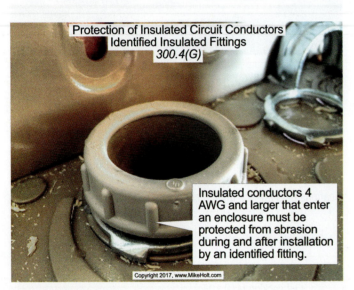

▶Figure 300–20

Author's Comment:

- If IMC or RMC conduit enters an enclosure without a connector, a bushing must be provided, regardless of the conductor size [342.46 and 344.46].
- An insulated fitting isn't required for a bare grounding electrode conductor.

Ex: Insulating bushings aren't required if a raceway terminates in a threaded raceway entry that provides a smooth, rounded, or flared surface for the conductors, such as a hub.

(H) Structural Joints. A listed expansion/deflection fitting or other means approved by the authority having jurisdiction must be used where a raceway crosses a structural joint intended for expansion, contraction or deflection.

300.5 Underground Installations

(A) Minimum Burial Depths. When cables or raceways are installed underground, they must have a minimum cover in accordance with Table 300.5. ▶Figure 300–21

Underground Installations, Minimum Cover Depths
Table 300.5

Location	Column 1 UF or USE Cables or Conductors	Column 2 RMC or IMC	Column 3 Nonmetallic Raceways not Encased in Concrete	Column 4 Residential 15A & 20A GFCI 120V Branch Ckts
Dwelling Unit	24 in.	6 in.	18 in.	12 in.
Dwelling Unit Driveway and Parking Area	18 in.	18 in.	18 in.	12 in.
Under Roadway Driveway Parking Lot	24 in.	24 in.	24 in.	24 in.
Other Locations	24 in.	6 in.	18 in.	12 in.

▶Figure 300–21

Table 300.5 Minimum Cover Requirements in Inches

Location	Column 1 Buried Cables	Column 2 RMC or IMC	Column 3 Nonmetallic Raceway
Under Building	0	0	0
Dwelling Unit	24/12*	6	18
Dwelling Unit Driveway	18/12*	6	18/12*
Under Roadway	24	24	24
Other Locations	24	6	18

*Residential branch circuits rated 120V or less with GFCI protection and maximum protection of 20A.

See the table in the NEC for full details.

General Requirements for Wiring Methods and Materials | 300.5

Table 300.5 Minimum Cover Requirements in Inches
(continued)

a. Lesser depth is permitted where specified in the installation instructions of a listed low-voltage lighting system. ▶Figure 300–22

b. A depth of 6 in. is permitted for pool, spa, and fountain lighting wiring installed in a nonmetallic raceway, where part of a listed 30V lighting system. ▶Figure 300–23

Note 1 to Table 300.5 defines "Cover" as the distance from the top of the underground cable or raceway to the top surface of finished grade. ▶Figure 300–24

Author's Comment:

- Table 300.5 Notes a and b only pertain to Column 5. Refer to the *NEC* for the complete table.

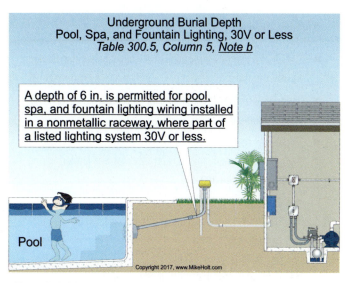
▶Figure 300–23

▶Figure 300–22

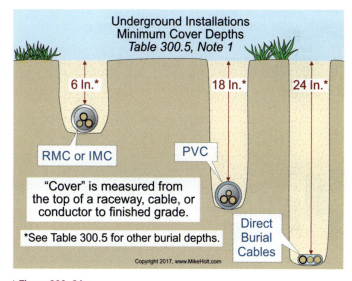
▶Figure 300–24

300.5 | General Requirements for Wiring Methods and Materials

Author's Comment:

- Circuits for control of irrigation and landscape lighting limited to 30V require a minimum of 6 in. of cover: ▶Figure 300–25
- There are no cover requirements for raceways under a building: ▶Figure 300–26
- The cover requirements contained in 300.5 don't apply to signaling, communications, and other power-limited wiring systems: ▶Figure 300–27
    - Class 2 and 3 Circuits, 725.3
    - Communications Cables and Raceways, 90.3
    - Coaxial Cable, 90.3
    - Fire Alarm Circuits, 760.3
    - Optical Fiber Cables and Raceways, 770.3

▶Figure 300–26

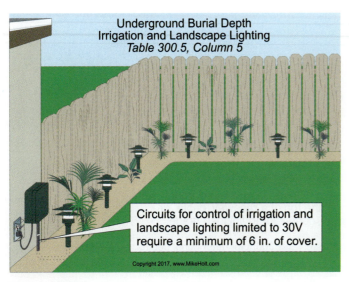

▶Figure 300–25

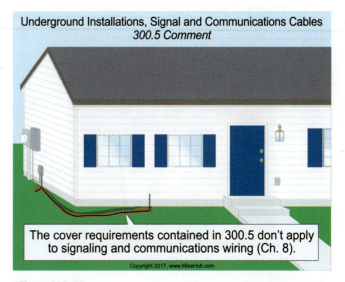

▶Figure 300–27

(B) Wet Locations. The interior of enclosures or raceways installed in an underground installation are considered to be a wet location. Cables and insulated conductors installed in underground enclosures or raceways must comply with 310.10(C).

Author's Comment:

- The definition of a "Wet Location" as contained in Article 100, includes installations underground, in concrete slabs in direct contact with the earth, locations subject to saturation with water, and unprotected locations exposed to weather. If raceways are installed in wet locations above grade, the interior of these raceways is also considered to be a wet location [300.9].

(C) Cables and Conductors Under Buildings. Cables and conductors installed under a building must be installed within a raceway that extends past the outside walls of the building. ▶Figure 300–28

Ex 2: Type MC Cable listed for direct burial is permitted under a building without installation within a raceway [330.10(A)(5)]. ▶Figure 300–29

(D) Protecting Underground Cables and Conductors. Direct-buried conductors and cables such as Types MC, UF, and USE installed underground must be protected from damage in accordance with (1) through (4).

General Requirements for Wiring Methods and Materials | 300.5

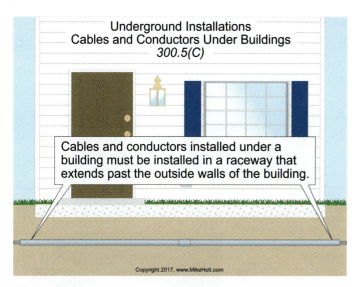
▶Figure 300–28

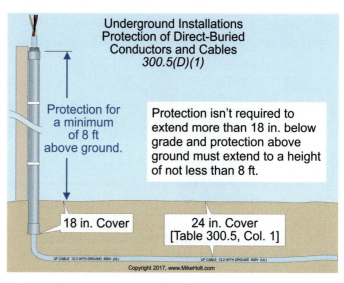
▶Figure 300–30

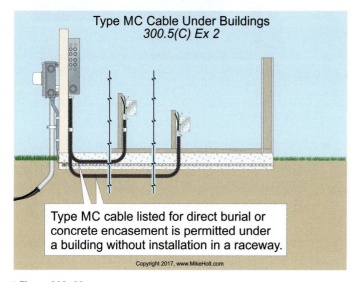
▶Figure 300–29

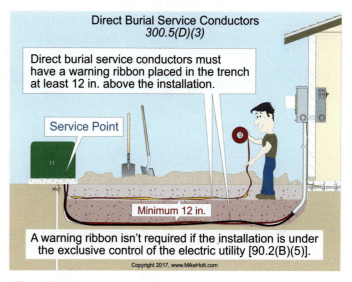
▶Figure 300–31

(1) Emerging from Grade. Direct-buried cables or conductors that emerge from grade must be installed in an enclosure or raceway to protect against physical damage. Protection isn't required to extend more than 18 in. below grade, and protection above ground must extend to a height of not less than 8 ft. ▶Figure 300–30

(2) Conductors Entering Buildings. Underground conductors and cables that enter a building must be protected to the point of entrance.

(3) Service Conductors. Underground service conductors must have their location identified by a warning ribbon placed in the trench at least 12 in. above the underground conductor installation. ▶Figure 300–31

Author's Comment:

- Although a warning ribbon isn't required by the *NEC* if the underground service conductors are under the exclusive control of the utility, it may be required by the local utility.

(4) Raceway Damage. Where a raceway is subject to physical damage, the conductors must be installed in EMT, RMC, IMC, RTRC-XW, or Schedule 80 PVC conduit.

(E) Underground Splices and Taps. Direct-buried conductors or cables can be spliced or tapped underground without a splice box [300.15(G)], if the splice or tap is made in accordance with 110.14(B). ▶Figure 300–32

300.5 | General Requirements for Wiring Methods and Materials

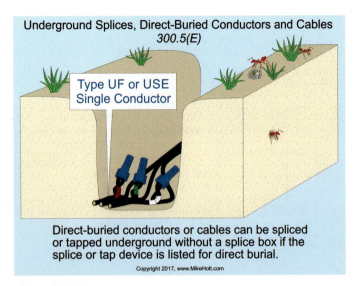

▶Figure 300–32

(F) Backfill. Backfill material for underground wiring must not damage underground raceways, cables, or conductors. ▶Figure 300–33

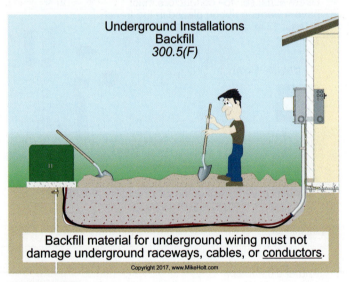

▶Figure 300–33

Author's Comment:

- Large rocks, chunks of concrete, steel rods, mesh, and other sharp-edged objects aren't permitted to be used for backfill material, because they can damage the underground conductors, cables, or raceways.

(G) Raceway Seals. If moisture could contact energized live parts from an underground raceway, including spare raceways, a seal identified for use with the cable or conductor insulation must be installed at either or both ends of the raceway [225.27 and 230.8]. ▶Figure 300–34

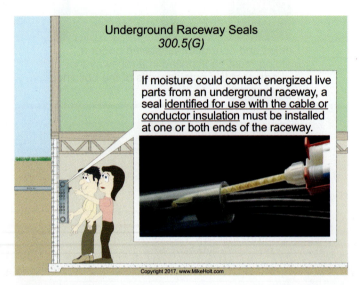

▶Figure 300–34

Author's Comment:

- This is a common problem for equipment located downhill from the supply, or in underground equipment rooms. See 230.8 for service raceway seals and 300.7(A) for different temperature area seals.

Note: Hazardous explosive gases or vapors make it necessary to seal underground raceways that enter the building in accordance with 501.15.

Author's Comment:

- It isn't the intent of this Note to imply that sealing fittings of the types required in hazardous locations be installed in unclassified locations, except as required in Chapter 5. This also doesn't imply that the sealing material provides a watertight seal, but only that it prevents moisture from entering the raceways.

(H) Bushing. Raceways that terminate underground must have a bushing or fitting at the end of the raceway to protect emerging cables or conductors.

General Requirements for Wiring Methods and Materials | 300.5

(I) Conductors Grouped Together. Underground conductors of the same circuit, including the equipment grounding conductor, must be inside the same raceway, or in close proximity to each other in the same trench. See 300.3(B). ▶Figure 300–35

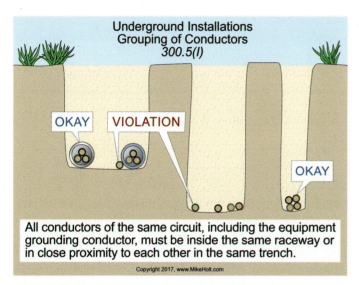

▶Figure 300–35

Ex 1: Conductors can be installed in parallel in raceways, multiconductor cables, or direct-buried single-conductor cables. Each raceway or multiconductor cable must contain all conductors of the same circuit including the equipment grounding conductor. Each direct-buried single-conductor cable must be located in close proximity in the trench to the other single-conductors cables in the same parallel set of conductors, including equipment grounding conductors.

Ex 2: Parallel circuit conductors installed in accordance with 310.10(H) of the same phase or neutral can be installed in underground PVC conduits, if inductive heating at raceway terminations is reduced by the use of aluminum locknuts and cutting a slot between the individual holes through which the conductors pass as required by 300.20(B). ▶Figure 300–36

Author's Comment:

- Installing ungrounded and neutral conductors in different PVC conduits makes it easier to terminate larger parallel sets of conductors, but it will result in higher levels of electromagnetic fields (EMF).

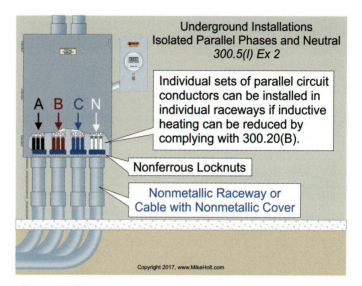

▶Figure 300–36

(J) Earth Movement. Direct-buried conductors, cables, or raceways that are subject to movement by settlement or frost must be arranged to prevent damage to conductors or equipment connected to the wiring. ▶Figure 300–37

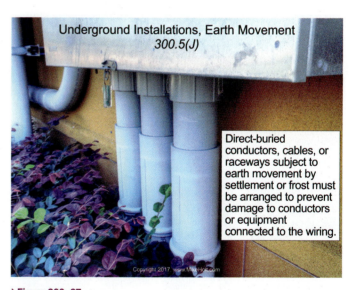

▶Figure 300–37

Note: "S" loops in underground direct burial cables and conductors, raceway expansion fittings, and flexible connections to equipment can serve this purpose.

(K) Directional Boring. Cables or raceways installed using directional boring equipment must be approved by the authority having jurisdiction for this purpose.

300.6 | General Requirements for Wiring Methods and Materials

Author's Comment:

- Directional boring technology uses a directional drill, which is steered continuously from point "A" to point "B." When the drill head comes out of the earth at point "B," it's replaced with a back-reamer and the duct or raceway being installed is attached to it. The size of the boring rig (hp, torque, and pull-back power) comes into play, along with the types of soil, in determining the type of raceways required. For telecommunications work, multiple poly innerducts are pulled in at one time. At major crossings, such as expressways, railroads, or rivers, outerduct may be installed to create a permanent sleeve for the innerducts.

- "Innerduct" and "outerduct" are terms usually associated with optical fiber cable installations, while "unitduct" comes with factory installed conductors. Galvanized rigid metal conduit, Schedule 40 and Schedule 80 PVC, HDPE conduit, and nonmetallic underground conduit with conductors (NUCC) are common wiring methods used with directional boring installations.

300.6 Protection Against Corrosion and Deterioration

Raceways, cable trays, cablebus, cable armor, boxes, cable sheathing, cabinets, elbows, couplings, fittings, supports, and support hardware must be suitable for the environment. ▶Figure 300–38

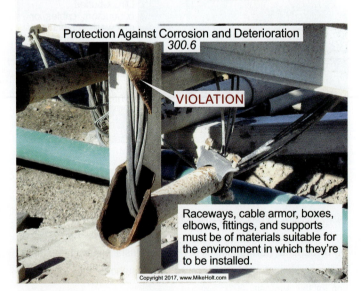

▶Figure 300–38

(A) Ferrous Metal Equipment. Ferrous metal raceways, enclosures, cables, cable trays, fittings, and support hardware must be protected against corrosion by a coating of listed corrosion-resistant material. Where conduit is threaded in the field, the threads must be coated with an approved electrically conductive, corrosion-resistant compound, such as cold zinc.

Note: Field-cut threads are those threads that are cut anywhere other than at the factory.

Author's Comment:

- Nonferrous metal raceways, such as aluminum rigid metal conduit, don't have to meet the provisions of this section.

(1) Protected from Corrosion Solely by Enamel. If ferrous metal parts are protected from corrosion solely by enamel, they aren't permitted to be used outdoors or in wet locations as described in 300.6(D).

(2) Organic Coatings on Boxes or Cabinets. Boxes or cabinets having a system of organic coatings marked "Raintight," "Rainproof," or "Outdoor Type," can be installed outdoors.

(3) In Concrete or in Direct Contact with the Earth. Ferrous metal raceways, cable armor, boxes, cable sheathing, cabinets, elbows, couplings, nipples, fittings, supports, and support hardware can be installed in concrete or in direct contact with the earth, or in areas subject to severe corrosive influences if made of material approved for the condition, or if provided with corrosion protection approved for the condition.

Author's Comment:

- Galvanized electrical metallic tubing can be installed in concrete at grade level and in direct contact with the earth, but supplementary corrosion protection is usually required (UL White Book, *Guide Information for Electrical Equipment*). Electrical metallic tubing can be installed in concrete above the ground floor slab generally without supplementary corrosion protection.

(B) Aluminum Equipment. Aluminum raceways, cable trays, cablebus, cable armor, boxes, cable sheathing, cabinets, elbows, couplings, nipples, fittings, supports, and support hardware embedded or encased in concrete or in direct contact with the earth must be provided with supplementary corrosion protection.

General Requirements for Wiring Methods and Materials | 300.7

(C) Nonmetallic Equipment. Nonmetallic raceways, cable trays, cablebus, boxes, cables with a nonmetallic outer jacket and internal metal armor or jacket, cable sheathing, cabinets, elbows, couplings, nipples, fittings, supports, and support hardware must be made of material identified for the condition, and must comply with (1) and (2). ▶Figure 300–39

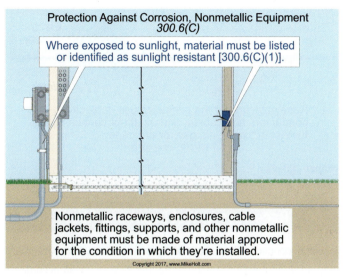

▶Figure 300–39

(1) Exposed to Sunlight. If exposed to sunlight, the materials must be listed or identified as sunlight resistant.

(2) Chemical Exposure. If subject to exposure to chemical solvents, vapors, splashing, or immersion, materials or coatings must either be inherently resistant to chemicals based upon their listing, or be identified for the specific chemical.

(D) Indoor Wet Locations. In portions of dairy processing facilities, laundries, canneries, and other indoor wet locations, and in locations where walls are frequently washed or where there are surfaces of absorbent materials, such as damp paper or wood, the entire wiring system, where installed exposed, including all boxes, fittings, raceways, and cables, must be mounted so there's at least ¼ in. of airspace between it and the wall or supporting surface.

Author's Comment:

- See the definitions of "Exposed" and "Location, Wet" in Article 100.

Ex: Nonmetallic raceways, boxes, and fittings are permitted without the airspace on a concrete, masonry, tile, or similar surface.

Note: Areas where acids and alkali chemicals are handled and stored may present corrosive conditions, particularly when wet or damp. Severe corrosive conditions may also be present in portions of meatpacking plants, tanneries, glue houses, and some stables; in installations immediately adjacent to a seashore or swimming pool, spa, hot tub, and fountain areas; in areas where chemical deicers are used; and in storage cellars or rooms for hides, casings, fertilizer, salt, and bulk chemicals.

300.7 Raceways Exposed to Different Temperatures

(A) Sealing. If a raceway is subjected to different temperatures, and where condensation is known to be a problem, the raceway must be filled with a material approved by the authority having jurisdiction that will prevent the circulation of warm air to a colder section of the raceway. An explosionproof seal isn't required for this purpose. ▶Figure 300–40

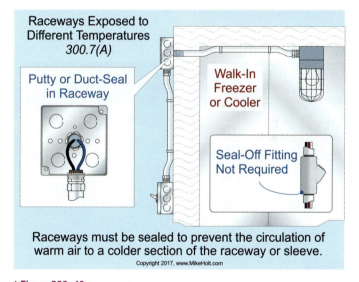

▶Figure 300–40

(B) Expansion, Expansion-Deflection, and Deflection Fittings. Raceways must be provided with expansion, expansion-deflection, and deflection fittings where necessary to compensate for thermal expansion, deflection, and contraction. ▶Figure 300–41

300.8 | General Requirements for Wiring Methods and Materials

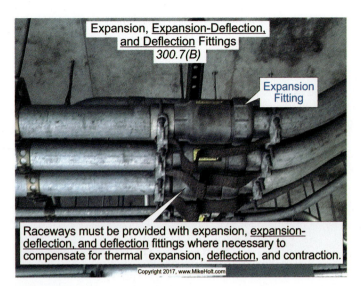

▶Figure 300–41

Note: Table 352.44 provides the expansion characteristics for PVC conduit. The expansion characteristics for steel conduit are determined by multiplying the values from Table 352.44 by 0.20, and the expansion characteristics for aluminum raceways are determined by multiplying the values from Table 352.44 by 0.40. Table 354.44 provides the expansion characteristics for reinforced thermosetting resin conduit (RTRC). ▶Figure 300–42

▶Figure 300–42

300.8 Not Permitted in Raceways

Raceways are designed for the exclusive use of electrical conductors and cables, and aren't permitted to contain nonelectrical components, such as pipes or tubes for steam, water, air, gas, drainage, and so forth.
▶Figure 300–43

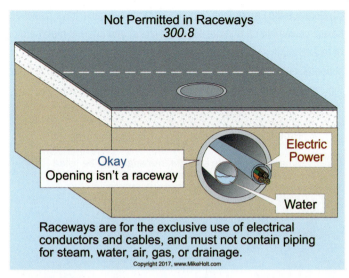

▶Figure 300–43

300.9 Raceways in Wet Locations Above Grade

Insulated conductors and cables installed in raceways in aboveground wet locations must be listed for use in wet locations in accordance with 310.10(C).

300.10 Electrical Continuity

Metal raceways, cable armor, and other metal enclosures must be metallically joined together into a continuous electrical conductor to provide effective electrical continuity [110.10 and 250.4(A)(3)]. ▶Figure 300–44

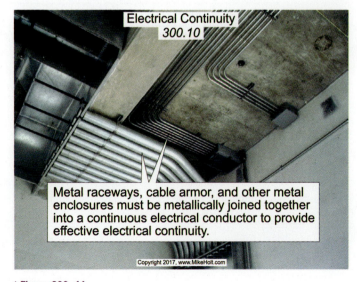

▶Figure 300–44

General Requirements for Wiring Methods and Materials | 300.11

Author's Comment:

- The purpose of effective electrical continuity is to establish an effective ground-fault current path necessary to facilitate the operation of the circuit overcurrent protection device in the event of a ground fault [250.4(A)(3)]. ▶Figure 300–45

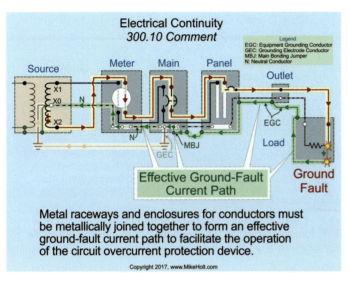

▶Figure 300–45

Ex 1: Short lengths of metal raceways used for the support or protection of cables aren't required to be electrically continuous, nor are they required to be connected to an equipment grounding conductor [250.86 Ex 2 and 300.12 Ex]. ▶Figure 300–46

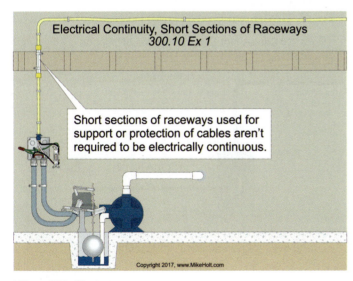

▶Figure 300–46

300.11 Securing and Supporting

(A) Secured in Place. Raceways, cable assemblies, and enclosures must be securely fastened in place.

(B) Wiring Systems Installed Above Suspended Ceilings. The ceiling-support wires or ceiling grid aren't permitted to be used to support raceways and cables (power, signaling, or communications). However, independent support wires that are secured at both ends and provide secure support are permitted. ▶Figure 300–47

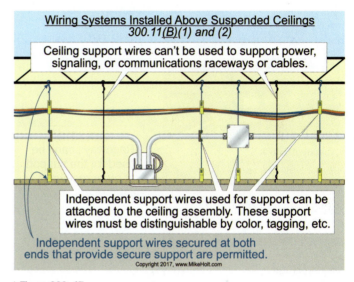

▶Figure 300–47

Author's Comment:

- Outlet boxes [314.23(D)] and luminaires can be secured to the suspended-ceiling grid if securely fastened to the ceiling-framing members by mechanical means such as bolts, screws, or rivets, or by the use of clips or other securing means identified for use with the type of ceiling-framing member(s) used [410.36(B)].

(1) Fire-Rated Ceiling Assembly. Electrical wiring within the cavity of a fire-rated floor-ceiling or roof-ceiling assembly can be supported by independent support wires attached to the ceiling assembly. The independent support wires must be distinguishable from the suspended-ceiling support wires by color, tagging, or other effective means.

300.11 | General Requirements for Wiring Methods and Materials

(2) Nonfire-Rated Ceiling Assembly. Wiring in a nonfire-rated floor-ceiling or roof-ceiling assembly can be supported by independent support wires attached to the ceiling assembly. The independent support wires must be distinguishable from the suspended-ceiling support wires by color, tagging, or other effective means.

(C) Raceways Used for Support. Raceways aren't permitted to be used as a means of support for other raceways, cables, or nonelectrical equipment, except as permitted in (1) through (3). ▶Figure 300–48 and ▶Figure 300–49.

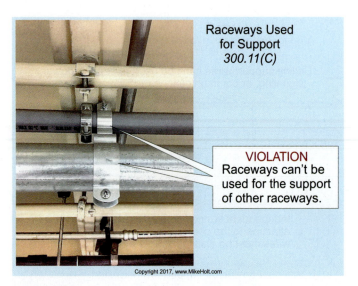

▶Figure 300–48

(1) Identified. If the raceway or means of support is identified as a means of support.

(2) Class 2 and 3 Circuits. Class 2 and 3 cables can be supported by the raceway that supplies power to the equipment controlled by the Class 2 or 3 circuit. ▶Figure 300–50

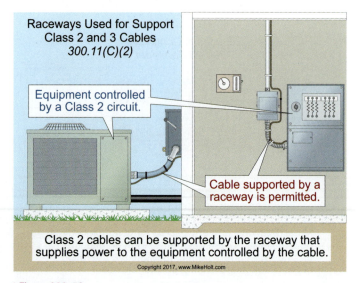

▶Figure 300–50

(3) Boxes Supported by Raceways. Raceways are permitted as a means of support for threaded boxes and conduit bodies in accordance with 314.23(E) and (F), or to support luminaires in accordance with 410.36(E).

(D) Cables Not Used as Means of Support. Cables aren't permitted to be used to support other cables, raceways, or nonelectrical equipment. ▶Figure 300–51

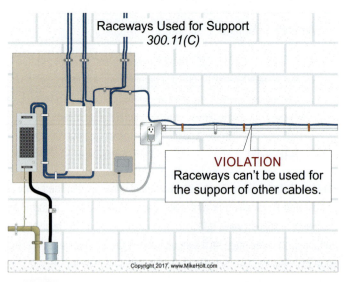

▶Figure 300–49

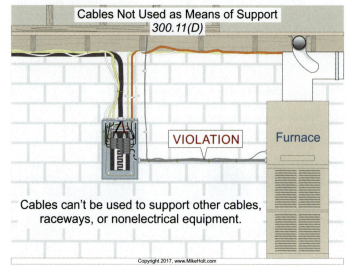

▶Figure 300–51

General Requirements for Wiring Methods and Materials | 300.13

300.12 Mechanical Continuity

Raceways and cable sheaths must be mechanically continuous between boxes, cabinets, and fittings. ▶Figure 300–52 and ▶Figure 300–53

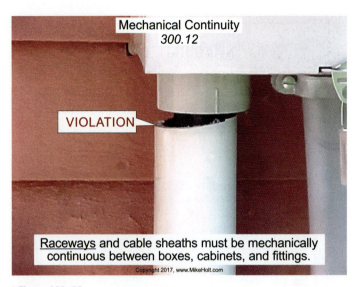
▶Figure 300–52

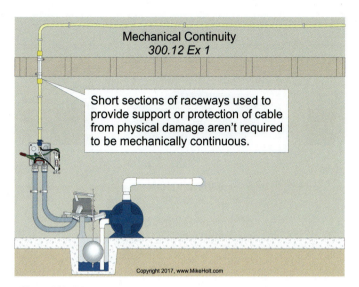
▶Figure 300–54

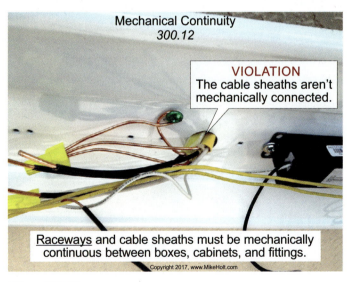
▶Figure 300–53

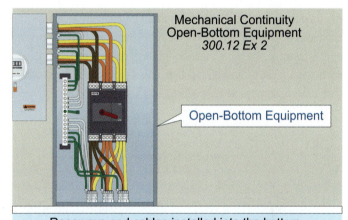
▶Figure 300–55

Ex 1: Short sections of raceways used to provide support or protection of cable from physical damage aren't required to be mechanically continuous [250.86 Ex 2 and 300.10 Ex 1]. ▶Figure 300–54

Ex 2: Raceways at the bottom of open-bottom equipment, such as switchboards, motor control centers, and transformers, aren't required to be mechanically secured to the equipment. ▶Figure 300–55

Author's Comment:

- When raceways are stubbed into an open-bottom switchboard, the raceway, including the end fitting, can't rise more than 3 in. above the bottom of the switchboard enclosure [408.5].

300.13 Splices and Pigtails

(A) Conductor Splices. Splices must be in enclosures in accordance with 300.15 and aren't permitted in raceways, except as permitted by 376.56, 386.56, or 388.56. ▶Figure 300–56

300.13 | General Requirements for Wiring Methods and Materials

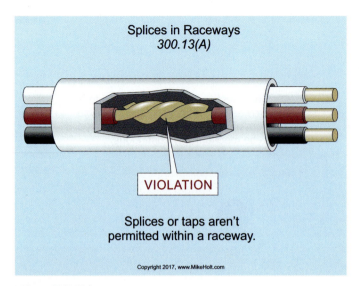

▶Figure 300–56

(B) Device Removal—Neutral Continuity. Continuity of the neutral conductor of a multiwire branch circuit isn't permitted to be interrupted by the removal of a wiring device. In these applications, the neutral conductors must be spliced together, and a pigtail must be provided for the wiring device. ▶Figure 300–57

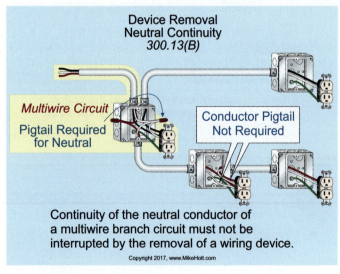

▶Figure 300–57

Author's Comment:

- The opening of the ungrounded conductors, or the neutral conductor of a 2-wire circuit during the replacement of a device doesn't cause a safety hazard, so pigtailing these conductors isn't required [110.14(B)].

⚠ **CAUTION:** If the continuity of the neutral conductor of a multiwire circuit is interrupted (opened), the resultant over- or undervoltage can cause a fire and/or destruction of electrical equipment.

▶ **Hazard of Open Neutral**

Example: If the neutral conductor is interrupted on a 3-wire, 120/240V multiwire circuit that supplies a 1,200W, 120V hair dryer and a 600W, 120V television, it will cause the 120V television to operate at 160V for an instant before it burns up. We can determine this as follows: ▶Figure 300–58 and ▶Figure 300–59

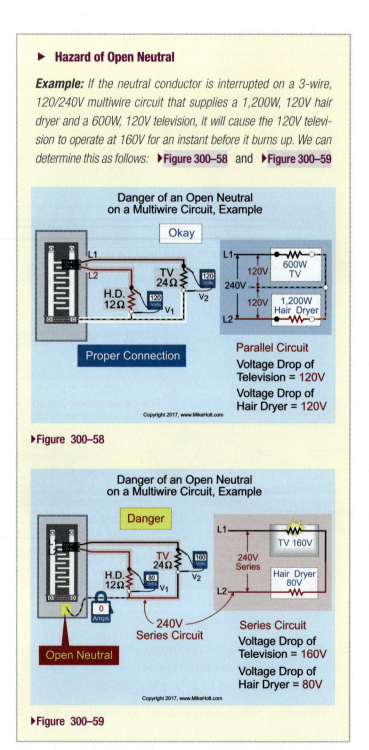

▶Figure 300–58

▶Figure 300–59

Step 1: Determine the resistance of each appliance:

$R = E^2/P$

R of the hair dryer = $120V^2/1{,}200W$
R of the hair dryer = 12 ohms
R of the television = $120V^2/600W$
R of the television = 24 ohms

Step 2: Determine the current of the circuit:

$I = E/R$

E = 240V
R = 36 ohms (12 ohms + 24 ohms)
I = 240V/36 ohms
I = 6.70A

Step 3: Determine the operating voltage for each appliance:

$E = I \times R$

I = 6.70A
R = 12 ohms for hair dryer and 24 ohms for TV
Voltage of hair dryer = 6.70A × 12 ohms
Voltage of hair dryer = 80V
Voltage of television = 6.70A × 24 ohms
Voltage of television = 160V

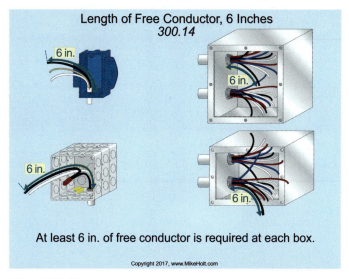
▶ Figure 300–60

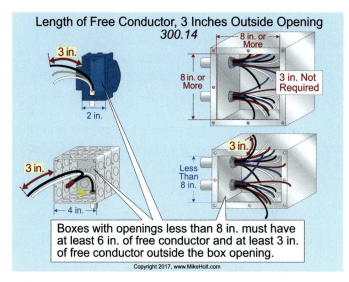
▶ Figure 300–61

300.14 Length of Free Conductors

At least 6 in. of free conductor, measured from the point in the box where the conductors enter the enclosure, must be left at each outlet, junction, and switch point for splices or terminations of luminaires or devices. ▶Figure 300–60

Boxes that have openings less than 8 in. in any dimension, must have at least 6 in. of free conductor, measured from the point where the conductors enter the box, and at least 3 in. of free conductor outside the box opening. ▶Figure 300–61

Ex: Six in. of free conductor aren't required for conductors that pass through a box without a splice or termination.

300.15 Boxes or Conduit Bodies

Fittings can only be used with the specific wiring methods for which they're listed and designed. For example, Type NM cable connectors aren't permitted to be used with Type AC cable, and electrical metallic tubing fittings aren't permitted to be used with rigid metal conduit or intermediate metal conduit, unless listed for the purpose. ▶Figure 300–62

300.15 | General Requirements for Wiring Methods and Materials

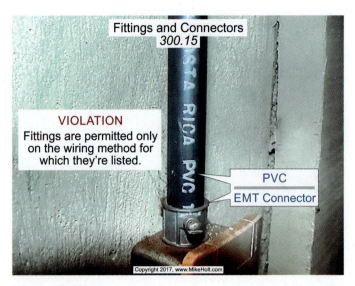

▶Figure 300–62

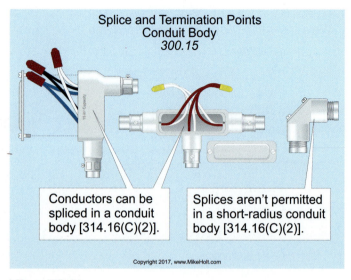

▶Figure 300–64

Author's Comment:

- PVC conduit couplings and connectors are permitted with electrical nonmetallic tubing if the proper glue is used in accordance with manufacturer's instructions [110.3(B)]. See 362.48.

A box or conduit body must be installed at each splice or termination point, except as permitted for by 310.15(A) through (L): ▶Figure 300–63 and ▶Figure 300–64

- Cabinets, 312.8
- Luminaires, 410.64
- Surface Raceways, 386.56 and 388.56
- Wireways, 376.56

Author's Comment:

- Boxes aren't required for the following signaling and communications cables or raceways: ▶Figure 300–65
  ◆ Class 2 and 3 Control and Signaling, 725.3
  ◆ Communications, 90.3
  ◆ Coaxial Cable, 90.3
  ◆ Optical Fiber, 770.3

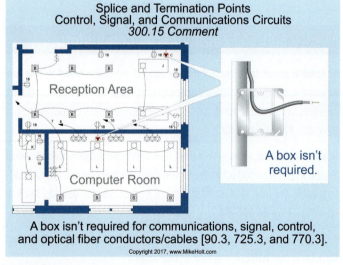

▶Figure 300–65

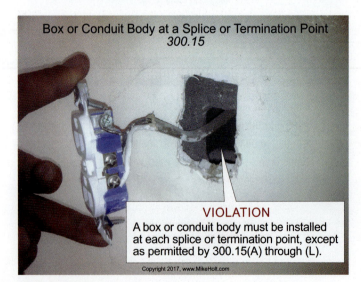

▶Figure 300–63

(C) Raceways for Support or Protection. When a raceway is used for the support or protection of cables, a fitting to reduce the potential for abrasion must be placed at the location the cables enter the raceway.
▶Figure 300–66

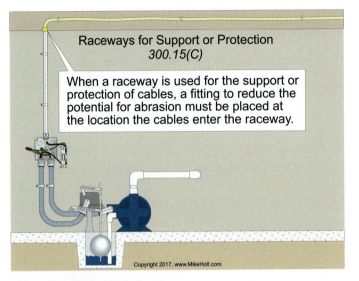
▶Figure 300–66

(F) Fitting. A fitting is permitted in lieu of a box or conduit body where conductors aren't spliced or terminated within the fitting if it's accessible after installation. ▶Figure 300–67

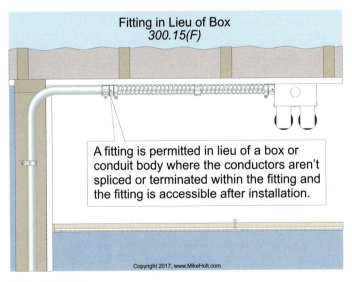
▶Figure 300–67

(G) Underground Splices. A box or conduit body isn't required where a splice is made underground if the conductors are spliced with a splicing device listed for direct burial. See 110.14(B) and 300.5(E).

Author's Comment:

- See the definition of "Conduit Body" in Article 100.

(H) NM Cable Interconnection Devices. A box or conduit body isn't required where a listed nonmetallic-sheathed cable interconnector device is used for any exposed cable wiring or for concealed cable wiring in existing buildings in accordance with 334.40(B). ▶Figure 300–68

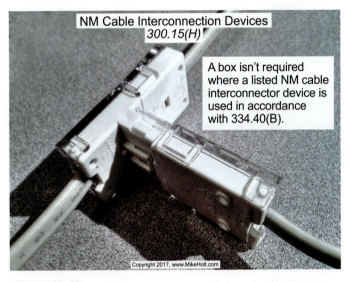
▶Figure 300–68

(I) Enclosures. A box or conduit body isn't required where a splice is made in a cabinet containing switches or overcurrent protection devices if the splices or taps don't fill the wiring space at any cross section to more than 75 percent, and the wiring at any cross section doesn't exceed 40 percent. See 312.8 and 404.3(B). ▶Figure 300–69

(L) Handhole Enclosures. A box or conduit body isn't required for conductors installed in a handhole enclosure. Splices must be made in accordance with 314.30. ▶Figure 300–70

Author's Comment:

- Splices or terminations within a handhole must be accomplished using fittings listed as suitable for wet locations [110.14(B) and 314.30(C)].

300.16 | General Requirements for Wiring Methods and Materials

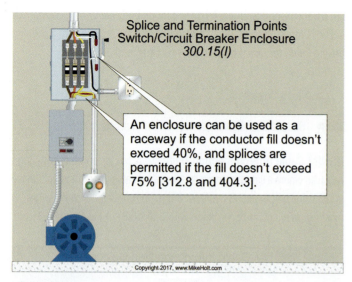

▶Figure 300–69

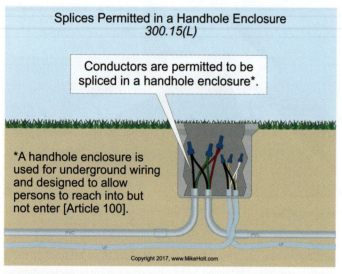

▶Figure 300–70

300.16 Raceway or Cable to Open or Concealed Wiring

(B) Bushing. A bushing is permitted in lieu of a box or terminal where the conductors emerge from a raceway and enter or terminate at equipment such as open switchboards, unenclosed control equipment, or similar equipment.

300.17 Raceway Sizing

Raceways must be large enough to permit the installation and removal of conductors without damaging the conductors' insulation.

Author's Comment:

- When all conductors within a raceway are the same size and of the same insulation type, the number of conductors permitted can be determined by Annex C.

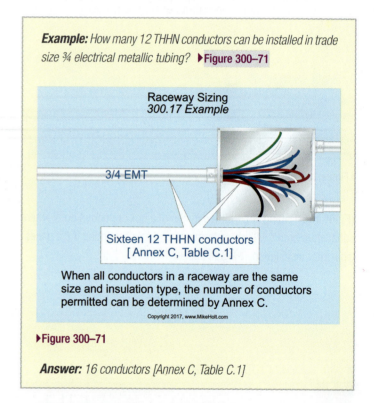

Example: How many 12 THHN conductors can be installed in trade size ¾ electrical metallic tubing? ▶Figure 300–71

▶Figure 300–71

Answer: 16 conductors [Annex C, Table C.1]

Author's Comment:

- When different size conductors are installed within a raceway, conductor fill is limited to the percentages in Table 1 of Chapter 9. ▶Figure 300–72

Table 1, Chapter 9	
Number	Percent Fill
1 Conductor	53%
2 Conductors	31%
3 or More	40%

General Requirements for Wiring Methods and Materials | 300.17

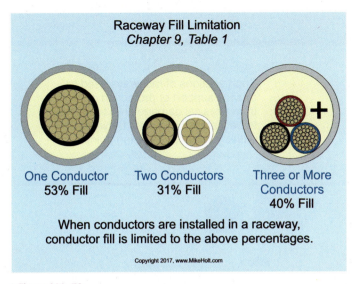

▸Figure 300–72

The above percentages are based on conditions where the length of the conductor and number of raceway bends are within reasonable limits [Chapter 9, Table 1, Note 1].

Author's Comment:

- Follow these steps for sizing raceways:
  - Step 1: When sizing a raceway, first determine the total area of conductors (Chapter 9, Table 5 for insulated conductors and Chapter 9, Table 8 for bare conductors).
    ▸Figure 300–73

▸Figure 300–73

- Step 2: Select the raceway from Chapter 9, Table 4, in accordance with the percent fill listed in Chapter 9, Table 1.
  ▸Figure 300–74

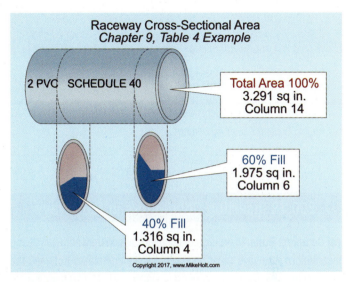

▸Figure 300–74

Example: What trade size Schedule 40 PVC conduit is required for the following conductors? ▸Figure 300–75

3—500 THHN
1—250 THHN
1—3 THHN

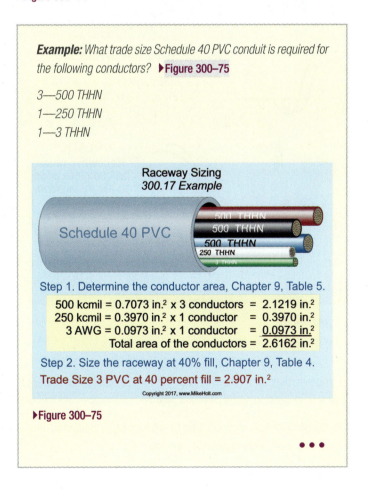

Step 1. Determine the conductor area, Chapter 9, Table 5.

500 kcmil = 0.7073 in.² x 3 conductors	= 2.1219 in.²
250 kcmil = 0.3970 in.² x 1 conductor	= 0.3970 in.²
3 AWG = 0.0973 in.² x 1 conductor	= 0.0973 in.²
Total area of the conductors	= 2.6162 in.²

Step 2. Size the raceway at 40% fill, Chapter 9, Table 4.
Trade Size 3 PVC at 40 percent fill = 2.907 in.²

▸Figure 300–75

Solution:

Step 1: Determine the total area of conductors [Chapter 9, Table 5]:
- 500 THHN $0.7073 \times 3 =$ $2.1219\ in^2$
- 250 THHN $0.3970 \times 1 =$ $0.3970\ in^2$
- 3 THHN $0.0973 \times 1 =$ $+\ 0.0973\ in^2$
- Total Area = $2.6162\ in^2$

Step 2: Select the raceway at 40 percent fill [Chapter 9, Table 4]

Answer: Trade size 3 Schedule 40 PVC because there's 2.907 sq in. of conductor fill at 40 percent.

300.18 Inserting Conductors in Raceways

(A) Complete Runs. To protect conductor insulation from abrasion during installation, raceways must be mechanically completed between the pulling points before conductors are installed. See 300.10 and 300.12.
▶Figure 300–76

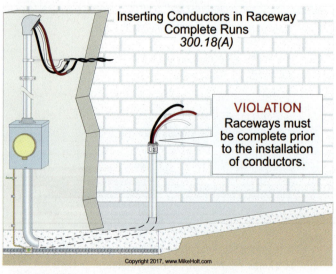
▶Figure 300–76

Ex: Short sections of raceways used for the protection of cables from physical damage aren't required to be installed complete between outlet, junction, or splicing points. ▶Figure 300–77

(B) Welding. Metal raceways aren't permitted to be supported, terminated, or connected by welding to the raceway.

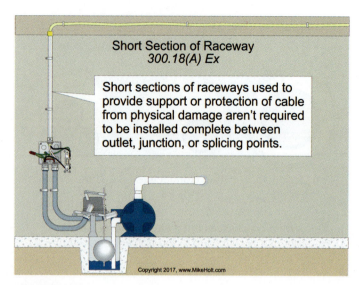
▶Figure 300–77

300.19 Supporting Conductors in Vertical Raceways

(A) Spacing Intervals. If the vertical rise of a raceway exceeds the values of Table 300.19(A), each conductor must be supported at the top, or as close to the top as practical. Intermediate support must also be provided in increments that don't exceed the values of Table 300.19(A). ▶Figure 300–78

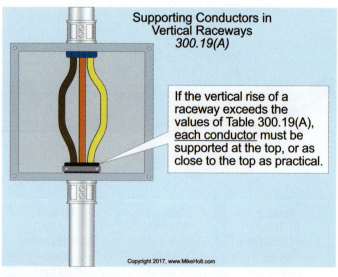
▶Figure 300–78

General Requirements for Wiring Methods and Materials | 300.20

Author's Comment:

- The weight of long vertical runs of conductors can cause the conductors to actually drop out of the raceway if they aren't properly secured. There've been many cases where conductors in a vertical raceway were released from the pulling "basket" or "grip" (at the top) without being secured, and the conductors fell down and out of the raceway, injuring those at the bottom of the installation.

300.20 Induced Currents in Ferrous Metal Enclosures and Raceways

(A) Conductors Grouped Together. To minimize induction heating of ferrous metal raceways and ferrous metal enclosures for alternating-current circuits, and to maintain an effective ground-fault current path, all conductors of a circuit must be installed in the same raceway, cable, trench, cord, or cable tray. See 250.102(E), 300.3(B), 300.5(I), and 392.8(D). ▶Figure 300–79 and ▶Figure 300–80

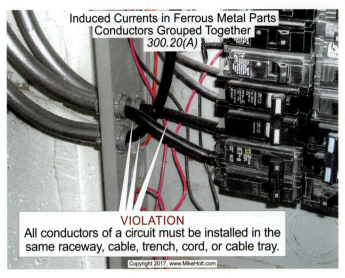

▶Figure 300–80

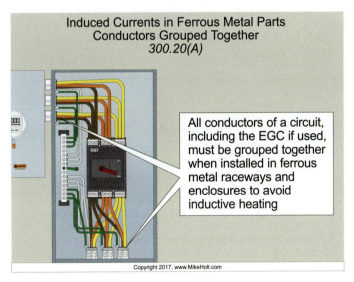

▶Figure 300–79

Author's Comment:

- When alternating current (ac) flows through a conductor, a pulsating or varying magnetic field is created around the conductor. This magnetic field is constantly expanding and contracting with the amplitude of the ac current. In the United States, the frequency is 60 cycles per second (Hz). Since ac reverses polarity 120 times per second, the magnetic field that surrounds the conductor also reverses its direction 120 times per second. This expanding and collapsing magnetic field induces eddy currents in the ferrous metal parts that surround the conductors, causing them to heat up from hysteresis heating.

- Magnetic materials naturally resist the rapidly changing magnetic fields. The resulting friction produces its own heat—hysteresis heating—in addition to eddy current heating. A metal which offers high resistance is said to have high magnetic "permeability." Permeability can vary on a scale of 100 to 500 for magnetic materials; nonmagnetic materials have a permeability of one.

- Simply put, the molecules of steel and iron align to the polarity of the magnetic field and when the magnetic field reverses, the molecules reverse their polarity as well. This back-and-forth alignment of the molecules heats up the metal, and the more the current flows, the more the heat rises in the ferrous metal parts. ▶Figure 300–81

- When conductors of the same circuit are grouped together, the magnetic fields of the different conductors tend to cancel each other out, resulting in a reduced magnetic field around them. The lower magnetic field reduces induced currents in the ferrous metal raceways or enclosures, which reduces the hysteresis heating of the surrounding metal enclosure.

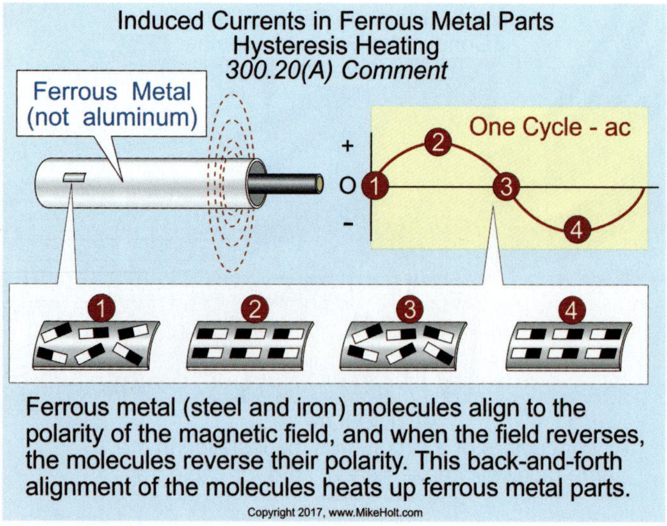

300.21 | General Requirements for Wiring Methods and Materials

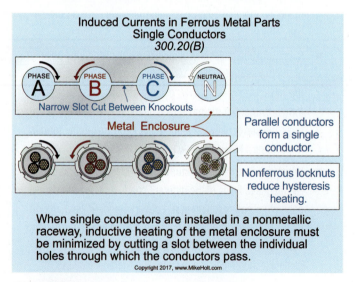

▶Figure 300–81

WARNING: There's been much discussion in the press on the effects of electromagnetic fields on humans. According to the Institute of Electrical and Electronics Engineers (IEEE), there's insufficient information at this time to define an unsafe electromagnetic field level.

(B) Single Conductors. When single conductors are installed in nonmetallic raceways as permitted in 300.5(I) Ex 2, the inductive heating of the metal enclosure must be minimized using aluminum locknuts and by cutting a slot between the individual holes through which the conductors pass. ▶Figure 300–82

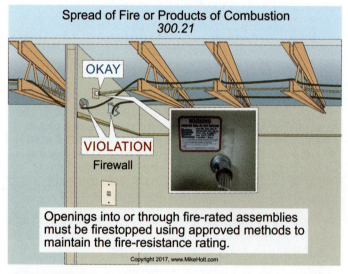

▶Figure 300–82

Note: Because aluminum is a nonmagnetic metal, aluminum parts don't heat up due to hysteresis heating.

Author's Comment:

- Aluminum conduit, locknuts, and enclosures carry eddy currents, but because aluminum is nonferrous, it doesn't heat up [300.20(B) Note].

300.21 Spread of Fire or Products of Combustion

Electrical circuits and equipment must be installed in such a way that the spread of fire or products of combustion won't be substantially increased. Openings into or through fire-rated walls, floors, and ceilings for electrical equipment must be fire-stopped using methods approved by the authority having jurisdiction to maintain the fire-resistance rating of the fire-rated assembly. ▶Figure 300–83

▶Figure 300–83

Author's Comment:

- Fire-stopping materials are listed for the specific types of wiring methods and the construction of the assembly that they penetrate. ▶Figure 300–84

General Requirements for Wiring Methods and Materials | 300.22

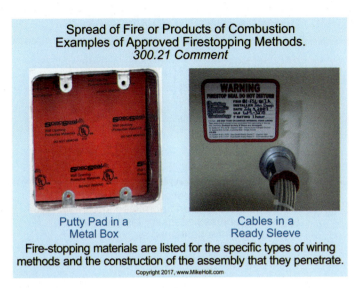
▶Figure 300–84

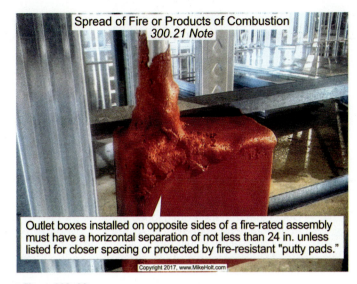
▶Figure 300–86

Note: Directories of electrical construction materials published by qualified testing laboratories contain listing and installation restrictions necessary to maintain the fire-resistive rating of assemblies. Outlet boxes must have a horizontal separation of not less than 24 in. when installed in a fire-rated assembly, unless an outlet box is listed for closer spacing or protected by fire-resistant "putty pads" in accordance with manufacturer's instructions. ▶Figure 300–85 and ▶Figure 300–86

Author's Comment:

- Boxes installed in fire-resistance-rated assemblies must be listed for the purpose. If steel boxes are used, they must be secured to the framing member, so cut-in type boxes aren't permitted (UL White Book, *Guide Information for Electrical Equipment*).

- This rule also applies to control, signaling, and communications cables or raceways.
    - Communications, 800.26
    - Control and Signaling, 725.25
    - Coaxial Cable, 820.26
    - Fire Alarm, 760.3(A)
    - Optical Fiber, 770.26
    - Sound Systems, 640.3(A)

300.22 Wiring in Ducts and Plenum Spaces

This section applies to the installation and uses of electrical wiring and equipment in ducts used for dust, loose stock, or vapor removal; ducts specifically fabricated for environmental air; and plenum spaces used for environmental air.

(A) Ducts Used for Dust, Loose Stock, or Vapor. Ducts that transport dust, loose stock, or vapors must not have any wiring method installed within them. ▶Figure 300–87

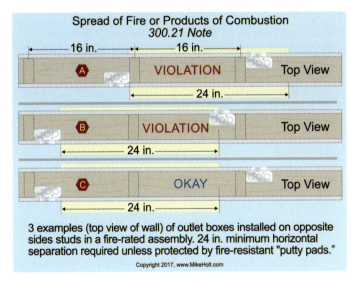
▶Figure 300–85

300.22 | General Requirements for Wiring Methods and Materials

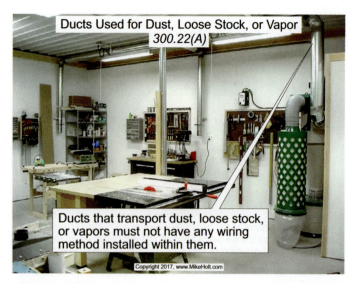

▸Figure 300–87

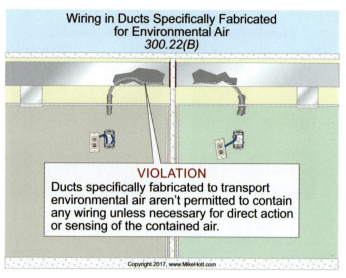

▸Figure 300–88

(B) Ducts Specifically Fabricated for Environmental Air. If necessary for direct action upon, or sensing of, the contained air, Type MC cable that has a smooth or corrugated impervious metal sheath without an overall nonmetallic covering, electrical metallic tubing, flexible metallic tubing, intermediate metal conduit, or rigid metal conduit without an overall nonmetallic covering can be installed in ducts specifically fabricated to transport environmental air. Flexible metal conduit in lengths not exceeding 4 ft can be used to connect physically adjustable equipment and devices within the fabricated duct.

Equipment is only permitted within the duct specifically fabricated to transport environmental air if necessary for the direct action upon, or sensing of, the contained air. Equipment, devices, and/or illumination are only permitted to be installed in the duct if necessary to facilitate maintenance and repair. ▸Figure 300–88

Ex: Wiring methods and cables listed for plenum spaces can be installed in ducts specifically fabricated for environmental air-handling purposes under the following conditions: ▸Figure 300–89

(1) The wiring method or cabling is necessary to connect to equipment or devices associated with the direct action upon or sensing of the contained air, and

(2) The total length of such wiring method or cabling doesn't exceed 4 ft.

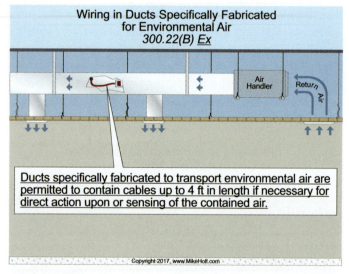

▸Figure 300–89

Author's Comment:

- Class 2 and Class 3 cables selected in accordance with Table 725.154 and installed in accordance with 725.135(B) are permitted to be installed in ducts specifically fabricated for environmental air [725.3(C) Ex. 1].

- Power-limited fire alarm cables selected in accordance with Table 760.154 and installed in accordance with 760.135(B) are permitted to be installed in ducts specifically fabricated for environmental air [760.3(C) Ex. 1].

(C) Plenum Space for Environmental Air. This subsection applies only to plenum spaces (space above a suspended ceiling or below a raised floor used for environmental air), it doesn't apply to habitable rooms or areas of buildings, the prime purpose of which isn't air handling. ▶Figure 300–90

Ex: In a dwelling unit, this section doesn't apply to the space between joists or studs where the wiring passes through that space perpendicular to the long dimension of that space. ▶Figure 300–92

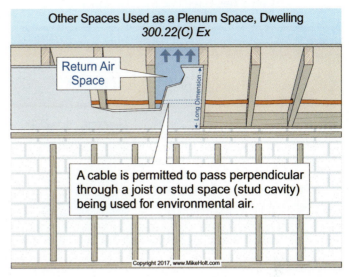

▶Figure 300–92

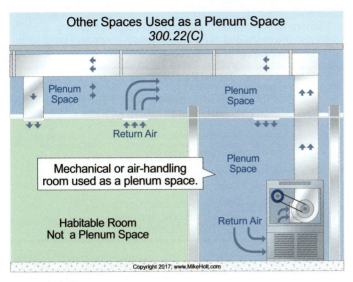

▶Figure 300–90

Note 1: The spaces above a suspended ceiling or below a raised floor used for environmental air are examples of the type of plenum spaces to which this section applies. ▶Figure 300–91

(1) Wiring Methods. Electrical metallic tubing, rigid metal conduit, intermediate metal conduit, armored cable, metal-clad cable without a nonmetallic cover, and flexible metal conduit can be installed in a plenum space. Surface metal raceways or metal wireways with metal covers can be installed in a plenum space. ▶Figure 300–93

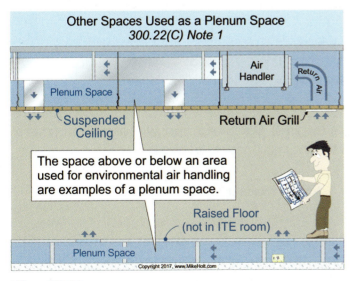

▶Figure 300–91

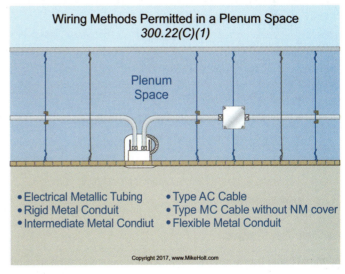

▶Figure 300–93

300.22 | General Requirements for Wiring Methods and Materials

Cable ties for securing and supporting must be listed for use in a plenum space. ▶Figure 300–94

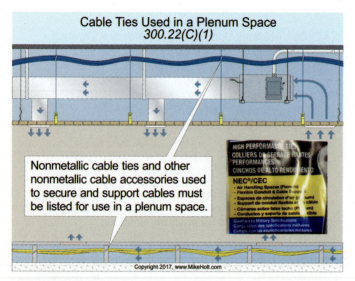
▶Figure 300–94

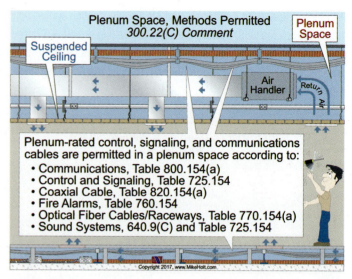
▶Figure 300–95

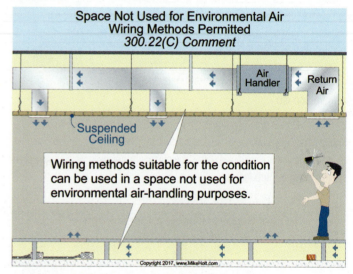
▶Figure 300–96

Author's Comment:

- PVC conduit [Article 352], electrical nonmetallic tubing [Article 362], liquidtight flexible conduit, and nonmetallic cables aren't permitted to be installed in plenum spaces because they give off deadly toxic fumes when burned or superheated.

- Plenum-rated control, signaling, and communications cables and raceways are permitted in plenum spaces according to the following: ▶Figure 300–95
    ♦ Communications, Table 800.154(a)
    ♦ Control and Signaling, 725.3(C) Ex 2
    ♦ Coaxial Cable, Table 820.154(a)
    ♦ Fire Alarm, Table 760.3(C) Ex 2
    ♦ Optical Fiber Cables and Raceways, Table 770.154(a)
    ♦ Sound Systems, 640.9(C) and Table 725.154

- Any wiring method suitable for the condition can be used in a space not used for environmental air-handling purposes. ▶Figure 300–96

(2) Cable Tray Systems.

(a) Metal Cable Tray Systems. Metal cable tray systems can be installed to support the wiring methods and equipment permitted to be installed in a plenum space. ▶Figure 300–97

(3) Equipment. Electrical equipment with a metal enclosure can be installed in a plenum space. ▶Figure 300–98

Author's Comment:

- Examples of electrical equipment permitted in plenum spaces are air-handlers, junction boxes, and dry-type transformers; however, transformers must not be rated over 50 kVA when located in hollow spaces [450.13(B)].

(D) Information Technology Equipment. Wiring methods beneath raised floors for information technology equipment can be installed as permitted in Article 645. ▶Figure 300–99

General Requirements for Wiring Methods and Materials | 300.23

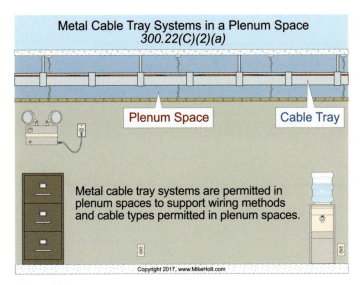
▶Figure 300–97

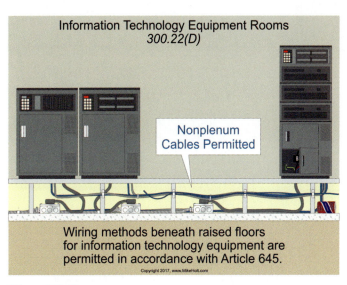
▶Figure 300–99

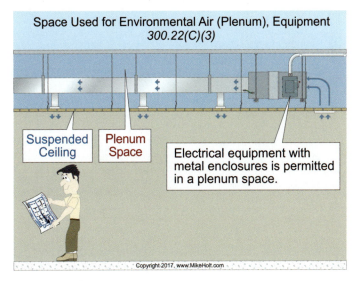
▶Figure 300–98

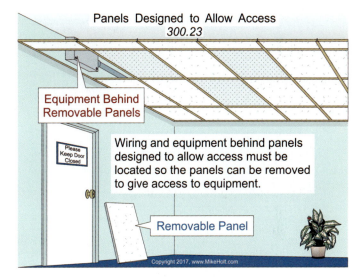
▶Figure 300–100

300.23 Panels Designed to Allow Access

Wiring, cables, and equipment installed behind panels must be located so the panels can be removed to give access to electrical equipment.
▶Figure 300–100

Author's Comment:

- Access to equipment must not be hindered by an accumulation of cables that prevents the removal of suspended-ceiling panels. Control, signaling, and communications cables must be located and supported so the suspended-ceiling panels can be moved to provide access to electrical equipment.

  ◆ Communications Cable, 800.21
  ◆ Control and Signaling Cable, 725.21
  ◆ Coaxial Cable, 820.21
  ◆ Fire Alarm Cable, 760.21
  ◆ Optical Fiber Cable, 770.21
  ◆ Audio Cable, 640.5

Notes

ARTICLE 310
CONDUCTORS FOR GENERAL WIRING

Introduction to Article 310—Conductors for General Wiring

This article contains the general requirements for conductors, such as insulation markings, ampacity ratings, and conditions of use. Article 310 doesn't apply to conductors that are part of flexible cords, fixture wires, or to conductors that are an integral part of equipment [90.7 and 300.1(B)].

People often make mistakes in applying the ampacity tables contained in Article 310. If you study the explanations carefully, you'll avoid common errors such as applying Table 310.15(B)(17) when you should be applying Table 310.15(B)(16).

Why so many tables? Why does Table 310.15(B)(17) list the ampacity of 6 THHN as 105A, while Table 310.15(B)(16) lists the same conductor as having an ampacity of only 75A? To answer that, go back to Article 100 and review the definition of ampacity. Notice the phrase "conditions of use." These tables set a maximum current value at which premature failure of the conductor insulation shouldn't occur during normal use, under the conditions described in the tables.

The designations THHN, THHW, RHH, and so on, are insulation types. Every type of insulation has a limit as to how much heat it can withstand. When current flows through a conductor, it creates heat. How well the insulation around a conductor can dissipate that heat depends on factors such as whether the conductor is in free air or not. Think about what happens when you put on a sweater, a jacket, and then a coat—all at the same time. You heat up. Your skin can't dissipate heat with all that clothing on nearly as well as it dissipates heat in free air. The same principle applies to conductors.

Conductor insulation also fails with age. That's why we conduct cable testing and take other measures to predict failure and replace certain conductors (for example, feeders or critical equipment conductors) while they're still within design specifications. But conductor insulation failure takes decades under normal use—and it's a maintenance issue. However, if a conductor is forced to exceed the ampacity listed in the appropriate table, and as a result its design temperature is exceeded, insulation failure happens much more rapidly—often catastrophically. Consequently, exceeding the allowable ampacity of a conductor is a serious safety issue.

Part I. General

310.1 Scope

Article 310 contains the general requirements for conductors, such as insulation markings, ampacity ratings, and their use. ▶Figure 310–1

Part II. Installation

310.10 Uses Permitted

(B) Dry and Damp Locations. Insulated conductors typically used in dry and damp locations include THHN, THHW, THWN, or THWN-2.

310.10 | Conductors for General Wiring

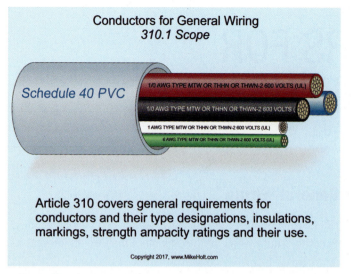

▶Figure 310–1

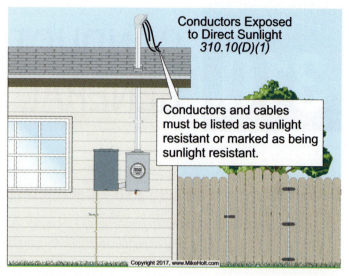

▶Figure 310–2

Author's Comment:

- Refer to Table 310.104(A) for a complete list of conductors that may be installed in dry or damp locations.

(C) Wet Locations. Insulated conductors typically used in wet locations include:

(2) Types THHW, THWN, THWN-2, XHHW, or XHHW-2

Author's Comment:

- Refer to Table 310.104 for a complete list of conductors that may be installed in wet locations.

(D) Locations Exposed to Direct Sunlight. Insulated conductors and cables exposed to the direct rays of the sun must be:

(1) Listed as sunlight resistant or marked as being sunlight resistant. ▶Figure 310–2

Author's Comment:

- SE cable and the conductors contained in the cable are listed as sunlight resistant. However, according to the UL listing standard, the conductors contained in SE cable aren't required to be marked as sunlight resistant.

(2) Covered with insulating material, such as tape or sleeving materials that are listed as being sunlight resistant or marked as being sunlight resistant.

(G) Corrosive Conditions. Conductor insulation must be suitable for any substance to which it may be exposed that may have a detrimental effect on the conductor's insulation, such as oil, grease, vapor, gases, fumes, liquids, or other substances. See 110.11.

(H) Conductors in Parallel.

(1) General. Ungrounded and neutral conductors can be connected in parallel only in sizes 1/0 AWG and larger where installed in accordance with (H)(2) through (H)(6). ▶Figure 310–3

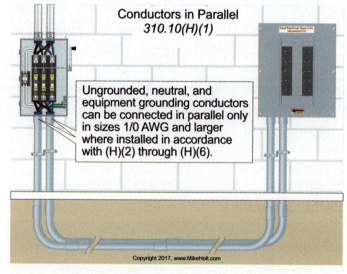

▶Figure 310–3

(2) Conductor and Installation Characteristics. When circuit conductors are installed in parallel, the conductors must be connected so the current will be evenly distributed between the individual parallel conductors by requiring all circuit conductors within each parallel set to: ▶Figure 310–4

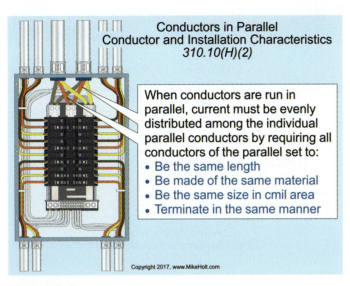
▶Figure 310–4

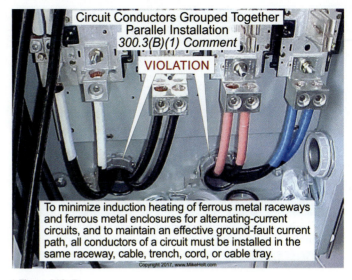
▶Figure 310–5

(1) Be the same length.

(2) Consist of the same conductor material (copper/aluminum).

(3) Be the same size in circular mil area (minimum 1/0 AWG).

(4) Have the same type of insulation (like THHN).

(5) Terminate using the same method (set screw fitting versus compression fitting).

Author's Comment:

- When installed in raceways or enclosures, paralleled conductors must be grouped to prevent inductive heating. ▶Figure 310–5

(3) Separate Raceways or Cables. Raceways or cables containing parallel conductors must have the same electrical characteristics. ▶Figure 310–6

Conductors of one phase, neutral, or equipment grounding conductor are not required to have the same physical characteristics as those of another phase, neutral, or equipment grounding conductor.

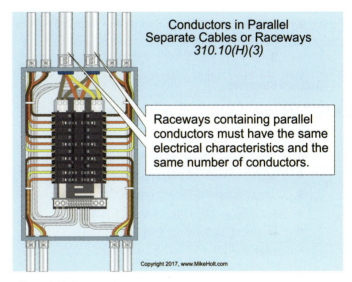
▶Figure 310–6

Author's Comment:

- If one set of parallel conductors is installed in a metal raceway and the other conductors are installed in PVC conduit, the conductors in the metal raceway will have an increased opposition to current flow (impedance) as compared to the conductors in the nonmetallic raceway. This results in an unbalanced distribution of current between the parallel conductors.

- Parallel conductor sets must have all circuit conductors within the same raceway [300.3(B)(1)]. ▶Figure 310–7

310.10 | Conductors for General Wiring

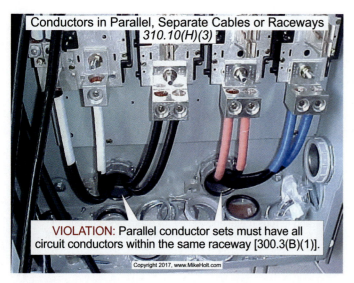

▶Figure 310–7

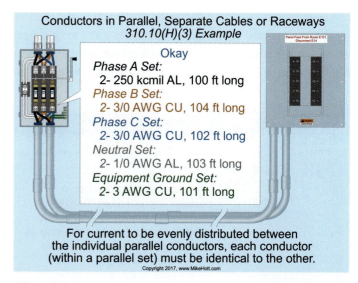

▶Figure 310–8

Parallel sets of conductors aren't required to have the same physical characteristics as those of another set to achieve balance.

Author's Comment:

- For example, a 400A feeder with a neutral load of 240A can be paralleled as follows: ▶Figure 310–8

  ◆ Phase A, Two—250 kcmil THHN aluminum, 100 ft
  ◆ Phase B, Two—3/0 THHN copper, 104 ft
  ◆ Phase C, Two—3/0 THHN copper, 102 ft
  ◆ Neutral, Two—1/0 THHN aluminum, 103 ft
  ◆ Equipment Grounding Conductor, Two—3 AWG copper, 101 ft*

  *The minimum 1/0 AWG requirement doesn't apply to equipment grounding conductors [310.10(H)(5)].

(4) Conductor Ampacity Adjustment. Each current-carrying conductor of a paralleled set of conductors must be counted as a current-carrying conductor for the purpose of conductor ampacity adjustment, in accordance with 310.15(B)(3)(a). ▶Figure 310–9

(5) Equipment Grounding Conductors. The equipment grounding conductors for circuits in parallel must be sized in accordance with 250.122(F). Sectioned equipment grounding conductors smaller than 1/0 AWG are permitted in multiconductor cables, if the combined circular mil area of the sectioned equipment grounding conductor in each cable complies with 250.122. ▶Figure 310–10

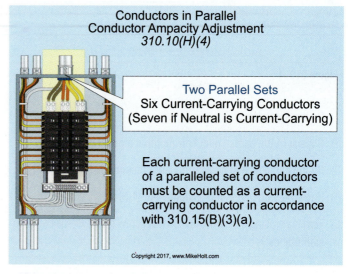

▶Figure 310–9

Author's Comment:

- The minimum 1/0 AWG parallel conductor size rule of 310.10(H) doesn't apply to equipment grounding conductors.

(6) Bonding Jumpers. Equipment bonding jumpers and supply-side bonding jumpers are sized in accordance with 250.102.

Author's Comment:

- The equipment bonding jumper isn't required to be larger than the largest ungrounded circuit conductors supplying the equipment.

Conductors for General Wiring | 310.15

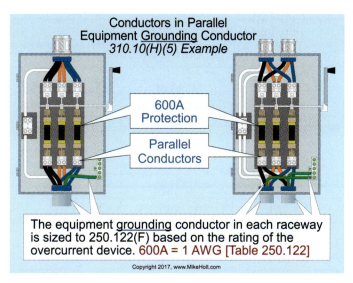

▶Figure 310–10

310.15 Conductor Ampacity

(A) General Requirements.

(1) Tables or Engineering Supervision. The ampacity of a conductor can be determined either by using the tables in accordance with 310.15(B), or under engineering supervision as provided in 310.15(C).

Note 1: Ampacities provided by this section don't take voltage drop into consideration. See 210.19(A) Note 4, for branch circuits and 215.2(D) Note 2, for feeders.

(2) Conductor Ampacity—Lower Rating. Where more than one ampacity applies for a given circuit length, the lowest ampacity value is to be used for the circuit. ▶Figure 310–11

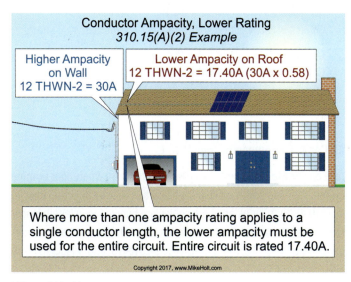

▶Figure 310–11

Ex: When different ampacities apply to a length of conductor because of temperature correction [310.15(B)(2)(a)] or conductor bundling [310.15(B)(3)(a)], the higher ampacity can apply for the entire circuit if length of the corrected or adjusted ampacity doesn't exceed the lesser of 10 ft or 10 percent of the length of the total circuit. ▶Figure 310–12

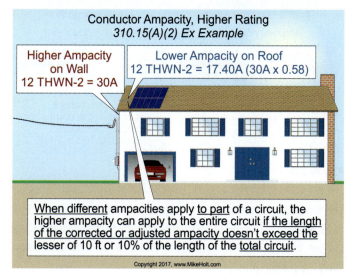

▶Figure 310–12

(3) Insulation Temperature Limitation. Conductors aren't permitted to be used where the operating temperature exceeds that designated for the type of insulated conductor involved.

Note 1: The insulation temperature rating of a conductor [Table 310.104(A)] is the maximum temperature a conductor can withstand over a prolonged time period without serious degradation. The main factors to consider for conductor operating temperature include:

(1) Ambient temperature may vary along the conductor length as well as from time to time [Table 310.15(B)(2)(a)].

(2) Heat generated internally in the conductor—load current flow.

(3) The rate at which generated heat dissipates into the ambient medium.

(4) Adjacent load-carrying conductors have the effect of raising the ambient temperature and impeding heat dissipation [Table 310.15(B)(3)(a)].

Note 2: See 110.14(C)(1) for the temperature limitation of terminations.

(B) Ampacity Table. The allowable conductor ampacities listed in Table 310.15(B)(16) are based on conditions where the ambient temperature is between 78°F and 86°F, and no more than three current-carrying conductors are bundled together. ▶Figure 310–13

310.15 | Conductors for General Wiring

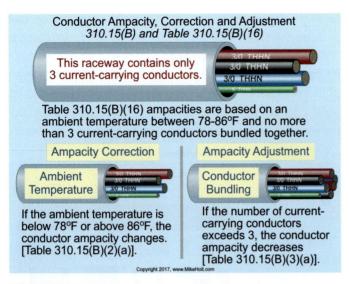

▶Figure 310–13

Table 310.15(B)(2)(a) Ambient Temperature Correction		
Ambient Temperature °F	Ambient Temperature °C	Correction Factor 90°C Conductors
50 or less	10 or less	1.15
51–59°F	11–15°C	1.12
60–68°F	16–20°C	1.08
69–77°F	21–25°C	1.04
78–86°F	26–30°C	1.00
87–95°F	31–35°C	0.96
96–104°F	36–40°C	0.91
105–113°F	41–45°C	0.87
114–122°F	46–50°C	0.82
123–131°F	51–55°C	0.76
132–140°F	56–60°C	0.71
141–149°F	61–65°C	0.65
150–158°F	66–70°C	0.58
159–167°F	71–75°C	0.50

The temperature correction [310.15(B)(2)(a)] and adjustment factors [310.15(B)(3)(a)] apply to the conductor ampacity, based on the temperature rating of the conductor insulation in accordance with Table 310.15(B)(16).

(2) Conductor Ampacity Ambient Temperature Correction. When conductors are installed in an ambient temperature other than 78°F to 86°F, the ampacities listed in Table 310.15(B)(16) must be corrected in accordance with the multipliers listed in Table 310.15(B)(2)(a).

▶Figure 310–14

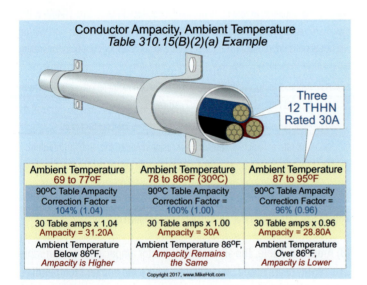

▶Figure 310–14

Example: What's the corrected ampacity of 3/0 THHN conductors if the ambient temperature is 108°F?

Solution:

Conductor Ampacity [90°C] = 225A

Correction Factor [Table 310.15(B)(2)(a)] = 0.87

Corrected Ampacity = 225A × 0.87

Corrected Ampacity = 196A

Answer: 196A

(3) Conductor Ampacity Adjustment.

(a) Four or More Current-Carrying Conductors. Where four or more current-carrying power conductors are within a raceway longer than 24 in. [310.15(B)(3)(a)(2)], or where cables are bundled for a length longer than 24 in., the ampacity of each conductor must be reduced in accordance with Table 310.15(B)(3)(a). ▶Figure 310–15 and ▶Figure 310–16

Conductors for General Wiring | 310.15

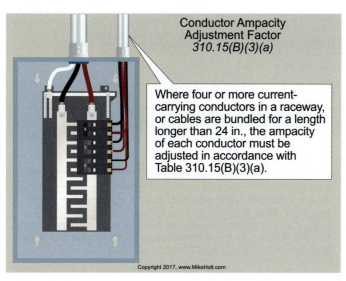

▶Figure 310–15

Table 310.15(B)(3)(a) Conductor Ampacity Adjustment for More Than Three Current–Carrying Conductors
(continued)

Number of Conductors[1]	Adjustment
31–40	0.40 or 40%
41 and above	0.35 or 35%

[1] Number of conductors is the total number of conductors, including spare conductors, adjusted in accordance with 310.15(B)(5) and (B)(6). It doesn't include conductors that can't be energized at the same time.

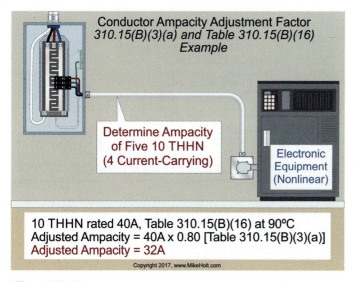

▶Figure 310–16

Author's Comment:

- Conductor ampacity reduction is required when four or more current-carrying conductors are bundled together because heat generated by current flow isn't able to dissipate as quickly as when there are three or fewer current-carry conductors.

(1) Conductor ampacity adjustment of Table 310.15(B)(3)(a) doesn't apply to conductors installed in cable trays, 392.80 applies.

(2) Conductor ampacity adjustment of Table 310.15(B)(3)(a) doesn't apply to conductors in raceways having a length not exceeding 24 in. ▶Figure 310–17

Table 310.15(B)(3)(a) Conductor Ampacity Adjustment for More Than Three Current–Carrying Conductors

Number of Conductors[1]	Adjustment
4–6	0.80 or 80%
7–9	0.70 or 70%
10–20	0.50 or 50%
21–30	0.45 or 45%

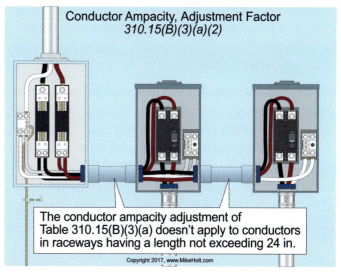

▶Figure 310–17

310.15 | Conductors for General Wiring

(4) Conductor ampacity adjustment of Table 310.15(B)(3)(a) doesn't apply to conductors within Type AC or Type MC cable under the following conditions: ▶Figure 310–18

a. The cables don't have an outer jacket,

b. Each cable has no more than three current-carrying conductors,

c. The conductors are 12 AWG copper, and

d. No more than 20 current-carrying conductors (ten 2-wire cables or six 3-wire cables) are installed without maintaining spacing for a continuous length longer than 24 in.

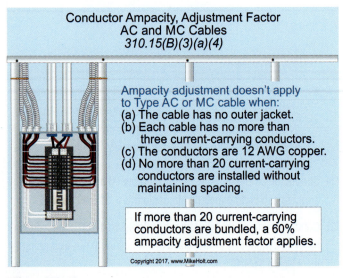

▶Figure 310–18

Ex to (4): A 60 percent adjustment factor applies if the number of current-carrying conductors in these cables exceed 20 and are stacked or bundled together for more than 24 in.

(c) **Raceways and Cables Exposed to Sunlight on Rooftops.** Where raceways or cables are exposed to direct sunlight and located less than ⅞ in. above the roof, a temperature adder of 60°F/33°C is to be added to the outdoor ambient temperature to determine the ambient temperature for the application of the ampacity correction in accordance with Table 310.15(B)(2)(a). ▶Figure 310–19 and ▶Figure 310–20

Ex: Type XHHW-2 insulated conductors aren't subject to the temperature adder of 60°F/33°C.

Note 1: See the *ASHRAE Handbook—Fundamentals* (www.ashrae.org) as a source for the ambient temperatures in various locations.

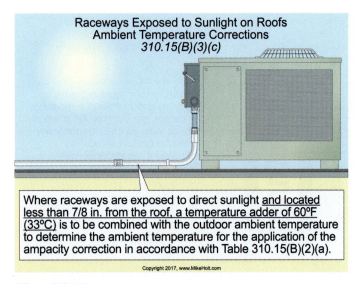

▶Figure 310–19

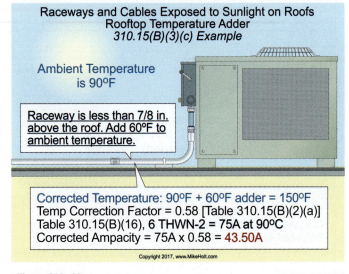

▶Figure 310–20

Author's Comment:

- This rule requires the ambient temperature used for ampacity correction to be adjusted where conductors or cables are installed within a raceway or cable on or above a rooftop and the raceway is exposed to direct sunlight. The reasoning is that the air inside raceways and cables that are in direct sunlight is significantly hotter than the surrounding air, and appropriate ampacity corrections must be made in order to comply with 310.10.

Conductors for General Wiring | 310.15

(5) Neutral Conductors.

(a) The neutral conductor of a 3-wire, single-phase, 120/240V system, or 4-wire, three-phase, 120/208V or 277/480V wye-connected system, isn't considered a current-carrying conductor for conductor ampacity adjustment of 310.15(B)(3)(a). ▶Figure 310–21

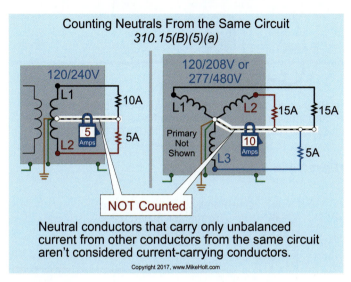

▶Figure 310–21

(b) The neutral conductor of a 3-wire circuit from a 4-wire, three-phase, 120/208V or 277/480V wye-connected system is considered a current-carrying conductor for conductor ampacity adjustment of 310.15(B)(3)(a).

Author's Comment:

- When a 3-wire circuit is supplied from a 4-wire, three-phase, 120/208V or 277/480V wye-connected system, the neutral conductor carries approximately the same current as the ungrounded conductors. ▶Figure 310–22

(c) On a 4-wire, 3-phase wye circuit where the major portion of the load consists of nonlinear loads, harmonic currents are present in the neutral conductor; the neutral conductor is to be considered a current-carrying conductor. ▶Figure 310–23

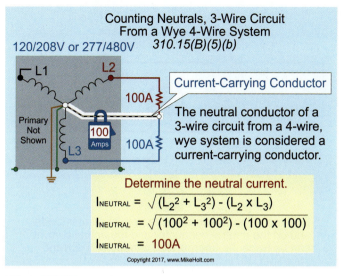

▶Figure 310–22

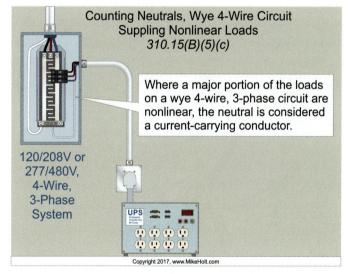

▶Figure 310–23

Author's Comment:

- Nonlinear loads supplied by a 4-wire, three-phase, 120/208V or 277/480V wye-connected system can produce unwanted and potentially hazardous odd triplen harmonic currents (3rd, 9th, 15th, and so on) that can add current on the neutral conductor. To prevent fire or equipment damage from excessive harmonic neutral current, the designer should consider increasing the size of the neutral conductor or installing a separate neutral for each phase. For more information, visit www.MikeHolt.com, click on the "Technical" link, then the "Power Quality" link. Also see 210.4(A) Note, 220.61 Note 2, and 450.3 Note 2. ▶Figure 310–24

310.15 | Conductors for General Wiring

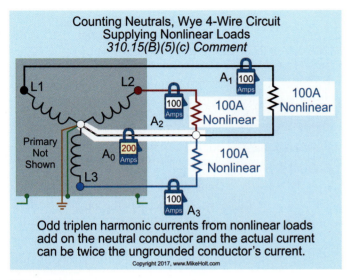

▶Figure 310–24

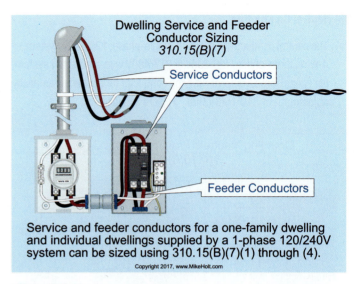

▶Figure 310–26

(6) Equipment Grounding Conductor. Grounding and bonding conductors aren't considered current carrying. ▶Figure 310–25

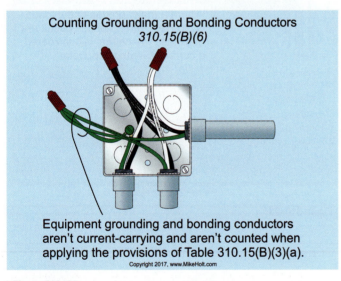

▶Figure 310–25

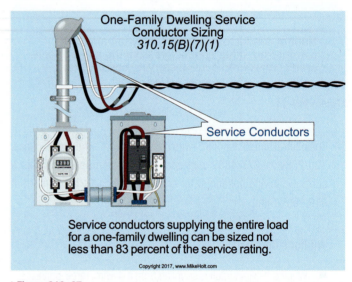

▶Figure 310–27

Example: What size service conductors are required if the calculated load for a dwelling unit equals 195A, and the service disconnect is rated 200A? ▶Figure 310–28

Solution: 200A rated circuit breaker multiplied by 83% = 166A

Answer: 2/0 AWG service conductors rated 175A at 75°C [Table 310.15(B)(16)] are required.

(7) Single-Phase Dwelling Services and Feeders.

For dwelling units, service and feeder conductors supplied by a single-phase, 120/240V and 120/208V system can be sized in accordance with the requirements contained in 310.15(B)(7)(1) through (3). ▶Figure 310–26

(1) Service Conductors. Service conductors supplying the entire load of a one-family dwelling or an individual dwelling unit in a two-family or multifamily dwelling can have the conductor ampacity sized to 83 percent of the service overcurrent protection device rating. ▶Figure 310–27

Conductors for General Wiring | 310.15

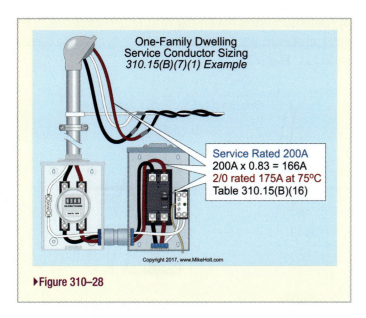
▶Figure 310–28

Author's Comment:

- Section 310.15(B)(7) can't be used for service conductors for two-family or multifamily dwelling buildings. ▶Figure 310–29

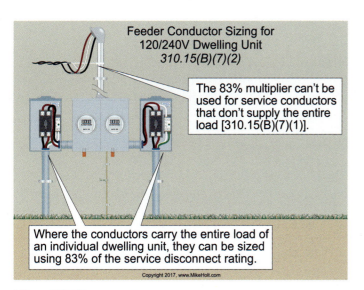
▶Figure 310–29

(2) Feeder Conductors. Ungrounded feeder conductors not over 400A supplying the entire load of a one-family dwelling, or an individual dwelling unit in a two-family or multifamily dwelling, can have the ungrounded feeder conductors sized to 83 percent of the feeder overcurrent protection device rating. ▶Figure 310–30 and ▶Figure 310–31

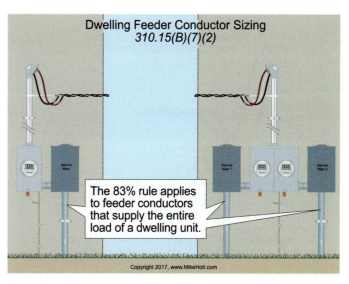
▶Figure 310–30

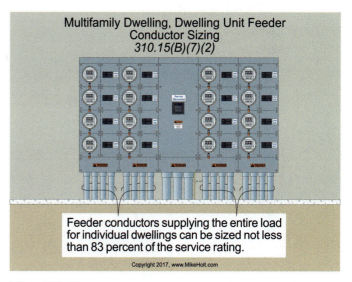
▶Figure 310–31

Example: What size feeder conductors are required if the calculated load for a dwelling unit equals 195A, the service disconnect is rated 200A, and the feeder conductors carry the entire load of the dwelling unit? ▶Figure 310–32

Solution: 200A rated circuit breaker multiplied by 83% = 166A

Answer: 2/0 AWG feeder conductors rated 175A at 75°C [Table 310.15(B)(16)] are required.

310.15 | Conductors for General Wiring

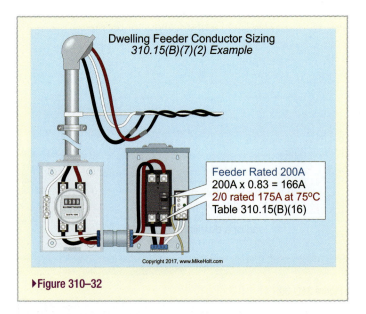
▶Figure 310–32

(3) Feeder Conductors Not Greater Than. Feeders conductors for an individual dwelling unit aren't required to be larger than the service conductors. ▶Figure 310–34

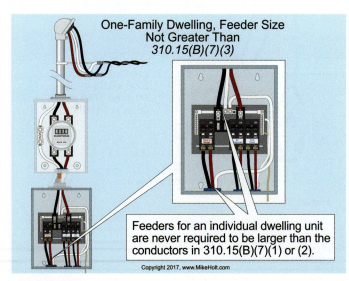
▶Figure 310–34

Author's Comment:

- Section 310.15(B)(7)(2) can't be used to size feeder conductors where a feeder doesn't carry the entire load of the dwelling unit, except as permitted in 310.15(B)(7)(3). ▶Figure 310–33

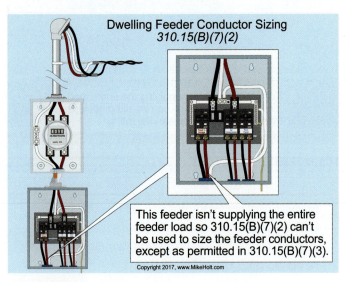
▶Figure 310–33

Table 310.15(B)(16) Allowable Ampacities of Insulated Conductors Based on Not More Than Three Current–Carrying Conductors and Ambient Temperature of 30°C (86°F)*

Size AWG kcmil	Copper			Aluminum			Size AWG kcmil
	60°C (140°F)	75°C (167°F)	90°C (194°F)	60°C (140°F)	75°C (167°F)	90°C (194°F)	
	TW UF	RHW THHW THW THWN XHHW USE	RHH RHW-2 THHN THHW THW-2 THWN-2 USE-2 XHHW XHHW-2	TW UF	THHN THW THWN XHHW	THHN THW-2 THWN-2 THHW XHHW XHHW-2	
14*	15	20	25				14*
12*	20	25	30	15	20	25	12*
10*	30	35	40	25	30	35	10*
8	40	50	55	35	40	45	8
6	55	65	75	40	50	55	6
4	70	85	95	55	65	75	4
3	85	100	115	65	75	85	3
2	95	115	130	75	90	100	2
1	110	130	145	85	100	115	1
1/0	125	150	170	100	120	135	1/0
2/0	145	175	195	115	135	150	2/0
3/0	165	200	225	130	155	175	3/0
4/0	195	230	260	150	180	205	4/0
250	215	255	290	170	205	230	250
300	240	285	320	195	230	260	300
350	260	310	350	210	250	280	350
400	280	335	380	225	270	305	400
500	320	380	430	260	310	350	500

*See 240.4(D)

Part III. Construction Specifications

310.104 Conductor Construction and Application

Only conductors in Tables 310.104(A) though 310.104(G) can be installed, and only for the application identified in the tables.

Author's Comment:

- The following explains the lettering on conductor insulation: ▶Figure 310–35

    - F — Fixture wires (solid or 7 strands) [Table 402.3]
    - FF — Flexible fixture wire (19 strands) [Table 402.3]
    - No H — 60°C insulation rating [Table 310.104(A)]
    - H — 75°C insulation rating [Table 310.104(A)]
    - HH — 90°C insulation rating [Table 310.104(A)]
    - N — Nylon outer cover [Table 310.104(A)]
    - R — Thermoset insulation [Table 310.104(A)]
    - T — Thermoplastic insulation [Table 310.104(A)]
    - U — Underground [Table 310.104(A)]
    - W — Wet or damp locations [Table 310.104(A)]
    - X — Cross-linked polyethylene insulation [Table 310.104(A)]
    - -2 — 90°C in dry and wet locations [Table 310.104(A)]

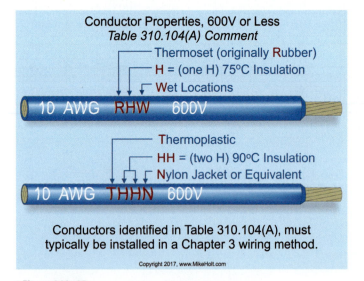

▶Figure 310–35

310.106 Conductors

(A) Minimum Size Conductors. The smallest conductor permitted for branch circuits for residential, commercial, and industrial locations is 14 AWG copper, except as permitted elsewhere in this *Code*. ▶Figure 310–36

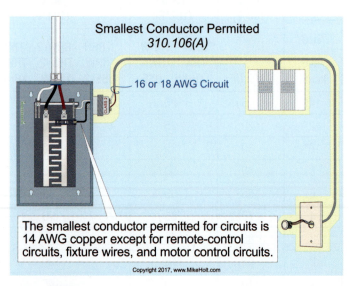

▶Figure 310–36

Author's Comment:

- There's a misconception that 12 AWG copper is the smallest conductor permitted for commercial or industrial facilities. Although this isn't true based on *NEC* rules, it may be a local code requirement.

(C) Stranded Conductors. Conductors 8 AWG and larger must be stranded when installed within a raceway. ▶Figure 310–37

Author's Comment:

- Solid conductors are often used for the grounding electrode conductor [250.62] and for the bonding of pools, spas, and outdoor hot tubs [680.26(C)].

(D) Insulated. Conductors must be insulated except where specific permission allows them to be covered or bare.

Author's Comment:

- Equipment grounding conductors are permitted to be bare, see 250.118(1).

Conductors for General Wiring | 310.110

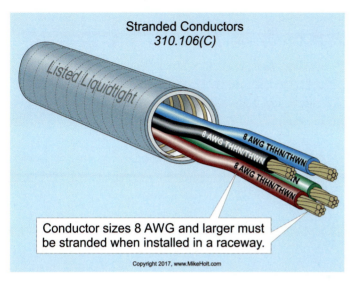

▶Figure 310–37

310.110 Conductor Identification

(A) Grounded [Neutral] Conductor. Grounded [neutral] conductors must be identified in accordance with 200.6.

(B) Equipment Grounding Conductor. Equipment grounding conductors must be identified in accordance with 250.119.

(C) Ungrounded Conductors. Ungrounded conductors must be clearly distinguishable from neutral and equipment grounding conductors.
▶Figure 310–38

▶Figure 310–38

Author's Comment:

- If the premises wiring system has branch circuits or feeders supplied from more than one nominal voltage system, each ungrounded conductor of the branch circuit or feeder, if accessible, must be identified by system. The means of identification can be by separate color coding, marking tape, tagging, or other means approved by the authority having jurisdiction. Such identification must be permanently posted at each panelboard [210.5(C) and 215.12].

- The *NEC* doesn't require color coding of ungrounded conductors, except for the high-leg conductor when a neutral conductor is present [110.15 and 230.56]. Although not required, electricians often use the following color system for power and lighting conductor identification: ▶Figure 310–39

    ◆ 120/240V, single-phase—black, red, and white
    ◆ 120/208V, three-phase—black, red, blue, and white
    ◆ 120/240V, three-phase, delta-connected system—black, orange, blue, and white
    ◆ 277/480V, three-phase, wye-connected system—brown, orange, yellow, and gray; or, brown, purple, yellow, and gray

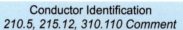

Although the *NEC* doesn't require a specific color code for ungrounded conductors, electricians often use the following color system for power and lighting conductor identification:
- 120/240V, single-phase–black, red, and white
- 120/208V, three-phase–black, red, blue, and white
- 120/240V, three-phase–black, orange, blue, and white
- 277/480V, three-phase–brown, orange, yellow, and gray; or, brown, purple, yellow, and gray

▶Figure 310–39

Notes

ARTICLE 312
CABINETS, CUTOUT BOXES, AND METER SOCKET ENCLOSURES

Introduction to Article 312—Cabinets, Cutout Boxes, and Meter Socket Enclosures

This article addresses the installation and construction specifications for the items mentioned in its title. In Article 310, we observed that the conditions of use have an effect on the ampacity of a conductor. Likewise, the conditions of use have an effect on the selection and application of cabinets. For example, you can't use just any enclosure in a wet location or in a hazardous location. The conditions of use impose special requirements for these situations.

For all such enclosures, certain requirements apply—regardless of the use. For example, you must cover any openings, protect conductors from abrasion, and allow sufficient bending room for conductors.

Notice that Article 408 covers switchboards and panelboards, with primary emphasis on the interior, or "guts," while the cabinet that would be used to enclose a panelboard is covered here in Article 312. Therefore, you'll find that some important considerations such as wire-bending space at terminals of panelboards are included in this article.

Part I. Scope and Installation

312.1 Scope

Article 312 covers the installation and construction specifications for cabinets, cutout boxes, and meter socket enclosures. ▶Figure 312–1

Author's Comment:

- A cabinet is an enclosure for either surface mounting or flush mounting and provided with a frame in which a door may be hung.

312.2 Damp or Wet Locations

Enclosures in damp or wet locations must prevent moisture or water from entering or accumulating within the enclosure, and must be weatherproof. When the enclosure is surface mounted in a wet location, the enclosure must be mounted with not less than a ¼ in. air space between it and the mounting surface. See 300.6(D).

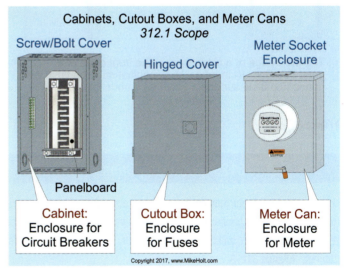

▶Figure 312–1

If raceways or cables enter above the level of uninsulated live parts of an enclosure in a wet location, a fitting listed for wet locations must be used for termination.

312.3 | Cabinets, Cutout Boxes, and Meter Socket Enclosures

Author's Comment:

- A fitting listed for use in a wet location with a sealing locknut is suitable for this application.

Ex: The ¼ in. air space isn't required for nonmetallic equipment, raceways, or cables.

312.3 Installed in Walls

Cabinets installed in walls of noncombustible material must be installed so that the front edge of the enclosure is set back no more than ¼ in. from the finished surface. In walls constructed of wood or other combustible material, cabinets must be flush with the finished surface or project outward. ▶Figure 312–2

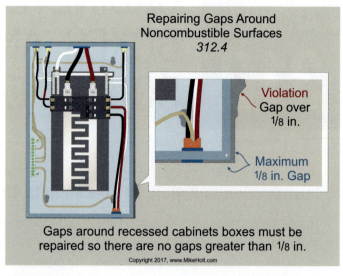

▶Figure 312–3

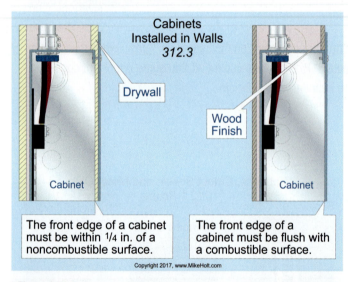

▶Figure 312–2

312.4 Repairing Gaps

Gaps around cabinets that are recessed in noncombustible surfaces (plaster, drywall, or plasterboard) having a flush-type cover, must be repaired so that there will be no gap more than ⅛ in. at the edge of the cabinet. ▶Figure 312–3

312.5 Enclosures

(A) Unused Openings. Openings in cabinet and cutout boxes intended to provide entry for conductors must be closed in an approved manner. ▶Figure 312–4

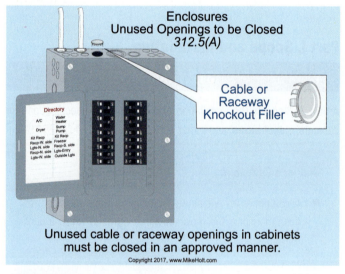

▶Figure 312–4

Author's Comment:

- Unused openings for circuit breakers must be closed by means that provide protection substantially equivalent to the wall of the enclosure [408.7]. ▶Figure 312–5

Cabinets, Cutout Boxes, and Meter Socket Enclosures | 312.5

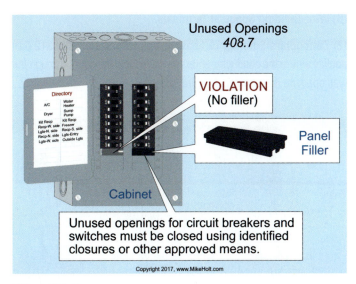

▶Figure 312–5

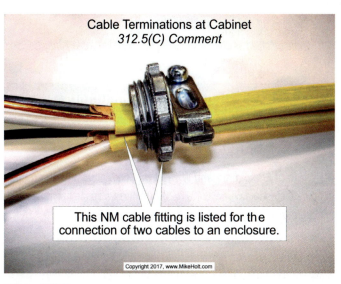

▶Figure 312–7

(C) Cable Termination. Cables must be secured to the cabinet or cutout box with fittings designed and listed for the cable. See 300.12 and 300.15. ▶Figure 312–6

Ex: Cables with nonmetallic sheaths aren't required to be secured to the cabinet if the cables enter the top of a surface-mounted cabinet through a nonflexible raceway not less than 18 in. or more than 10 ft long, if all of the following conditions are met: ▶Figure 312–8

▶Figure 312–6

Author's Comment:

- Cable clamps or cable connectors must be used with only one cable, unless that clamp or fitting is identified for more than one cable. Some Type NM cable clamps are listed for two Type NM cables within a single fitting (UL White Book, *Guide Information for Electrical Equipment*). ▶Figure 312–7

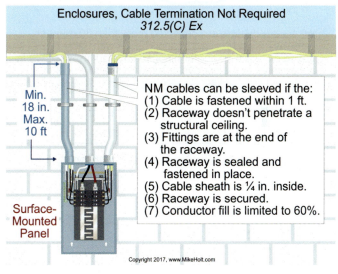

▶Figure 312–8

(1) Each cable is fastened within 1 ft from the raceway.

(2) The raceway doesn't penetrate a structural ceiling.

(3) Fittings are provided on the raceway to protect the cables from abrasion.

(4) The raceway is sealed.

(5) Each cable sheath extends not less than ¼ in. into the panelboard.

317

(6) The raceway is properly secured.

(7) Where installed as conduit or tubing so Chapter 9 Table 1 may be used.

312.6 Deflection of Conductors

Conductors entering or leaving enclosures and wireways must comply with 312.6(A) and 312.6(B).

(A) Width of Enclosures and Wireways. Conductors aren't permitted to be deflected in a wireway [376.23(A)] unless a space having a width in accordance with Table 312.6(A) is provided. ▶Figure 312–9

(B) Wire-Bending Space at Terminals.

(2) Conductors Entering or Leaving Opposite Wall. Table 312.6(B) applies where the conductor enters or leaves the enclosure through the wall opposite its terminal. ▶Figure 312–10

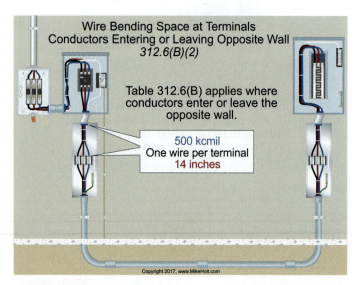

▶Figure 312–10

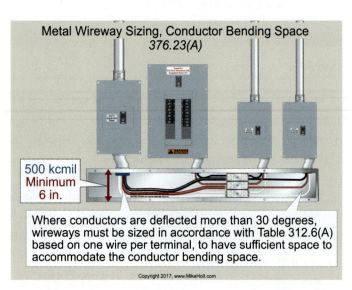

▶Figure 312–9

Table 312.6(A) Minimum Wire–Bending Space

Wire Size (AWG or kcmil)	Inches
8–6	1½
4–3	2
2	2½
1	3
1/0–2/0	3½
3/0–4/0	4
250	4½
300–350	5
400–500	6
600–700	8

Table 312.6(B) Minimum Wire–Bending Space

Wire Size (AWG or kcmil)	Inches
2	3½
1	4½
1/0	5½
3/0	6½
250	8½
350	12
500	14
600	15

312.8 Overcurrent Protection Device Enclosures

Cabinets are permitted to contain overcurrent protection devices and other wiring and equipment as provided in (A) and (B).

(A) Splices, Taps, and Feed-Through Conductors. The wiring space within cabinets can be used for conductors feeding through, spliced, or tapping where all of the following conditions are met:

(1) The area of conductors at any cross section doesn't exceed 40 percent of the cross-sectional area of the space. ▶Figure 312–11

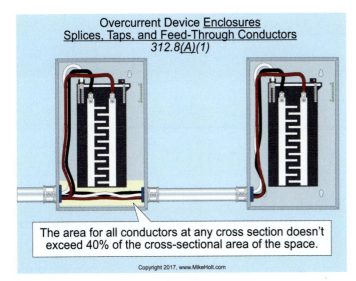

▶Figure 312–11

(2) The area of conductors, splices, and taps installed at any cross section doesn't exceed 75 percent of the cross-sectional area of that space. ▶Figure 312–12

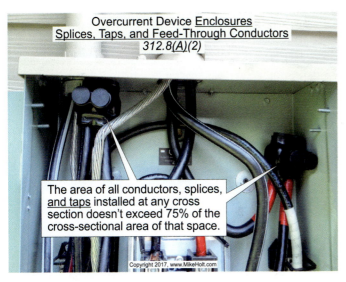

▶Figure 312–12

(3) A permanently affixed warning label having sufficient durability to withstand the environment involved and comply with 110.21(B), must be applied on the cabinet to identify the location of the disconnecting means for the feed-through conductors. ▶Figure 312–13

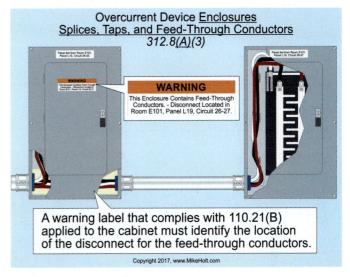

▶Figure 312–13

(B) Power Monitoring Equipment. The wiring space within cabinets can contain power monitoring equipment where all of the following conditions are met:

(1) The power monitoring equipment is identified as a field installable accessory as part of listed equipment, or a listed kit for field installation in the overcurrent protection device enclosures.

(2) The area of all conductors, splices, taps, and equipment at any cross section doesn't exceed 75 percent of the cross-sectional area of that space.

Notes

ARTICLE 314 — OUTLET, DEVICE, PULL, AND JUNCTION BOXES; CONDUIT BODIES; AND HANDHOLE ENCLOSURES

Introduction to Article 314—Outlet, Device, Pull, and Junction Boxes; Conduit Bodies; and Handhole Enclosures

Article 314 contains installation requirements for outlet boxes, pull and junction boxes, conduit bodies, and handhole enclosures. As with the cabinets covered in Article 312, the conditions of use have a bearing on the type of material and equipment selected for a particular installation. If a raceway is installed in a wet location, for example, the correct fittings and the proper installation methods must be used.

The information here will help you size an outlet box using the proper cubic-inch capacity as well as calculating the minimum dimensions for larger pull boxes. There are limits on the amount of weight that can be supported by an outlet box and rules on how to support a device or outlet box to various surfaces. Article 314 will help you understand these types of rules so that your installation will be compliant with the *NEC*. As always, the clear illustrations in this article will help you visualize the finished installation.

Part I. Scope and General

314.1 Scope

Article 314 contains the installation requirements for outlet boxes, conduit bodies, pull and junction boxes, and handhole enclosures. ▶Figure 314–1

314.3 Nonmetallic Boxes

Nonmetallic boxes can only be used with nonmetallic cables and raceways.

Ex 1: Metal raceways and metal cables can be used with nonmetallic boxes if all raceways are bonded together in the nonmetallic box.
▶Figure 314–2

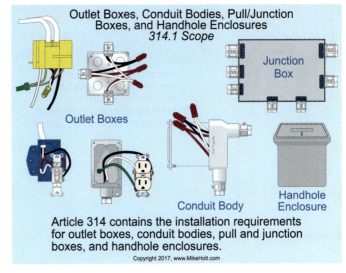

▶Figure 314–1

314.4 | Outlet, Device, Pull, and Junction Boxes; Conduit Bodies; and Handhole Enclosures

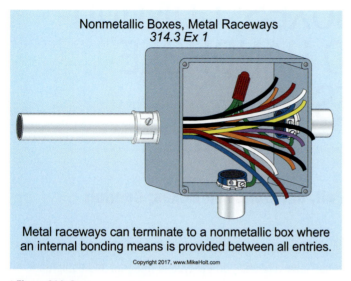

▶Figure 314–2

314.4 Metal Boxes

Metal boxes containing circuits that operate at 50V or more must be connected to an equipment grounding conductor of a type listed in 250.118 [250.112(I) and 250.148]. ▶Figure 314–3

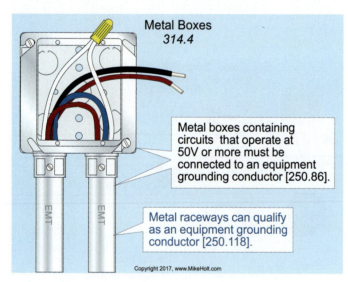

▶Figure 314–3

Part II. Installation

314.15 Damp or Wet Locations

Boxes, conduit bodies, and fittings in damp or wet locations must be listed for wet locations and prevent moisture or water from entering or accumulating within the enclosure. ▶Figure 314–4 and ▶Figure 314–5

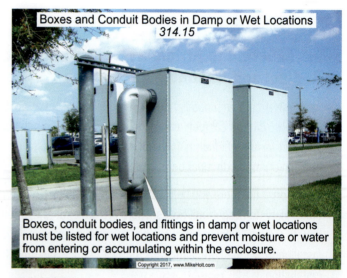

▶Figure 314–4

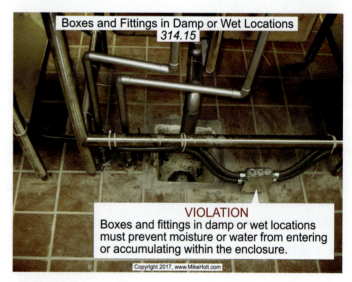

▶Figure 314–5

Approved drainage openings can be created in the field if they aren't smaller than ⅛ in. in diameter and not larger than ¼ in. in diameter.

Outlet, Device, Pull, and Junction Boxes; Conduit Bodies; and Handhole Enclosures | 314.16

Author's Comment:

- If handhole enclosures without bottoms are installed, all enclosed conductors and any splices or terminations must be listed as suitable for wet locations [314.30(C)].

314.16 Number of Conductors in Boxes and Conduit Bodies

Boxes containing 6 AWG and smaller conductors must be sized in an approved manner to provide free space for all conductors, devices, and fittings. In no case can the volume of the box, as calculated in 314.16(A), be less than the volume requirement as calculated in 314.16(B). ▶Figure 314–6

Conduit bodies must be sized in accordance with 314.16(C).

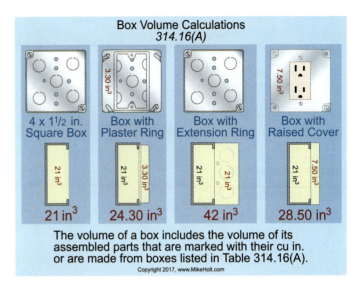
▶Figure 314–7

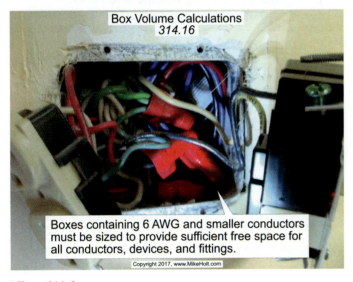
▶Figure 314–6

Author's Comment:

- The requirements for sizing boxes and conduit bodies containing conductors 4 AWG and larger are contained in 314.28. The requirements for sizing handhole enclosures are contained in 314.30(A).

(A) Box Volume Calculations. The volume of a box includes plaster rings, extension rings, and domed covers that are either marked with their volume in cubic inches (cu in.), or are made from boxes listed in Table 314.16(A). ▶Figure 314–7 and ▶Figure 314–8

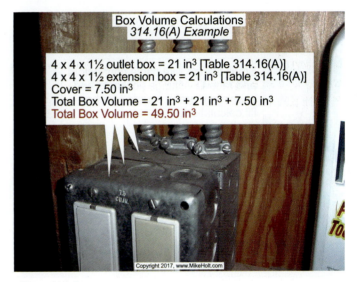
▶Figure 314–8

Where a box is provided with barriers, the volume is apportioned to each of the resulting spaces. Each barrier, if not marked with its volume, is considered to take up ½ cu in. if metal and 1 cu in. if nonmetallic. ▶Figure 314–9

(B) Box Fill Calculations. The calculated conductor volume as determined by 314.16(B)(1) through (5) and Table 314.16(B) determine the total volume of the conductors, devices, and fittings. Raceway and cable fittings, including locknuts and bushings, aren't counted for box fill calculations. ▶Figure 314–10

314.16 | Outlet, Device, Pull, and Junction Boxes; Conduit Bodies; and Handhole Enclosures

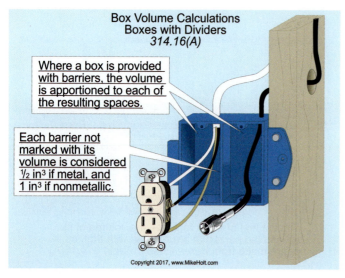

▶Figure 314–9

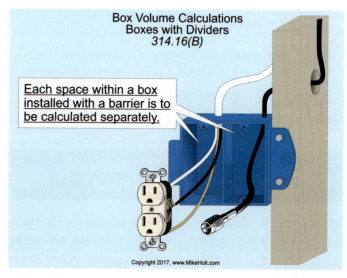

▶Figure 314–11

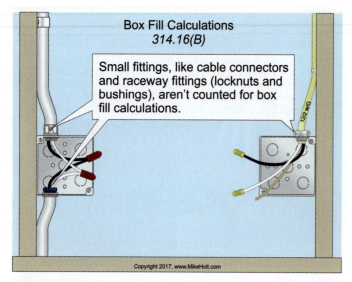

▶Figure 314–10

The volume of a box that's provided with barriers, is apportioned to each of the resulting spaces. ▶Figure 314–11

Table 314.16(B) Volume Allowance Required per Conductor	
Conductor AWG	Volume cu in.
18	1.50
16	1.75
14	2.00
12	2.25
10	2.50
8	3.00
6	5.00

(1) Conductor Volume. Each unbroken conductor that runs through a box, and each conductor that terminates in a box, is counted as a single conductor volume in accordance with Table 314.16(B). ▶Figure 314–12 and ▶Figure 314–13

Outlet, Device, Pull, and Junction Boxes; Conduit Bodies; and Handhole Enclosures | 314.16

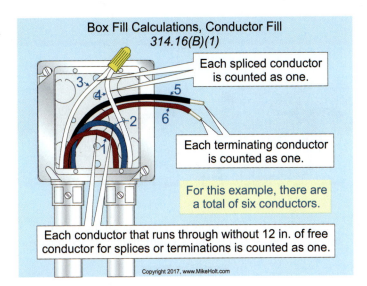

▶Figure 314–12

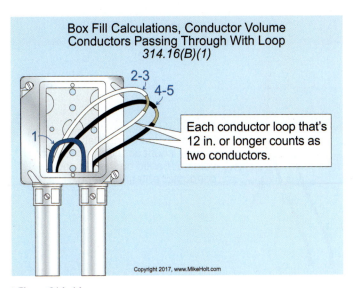

▶Figure 314–14

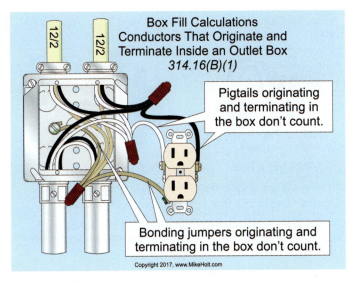

▶Figure 314–13

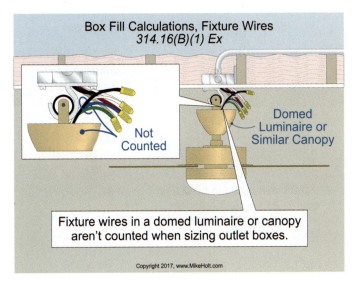

▶Figure 314–15

Each loop or coil of unbroken conductor having a length of at least twice the minimum length required for free conductors in 300.14 must be counted as two conductor volumes. Conductors that originate and terminate within the box, such as pigtails, aren't counted at all. ▶Figure 314–14

Ex: Equipment grounding conductors, and up to four 16 AWG and smaller fixture wires, can be omitted from box fill calculations if they enter the box from a domed luminaire or similar canopy, such as a ceiling paddle fan canopy. ▶Figure 314–15

(2) Cable Clamp Volume. One or more internal cable clamps count as a single conductor volume in accordance with Table 314.16(B), based on the largest conductor that enters the box. Cable connectors that have their clamping mechanism outside the box aren't counted. ▶Figure 314–16

(3) Support Fitting Volume. Each luminaire stud or luminaire hickey counts as a single conductor volume in accordance with Table 314.16(B), based on the largest conductor that enters the box. ▶Figure 314–17

314.16 | Outlet, Device, Pull, and Junction Boxes; Conduit Bodies; and Handhole Enclosures

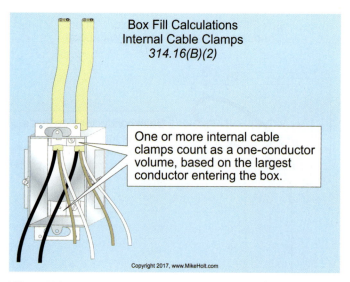
▶Figure 314–16

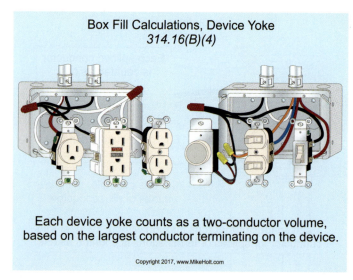
▶Figure 314–18

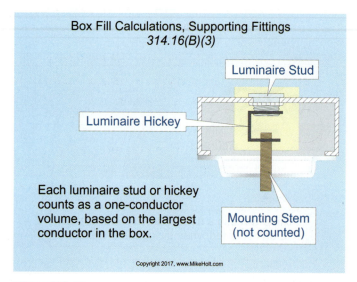
▶Figure 314–17

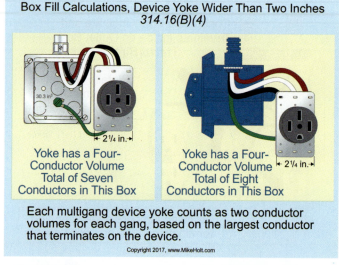
▶Figure 314–19

Author's Comment:

- Luminaire stems don't need to be counted as a conductor volume.

(4) Device Yoke Volume. Each single-gang device yoke (regardless of the ampere rating of the device) counts as two conductor volumes, based on the largest conductor that terminates on the device in accordance with Table 314.16(B). ▶Figure 314–18

Each multigang device yoke counts as two conductor volumes for each gang, based on the largest conductor that terminates on the device in accordance with Table 314.16(B). ▶Figure 314–19

Author's Comment:

- A device that's too wide for mounting in a single-gang box, as described in Table 314.16(A), is counted based on the number of gangs required for the device.

(5) Equipment Grounding Conductor Volume. Equipment grounding conductors in a box count as a single conductor volume in accordance with Table 314.16(B), based on the largest equipment grounding conductor that enters the box. Insulated equipment grounding conductors for receptacles having insulated grounding terminals (isolated ground receptacles) [250.146(D)], count as a single conductor volume in accordance with Table 314.16(B). ▶Figure 314–20

Outlet, Device, Pull, and Junction Boxes; Conduit Bodies; and Handhole Enclosures | 314.16

Figure 314–20

Author's Comment:

- Conductor insulation isn't a factor that's considered when determining box volume calculations.

Example: How many 14 AWG conductors can be pulled through a 4 in. square × 2⅛ in. deep box with a plaster ring with a marking of 3.60 cu in.? The box contains two receptacles, five 12 AWG conductors, and two 12 AWG equipment grounding conductors.
▶Figure 314–21

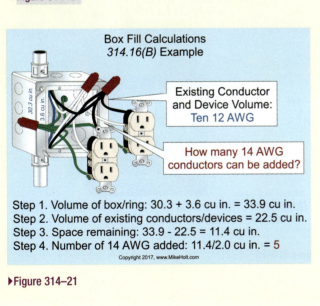

▶Figure 314–21

Solution:

Step 1: Determine the volume of the box assembly [314.16(A)]:
Box 30.30 cu in. + 3.60 cu in. plaster ring = 33.90 cu in.

A 4 × 4 × 2⅛ in. box has a volume of 30.30 cu in., as listed in Table 314.16(A).

Step 2: Determine the volume of the devices and conductors in the box:

Two—receptacles	4—12 AWG
Five—12 AWG	5—12 AWG
Two—12 AWG Grounds	1—12 AWG

Total Ten—12 AWG × 2.25 cu in. = 22.50 cu in.

Step 3: Determine the remaining volume permitted for the 14 AWG conductors (volume of box less volume of conductors):
33.90 cu in. − 22.50 cu in. = 11.40 cu in.

Step 4: Determine the number of 14 AWG conductors (at 2.00 cu in. each) permitted in the remaining volume of 11.40 cu in:
14 AWG = 2.00 cu in. each [Table 314.16(B)]
11.40 cu in./2.00 cu in. = 5 conductors

Answer: Five 14 AWG conductors can be pulled through.

(C) Conduit Bodies.

(2) Splices. Splices are permitted in conduit bodies that are legibly marked by the manufacturer with their volume, and the maximum number of conductors permitted in a conduit body is limited in accordance with 314.16(B).

Example: How many 12 AWG conductors can be spliced in an 11.80 cu in. conduit body? ▶Figure 314–22

Solution:

12 AWG = 2.25 cu in. [Table 314.16(B)]
11.80 cu in./2.25 cu in. = 5.40 conductors

Answer: A maximum of five 12 AWG conductors (round down) can be spliced in this conduit body.

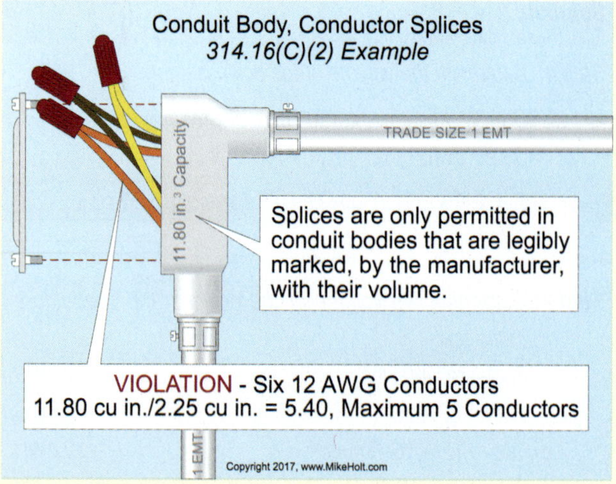

314.17 | Outlet, Device, Pull, and Junction Boxes; Conduit Bodies; and Handhole Enclosures

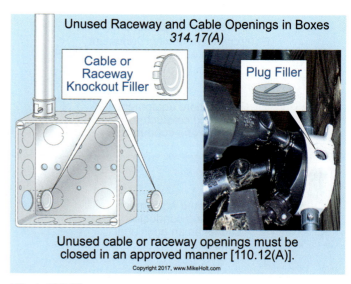

▶Figure 314–22

(3) Short-Radius Conduit Bodies. Capped elbows, handy ells, and service-entrance elbows aren't permitted to contain any splices.
▶Figure 314–23

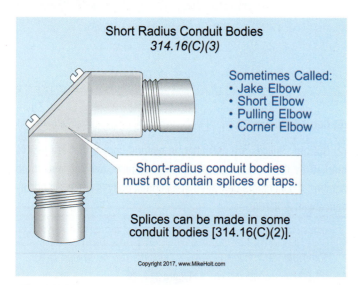

▶Figure 314–23

314.17 Conductors That Enter Boxes or Conduit Bodies

(A) Openings to be Closed. Unused openings through which cables or raceways enter must be closed in an approved manner. ▶Figure 314–24

▶Figure 314–24

Author's Comment:

- Unused cable or raceway openings in electrical equipment must be effectively closed by fittings that provide protection substantially equivalent to the wall of the equipment [110.12(A)].

(B) Metal Boxes. Nonmetallic-sheathed cable and multiconductor Type UF cable must extend at least ¼ in. inside the box. ▶Figure 314–25

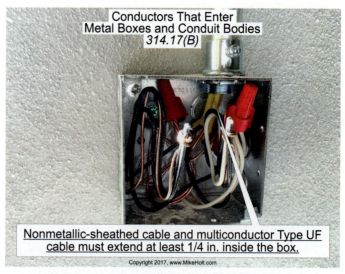

▶Figure 314–25

(C) Nonmetallic Boxes and Conduit Bodies. Raceways and cables must be securely fastened to nonmetallic boxes or conduit bodies by fittings designed for the wiring method [300.12 and 300.15]. ▶Figure 314–26

Outlet, Device, Pull, and Junction Boxes; Conduit Bodies; and Handhole Enclosures | 314.20

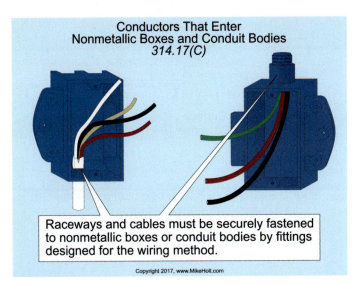

▶Figure 314–26

The sheath of type NM cable must extend not less than ¼ in. into the nonmetallic box.

Author's Comment:

- Two Type NM cables can terminate in a single cable clamp, if the clamp is listed for this purpose.

Ex: Type NM cable terminating to a single-gang (2¼ in. × 4 in.) device box isn't required to be secured to the box if the cable is securely fastened within 8 in. of the box. ▶Figure 314–27

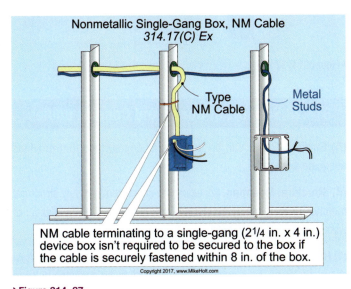

▶Figure 314–27

314.20 Flush-Mounted Box Installations

Installation within or behind walls or ceilings that are constructed of noncombustible material must have the front edge of the flush-mounted box, plaster ring, extension ring, or listed extender set back no more than ¼ in. from the finished surface. ▶Figure 314–28

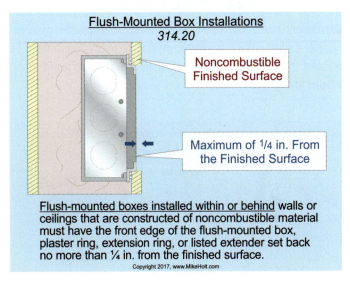

▶Figure 314–28

Installation within or behind walls or ceilings constructed of wood or other combustible material must have the front edge of the flush-mounted box, plaster ring, extension ring, or listed extender extend to the finished surface or project out from the finished surface. ▶Figure 314–29

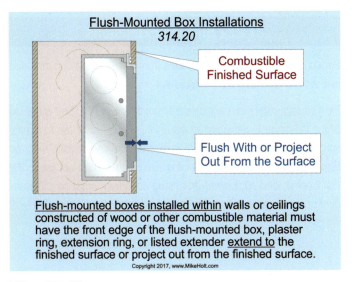

▶Figure 314–29

314.21 | Outlet, Device, Pull, and Junction Boxes; Conduit Bodies; and Handhole Enclosures

Author's Comment:

- Plaster rings and extension rings are available in a variety of depths to meet the above requirements.

314.21 Repairing Noncombustible Surfaces

Gaps around boxes with flush-type covers that are recessed in noncombustible surfaces (such as plaster, drywall, or plasterboard) must be repaired so there will be no gap more than 1/8 in. at the edge of the box.
▶Figure 314–30

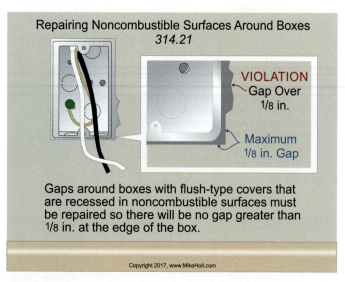

▶Figure 314–30

314.22 Surface Extensions

Surface extensions can only be made from an extension ring mounted over a flush-mounted box. ▶Figure 314–31

Ex: A surface extension can be made from the cover of a flush-mounted box if the cover is designed so it's unlikely to fall off if the mounting screws become loose. The surface extension wiring method must be flexible to permit the removal of the cover and provide access to the box interior, and equipment grounding continuity must be independent of the connection between the box and the cover. ▶Figure 314–32

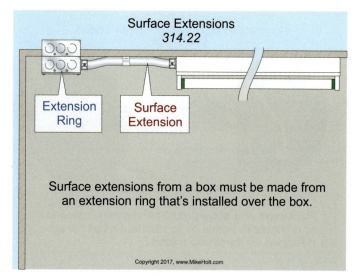

▶Figure 314–31

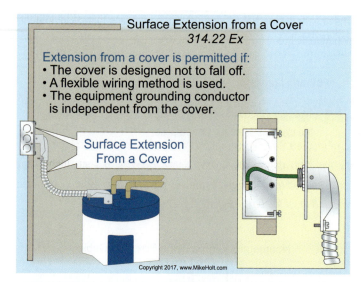

▶Figure 314–32

314.23 Support of Boxes and Conduit Bodies

(A) Surface. Boxes can be fastened to any surface that provides adequate support.

(B) Structural Mounting. Boxes can be supported from any structural member, or they can be supported from grade by a metal, plastic, or wood brace. ▶Figure 314–33

(1) Nails and Screws. Nails or screws used as a fastening means, must secure boxes by using outside brackets or by using mounting holes in the back or in a single side of the box, or pass through the interior within 1/4 in. of the back or ends of the box. Screws aren't permitted to pass

▶Figure 314–33

through the box unless the exposed threads in the box are protected using approved means to avoid abrasion of conductor insulation. Mounting holes made in the field to support boxes must be approved by the authority having jurisdiction.

(2) Braces. Metal braces no less than 0.02 in. thick and wood braces not less than a nominal 1 in. × 2 in. can support a box.

(C) Finished Surface Support. Boxes can be secured to a finished surface (drywall or plaster walls, or ceilings) by clamps, anchors, or fittings identified for the purpose. ▶Figure 314–34

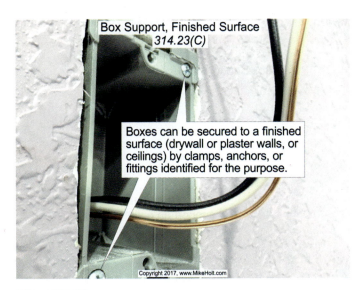

▶Figure 314–34

(D) Suspended-Ceiling Support. Outlet boxes can be supported to the structural or supporting elements of a suspended ceiling, if securely fastened by any of the following methods:

(1) Ceiling-Framing Members. An outlet box can be secured to suspended-ceiling framing members by bolts, screws, rivets, clips, or other means identified for the suspended-ceiling framing member(s). ▶Figure 314–35

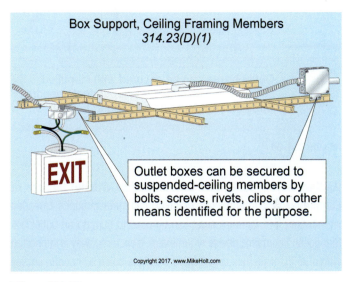

▶Figure 314–35

Author's Comment:

- If framing members of suspended-ceiling systems are used to support luminaires, they must be securely fastened to each other and must be securely attached to the building structure at appropriate intervals. In addition, luminaires must be attached to the suspended-ceiling framing members with screws, bolts, rivets, or clips listed and identified for such use [410.36(B)].

(2) Independent Support Wires. Outlet boxes can be secured with identified fittings to the ceiling-support wires. If independent support wires are used for outlet box support, they must be taunt and secured at both ends [300.11(B)]. ▶Figure 314–36

Author's Comment:

- See 300.11(B) on the use of independent support wires to support raceways and cables.

314.23 | Outlet, Device, Pull, and Junction Boxes; Conduit Bodies; and Handhole Enclosures

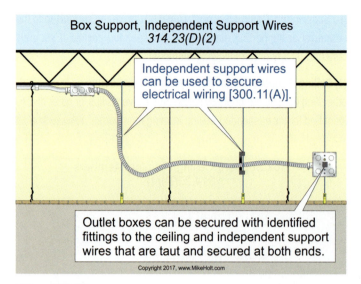

▶Figure 314–36

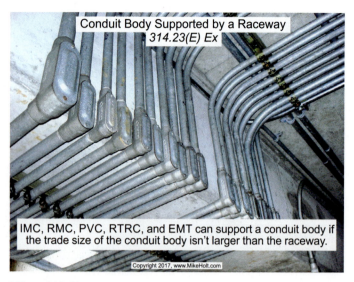

▶Figure 314–38

(E) Raceways—Boxes and Conduit Bodies Without Devices or Luminaires. Two intermediate metal or rigid metal conduits, threaded wrenchtight into the enclosure, can be used to support an outlet box that doesn't contain a device or luminaire, if each raceway is supported within 36 in. of the box or within 18 in. of the box if all conduit entries are on the same side. ▶Figure 314–37

(1) Intermediate metal conduit, Type IMC

(2) Rigid metal conduit, Type RMC

(3) Rigid polyvinyl chloride conduit, Type PVC

(4) Reinforced thermosetting resin conduit, Type RTRC

(5) Electrical metallic tubing, Type EMT

(F) Raceways—Boxes and Conduit Bodies with Devices or Luminaires. Two intermediate metal or rigid metal conduits, threaded wrenchtight into the enclosure, can be used to support an outlet box containing devices or luminaires, if each raceway is supported within 18 in. of the box. ▶Figure 314–39 and ▶Figure 314–40

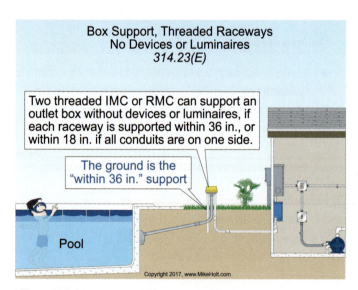

▶Figure 314–37

Ex: Conduit bodies are permitted to be supported by any of the following wiring methods: ▶Figure 314–38

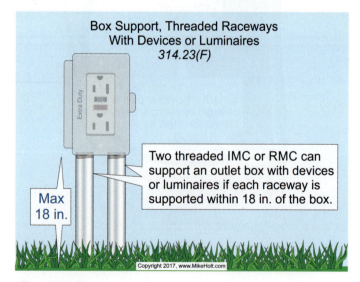

▶Figure 314–39

(1) The area of conductors at any cross section doesn't exceed 40 percent of the cross-sectional area of the space. ▶Figure 312–11

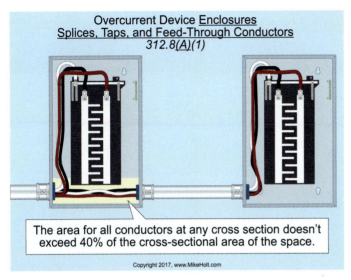

▶Figure 312–11

(2) The area of conductors, splices, and taps installed at any cross section doesn't exceed 75 percent of the cross-sectional area of that space. ▶Figure 312–12

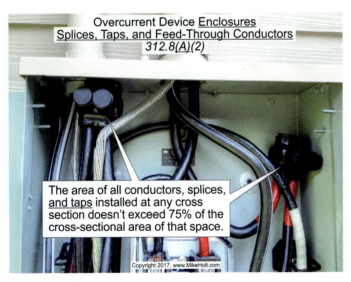

▶Figure 312–12

(3) A permanently affixed warning label having sufficient durability to withstand the environment involved and comply with 110.21(B), must be applied on the cabinet to identify the location of the disconnecting means for the feed-through conductors. ▶Figure 312–13

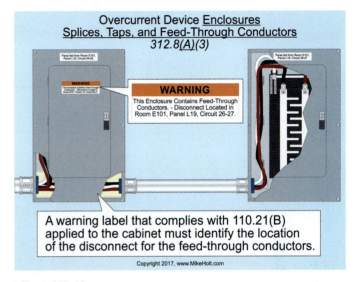

▶Figure 312–13

(B) Power Monitoring Equipment. The wiring space within cabinets can contain power monitoring equipment where all of the following conditions are met:

(1) The power monitoring equipment is identified as a field installable accessory as part of listed equipment, or a listed kit for field installation in the overcurrent protection device enclosures.

(2) The area of all conductors, splices, taps, and equipment at any cross section doesn't exceed 75 percent of the cross-sectional area of that space.

Notes

Author's Comment:

- If handhole enclosures without bottoms are installed, all enclosed conductors and any splices or terminations must be listed as suitable for wet locations [314.30(C)].

314.16 Number of Conductors in Boxes and Conduit Bodies

Boxes containing 6 AWG and smaller conductors must be sized in an approved manner to provide free space for all conductors, devices, and fittings. In no case can the volume of the box, as calculated in 314.16(A), be less than the volume requirement as calculated in 314.16(B). ▶Figure 314–6

Conduit bodies must be sized in accordance with 314.16(C).

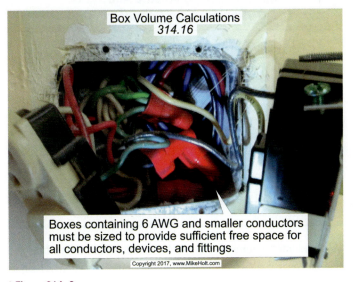
▶Figure 314–6

Author's Comment:

- The requirements for sizing boxes and conduit bodies containing conductors 4 AWG and larger are contained in 314.28. The requirements for sizing handhole enclosures are contained in 314.30(A).

(A) Box Volume Calculations. The volume of a box includes plaster rings, extension rings, and domed covers that are either marked with their volume in cubic inches (cu in.), or are made from boxes listed in Table 314.16(A). ▶Figure 314–7 and ▶Figure 314–8

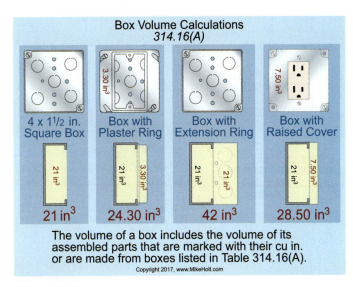
▶Figure 314–7

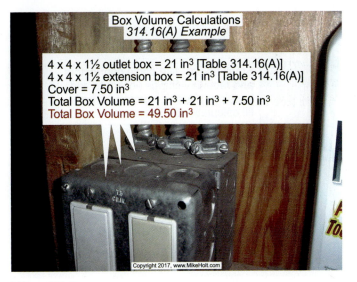
▶Figure 314–8

Where a box is provided with barriers, the volume is apportioned to each of the resulting spaces. Each barrier, if not marked with its volume, is considered to take up ½ cu in. if metal and 1 cu in. if nonmetallic.
▶Figure 314–9

(B) Box Fill Calculations. The calculated conductor volume as determined by 314.16(B)(1) through (5) and Table 314.16(B) determine the total volume of the conductors, devices, and fittings. Raceway and cable fittings, including locknuts and bushings, aren't counted for box fill calculations. ▶Figure 314–10

314.16 | Outlet, Device, Pull, and Junction Boxes; Conduit Bodies; and Handhole Enclosures

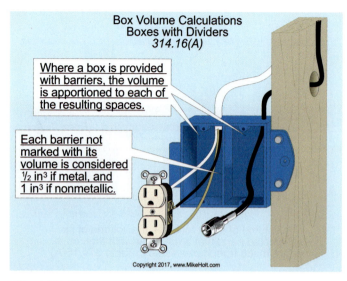

▶Figure 314–9

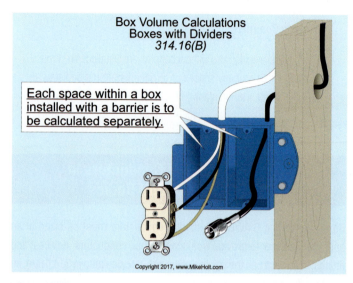

▶Figure 314–11

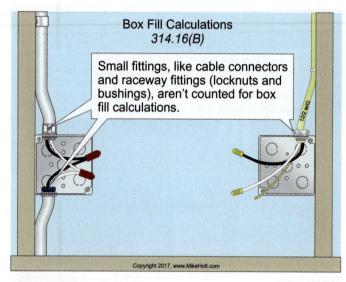

▶Figure 314–10

Table 314.16(B) Volume Allowance Required per Conductor

Conductor AWG	Volume cu in.
18	1.50
16	1.75
14	2.00
12	2.25
10	2.50
8	3.00
6	5.00

The volume of a box that's provided with barriers, is apportioned to each of the resulting spaces. ▶Figure 314–11

(1) Conductor Volume. Each unbroken conductor that runs through a box, and each conductor that terminates in a box, is counted as a single conductor volume in accordance with Table 314.16(B). ▶Figure 314–12 and ▶Figure 314–13

Outlet, Device, Pull, and Junction Boxes; Conduit Bodies; and Handhole Enclosures | 314.25

▶Figure 314–40

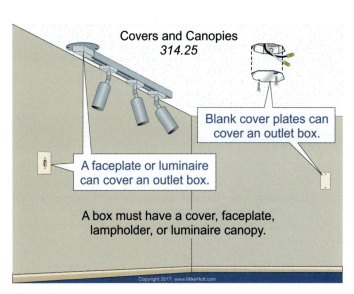
▶Figure 314–42

(H) Pendant Boxes.

(1) Flexible Cord. Boxes containing a hub can be supported from a flexible cord connected to fittings that prevent tension from being transmitted to joints or terminals [400.10]. ▶Figure 314–41

Screws used for attaching covers or other equipment to the box must be machine screws that match the thread gage or size of the screw holes in the box or they must be in accordance with the manufacturer's instructions. ▶Figure 314–43

▶Figure 314–41

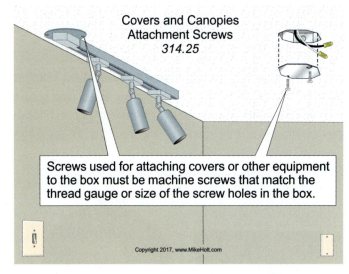
▶Figure 314–43

314.25 Covers and Canopies

When the installation is complete, each outlet box must be provided with a cover or faceplate, unless covered by a fixture canopy, lampholder, or similar device. ▶Figure 314–42

(A) Metal Covers. Metal covers are only permitted if they can be connected to an equipment grounding conductor of a type recognized in 250.118 [250.110]. ▶Figure 314–44

314.27 | Outlet, Device, Pull, and Junction Boxes; Conduit Bodies; and Handhole Enclosures

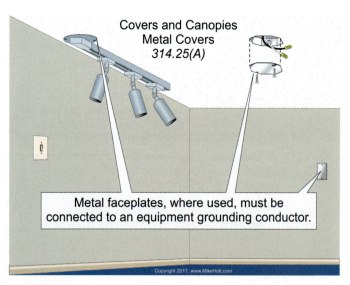

▶Figure 314–44

Author's Comment:

- Metal switch faceplates [404.9(B)] and metal receptacle faceplates [406.6(A)] must be connected to an equipment grounding conductor.

314.27 Outlet Box

(A) Boxes at Luminaire Outlets.

(1) Luminaire Outlets in or on Vertical Surfaces. Boxes or fittings designed for the support of luminaires in or on a wall or other vertical surface must be identified and marked on the interior of the box to indicate the maximum weight of the luminaire if other than 50 lb. ▶Figure 314–45

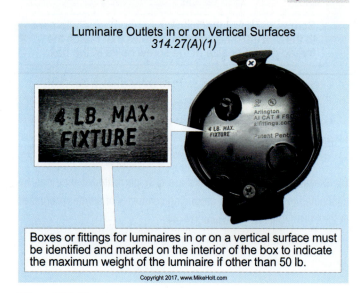

▶Figure 314–45

Ex: A vertically mounted luminaire weighing no more than 6 lb can be supported to a device box or plaster ring secured to a device box, provided the luminaire or its supporting yoke, or the lampholder, is secured to the box with no fewer than two No. 6 or larger screws. ▶Figure 314–46

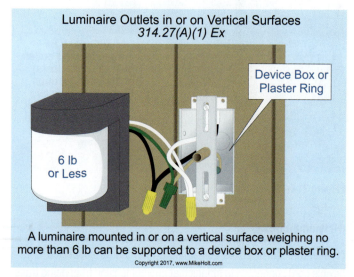

▶Figure 314–46

(2) Luminaire Outlets in the Ceiling. Boxes for ceiling luminaires must be listed and marked to support a luminaire weighing a minimum of 50 lb. Luminaires weighing more than 50 lb must be supported independently of the outlet box unless the outlet box is listed and marked on the interior of the box by the manufacturer for the maximum weight the box can support. ▶Figure 314–47

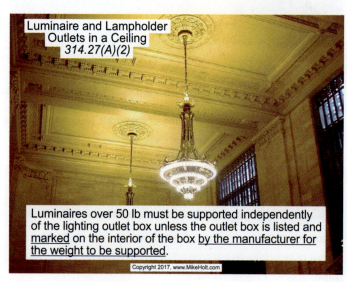

▶Figure 314–47

(B) Floor Box. Floor boxes must be specifically listed for the purpose. ▶Figure 314–48

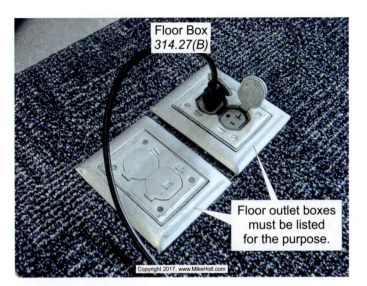

▶Figure 314–48

(C) Ceiling Paddle Fan Box. Outlet boxes for a ceiling paddle fan must be listed and marked as suitable for the purpose, and must not support a fan weighing more than 70 lb. Outlet boxes for a ceiling paddle fan that weighs more than 35 lb must include the maximum weight to be supported in the required marking. ▶Figure 314–49

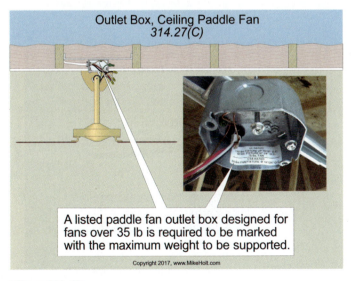

▶Figure 314–49

Author's Comment:

- If the maximum weight isn't marked on the box, and the fan weighs over 35 lb, it must be supported independently of the outlet box. Ceiling paddle fans over 70 lb must be supported independently of the outlet box. ▶Figure 314–50

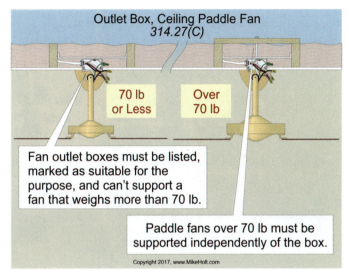

▶Figure 314–50

Where spare, separately switched, ungrounded conductors are provided to a ceiling-mounted outlet box, in a location acceptable for a ceiling-suspended (paddle) fan in one-family, two-family, or multifamily dwellings, the outlet box or outlet box system must be listed for the support of a ceiling-suspended (paddle) fan. ▶Figure 314–51

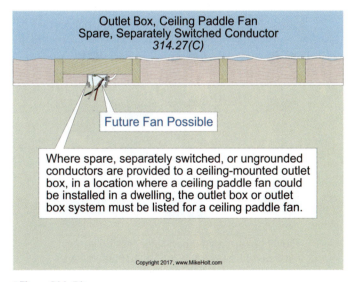

▶Figure 314–51

314.28 | Outlet, Device, Pull, and Junction Boxes; Conduit Bodies; and Handhole Enclosures

(D) Utilization Equipment. Boxes used for the support of utilization equipment must be designed to support equipment that weighs a minimum of 50 lb [314.27(A)].

Ex: Utilization equipment weighing 6 lb or less can be supported by any box or plaster ring secured to a box, provided the equipment is secured with no fewer than two No. 6 or larger screws. ▶Figure 314–52

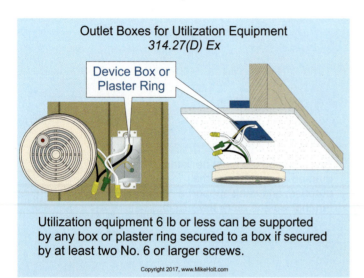

▶Figure 314–52

(E) Separable Attachment Fittings. Outlet boxes are permitted to support listed locking support and mounting receptacles (SQL receptacles) used in combination with compatible attachment fittings. The combination must be identified for the support of equipment within the weight and mounting orientation limits of the listing. ▶Figure 314–53

▶Figure 314–53

Author's Comment:

- See the Article 100 definition of "Receptacle" and visit http://www.safetyquicklight.com/ for additional information on SQL receptacles.

314.28 Sizing Conductors 4 AWG and Larger

Boxes containing conductors 4 AWG and larger that are required to be insulated must be sized so the conductor insulation won't be damaged.

Author's Comment:

- The requirements for sizing boxes containing conductors 6 AWG and smaller are contained in 314.16.
- If conductors 4 AWG and larger enter a box or other enclosure, a fitting that provides a smooth, rounded, insulating surface, such as a bushing or adapter, is required to protect the conductors from abrasion during and after installation [300.4(G)].

(A) Minimum Size. For raceways containing conductors 4 AWG and larger, the minimum dimensions of boxes must comply with the following:

(1) Straight Pulls. The minimum distance from where the conductors enter the box to the opposite wall isn't permitted to be less than eight times the trade size of the largest raceway. ▶Figure 314–54

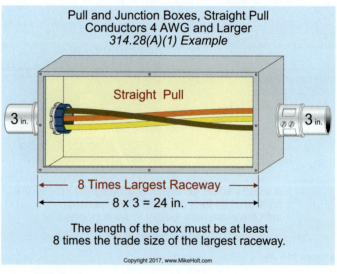

▶Figure 314–54

Outlet, Device, Pull, and Junction Boxes; Conduit Bodies; and Handhole Enclosures | 314.28

(2) Angle Pulls, U Pulls, or Splices.

Angle Pulls. The distance from the raceway entry of the box to the opposite wall isn't permitted to be less than six times the trade size of the largest raceway, plus the sum of the trade sizes of the remaining raceways on the same wall and row. ▶Figure 314–55

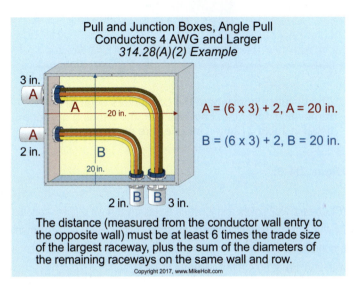

▶Figure 314–55

U Pulls. When a conductor enters and leaves from the same wall of the box, the distance from where the raceways enter to the opposite wall isn't permitted to be less than six times the trade size of the largest raceway, plus the sum of the trade sizes of the remaining raceways on the same wall and row. ▶Figure 314–56

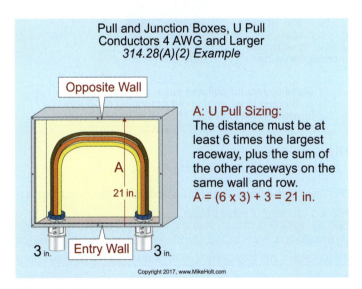

▶Figure 314–56

Splices. When conductors are spliced, the distance from where the raceways enter to the opposite wall isn't permitted to be less than six times the trade size of the largest raceway, plus the sum of the trade sizes of the remaining raceways on the same wall and row. ▶Figure 314–57

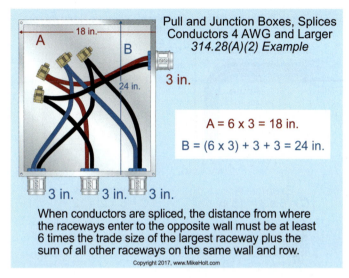

▶Figure 314–57

Rows. If there are multiple rows of raceway entries, each row is calculated individually and the row with the largest distance must be used.
▶Figure 314–58

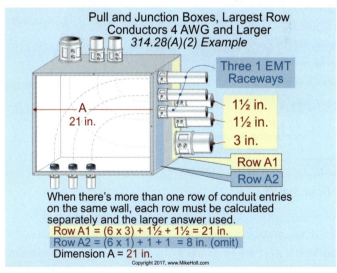

▶Figure 314–58

314.28 | Outlet, Device, Pull, and Junction Boxes; Conduit Bodies; and Handhole Enclosures

Distance Between Raceways. The distance between raceways enclosing the same conductor isn't permitted to be less than six times the trade size of the largest raceway, measured from the raceways' nearest edge-to-nearest edge. ▶Figure 314–59 and ▶Figure 314–60

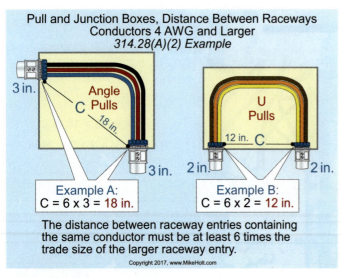

▶Figure 314–59

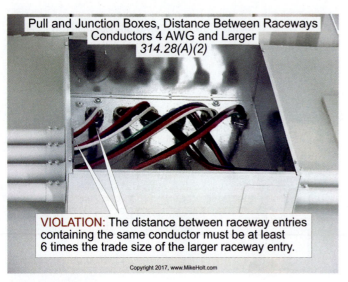

▶Figure 314–60

Ex: When conductors enter an enclosure with a removable cover, the distance from where the conductors enter to the removable cover isn't permitted to be less than the bending distance as listed in Table 312.6(A) for one conductor per terminal. ▶Figure 314–61

(B) Conductors in Pull or Junction Boxes. Pull boxes or junction boxes with any dimension over 6 ft must have all conductors cabled or racked in an approved manner.

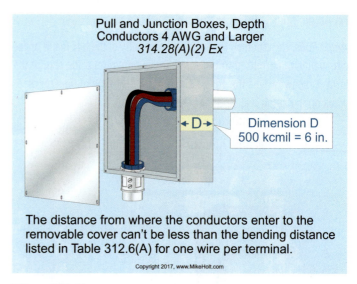

▶Figure 314–61

(C) Covers. Pull boxes and junction boxes must have a cover suitable for the conditions. Metal covers must be connected to an equipment grounding conductor of a type recognized in 250.118, in accordance with 250.110 [250.4(A)(3)]. ▶Figure 314–62

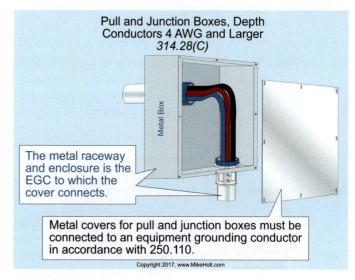

▶Figure 314–62

(E) Power Distribution Block. Power distribution blocks must comply with the following: ▶Figure 314–63

(1) Installation. Power distribution blocks must be listed; if installed on the line side of the service equipment, power distribution blocks must be listed and marked "suitable for use on the line side of service equipment" or equivalent. ▶Figure 314–64

Outlet, Device, Pull, and Junction Boxes; Conduit Bodies; and Handhole Enclosures | 314.29

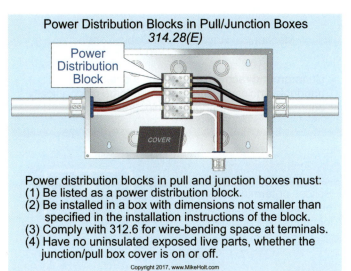

▶Figure 314–63

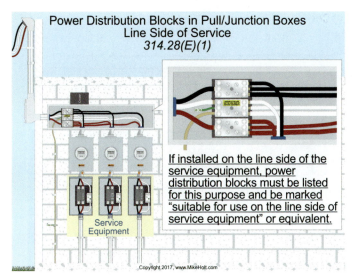

▶Figure 314–64

(2) Size. Be installed in a box not smaller than required by the installation instructions of the power distribution block.

(3) Wire-Bending Space. The junction box is sized so the wire-bending space requirements of 312.6 can be met.

(4) Live Parts. Exposed live parts on the power distribution block aren't present when the junction box cover is removed.

(5) Through Conductors. Where the junction box has conductors that don't terminate on the power distribution block(s), the through conductors must be arranged so the power distribution block terminals are unobstructed following installation.

314.29 Wiring to be Accessible

Boxes, conduit bodies, and handhole enclosures must be installed so the wiring is accessible without removing any part of the building or structure, sidewalks, paving, or earth. ▶Figure 314–65 and ▶Figure 314–66

Ex: Listed boxes and handhole enclosures can be buried if covered by gravel, light aggregate, or noncohesive granulated soil, and their location is effectively identified and accessible for excavation.

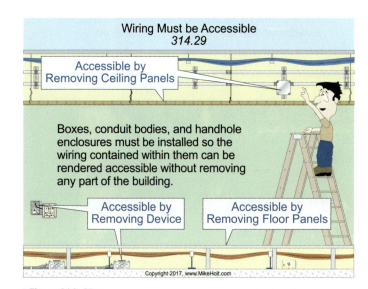

▶Figure 314–65

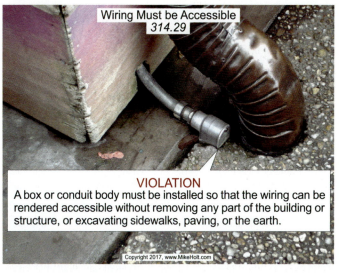

▶Figure 314–66

314.30 | Outlet, Device, Pull, and Junction Boxes; Conduit Bodies; and Handhole Enclosures

314.30 Handhole Enclosures

Handhole enclosures must be identified for underground use, and be designed and installed to withstand all loads likely to be imposed on them. ▶Figure 314–67

▶Figure 314–68

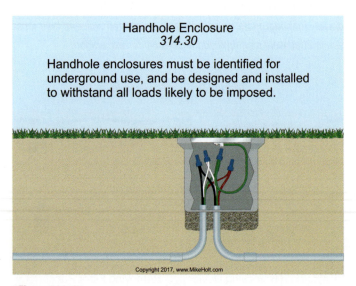

▶Figure 314–67

(A) Size. Handhole enclosures must be sized in accordance with 314.28(A). For handhole enclosures without bottoms, the measurement to the removable cover is taken from the end of the raceway or cable assembly. When the measurement is taken from the end of the raceway or cable assembly, the values in Table 312.6(A) for one wire to terminal can be used [314.28(A)(2) Ex].

(B) Mechanical Raceway and Cable Connection. Underground raceways and cables entering a handhole enclosure aren't required to be mechanically connected to the handhole enclosure. ▶Figure 314–68

(C) Enclosure Wiring. Splices or terminations within a handhole must be listed as suitable for wet locations [110.14(B)].

(D) Covers. Handhole enclosure covers must have an identifying mark or logo that prominently identifies the function of the enclosure, such as "electric." Handhole enclosure covers must require the use of tools to open, or they must weigh over 100 lb. ▶Figure 314–69 and ▶Figure 314–70

Metal covers and exposed conductive surfaces of handhole enclosures containing branch-circuit or feeder conductors must be connected to an equipment grounding conductor sized in accordance with 250.122, based on the rating of the overcurrent protection device [250.102(D)]. ▶Figure 314–71

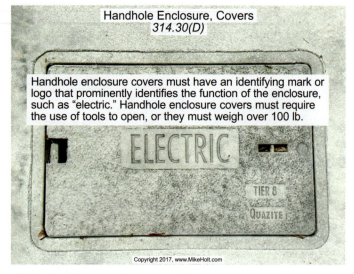

▶Figure 314–69

Metal covers and exposed conductive surfaces of handhole enclosures containing service conductors must be connected to a supply-side bonding jumper sized in accordance with Table 250.102(C)(1), based on the size of service conductors [250.92 and 250.102(C)].

Outlet, Device, Pull, and Junction Boxes; Conduit Bodies; and Handhole Enclosures | 314.30

▶Figure 314–70

▶Figure 314–71

Notes

ARTICLE 320 ARMORED CABLE (TYPE AC)

Introduction to Article 320—Armored Cable (Type AC)

Armored cable is an assembly of insulated conductors, 14 AWG through 1 AWG, individually wrapped within waxed paper and contained within a flexible spiral metal sheath. The outside appearance of armored cable looks like flexible metal conduit as well as metal-clad cable to the casual observer. This cable has been referred to as "BX®" cable over the years and used in residential wiring in some areas of the country.

Part I. General

320.1 Scope

This article covers the use, installation, and construction specifications of armored cable, Type AC. ▶Figure 320–1

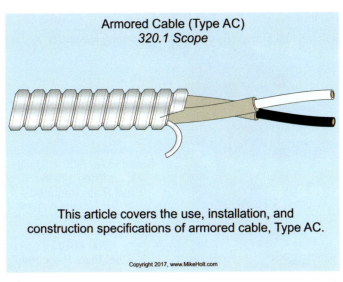

▶Figure 320–1

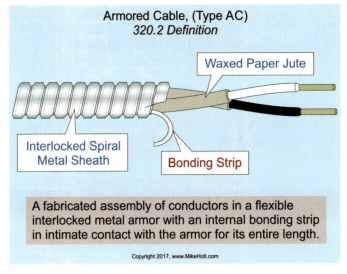

▶Figure 320–2

320.2 Definition

Armored Cable (Type AC). A fabricated assembly of conductors in a flexible interlocked metal armor with an internal bonding strip in intimate contact with the armor for its entire length. ▶Figure 320–2

Author's Comment:

- The conductors are contained within a flexible metal sheath that interlocks at the edges with an internal aluminum bonding strip, giving the cable an outside appearance similar to that of flexible metal conduit. Many electricians call this metal cable "BX®." The advantages the use of any flexible cables, as compared to raceway wiring methods, are that there's no limit to the number of bends between terminations and the cable can be quickly installed.

320.6 Listing Requirements

Type AC cable and associated fittings must be listed.

Part II. Installation

320.10 Uses Permitted

Type AC cable can be used or installed as follows:

(1) Feeders and branch circuits in both exposed and concealed installations.

(2) Cable trays.

(3) Dry locations.

(4) Embedded in plaster or brick, except in damp or wet locations.

(5) In air voids where not exposed to excessive moisture or dampness.

Note: The "Uses Permitted" isn't an all-inclusive list, which indicates that other suitable uses are permitted if approved by the authority having jurisdiction.

Author's Comment:

- Type AC cable is also permitted to be installed in a plenum space [300.22(C)(1)].

320.12 Uses Not Permitted

Type AC cable isn't permitted to be installed:

(1) Where subject to physical damage.

(2) In damp or wet locations.

(3) In air voids of masonry block or tile walls where such walls are exposed or subject to excessive moisture or dampness.

(4) Where exposed to corrosive conditions.

320.15 Exposed Work

Exposed Type AC cable must closely follow the surface of the building finish or running boards. Type AC cable installed on the bottom of floor or ceiling joists must be secured at every joist, and isn't permitted to be subject to physical damage. ▶Figure 320–3

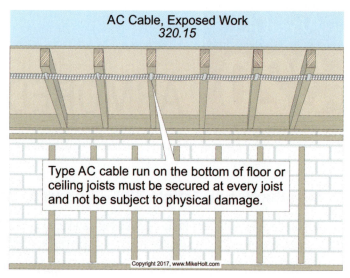

▶Figure 320–3

320.17 Through or Parallel to Framing Members

Type AC cable installed through, or parallel to, framing members or furring strips must be protected against physical damage from penetration by screws or nails by maintaining 1¼ in. of separation of the cable to the framing member or furring strip, or by a suitable metal plate in accordance with 300.4(A) and (D). ▶Figure 320–4 and ▶Figure 320–5

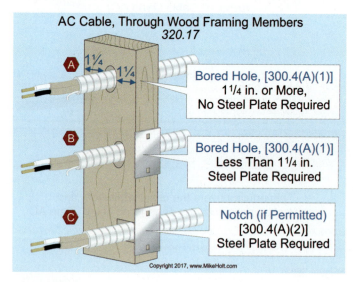

▶Figure 320–4

Armored Cable (Type AC) | 320.30

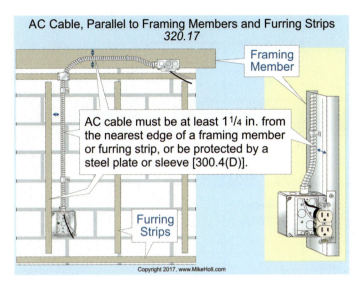

▶Figure 320–5

320.23 In Accessible Attics or Roof Spaces

(A) Cables Run Across the Top of Floor Joists. Where run across the top of floor joists, or across the face of rafters or studding within 7 ft of the floor or floor joists, the cable must be protected by guard strips that are at least as high as the cable. If this space isn't accessible by permanent stairs or ladders, protection is required only within 6 ft of the nearest edge of the scuttle hole or attic entrance. ▶Figure 320–6

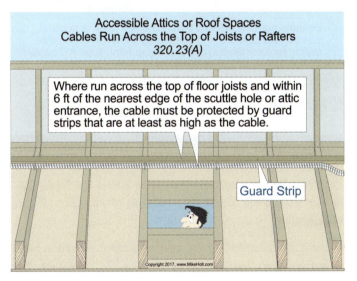

▶Figure 320–6

(B) Cable Installed Parallel to Framing Members. Where Type AC cable is installed on the side of rafters, studs, ceiling joists, or floor joists, no protection is required if the cable is installed and supported so the nearest outside surface of the cable or raceway is at least 1¼ in. from the nearest edge of the framing member [300.4(D)].

320.24 Bends

Type AC cable isn't permitted to be bent in a manner that will damage the cable. This is accomplished by limiting bending of the inner edge of the cable to a radius of not less than five times the diameter of the cable. ▶Figure 320–7

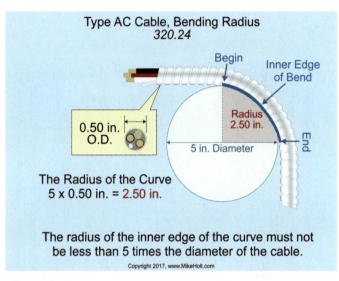

▶Figure 320–7

320.30 Securing and Supporting

(A) General. Type AC cable must be supported and secured by staples, cable ties listed and identified for securing and supporting; straps, hangers, or similar fittings; or other approved means designed and installed so as not to damage the cable. ▶Figure 320–8

(B) Securing. Type AC cable must be secured within 12 in. of every outlet box, junction box, cabinet, or fitting, and at intervals not exceeding 4½ ft. ▶Figure 320–9

Author's Comment:

- Type AC cable is considered secured when installed horizontally through openings in wooden or metal framing members [320.30(C)].

320.40 | Armored Cable (Type AC)

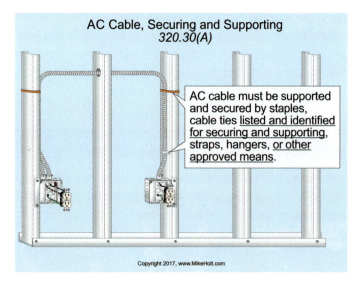
▶Figure 320–8

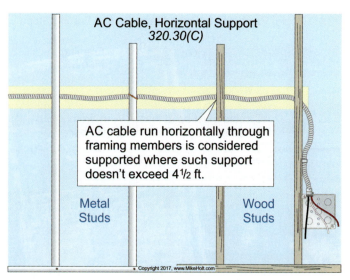
▶Figure 320–10

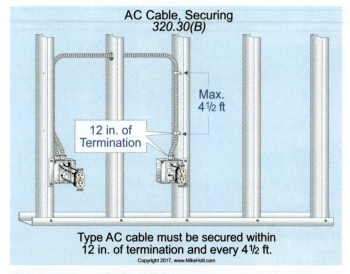
▶Figure 320–9

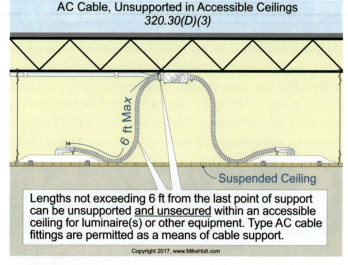
▶Figure 320–11

(C) Supporting. Type AC cable must be supported at intervals not exceeding 4½ ft. Cables installed horizontally through wooden or metal framing members are considered supported if support doesn't exceed 4½ ft. ▶Figure 320–10

(D) Unsupported Cables. Type AC cable can be unsupported and unsecured where:

(1) Fished through concealed spaces

(2) Not more than 2 ft long at terminals where flexibility is necessary

(3) Not more than 6 ft long from the last point of cable support or Type AC cable fitting to the point of connection to a luminaire or electrical equipment within an accessible ceiling. ▶Figure 320–11

320.40 Boxes and Fittings

Type AC cable must terminate in boxes or fittings specifically listed for Type AC cable to protect the conductors from abrasion [300.15]. ▶Figure 320–12

An insulating anti-short bushing, sometimes called a "redhead," must be installed at all Type AC cable terminations. The termination fitting must permit the visual inspection of the anti-short bushing once the cable has been installed. ▶Figure 320–13

Armored Cable (Type AC) | 320.100

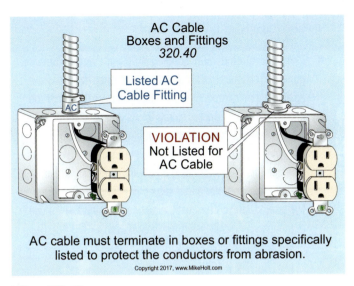

▶Figure 320–12

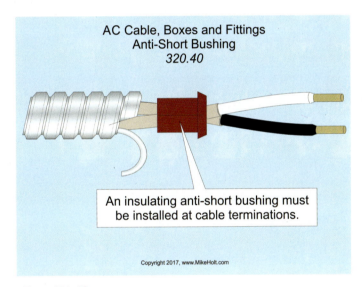

▶Figure 320–13

Author's Comment:

- The internal aluminum bonding strip within the cable serves no electrical purpose once its outside the cable, and can be cut off, but many electricians use it to secure the anti-short bushing to the cable. See 320.108.
- Conductors 4 AWG and larger that enter an enclosure must be protected from abrasion during and after installation by a fitting that provides a smooth, rounded, insulating surface, such as an insulating bushing unless the design of the box, fitting, or enclosure provides equivalent protection in accordance with 300.4(G).

320.80 Conductor Ampacity

(A) Thermal Insulation. Conductor ampacity is calculated on the 90°C insulation rating of the conductors, however the conductors must be sized to the termination temperature rating in accordance with 110.14(C)(1) and Table 310.15(B)(16). ▶Figure 320–14

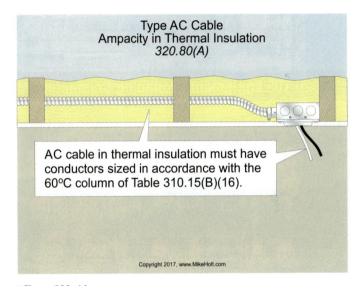

▶Figure 320–14

Example: What's the ampacity of four 12 THHN current-carrying conductors installed in Type AC cable?

Solution:

Table 310.15(B)(16) ampacity if 12 THHN is 30A

Conductor Adjusted Ampacity = 30A × 0.80 [Table 310.15(B)(3)(a)]
Conductor Adjusted Ampacity = 24A

Answer: 24A

Part III. Construction Specifications

320.100 Construction

Type AC cable has an armor of flexible metal tape with an internal aluminum bonding strip in intimate contact with the armor for its entire length.

320.108 | Armored Cable (Type AC)

Author's Comment:

- The best method of cutting Type AC cable is to use a tool specifically designed for the purpose, such as a rotary armor cutter.
- When cutting Type AC cable with a hacksaw, be sure to cut only one spiral of the cable and be careful not to nick the conductors; this is done by cutting the cable at an angle. Breaking the cable spiral (bending the cable very sharply), then cutting the cable with a pair of dikes isn't a good practice.

Author's Comment:

- The internal aluminum bonding strip isn't an equipment grounding conductor, but it allows the interlocked armor to serve as an equipment grounding conductor because it reduces the impedance of the armored spirals to ensure that a ground fault will be cleared. It's the combination of the aluminum bonding strip and the cable armor that creates the equipment grounding conductor. Once the bonding strip exits the cable, it can be cut off because it no longer serves any purpose. The effective ground-fault current path must be maintained by the use of fittings specifically listed for Type AC cable [320.40]. See 300.12, 300.15, and 300.10.

320.108 Equipment Grounding Conductor

Type AC cable can serve as an equipment grounding conductor [250.118(8)]. ▶Figure 320–15

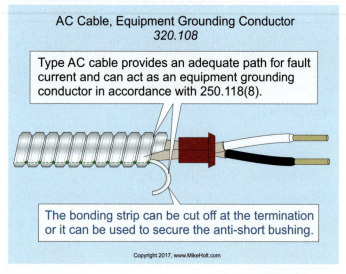

▶Figure 320–15

ARTICLE 330 METAL-CLAD CABLE (TYPE MC)

Introduction to Article 330—Metal-Clad Cable (Type MC)

Metal-clad cable encloses insulated conductors in a metal sheath of either corrugated or smooth copper or aluminum tubing, or spiral interlocked steel or aluminum. The physical characteristics of Type MC cable make it a versatile wiring method that you can use in almost any location, and for almost any application. The most commonly used Type MC cable is the interlocking kind, which looks similar to armored cable or flexible metal conduit. Traditional interlocked Type MC cable isn't permitted to serve as an equipment grounding conductor, therefore this cable must contain an equipment grounding conductor in accordance with 250.118(1). There's a fairly new product available called interlocked Type MC$^{AP®}$ cable that contains a bare aluminum grounding/bonding conductor running just below the metal armor, which allows the sheath to serve as an equipment grounding conductor [250.118(10)(b)].

Part I. General

330.1 Scope

Article 330 covers the use, installation, and construction specifications of metal-clad cable. ▶Figure 330–1

330.2 Definition

Metal-Clad Cable (Type MC). A factory assembly of insulated circuit conductors, with or without optical fiber members, enclosed in an armor of interlocking metal tape; or a smooth or corrugated metallic sheath. ▶Figure 330–2

Author's Comment:

- Because the outer sheath of interlocked Type MC cable isn't listed as an equipment grounding conductor, it contains an equipment grounding conductor [330.108].

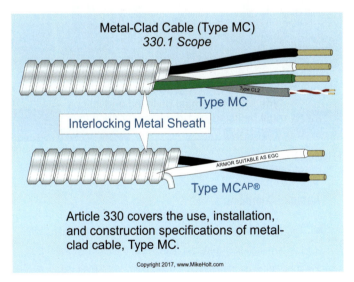

▶Figure 330–1

330.6 Listing Requirements

Type MC cable must be listed and the fittings must be listed and identified for the use. ▶Figure 330–3

330.10 | Metal-Clad Cable (Type MC)

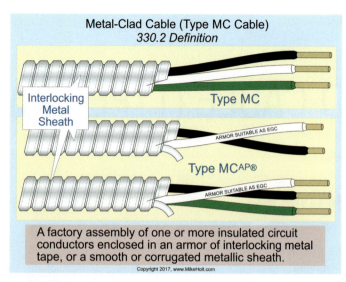

▶Figure 330–2

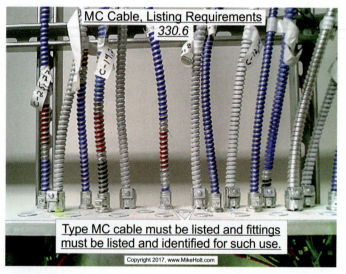

▶Figure 330–3

Author's Comment:

- The *NEC* doesn't require anti-short bushings (red heads) at the termination of Type MC cable, but if they're supplied it's considered by many to be a good practice to use them.

Part II. Installation

330.10 Uses Permitted

(A) General Uses.

(1) In branch circuits, feeders, and services

(2) In power, lighting, control, and signal circuits

(3) Indoors or outdoors

(4) Exposed or concealed

(5) Directly buried (if identified for the purpose)

(6) In a cable tray

(7) In a raceway

(8) As aerial cable on a messenger

(9) In hazardous locations as permitted in 501.10(B), 502.10(B), and 503.10

(10) Embedded in plaster or brick in dry locations

(11) In wet locations, where a corrosion-resistant jacket is provided over the metal sheath and any of the following are met:

　a. The metallic covering is impervious to moisture.

　b. A jacket is provided under the metal covering that's moisture resistant. ▶Figure 330–4

　c. The insulated conductors under the metallic covering are listed for use in wet locations.

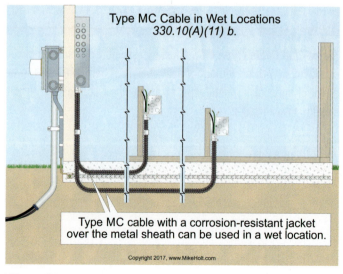

▶Figure 330–4

(12) If single-conductor cables are used, all circuit conductors must be grouped together to minimize induced voltage on the sheath [300.3(B)].

(B) Specific Uses.

(1) Cable Tray. Type MC cable installed in a cable tray in accordance with Article 392.

(2) Direct Buried. Direct-buried cables must be protected in accordance with 300.5.

(3) Installed as Service-Entrance Cable. Type MC cable is permitted for service entrances when installed in accordance with 230.43.

(4) Installed Outside of Buildings. Type MC cable installed outside of buildings must comply with 225.10, 396.10, and 396.12.

Note: The "Uses Permitted" isn't an all-inclusive list, which indicates that other suitable uses are permitted if approved by the authority having jurisdiction.

330.12 Uses Not Permitted

Type MC cable isn't permitted to be used where:

(1) Subject to physical damage.

(2) Exposed to the destructive corrosive conditions in (a) or (b), unless the metallic sheath or armor is resistant to the conditions, or protected by material resistant to the conditions:

　a. Direct burial in the earth or embedded in concrete unless identified for the application.

　b. Exposed to cinder fills, strong chlorides, caustic alkalis, or vapors of chlorine or of hydrochloric acids.

330.15 Exposed Work

Exposed runs of Type MC cable must closely follow the surface of the building finish or running boards. Type MC cable installed on the bottom of floor or ceiling joists must be secured at every joist and not be subject to physical damage. ▶Figure 330–5

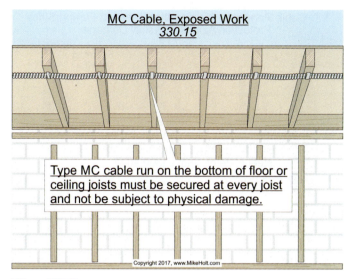

▶Figure 330–5

330.17 Through or Parallel to Framing Members

Type MC cable installed through or parallel to framing members or furring strips must be protected against physical damage from penetration of screws or nails by maintaining a 1¼ in. separation, or by installing a suitable metal plate in accordance with 300.4(A) and (D). ▶Figure 330–6 and ▶Figure 330–7

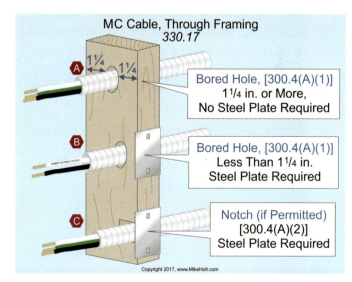

▶Figure 330–6

330.23 | Metal-Clad Cable (Type MC)

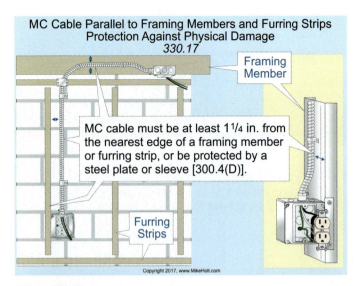

▶Figure 330–7

330.23 In Accessible Attics or Roof Spaces

Type MC cable installed in accessible attics or roof spaces must comply with 320.23.

Author's Comment:

- **On the Surface of Floor Joists, Rafters, or Studs.** In attics and roof spaces that are accessible, substantial guards must protect cables installed across the top of floor joists, or across the face of rafters or studding within 7 ft of the floor or floor joists. If this space isn't accessible by permanent stairs or ladders, protection is required only within 6 ft of the nearest edge of the scuttle hole or attic entrance [320.23(A)].

- **Along the Side of Framing Members [320.23(B)].** When Type MC cable is installed on the side of rafters, studs, or floor joists, no protection is required if the cable is installed and supported so the nearest outside surface of the cable or raceway is at least 1¼ in. from the nearest edge of the framing member where nails or screws are likely to penetrate [300.4(D)].

330.24 Bends

Bends must be made so the cable won't be damaged, and the radius of the curve of any bend at the inner edge of the cable isn't permitted to be less than what's dictated in each of the following instances:

(A) Smooth-Sheath Cables.

(1) Smooth-sheath Type MC cables aren't permitted to be bent so the bending radius of the inner edge of the cable is less than 10 times the external diameter of the metallic sheath for cable up to ¾ in. in external diameter.

(B) Interlocked or Corrugated Sheath. Interlocked- or corrugated-sheath Type MC cable isn't permitted to be bent so the bending radius of the inner edge of the cable is less than seven times the external diameter of the cable. ▶Figure 330–8

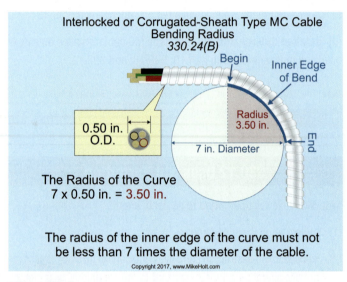

▶Figure 330–8

330.30 Securing and Supporting

(A) General. Type MC cable must be supported and secured by staples, cable ties listed and identified for securing and supporting; straps, hangers, or similar fittings; or other approved means designed and installed so as not to damage the cable. ▶Figure 330–9 and ▶Figure 330–10

Author's Comment:

- Secured is "fastened" such as with a strap or tie wrap; supported is "held" such with as a hanger or through a hole in a stud, joist, or rafter. ▶Figure 330–11

(B) Securing. Type MC cable with four or fewer conductors sized no larger than 10 AWG, must be secured within 12 in. of every outlet box, junction box, cabinet, or fitting and at intervals not exceeding 6 ft. ▶Figure 330–12

Listed cables with ungrounded conductors 250 kcmil and larger can be secured at 10-ft intervals when installed vertically.

Metal-Clad Cable (Type MC) | 330.30

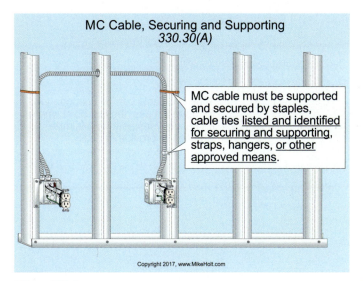

▶Figure 330–9

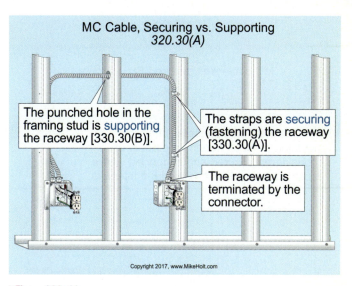

▶Figure 330–11

▶Figure 330–10

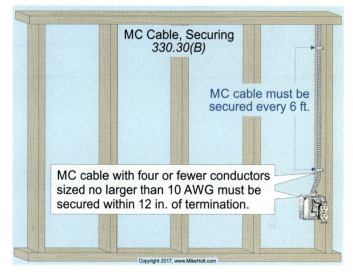

▶Figure 330–12

(C) Supporting. Type MC cable must be supported at intervals not exceeding 6 ft. Cables installed horizontally through wooden or metal framing members are considered secured and supported if such support doesn't exceed 6-ft intervals. ▶Figure 330–13

(D) Unsupported Cables. Type MC cable can be unsupported and unsecured where:

(1) Fished through concealed spaces

(2) Not more than 6 ft long from the last point of cable support to the point of connection to a luminaire or electrical equipment within an accessible ceiling. For the purposes of this section, Type MC cable fittings are permitted as a means of cable support. ▶Figure 330–14

(3) Not more than 3 ft from the last point where it's securely fastened to provide flexibility for equipment that requires movement after installation, or to connect equipment where flexibility is necessary to minimize the transmission of vibration from the equipment. ▶Figure 330–15

330.80 | Metal-Clad Cable (Type MC)

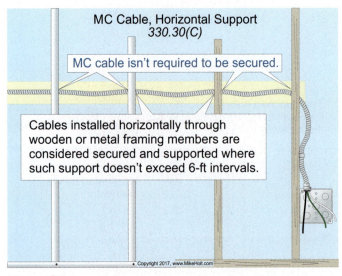

▶Figure 330–13

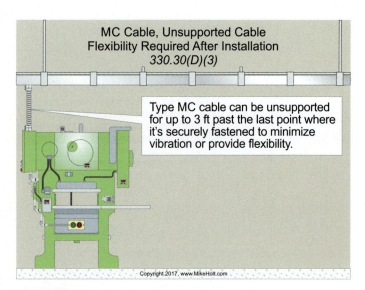

▶Figure 330–15

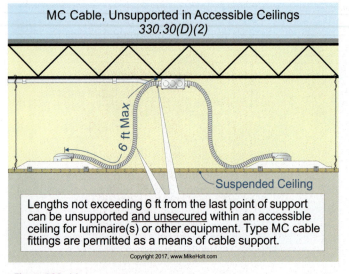

▶Figure 330–14

330.80 Conductor Ampacities

Conductor ampacity is calculated on the 90°C insulation rating of the conductors; however, the conductors must be sized to the termination temperature rating in accordance with 110.14(C)(1).

Part III. Construction Specifications

330.108 Equipment Grounding Conductor

If Type MC cable is to serve as an equipment grounding conductor, it must comply with 250.118 and 250.122.

Author's Comment:

- The outer sheath of:
  ◆ Traditional interlocked Type MC cable isn't permitted to serve as an equipment grounding conductor, therefore this cable must contain an insulated equipment grounding conductor in accordance with 250.118(1). ▶Figure 330–16
  ◆ Interlocked Type MC^{AP} cable containing an aluminum grounding/bonding conductor running just below the metal armor is listed to serve as an equipment grounding conductor [250.118(10)(b)]. ▶Figure 330–17
  ◆ Smooth or corrugated-tube Type MC cable is listed to serve as an equipment grounding conductor [250.118(10)(c)].

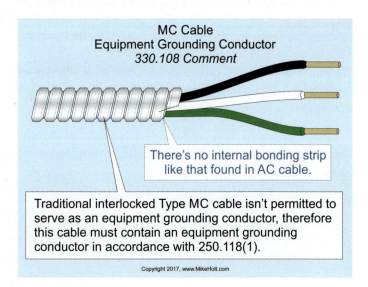

▶Figure 330–16

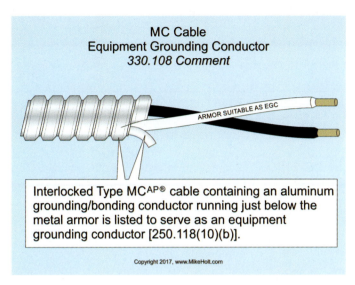
▶Figure 330–17

Notes

ARTICLE 334

NONMETALLIC-SHEATHED CABLE (TYPES NM AND NMC)

Introduction to Article 334—Nonmetallic-Sheathed Cable (Types NM and NMC)

Nonmetallic-sheathed cable is flexible, inexpensive, and easily installed. It provides very limited physical protection for the conductors, so the installation restrictions are stringent. Its low cost and relative ease of installation make it a common wiring method for residential and commercial branch circuits. In the field, Type NM cable is typically referred to as "Romex®."

Part I. General

334.1 Scope

Article 334 covers the use, installation, and construction specifications of nonmetallic-sheathed cable. ▶Figure 334–1

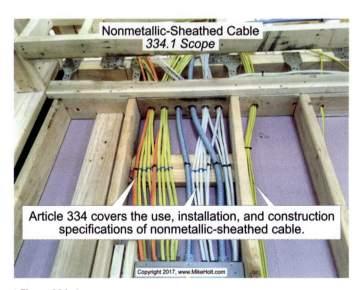

▶Figure 334–1

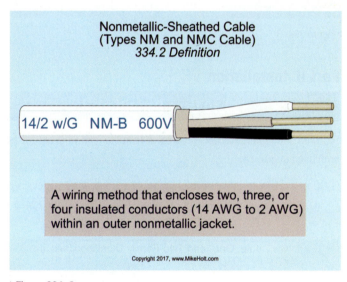

▶Figure 334–2

- NM cable has insulated conductors enclosed within an overall nonmetallic jacket.
- NMC cable has insulated conductors enclosed within an overall, corrosion-resistant, nonmetallic jacket.

Author's Comment:

- It's the generally accepted practice in the electrical industry to call Type NM cable "Romex®," a registered trademark of the Southwire Company.

334.2 Definition

Nonmetallic-Sheathed Cable (Types NM and NMC). A wiring method that encloses two or more insulated conductors, 14 AWG through 2 AWG, within a nonmetallic jacket. ▶Figure 334–2

334.6 | Nonmetallic-Sheathed Cable (Types NM and NMC)

334.6 Listing Requirements

Type NM cable and associated fittings must be listed. ▶Figure 334–3

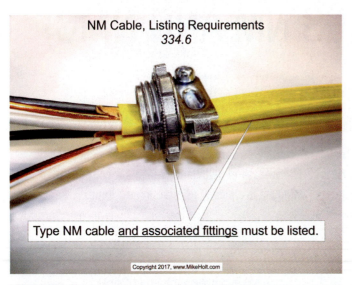

▶Figure 334–3

Part II. Installation

334.10 Uses Permitted

Type NM and Type NMC cables can be used in the following, except as prohibited in 334.12:

(1) One- and two-family dwellings of any height, and their attached/detached garages or storage buildings. ▶Figure 334–4 and ▶Figure 334–5

▶Figure 334–4

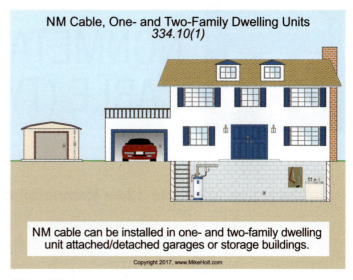

▶Figure 334–5

(2) Multifamily dwellings permitted to be of Types III, IV, and V construction. ▶Figure 334–6

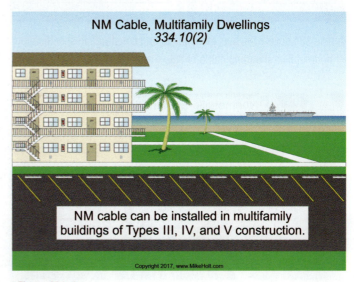

▶Figure 334–6

(3) Other structures permitted to be of Types III, IV, and V construction. Cables must be concealed within walls, floors, or ceilings that provide a thermal barrier of material with at least a 15-minute finish rating, as identified in listings of fire-rated assemblies. ▶Figure 334–7

Author's Comment:

- See the definition of "Concealed" in Article 100.

Nonmetallic-Sheathed Cable (Types NM and NMC) | 334.12

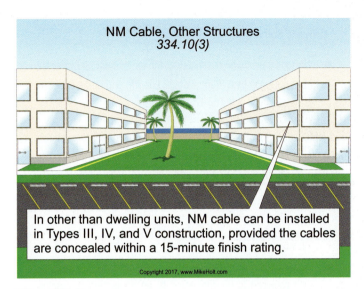

▶Figure 334–7

Note 1: Building constructions are defined in NFPA 220-2006, *Standard on Types of Building Construction*, the applicable building code, or both.

Note 2: See Annex E for the determination of building types [NFPA 220, Table 3-1].

334.12 Uses Not Permitted

(A) Types NM and NMC. Types NM and NMC cables aren't permitted.

(1) In any dwelling or structure not specifically permitted in 334.10(1), (2), (3), and (5).

(2) Exposed within a dropped or suspended ceiling cavity in other than one- and two-family, and multifamily dwellings. ▶Figure 334–8

(3) As service-entrance cable.

(4) In commercial garages having hazardous locations, as defined in 511.3.

(5) In theaters and similar locations, except where permitted in 518.4(B).

(6) In motion picture studios.

(7) In storage battery rooms.

(8) In hoistways, or on elevators or escalators.

(9) Embedded in poured cement, concrete, or aggregate.

(10) In any hazardous location, except where permitted by other sections in the *Code*.

(B) Type NM. Type NM cables aren't permitted to be used under the following conditions, or in the following locations:

(1) If exposed to corrosive fumes or vapors.

(2) If embedded in masonry, concrete, adobe, fill, or plaster.

(3) In a shallow chase in masonry, concrete, or adobe and covered with plaster, adobe, or similar finish.

(4) In wet or damp locations. ▶Figure 334–9

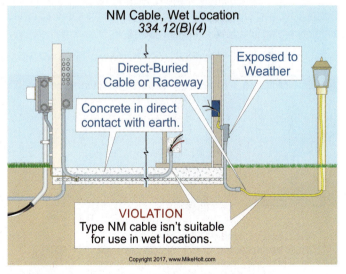

▶Figure 334–9

Author's Comment:

- A raceway in a ground floor slab is considered a wet location.
  ▶Figure 334–10

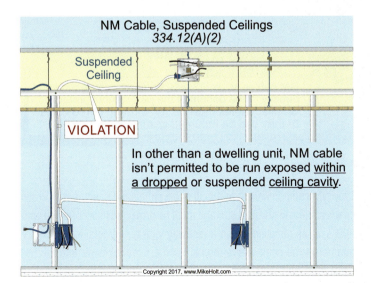

▶Figure 334–8

359

334.15 | Nonmetallic-Sheathed Cable (Types NM and NMC)

▶Figure 334–10

334.15 Exposed Work

(A) Surface of the Building. Exposed Type NM cable must closely follow the surface of the building.

(B) Protected from Physical Damage. Nonmetallic-sheathed cable must be protected from physical damage by rigid metal conduit, intermediate metal conduit, Schedule 80 PVC conduit, Type RTRC-XW conduit, electrical metallic tubing, guard strips, or other means approved by the authority having jurisdiction. ▶Figure 334–11

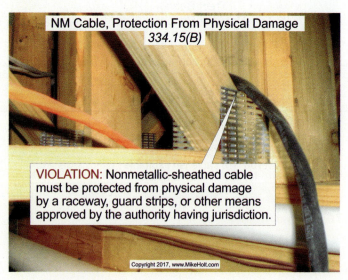

▶Figure 334–11

Author's Comment:

- When installed within a raceway, the cable must be protected from abrasion by a fitting installed on the end of the raceway [300.15(C)].

Type NMC cable installed in shallow chases in masonry, concrete, or adobe, must be protected against nails or screws by a steel plate not less than 1/16 in. thick [300.4(F)] and covered with plaster, adobe, or similar finish.

Author's Comment:

- If Type NM cable is installed in a metal raceway, the raceway isn't required to be connected to an equipment grounding conductor [250.86 Ex 2 and 300.12 Ex].

(C) In Unfinished Basements and Crawl Spaces. If Type NM cable is installed at angles with joists in unfinished basements and crawl spaces, it's permissible to secure cables containing conductors not smaller than two 6 AWG or three 8 AWG conductors directly to the lower edges of the joists. Smaller cables must be installed through bored holes in joists or on running boards. ▶Figure 334–12

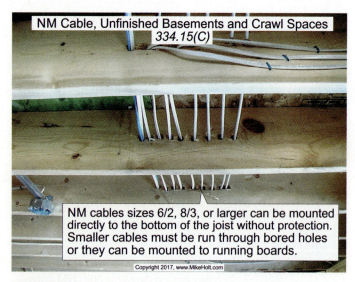

▶Figure 334–12

Type NM cable installed on a wall of an unfinished basement or crawl space subject to physical damage must be protected in accordance with 300.4, or be installed within a raceway with a nonmetallic bushing or adapter at the point where the cable enters the raceway, and the NM cable must be secured within 12 in. of the point where the cable enters the raceway. ▶Figure 334–13

Nonmetallic-Sheathed Cable (Types NM and NMC) | 334.17

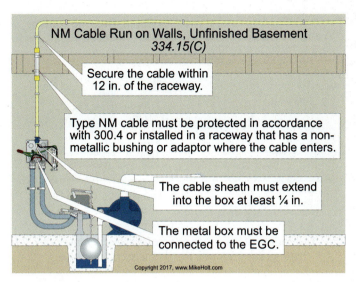
▶Figure 334–13

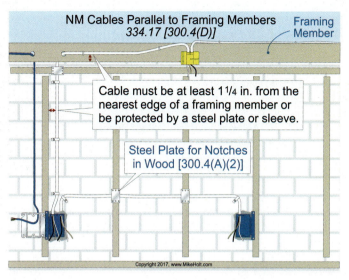
▶Figure 334–15

334.17 Through or Parallel to Framing Members

Type NM cable installed through or parallel to framing members or furring strips must be protected against physical damage from penetration by screws or nails by maintaining 1¼ in. of separation of the cable to the framing member or furring strip, or by a suitable metal plate in accordance with 300.4(A) and (D). ▶Figure 334–14 and ▶Figure 334–15

If Type NM cables pass through factory or field openings in metal framing members, the cable must be protected by listed bushings or listed grommets that cover all metal edges. The protection fitting must be securely fastened in the opening before the installation of the cable.
▶Figure 334–16

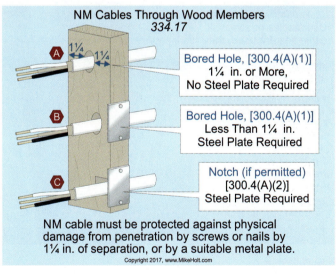
▶Figure 334–14

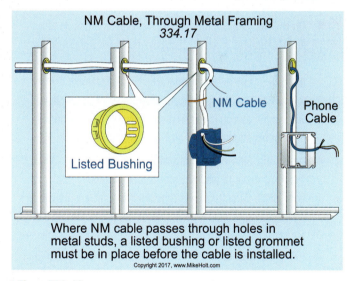
▶Figure 334–16

334.23 Attics and Roof Spaces

Type NM cable installed in accessible attics or roof spaces must comply with 320.23. ▶Figure 334–17

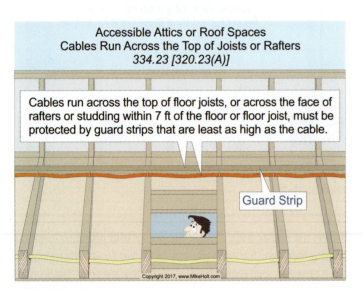

▶Figure 334–17

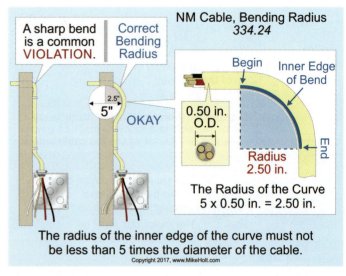

▶Figure 334–18

Author's Comment:

- **On the Surface of Floor Joists, Rafters, or Studs.** In attics and roof spaces that are accessible, substantial guards must protect cables installed across the top of floor joists, or across the face of rafters or studding within 7 ft of the floor or floor joists. If this space isn't accessible by permanent stairs or ladders, protection is required only within 6 ft of the nearest edge of the scuttle hole or attic entrance [320.23(A)].

- **Along the Side of Framing Members [320.23(B)].** When Type NM cable is installed on the side of rafters, studs, or floor joists, no protection is required if the cable is installed and supported so the nearest outside surface of the cable or raceway is at least 1¼ in. from the nearest edge of the framing member if nails or screws are likely to penetrate [300.4(D)].

334.24 Bends

When the cable is bent, it isn't permitted to be damaged and the radius of the curve of the inner edge of any bend isn't permitted to be less than five times the diameter of the cable. ▶Figure 334–18

334.30 Securing and Supporting

Nonmetallic-sheathed cable must be supported and secured by staples, straps, cable ties listed and identified for securing and supporting; hangers, or similar fittings, at intervals not exceeding 4½ ft and within 12 in. of the cable entry into enclosures or fittings. ▶Figure 334–19

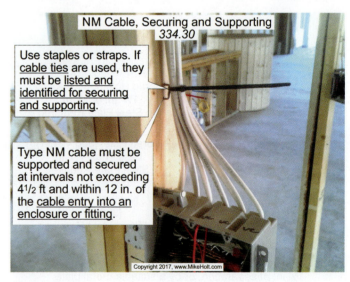

▶Figure 334–19

Two-wire (flat) Type NM cable isn't permitted to be stapled on edge. ▶Figure 334–20

Type NM cable installed within a raceway isn't required to be secured within the raceway. ▶Figure 334–21

Nonmetallic-Sheathed Cable (Types NM and NMC) | 334.40

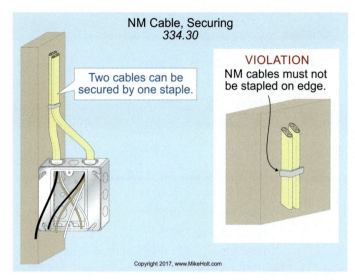

▶Figure 334–20

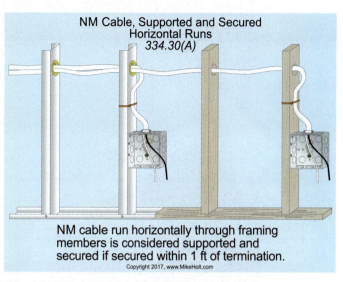

▶Figure 334–22

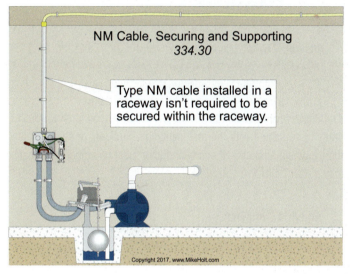

▶Figure 334–21

(A) Horizontal Runs. Type NM cable installed horizontally in bored or punched holes in wood or metal framing members, or notches in wooden members is considered secured and supported, but the cable must be secured within 1 ft of termination. ▶Figure 334–22

Note: See 314.17(C) for support where nonmetallic boxes are used.

(B) Unsupported. Type NM cable can be unsupported in the following situations:

(1) If Type NM cable is fished between concealed access points in finished buildings, and support is impracticable.

(2) Not more than 4½ ft of unsupported cable is permitted from the last point of support within an accessible ceiling for the connection of luminaires or equipment in one-, two-, or multifamily dwellings.

Author's Comment:

- Type NM cable isn't permitted as a wiring method above accessible ceilings, except in dwellings [334.12(A)(2)].

334.40 Boxes and Fittings

(B) NM Cable Interconnection Devices. A box or conduit body isn't required where a listed nonmetallic-sheathed cable interconnector device is used for any exposed cable wiring or for concealed cable wiring in existing buildings in accordance with 300.15(H). ▶Figure 334–23

Author's Comment:

- According to UL (QAAV), interconnection devices have been investigated for equivalency to Type NM cable in insulation and temperature rise, and for capability to withstand fault currents, vibration, and mechanical shock that may occur during transport. The interconnects are intended for use with 14 AWG and 12 AWG solid or stranded copper conductors.

334.80 | Nonmetallic-Sheathed Cable (Types NM and NMC)

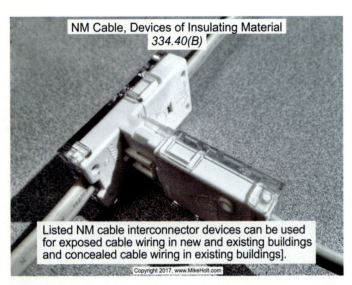

▶Figure 334–23

334.80 Conductor Ampacity

Adjusted and corrected conductor ampacity for Type NM cable is based on the 90°C insulation rating in accordance with Table 310.15(B)(16); however, conductors are sized in accordance with that of the 60°C termination temperature rating in accordance with Table 310.15(B)(16).

Example: What size Type NM cable is required to supply a 9,600W, 240V, single-phase fixed space heater with a 3A blower motor?
▶Figure 334–24

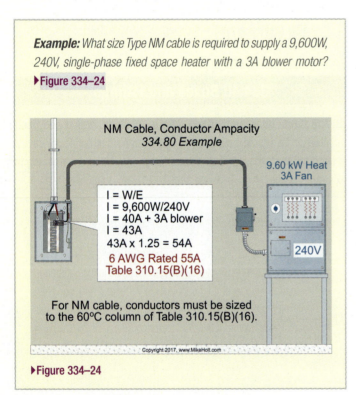

▶Figure 334–24

Solution:

Step 1: Determine the load for the heater:

$I = W/E$

$I = 9,600 \text{ VA}/240\text{V}$

$I = 40\text{A} + 3\text{A blower}$

$I = 43\text{A}$

Step 2: Size the conductors at 125 percent of the total current load [110.14(C)(1) and 210.19(A)(1)]:

Conductor Size = 43A × 1.25

Conductor Size = 53.75A

Conductor Size = 53.75A, 6 AWG, rated 55A at 60°C [Table 310.15(B)(16)]

Conductor/Protection Size = Load × 1.25

Conductor/Protection Size = 43A × 1.25

Conductor/Protection Size = 53.75A

Answer: A 6 AWG conductor rated 55A at 60°C [Table 310.15(B)(16)], protected with a 60A overcurrent protection device [240.6(A)].

If multiple Type NM cables pass through the same wood framing opening that's to be sealed with thermal insulation, caulking, or sealing foam, the allowable ampacity of each conductor must be adjusted in accordance with Table 310.15(B)(3)(a).

Author's Comment:

- This requirement has no effect on conductor sizing if you bundle no more than nine current-carrying 14 AWG or 12 AWG conductors together. For example, if three 14/2 cables and one 14/3 cable (eight current-carrying 14 THHN conductors) are bundled together in a dry location, the ampacity for each conductor (25A at 90°C, Table 310.15(B)(16)) is adjusted by a 70 percent adjustment factor [Table 310.15(B)(3)(a)].
  - ◆ Adjusted Conductor Ampacity = 25A × 0.70
  - ◆ Adjusted Conductor Ampacity = 17.50A

Where more than two NM cables are installed in contact with thermal insulation without maintaining spacing between cables, the allowable ampacity of each conductor must be adjusted in accordance with Table 310.15(B)(3)(a).

Part III. Construction Specifications

334.100 Construction

The outer cable sheath of Type NM cable must be constructed with nonmetallic material.

334.104 Conductors

The conductors must be 14 AWG through 2 AWG copper, or 12 AWG through 2 AWG aluminum or copper-clad aluminum.

334.108 Equipment Grounding Conductor

Type NM cable must have an insulated, covered, or bare equipment grounding conductor. ▶Figure 334–25

334.112 Insulation

NM conductor insulation must be rated 90°C (194°F).

Note: Type NM cable identified by the markings NM-B meets this requirement.

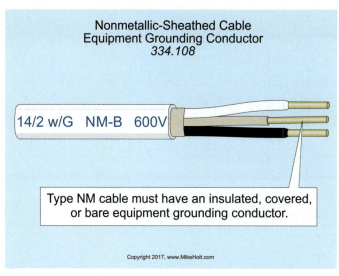

▶Figure 334–25

Notes

ARTICLE 336 — POWER AND CONTROL TRAY CABLE (TYPE TC)

Introduction to Article 336—Power and Control Tray Cable (Type TC)

Power and control tray cable is flexible, inexpensive, and easily installed. It provides very limited physical protection for the conductors, so the installation restrictions are stringent. Its low cost and relative ease of installation make it a common wiring method for industrial applications.

Part I. General

336.1 Scope

This article covers the use and installation for power and control tray cable, Type TC.

336.2 Definition

Power and Control Tray Cable, Type TC. A factory assembly of two or more insulated conductors under a nonmetallic jacket.

336.6 Listing Requirements

Type TC cable and associated fittings must be listed. ▶Figure 336–1

▶Figure 336–1

Part II. Installation

336.10 Uses Permitted

(1) Power, lighting, control, and signal circuits.

(2) In cable trays including those with mechanically discontinuous segments up to 1 ft.

(3) In raceways.

(4) Outdoor locations supported by a messenger wire.

(5) Class 1 circuits as permitted in Parts II and III of Article 725.

(6) Nonpower-limited fire alarm circuits in accordance with if 760.49.

(7) Industrial establishments where the conditions of maintenance and supervision ensure that only qualified persons service the installation.

(8) In wet locations where the cable is resistant to moisture and corrosive agents.

(9) In one- and two-family dwellings, Type TC-ER cable is permitted in accordance with Part II of Article 334. ▶Figure 336–2

336.12 | Power and Control Tray Cable (Type TC)

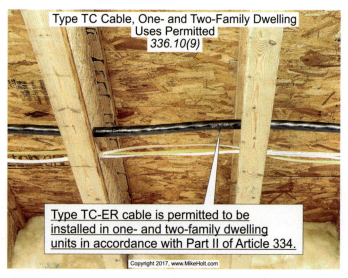

▶Figure 336–2

Author's Comment:

- The "ER" marking on Type TC-ER cable identifies the cable as suitable for exposed run use in accordance with UL 1277.

Ex: Where Type TC cable is used to connect a generator and its associated equipment, the cable ampacity limitations of 334.80 don't apply.

Note 1: Type TC cable that's suitable for pulling through structural members of a dwelling unit will be marked "TC-ER-JP." ▶Figure 336–3

▶Figure 336–3

Author's Comment:

- The "JP" marking on Type TC-ER-JP cable identifies the cable as suitable to be pulled through wood framing members because the cable has met the joist pull testing requirements of UL 1277.

Note 2: Control and Class 1 power conductors within the same Type TC cable are only permitted where the conductors are functionally associated with each other in accordance with 725.136.

(10) Direct buried where identified for direct burial.

336.12 Uses Not Permitted

Type TC tray cables aren't permitted:

(1) Where exposed to physical damage

(2) Outside a raceway or cable tray system, except as permitted in 336.10(4), 336.10(7), 336.10(9), and 336.10(10)

(3) Exposed to direct rays of the sun, unless identified as sunlight resistant

336.24 Bending Radius

Bends in Type TC cable must be made so as not to damage the cable. Type TC cable without metal shielding must have a minimum bending radius as follows:

(1) Four times the overall diameter for cables 1 in. or less in diameter

(2) Five times the overall diameter for cables larger than 1 in. but not more than 2 in. in diameter

336.80 Ampacity

The ampacity of Type TC tray cable is in accordance with 310.15(B)(16) as limited by 110.14(C)(1).

ARTICLE 338

SERVICE-ENTRANCE CABLE (TYPES SE AND USE)

Introduction to Article 338—Service-Entrance Cable (Types SE and USE)

Service-entrance cable is a single conductor or multiconductor assembly with or without an overall moisture-resistant covering. This cable is used primarily for services, but can also be used for feeders and branch circuits when the limitations of this article are observed.

Part I. General

338.1 Scope

Article 338 covers the use, installation, and construction specifications of service-entrance cable, Types SE and USE. ▶Figure 338–1

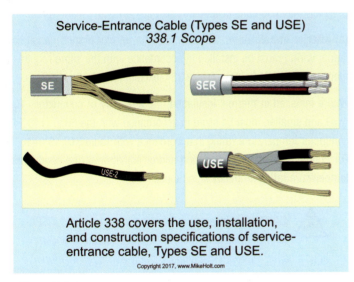

▶Figure 338–1

338.2 Definitions

Service-Entrance Cable. Service-entrance cable is a single or multi-conductor assembly, with or without an overall covering, used primarily for services. ▶Figure 338–2

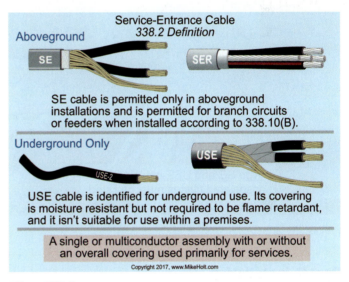

▶Figure 338–2

Type SE. SE and SER cables have a flame-retardant, moisture-resistant covering and are permitted only in aboveground installations. These cables are permitted for branch circuits or feeders when installed in accordance with 338.10(B).

Author's Comment:

■ SER cable is SE cable with an insulated neutral, resulting in three insulated conductors with an uninsulated equipment grounding conductor. SER cable is round, while 2-wire SE cable is flat.

338.6 | Service-Entrance Cable (Types SE and USE)

Type USE. USE cable is identified as a wiring method permitted for underground use; its covering is moisture resistant, but not flame retardant.

Author's Comment:

- USE cable isn't permitted to be installed indoors [338.10(B)], except single-conductor USE dual rated as RHH/RHW.

338.6 Listing Requirements

Type SE and USE cables and associated fittings must be listed.
▶Figure 338–3

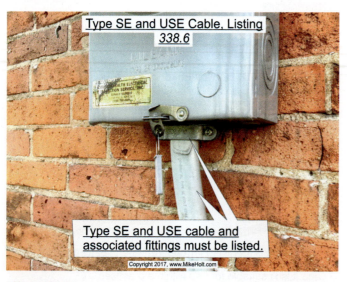

▶Figure 338–3

Part II. Installation

338.10 Uses Permitted

(A) Service-Entrance Conductors. Service-entrance cable used as service-entrance conductors must be installed in accordance with Article 230.

(B) Branch Circuits or Feeders.

(1) Insulated Conductor. Type SE service-entrance cable is permitted for branch circuits and feeders where the circuit conductors are insulated.

(2) Uninsulated Conductor. SE cable is permitted for branch circuits and feeders if the insulated conductors are used for circuit wiring, and the uninsulated conductor is only used for equipment grounding purposes. ▶Figure 338–4

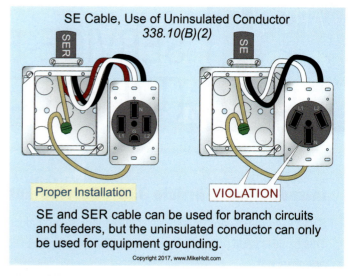

▶Figure 338–4

Ex: In existing installations, uninsulated conductors may be used for the neutral conductor if the uninsulated neutral conductor of the cable originates in service equipment.

(3) Temperature Limitations. SE cable isn't permitted to be subjected to conductor temperatures exceeding its insulation rating.

(4) Installation Methods for Branch Circuits and Feeders. SE cable used for branch circuits or feeders must comply with (a) and (b).

(a) Interior Installations. SE cable used for interior branch-circuit or feeder wiring must be installed in accordance with the same requirements as Type NM Cable—Article 334, excluding 334.80.

Where installed in thermal insulation, the ampacity of conductors 10 AWG and smaller, must be sized in accordance with the 60°C (140°F) conductor temperature rating in accordance with Table 310.15(B)(16). For conductor ampacity correction and/or adjustment, the conductor temperature rating ampacity is to be used.

CAUTION: Underground service-entrance cable (USE) isn't permitted for interior wiring because it doesn't have a flame-retardant insulation. It's only permitted in interior wiring when listed as both a cable (USE) and a conductor, such as RHH, in accordance with Table 310.104.

(b) Exterior Installations. The cable must be supported in accordance with 334.30 and where run underground, the cable must comply with Part II of Article 340.

338.12 Uses Not Permitted

(A) Service-Entrance Cable. SE cable isn't permitted under the following conditions or locations:

(1) If subject to physical damage unless protected in accordance with 230.50(A).

(2) Underground with or without a raceway.

(B) Underground Service-Entrance Cable. USE cable isn't permitted:

(1) For interior wiring.

(2) Above ground, except where protected against physical damage in accordance with 300.5(D).

338.24 Bends

Bends in cable must be made so the protective coverings of the cable aren't damaged, and the radius of the curve of the inner edge is at least five times the diameter of the cable. ▶Figure 338–5

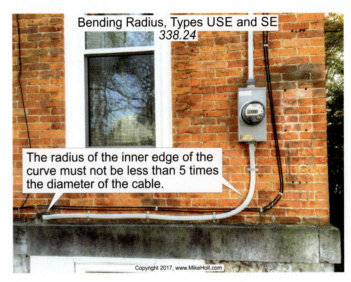

▶Figure 338–5

Notes

ARTICLE 340 — UNDERGROUND FEEDER AND BRANCH-CIRCUIT CABLE (TYPE UF)

Introduction to Article 340—Underground Feeder and Branch-Circuit Cable (Type UF)

UF cable is a moisture-, fungus-, and corrosion-resistant cable suitable for direct burial in the earth.

Part I. General

340.1 Scope

Article 340 covers the use, installation, and construction specifications of underground feeder and branch-circuit cable, Type UF. ▶Figure 340–1

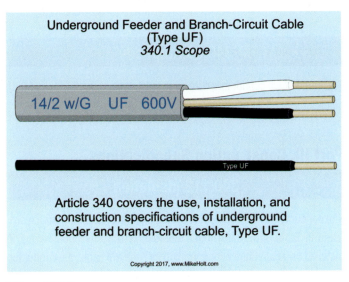

▶Figure 340–1

340.2 Definition

Underground Feeder and Branch-Circuit Cable (Type UF). A factory assembly of insulated conductors with an integral or an overall covering of nonmetallic material suitable for direct burial in the earth. Notice that Type UF isn't allowed as a service cable. ▶Figure 340–2

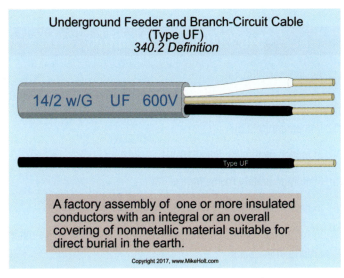

▶Figure 340–2

Author's Comment:

- UF cable is a moisture-, fungus-, and corrosion-resistant cable suitable for direct burial in the earth. It comes in sizes 14 AWG through 4/0 AWG [340.104]. The covering of multiconductor Type UF cable is molded plastic that encases the insulated conductors.

- Because the covering of Type UF cable encapsulates the insulated conductors, it's difficult to strip off the outer jacket to gain access to the conductors, but this covering provides excellent corrosion protection. Be careful not to damage the conductor insulation or cut yourself when you remove the outer cover.

340.10 | Underground Feeder and Branch-Circuit Cable (Type UF)

Part II. Installation

340.10 Uses Permitted

(1) Underground, in accordance with 300.5.

(2) As a single conductor in the same trench or raceway with circuit conductors.

(3) As interior or exterior wiring in wet, dry, or corrosive locations.

(4) As Type NM cable, when installed in accordance with Article 334.

(5) For solar PV systems, in accordance with 690.31.

(6) As single-conductor cables for nonheating leads for heating cables, as provided in 424.43.

(7) Supported by cable trays.

340.12 Uses Not Permitted

(1) As services [230.43].

(2) In commercial garages [511.3].

(3) In theaters [520.5].

(4) In motion picture studios [530.11].

(5) In storage battery rooms [Article 480].

(6) In hoistways [Article 620].

(7) In hazardous locations, except as specifically permitted by other articles in the *Code*.

(8) Embedded in concrete.

(9) Exposed to direct sunlight unless identified.

(10) If subject to physical damage. ▶Figure 340–3

(11) As overhead messenger-supported wiring.

Author's Comment:

- UF cable isn't permitted in ducts or plenum spaces [300.22], or in patient care spaces [517.13].

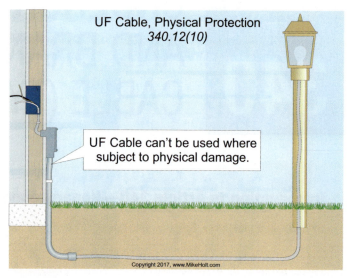

▶Figure 340–3

340.24 Bends

Bends in cables must be made so the protective coverings of the cable aren't damaged, and the radius of the curve of the inner edge isn't permitted to be less than five times the diameter of the cable.

340.80 Ampacity

The ampacity of conductors contained in UF cable is based on the 60°C insulation rating listed in Table 310.15(B)(16).

Part III. Construction Specifications

340.112 Insulation

The conductors of UF cable must be one of the moisture-resistant types listed in Table 310.104(A) that's suitable for branch-circuit wiring. If installed as a substitute wiring method for Type NM cable, the conductor insulation must be rated 90°C (194°F).

ARTICLE 342 — INTERMEDIATE METAL CONDUIT (TYPE IMC)

Introduction to Article 342—Intermediate Metal Conduit (Type IMC)

Intermediate metal conduit is a circular metal raceway with an outside diameter equal to that of rigid metal conduit. The wall thickness of intermediate metal conduit is less than that of rigid metal conduit, so it has a greater interior cross-sectional area for containing conductors. Intermediate metal conduit is lighter and less expensive than rigid metal conduit, and it can be used in all of the same locations as rigid metal conduit. Intermediate metal conduit also uses a different steel alloy that makes it stronger than rigid metal conduit, even though the walls are thinner. Intermediate metal conduit is manufactured in both galvanized steel and aluminum; the steel type is much more common.

Part I. General

342.1 Scope

Article 342 covers the use, installation, and construction specifications of intermediate metal conduit and associated fittings. ▶Figure 342–1

▶Figure 342–1

342.2 Definition

Intermediate Metal Conduit (Type IMC). A listed steel raceway of circular cross section that can be threaded with integral or associated couplings. It's listed for the installation of electrical conductors, and is used with listed fittings to provide electrical continuity. ▶Figure 342–2

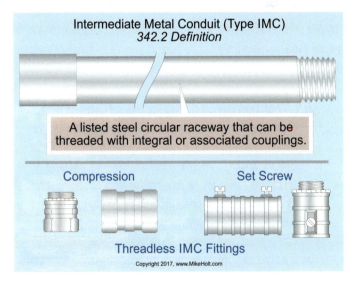

▶Figure 342–2

342.6 | Intermediate Metal Conduit (Type IMC)

Author's Comment:

- The type of steel from which intermediate metal conduit is manufactured, the process by which it's made, and the corrosion protection applied are all equal, or superior, to that of rigid metal conduit.

342.6 Listing Requirements

Intermediate metal conduit and its associated fittings, such as elbows and couplings, must be listed.

Part II. Installation

342.10 Uses Permitted

(A) Atmospheric Conditions and Occupancies. Intermediate metal conduit is permitted in all atmospheric conditions and occupancies.

(B) Corrosive Environments. Intermediate metal conduit, elbows, couplings, and fittings can be installed in concrete, in direct contact with the earth, or in areas subject to severe corrosive influences if provided with supplementary corrosion protection approved for the condition.

Author's Comment:

- See 300.6 for additional details.

(D) Wet Locations. Support fittings, such as screws, straps, and so forth, installed in a wet location must be made of corrosion-resistant material, or be protected by corrosion-resistant coatings in accordance with 300.6.

> ⚠ **CAUTION:** Supplementary coatings for corrosion protection haven't been investigated by a product testing and listing agency, and these coatings are known to cause cancer in laboratory animals. There's a documented case where an electrician was taken to the hospital for lead poisoning after using a supplemental coating product (asphalted paint) in a poorly ventilated area. As with all products, be sure to read and follow all product instructions, including material data safety sheets, particularly when petroleum-based chemicals (volatile organic compounds) may be in the material.

342.14 Dissimilar Metals

If practical, contact with dissimilar metals should be avoided to prevent the deterioration of the metal because of galvanic action. Aluminum fittings and enclosures are permitted to be used with galvanized steel intermediate metal conduit where not subject to severe corrosive influences.

342.20 Trade Size

(A) Minimum. Intermediate metal conduit smaller than trade size ½ isn't permitted.

(B) Maximum. Intermediate metal conduit larger than trade size 4 isn't permitted to be used.

342.22 Number of Conductors

The number of conductors in IMC isn't permitted to exceed the percentage fill specified in Table 1, Chapter 9. Raceways must be large enough to permit the installation and removal of conductors without damaging the conductor insulation. When all conductors within a raceway are the same size and insulation, the number of conductors permitted can be found in Annex C for the raceway type.

> **Example:** How many 10 THHN conductors can be installed in trade size 1 IMC?
>
> **Answer:** 18 conductors [Annex C, Table C.4]

Author's Comment:

- See 300.17 for additional examples on how to size raceways when conductors aren't all the same size.

Cables can be installed in intermediate metal conduit, if the number of cables doesn't exceed the allowable percentage fill specified in Table 1, Chapter 9.

342.24 Bends

Raceway bends aren't permitted to be made in any manner that would damage the raceway, or significantly change its internal diameter (no kinks). The radius of the curve of the inner edge of any field bend isn't permitted to be less than shown in Table 2, Chapter 9.

Author's Comment:

- This usually isn't a problem because benders are made to comply with this table. However, when using a hickey bender (short-radius bender), be careful not to over-bend the raceway.

342.26 Number of Bends (360°)

To reduce the stress and friction on conductor insulation, the total amount of bends (including offsets) between pull points must not exceed 360°. ▶Figure 342–3

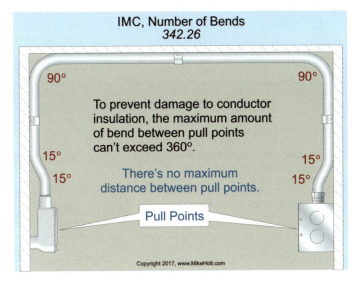

▶Figure 342–3

Author's Comment:

- There's no maximum distance between pull boxes because this is a design issue rather than a safety issue.

342.28 Reaming

When the raceway is cut in the field, reaming is required to remove the burrs and rough edges.

Author's Comment:

- It's a commonly accepted practice to ream small raceways with a screwdriver or the backside of pliers. However, when the raceway is cut with a three-wheel pipe cutter, a reaming tool is required to remove the sharp edge of the indented raceway. When conduits are threaded in the field, the threads must be coated with an electrically conductive, corrosion-resistant compound approved by the authority having jurisdiction, in accordance with 300.6(A).

342.30 Securing and Supporting

Intermediate metal conduit must be installed as a complete system in accordance with 300.18 [300.10 and 300.12], and it must be securely fastened in place and supported in accordance with (A) and (B).

(A) Securely Fastened. IMC must be secured in accordance with any of the following:

(1) Fastened within 3 ft of each outlet box, junction box, device box, cabinet, conduit body, or other conduit termination. ▶Figure 342–4

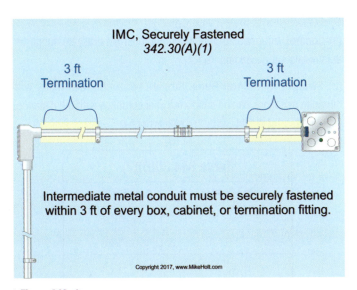

▶Figure 342–4

342.30 | Intermediate Metal Conduit (Type IMC)

Author's Comment:

- Fastening is required within 3 ft of terminations, not within 3 ft of each coupling.

(2) When structural members don't permit the raceway to be secured within 3 ft of a box or termination fitting, the raceway must be secured within 5 ft of the termination. ▶Figure 342–5

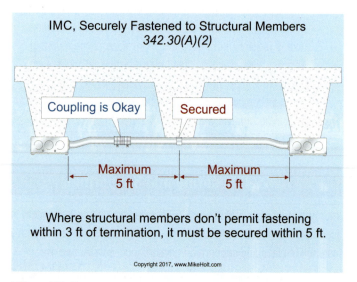
▶Figure 342–5

(3) Conduits aren't required to be securely fastened within 3 ft of the service head for an above-the-roof termination of a mast.

(B) Supports.

(1) General. Intermediate metal conduit must generally be supported at intervals not exceeding 10 ft

(2) Straight Horizontal Runs. Straight horizontal runs made with threaded couplings can be supported in accordance with the distances contained in Table 344.30(B)(2). ▶Figure 342–6

Table 344.30(B)(2)	
Trade Size	Support Spacing
½ – ¾	10 ft
1	12 ft
1¼ – 1½	14 ft
2 – 2½	16 ft
3 and larger	20 ft

▶Figure 342–6

(3) Vertical Risers. Exposed vertical risers for fixed equipment can be supported at intervals not exceeding 20 ft, if the conduit is made up with threaded couplings, firmly supported, securely fastened at the top and bottom of the riser, and if no other means of support is available. ▶Figure 342–7

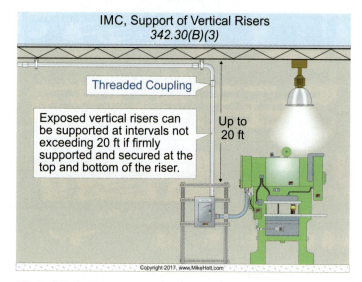
▶Figure 342–7

(4) Horizontal Runs. Conduits installed horizontally in bored or punched holes in wood or metal framing members, or notches in wooden members are considered supported, but the raceway must be secured within 3 ft of termination.

Intermediate Metal Conduit (Type IMC) | 342.46

Author's Comment:

- IMC must be provided with expansion fittings if necessary to compensate for thermal expansion and contraction [300.7(B)]. The expansion characteristics for metal raceways are determined by multiplying the values from Table 352.44 by 0.20, and the expansion characteristics for aluminum raceways are determined by multiplying the values from Table 352.44 by 0.40 [300.7 Note].

342.42 Couplings and Connectors

(A) Installation. Threadless couplings and connectors must be made up tight to maintain an effective ground-fault current path to safely conduct fault current in accordance with 250.4(A)(5), 250.96(A), and 300.10.

Author's Comment:

- Loose locknuts have been found to burn clear before a fault was cleared because loose termination fittings increase the impedance of the ground-fault current path.

If buried in masonry or concrete, threadless fittings must be the concrete-tight type. Fittings installed in wet locations must be listed for use in wet locations to prevent moisture or water from entering or accumulating within the enclosure as required by 314.15. ▶Figure 342–8

▶Figure 342–8

Threadless couplings and connectors aren't permitted to be used on threaded conduit ends unless listed for the purpose.

(B) Running Threads. Running threads aren't permitted for the connection of couplings, but they're permitted at other locations. ▶Figure 342–9

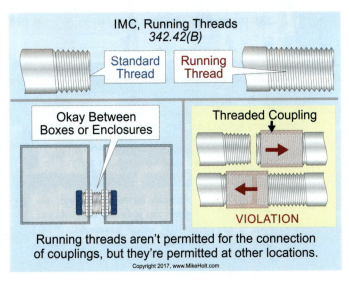

▶Figure 342–9

342.46 Bushings

To protect conductors from abrasion, a metal or plastic bushing must be installed on conduit termination threads, regardless of conductor size, unless the box, fitting, or enclosure is designed to provide this protection.

Note: Conductors 4 AWG and larger that enter an enclosure must be protected from abrasion, during and after installation, by a fitting that provides a smooth, rounded, insulating surface, such as an insulating bushing, unless the design of the box, fitting, or enclosure provides equivalent protection, in accordance with 300.4(G). ▶Figure 342–10

342.46 | Intermediate Metal Conduit (Type IMC)

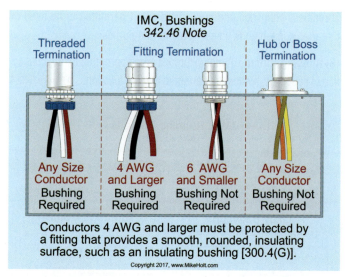

▶Figure 342–10

ARTICLE 344 — RIGID METAL CONDUIT (TYPE RMC)

Introduction to Article 344—Rigid Metal Conduit (Type RMC)

Rigid metal conduit, commonly called "rigid," has long been the standard raceway for providing protection from physical impact and from difficult environments. The outside diameter of rigid metal conduit is the same as intermediate metal conduit. However, the wall thickness of rigid metal conduit is greater than intermediate metal conduit; therefore the interior cross-sectional area is smaller. Rigid metal conduit is heavier and more expensive than intermediate metal conduit, and it can be used in any location. It's manufactured in both galvanized steel and aluminum; the steel type is much more common.

Part I. General

344.1 Scope

Article 344 covers the use, installation, and construction specifications of rigid metal conduit and associated fittings. ▶Figure 344–1

344.2 Definition

Rigid Metal Conduit (Type RMC). A listed metal raceway of circular cross section with integral or associated couplings, listed for the installation of electrical conductors, and used with listed fittings to provide electrical continuity. ▶Figure 344–2

▶Figure 344–1

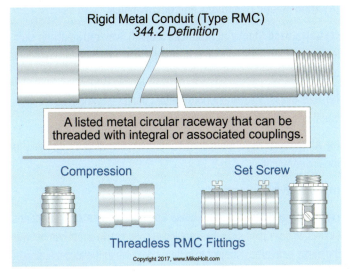

▶Figure 344–2

344.6 | Rigid Metal Conduit (Type RMC)

> **Author's Comment:**
>
> ■ When the mechanical and physical characteristics of rigid metal conduit are desired and a corrosive environment is anticipated, a PVC-coated raceway system is commonly used. This type of raceway is frequently used in the petro-chemical industry. The common trade name of this coated raceway is "Plasti-Bond®," and it's commonly referred to as "Rob Roy conduit." The benefits of the improved corrosion protection can be achieved only when the system is properly installed. Joints must be sealed in accordance with the manufacturer's instructions, and coated to prevent corrosion where damaged with tools such as benders, pliers, and pipe wrenches. Couplings are available with an extended skirt that can be properly sealed after installation.

▶Figure 344–3

344.6 Listing Requirements

Rigid metal conduit, elbows, couplings, and associated fittings must be listed.

Part II. Installation

344.10 Uses Permitted

(A) Atmospheric Conditions and Occupancies.

(1) Galvanized Steel and Stainless Steel. Galvanized steel and stainless steel rigid metal conduit is permitted in all atmospheric conditions and occupancies.

(2) Red Brass. Red brass rigid metal conduit is permitted for direct burial and swimming pool applications.

(3) Aluminum. Rigid aluminum conduit is permitted if approved for the environment.

(B) Corrosive Environments.

(1) Galvanized Steel and Stainless Steel. Rigid metal conduit fittings, elbows, and couplings can be installed in concrete, in direct contact with the earth, or in areas subject to severe corrosive influences if approved for the condition. ▶Figure 344–3

(2) Aluminum. Rigid aluminum conduit must be provided with supplementary corrosion protection approved by the authority having jurisdiction if encased in concrete or in direct contact with the earth.

(D) Wet Locations. Support fittings, such as screws, straps, and so forth, installed in a wet location must be made of corrosion-resistant material or protected by corrosion-resistant coatings in accordance with 300.6.

> ⚡ **CAUTION:** *Supplementary coatings (asphalted paint) for corrosion protection haven't been investigated by a product testing and listing agency, and these coatings are known to cause cancer in laboratory animals.*

344.14 Dissimilar Metals

If practical, contact with dissimilar metals should be avoided to prevent the deterioration of the metal because of galvanic action. Aluminum fittings and enclosures are permitted to be used with galvanized steel intermediate metal conduit where not subject to severe corrosive influences.

344.20 Trade Size

(A) Minimum. Rigid metal conduit smaller than trade size ½ isn't permitted.

(B) Maximum. Rigid metal conduit larger than trade size 6 isn't permitted to be used.

344.22 Number of Conductors

Raceways must be large enough to permit the installation and removal of conductors without damaging the conductors' insulation. When all conductors within a raceway are the same size and insulation, the number of conductors permitted can be found in Annex C for the raceway type.

Example: *How many 8 THHN conductors can be installed in trade size 1½ RMC?*

Answer: *22 conductors [Annex C, Table C.9]*

Author's Comment:

- See 300.17 for additional examples on how to size raceways when conductors aren't all the same size.

Cables can be installed in rigid metal conduit, if the number of cables doesn't exceed the allowable percentage fill specified in Table 1, Chapter 9.

344.24 Bends

Raceway bends aren't permitted to be made in any manner that would damage the raceway, or significantly change its internal diameter (no kinks). The radius of the curve of the inner edge of any field bend isn't permitted to be less than shown in Table 2, Chapter 9.

Author's Comment:

- This usually isn't a problem because benders are made to comply with this table. However, when using a hickey bender (short-radius bender), be careful not to over-bend the raceway.

344.26 Number of Bends (360°)

To reduce the stress and friction on conductor insulation, the total amount of bends (including offsets) between pull points must not exceed 360°.
▶Figure 344–4 and ▶Figure 344–5

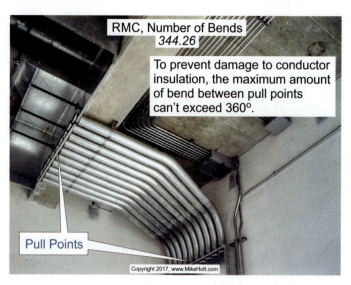
▶Figure 344–4

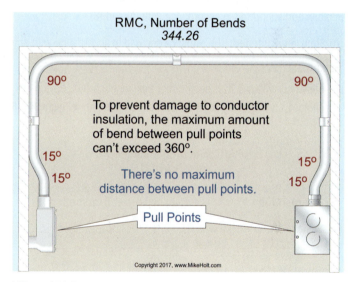
▶Figure 344–5

Author's Comment:

- There's no maximum distance between pull boxes because this is a design issue, not a safety issue.

344.28 Reaming

When the raceway is cut in the field, reaming is required to remove the burrs and rough edges.

344.30 | Rigid Metal Conduit (Type RMC)

Author's Comment:

- It's a commonly accepted practice to ream small raceways with a screwdriver or the backside of pliers. However, when the raceway is cut with a three-wheel pipe cutter, a reaming tool is required to remove the sharp edge of the indented raceway. When conduit is threaded in the field, the threads must be coated with an electrically conductive, corrosion-resistant compound approved by the authority having jurisdiction, in accordance with 300.6(A).

344.30 Securing and Supporting

Rigid metal conduit must be installed as a complete system in accordance with 300.18 [300.10 and 300.12], and it must be securely fastened in place and supported in accordance with (A) and (B).

(A) Securely Fastened. RMC must be secured in accordance with any of the following:

(1) Fastened within 3 ft of each outlet box, junction box, device box, cabinet, conduit body, or other conduit termination. ▶Figure 344–6

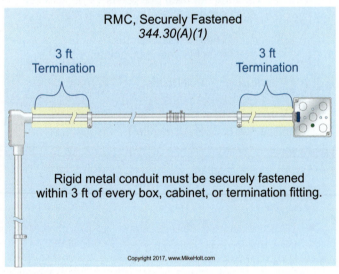

▶Figure 344–6

Author's Comment:

- Fastening is required within 3 ft of terminations, not within 3 ft of each coupling.

(2) When structural members don't permit the raceway to be secured within 3 ft of a box or termination fitting, the raceway must be secured within 5 ft of the termination. ▶Figure 344–7

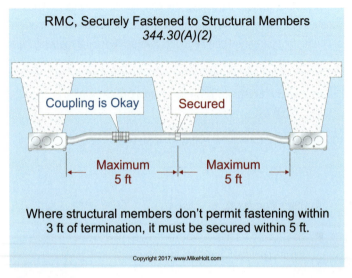

▶Figure 344–7

(3) Conduits aren't required to be securely fastened within 3 ft of the service head for an above-the-roof termination of a mast. ▶Figure 344–8

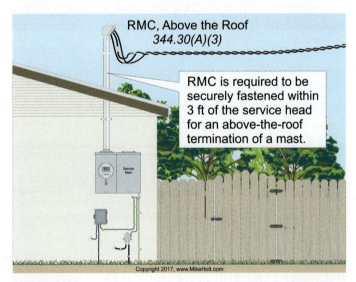

▶Figure 344–8

(B) Supports.

(1) General. Rigid metal conduit must be supported at intervals not exceeding 10 ft.

(2) Straight Horizontal Runs. Straight horizontal runs made with threaded couplings can be supported in accordance with the distances contained in Table 344.30(B)(2). ▶Figure 344–9

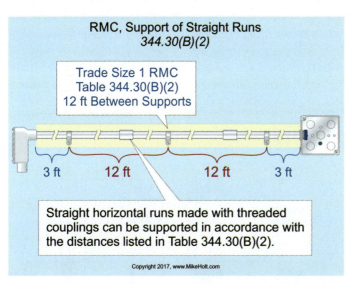

▶Figure 344–9

Table 344.30(B)(2)	
Trade Size	Support Spacing
½–¾	10 ft
1	12 ft*
1¼–1½	14 ft
2–2½	16 ft
3 and larger	20 ft

(3) Vertical Risers. Exposed vertical risers for fixed equipment can be supported at intervals not exceeding 20 ft, if the conduit is made up with threaded couplings, firmly supported, securely fastened at the top and bottom of the riser, and if no other means of support is available. ▶Figure 344–10

(4) Horizontal Runs. Conduits installed horizontally in bored or punched holes in wood or metal framing members, or notches in wooden members, are considered supported, but the raceway must be secured within 3 ft of termination.

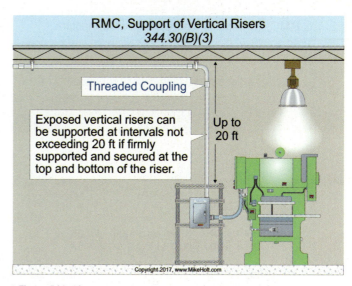

▶Figure 344–10

Author's Comment:

- Rigid metal conduit must be provided with expansion fittings if necessary to compensate for thermal expansion and contraction [300.7(B)]. The expansion characteristics for metal raceways are determined by multiplying the values from Table 352.44 by 0.20, and the expansion characteristics for aluminum raceways is determined by multiplying the values from Table 352.44 by 0.40 [300.7 Note].

344.42 Couplings and Connectors

(A) Installation. Threadless couplings and connectors must be made up tight to maintain an effective ground-fault current path to safely conduct fault current in accordance with 250.4(A)(5), 250.96(A), and 300.10.

Author's Comment:

- Loose locknuts have been found to burn clear before a fault was cleared because loose connections increase the impedance of the ground-fault current path.

If buried in masonry or concrete, threadless fittings must be the concrete-tight type. If installed in wet locations, fittings must be listed for use in wet locations and prevent moisture or water from entering or accumulating within the enclosure in accordance with 314.15. ▶Figure 344–11

Threadless couplings and connectors aren't permitted to be used on threaded conduit ends, unless listed for the purpose.

344.46 | Rigid Metal Conduit (Type RMC)

▶Figure 344–11

(B) Running Threads. Running threads aren't permitted for the connection of couplings, but they're permitted at other locations. ▶Figure 344–12

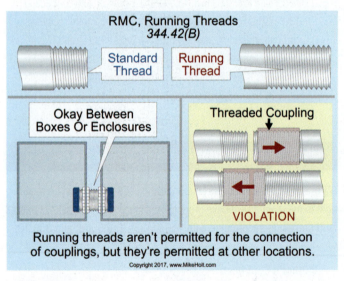

▶Figure 344–12

344.46 Bushings

To protect conductors from abrasion, a metal or plastic bushing must be installed on conduit threads at terminations, regardless of conductor size, unless the box, fitting, or enclosure is designed to provide this protection.

Note: Conductors 4 AWG and larger that enter an enclosure must be protected from abrasion, during and after installation, by a fitting that provides a smooth, rounded, insulating surface, such as an insulating bushing, unless the design of the box, fitting, or enclosure provides equivalent protection, in accordance with 300.4(G). ▶Figure 344–13

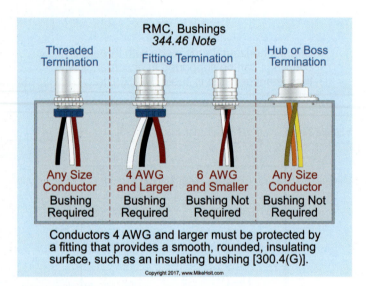

▶Figure 344–13

ARTICLE 348

FLEXIBLE METAL CONDUIT (TYPE FMC)

Introduction to Article 348—Flexible Metal Conduit (Type FMC)

Flexible metal conduit (FMC), commonly called "Greenfield" or "flex," is a raceway of an interlocked metal strip of either steel or aluminum. It's primarily used for the final 6 ft or less of raceways between a more rigid raceway system and equipment that moves, shakes, or vibrates. Examples of such equipment include pump motors and industrial machinery.

Part I. General

348.1 Scope

Article 348 covers the use, installation, and construction specifications for flexible metal conduit and associated fittings. ▶Figure 348–1

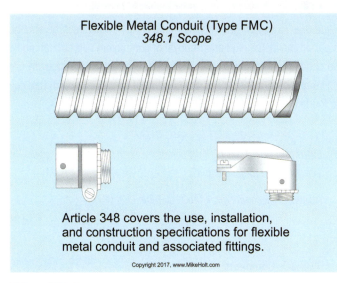

▶Figure 348–1

348.2 Definition

Flexible Metal Conduit (Type FMC). A raceway of circular cross section made of a helically wound, formed, interlocked metal strip. ▶Figure 348–2

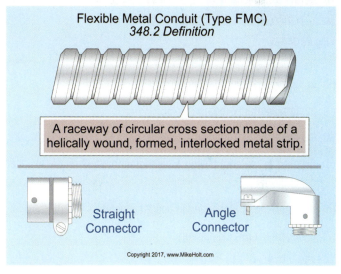

▶Figure 348–2

348.6 Listing Requirements

Flexible metal conduit and associated fittings must be listed.

Part II. Installation

348.10 Uses Permitted

Flexible metal conduit is permitted exposed or concealed.

348.12 | Flexible Metal Conduit (Type FMC)

348.12 Uses Not Permitted

(1) In wet locations. ▶Figure 348–3

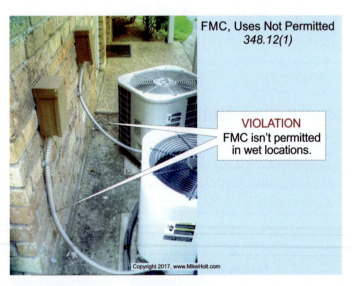

▶Figure 348–3

(2) In hoistways, other than as permitted in 620.21(A)(1).

(3) In storage battery rooms.

(4) In any hazardous location, except as permitted by 501.10(B).

(5) Exposed to material having a deteriorating effect on the installed conductors.

(6) Underground or embedded in poured concrete.

(7) If subject to physical damage.

348.20 Trade Size

(A) Minimum. Flexible metal conduit smaller than trade size ½ isn't permitted to be used, except trade size ⅜ can be used for the following applications:

(1) For enclosing the leads of motors.

(2) Not exceeding 6 ft in length: ▶Figure 348–4

   a. For utilization equipment,

   b. As part of a listed assembly, or

   c. For luminaire tap connections, in accordance with 410.117(C).

(3) In manufactured wiring systems, 604.100(A).

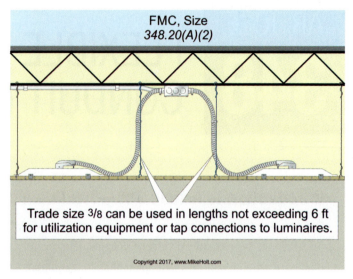

▶Figure 348–4

(4) In hoistways, 620.21(A)(1).

(5) As part of a listed luminaire assembly in accordance with 410.137(C).

(B) Maximum. Flexible metal conduit larger than trade size 4 isn't permitted to be used.

348.22 Number of Conductors

Trade Size ½ and Larger. Flexible metal conduit must be large enough to permit the installation and removal of conductors without damaging the conductors' insulation. When all conductors within a raceway are the same size and insulation, the number of conductors permitted can be found in Annex C for the raceway type.

Example: How many 6 THHN conductors can be installed in trade size 1 flexible metal conduit?

Answer: Six conductors [Annex C, Table C.3]

Author's Comment:

- See 300.17 for additional examples on how to size raceways when conductors aren't all the same size.

Trade Size ⅜. The number and size of conductors in trade size ⅜ flexible metal conduit must comply with Table 348.22.

Flexible Metal Conduit (Type FMC) | 348.30

> **Example:** How many 12 THHN conductors can be installed in trade size ⅜ flexible metal conduit that uses outside fittings?
>
> **Answer:** Three conductors [Table 348.22]. One insulated, covered, or bare equipment grounding conductor of the same size is permitted with the circuit conductors. See the "*" note at the bottom of Table 348.22.

Cables can be installed in flexible metal conduit if the number of cables doesn't exceed the allowable percentage fill specified in Table 1, Chapter 9.

348.24 Bends

Bends must be made so the conduit won't be damaged, and its internal diameter won't be effectively reduced. The radius of the curve of the inner edge of any field bend isn't permitted to be less than shown in Table 2, Chapter 9 using the column "Other Bends."

348.26 Number of Bends (360°)

To reduce the stress and friction on conductor insulation, the total amount of bends (including offsets) between pull points must not exceed 360°.

> **Author's Comment:**
> - There's no maximum distance between pull boxes because this is a design issue, not a safety issue.

348.28 Trimming

The cut ends of flexible metal conduit must be trimmed to remove the rough edges, but this isn't necessary if fittings are threaded into the convolutions.

348.30 Securing and Supporting

(A) Securely Fastened. Flexible metal conduit must be securely fastened by a means approved by the authority having jurisdiction within 1 ft of termination, and it must be secured and supported at intervals not exceeding 4½ ft. ▶Figure 348–5

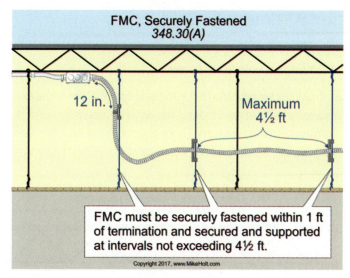

▶Figure 348–5

Where cable ties are to be used to secure and support flexible metal conduit, cable ties must be listed and identified for securing and supporting.

Ex 1: Flexible metal conduit isn't required to be securely fastened or supported where fished between access points through concealed spaces and supporting is impracticable.

Ex 2: If flexibility is necessary after installation, unsecured lengths from the last point the raceway is securely fastened must not exceed:
▶Figure 348–6

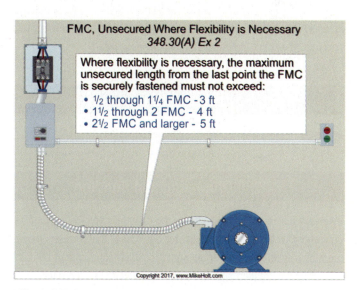

▶Figure 348–6

348.42 | Flexible Metal Conduit (Type FMC)

(1) 3 ft for trade sizes ½ through 1¼

(2) 4 ft for trade sizes 1½ through 2

(3) 5 ft for trade sizes 2½ and larger

Ex 4: Lengths not exceeding 6 ft from the last point where the raceway is securely fastened can be unsecured within an accessible ceiling for luminaire(s) or other equipment. For the purposes of this exception, listed fittings are considered a means of securement and support. ▶Figure 348–7

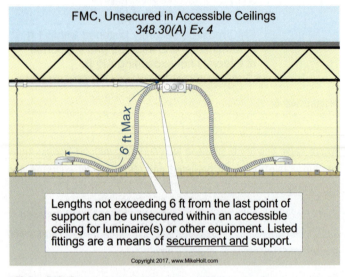

▶Figure 348–7

(B) Horizontal Runs. Flexible metal conduit installed horizontally in bored or punched holes in wood or metal framing members, or notches in wooden members, is considered supported, but the raceway must be secured within 1 ft of terminations. ▶Figure 348–8

348.42 Fittings

Angle connectors aren't permitted to be concealed.

348.60 Grounding and Bonding

If flexibility is necessary to minimize the transmission of vibration from equipment or to provide flexibility for equipment that requires movement after installation, an equipment grounding conductor of the wire type must be installed with the circuit conductors in accordance with 250.118(5), sized in accordance with 250.122, based on the rating of the overcurrent protection device. ▶Figure 348–9

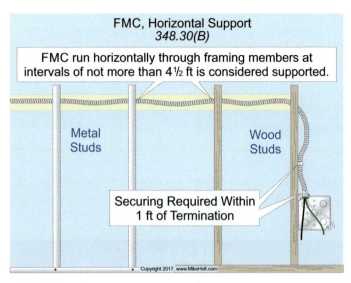

▶Figure 348–8

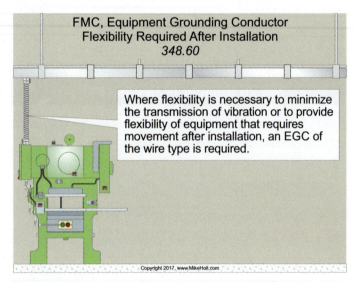

▶Figure 348–9

If flexibility isn't necessary after installation, and vibration isn't a concern, the metal armor of flexible metal conduit can serve as an equipment grounding conductor if the circuit conductors contained in the raceway are protected by an overcurrent protection device rated 20A or less, and the combined length of the flexible metal raceway in the same ground-fault return path doesn't exceed 6 ft [250.118(5)]. ▶Figure 348–10

If an equipment bonding jumper is installed outside of a raceway, the length of the equipment bonding jumper must not exceed 6 ft, and it must be routed with the raceway or enclosure in accordance with 250.102(E)(2).

Flexible Metal Conduit (Type FMC) | 348.60

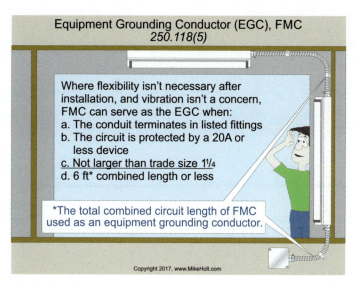

▸Figure 348–10

Notes

ARTICLE 350 — LIQUIDTIGHT FLEXIBLE METAL CONDUIT (TYPE LFMC)

Introduction to Article 350—Liquidtight Flexible Metal Conduit (Type LFMC)

Liquidtight flexible metal conduit (LFMC), with its associated connectors and fittings, is a flexible raceway commonly used for connections to equipment that vibrates or is required to move occasionally. Liquidtight flexible metal conduit is commonly called "Sealtight®" or "liquidtight." Liquidtight flexible metal conduit is of similar construction to flexible metal conduit, but it also has an outer liquidtight thermoplastic covering. It has the same primary purpose as flexible metal conduit, but it also provides protection from moisture and some corrosive effects.

Part I. General

350.1 Scope

Article 350 covers the use, installation, and construction specifications of liquidtight flexible metal conduit and associated fittings. ▶Figure 350–1

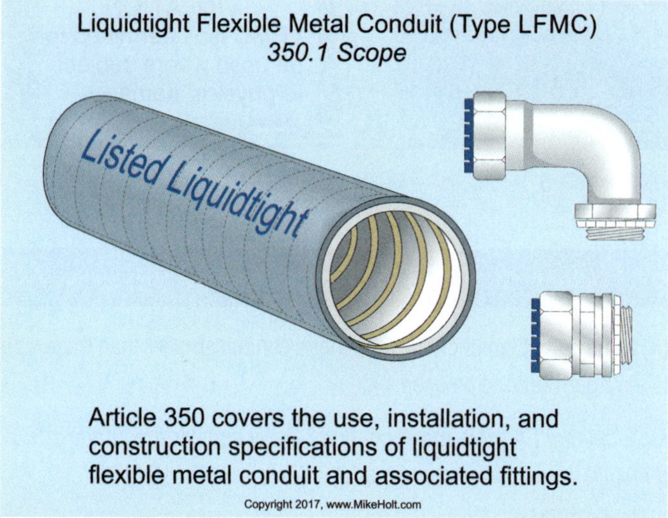

▶Figure 350–1

350.2 Definition

Liquidtight Flexible Metal Conduit (Type LFMC). A raceway of circular cross section, having an outer liquidtight, nonmetallic, sunlight-resistant jacket over an inner flexible metal core, with associated connectors and fittings for the installation of electric conductors. ▶Figure 350–2

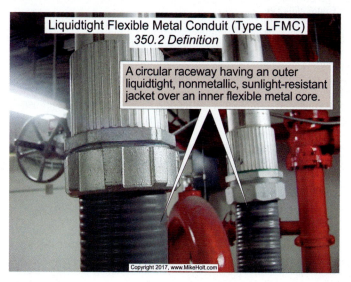

▶Figure 350–2

350.6 | Liquidtight Flexible Metal Conduit (Type LFMC)

350.6 Listing Requirements

Liquidtight flexible metal conduit and its associated fittings must be listed.

Part II. Installation

350.10 Uses Permitted

Listed liquidtight flexible metal conduit is permitted, either exposed or concealed, at any of the following locations: ▶Figure 350–3

▶Figure 350–3

(1) If flexibility or protection from liquids, vapors, or solids is required.

(2) In hazardous locations as permitted in Chapter 5.

(3) For direct burial, if listed and marked for this purpose. ▶Figure 350–4

350.12 Uses Not Permitted

Liquidtight flexible metal conduit is not to be used as follows:

(1) If subject to physical damage. ▶Figure 350–5

(2) If the combination of the ambient and conductor operating temperatures exceeds the rating of the raceway.

▶Figure 350–4

▶Figure 350–5

350.20 Trade Size

(A) Minimum. Liquidtight flexible metal conduit smaller than trade size ½ isn't permitted to be used.

Ex: Liquidtight flexible metal conduit can be smaller than trade size ½ if installed in accordance with 348.20(A).

(B) Maximum. Liquidtight flexible metal conduit larger than trade size 4 isn't permitted to be used.

Liquidtight Flexible Metal Conduit (Type LFMC) | 350.30

350.22 Number of Conductors

(A) Raceway Trade Size ½ and Larger. Raceways must be large enough to permit the installation and removal of conductors without damaging the insulation. When all conductors within a raceway are the same size and insulation, the number of conductors permitted can be found in Annex C for the raceway type.

Example: How many 6 THHN conductors can be installed in trade size 1 LFMC? ▶Figure 350–6

▶Figure 350–6

Answer: Seven conductors [Annex C, Table C.8]

Author's Comment:

- See 300.17 for additional examples on how to size raceways when conductors aren't all the same size.

Cables can be installed in liquidtight flexible metal conduit if the number of cables doesn't exceed the allowable percentage fill specified in Table 1, Chapter 9.

(B) Raceway Trade Size ⅜. The number and size of conductors in a trade size ⅜ liquidtight flexible metal conduit must comply with Table 348.22.

Example: How many 12 THHN conductors can be installed in trade size ⅜ LFMC that uses outside fittings?

Answer: Three conductors [Table 348.22]. One insulated, covered, or bare equipment grounding conductor of the same size is permitted with the circuit conductors. See the "*" note at the bottom of Table 348.22.

350.24 Bends

Bends must be made so the conduit won't be damaged and the internal diameter of the conduit won't be effectively reduced. The radius of the curve of the inner edge of any field bend isn't permitted to be less than shown in Table 2, Chapter 9 using the column "Other Bends."

350.26 Number of Bends (360°)

To reduce the stress and friction on conductor insulation, the total amount of bends (including offsets) between pull points must not exceed 360°.

Author's Comment:

- There's no maximum distance between pull boxes because this is a design issue, not a safety issue.

350.28 Trimming

Cut ends of liquidtight flexible metal conduit must be trimmed both inside and outside the raceway to remove rough edges from the cut ends.

350.30 Securing and Supporting

Liquidtight flexible metal conduit must be securely fastened in place and supported in accordance with (A) and (B).

(A) Securely Fastened. Liquidtight flexible metal conduit must be securely fastened by a means approved by the authority having jurisdiction within 1 ft of termination, and must be secured and supported at intervals not exceeding 4½ ft. ▶Figure 350–7

Where cable ties are used for securing liquidtight flexible metal conduit, the cable ties must be listed and identified for securement and support.

350.42 | Liquidtight Flexible Metal Conduit (Type LFMC)

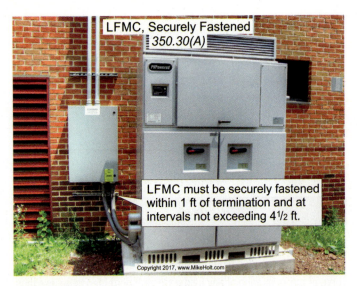

▶Figure 350–7

Ex 1: Liquidtight flexible metal conduit isn't required to be securely fastened or supported where fished between access points through concealed spaces and supporting is impracticable.

Ex 2: If flexibility is necessary after installation, unsecured lengths from the last point where the raceway is securely fastened must not exceed:
▶Figure 350–8

(1) 3 ft for trade sizes ½ through 1¼

(2) 4 ft for trade sizes 1½ through 2

(3) 5 ft for trade sizes 2½ and larger

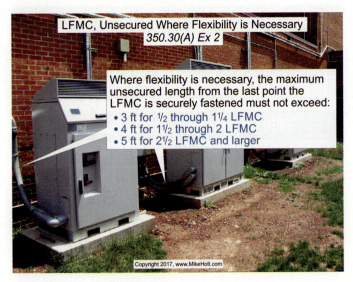

▶Figure 350–8

Ex 4: Lengths not exceeding 6 ft from the last point where the raceway is securely fastened can be unsecured within an accessible ceiling for luminaire(s) or other equipment. For the purposes of this exception, listed fittings are considered a means of securement and support. ▶Figure 350–9

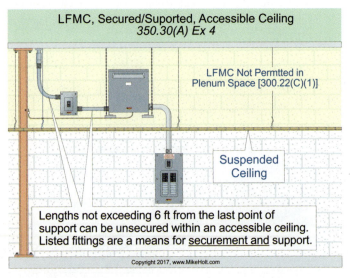

▶Figure 350–9

(B) Horizontal Runs. Liquidtight flexible metal conduit installed horizontally in bored or punched holes in wood or metal framing members, or notches in wooden members, is considered supported, but the raceway must be secured within 1 ft of termination.

350.42 Fittings

Fittings used with LFMC must be listed. Angle connectors aren't permitted to be concealed. Straight fittings can be buried where marked as suitable for direct burial.

350.60 Grounding and Bonding

If flexibility is necessary to minimize the transmission of vibration from equipment or to provide flexibility for equipment that requires movement after installation, an equipment grounding conductor of the wire type must be installed with the circuit conductors in accordance with 250.118(6), sized in accordance with 250.122, based on the rating of the overcurrent protection device. ▶Figure 350–10

Liquidtight Flexible Metal Conduit (Type LFMC) | 350.60

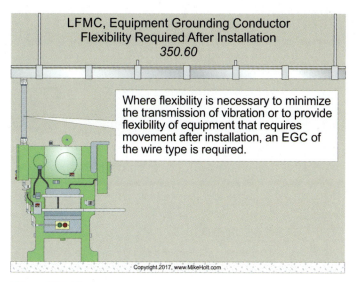

▶Figure 350–10

If flexibility isn't necessary after installation, and vibration isn't a concern, the metal armor of flexible metal conduit can serve as an equipment grounding conductor if the circuit conductors contained in the raceway are protected by an overcurrent protection device rated 20A or less, and the combined length of the flexible metal raceway in the same ground-fault return path doesn't exceed 6 ft [250.118(6)]. ▶Figure 350–11

If an equipment bonding jumper is installed outside of a raceway, the length of the equipment bonding jumper must not exceed 6 ft, and it must be routed with the raceway or enclosure in accordance with 250.102(E)(2). ▶Figure 350–12

▶Figure 350–12

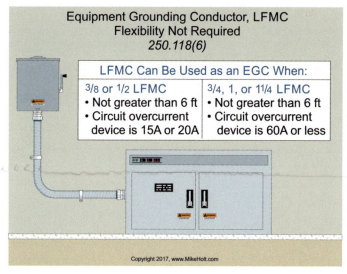

▶Figure 350–11

Notes

ARTICLE 352 — RIGID POLYVINYL CHLORIDE CONDUIT (TYPE PVC)

Introduction to Article 352—Rigid Polyvinyl Chloride Conduit (Type PVC)

Rigid polyvinyl chloride conduit is a rigid nonmetallic conduit that provides many of the advantages of rigid metal conduit, while allowing installation in areas that are wet or corrosive. It's an inexpensive raceway, and easily installed. It's lightweight, easily cut and glued together, and relatively strong. However, conduits manufactured from polyvinyl chloride (PVC) are brittle when cold, and they sage when hot. This type of conduit is commonly used as an underground raceway because of its low cost, ease of installation, and resistance to corrosion and decay.

Part I. General

352.1 Scope

Article 352 covers the use, installation, and construction specifications of PVC conduit and associated fittings. ▶Figure 352–1

352.2 Definition

Rigid Polyvinyl Chloride Conduit (PVC). A rigid nonmetallic raceway of circular cross section with integral or associated couplings, listed for the installation of electrical conductors and cables. ▶Figure 352–2

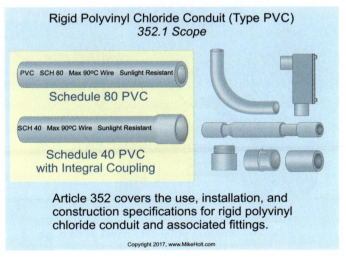

▶Figure 352–1

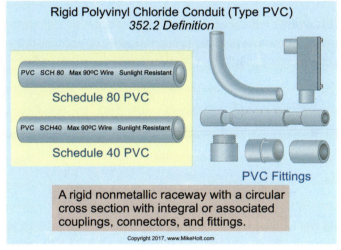

▶Figure 352–2

352.10 | Rigid Polyvinyl Chloride Conduit (Type PVC)

Part II. Installation

352.10 Uses Permitted

Note: In extreme cold, PVC conduit can become brittle, and is more susceptible to physical damage.

(A) Concealed. PVC conduit can be concealed within walls, floors, or ceilings, directly buried or embedded in concrete in buildings of any height. ▶Figure 352–3

▶Figure 352–3

(B) Corrosive Influences. PVC conduit is permitted in areas subject to severe corrosion for which the material is specifically approved by the authority having jurisdiction.

Author's Comment:

- If subject to exposure to chemical solvents, vapors, splashing, or immersion, materials or coatings must either be inherently resistant to chemicals based upon their listing, or be identified for the specific chemical reagent [300.6(C)(2)].

(D) Wet Locations. PVC conduit is permitted in wet locations such as dairies, laundries, canneries, car washes, and other areas frequently washed or in outdoor locations. Support fittings such as straps, screws, and bolts must be made of corrosion-resistant materials, or must be protected with a corrosion-resistant coating, in accordance with 300.6(A).

(E) Dry and Damp Locations. PVC conduit is permitted in dry and damp locations, except where limited in 352.12.

(F) Exposed. Schedule 40 PVC conduit is permitted for exposed locations where not subject to physical damage. If PVC conduit is exposed to physical damage, the raceway must be identified for the application. ▶Figure 352–4

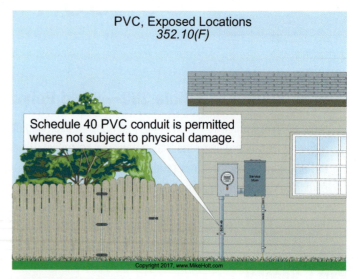

▶Figure 352–4

Note: PVC Schedule 80 conduit is identified for use in areas subject to physical damage. ▶Figure 352–5

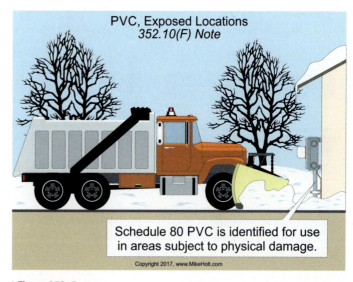

▶Figure 352–5

(G) Underground. PVC conduit installed underground must comply with the burial requirements of 300.5.

(H) Support of Conduit Bodies. PVC conduit can support nonmetallic conduit bodies that aren't larger than the largest trade size of an entering raceway. These conduit bodies can't support luminaires or other equipment, and aren't permitted to contain devices other than splicing devices permitted by 110.14(B) and 314.16(C)(2).

352.12 Uses Not Permitted

(A) Hazardous Locations. PVC conduit isn't permitted to be used in hazardous locations except as permitted by 501.10(A)(1)(a) Ex, 503.10(A), 504.20, 514.8 Ex 2, and 515.8.

(2) In Class I, Division 2 locations, except as permitted in 501.10(B)(7).

(B) Support of Luminaires. PVC conduit isn't permitted to be used for the support of luminaires or other equipment not described in 352.10(H).

Author's Comment:

- PVC conduit can support conduit bodies in accordance with 314.23(E) Ex.

(C) Physical Damage. Schedule 40 PVC conduit isn't permitted to be installed if subject to physical damage, unless identified for the application. ▶Figure 352–6

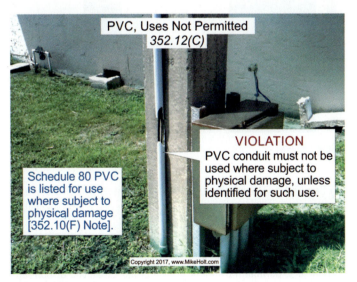

▶Figure 352–6

Author's Comment:

- PVC Schedule 80 conduit is identified for use in areas subject to physical damage [352.10(F) Note].

(D) Ambient Temperature. PVC conduit isn't permitted to be installed if the ambient temperature exceeds 50°C (122°F).

352.20 Trade Size

(A) Minimum. PVC conduit smaller than trade size ½ isn't permitted to be used.

(B) Maximum. PVC conduit larger than trade size 6 isn't permitted to be used.

352.22 Number of Conductors

Raceways must be large enough to permit the installation and removal of conductors without damaging the conductors' insulation, and the number of conductors must not exceed that permitted by the percentage fill specified in Table 1, Chapter 9.

When all conductors within a raceway are the same size and insulation, the number of conductors permitted can be found in Annex C for the raceway type.

Example: How many 4/0 THHN conductors can be installed in trade size 2 Schedule 40 PVC?

Answer: Four conductors [Annex C, Table C.11]

Author's Comment:

- Schedule 80 PVC conduit has the same outside diameter as Schedule 40 PVC conduit, but the wall thickness of Schedule 80 PVC conduit is greater, which results in a reduced interior area for conductor fill.

Example: How many 4/0 THHN conductors can be installed in trade size 2 Schedule 80 PVC conduit?

Answer: Three conductors [Annex C, Table C.10]

352.24 | Rigid Polyvinyl Chloride Conduit (Type PVC)

Author's Comment:

- See 300.17 for additional examples on how to size raceways when conductors aren't all the same size.

Cables can be installed in PVC conduit, if the number of cables doesn't exceed the allowable percentage fill specified in Table 1, Chapter 9.

352.24 Bends

Raceway bends aren't permitted to be made in any manner that would damage the raceway, or significantly change its internal diameter (no kinks). The radius of the curve of the inner edge of any field bend isn't permitted to be less than shown in Table 2, Chapter 9.

Author's Comment:

- Be sure to use equipment designed for heating the nonmetallic raceway so it's pliable for bending (for example, a "hot box"). Don't use open-flame torches.

352.26 Number of Bends (360°)

To reduce the stress and friction on conductor insulation, the total amount of bends (including offsets) between pull points must not exceed 360°. ▶Figure 352–7

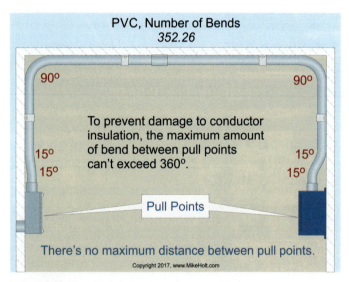

▶Figure 352–7

352.28 Trimming

The cut ends of PVC conduit must be trimmed (inside and out) to remove the burrs and rough edges.

Author's Comment:

- Trimming PVC conduit is very easy; most of the burrs will rub off with your fingers, and a knife will smooth the rough edges.

352.30 Securing and Supporting

PVC conduit must be fastened and supported in accordance with (A) and (B) so movement from thermal expansion and contraction is permitted. ▶Figure 352–8

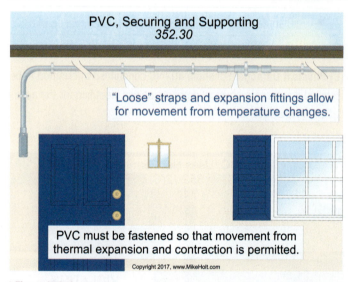

▶Figure 352–8

(A) Secured. PVC conduit must be secured within 3 ft of every box, cabinet, or termination fitting, such as a conduit body. ▶Figure 352–9

(B) Supports. PVC conduit must be supported at intervals not exceeding the values in Table 352.30, and the raceway must be fastened in a manner that permits movement from thermal expansion or contraction. ▶Figure 352–10

Rigid Polyvinyl Chloride Conduit (Type PVC) | 352.44

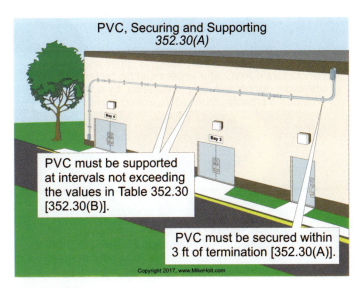

▶Figure 352–9

PVC conduit installed horizontally in bored or punched holes in wood or metal framing members, or notches in wooden members, is considered supported, but the raceway must be secured within 3 ft of termination.

352.44 Expansion Fittings

If PVC conduit is installed in a straight run between securely mounted items, such as boxes, cabinets, elbows, or other conduit terminations, expansion fittings must be provided if the expansion or contraction length change, in accordance with Table 352.44 is expected to be ¼ in. or greater. ▶Figure 352–11

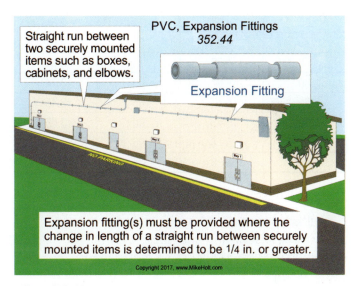

▶Figure 352–11

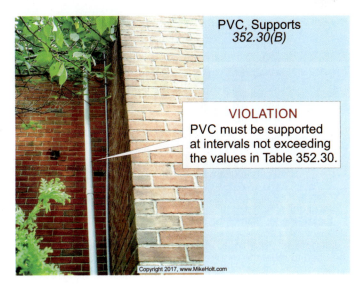

▶Figure 352–10

Table 352.30

Trade Size	Support Spacing
½–1	3 ft
1¼–2	5 ft
2½–3	6 ft
3½–5	7 ft
6	8 ft

Table 352.44 Expansion Characteristics of PVC Rigid Nonmetallic Conduit Coefficient of Thermal Expansion

Temperature Change (°C)	Length of Change of PVC Conduit (mm/m)	Temperature Change (°F)	Length Change of PVC Conduit (in./100 ft)
5	0.30	5	0.20
10	0.61	10	0.41
15	0.91	15	0.61
20	1.22	20	0.81
25	1.52	25	1.01
30	1.83	30	1.22
35	2.13	35	1.42
40	2.43	40	1.62

352.46 | Rigid Polyvinyl Chloride Conduit (Type PVC)

Table 352.44 Expansion Characteristics of PVC Rigid Nonmetallic Conduit Coefficient of Thermal Expansion
(continued)

Temperature Change (°C)	Length of Change of PVC Conduit (mm/m)	Temperature Change (°F)	Length Change of PVC Conduit (in./100 ft)
45	2.74	45	1.83
50	3.04	50	2.03
55	3.35	55	2.23
60	3.65	60	2.43
65	3.95	65	2.64
70	4.26	70	2.84
75	4.56	75	3.04
80	4.87	80	3.24
85	5.17	85	3.45
90	5.48	90	3.65
95	5.78	95	3.85
100	6.08	100	4.06

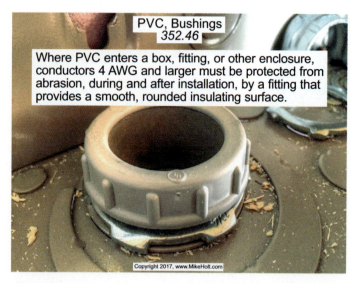

▶Figure 352–12

Author's Comment:

- When determining the number and setting of expansion fittings, you must be sure to actually read the manufacturer's documentation. For example, instructions for Carlon® expansion fittings for PVC states that when the PVC has sunlight exposure, we must add 30°F to the high ambient temperature.

352.46 Bushings

Where PVC enters a box, fitting, or other enclosure, conductors 4 AWG and larger must be protected from abrasion, during and after installation, by a fitting that provides a smooth, rounded insulating surface [300.4(G)]. ▶Figure 352–12

Note: Conductors 4 AWG and larger that enter an enclosure must be protected from abrasion, during and after installation, by a fitting that provides a smooth, rounded insulating surface, such as an insulating bushing, unless the design of the box, fitting, or enclosure provides equivalent protection, in accordance with 300.4(G). ▶Figure 352–13

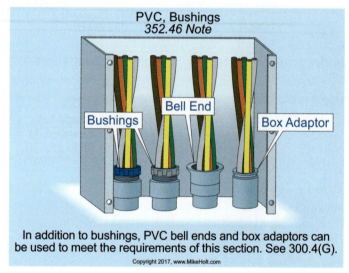

▶Figure 352–13

Author's Comment:

- When PVC conduit is stubbed into an open-bottom switchboard, the raceway, including the end fitting (bell-end), must not rise more than 3 in. above the bottom of the switchboard enclosure [300.16(B) and 408.5].

352.48 Joints

Joints, such as couplings and connectors, must be made in a manner approved by the authority having jurisdiction.

Author's Comment:

- Follow the manufacturers' instructions for the raceway, fittings, and glue. Some glue requires the raceway surface to be cleaned with a solvent before it's applied. After applying glue to both surfaces, a quarter turn of the fitting is required.

352.60 Equipment Grounding Conductor

If equipment grounding is required, a separate equipment grounding conductor of the wire type must be installed within the conduit [300.2(B)].
▶Figure 352–14

Ex 2: An equipment grounding conductor isn't required in PVC conduit if the neutral conductor is used to ground service equipment, as permitted in 250.142(A) [250.24(C)]. ▶Figure 352–15

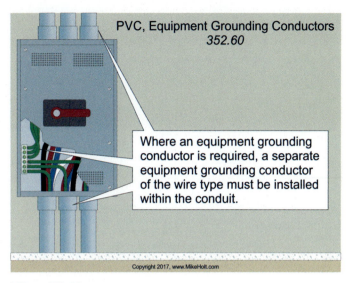

▶Figure 352–14

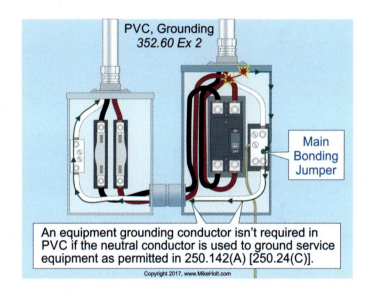

▶Figure 352–15

Notes

ARTICLE 356 — LIQUIDTIGHT FLEXIBLE NONMETALLIC CONDUIT (TYPE LFNC)

Introduction to Article 356—Liquidtight Flexible Nonmetallic Conduit (Type LFNC)

Liquidtight flexible nonmetallic conduit (LFNC) is a listed raceway of circular cross section having an outer liquidtight, nonmetallic, sunlight-resistant jacket over an inner flexible core with associated couplings, connectors, and fittings.

Part I. General

356.1 Scope

Article 356 covers the use, installation, and construction specifications of liquidtight flexible nonmetallic conduit and associated fittings. ▶Figure 356–1

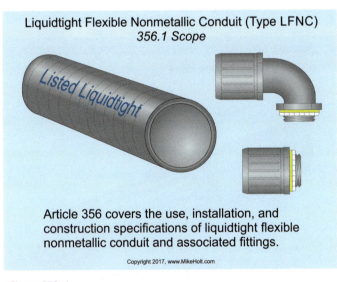

▶Figure 356–1

356.2 Definition

Liquidtight Flexible Nonmetallic Conduit (Type LFNC). A listed raceway of circular cross section, having an outer liquidtight, nonmetallic, sunlight-resistant jacket over a flexible inner core, with associated couplings, connectors, and fittings, listed for the installation of electrical conductors. ▶Figure 356–2

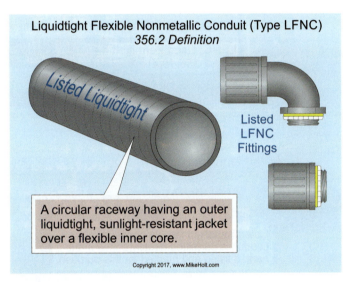

▶Figure 356–2

(1) **Type LFNC-A (orange color).** A smooth seamless inner core and cover having reinforcement layers between the core and cover.

(2) **Type LFNC-B (gray color).** A smooth inner surface with integral reinforcement within the raceway wall.

(3) **Type LFNC-C (black color).** A corrugated internal and external surface without integral reinforcement.

356.6 Listing Requirements

Liquidtight flexible nonmetallic conduit and its associated fittings must be listed.

356.10 | Liquidtight Flexible Nonmetallic Conduit (Type LFNC)

Part II. Installation

356.10 Uses Permitted

Listed liquidtight flexible nonmetallic conduit is permitted, either exposed or concealed, at any of the following locations:

Note: Extreme cold can cause nonmetallic conduits to become brittle and more susceptible to damage from physical contact.

(1) If flexibility is required.

(2) If protection from liquids, vapors, or solids is required.

(3) Outdoors, if listed and marked for this purpose.

(4) Directly buried in the earth, if listed and marked for this purpose.
▶ Figure 356–3

▶ Figure 356–3

(5) LFNC (gray color) is permitted in lengths over 6 ft if secured in accordance with 356.30.

(6) LFNC, Type B (black color) as a listed manufactured prewired assembly.

(7) Encasement in concrete if listed for direct burial.

356.12 Uses Not Permitted

(1) If subject to physical damage.

(2) If the ambient temperature and/or conductor temperature is in excess of its listing.

(3) Longer than 6 ft, except if approved by the authority having jurisdiction as essential for a required degree of flexibility.

(4) In any hazardous location, except as permitted by 501.10(B), 502.10(A) and (B), and 504.20.

356.20 Trade Size

(A) Minimum. Liquidtight flexible nonmetallic conduit smaller than trade size ½ isn't permitted, except as in the following:

(1) Enclosing the leads of motors, 430.245(B).

(2) For tap connections to lighting fixtures as permitted by 410.117(C).

(B) Maximum. Liquidtight flexible nonmetallic conduit larger than trade size 4 isn't permitted.

356.22 Number of Conductors

Raceways must be large enough to permit the installation and removal of conductors without damaging the insulation. When all conductors within a raceway are the same size and insulation, the number of conductors permitted can be found in Annex C for the raceway type.

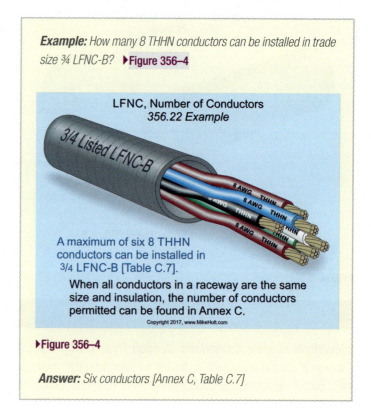

Example: How many 8 THHN conductors can be installed in trade size ¾ LFNC-B? ▶ Figure 356–4

▶ Figure 356–4

Answer: Six conductors [Annex C, Table C.7]

Author's Comment:

- See 300.17 for additional examples on how to size raceways when conductors aren't all the same size.

Cables can be installed in liquidtight flexible nonmetallic conduit if the number of cables doesn't exceed the allowable percentage fill specified in Table 1, Chapter 9.

356.24 Bends

Raceway bends aren't permitted to be made in any manner that would damage the raceway or significantly change its internal diameter (no kinks). The radius of the curve of the inner edge of any field bend isn't permitted to be less than shown in Table 2, Chapter 9 using the column "Other Bends."

356.26 Number of Bends (360°)

To reduce the stress and friction on conductor insulation, the total amount of bends (including offsets) between pull points must not exceed 360°.

Author's Comment:

- There's no maximum distance between pull boxes because this is a design issue, not a safety issue.

356.30 Securing and Supporting

LFNC (gray color) must be securely fastened and supported in accordance with any of the following:

(1) The conduit must be securely fastened at intervals not exceeding 3 ft, and within 1 ft of termination when installed in lengths longer than 6 ft. ▶Figure 356–5

Where cable ties are to be used to secure and support LFNC, they must be listed as suitable for the application and for securing and supporting.

(2) Securing or supporting isn't required if it's fished, installed in lengths not exceeding 3 ft at terminals if flexibility is required, or installed in lengths not exceeding 6 ft for tap conductors to luminaires, as permitted in 410.117(C).

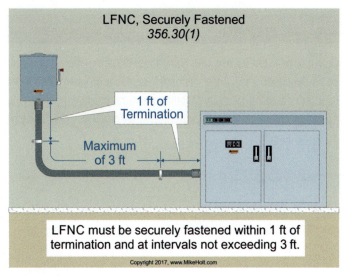

▶Figure 356–5

(3) Horizontal runs of liquidtight flexible nonmetallic conduit installed horizontally in bored or punched holes in wood or metal framing members, or notches in wooden members, are considered supported, but the raceway must be secured within 1 ft of termination.

(4) Securing or supporting of LFNC (gray color) isn't required if installed in lengths not exceeding 6 ft from the last point where the raceway is securely fastened for connections within an accessible ceiling to luminaire(s) or other equipment. For the purposes of this allowance, listed fittings are considered support. ▶Figure 356–6

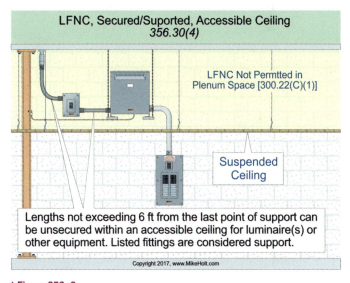

▶Figure 356–6

356.42 | Liquidtight Flexible Nonmetallic Conduit (Type LFNC)

356.42 Fittings

Only fittings listed for use with liquidtight flexible nonmetallic conduit can be used [300.15]. Angle connector fittings aren't permitted to be used in concealed raceway installations. Straight liquidtight flexible nonmetallic conduit fittings are permitted for direct burial or encasement in concrete.

Author's Comment:

- Conductors 4 AWG and larger that enter an enclosure must be protected from abrasion, during and after installation, by a fitting that provides a smooth, rounded, insulating surface, such as an insulating bushing, unless the design of the box, fitting, or enclosure provides equivalent protection, in accordance with 300.4(G).

356.60 Equipment Grounding Conductor

If equipment grounding is required, a separate equipment grounding conductor of the wire type must be installed within the conduit [250.134(B)]. ▶Figure 356–7

▶Figure 356–7

Author's Comment:

- An equipment grounding conductor is not required to be installed in a nonmetallic raceway supplying nonmetallic equipment.

If an equipment bonding jumper is installed outside of a raceway, the length of the equipment bonding jumper must not exceed 6 ft, and it must be routed with the raceway or enclosure in accordance with 250.102(E)(2).

ARTICLE 358 — ELECTRICAL METALLIC TUBING (TYPE EMT)

Introduction to Article 358—Electrical Metallic Tubing (Type EMT)

Electrical metallic tubing is a lightweight raceway that's relatively easy to bend, cut, and ream. Because it isn't threaded, all connectors and couplings are of the threadless type and provide quick, easy, and inexpensive installation when compared to other metallic conduit systems, which makes it very popular. Electrical metallic tubing is manufactured in both galvanized steel and aluminum; the steel type is used the most.

Part I. General

358.1 Scope

Article 358 covers the use, installation, and construction specifications of electrical metallic tubing and associated fittings. ▶Figure 358–1

▶Figure 358–1

358.2 Definition

Electrical Metallic Tubing (Type EMT). A metallic tubing of circular cross section used for the installation and physical protection of electrical conductors when joined together with fittings. ▶Figure 358–2

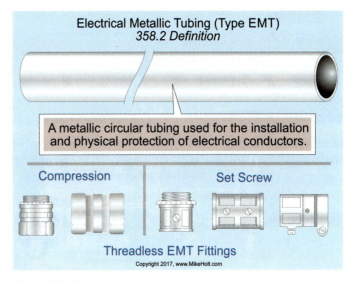

▶Figure 358–2

358.6 Listing Requirements

Electrical metallic tubing, elbows, and associated fittings must be listed.

Part II. Installation

358.10 Uses Permitted

(A) Exposed and Concealed. Electrical metallic tubing is permitted exposed or concealed for the following applications: ▶Figure 358–3

358.12 | Electrical Metallic Tubing (Type EMT)

▶Figure 358–3

(1) In concrete in direct contact with the earth in accordance with 358.10(B).

(2) In wet, dry, or damp locations.

(3) In any hazardous (classified) location as permitted by other articles in this *Code*.

(B) Corrosive Environments.

(1) Galvanized Steel. Electrical metallic tubing, elbows, and fittings can be installed in concrete, in direct contact with the earth, or in areas subject to severe corrosive influences if protected by corrosion protection and approved as suitable for the condition [300.6(A)].

(D) Wet Locations. Support fittings, such as screws, straps, and so on, installed in a wet location must be made of corrosion-resistant material.

Author's Comment:

- If installed in wet locations, fittings for EMT must be listed for use in wet locations and prevent moisture or water from entering or accumulating within the enclosure in accordance with 314.15 [358.42].

358.12 Uses Not Permitted

EMT isn't permitted to be used under the following conditions:

(1) Where subject to severe physical damage.

(2) For the support of luminaires or other equipment (like boxes), except conduit bodies no larger than the largest trade size of the tubing that can be supported by the raceway. ▶Figure 358–4

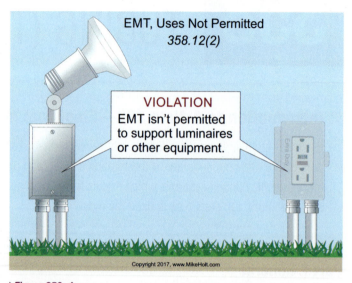

▶Figure 358–4

358.20 Trade Size

(A) Minimum. Electrical metallic tubing smaller than trade size ½ isn't permitted.

(B) Maximum. Electrical metallic tubing larger than trade size 4 isn't permitted.

358.22 Number of Conductors

Raceways must be large enough to permit the installation and removal of conductors without damaging the conductor insulation. When all conductors within a raceway are the same size and insulation, the number of conductors permitted can be found in Annex C for the raceway type.

Example: How many 12 THHN conductors can be installed in trade size 1 EMT? ▶Figure 358–5

Answer: 26 conductors [Annex C, Table C.1]

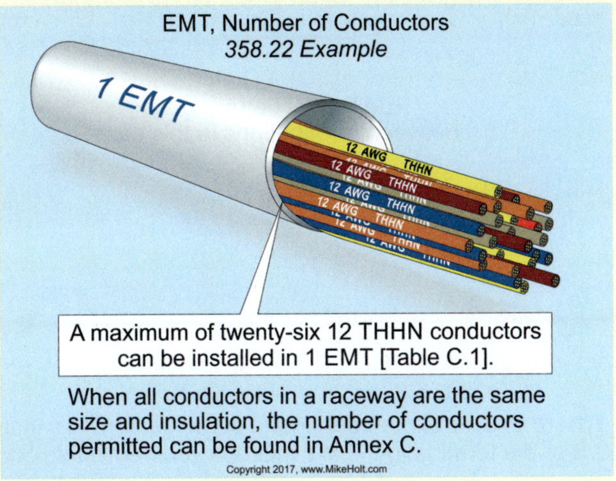

Electrical Metallic Tubing (Type EMT) | 358.28

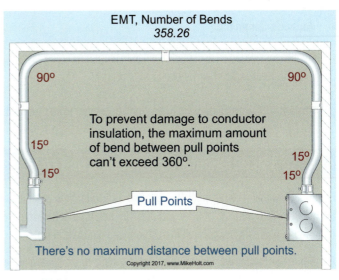
▶Figure 358–5

Author's Comment:

- See 300.17 for additional examples on how to size raceways when conductors aren't all the same size.

Cables can be installed in electrical metallic tubing, if the number of cables doesn't exceed the allowable percentage fill specified in Table 1, Chapter 9.

358.24 Bends

Raceway bends aren't permitted to be made in any manner that would damage the raceway, or significantly change its internal diameter (no kinks). The radius of the curve of the inner edge of any field bend isn't permitted to be less than shown in Chapter 9, Table 2 for one-shot and full shoe benders.

Author's Comment:

- This typically isn't a problem, because most benders are made to comply with this table.

358.26 Number of Bends (360°)

To reduce the stress and friction on conductor insulation, the total amount of bends (including offsets) between pull points can't exceed 360°. ▶Figure 358–6

▶Figure 358–6

Author's Comment:

- There's no maximum distance between pull boxes because this is a design issue, not a safety issue.

358.28 Reaming and Threading

(A) Reaming. Reaming to remove the burrs and rough edges is required when the raceway is cut. ▶Figure 358–7

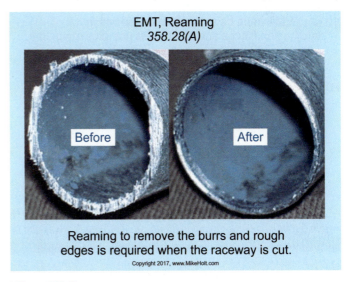
▶Figure 358–7

358.30 | Electrical Metallic Tubing (Type EMT)

Author's Comment:

- It's considered an accepted practice to ream small raceways with a screwdriver or the backside of pliers.

(B) Threading. Electrical metallic tubing isn't permitted to be threaded.

358.30 Securing and Supporting

Electrical metallic tubing must be installed as a complete system in accordance with 300.18 [300.10 and 300.12], and it must be securely fastened in place and supported in accordance with (A) and (B).

(A) Securely Fastened. Electrical metallic tubing must generally be securely fastened within 3 ft of every box, cabinet, or termination fitting, and at intervals not exceeding 10 ft. ▶Figure 358–8

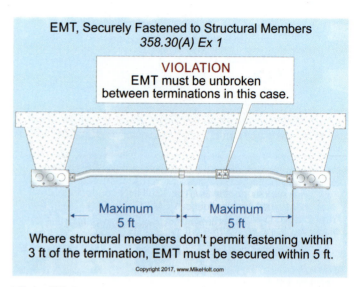

▶Figure 358–9

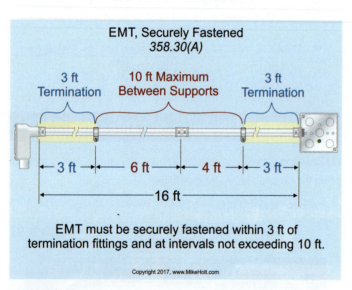

▶Figure 358–8

Author's Comment:

- Fastening is required within 3 ft of termination, not within 3 ft of a coupling.

Ex 1: When structural members don't permit the raceway to be secured within 3 ft of a box or termination fitting, an unbroken raceway can be secured within 5 ft of a box or termination fitting. ▶Figure 358–9

(B) Horizontal Runs. Electrical metallic tubing installed horizontally in bored or punched holes in wood or metal framing members, or notches in wooden members, is considered supported, but the raceway must be secured within 3 ft of termination. ▶Figure 358–10

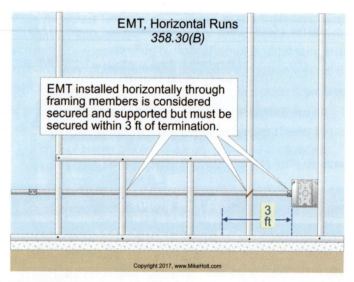

▶Figure 358–10

358.42 Couplings and Connectors

Couplings and connectors must be made up tight to maintain an effective ground-fault current path to safely conduct fault current in accordance with 250.4(A)(5), 250.96(A), and 300.10.

If buried in masonry or concrete, threadless electrical metallic tubing fittings must be of the concrete-tight type. If installed in wet locations, fittings must be listed for use in wet locations and prevent moisture or water from entering or accumulating within the enclosure in accordance with 314.15. ▶Figure 358–11

Electrical Metallic Tubing (Type EMT) | 358.60

▶Figure 358–11

▶Figure 358–12

Author's Comment:

- Conductors 4 AWG and larger that enter an enclosure must be protected from abrasion, during and after installation, by a fitting that provides a smooth, rounded, insulating surface, such as an insulating bushing, unless the design of the box, fitting, or enclosure provides equivalent protection, in accordance with 300.4(G).

358.60 Grounding

EMT can serve as an equipment grounding conductor [250.118(4)].
▶Figure 358–12 and ▶Figure 358–13

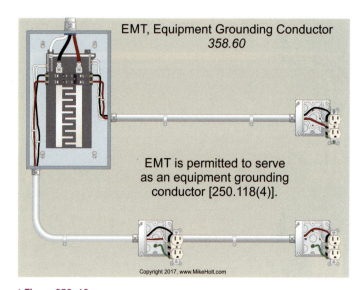

▶Figure 358–13

Notes

ARTICLE 362 — ELECTRICAL NONMETALLIC TUBING (TYPE ENT)

Introduction to Article 362—Electrical Nonmetallic Tubing (Type ENT)

Electrical nonmetallic tubing (ENT) is a pliable, corrugated, circular raceway made of polyvinyl chloride. In some parts of the country, the field name for electrical nonmetallic tubing is "Smurf Pipe" or "Smurf Tube," because it was only available in blue when it originally came out when the children's cartoon characters "The Smurfs" were most popular. Today, the raceway is available in many colors such as white, yellow, red, green, and orange, and is sold in both fixed lengths and on reels.

Part I. General

362.1 Scope

Article 362 covers the use, installation, and construction specifications of electrical nonmetallic tubing and associated fittings. ▶Figure 362–1

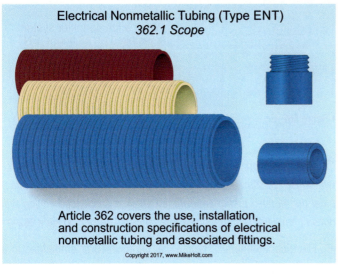
▶Figure 362–1

362.2 Definition

Electrical Nonmetallic Tubing (Type ENT). A pliable corrugated raceway of circular cross section, with integral or associated couplings, connectors, and fittings listed for the installation of electrical conductors. ENT is composed of a material that's resistant to moisture and chemical atmospheres and is flame retardant. ▶Figure 362–2

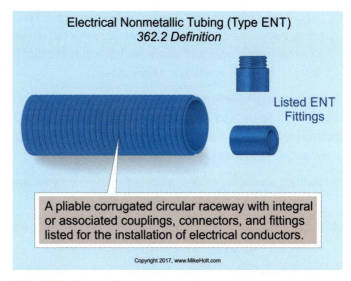
▶Figure 362–2

Electrical nonmetallic tubing can be bent by hand with a reasonable force, but without other assistance.

362.10 | Electrical Nonmetallic Tubing (Type ENT)

Part II. Installation

362.10 Uses Permitted

Electrical nonmetallic tubing is permitted as follows:

(1) In buildings not exceeding three floors. ▶Figure 362–3

    a. Exposed, where not prohibited by 362.12.

    b. Concealed within walls, floors, and ceilings.

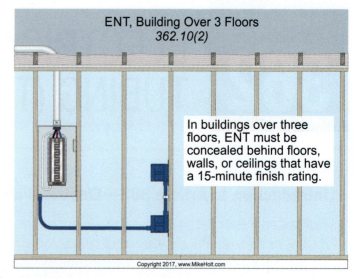

▶Figure 362–4

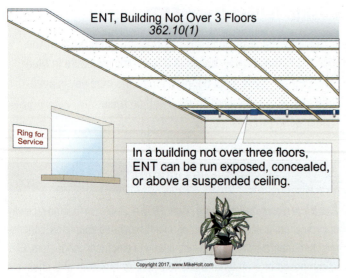

▶Figure 362–3

(2) In buildings exceeding three floors, electrical nonmetallic tubing can be installed concealed in walls, floors, or ceilings that provide a thermal barrier having a 15-minute finish rating, as identified in listings of fire-rated assemblies. ▶Figure 362–4

Ex to (2): If a fire sprinkler system is installed on all floors, in accordance with NFPA 13, Standard for the Installation of Sprinkler Systems, electrical nonmetallic tubing is permitted exposed or concealed in buildings of any height. ▶Figure 362–5

(3) Electrical nonmetallic tubing is permitted in severe corrosive and chemical locations, when identified for this use.

(4) Electrical nonmetallic tubing is permitted in dry and damp concealed locations, if not prohibited by 362.12.

(5) Electrical nonmetallic tubing is permitted above a suspended ceiling, if the suspended ceiling provides a thermal barrier having a 15-minute finish rating, as identified in listings of fire-rated assemblies. ▶Figure 362–6

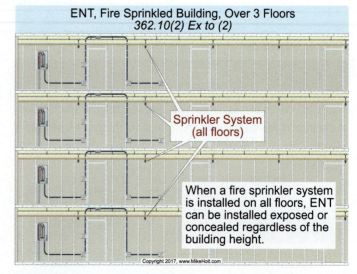

▶Figure 362–5

Ex to (5): If a fire sprinkler system is installed on all floors, in accordance with NFPA 13, Standard for the Installation of Sprinkler Systems, electrical nonmetallic tubing is permitted above a suspended ceiling that doesn't have a 15-minute finish rated thermal barrier. ▶Figure 362–7

(6) Electrical nonmetallic tubing can be encased or embedded in a concrete slab provided fittings identified for the purpose are used.

Author's Comment:

■ Electrical nonmetallic tubing isn't permitted in the earth [362.12(5)].

Electrical Nonmetallic Tubing (Type ENT) | 362.12

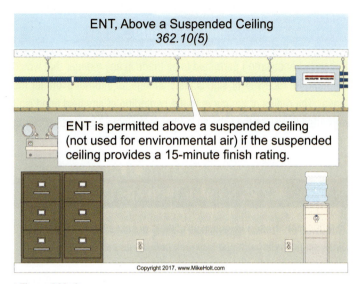

▶Figure 362–6

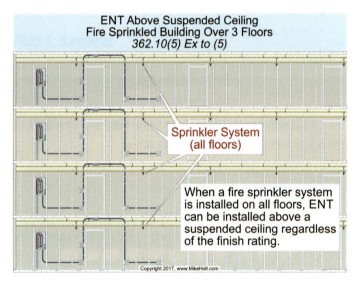

▶Figure 362–7

(7) Electrical nonmetallic tubing is permitted in wet locations indoors, or in a concrete slab on or below grade, with fittings listed for the purpose.

(8) Listed prewired electrical nonmetallic tubing with conductors is permitted in trade sizes ½, ¾, and 1.

362.12 Uses Not Permitted

ENT isn't permitted to be used in the following:

(1) In any hazardous location, except as permitted by 504.20 and 505.15(A)(1).

(2) For the support of luminaires or equipment. See 314.2.

(3) If the ambient temperature exceeds 50°C (122°F).

(4) For direct earth burial.

Author's Comment:

- Electrical nonmetallic tubing can be encased in concrete [362.10(6)].

(5) Exposed in buildings over three floors, except as permitted by 362.10(2) and (5) Ex.

(6) In assembly occupancies or theaters, except as permitted by 518.4 and 520.5.

(7) Exposed to the direct rays of the sun for an extended period, unless listed as sunlight resistant. ▶Figure 362–8

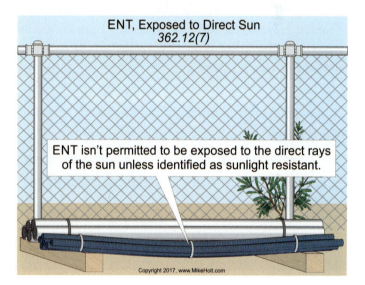

▶Figure 362–8

Author's Comment:

- Exposing electrical nonmetallic tubing to the direct rays of the sun for an extended time may result in the product becoming brittle, unless it's listed to resist the effects of ultraviolet (UV) radiation.

(8) If subject to physical damage.

362.20 | Electrical Nonmetallic Tubing (Type ENT)

Author's Comment:

- Electrical nonmetallic tubing is prohibited in ducts, plenum spaces [300.22(C)], and patient care space circuits in health care facilities [517.13(A)].

362.20 Trade Sizes

(A) Minimum. Electrical nonmetallic tubing smaller than trade size ½ isn't permitted.

(B) Maximum. Electrical nonmetallic tubing larger than trade size 2½ isn't permitted.

362.22 Number of Conductors

Raceways must be large enough to permit the installation and removal of conductors without damaging the conductors' insulation, and the number of conductors must not exceed that permitted by the percentage fill specified in Table 1, Chapter 9.

When all conductors within a raceway are the same size and insulation, the number of conductors permitted can be found in Annex C for the raceway type.

> **Example:** How many 12 THHN conductors can be installed in trade size ½ ENT?
>
> **Answer:** Seven conductors [Annex C, Table C.2]

Author's Comment:

- See 300.17 for additional examples on how to size raceways when conductors aren't all the same size.

Cables can be installed in electrical nonmetallic tubing, if the cables don't exceed the allowable percentage fill specified in Table 1, Chapter 9.

362.24 Bends

Raceway bends aren't permitted to be made in any manner that would damage the raceway, or significantly change its internal diameter (no kinks). The radius of the curve to the centerline of any field bend isn't permitted to be less than shown in Chapter 9, Table 2, using the column "Other Bends."

362.26 Number of Bends (360°)

To reduce the stress and friction on conductor insulation, the total amount of bends (including offsets) between pull points can't exceed 360°.

Author's Comment:

- There's no maximum distance between pull boxes because this is a design issue, not a safety issue.

362.28 Trimming

The cut ends of electrical nonmetallic tubing must be trimmed (inside and out) to remove the burrs and rough edges.

Author's Comment:

- Trimming electrical nonmetallic tubing is very easy; most of the burrs will rub off with your fingers, and a knife will smooth the rough edges.

362.30 Securing and Supporting

Electrical nonmetallic tubing must be installed as a complete system in accordance with 300.18 [300.10 and 300.12], and it must be securely fastened in place by an approved means and supported in accordance with (A) and (B).

(A) Securely Fastened. Electrical nonmetallic tubing must be secured within 3 ft of every box, cabinet, or termination fitting, such as a conduit body, and at intervals not exceeding 3 ft. ▶Figure 362–9

Where cable ties are to be used to secure and support electrical nonmetallic tubing, they must be listed as suitable for the application and for securing and supporting. ▶Figure 362–10

Electrical Nonmetallic Tubing (Type ENT) | 362.48

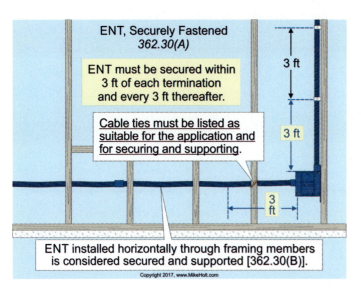

▶Figure 362–9

▶Figure 362–10

Ex 2: Lengths not exceeding 6 ft from the last point if the raceway is securely fastened within an accessible ceiling to luminaire(s) or other equipment.

Ex 3: If fished between access points through concealed spaces and supporting is impractical.

(B) Horizontal Runs. Electrical nonmetallic tubing installed horizontally in bored or punched holes in wood or metal framing members, or notches in wooden members, is considered supported, but the raceway must be secured within 3 ft of terminations.

362.46 Bushings

Conductors 4 AWG and larger that enter an enclosure from a fitting must be protected from abrasion, during and after installation, by a fitting that provides a smooth, rounded, insulating surface, such as an insulating bushing, unless the design of the box, fitting, or enclosure provides equivalent protection, in accordance with 300.4(G).

362.48 Joints

Joints, such as couplings and connectors, must be made in a manner approved by the authority having jurisdiction.

Author's Comment:

- Follow the manufacturers' instructions for the raceway, fittings, and glue. According to product listings, PVC conduit fittings are permitted with electrical nonmetallic tubing.

⚠ **CAUTION:** *Glue used with electrical nonmetallic tubing must be listed for ENT. Glue for PVC conduit must not be used with electrical nonmetallic tubing because it damages the plastic from which ENT is manufactured.*

362.60 | Electrical Nonmetallic Tubing (Type ENT)

362.60 Equipment Grounding Conductor

If equipment grounding is required, a separate equipment grounding conductor of the wire type must be installed within the raceway.

▶Figure 362–11

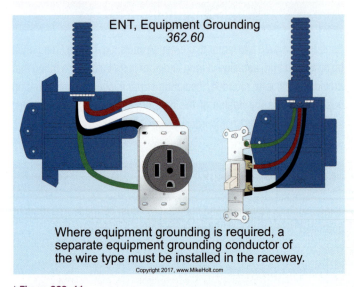

▶Figure 362–11

ARTICLE 376 METAL WIREWAYS

Introduction to Article 376—Metal Wireways

Metal wireways are commonly used where access to the conductors within a raceway is required to make terminations, splices, or taps to several devices at a single location. High cost precludes their use for other than short distances, except in some commercial or industrial occupancies where the wiring is frequently revised.

Author's Comment:

- Both metal wireways and nonmetallic wireways are often incorrectly called "troughs," "auxiliary gutters," "auxiliary wireways," or "gutters" in the field.

Part I. General

376.1 Scope

Article 376 covers the use, installation, and construction specifications of metal wireways and associated fittings. ▶Figure 376–1

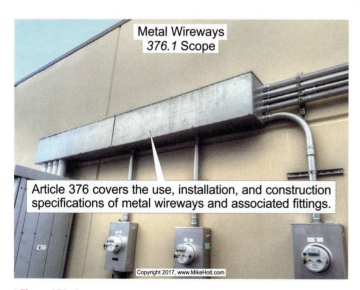

▶Figure 376–1

376.2 Definition

Metal Wireway. A sheet metal trough with hinged or removable covers for housing and protecting electric conductors and cable, and in which conductors are placed after the raceway has been installed. ▶Figure 376–2

▶Figure 376–2

Part II. Installation

376.10 Uses Permitted

(1) Exposed.

(2) In any hazardous locations, as permitted by other articles in the *Code*.

(3) Wet locations where listed for the purpose.

(4) Unbroken through walls, partitions, and floors.

Author's Comment:

- See 501.10(B), 502.10(B), and 504.20 for metal wireways used in hazardous locations.

376.12 Uses Not Permitted

(1) Where subject to severe physical damage.

(2) Where subject to corrosive environments.

376.20 Conductors Connected in Parallel

Where conductors are installed in parallel as permitted in 310.10(H), the parallel conductor sets must be installed in groups consisting of not more than one conductor per phase or neutral conductor to prevent current imbalance in the paralleled conductors due to inductive reactance. ▶Figure 376–3

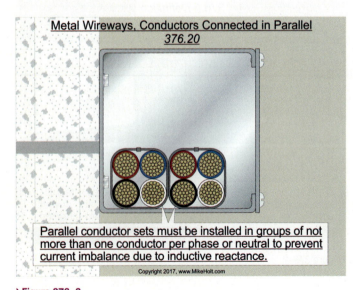

▶Figure 376–3

376.21 Conductors—Maximum Size

The maximum size conductor permitted in a wireway isn't permitted to be larger than that for which the wireway is designed.

376.22 Number of Conductors and Ampacity

(A) Number of Conductors. The maximum number of conductors or cables permitted in a wireway is limited to 20 percent of the cross-sectional area of the wireway. ▶Figure 376–4

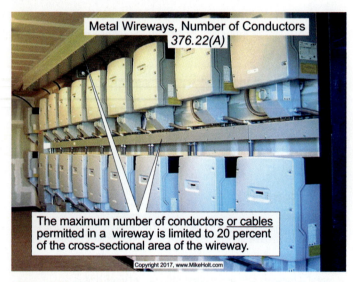

▶Figure 376–4

Author's Comment:

- Splices and taps must not fill more than 75 percent of the wiring space at any cross section [376.56].

(B) Conductor Ampacity Adjustment Factors. When more than 30 current-carrying conductors are installed in any cross-sectional area of the wireway, the conductor ampacity, as listed in Table 310.15(B)(16), must be adjusted in accordance with Table 310.15(B)(3)(a). ▶Figure 376–5

Signaling and motor-control conductors between a motor and its starter used only for starting duty aren't considered current carrying for conductor ampacity adjustment.

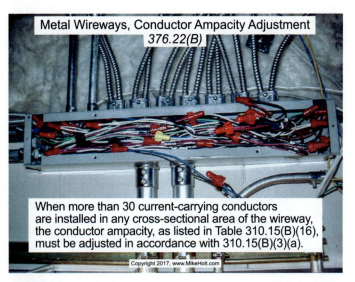

▶Figure 376–5

376.23 Wireway Sizing

(A) Sizing for Conductor Bending Radius. Where conductors are bent within a metal wireway, the wireway must be sized to meet the conductor bending space requirements contained in Table 312.6(A), based on one wire per terminal. ▶Figure 376–6

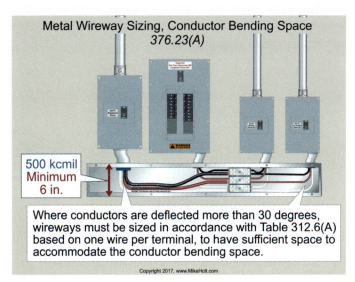

▶Figure 376–6

376.30 Supports

Wireways must be supported in accordance with (A) and (B).

(A) Horizontal Support. If installed horizontally, metal wireways must be supported at each end and at intervals not exceeding 5 ft.

(B) Vertical Support. If installed vertically, metal wireways must be securely supported at intervals not exceeding 15 ft, with no more than one joint between supports.

376.56 Splices, Taps, and Power Distribution Blocks

(A) Splices and Taps. Splices and taps in metal wireways must be accessible, and they must not fill the wireway to more than 75 percent of its cross-sectional area. ▶Figure 376–7

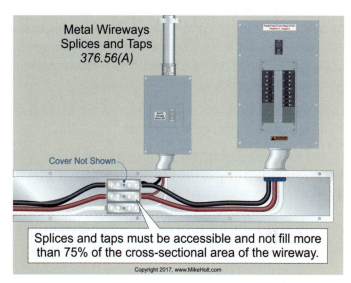

▶Figure 376–7

Author's Comment:

- The maximum number of conductors permitted in a metal wireway is limited to 20 percent of its cross-sectional area at any point [376.22(A)].

(B) Power Distribution Blocks.

(1) Installation. Power distribution blocks installed in wireways must be listed; if installed on the supply side of the service disconnect, they must be marked "suitable for use on the line side of service equipment" or equivalent. ▶Figure 376–8

376.100 | Metal Wireways

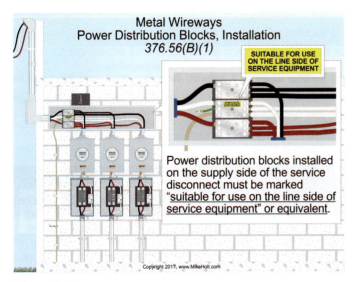
▶Figure 376–8

(2) Size of Enclosure. In addition to the wiring space requirements [376.56(A)], the power distribution block must be installed in a metal wireway not smaller than specified in the installation instructions of the power distribution block.

(3) Wire-Bending Space. Wire-bending space at the terminals of power distribution blocks must comply with 312.6(B).

(4) Live Parts. Power distribution blocks must not have uninsulated exposed live parts in the metal wireway after installation, whether or not the wireway cover is installed. ▶Figure 376–9

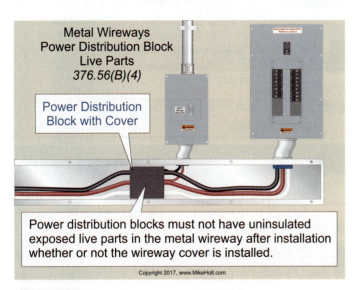
▶Figure 376–9

(5) Conductors. Conductors must be installed so that the terminals of the power distribution block aren't obstructed. ▶Figure 376–10

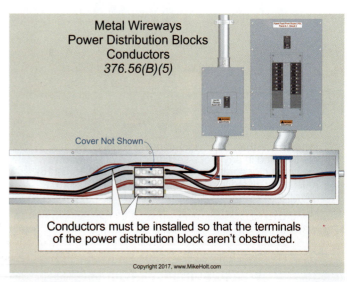
▶Figure 376–10

Part III. Construction Specifications

376.100 Construction

(A) Electrical and Mechanical Continuity. Wireways shall be constructed and installed so that electrical and mechanical continuity of the complete system are assured. ▶Figure 376–11

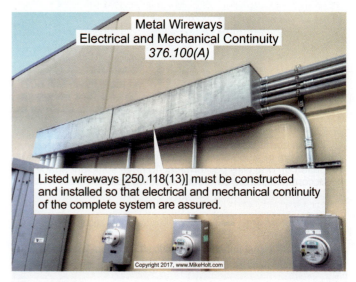
▶Figure 376–11

ARTICLE 392 — CABLE TRAYS

Introduction to Article 392—Cable Trays

A cable tray system is a unit or an assembly of units or sections with associated fittings that forms a structural system used to securely fasten or support cables and raceways. A cable tray isn't a raceway.

Cable tray systems include ladder, ventilated trough, ventilated channel, solid bottom, and other similar structures. Cable trays are manufactured in many forms, from a simple hanger or wire mesh to a substantial, rigid, steel support system. Cable trays are designed and manufactured to support specific wiring methods, as identified in 392.10(A).

Part I. General

392.1 Scope

Article 392 covers cable tray systems, including ladder, ventilated trough, ventilated channel, solid bottom, and other similar structures. ▶Figure 392–1

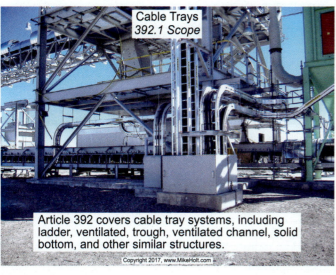

▶Figure 392–1

392.2 Definition

Cable Tray System. A unit or assembly of units or sections with associated fittings forming a rigid structural system used to securely fasten or support cables, raceways, and boxes. ▶Figure 392–2

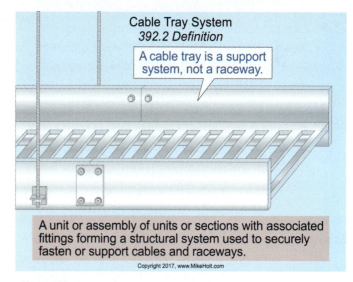

▶Figure 392–2

Author's Comment:

- Cable tray isn't a type of raceway. It's a support system for cables and raceways.

392.10 | Cable Trays

Part II. Installation

392.10 Uses Permitted

Cable trays can be used as a support system for service, feeder, or branch-circuit conductors, as well as communications circuits, control circuits, and signaling circuits. ▶Figure 392–3

- Class 2 and 3 Cables, 725.136(B) and 725.136(I)
- Communications Cables, 800.133(A)(2) Ex 1
- Fire Alarm Cables, 760.136(G)
- Optical Fiber Cables, 770.133(B)
- Intrinsically Safe Systems Cables, 504.30(A)(2) Ex 1
- Radio and Television Cables, 810.18(B) Ex 1

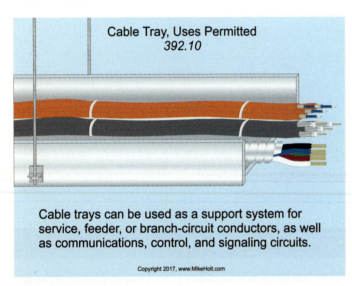

▶Figure 392–3

Author's Comment:

- Cable trays used to support service-entrance conductors must contain only service-entrance conductors unless a solid fixed barrier separates the service-entrance conductors from other conductors [230.44].
- Cable tray installations aren't limited to industrial establishments.
- If exposed to the direct rays of the sun, insulated conductors and jacketed cables must be identified as being sunlight resistant. The manufacturer must identify cable trays and associated fittings for their intended use.

(A) Wiring Methods. Any wiring methods listed in Table 392.10(A) can be installed in a cable tray.

Author's Comment:

- Control, signal, and communications cables must be separated from the power conductors by a barrier or maintain a 2-in. separation.
  - ◆ Coaxial Cables, 820.133(A)(1)(b) Ex 1

Table 392.10(A) Wiring Methods

Wiring Method	Article/Section
Armored cable	320
Coaxial cables	820
Class 2 & 3 cables	725
Communications cables	800
Communications raceways	725, 770, and 800
Electrical metallic tubing	358
Electrical nonmetallic tubing	362
Fire alarm cables	760
Flexible metal conduit	348
Instrumentation tray cable	727
Intermediate metal conduit	342
Liquidtight flexible metal conduit	350
Liquidtight flexible nonmetallic conduit	356
Metal-clad cable	330
Nonmetallic-sheathed cable	334
Nonpower-limited fire alarm cable	760
Polyvinyl chloride (PVC) conduit	352
Power and control tray cable	336
Power-limited fire alarm cable	760
Power-limited tray cable	Table 725.154 and 725.179(E) and 725.71(F)
Rigid metal conduit	344
Service-entrance cable	338
Signaling raceway	725
Underground feeder and branch-circuit cable	340

(B) In Industrial Establishments.

(1) Where conditions of maintenance and supervision ensure that only qualified persons service the installed cable tray system, single-conductor cables can be installed in accordance with the following: ▶Figure 392–4

(a) 1/0 AWG and larger listed and marked for use in cable trays.

(c) Equipment grounding conductors must be 4 AWG and larger.

392.18 Cable Tray Installations

(A) Complete System. Cable trays must be installed as a complete system, except mechanically discontinuous segments between cable tray runs, or between cable tray runs and equipment are permitted. The system must provide for the support of the cables and raceways in accordance with their corresponding articles. ▶Figure 392–5

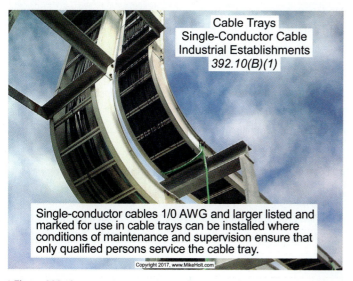

▶Figure 392–4

▶Figure 392–5

A bonding jumper, sized in accordance with 250.102 and installed in accordance with 250.96, must bond the sections of cable tray, or the cable tray and the raceway or equipment.

(B) Completed Before Installation. Each run of cable tray must be completed before the installation of cables or conductors.

(C) Hazardous Locations. Cable trays in hazardous locations must contain only the cable types and raceways permitted by the *Code* for the application.

(D) Through Partitions and Walls. Cable trays can extend through partitions and walls, or vertically through platforms and floors if the installation is made in accordance with the firestopping requirements of 300.21.

Author's Comment:

- For permitted cable types, see 501.10, 502.10, 503.10, 504.20, and 505.15.

(E) Exposed and Accessible. Cable trays must be exposed and accessible, except as permitted by 392.18(D).

(F) Adequate Access. Sufficient space must be provided and maintained about cable trays to permit adequate access for installing and maintaining the cables.

(D) Nonmetallic Cable Trays. In addition to the uses permitted elsewhere in Article 392, nonmetallic cable trays can be installed in corrosive areas, and in areas requiring voltage isolation.

(G) Raceways, Cables, and Boxes Supported from Cable Trays. In industrial facilities where conditions of maintenance and supervision ensure only qualified persons will service the installation, and if the cable tray system is designed and installed to support the load, cable tray systems can support raceways, cables, boxes, and conduit bodies. ▶Figure 392–6

392.12 Uses Not Permitted

Cable tray systems aren't permitted in hoistways, or where subject to severe physical damage.

392.20 | Cable Trays

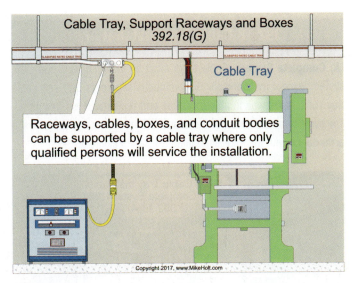
▶Figure 392–6

For raceways terminating at the tray, a listed cable tray clamp or adapter must be used to securely fasten the raceway to the cable tray system. The raceway must be supported in accordance with the appropriate raceway article.

Raceways or cables running parallel to the cable tray system can be attached to the bottom or side of a cable tray system. The raceway or cable must be fastened and supported in accordance with the appropriate raceway or cable's *Code* article.

Boxes and conduit bodies attached to the bottom or side of a cable tray system must be fastened and supported in accordance with 314.23.

392.20 Cable and Conductor Installation

(C) Connected in Parallel. To prevent unbalanced current in the parallel conductors due to inductive reactance, all circuit conductors of a parallel set [310.10(H)] must be bundled together and secured to prevent excessive movement due to fault-current magnetic forces.

(D) Single Conductors. Single conductors of a circuit not connected in parallel must be installed in a single layer, unless the conductors are bound together.

392.22 Number of Conductors or Cables

(A) Number of Multiconductor Cables in Cable Trays. The number of multiconductor cables, rated 2,000V or less, permitted in a single cable tray must not exceed the requirements of this section. The conductor sizes herein apply to both aluminum and copper conductors. Where dividers are used, fill calculations apply to each divided section of the cable tray.

(1) Any Mixture of Cables. If ladder or ventilated trough cable trays contain multiconductor power or lighting cables, the maximum number of cables must conform to the following:

(a) If all of the cables are 4/0 AWG and larger, the sum of the diameters of all cables must not exceed the cable tray width, and the cables must be installed in a single layer.

392.30 Securing and Supporting

(A) Fastened Securely. Cables installed vertically must be securely fastened to transverse members of the cable tray.

(B) Support. Supports for cable trays must be provided to prevent stress on cables where they enter raceways or other enclosures from cable tray systems. Cable trays must be supported in accordance with the manufacturer's installation instructions.

392.46 Bushed Raceway

A box isn't required where cables or conductors exit a bushed raceway used for the support or protection of the conductors. ▶Figure 392–7

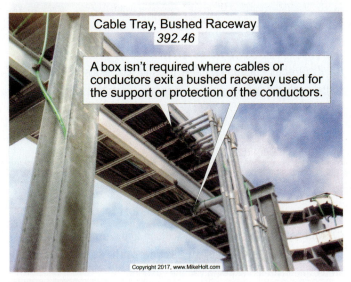
▶Figure 392–7

392.56 Cable Splices

Splices are permitted in a cable tray if the splice is accessible and insulated by a method approved by the authority having jurisdiction. Splices can project above the side rails of the cable tray if not subject to physical damage. ▶Figure 392–8

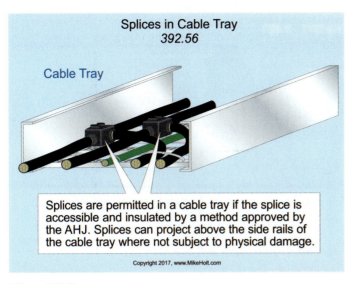

▶Figure 392–8

392.60 Equipment Grounding Conductor

(A) Used As Equipment Grounding Conductor. Metal cable trays can be used as equipment grounding conductors where continuous maintenance and supervision ensure that only qualified persons service the cable tray system. ▶Figure 392–9

▶Figure 392–9

Metal cable trays containing single conductors must be bonded together to ensure they have the capacity to conduct safely any fault current likely to be imposed in accordance with 250.96(A).

Metal cable trays containing communications, data, and signaling conductors and cables must be electrically continuous through approved connections or the use of a bonding jumper. ▶Figure 392–10

▶Figure 392–10

(B) Serve as Equipment Grounding Conductor. Metal cable trays can serve as equipment grounding conductors where the following requirements have been met [392.10(C)]:

(1) Metal cable trays and fittings are identified as an equipment grounding conductor. ▶Figure 392–11

▶Figure 392–11

392.60 | Cable Trays

(4) Cable tray sections, fittings, and connected raceways are effectively bonded to each other to ensure electrical continuity and the capacity to conduct safely any fault current likely to be imposed on them [250.96(A)]. This is accomplished by using bolted mechanical connectors or bonding jumpers sized in accordance with 250.102. ▶Figure 392–12

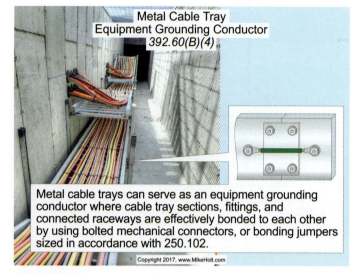

▶Figure 392–12

CHAPTER 3

PRACTICE QUESTIONS

Please use the 2017 *Code* book to answer the following questions.

Article 300. General Requirements for Wiring Methods and Materials

1. What is the minimum cover requirement for direct burial Type UF cable installed outdoors that supplies a 120V, 30A circuit?

    (a) 6 in.
    (b) 12 in.
    (c) 18 in.
    (d) 24 in.

2. "____" is defined as the area between the top of direct-burial cable and the top surface of the finished grade.

    (a) Notch
    (b) Cover
    (c) Gap
    (d) none of these

3. Direct-buried conductors or cables can be spliced or tapped without the use of splice boxes when the splice or tap is made in accordance with 110.14(B).

    (a) True
    (b) False

4. Raceways, cable trays, cablebus, auxiliary gutters, cable armor, boxes, cable sheathing, cabinets, elbows, couplings, fittings, supports, and support hardware shall be of materials suitable for ____.

    (a) corrosive locations
    (b) wet locations
    (c) the environment in which they are to be installed
    (d) none of these

5. Which of the following metal parts shall be protected from corrosion?

    (a) Ferrous metal raceways.
    (b) Ferrous metal elbows.
    (c) Ferrous boxes.
    (d) all of these

6. Aluminum raceways, cable trays, cablebus, auxiliary gutters, cable armor, boxes, cable sheathing, cabinets, elbows, couplings, nipples, fittings, supports, and support hardware ____ shall be provided with supplementary corrosion protection.

    (a) embedded or encased in concrete
    (b) in direct contact with the earth
    (c) likely to become energized
    (d) a or b

Chapter 3 | Practice Questions

7. Where nonmetallic wiring methods are subject to exposure to chemical solvents or vapors, they shall be inherently resistant to chemicals based upon their being _____ for the specific chemical reagent.

    (a) listed
    (b) identified
    (c) a and b
    (d) a or b

8. The independent support wires for supporting electrical wiring methods in a fire-rated ceiling assembly shall be distinguishable from fire-rated suspended-ceiling framing support wires by _____.

    (a) color
    (b) tagging
    (c) other effective means
    (d) any of these

9. Independent support wires used for the support of electrical raceways and cables within nonfire-rated assemblies shall be distinguishable from the suspended-ceiling framing support wires.

    (a) True
    (b) False

10. Cable wiring methods shall not be used as a means of support for _____.

    (a) other cables
    (b) raceways
    (c) nonelectrical equipment
    (d) all of these

11. A box or conduit body shall not be required where cables enter or exit from conduit or tubing that is used to provide cable support or protection against physical damage.

    (a) True
    (b) False

12. At least _____ support method(s) shall be provided for each conductor at the top of the vertical raceway or as close to the top as practical if the vertical rise exceeds the values in Table 300.19(A).

    (a) one
    (b) two
    (c) three
    (d) four

Article 310. Conductors for General Wiring

13. Insulated conductors used in wet locations shall be _____.

    (a) moisture-impervious metal-sheathed
    (b) MTW, RHW, RHW-2, TW, THW, THW-2, THHW, THWN, THWN-2, XHHW, XHHW-2, or ZW
    (c) listed for wet locations
    (d) any of these

14. Where raceways or cables are exposed to direct sunlight on or above rooftops, raceways or cables shall be installed a minimum distance of _____ in. above the roof to the bottom of the raceway or cable.

    (a) ¼
    (b) ⅓
    (c) ½
    (d) ⅞

15. Type _____ insulated conductors shall not be subject to the ampacity adjustment provisions of 310.15(B)(3)(c).

    (a) THW-2
    (b) XHHW-2
    (c) THWN-2
    (d) RHW-2

16. When determining the number of current-carrying conductors, a grounding or bonding conductor shall not be counted when applying the provisions of 310.15(B)(3)(a).

    (a) True
    (b) False

17. Where correction or adjustment factors are required by 310.15(B)(2) or (3), for single-phase feeder conductors installed for _____ dwellings, they shall be permitted to be applied to the ampacity associated with the temperature rating of the conductor.

    (a) one-family
    (b) the individual dwelling units of two-family
    (c) the individual dwelling units of multifamily
    (d) all of these

18. Where installed in raceways, conductors _____ AWG and larger shall be stranded, unless specifically permitted or required elsewhere in the *NEC*.

    (a) 10
    (b) 8
    (c) 6
    (d) 4

Article 312. Cabinets, Cutout Boxes, and Meter Socket Enclosures

19. Surface-type cabinets, cutout boxes, and meter socket enclosures in damp or wet locations shall be mounted so there is at least _____-in. airspace between the enclosure and the wall or supporting surface.

    (a) ¹⁄₁₆
    (b) ¼
    (c) 1¼
    (d) 6

20. Where raceways or cables enter above the level of uninsulated live parts of cabinets, cutout boxes, and meter socket enclosures in a wet location, a(n) _____ shall be used.

    (a) fitting listed for wet locations
    (b) explosionproof seal
    (c) fitting listed for damp locations
    (d) insulated fitting

21. Noncombustible surfaces that are broken or incomplete shall be repaired so there will be no gaps or open spaces greater than _____ in. at the edge of a cabinet or cutout box employing a flush-type cover.

    (a) ¹⁄₃₂
    (b) ¹⁄₁₆
    (c) ⅛
    (d) ¼

22. The wiring space of enclosures for switches or overcurrent devices shall be permitted to contain power monitoring equipment where the _____.

    (a) power monitoring equipment is identified as a field installable accessory as part of the listed equipment, or is a listed kit evaluated for field installation in switch or overcurrent device enclosures
    (b) total area of all conductors, splices, taps, and equipment at any cross section of the wiring space does not exceed 75 percent of the cross-sectional area of that space.
    (c) a and b
    (d) none of these

Article 314. Outlet, Device, Pull, and Junction Boxes; Conduit Bodies; and Handhole Enclosures

23. _____ drainage openings not smaller than ⅛ in. and not larger than ¼ in. in diameter shall be permitted to be installed in the field in boxes or conduit bodies listed for use in damp or wet locations.

    (a) Listed
    (b) Approved
    (c) Labeled
    (d) Identified

24. Conduit bodies that are durably and legibly marked by the manufacturer with their volume can contain splices, taps, or devices.

    (a) True
    (b) False

25. Where nonmetallic-sheathed cable or multiconductor Type UF cable is used, the sheath shall extend not less than _____ in. inside the box and beyond any cable clamp.

    (a) ¼
    (b) ⅜
    (c) ½
    (d) ¾

Chapter 3 | Practice Questions

26. Unless otherwise specified, the applicable product standards evaluate the fill markings covered in 314.28(A)(3), based on conductors with Type _____ insulation.

    (a) THHW
    (b) RHW
    (c) THHN
    (d) XHHW

27. Bends made in interlocked or corrugated sheath Type MC cable shall have a radius of at least _____ times the external diameter of the metallic sheath.

    (a) five
    (b) seven
    (c) ten
    (d) twelve

28. Type MC cable shall be supported and secured by staples; cable ties _____ for securement and support; straps, hangers, or similar fittings; or other approved means designed and installed so as not to damage the cable.

    (a) listed
    (b) identified
    (c) a and b
    (d) none of these

Article 334. Nonmetallic-Sheathed Cable (Types NM and NMC)

29. Type NM cable can be installed as open runs in dropped or suspended ceilings in other than one- and two-family and multi-family dwellings.

    (a) True
    (b) False

30. Type NM cable shall not be used _____.

    (a) in other than dwelling units
    (b) in the air void of masonry block not subject to excessive moisture
    (c) for exposed work
    (d) embedded in poured cement, concrete, or aggregate

31. Where more than two Type NM cables are installed through the same opening in wood framing that is to be sealed with thermal insulation, caulk, or sealing foam, the allowable ampacity of each conductor shall be _____.

    (a) no more than 20A
    (b) adjusted in accordance with Table 310.15(B)(3)(a)
    (c) limited to 30A
    (d) calculated by an engineer

Article 336. Power and Control Tray Cable (Type TC)

32. Type TC cable can be used in one- and two-family dwelling units.

    (a) True
    (b) False

33. Where Type TC cable is installed in one- and two-family dwelling units, 725.136 provides rules for limitations on Class 2 or 3 circuits contained within the same cable with conductors of electric light, power, or Class 1 circuits.

    (a) True
    (b) False

Article 338. Service-Entrance Cable (Types SE and USE)

34. Type SE cable shall be permitted to be used as _____ in wiring systems where all of the circuit conductors of the cable are of the thermoset or thermoplastic type.

    (a) branch circuits
    (b) feeders
    (c) a or b
    (d) none of these

Article 340. Underground Feeder and Branch-Circuit Cable (Type UF)

35. Type UF cable can be used for service conductors.

    (a) True
    (b) False

36. Type UF cable shall not be used in _____.

    (a) motion picture studios
    (b) storage battery rooms
    (c) hoistways
    (d) all of these

37. The ampacity of Type UF cable shall be that of _____ conductors in accordance with 310.15.

    (a) 60°C
    (b) 75°C
    (c) 90°C
    (d) 105°C

Article 344. Rigid Metal Conduit (Type RMC)

38. Aluminum RMC shall be permitted to be installed where approved for the environment.

    (a) True
    (b) False

39. Aluminum fittings and enclosures shall be permitted to be used with galvanized steel RMC, and galvanized steel fittings and enclosures shall be permitted to be used with aluminum RMC where not subject to _____.

    (a) physical damage
    (b) severe corrosive influences
    (c) excessive moisture
    (d) all of these

Article 348. Flexible Metal Conduit (Type FMC)

40. When FMC is used where flexibility is necessary to minimize the transmission of vibration from equipment or to provide flexibility for equipment that requires movement after installation, _____ shall be installed.

    (a) an equipment grounding conductor
    (b) an expansion fitting
    (c) flexible nonmetallic connectors
    (d) none of these

Article 350. Liquidtight Flexible Metal Conduit (Type LFMC)

41. The use of LFMC shall be permitted for _____.

    (a) direct burial where listed and marked for the purpose
    (b) exposed work
    (c) concealed work
    (d) all of these

42. Liquidtight flexible metal conduit shall be securely fastened by a means approved by the authority having jurisdiction within _____ of termination.

    (a) 6 in.
    (b) 10 in.
    (c) 1 ft
    (d) 10 ft

Article 352. Rigid Polyvinyl Chloride Conduit (Type PVC)

43. PVC conduit shall be securely fastened within _____ in. of each box.

    (a) 6
    (b) 12
    (c) 24
    (d) 36

Article 356. Liquidtight Flexible Nonmetallic Conduit (Type LFNC)

44. LFNC shall be permitted for _____.

    (a) direct burial where listed and marked for the purpose
    (b) exposed work
    (c) outdoors where listed and marked for this purpose
    (d) all of these

Article 358. Electrical Metallic Tubing (Type EMT)

45. The use of EMT shall be permitted for both exposed and concealed work in _____.

    (a) concrete, in direct contact with the earth or in areas subject to severe corrosive influences where installed in accordance with 358.10(B)
    (b) dry, damp, and wet locations
    (c) any hazardous (classified) location as permitted by other articles in this *Code*
    (d) all of these

Article 362. Electrical Nonmetallic Tubing (Type ENT)

46. ENT is composed of a material resistant to moisture and chemical atmospheres, and is _____.

    (a) flexible
    (b) flame retardant
    (c) fireproof
    (d) flammable

47. Unbroken lengths of electric nonmetallic tubing shall not be required to be secured where fished between access points for _____ work in finished buildings or structures and securing is impractical.

    (a) concealed
    (b) exposed
    (c) hazardous
    (d) completed

Article 376. Metal Wireways

48. Metal wireways can pass transversely through a wall _____.

    (a) if the length passing through the wall is unbroken
    (b) if the wall is of fire-rated construction
    (c) in hazardous (classified) locations
    (d) if the wall is not of fire-rated construction

49. Conductors larger than that for which the metal wireway is designed can be installed in any metal wireway.

    (a) True
    (b) False

Article 392. Cable Trays

50. Each run of cable tray shall be _____ before the installation of cables.

    (a) tested for 25 ohms resistance
    (b) insulated
    (c) completed
    (d) all of these

CHAPTER 4
EQUIPMENT FOR GENERAL USE

Introduction to Chapter 4—Equipment for General Use

With the first three chapters behind you, the final chapter in the *NEC* necessary for building a solid foundation in general work is Chapter 4. This chapter helps you apply the first three to installations involving general equipment. These first four chapters follow a natural sequential progression. Each of the next four chapters—5, 6, 7, and 8—build upon the first four, but in no particular order. You need to understand all of the first four chapters to properly apply any of the next ones.

As in the preceding chapters, Chapter 4 is also arranged logically. Here are the groupings:

- Flexible cords and flexible cables, and fixture wires.
- Switches and receptacles.
- Switchboards, switchgear, and panelboards.
- Lamps and luminaires.
- Appliances and space heaters.
- Motors, refrigeration equipment, generators, and transformers.
- Batteries, capacitors, and other components.

This logical arrangement of the *NEC* is something to keep in mind when you're searching for a particular item. You know, for example, that transformers are general equipment. So you'll find the *Code* requirements for them in Chapter 4. You know they're wound devices, so you'll find transformer requirements located somewhere near motor requirements.

- **Article 400—Flexible Cords and Flexible Cables.** Article 400 covers the general requirements, applications, and construction specifications for flexible cords and flexible cables.

- **Article 402—Fixture Wires.** This article covers the general requirements and construction specifications for fixture wires.

- **Article 404—Switches.** The requirements of Article 404 apply to switches of all types. These include snap (toggle) switches, dimmer switches, fan switches, knife switches, circuit breakers used as switches, and automatic switches such as time clocks, timers, and switches and circuit breakers used for disconnecting means.

- **Article 406—Receptacles, Cord Connectors, and Attachment Plugs (Caps).** This article covers the rating, type, and installation of receptacles, cord connectors, and attachment plugs (cord caps). It also covers flanged surface inlets.

- **Article 408—Switchboards, Switchgear, and Panelboards.** Article 408 covers specific requirements for switchboards, panelboards, switchgear, and distribution boards that supply lighting and power circuits.

Chapter 4 | Equipment for General Use

Author's Comment:

- See Article 100 for the definitions of "Panelboard," "Switchboard," and "Switchgear."

- **Article 410—Luminaires, Lampholders, and Lamps.** This article contains the requirements for luminaires, lampholders, and lamps. Because of the many types and applications of luminaires, manufacturer's instructions are very important and helpful for proper installation. Underwriters Laboratories produces a pamphlet called the *Luminaire Marking Guide*, which provides information for properly installing common types of incandescent, fluorescent, and high-intensity discharge (HID) luminaires.

- **Article 411—Low-Voltage Lighting.** Article 411 covers lighting systems, and their associated components, that operate at no more than 30V alternating current, or 60V direct current.

- **Article 422—Appliances.** This article covers electric appliances used in any occupancy.

- **Article 424—Fixed Electric Space-Heating Equipment.** Article 424 covers fixed electric equipment used for space heating. For the purpose of this article, heating equipment includes heating cable, unit heaters, boilers, central systems, and other fixed electric space-heating equipment. Article 424 doesn't apply to process heating and room air-conditioning.

- **Article 430—Motors, Motor Circuits, and Controllers.** This article contains the specific requirements for conductor sizing, overcurrent protection, control circuit conductors, motor controllers, and disconnecting means. The installation requirements for motor control centers are covered in Article 430, Part VIII.

- **Article 440—Air-Conditioning and Refrigeration Equipment.** Article 440 applies to electrically driven air-conditioning and refrigeration equipment with a motorized hermetic refrigerant compressor. The requirements in this article are in addition to, or amend, the requirements in Article 430 and others.

- **Article 445—Generators.** Article 445 contains the electrical installation requirements for generators and other requirements, such as where they can be installed, nameplate markings, conductor ampacity, and disconnecting means.

- **Article 450—Transformers.** This article covers the installation of transformers.

- **Article 480—Storage Batteries.** Article 480 covers stationary installations of storage batteries.

ARTICLE 400 — FLEXIBLE CORDS AND FLEXIBLE CABLES

Introduction to Article 400—Flexible Cords and Flexible Cables

This article covers the general requirements, applications, and construction specifications for flexible cords and flexible cables. The *NEC* doesn't consider flexible cords to be wiring methods like those defined in Chapter 3.

Always use a flexible cord (and fittings) identified for the application. Table 400.4 will help you in that regard. For example, use cords listed for a wet location if you're using them outdoors. The jacket material of any flexible cord is tested to maintain its insulation properties and other characteristics in the environments for which it's been listed. Tables 400.5(A)(1) and 400.5(A)(2) are also important tables to turn to when looking for the ampacity of flexible cords.

Part I. General

400.1 Scope

Article 400 covers the general requirements, applications, and construction specifications for flexible cords and flexible cables as contained in Table 400.4. ▶Figure 400–1

Note: Extension cords and power-supply cords are restricted in use by the requirements contained in Article 400.

▶Figure 400–1

400.3 Suitability

Flexible cords and flexible cables, as well as their fittings, must be suitable for the use and location. ▶Figure 400–2

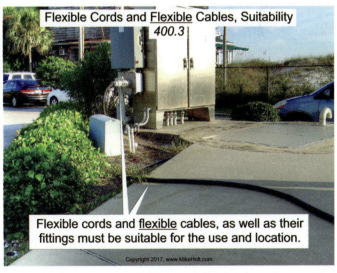

▶Figure 400–2

400.4 Types of Flexible Cords and Flexible Cables

The use of flexible cords and flexible cables must conform to the descriptions contained in Table 400.4. ▶Figure 400–3

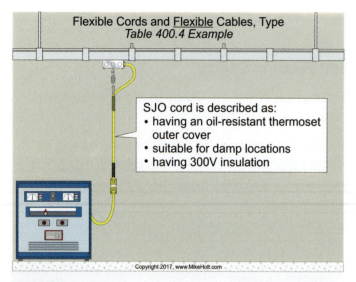

▶Figure 400–3

Author's Comment:

- The suffix "W" at the end of a flexible cord type designates that the flexible cord is water and sunlight resistant [Table 400.4, Note 15].

400.5 Ampacity of Flexible Cords and Flexible Cables

(A) Ampacity Tables. Table 400.5(A)(1) lists the allowable ampacity for copper conductors in flexible cords and Table 400.5(A)(2) lists the allowable ampacity for copper conductors in flexible cords with not more than three current-carrying conductors at an ambient temperature of 86ºF.

Where the number of current-carrying conductors in a cable or raceway exceeds three, the allowable ampacity of each conductor must be adjusted in accordance with the following multipliers:

Table 400.5 Adjustment Factor

Current Carrying	Ampacity Multiplier
4–6 Conductors	0.80
7–9 Conductors	0.70
10–20 Conductors	0.50

If the ambient temperature is other than 86°F, the flexible cord or flexible cable ampacity, as listed in Table 400.5(A)(1) or 400.5(A)(2), must be adjusted by using the ambient temperature correction factors listed in Table 310.15(B)(2)(a).

Author's Comment:

- Temperature ratings for flexible cords aren't contained in the *NEC*, but UL listing standards state that flexible cords are rated for 60°C unless marked otherwise.

400.10 Uses Permitted

(A) Uses Permitted. Flexible cords within the scope of this article can be used for the following applications:

(1) Pendants [receptacles—210.50(A) and boxes—314.23(H)].

(2) Wiring of luminaires [410.24(A) and 410.62(B)].

(3) Connection of portable luminaires, portable and mobile signs, or appliances [422.16].

(4) Elevator cables.

(5) Wiring of cranes and hoists.

(6) Connection of utilization equipment to facilitate frequent interchange [422.16]. ▶Figure 400–4

(7) Prevention of the transmission of noise or vibration [422.16].

(8) Appliances where the fastening means and mechanical connections are specifically designed to permit ready removal for maintenance and repair, and the appliance is intended or identified for flexible cord connections [422.16]. ▶Figure 400–5

(9) Connection of moving parts.

Flexible Cords and Flexible Cables | 400.12

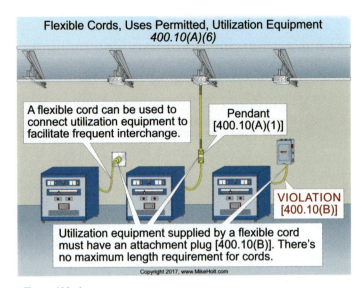
▶Figure 400–4

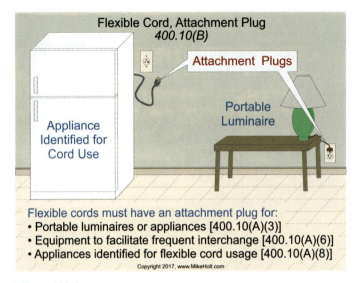
▶Figure 400–6

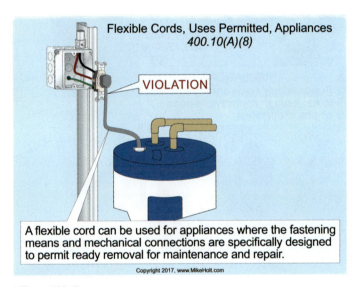
▶Figure 400–5

Author's Comment:

- Flexible cords are permitted for fixed permanent wiring by 501.10(A)(2) and (B)(2), 501.140, 502.4(A)(1)(e), 502.4(B)(2), 503.3(A)(2), 550.10(B), 553.7(B), and 555.13(A)(2).

(B) Attachment Plugs. Attachment plugs are required for flexible cords used in any of the following applications: ▶Figure 400–6

- Portable luminaires, portable and mobile signs, or appliances [400.10(A)(3)].

- Stationary equipment to facilitate its frequent interchange [400.10(A)(6) and 422.16].

- Appliances specifically designed to permit ready removal for maintenance and repair, and identified for flexible cord connection [400.10(A)(8)].

Author's Comment:

- An attachment plug can serve as the disconnecting means for stationary appliances [422.33] and room air conditioners [440.63].

400.12 Uses Not Permitted

Unless specifically permitted in 400.10, flexible cords sets (extension cords) and power-supply cords aren't permitted for the following:

(1) Flexible cord sets (extension cords) and power-supply cords aren't permitted to be a substitute for the fixed wiring of a structure. ▶Figure 400–7

(2) Flexible cord sets (extension cords) and power-supply cords aren't permitted to be run through holes in walls, structural ceilings, suspended or dropped ceilings, or floors. ▶Figure 400–8

400.12 | Flexible Cords and Flexible Cables

▶Figure 400–7

▶Figure 400–9

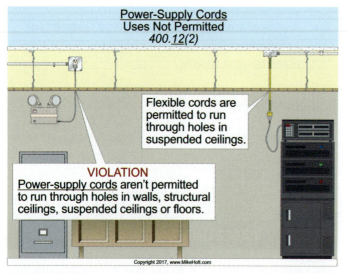

▶Figure 400–8

▶Figure 400–10

Author's Comment:

- Flexible cords are permitted to run through holes in suspended ceilings. ▶Figure 400–9

(3) Flexible cord sets (extension cords) and power-supply cords aren't permitted to be run through doorways, windows, or similar openings. ▶Figure 400–10

(4) Flexible cord sets (extension cords) and power-supply cords aren't permitted to be attached to building surfaces.

(5) Flexible cord sets (extension cords) and power-supply cords aren't permitted to be concealed by walls, floors, or ceilings, or located above suspended or dropped ceilings. ▶Figure 400–11

Ex: Flexible cords can be located above suspended or dropped ceilings if installed in a metal enclosure in accordance with 300.22(C)(3).

(6) Flexible cord sets (extension cords) and power-supply cords aren't permitted to be installed in raceways, except as permitted by 400.17 for industrial establishments where the conditions of maintenance and supervision ensure that only qualified persons will service the installation.

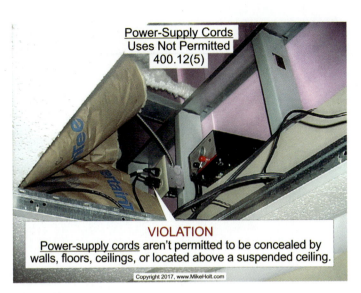

▶Figure 400–11

(7) Flexible cord sets (extension cords) and power-supply cords aren't permitted where they're subject to physical damage.

Author's Comment:

- Even cords listed as "extra-hard usage" must not be used where subject to physical damage.

400.14 Pull at Joints and Terminals

Flexible cords must be installed so tension won't be transmitted to the conductor terminals. ▶Figure 400–12

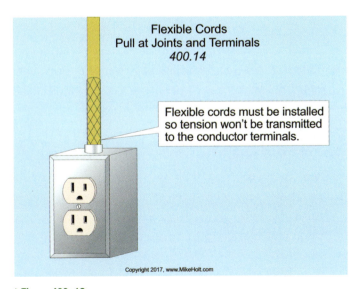

▶Figure 400–12

Note: This can be accomplished by knotting the cord, winding the flexible cord with tape, or by using support or strain-relief fittings. ▶Figure 400–13

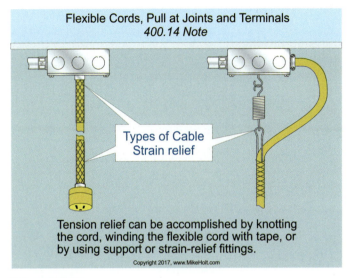

▶Figure 400–13

Author's Comment:

- When critical health and economic activities are dependent on flexible cord-supplied equipment, the best method is a factory-made, stress-relieving, listed device, not an old-timer's knot.

400.17 Protection from Damage

Flexible cords must be protected by bushings or fittings where passing through holes in covers, outlet boxes, or similar enclosures.

In industrial establishments where the conditions of maintenance and supervision ensure that only qualified persons will service the installation, flexible cords or flexible cables not exceeding 50 ft can be installed in aboveground raceways.

400.23 Equipment Grounding Conductor Identification

A conductor intended to be used as an equipment grounding conductor must have a continuous green color or a continuous identifying marker distinguishing it from the other conductor(s). Conductors with green insulation, or green with one or more yellow stripes aren't permitted to be used for an ungrounded or neutral conductor [250.119].

Notes

ARTICLE 404 SWITCHES

Introduction to Article 404—Switches

The requirements of Article 404 apply to switches of all types, including snap (toggle) switches, dimmer switches, fan switches, knife switches, circuit breakers used as switches, and automatic switches, such as time clocks and timers.

Part I. Installation

404.1 Scope

The requirements of Article 404 apply to all types of switches, switching devices, and circuit breakers used as switches. ▶Figure 404–1

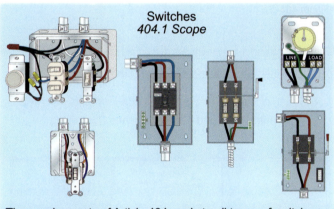

The requirements of Article 404 apply to all types of switches, such as snap (toggle) switches, knife switches, circuit breakers used as switches, and automatic switches such as time clocks.
Copyright 2017, www.MikeHolt.com

▶Figure 404–1

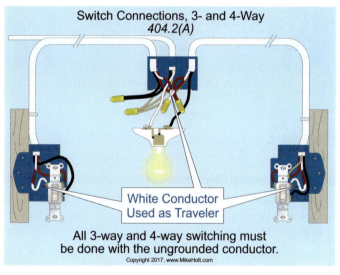

Switch Connections, 3- and 4-Way
404.2(A)

White Conductor Used as Traveler

All 3-way and 4-way switching must be done with the ungrounded conductor.
Copyright 2017, www.MikeHolt.com

▶Figure 404–2

Author's Comment:

▪ In other words, the neutral conductor must not be switched. The white insulated conductor within a cable assembly can be used for single-pole, 3-way, or 4-way switch loops if it's permanently reidentified to indicate its use as an ungrounded conductor at each location where the conductor is visible and accessible [200.7(C)(2)].

404.2 Switch Connections

(A) Three-Way and Four-Way Switches. Wiring for 3-way and 4-way switching must be done so that only the ungrounded conductors are switched. ▶Figure 404–2

404.2 | Switches

If a metal raceway or metal-clad cable contains the ungrounded conductors for switches, the wiring must be arranged to avoid heating the surrounding metal by induction. This is accomplished by installing all circuit conductors in the same raceway in accordance with 300.3(B) and 300.20(A), or ensuring that they're all within the same cable.

Ex: A neutral conductor isn't required in the same raceway or cable with travelers and switch leg (switch loop) conductors. ▶Figure 404–3

Ex: A switch or circuit breaker can disconnect a grounded circuit conductor where it disconnects all circuit conductors simultaneously.

(C) Switches Controlling Lighting Loads. Switches controlling line-to-neutral lighting loads must have a neutral conductor installed at a switch serving bathrooms, hallways, stairways, or rooms suitable for human habitation or occupancy as defined in the applicable building code. ▶Figure 404–5

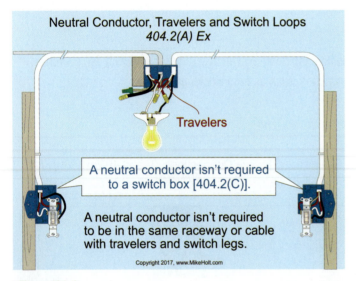

▶Figure 404–3

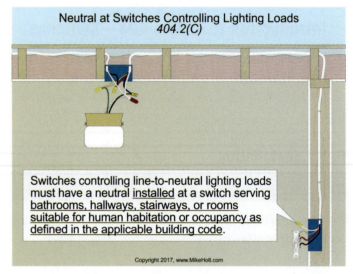

▶Figure 404–5

(B) Switching Neutral Conductors. Only the ungrounded conductor can be used for switching, and the grounded [neutral] conductor isn't permitted to be disconnected by switches or circuit breakers. ▶Figure 404–4

Where 3-way and 4-way switches are visible in a room, only one of the switches requires a neutral conductor. ▶Figure 404–6

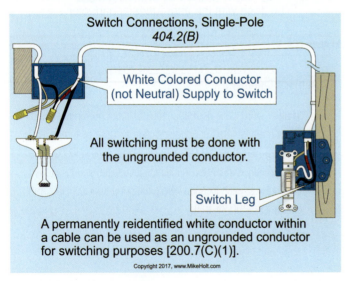

▶Figure 404–4

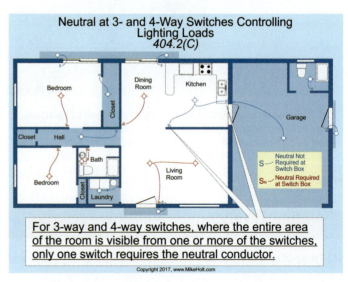

▶Figure 404–6

A neutral conductor isn't required under any of the following conditions:

(1) Where conductors enter the box through a raceway with sufficient cross-sectional area to accommodate a neutral conductor. ▶Figure 404–7

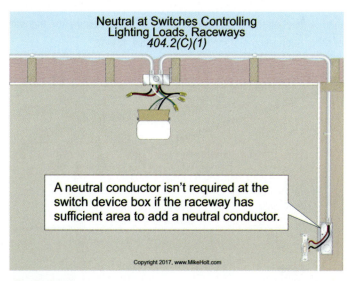

▶Figure 404–7

(2) Where the switch box can be accessed to add or replace a cable without damaging the building finish. ▶Figure 404–8

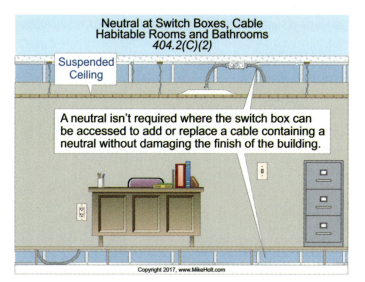

▶Figure 404–8

(3) Snap switches with integral enclosures [300.15(E)].

(4) Where the lighting is controlled by automatic means.

(5) Switches controlling receptacles. ▶Figure 404–9

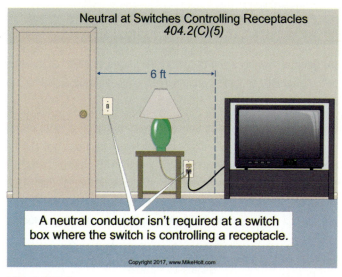

▶Figure 404–9

The neutral conductor must be run to any replacement switch that requires line-to-neutral voltage [404.22] to operate the electronics of the switch in the standby mode. ▶Figure 404–10

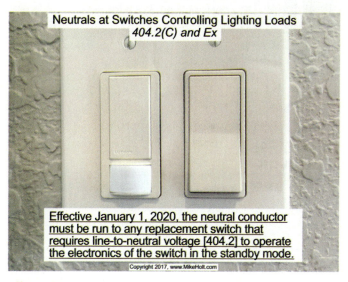

▶Figure 404–10

Ex: The connection requirements become effective January 1, 2020. A neutral conductor isn't required for replacement switches installed in locations wired prior to the adoption of 404.2(C) where the neutral conductor can't be extended without removing finish materials. The number of electronic lighting control switches without a neutral conductor on a branch circuit must not exceed five switches, and the number connected to any feeder must not exceed twenty-five switches.

Note: The purpose of the neutral conductor at a switch is to complete a circuit path for electronic lighting control devices that require a neutral conductor.

404.3 | Switches

404.3 Switch Enclosures

(A) General. Switches and circuit breakers used as switches must be of the externally operable type mounted in an enclosure listed for the intended use.

(B) Used for Raceways or Splices. Switch or circuit-breaker enclosures can contain splices and taps if the splices and/or taps don't fill the wiring space at any cross section to more than 75 percent. Switch or circuit-breaker enclosures can have conductors feed through them if the wiring doesn't fill the wiring space at any cross section to more than 40 percent in accordance with 312.8. ▶Figure 404–11 and ▶Figure 404–12

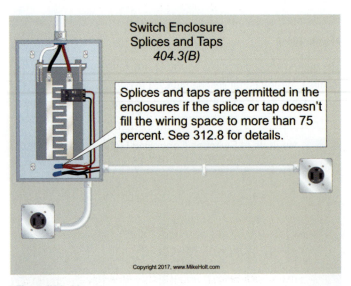

▶Figure 404–11

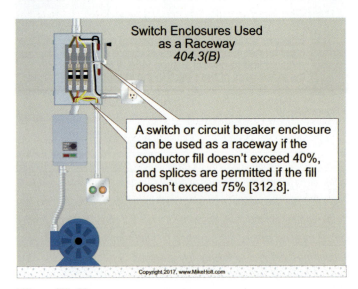

▶Figure 404–12

404.4 Damp or Wet Locations

(A) Surface-Mounted Switches or Circuit Breakers. Surface-mounted switches and circuit breakers in a damp or wet location must be installed in a weatherproof enclosure. The enclosure must be installed so not less than ¼ in. of airspace is provided between the enclosure and the wall or other supporting surface [312.2]. ▶Figure 404–13

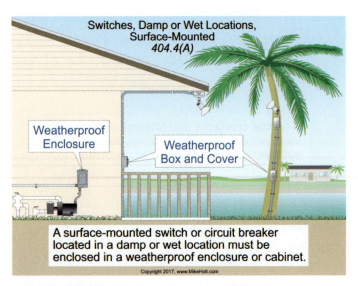

▶Figure 404–13

(B) Flush-Mounted Switches or Circuit Breakers. A flush-mounted switch or circuit breaker in a damp or wet location must have a weatherproof cover. ▶Figure 404–14

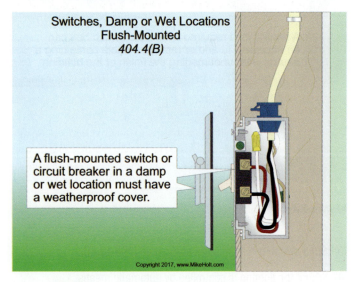

▶Figure 404–14

(C) Switches in Bathtub or Shower Spaces. Switches can be located next to but not within a bathtub, hydromassage bathtub, or shower space unless installed as part of a listed tub or shower assembly. ▶Figure 404–15

▶Figure 404–15

404.6 Position of Knife Switches

(A) Single-Throw Knife Switch. Single-throw knife switches must be installed so gravity won't tend to close them.

(C) Connection of Switches. Single-throw knife switches, molded case switches, and circuit breakers used as switches must have the terminals supplying the load de-energize when the switch is in the open position.

Ex: Terminals of a backfed switch or circuit breaker must be identified to indicate the terminals will be energized when the switch is in the open position. A permanent affixed warning label having sufficient durability to withstand the environment involved and comply with 110.21(B) must be on the switch enclosure or immediately adjacent to open switches, and read:

WARNING—LOAD SIDE TERMINALS MAY BE ENERGIZED BY BACKFEED.

404.7 Indicating

Switches, motor circuit switches, and circuit breakers used as switches must be marked to indicate whether they're in the "on" or "off" position. When the switch is operated vertically, it must be installed so the "up" position is the "on" position [240.81]. ▶Figure 404–16

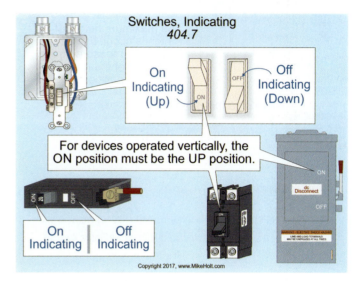

▶Figure 404–16

Ex 1: Double-throw switches, such as 3-way and 4-way switches, aren't required to be marked "on" or "off."

Ex 2: On busway installations, tap switches employing a center-pivoting handle can be open or closed with either end of the handle in the up or down position. The switch position must be clearly indicated and must be visible from the floor or from the usual point of operation.

404.8 Accessibility and Grouping

(A) Location. Switches and circuit breakers used as switches must be capable of being operated from a readily accessible location with the center of the grip of the operating handle of the switch or circuit breaker, when in its highest position, not more than 6 ft 7 in. above the floor or working platform [240.24(A)]. ▶Figure 404–17

404.8 | Switches

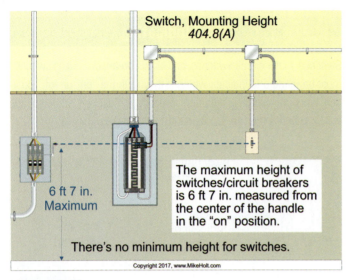

▶Figure 404–17

Author's Comment:

- There isn't a minimum height above the floor or working platform for a switch or electrical equipment. ▶Figure 404–18

▶Figure 404–18

Ex 1: On busways, fusible switches and circuit breakers can be located at the same level as the busway where suitable means is provided to operate the handle of the device from the floor. ▶Figure 404–19

Ex 2: Switches and circuit breakers used as switches can be mounted above 6 ft 7 in. if they're next to the equipment they supply, and are accessible by portable means [240.24(A)(4)]. ▶Figure 404–20

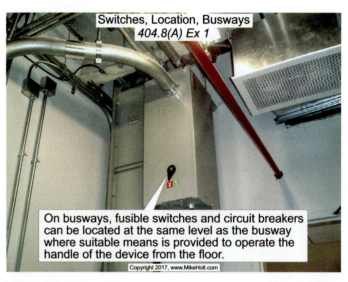

▶Figure 404–19

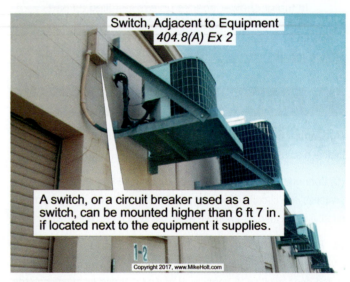

▶Figure 404–20

(B) Voltage Between Devices. Snap switches aren't permitted to be grouped or ganged in enclosures with other snap switches, receptacles, or similar devices if the voltage between devices exceeds 300V, unless the devices are separated by barriers. ▶Figure 404–21

Author's Comment:

- The voltage between devices is a function of the difference in voltage between the conductors. When adjacent devices are connected to different systems such as 120/208V and 277/480V, the voltage difference between the devices can be as much as 381V. ▶Figure 404–22

Switches | 404.9

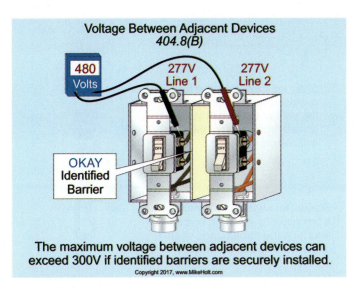

▶Figure 404–21

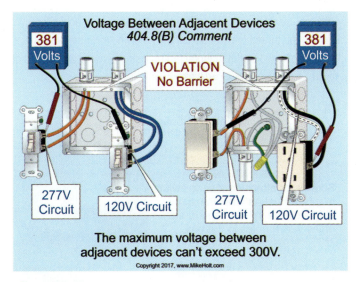

▶Figure 404–22

(1) Metal Boxes. The switch is mounted with metal screws to a metal box or a metal cover that's connected to an equipment grounding conductor in accordance with 250.148. ▶Figure 404–23

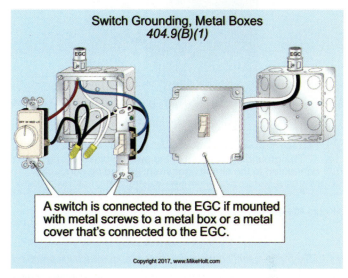

▶Figure 404–23

Author's Comment:

- Direct metal-to-metal contact between the device yoke of a switch and the box isn't required. ▶Figure 404–24

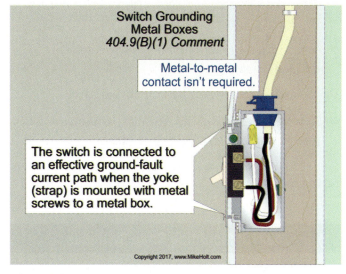

▶Figure 404–24

404.9 Switch Faceplates

(A) Mounting. Faceplates for switches must be installed so they completely cover the outlet box opening and, where flush mounted, the faceplate must seat against the wall surface.

(B) Grounding. The metal mounting yokes for switches, dimmers, and similar control switches must be connected to an equipment grounding conductor. Metal faceplates must be grounded. Snap switches are considered to be part of an effective ground-fault current path if either of the following conditions is met:

(2) Nonmetallic Boxes. The grounding terminal of the switch yoke must be connected to the circuit equipment grounding conductor. ▶Figure 404–25

404.10 | Switches

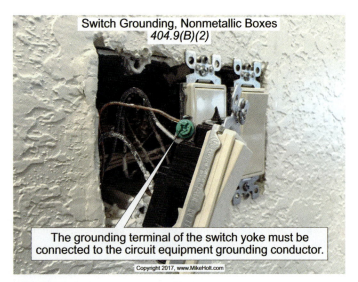

▶Figure 404–25

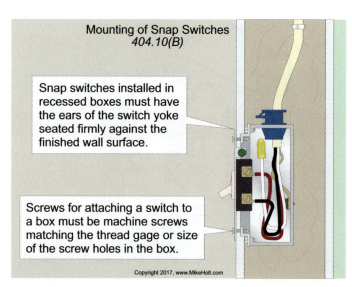

▶Figure 404–26

Ex 1: The metal mounting yoke of a replacement switch isn't required to be connected to an equipment grounding conductor if the wiring at the existing switch doesn't contain an equipment grounding conductor and the switch faceplate is nonmetallic with nonmetallic screws, or the replacement switch is GFCI protected.

Ex 2: Listed assemblies aren't required to be connected to an equipment grounding conductor if all of the following conditions are met:

(1) The device is provided with a nonmetallic faceplate that can't be installed on any other type of device,

(2) The device doesn't have mounting means to accept other configurations of faceplates,

(3) The device is equipped with a nonmetallic yoke, and

(4) Parts of the device that are accessible after installation of the faceplate are manufactured of nonmetallic material.

Ex 3: A snap switch with an integral nonmetallic enclosure complying with 300.15(E).

404.10 Mounting Snap Switches

(B) Mounting of Snap Switches. Snap switches installed in recessed boxes must have the ears of the switch yoke seated firmly against the finished wall surface. ▶Figure 404–26

Screws for attaching a snap switch to a box must be machine screws matching the thread gage or size of the screw holes in the box, unless otherwise allowed by the manufacturer's instructions, or unless part of a listed assembly. ▶Figure 404–27

▶Figure 404–27

Author's Comment:

- In walls or ceilings of noncombustible material, such as drywall, boxes aren't permitted to be set back more than ¼ in. from the finished surface. In combustible walls or ceilings, boxes must be flush with, or project slightly from, the finished surface [314.20]. There must not be any gaps more than ⅛ in. at the edge of the box [314.21].

404.11 Circuit Breakers Used as Switches

A manually operable circuit breaker used as a switch must show when it's in the "on" (closed) or "off" (open) position [404.7]. ▶Figure 404–28

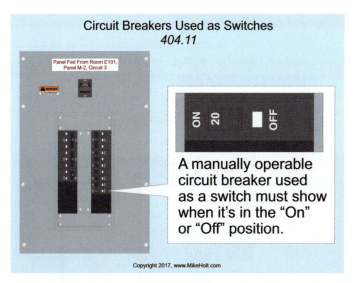

▶Figure 404–28

Author's Comment:

- Circuit breakers used to switch fluorescent lighting must be listed and marked "SWD" or "HID." Circuit breakers used to switch high-intensity discharge lighting must be listed and must be marked "HID" [240.83(D)]. ▶Figure 404–29

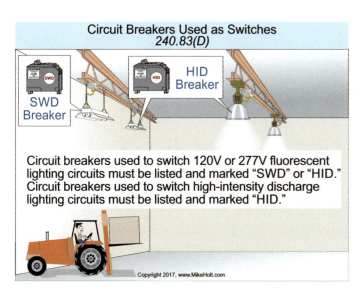

▶Figure 404–29

404.12 Grounding of Enclosures

Metal enclosures for switches and circuit breakers used as switches must be connected to an equipment grounding conductor of a type recognized in 250.118 [250.4(A)(3)]. Nonmetallic boxes for switches must be installed using a wiring method that includes an equipment grounding conductor.

404.14 Rating and Use of Snap Switches

(A) Alternating-Current General-Use Snap Switches. Alternating-current general-use snap switches can control:

(1) Resistive and inductive loads, including electric-discharge lamps that don't exceed the ampere rating of the switch, at the voltage applied.

(2) Tungsten-filament lamp loads not exceeding the ampere rating of the switch at 120V.

(3) Motor loads rated 2 hp or less that don't exceed 80 percent of the ampere rating of the switch. See 430.109(C).

(B) Alternating-Current or Direct-Current General-Use Snap Switch. A form of general-use snap switch suitable for use on either alternating-current or direct-current circuits for controlling:

(1) Resistive loads not exceeding the ampere rating of the switch at the voltage applied.

(2) Inductive loads not exceeding 50 percent of the ampere rating of the switch at the applied voltage or rated in horsepower for motor loads.

(3) Tungsten-filament lamp loads not exceeding the ampere rating of the switch at the applied voltage if T-rated.

(C) CO/ALR Snap Switches. Snap switches rated 20A or less connected to aluminum wire must be marked CO/ALR. See 406.3(C).

Author's Comment:

- According to UL listing requirements, aluminum conductors must not terminate in screwless (push-in) terminals of a snap switch (UL White Book, *Guide Information for Electrical Equipment*).

(E) Dimmers. General-use dimmer switches are only permitted to control permanently installed incandescent luminaires. ▶Figure 404–30

404.20 | Switches

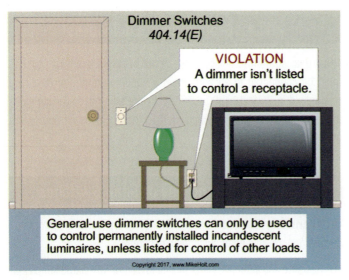

▶Figure 404–30

Part II. Construction Specifications

404.20 Switch Marking

(A) Markings. Switches must be marked with the current, voltage, and if horsepower rated, the maximum rating for which they're designed.
▶Figure 404–31

▶Figure 404–31

(B) Off Indication. If in the off position, a switching device with a marked "off" position must completely disconnect all ungrounded conductors of the load it controls.

Author's Comment:

- If an electronic occupancy sensor is used for switching, voltage will be present and a small current of 0.05 mA can flow through the circuit when the switch is in the "off" position. This small amount of current can startle a person, perhaps causing a fall. To solve this problem, manufacturers have simply removed the word "off" from the switch. ▶Figure 404–32

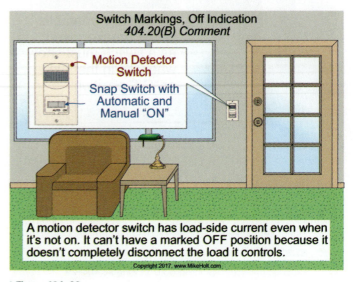

▶Figure 404–32

456 Mike Holt's Illustrated Guide to Understanding 2017 NEC Requirements for Solar Photovoltaic Systems

404.22 Electronic Lighting Switches

Effective January 1, 2020, electronic lighting control switches must be listed to not introduce current on the equipment grounding conductor during normal operation. ▶Figure 404–33

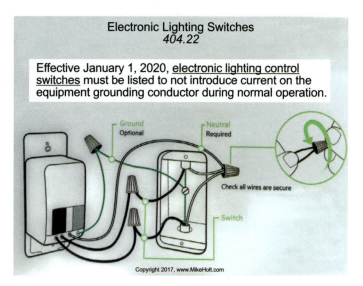

▶Figure 404–33

Ex: Electronic lighting control switches that put current on the equipment grounding conductor [404.2(C) Ex] must be listed and marked for use only for replacement or retrofit applications.

Notes

ARTICLE 408 — SWITCHBOARDS, SWITCHGEAR, AND PANELBOARDS

Introduction to Article 408—Switchboards, Switchgear, and Panelboards

Article 408 covers the specific requirements for switchboards, switchgear, and panelboards that control power and lighting circuits. There's a tendency among some people in the industry to use the terms switchboard and switchgear interchangeably. Switchgear is manufactured and tested to more exacting standards and is configured differently than switchboards. For example, in switchgear there are physical barriers between breakers, and between the breakers and the bus. Switchgear is more durable and fault resistant, and is commonly selected for larger applications where low-voltage power circuit breakers and selective coordination are applied, such as computer data centers, manufacturing, and process facilities [Source NCCER].

As you study this article, remember some of these key points:

- One objective of Article 408 is that the installation prevents contact between current-carrying conductors and people or equipment.
- The circuit directory of a panelboard must clearly identify the purpose or use of each circuit that originates in the panelboard.
- You must understand the detailed grounding and overcurrent protection requirements for panelboards.

Part I. General

408.1 Scope

Article 408 covers the specific requirements for switchboards, switchgear, and panelboards that control power and lighting circuits. ▶Figure 408–1

408.3 Arrangement of Busbars and Conductors

(A) Switchboard, Switchgear, or Panelboard

(2) Service Equipment. Barriers must be placed on ungrounded service parts exposed to inadvertent contact by persons servicing load terminations of switchboards, switchgear, or panelboards. ▶Figure 408–2

Ex: This requirement doesn't apply to panelboards with provisions for more than one service disconnect within a single enclosure as permitted in 408.36, Ex 1, 2, and 3.

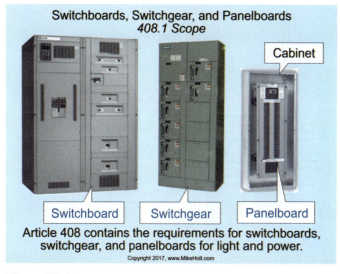

▶Figure 408–1

408.3 | Switchboards, Switchgear, and Panelboards

▶Figure 408–2

(D) Terminals. In switchboards, switchgear, and panelboards, terminals for neutral and equipment grounding conductors must be located so it's not necessary to reach beyond uninsulated live parts to make connections.

(E) Bus Arrangement

(1) Alternating-Current Phase Arrangement. Panelboards supplied by a 4-wire, delta-connected, three-phase (high-leg) system must have the high-leg conductor (which operates at 208V to ground) terminate to the "B" phase of the panelboard. ▶Figure 408–3

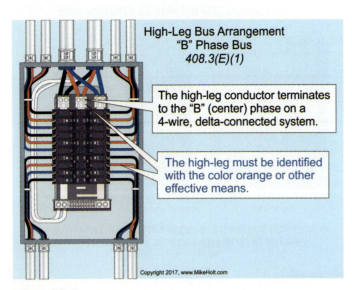

▶Figure 408–3

Ex: The high-leg conductor can terminate to the "C" phase when the meter is in the same section of a switchboard or panelboard.

Note: Orange identification, or some other effective means, is required for the high-leg conductor [110.15 and 230.56]. ▶Figure 408–4

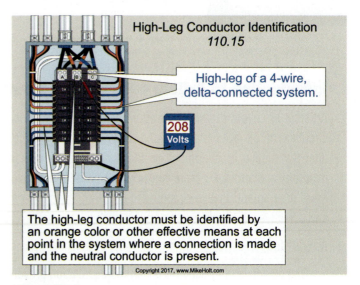

▶Figure 408–4

WARNING: The ANSI standard for meter equipment requires the high-leg conductor (208V to neutral) to terminate on the "C" (right) phase of the meter socket enclosure. This is because the demand meter needs 120V and it gets it from the "B" phase. ▶Figure 408–5

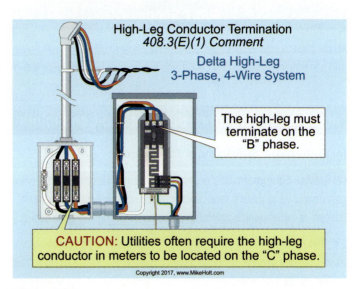

▶Figure 408–5

460 | Mike Holt's Illustrated Guide to Understanding 2017 NEC Requirements for Solar Photovoltaic Systems

Switchboards, Switchgear, and Panelboards | 408.4

⚠️ **WARNING:** When replacing equipment in existing facilities that contain a high-leg conductor, use care to ensure that the high-leg conductor is replaced in the original location. Prior to 1975, the high-leg conductor was required to terminate on the "C" phase of panelboards and switchboards. Failure to re-terminate the high-leg in accordance with the existing installation can result in 120V circuits being inadvertently connected to the 208V high-leg, with disastrous results.

(F) Switchboard, Switchgear, or Panelboard Identification. A permanently affixed caution label having sufficient durability to withstand the environment involved and comply with 110.21(B), must be installed and read:

(1) High-Leg Identification. A switchboard, switchgear, or panelboard containing a 4-wire, delta-connected system where the midpoint of one phase winding is grounded must be legibly and permanently field-marked as follows: ▶Figure 408–6

"CAUTION _____ PHASE HAS _____ VOLTS TO GROUND"

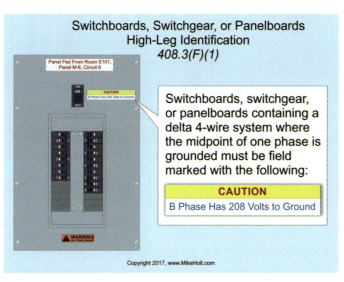
▶Figure 408–6

408.4 Field Identification

(A) Circuit Directory or Circuit Identification. Circuits, and circuit modifications, must be legibly identified as to their clear, evident, and specific purpose. Spare positions that contain unused overcurrent protection devices must also be identified. Identification must include an approved amount of detail to allow each circuit to be distinguished from all others, and the identification must be on a circuit directory located on the face or inside of the door of the panelboard. See 110.22. ▶Figure 408–7

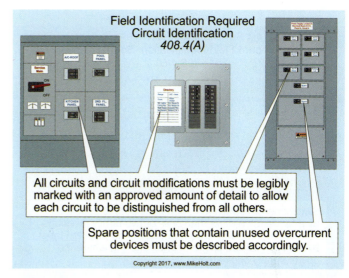
▶Figure 408–7

Circuit identification must not be based on transient conditions of occupancy, such as "Dad's Office Recp." ▶Figure 408–8

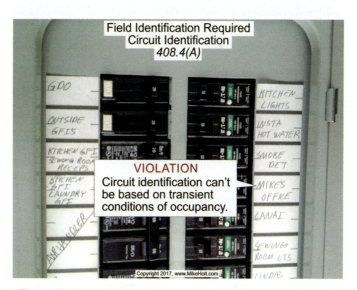
▶Figure 408–8

408.5 | Switchboards, Switchgear, and Panelboards

(B) Source of Supply. Switchboards, switchgear, and panelboards supplied by a feeder, in other than one- or two-family dwellings, must be marked with a permanent, not handwritten label that withstands the environment indicating where the power supply originates. ▶Figure 408–9

▶Figure 408–9

408.5 Clearance for Conductors Entering Bus Enclosures

If raceways enter a switchboard, switchgear, floor-standing panelboard, or similar enclosure, the raceways, including end fittings, must not rise more than 3 in. above the bottom of the enclosure.

408.7 Unused Openings

Unused openings for circuit breakers and switches must be closed using identified closures, or other means approved by the authority having jurisdiction, that provide protection substantially equivalent to the wall of the enclosure. ▶Figure 408–10

Part III. Panelboards

408.36 Protection of Panelboards

Each panelboard must be provided with overcurrent protection located within, or at any point on the supply side of, the panelboard. The overcurrent protection device must have a rating not greater than that of the panelboard, and it can be located within or on the supply side of the panelboard. ▶Figure 408–11

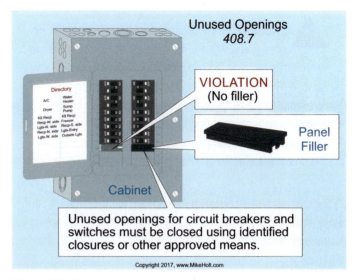

▶Figure 408–10

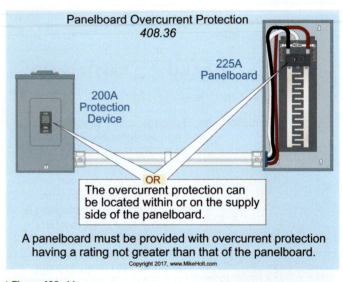

▶Figure 408–11

Ex 1: Individual overcurrent protection isn't required for panelboards used as service equipment where the service disconnect consists of up to six circuit breakers mounted in a single enclosure in accordance with 230.71. ▶Figure 408–12

Author's Comment:

- Always read the instructions provided with your equipment. Some panelboards require the field installation of a main overcurrent device for the equipment to be rated for use as service equipment.

Switchboards, Switchgear, and Panelboards | 408.37

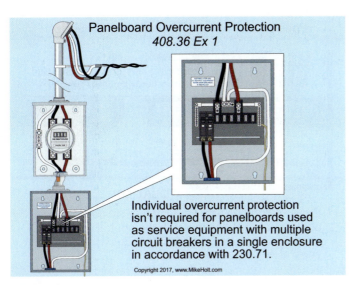

▶Figure 408–12

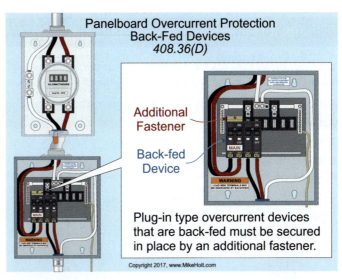

▶Figure 408–14

(B) Panelboards Supplied Through a Transformer. When a panelboard is supplied from a transformer, as permitted in 240.21(C), the overcurrent protection for the panelboard must be on the secondary side of the transformer. The required overcurrent protection can be in a separate enclosure ahead of the panelboard, or it can be in the panelboard. ▶Figure 408–13

Author's Comment:

- The purpose of the breaker fastener is to prevent the circuit breaker from being accidentally removed from the panelboard while energized, thereby exposing someone to dangerous voltage.

CAUTION: *Circuit breakers marked "Line" and "Load" must be installed in accordance with listing or labeling instructions [110.3(B)]; therefore, these types of devices aren't permitted to be back-fed.*

408.37 Panelboards in Damp or Wet Locations

The enclosures (cabinets) for panelboards must prevent moisture or water from entering or accumulating within the enclosure, and they must be weatherproof when located in a wet location. When the enclosure is surface mounted in a wet location, the enclosure must be mounted with not less than ¼ in. air space between it and the mounting surface [312.2].

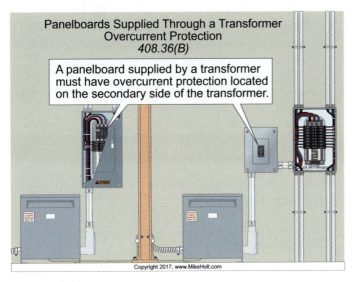

▶Figure 408–13

(D) Back-Fed Devices. Plug-in circuit breakers that are back-fed from field-installed conductors must be secured in place by an additional fastener that requires other than a pull to release the breaker from the panelboard. ▶Figure 408–14

408.40 | Switchboards, Switchgear, and Panelboards

408.40 Equipment Grounding Conductor

Metal panelboard cabinets and frames must be connected to an equipment grounding conductor of a type recognized in 250.118 [215.6 and 250.4(A)(3)]. Where a panelboard cabinet contains equipment grounding conductors, a terminal bar for the equipment grounding conductors must be bonded to the metal cabinet or be connected to the feeder equipment grounding conductor. ▶Figure 408–15

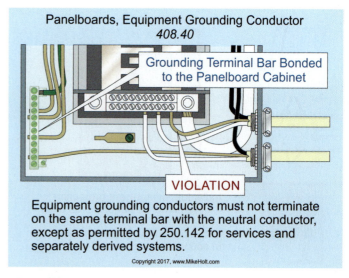

▶Figure 408–16

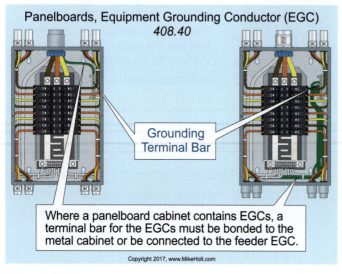

▶Figure 408–15

Ex: Insulated equipment grounding conductors for receptacles having insulated grounding terminals (isolated ground receptacles) [250.146(D)] are permitted to pass through the panelboard without terminating onto the equipment grounding terminal of the panelboard cabinet.

Equipment grounding conductors aren't permitted to terminate on the neutral terminal bar, and neutral conductors aren't permitted to terminate on the equipment grounding terminal bar, except as permitted by 250.142 for services and separately derived systems. ▶Figure 408–16

Author's Comment:

- See the definition of "Separately Derived System" in Article 100.

CAUTION: Most panelboards are rated for use as service equipment, which means they're supplied with a main bonding jumper [250.28]. This screw or strap must not be installed except when the panelboard is used for service equipment [250.24(A)(5)] or a separately derived system [250.30(A)(1)]. In addition, a panelboard marked "suitable only for use as service equipment" means the neutral bar or terminal of the panelboard has been bonded to the case at the factory, and this panelboard is restricted to being used only for service equipment or on separately derived systems in accordance with 250.142(A).

408.41 Neutral Conductor Terminations

Each neutral conductor within a panelboard must terminate to an individual terminal. ▶Figure 408–17

Author's Comment:

- If two neutral conductors are connected to the same terminal, and someone removes one of them, the other neutral conductor might unintentionally be removed as well. If that happens to the neutral conductor of a multiwire circuit, it can result in excessive line-to-neutral voltage for one of the circuits, as well as undervoltage for the other circuit. See 300.13(B) of this textbook for details. ▶Figure 408–18

Switchboards, Switchgear, and Panelboards | 408.54

Part IV. Construction Specifications

408.54 Maximum Number of Overcurrent Protection Devices

A panelboard must prevent the installation of more overcurrent protection devices than the number for which the panelboard was designed, rated, and listed. When applying this rule, a 2-pole circuit breaker is considered as two overcurrent protection devices, and a 3-pole circuit breaker is considered as three overcurrent protection devices.

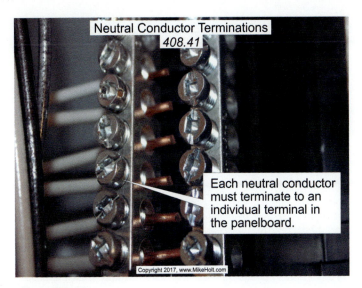

▶Figure 408–17

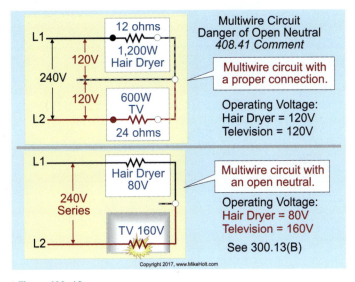

▶Figure 408–18

Notes

ARTICLE 445 GENERATORS

Introduction to Article 445—Generators

This article contains the electrical installation, and other requirements, for generators. These requirements include such things as where generators can be installed, nameplate markings, conductor ampacity, and disconnecting means.

Generators are basically motors that operate in reverse—they produce electricity when rotated, instead of rotating when supplied with electricity. Article 430, which covers motors, is the longest article in the *NEC*. Article 445, which covers generators, is one of the shortest. At first, this might not seem to make sense. But you don't need to size and protect conductors to a generator. You do need to size and protect them to a motor.

Generators need overload protection, and it's necessary to properly size the conductors that come from the generator. But these considerations are much more straightforward than the equivalent considerations for motors. Before you study Article 445, take a moment to read the definition of a "Separately Derived System" in Article 100.

445.1 Scope

Article 445 contains the installation and other requirements for generators. ▶Figure 445–1

▶Figure 445–1

Author's Comment:

- Generators, associated wiring, and equipment must be installed in accordance with the following requirements depending on their use:
    - Article 695, Fire Pumps
    - Article 700, Emergency Systems
    - Article 701, Legally Required Standby Systems
    - Article 702, Optional Standby Systems

445.12 Overcurrent Protection

(A) Generators. Generators must be protected from overload by inherent design, circuit breakers, fuses, or other identified overcurrent protective means.

445.13 | Generators

445.13 Ampacity of Conductors

(A) General. The ampacity of the conductors from the generator winding output terminals to the first overcurrent protection device, typically on the generator, must have an ampacity of not less than 115 percent of the nameplate current rating of the generator.

Author's Comment:

- Since the overcurrent protection device is typically part of the generator, this rule applies to the generator manufacturer, not the field installer.
- Conductors from the load side of the generator overcurrent protection device to the transfer switch are sized in accordance with 240.4.

Example: What size conductor is required from a 100A overcurrent protection device on a 20 kW, 120/240V single-phase generator to a 200A service rated transfer switch if the terminals are rated for 75°C conductor sizing? ▶Figure 445–2

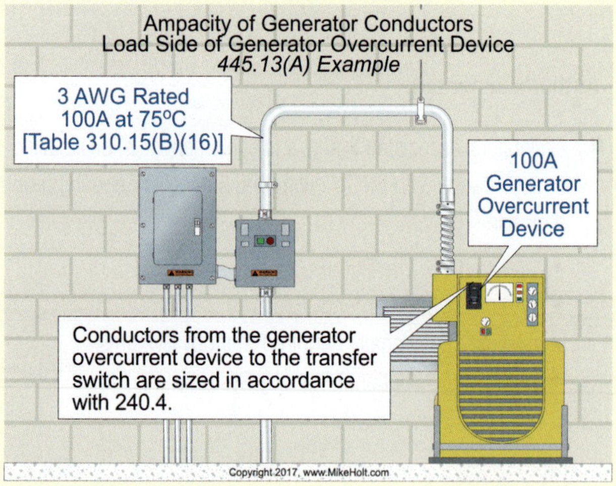

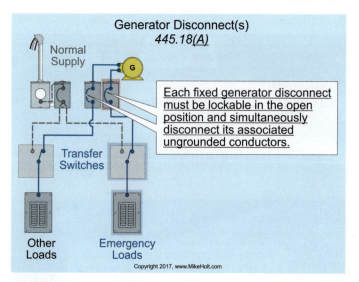

▶Figure 445–2

Answer: A 3 AWG conductor is required; Table 310.15(B)(16), rated 100A at 75°C [110.14(C)(1)(b)].

Generators that aren't a separately derived system must have the neutral conductor sized to carry the maximum unbalanced current as determined by 220.61, serve as part of the effective ground-fault current path, and not be smaller than required by 250.30. ▶Figure 445–3

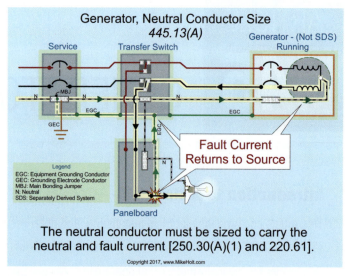

▶Figure 445–3

(B) Overcurrent Protection Provided. Conductors can be tapped from the load side of the generator overcurrent protected device in accordance with 240.21(B).

445.18 Disconnecting Means and Shutdown of Prime Mover

(A) Disconnecting Means. Each fixed generator disconnect must simultaneously disconnect all its associated ungrounded conductors and must be lockable in the open position in accordance with 110.25. ▶Figure 445–4

▶Figure 445–4

(B) Shutdown of Prime Mover. Generators must have provisions to shut down the prime mover; shutdown must comply with all of the following:

(1) Be equipped with provisions to disable all prime mover start control circuits to render the prime mover incapable of starting.

(2) Initiate a shutdown mechanism that requires a mechanical reset.

The provisions to shut down the prime mover can satisfy the requirements of 445.18(A) where the shutdown is capable of being locked in the open position in accordance with 110.25. Generators with greater than 15 kW rating must be provided with an additional shutdown means located outside the equipment room or generator and comply with 445.18(B)(1) and (B)(2).

Notes

ARTICLE 450 TRANSFORMERS

Introduction to Article 450—Transformers

Article 450 opens by saying, "This article covers the installation of all transformers." Then it lists eight exceptions. So what does it really cover? Essentially, Article 450 covers power transformers and most kinds of lighting transformers.

A major concern with transformers is preventing overheating. The *Code* doesn't completely address this issue. Article 90 explains that the *NEC* isn't a design manual, and it assumes that anyone using the *Code* has a certain level of expertise. Proper transformer selection is an important part of preventing it from overheating. The *NEC* assumes you've already selected a transformer suitable to the load characteristics. For the *Code* to tell you how to do that would push it into the realm of a design manual. Article 450 then takes you to the next logical step—providing overcurrent protection and the proper connections. But this article doesn't stop there; 450.9 provides ventilation requirements, and 450.13 contains accessibility requirements.

Part I contains the general requirements such as guarding, marking, and accessibility, Part II contains the requirements for different types of transformers, and Part III covers.

Part I. General

450.1 Scope

Article 450 covers the installation requirements of transformers.
▶Figure 450–1

▶Figure 450–1

450.3 Overcurrent Protection

(B) Overcurrent Protection for Transformers Not Over 1,000V. The primary winding of a transformer must be protected against overcurrent in accordance with the percentages listed in Table 450.3(B) and all applicable notes.

Table 450.3(B) Primary Overcurrent Protection Only	
Primary Current Rating	Maximum Protection
9A or More	125%, see Table Note 1
Less Than 9A	167%
Less Than 2A	300%

Note 1: If 125 percent of the primary current doesn't correspond to a standard rating of a fuse or nonadjustable circuit breaker, the next higher rating is permitted [240.6(A)]. ▶Figure 450–2

450.9 | Transformers

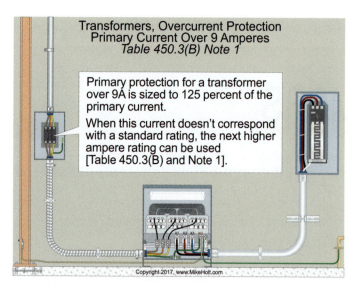

▶Figure 450–2

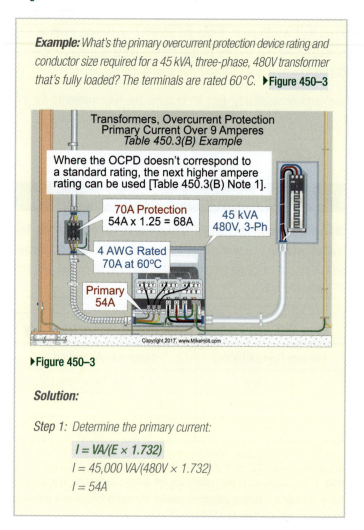

▶Figure 450–3

Solution:

Step 1: Determine the primary current:

I = VA/(E × 1.732)

I = 45,000 VA/(480V × 1.732)

I = 54A

Step 2: Determine the primary overcurrent protection device rating [240.6(A)]:

54A × 1.25 = 68A, next size up 70A, Table 450.3(B), Table Note 1

Answer: A 70A overcurrent protection device and 4 AWG conductors are required. The primary conductor must be sized to carry 54A continuously (54A × 1.25 = 68A) [215.2(A)(1)] and be protected by a 70A overcurrent protection device [240.4(B)]. A 4 AWG conductor rated 70A at 60°C meets all of the requirements [110.14(C)(1) and 310.15(B)(16)].

450.9 Ventilation

Transformers must be installed in accordance with the manufacturer's instructions, and their ventilating openings aren't permitted to be blocked [110.3(B)].

450.10 Grounding and Bonding

(A) Dry-Type Transformer Enclosures. Where separate equipment grounding conductors and supply-side bonding jumpers are installed, a terminal bar for these conductors must be installed inside the enclosure. The terminal bar must not cover any ventilation openings. ▶Figure 450–4

Ex: Where a dry-type transformer is equipped with wire-type connections (leads), the terminal bar isn't required.

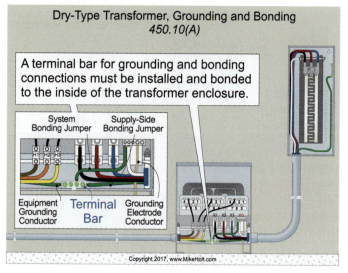

▶Figure 450–4

450.11 Marking

(A) General. Transformers must have a nameplate that provides the following information: ▶Figure 450–5

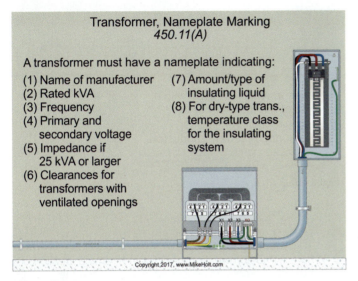

▶Figure 450–5

(1) The name of the manufacturer

(2) Rated kilovolt-amperes

(3) Frequency

(4) Primary and secondary voltage

(5) The impedance of transformers 25 kVA and larger

(6) Required clearances for transformers with ventilating openings

(7) The amount and kind of insulating liquid where used

(8) For dry-type transformers, the temperature class for the insulation system

450.13 Transformer Accessibility

Transformers must be readily accessible to qualified personnel for inspection and maintenance, except as permitted by (A) or (B).

(A) Open Installations. Dry-type transformers can be located in the open on walls, columns, or structures. ▶Figure 450–6

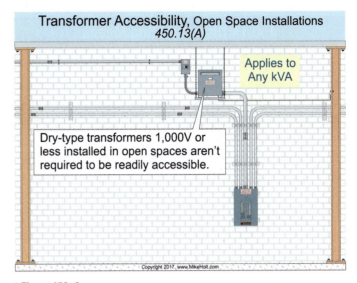

▶Figure 450–6

(B) Suspended Ceilings. Dry-type transformers, rated not more than 50 kVA, are permitted above suspended ceilings or in hollow spaces of buildings, if not permanently closed in by the structure. ▶Figure 450–7

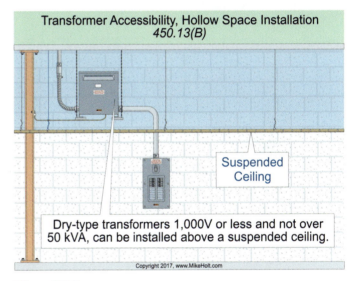

▶Figure 450–7

Author's Comment:

- Dry-type transformers not exceeding 50 kVA with a metal enclosure can be installed above a suspended-ceiling space used for environmental air-handling purposes (plenum) [300.22(C)(3)].

450.14 | Transformers

450.14 Disconnecting Means

A disconnecting means is required to disconnect all transformer ungrounded primary conductors, unless the transformer is Class 2 or Class 3. The disconnect must be located within sight of the transformer, unless the location of the disconnect is field marked on the transformer and the disconnect is lockable with provisions for locking to remain in place whether the lock is installed or not [110.25]. ▶Figure 450–8 and ▶Figure 450–9

Author's Comment:

- "Within Sight" means that it's visible and not more than 50 ft from one to the other [Article 100].

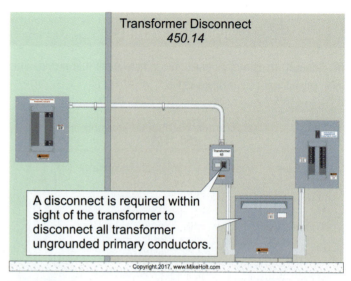

▶Figure 450–8

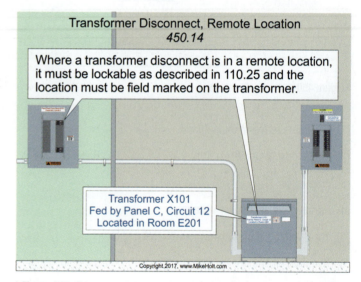

▶Figure 450–9

ARTICLE 480 STORAGE BATTERIES

Introduction to Article 480—Storage Batteries

The stationary battery is the heart of any uninterruptible power supply. Article 480 addresses stationary batteries for commercial and industrial grade power supplies; not the small, "point of use," UPS boxes.

Stationary batteries are also used in other applications, such as emergency power systems. Regardless of the application, if it uses stationary batteries, Article 480 applies.

Lead-acid stationary batteries fall into two general categories; flooded, and valve regulated (VRLA). These differ markedly in such ways as maintainability, total cost of ownership, and scalability. The *NEC* doesn't address these differences, as they're engineering issues and not fire safety or electrical safety matters [90.1].

The *Code* doesn't address such design issues as optimum tier height, distance between tiers, determination of charging voltage, or string configuration. Nor does it address battery testing, monitoring, or maintenance, which involve highly specialized areas of knowledge, and are required for optimizing operational efficiency. Standards other than the *NEC* address these topics.

What the *Code* does address, in Article 480, are issues related to preventing electrocution and the ignition of the gases that all stationary batteries (even "sealed" ones) emit.

480.1 Scope

Article 480 applies to stationary storage battery installations. ▶Figure 480–1

480.2 Definitions

Cell. The basic electrochemical unit, consisting of an anode and a cathode, which receives, stores, and delivers electrical energy.

Author's Comment:

- A battery is made up of one or more cells.

Container. An object that holds the elements of a single unit in a battery.

Note: Containers can be single-cell or multi-cell and are often called "jars."

▶Figure 480–1

480.3 | Storage Batteries

Intercell Connector. A conductive bar or cable that connects adjacent cells.

Intertier Connector. An electrical conductor that connects two cells on different tiers of the same rack, or different shelves of the same rack.

Nominal Voltage (Battery or Cell). The value assigned to a cell or battery for conveniently designating the voltage class. The operating voltage of the cell or battery can be higher or lower than the nominal voltage.

Note: The most common nominal cell voltages are 2V per cell for lead-acid, 1.20V per cell for alkali, and 3.60V to 3.80V per cell for lithium-ion. ▶Figure 480–2

▶Figure 480–2

Author's Comment:

- The voltage of a battery will decrease below the nominal voltage while it's being used (discharged) and the actual voltage will often be higher than nominal when the battery is fully charged.

Sealed Cell or Battery. A cell or battery with no provision for the routine addition of water or electrolytes.

Storage Battery. A battery consisting of one or more rechargeable cells.

480.3 Listing Requirement

Storage batteries, other than lead-acid batteries, and battery management equipment must be listed.

480.4 Battery and Cell Terminations

(A) Corrosion Prevention. Where connections between dissimilar metals occur, antioxidant material must be used as recommended by the battery manufacturer. ▶Figure 480–3

▶Figure 480–3

Note: The manufacturer's instructions may have guidance for acceptable materials.

(B) Intercell and Intertier Conductors and Connections. The ampacity of field-assembled intercell and intertier connectors and conductors must be sized so that the temperature rise under maximum load conditions and at maximum ambient temperature doesn't exceed the safe operating temperature of the conductor insulation.

Note: IEEE 1375, *Guide for the Overcurrent Protection of Stationary Battery Systems* provides guidance for overcurrent protection and associated cable sizing. Typical voltage-drop considerations for alternating-current circuits might not be adequate for battery systems.

480.5 Wiring and Equipment Supplied from Batteries

Wiring and equipment supplied from storage batteries must be in accordance with Chapters 1 through 4 unless otherwise permitted by 480.5.

480.7 Battery Disconnect

(A) Disconnecting Means. A readily accessible disconnect located within sight of the battery system must be provided for all ungrounded conductors derived from a stationary battery system having a nominal voltage over 60V dc.

Note: See 240.21(H) on the location of the overcurrent protection device for battery conductors.

(D) Notification. The disconnect must be legibly field marked and placed in a conspicuous location near the battery if a disconnect isn't provided. The marking must withstand the environment involved and include the following:

(1) Nominal battery voltage

(2) Maximum available short-circuit current derived from the stationary battery system

(3) Date the short-circuit calculation was performed

(4) The disconnect must be marked in accordance with 110.16

Note: Battery equipment suppliers can provide information about short-circuit current on any particular battery model.

480.9 Battery Support Systems

The structure that supports the battery must be resistant to deteriorating action by the electrolyte. Metal structures must be provided with nonconducting support members for the cells, or be constructed with a continuous insulating material. Painting alone isn't considered as an insulating material. ▶Figure 480–4

▶Figure 480–4

CHAPTER 4

PRACTICE QUESTIONS

Please use the 2017 *Code* book to answer the following questions.

Article 400. Flexible Cords and Flexible Cables

1. Article 400 covers general requirements, applications, and construction specifications for flexible cords and flexible cables.

    (a) True
    (b) False

2. HPD cord shall be permitted for _____.

    (a) not hard usage
    (b) hard usage
    (c) extra-hard usage
    (d) all of these

3. TPT and TST cords shall be permitted in lengths not exceeding _____ ft when attached directly to a portable appliance rated 50W or less.

    (a) 8
    (b) 10
    (c) 15
    (d) 20

4. A 3-conductor SJE cable (one conductor is used for grounding) has a maximum ampacity of _____ for each 16 AWG conductor.

    (a) 9A
    (b) 11A
    (c) 13A
    (d) 15A

5. Conductors within flexible cords and flexible cables shall not be associated together in such a way that the _____ temperature of the conductors is exceeded.

    (a) operating
    (b) governing
    (c) ambient
    (d) limiting

6. Unless specifically permitted in 400.10, flexible cables, flexible cord sets, and power-supply cords shall not be used where subject to physical damage.

    (a) True
    (b) False

7. Flexible cord sets and power-supply cords shall not be used where they are _____.

    (a) run through holes in walls, ceilings, or floors
    (b) run through doorways, windows, or similar openings
    (c) attached to building surfaces, unless permitted by 368.56(B)
    (d) all of these

8. Flexible cord sets and power-supply cords shall not be concealed behind building _____, or run through doorways, windows, or similar openings.

    (a) structural ceilings
    (b) suspended or dropped ceilings
    (c) floors or walls
    (d) all of these

9. Flexible cord sets and power-supply cords shall not be permitted above suspended or dropped ceilings even if contained within an enclosure for use in "other spaces used for environmental air."

   (a) True
   (b) False

10. Flexible cords and flexible cables shall be protected by _____ where passing through holes in covers, outlet boxes, or similar enclosures.

    (a) bushings
    (b) fittings
    (c) a or b
    (d) none of these

11. A flexible cord conductor intended to be used as a(n) _____ conductor shall have a continuous identifying marker readily distinguishing it from the other conductor or conductors. One means of identification is a braid finished to show a continuous green color or a green color with one or more yellow stripes on one conductor.

    (a) ungrounded
    (b) equipment grounding
    (c) service
    (d) high-leg

Article 402. Fixture Wires

12. Three-way and four-way switches shall be wired so that all switching is done only in the _____ circuit conductor.

    (a) ungrounded
    (b) grounded
    (c) equipment ground
    (d) neutral

Article 404. Switches

13. Switches or circuit breakers shall not disconnect the grounded conductor of a circuit unless the switch or circuit breaker _____.

    (a) can be opened and closed by hand levers only
    (b) simultaneously disconnects all conductors of the circuit
    (c) opens the grounded conductor before it disconnects the ungrounded conductors
    (d) none of these

14. As a general rule, the grounded circuit conductor for the controlled lighting circuit shall be installed at the location where switches control lighting loads that are supplied by a grounded general-purpose branch circuit serving bathrooms, hallways, stairways, or rooms suitable for human habitation or occupancy as defined in the applicable building code.

    (a) True
    (b) False

15. Which of the following switches shall indicate whether they are in the open (off) or closed (on) position?

    (a) General-use switches.
    (b) Motor-circuit switches.
    (c) Circuit breakers.
    (d) all of these

16. Switches and circuit breakers used as switches can be mounted _____ if they are installed adjacent to motors, appliances, or other equipment that they supply and are accessible by portable means.

    (a) not higher than 6 ft 7 in.
    (b) higher than 6 ft 7 in.
    (c) in the mechanical equipment room
    (d) up to 8 ft high

17. A multipole, general-use snap switch shall not be fed from more than a single circuit unless it is listed and marked as a _____ switch.

    (a) 2-circuit
    (b) 3-circuit
    (c) a or b
    (d) none of these

18. Metal faceplates for snap switches, including dimmer and similar control switches, shall be _____.

    (a) bonded to the grounded electrode
    (b) grounded
    (c) a and b
    (d) none of these

19. Snap switches are considered to be part of the effective ground-fault current path when _____.

    (a) the switch is connected to the intersystem bonding termination
    (b) the switch is mounted with metal screws to a metal box or a metal cover that is connected to an equipment grounding conductor
    (c) an equipment grounding conductor or equipment bonding jumper is connected to the equipment grounding termination of the snap switch
    (d) b or c

20. A snap switch that does not have means for connection to an equipment grounding conductor shall be permitted for replacement purposes only where the wiring method does not include an equipment grounding conductor and the switch is _____.

    (a) provided with a faceplate of nonconducting, noncombustible material with nonmetallic screws
    (b) GFCI protected
    (c) a or b
    (d) none of these

21. The metal mounting yoke of a replacement switch is not required to be connected to an equipment grounding conductor if the wiring at the existing switch does not contain an equipment grounding conductor, and the _____.

    (a) switch faceplate is nonmetallic with nonmetallic screws
    (b) replacement switch is GFCI protected
    (c) a or b
    (d) circuit is AFCI protected

22. A snap switch with an integral nonmetallic enclosure complying with 300.15(E) is required to be connected to an equipment grounding conductor.

    (a) True
    (b) False

23. Snap switches installed in boxes that are set back of the finished surface shall have the _____ seated against the finished wall surface.

    (a) extension plaster ears
    (b) body
    (c) toggle
    (d) all of these

24. Metal enclosures for switches or circuit breakers shall be connected to the circuit _____ conductor.

    (a) grounded
    (b) grounding
    (c) equipment grounding
    (d) any of these

25. Where in the off position, a switching device with a marked OFF position shall completely disconnect all _____ conductors of the load it controls.

    (a) grounded
    (b) ungrounded
    (c) grounding
    (d) all of these

Article 408. Switchboards, Switchgear, and Panelboards

26. In switchboards, switchgear, and panelboards, load terminals for field wiring shall be so located that it is not necessary to reach across or beyond a(n) _____ ungrounded bus in order to make connections.

    (a) insulated
    (b) uninsulated
    (c) grounded
    (d) high impedance

27. Panelboards supplied by a three-phase, 4-wire, delta-connected system shall have the phase with the higher voltage-to-ground (high-leg) connected to the _____ phase.

    (a) A
    (b) B
    (c) C
    (d) any of these

28. A switchboard, switchgear, or panelboard containing a 4-wire, _____ system where the midpoint of one phase winding is grounded, shall be legibly and permanently field-marked to caution that one phase has a higher voltage-to-ground.

    (a) wye-connected
    (b) delta-connected
    (c) solidly grounded
    (d) ungrounded

29. A switchboard or panelboard containing an ungrounded ac electrical system is required to be legibly and permanently field marked to caution that the system is ungrounded and include the _____.

    (a) contact information for the power supplier
    (b) contact information for emergency services
    (c) operating voltage between conductors
    (d) transformer impedance rating

30. The purpose or use of panelboard circuits and circuit _____, including spare positions, shall be legibly identified on a circuit directory located on the face or inside of the door of a panelboard, and at each switch or circuit breaker in a switchboard or switchgear.

    (a) manufacturers
    (b) conductors
    (c) feeders
    (d) modifications

31. All switchboards, switchgear, and panelboards supplied by a feeder(s) in _____ shall be permanently marked to indicate each device or equipment where the power supply originates.

    (a) other than one- or two-family dwellings
    (b) all dwelling units
    (c) all nondwelling units
    (d) b and c

32. Conduits and raceways, including end fittings, shall not rise more than _____ in. above the bottom of a switchboard enclosure.

    (a) 3
    (b) 4
    (c) 5
    (d) 6

33. Unused openings for circuit breakers and switches in switchboards and panelboards shall be closed using _____, or other approved means that provide protection substantially equivalent to the wall of the enclosure.

    (a) duct seal and tape
    (b) identified closures
    (c) exothermic welding
    (d) sheet metal

34. Panelboards equipped with snap switches rated at 30A or less shall have overcurrent protection not exceeding _____.

    (a) 30A
    (b) 50A
    (c) 100A
    (d) 200A

35. Plug-in-type back-fed circuit breakers used to terminate field-installed ungrounded supply conductors shall be _____ by an additional fastener that requires more than a pull to release.

    (a) grounded
    (b) secured in place
    (c) shunt tripped
    (d) none of these

36. When separate equipment grounding conductors are provided in panelboards, a _____ shall be secured inside the cabinet.

    (a) grounded conductor
    (b) terminal lug
    (c) terminal bar
    (d) none of these

37. Each _____ conductor shall terminate within the panelboard at an individual terminal that is not used for another conductor.

    (a) grounded
    (b) ungrounded
    (c) grounding
    (d) all of these

Chapter 4 | Practice Questions

Article 445. Generators

38. Constant-voltage generators, except ac generator exciters, shall be protected from overload by _____ or other acceptable overcurrent protective means suitable for the conditions of use.

    (a) inherent design
    (b) circuit breakers
    (c) fuses
    (d) any of these

39. The ampacity of the conductors from the generator output terminals to the first distribution device(s) containing overcurrent protection shall not be less than _____ percent of the nameplate current rating of the generator.

    (a) 75
    (b) 115
    (c) 125
    (d) 140

40. Separately derived system generators shall have the _____ conductor sized not smaller than required to carry the maximum unbalanced current as determined by 220.61.

    (a) neutral
    (b) grounding
    (c) a and b
    (d) none of these

41. Unbonded 15 kW or smaller portable generators with both 125V and 125/250V receptacle outlets shall have _____ GFCI protection for personnel integral to the generator or receptacle on all 125V, 15A and 20A receptacle outlets.

    (a) identified
    (b) labeled
    (c) listed
    (d) approved

42. GFCI protection for 15 kW or smaller portable generators shall not be required where the 125V receptacle outlets(s) is interlocked such that it is not available for use when any 125/250V receptacle(s) is in use.

    (a) True
    (b) False

43. Bonded 15 kW or smaller portable generators shall be provided with GFCI protection on all 125V, _____ receptacle outlets.

    (a) 15A
    (b) 20A
    (c) 30A
    (d) a and b

44. If the 15 kW or smaller portable generator was manufactured or remanufactured prior to _____, listed cord sets or devices incorporating listed GFCI protection for personnel identified for portable use shall be permitted.

    (a) January 1, 2012
    (b) January 1, 2013
    (c) January 1, 2014
    (d) January 1, 2015

Article 450. Transformers

45. A secondary tie of a transformer is a circuit operating at _____, nominal, or less, between phases that connects two power sources or power-supply points.

    (a) 600V
    (b) 1,000V
    (c) 12,000V
    (d) 35,000V

46. Transformers with ventilating openings shall be installed so that the ventilating openings are _____.

    (a) a minimum 18 in. above the floor
    (b) not blocked by walls or obstructions
    (c) aesthetically located
    (d) vented to the exterior of the building

47. For transformers, other than Class 2 and Class 3, a means is required to disconnect all transformer ungrounded primary conductors. The disconnecting means shall be located within sight of the transformer unless the disconnect _____.

    (a) location is field marked on the transformer
    (b) is lockable in accordance with 110.25
    (c) is nonfusible
    (d) a and b

Article 480. Storage Batteries

48. Nominal battery voltage is typically _____.

    (a) 2V per cell for lead-acid systems
    (b) 1.20V for per cell for alkali systems
    (c) 3.60 to 3.80V per cell for Li-ion systems
    (d) all of these

49. Wiring and equipment supplied from storage batteries shall be in accordance with Chapters 1 through 4 of the *NEC* unless otherwise permitted by 480.6.

    (a) True
    (b) False

50. A disconnecting means is required within sight of the storage battery for all ungrounded stationary battery system conductors operating at over _____ dc.

    (a) 30V
    (b) 40V
    (c) 50V
    (d) 60V

Notes

CHAPTER 6
SPECIAL EQUIPMENT

Introduction to Chapter 6—Special Equipment

Chapter 6, which covers special equipment, is the second of four *NEC* chapters that deal with special topics. Chapters 5 and 7 focus on special occupancies, and special conditions respectively. Remember, the first four chapters of the *Code* are sequential and form a foundation for each of the subsequent four. Chapter 8 covers communications systems (twisted wire, antennas, and coaxial cable) and isn't subject to the requirements of Chapters 1 through 7 except where the requirements are specifically referenced in Chapter 8. What exactly is "Special Equipment"? It's equipment that, by the nature of its use, construction, or by its unique nature creates a need for additional measures to ensure the "safeguarding of people and property" mission of the *NEC*, as stated in Article 90. While the *Code* groups the articles in this chapter logically, we'll only cover Articles 690 and 691 in this textbook.

- **Article 690—Solar Photovoltaic (PV) Systems.** Article 690 focuses on reducing the electrical hazards that may arise from installing and operating a solar PV system, to the point where it can be considered safe for property and people. The requirements of the *NEC* Chapters 1 through 4 apply to these installations, except as specifically modified by Article 690.

- **Article 691—Large-Scale Photovoltaic (PV) Electric Power Production Facility.** This article is new with the 2017 *Code*. It appends Article 690 for solar installations that aren't under exclusive utility control if they have a production capacity of 500 kW or greater. Articles 690 and 691 both apply to such installations.

Notes

ARTICLE 690 — SOLAR PHOTOVOLTAIC (PV) SYSTEMS

Introduction to Article 690—Solar Photovoltaic (PV) Systems

You've seen, or maybe own, devices powered by photovoltaic cells, such as night lights, car coolers, and toys. These generally consist of a small solar module powering a small device running on less than 10V direct current and drawing only a fraction of an ampere. A solar PV system that powers a house or interconnects with an electric utility to offset a building's energy consumption operates on the same principals but on a much larger scale.

Solar PV systems that provide electrical power to an electrical system are large, heavy, and complex. There are mechanical and site selection issues that require expert knowledge as well as complex structural and architectural concerns that must be addressed. In this textbook we'll only discuss these installations as they pertain to Articles 690, 691, 705, and 710 of the *NEC* and the installation of non-utility solar PV systems.

The purpose of the *NEC* is to safeguard persons and property from the hazards arising from the use of electricity [90.1(A)]. Article 690 keeps that theme by focusing on reducing the electrical hazards that may arise from installing and operating a PV system, to a point where it can be considered safe for people and property.

This article consists of eight Parts and the general requirements of Chapters 1 through 4 apply to these installations, except as specifically modified by Article 690.

Part I. General

690.1 Scope

 Scan this QR code for a video of Mike explaining this topic; it's a sample from the DVDs that accompany this textbook.

Article 690 applies to solar PV systems, array circuit(s), inverter(s), and charge controller(s) for PV systems not covered in Article 691. These solar PV systems may be interactive with other electrical power sources (electric utility power, wind, generator) or stand-alone, or both, and may or may not be connected to an energy storage system (batteries). ▶Figure 690–1

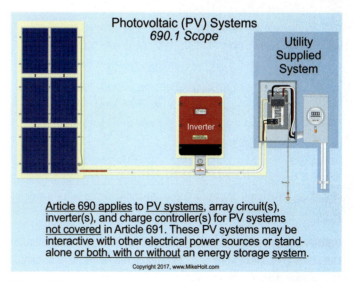

▶Figure 690–1

690.2 | Solar Photovoltaic (PV) Systems

690.2 Definitions

Alternating-Current PV Module. An alternating current PV module is a unit consisting of solar cells, and an integral micro-inverter that changes dc power to ac power when exposed to sunlight. ▶Figure 690–2

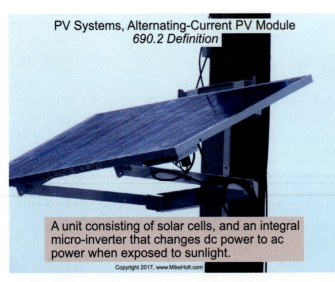

▶Figure 690–2

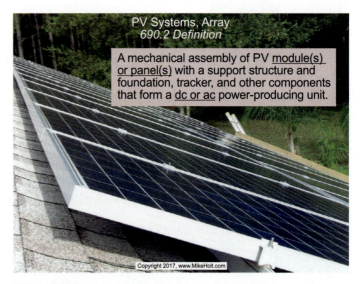

▶Figure 690–3

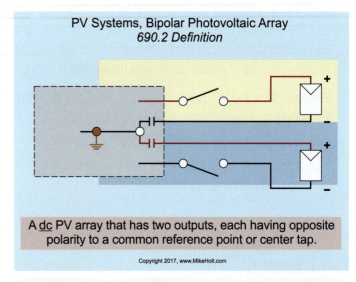

▶Figure 690–4

Author's Comment:

- A "Module" is only an "Alternating-Current PV Module" if it's listed as such.
- According to the UL White Book, ac modules provide single-phase power at 50/60 Hz when exposed to sunlight. Alternating-current modules are connected in parallel with each other and are evaluated to operate interactively (de-energize output upon loss of electric power) with electric utility power.
- Alternating-current modules are marked with the maximum size of the dedicated branch circuit on which they may be installed and the maximum number of modules which may be connected to each circuit.

Array. A mechanical assembly of PV module(s) or panel(s) consisting of support structures, trackers, and other components to form a dc or ac power-producing unit. ▶Figure 690–3

Bipolar Photovoltaic Array. A dc PV array that has two outputs, each having opposite polarity to a common reference point or center tap. ▶Figure 690–4

Author's Comment:

- Two monopole PV subarrays are used to form a bipolar PV array.

DC-to-DC Converter. A device installed in the PV source circuit or PV output circuit that provides output dc voltage and current at a higher or lower value than the input dc voltage and current. ▶Figure 690–5

Solar Photovoltaic (PV) Systems | 690.2

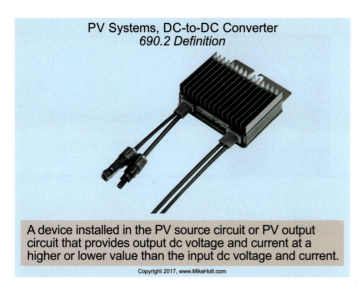
▶Figure 690–5

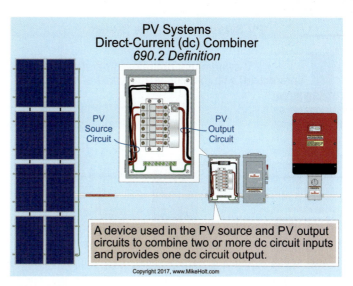
▶Figure 690–6

Author's Comment:

- These are components that are intended to maximize the output of independent modules and reduce losses due to variances between modules' outputs. They're directly wired to each module and are bolted to the module frame or the PV rack.

- A dc-to-dc convert enables the inverter to automatically maintain a fixed string voltage, at the optimal point for dc-ac conversion by the inverter, regardless of string length and individual module performance.

DC-to-DC Converter Output Circuit. The circuit conductors between the dc-to-dc converter and the inverter or dc utilization equipment.

DC-to-DC Converter Source Circuit. The conductors between dc-to-dc converter(s) and from dc-to-dc converters to the common connection point(s) of the dc system.

Direct-Current (dc) Combiner. A device that combines two or more dc circuit inputs and provides one dc circuit output. ▶Figure 690–6

Author's Comment:

- The dc combiner connects multiple PV source circuit conductors of PV modules together in parallel. Direct-current combiners can also combine two or more output circuits together into another "output circuit." These "array combiners" are used on large inverter systems where there are several tiers of combiners.

Functional Grounded PV System. A PV system that has an electrical reference to ground that's not solidly grounded. ▶Figure 690–7

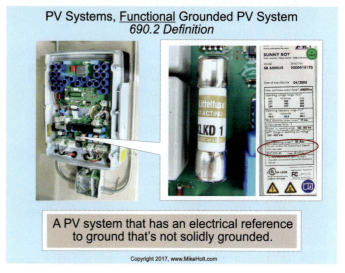
▶Figure 690–7

Note: A functional grounded PV system is grounded through a listed ground-fault protection system that's part of the inverter.

Generating Capacity. The sum of parallel-connected inverter maximum continuous output power at 40°C in kilowatts.

Interactive System. A PV system that operates in parallel (interactive) with the electric utility power source. ▶Figure 690–8

690.2 | Solar Photovoltaic (PV) Systems

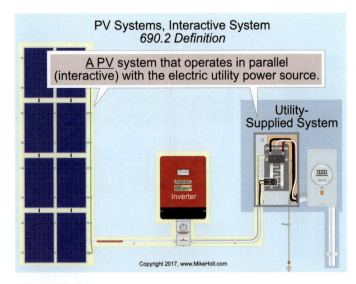
▶Figure 690–8

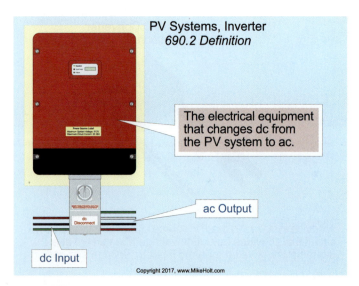
▶Figure 690–10

Author's Comment:

- A listed interactive inverter automatically ceases exporting power upon loss of utility voltage and automatically resumes exporting power once the voltage has been restored [705.40 Ex].

Interactive Inverter Output Circuit. The conductors between the interactive inverter and service or distribution network. ▶Figure 690–9

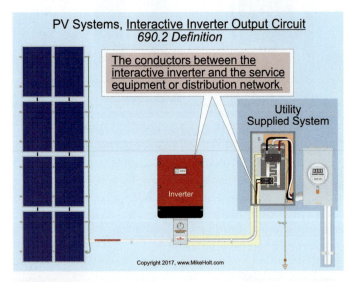
▶Figure 690–9

Inverter. Electrical equipment that changes dc power from the PV system to ac power. ▶Figure 690–10

Author's Comment:

- Inverters change direct current produced by the PV modules or batteries into alternating current. Grid-tied interactive inverters synchronize the ac output current with the utility's ac frequency, thus allowing the PV system to transfer current to the electric utility grid. Battery-based inverters for stand-alone systems often include a charge controller, which can charge a battery bank from a generator during cloudy weather.

Inverter Input Circuit. The conductors connected to the dc input of an inverter. ▶Figure 690–11

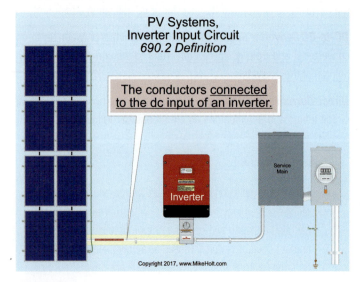
▶Figure 690–11

Solar Photovoltaic (PV) Systems | 690.2

Inverter Output Circuit. The conductors connected to the ac output of an inverter. ▶Figure 690–12

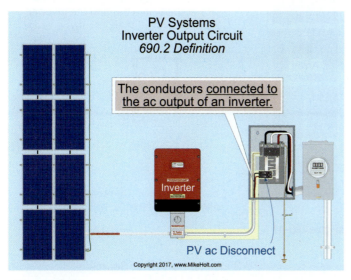

▶Figure 690–12

Author's Comment:

- The output conductors of an ac module are considered an inverter output circuit; see 690.6(B).

Module. A unit of environmentally protected solar cells and components designed to generate dc power when exposed to sunlight. ▶Figure 690–13

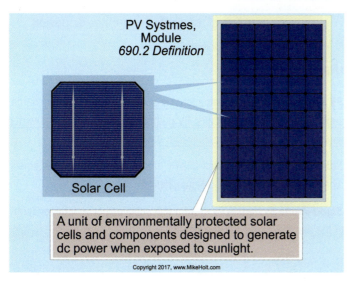

▶Figure 690–13

Author's Comment:

- PV modules are built of solar cells mounted to an environmentally sealed laminate.
- PV modules use sunlight to generate direct-current (dc) electricity by using light (photons) to move electrons in a semi-conductor. This is known as the "photovoltaic effect."

Monopole Subarray. A PV subarray with two output circuit conductors, one positive (+) and one negative (−). Two monopole PV subarrays are used to form a bipolar PV array. ▶Figure 690–14

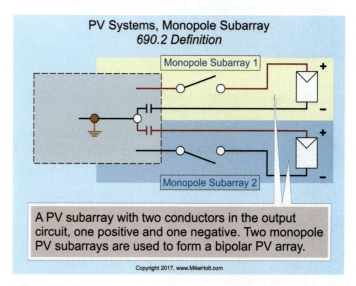

▶Figure 690–14

Multimode Inverter. An inverter having the capabilities of both interactive and stand-alone functions. ▶Figure 690–15 and ▶Figure 690–16

Author's Comment:

- Multimode inverters are also referred to as hybrid inverters. They're still interactive with the utility power source but are also connected to batteries and often a generator for use as part of a standby system.

Panel. A collection of solar modules mechanically fastened together, wired, and designed to provide a field-installable unit.

690.2 | Solar Photovoltaic (PV) Systems

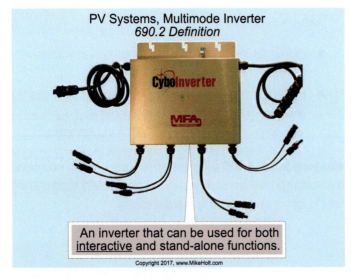
▶Figure 690–15

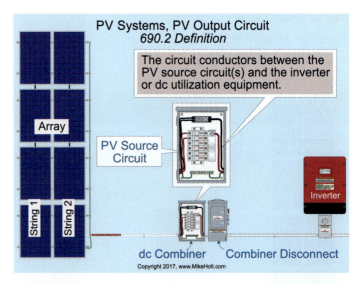
▶Figure 690–17

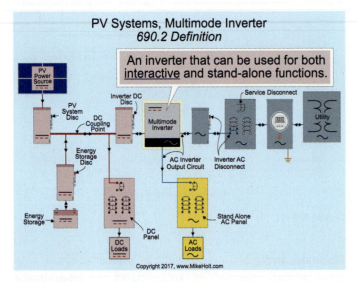
▶Figure 690–16

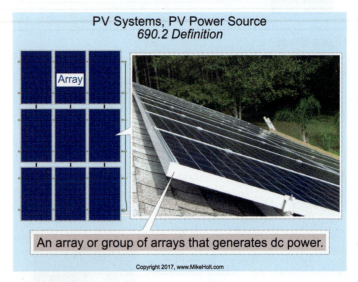
▶Figure 690–18

PV Output Circuit. The circuit conductors between the PV source circuit(s) and the inverter or dc utilization equipment. ▶Figure 690–17

PV Power Source. An array or group of arrays that generates dc power. ▶Figure 690–18

PV Source Circuit. The circuit conductors between PV dc modules, and from PV dc modules to a common connection point of the dc system. ▶Figure 690–19 and ▶Figure 690–20

PV System DC Circuit. Conductor(s) supplied by a PV dc power source, such as the PV source circuits, PV output circuits, dc-to-dc converter source circuits, or dc-to-dc converter output circuits.

Solar Cell. The building block of a PV module that generates dc power when exposed to sunlight. ▶Figure 690–21

Stand-Alone System. A PV system that supplies power independently of the electric utility. ▶Figure 690–22

Solar Photovoltaic (PV) Systems | 690.4

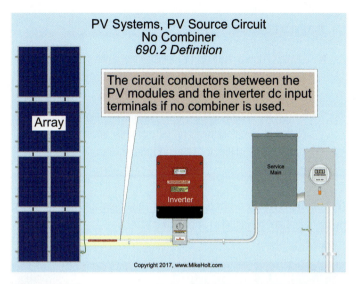
▶Figure 690–19

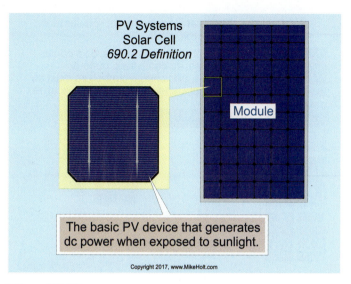
▶Figure 690–21

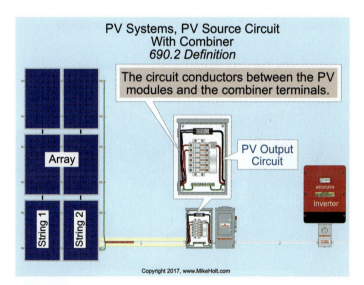
▶Figure 690–20

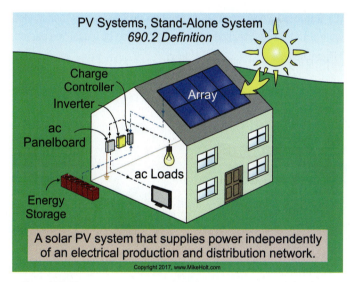
▶Figure 690–22

690.4 General Requirements

(A) PV Systems. A PV system is permitted to supply power to buildings, structures, or other electrical supply system(s).

(B) Listed or Field Labeled Equipment. Equipment for use in PV systems, such as inverters, dc modules, ac modules, dc combiners, dc-to-dc converters, and charge controllers must be listed or field labeled for the PV application. ▶Figure 690–23

Author's Comment:

- Listing means that the equipment is in a list published by a testing laboratory acceptable to the authority having jurisdiction [Article 100].

- Field labeled means that equipment or materials have been labeled or marked by a Field Evaluation Body indicating the equipment or materials comply with the requirements described in an accompanying field evaluation report.

690.6 | Solar Photovoltaic (PV) Systems

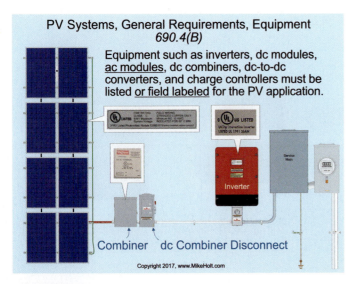

▶Figure 690–23

(C) Qualified Persons. The installation of PV systems, associated wiring, and interconnections must be performed by a qualified person.
▶Figure 690–24

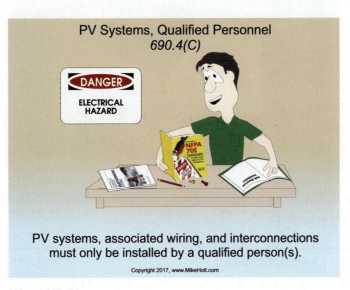

▶Figure 690–24

Note: A qualified person has the knowledge related to the construction and operation of PV equipment and installations; along with safety training to recognize and avoid hazards to persons and property [Article 100].

(D) Multiple PV Systems. Multiple PV systems are permitted to be installed on or in a single building or structure. Where multiple PV systems are located remotely from each other, a permanent plaque or directory must be provided in accordance with 705.10 at each PV system disconnecting means.

Author's Comment:

- Section 705.10 requires the installation of a permanent plaque or directory denoting the location of all electric power source disconnecting means at the disconnecting means location for service equipment and PV system disconnecting means. The plaque or directory must be permanently affixed and have sufficient durability to withstand the environment involved [110.21(B)].

(E) Locations Not Permitted. PV system equipment and disconnecting means must not be installed in bathrooms.

690.6 Alternating-Current Modules

(A) PV Source Circuits. The requirements of Article 690 pertaining to PV source circuits don't apply to ac modules. ▶Figure 690–25

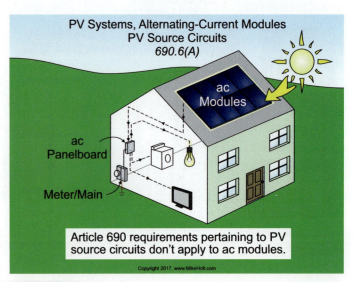

▶Figure 690–25

(B) Inverter Output Circuit. The output conductors of an ac module are considered the "Inverter Output Circuit" as defined in 690.2. ▶Figure 690–26

Part II. Circuit Requirements

690.7 Maximum Voltage

The maximum voltage of a PV system is considered as the highest voltage between any two circuit conductors or any conductor and grounded metal parts.

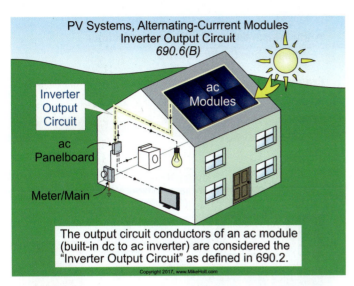

▶Figure 690–26

For one- and two-family dwellings, the maximum PV voltage is limited to 600V dc; for other types of buildings, the maximum PV voltage is limited to 1,000V dc. Where not on or in a building, the maximum PV voltage is limited to 1,500V dc. ▶Figure 690–27

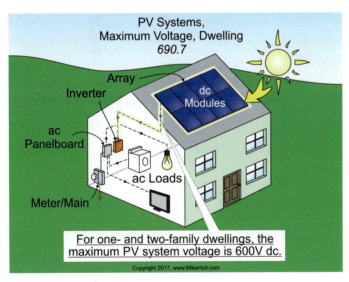

▶Figure 690–27

(A) PV Source and Output Circuits. The maximum PV system dc source and output circuit voltage can be determined by one of the three following methods:

Note: One source for lowest-expected, ambient temperature design data for various locations is the chapter titled *Extreme Annual Mean Minimum Design Dry Bulb Temperature* found in the ASHRAE *Handbook—Fundamentals*, 2013. This temperature data can be used to calculate maximum voltage.

(1) Instructions in listing or labeling of the module: The maximum PV system circuit voltage is equal to the sum of the PV module rated open-circuit voltage (Voc) of the series-connected modules as corrected for the lowest expected ambient temperature using the manufacturer's voltage temperature coefficient. ▶Figure 690–28 and ▶Figure 690–29

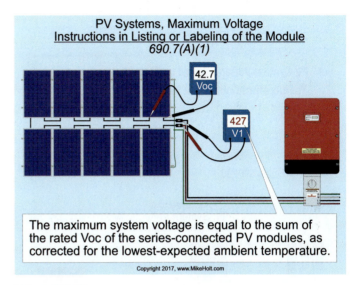

▶Figure 690–28

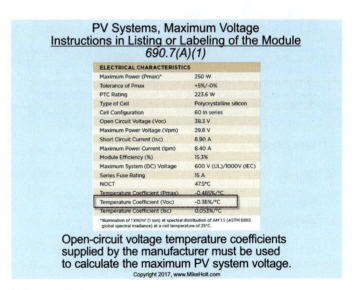

▶Figure 690–29

690.7 | Solar Photovoltaic (PV) Systems

Author's Comment:

- Open-circuit voltage (Voc) is the voltage when there's no load on the system.
- PV module voltage has an inverse relationship with temperature, which means that at lower temperatures, the PV modules' voltage increases; at higher temperatures, the PV modules' voltage decreases from the manufacturer's nameplate Voc values.

▶ **PV System Voltage Based on Manufacturer Temperature Coefficient %/°C**

Example: Using the manufacturer's temperature coefficient of -0.36%/°C, what's the maximum PV source circuit voltage for twelve modules each rated Voc 38.30, at a temperature of -7°C? ▶Figure 690–30

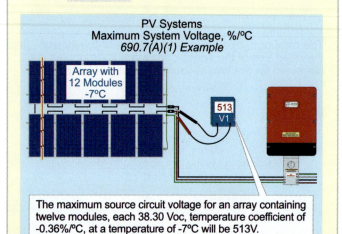

▶Figure 690–30

Solution:

PV Voc = Rated Voc × (1 + [(Temp. °C - 25°C) × Module Coefficient %/°C]) × # Modules per Series String]

Module Voc = 38.30 Voc × (1+ [(-7°C - 25°C) × -0.36%/°C]) × 12 Strings

Module Voc = 38.30 Voc × (1 + [-32°C × -0.36%/°C]) × 12 Strings

Module Voc = 38.30 Voc × (1 + 11.52%) × 12 Strings

Module Voc = 38.30 Voc × 1.1152 × 12 Strings

Module Voc = 42.71V × 12 Strings

PV Voltage = 42.71 × 12 Strings

Answer: PV Voltage = 513V

▶ **PV System Voltage Based on Manufacturer Temperature Coefficient V/°C**

Example: Using the manufacturer's temperature coefficient of -0.137V/°C, what's the maximum PV source circuit voltage for twelve modules each rated Voc 38.30, at a temperature of -7°C? ▶Figure 690–31

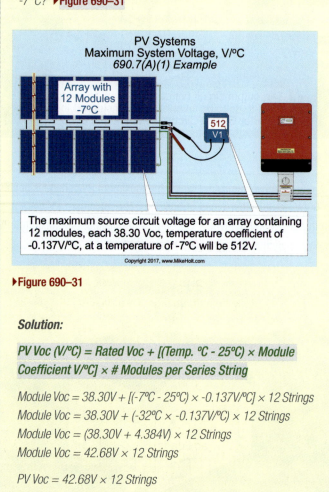

▶Figure 690–31

Solution:

PV Voc (V/°C) = Rated Voc + [(Temp. °C - 25°C) × Module Coefficient V/°C] × # Modules per Series String

Module Voc = 38.30V + [(-7°C - 25°C) × -0.137V/°C] × 12 Strings

Module Voc = 38.30V + (-32°C × -0.137V/°C) × 12 Strings

Module Voc = (38.30V + 4.384V) × 12 Strings

Module Voc = 42.68V × 12 Strings

PV Voc = 42.68V × 12 Strings

Answer: PV Voc = 512V

(2) <u>Crystalline and multicrystalline modules:</u> The maximum PV system circuit voltage is equal to the sum of the PV module-rated open-circuit voltage (Voc) of the series-connected modules as corrected for the lowest expected ambient temperature using the correction factor provided in Table 690.7(A).

Table 690.7(A) Voltage Correction Factors

Lowest-Expected Ambient Temperature °C	Lowest-Expected Ambient Temperature °F	Temperature Correction Factor
4 to 0	40 to 32	1.10
-5 to -1	31 to 23	1.12
-10 to -6	22 to 14	1.14
-15 to -11	13 to 5	1.16
-20 to -16	-4 to 4	1.18
-25 to -21	-13 to -5	1.20
-30 to -26	-22 to -14	1.21
-35 to -31	-31 to -23	1.23
-40 to -36	-40 to -32	1.25

CAUTION: Illumination at dawn, dusk, heavy overcast, and even on rainy days is sufficient to produce dangerous dc voltage. ▶Figure 690–32

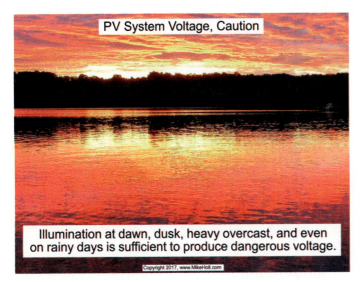
▶Figure 690–32

▶ **PV System Voltage Based on Table 690.7 Temperature Correction**

Example: Using Table 690.7, what's the maximum PV source circuit voltage for twelve modules each rated Voc 38.30, at a temperature of -7°C? ▶Figure 690–33

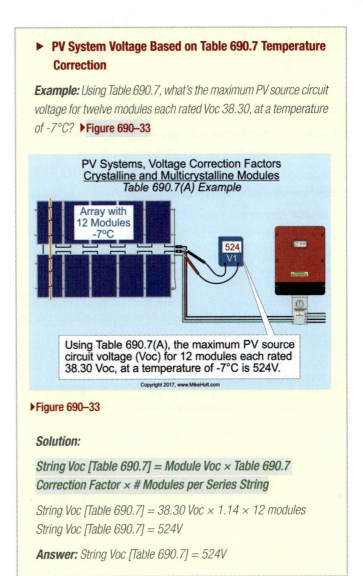
▶Figure 690–33

Solution:

String Voc [Table 690.7] = Module Voc × Table 690.7 Correction Factor × # Modules per Series String

String Voc [Table 690.7] = 38.30 Voc × 1.14 × 12 modules
String Voc [Table 690.7] = 524V

Answer: String Voc [Table 690.7] = 524V

(3) PV systems rated 100 kW or larger: The maximum PV system dc voltage can be determined in a documented and stamped PV system design, using an industry standard method provided by a licensed professional electrical engineer.

Note: One industry standard method for calculating maximum PV system voltage is published by Sandia National Laboratories, reference SAND 2004-3535, *Photovoltaic Array Performance Model.*

The maximum PV voltage value is used when selecting conductors, cables, disconnects, overcurrent protection devices, and other PV equipment.

(B) DC-to-DC Converter Source and Output Circuits. The maximum voltage for a dc-to-dc converter circuit can be determined by one of the two following methods:

690.8 | Solar Photovoltaic (PV) Systems

(1) Single DC-to-DC Converter. The maximum rated voltage of a single dc-to-dc converter is equal to the maximum rated output voltage of the dc-to-dc converter.

(2) Two or More Series-Connected DC-to-DC Converters. The maximum voltage for series-connected dc-to-dc converters is determined in accordance with the manufacturer's instructions. Where no manufacturer's instructions are provided, the maximum voltage for series-connected dc-to-dc converters is equal to the sum of the maximum rated voltage output of the dc-to-dc converters connected in series.

(C) Bipolar Source and Output Circuits. The maximum voltage for a 2-wire circuit connected to bipolar PV arrays is equal to the highest voltage between the two circuit conductors, where one circuit conductor is connected to the functional ground reference point (center tap).

To prevent overvoltage in the event of a ground-fault or arc-fault, the arrays must be isolated from the ground reference and isolated into two separate 2-wire circuits.

Author's Comment:

- A bipolar PV system has two output circuit conductors having opposite polarity to a common reference point or center tap [690.2].
- Two monopole PV subarrays are used to form a bipolar PV array and are usually connected together inside the inverter connection box.
- Where the combined voltages of the two monopole subarrays exceeds the conductor and connected equipment rating, the monopole subarray electrical output circuits must be physically separated in separate raceways until connected to the inverter [690.31(I)].

690.8 Circuit Current and Conductor Sizing

(A) Calculating Maximum Circuit Current. The maximum PV circuit current can be determined by one of the six following methods:

(1) PV Source Circuit Current. The maximum PV source circuit current is calculated by one of the two following methods:

Author's Comment:

- The PV source circuit consists of the circuit conductors between PV modules and from PV modules to a common connection point of the dc system [690.2].

(1) PV System Rated Less Than 100 kW. The maximum PV source circuit current is equal to the sum of parallel-connected PV module rated short-circuit currents multiplied by 125 percent. ▶Figure 690–34

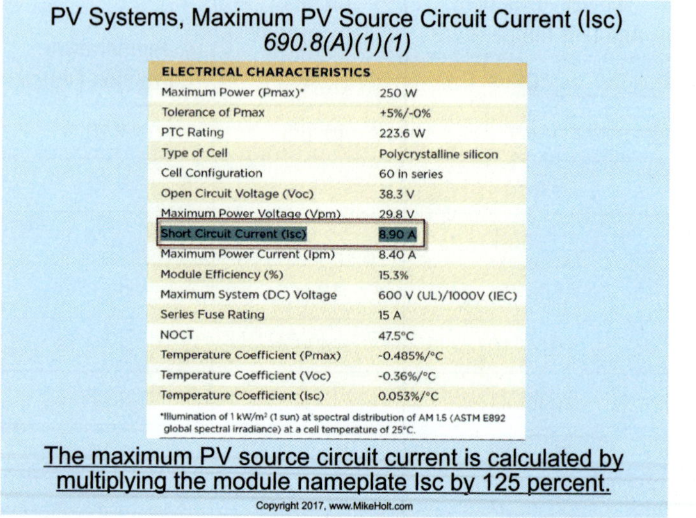

PV Systems, Maximum PV Source Circuit Current (Isc)
690.8(A)(1)(1)

ELECTRICAL CHARACTERISTICS	
Maximum Power (Pmax)*	250 W
Tolerance of Pmax	+5%/-0%
PTC Rating	223.6 W
Type of Cell	Polycrystalline silicon
Cell Configuration	60 in series
Open Circuit Voltage (Voc)	38.3 V
Maximum Power Voltage (Vpm)	29.8 V
Short Circuit Current (Isc)	**8.90 A**
Maximum Power Current (Ipm)	8.40 A
Module Efficiency (%)	15.3%
Maximum System (DC) Voltage	600 V (UL)/1000V (IEC)
Series Fuse Rating	15 A
NOCT	47.5°C
Temperature Coefficient (Pmax)	-0.485%/°C
Temperature Coefficient (Voc)	-0.36%/°C
Temperature Coefficient (Isc)	0.053%/°C

*Illumination of 1 kW/m² (1 sun) at spectral distribution of AM 1.5 (ASTM E892 global spectral irradiance) at a cell temperature of 25°C.

The maximum PV source circuit current is calculated by multiplying the module nameplate Isc by 125 percent.

Copyright 2017, www.MikeHolt.com

▶Figure 690–34

Author's Comment:

- The 125% current multiplier compensates for current produced by a PV source that exceeds the module's rating. A module is able to produce more than the rated current when the intensity of the sunlight is greater than the standard used to determine the module's short-circuit rating. This happens when sunlight intensity is affected by altitude, reflection due to snow or other buildings, refraction through clouds, or the dryness of the air.

▶ **Maximum PV Source Circuit Current**

Example: What's the maximum PV source circuit current for 12 series-connected dc modules having a module nameplate short-circuit current (Isc) of 8.90A? ▶Figure 690–35

Solution:

Maximum PV Source Circuit Current = Module Isc × 1.25
Maximum PV Source Circuit Current = 8.90A × 1.25

Answer: The maximum PV source circuit current = 11.13A

Solar Photovoltaic (PV) Systems | 690.8

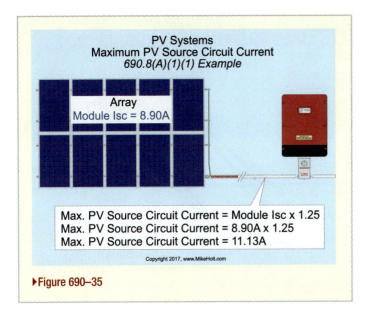

▶Figure 690–35

(2) PV System Rated 100 kW or Greater. For PV systems with a generating capacity of 100 kW or greater, a documented and stamped PV system design, using an industry standard method and provided by a licensed professional electrical engineer, is permitted.

The calculated maximum current value is based on the highest 3-hour current average resulting from the simulated local irradiance on the PV array accounting for elevation and orientation.

The current value used by this method must not be less than 70 percent of the value calculated using 690.8(A)(1)(1).

Author's Comment:

- The value determined in 690.8(A)(1)(1) is equal to 125% of the module Isc; seventy percent of this value would equal 90 percent of the module Isc (125% x 70% = 90%)

Note: One industry standard method for calculating maximum current of a PV system is available from Sandia National Laboratories, reference SAND 2004-3535, *Photovoltaic Array Performance Model*. This model is used by the System Advisor Model simulation program provided by the National Renewable Energy Laboratory.

(2) PV Output Circuit Current. The maximum PV output circuit current is equal to the sum of parallel-connected PV module-rated short-circuit currents multiplied by 125 percent [690.8(A)(1)(1)].

Author's Comment:

- The PV output circuit consists of the circuit conductors between the PV source circuit(s) and the inverter or dc utilization equipment [690.2].

▶ **Maximum PV Output Circuit Current**

Example: *What's the maximum PV output circuit current for two PV source circuits (strings), each containing 12 dc modules having a nameplate Isc of 8.90A?* ▶Figure 690–36

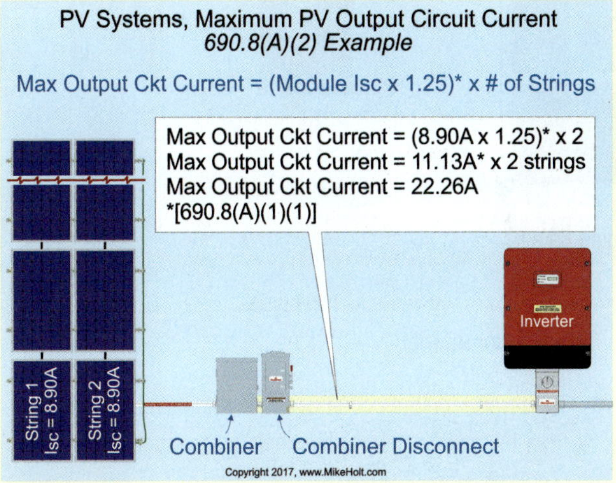

▶Figure 690–36

Solution:

Maximum PV Output Circuit Current =
(Module Isc × 1.25)* × Number of Strings

Maximum PV Output Circuit Current = (8.90A × 1.25)* × 2 strings
Maximum PV Output Circuit Current = 11.13A × 2 strings

Answer: *The maximum PV output circuit current = 22.26A*
*690.8(A)(1)(1)

690.8 | Solar Photovoltaic (PV) Systems

(3) Inverter Output Circuit Current. The maximum inverter output circuit current is equal to the maximum continuous inverter output current. ▶Figure 690–37

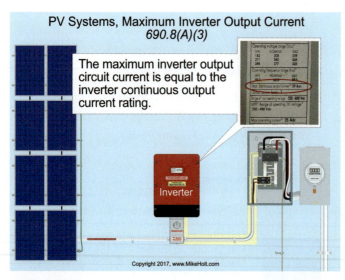

▶Figure 690–37

Author's Comment:

- The inverter output circuit consists of the circuit conductors from the inverter output terminals or ac modules to the ac premises wiring [690.2].

(4) Stand-Alone Inverter Input Circuit Current. The maximum current is the stand-alone continuous inverter input current rating when the inverter is producing rated power at the lowest input voltage.

(5) DC-to-DC Converter Source Circuit Current. The maximum output current for a dc-to-dc converter is equal to its continuous output current rating. ▶Figure 690–38

(6) DC-to-DC Converter Output Circuit Current. The maximum output current for a dc-to-dc converter is equal to the sum of parallel-connected dc-to-dc converter continuous output current ratings [690.8(A)(5)].

(B) Conductor Sizing. PV circuit conductors must be sized to the larger of 690.8(B)(1) or 690.8(B)(2), or where protected by a listed adjustable electronic overcurrent protective device in accordance 690.9(B)(3), not less than the current in 690.8(B)(3).

▶Figure 690–38

(1) Ampacity Before Correction and Adjustment. PV source circuit conductors, PV output circuit conductors, and PV inverter output circuits must have an ampacity of not less than 125 percent of the current as determined by 690.8(A) before the application of conductor ampacity correction [310.15(B)(2)(a)] and ampacity adjustment [310.15(B)(3)(a)]. ▶Figure 690–39

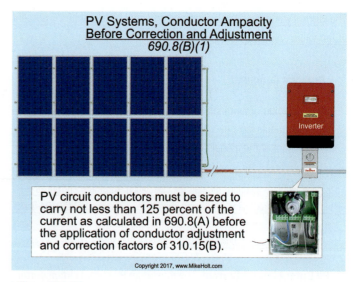

▶Figure 690–39

▶ **PV Source Circuit Ampacity Before Correction and Adjustment Example**

Example: What's the minimum PV source circuit conductor ampacity, before the application of conductor correction or adjustment, for the PV source circuit (string) conductors having a short-circuit current rating of 8.90A? ▶Figure 690–40

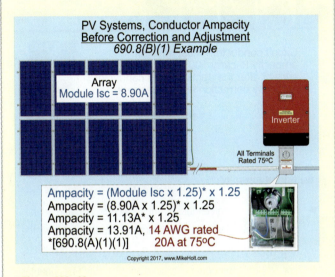

▶Figure 690–40

Solution:

Conductor Ampacity = (Module Isc × 1.25)* × 1.25

Conductor Ampacity = (8.90A × 1.25)* × 1.25

Conductor Ampacity = (11.13A)* × 1.25

Conductor Ampacity = 13.91A

Answer: The conductor ampacity = 13.91A, 14 AWG rated 20A at 75ºC [Table 310.15(B)(16)]

*690.8(A)(1)(1)

▶ **PV Output Circuit Ampacity Before Correction and Adjustment Example 1**

Example: What's the minimum PV output circuit conductor ampacity, before the application of conductor correction or adjustment, supplied by two PV source circuits, each having a short-circuit current rating of 8.90A? ▶Figure 690–41

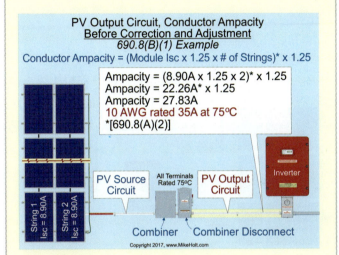

▶Figure 690–41

Solution:

Conductor Ampacity = (Module Isc × 1.25 × Number of Source Circuits)* × 1.25

Conductor Ampacity = (8.90A × 1.25 × 2 strings)* × 1.25

Conductor Ampacity = 22.26A* × 1.25

Conductor Ampacity = 27.83A

Answer: The conductor ampacity = 27.83A, 10 AWG rated 35A at 75ºC [Table 310.15(B)(16)]

*690.8(A)(1)(1)

690.8 | Solar Photovoltaic (PV) Systems

▶ **Inverter Output Circuit Ampacity Before Correction and Adjustment Example 2**

Example: What's the minimum inverter ac output circuit conductor ampacity, before the application of conductor correction or adjustment factors, if the maximum continuous nameplate ac rating of the inverter is 24A? ▶Figure 690–42

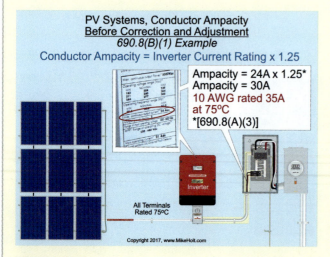

▶Figure 690–42

Solution:

Conductor Ampacity = Inverter Nameplate Rating [690.8(A)(3)] × 1.25

Conductor Ampacity = 24A × 1.25
Conductor Ampacity = 30A

Answer: The conductor ampacity = 30A, 10 AWG rated 35A at 75°C [310.15(B)(16)]

(2) Ampacity After Correction and Adjustment. PV source circuit conductors, PV output circuit conductors, and PV inverter output circuits must have an ampacity of not less than 100 percent of the current as determined by 690.8(A) after the application of conductor ampacity correction [310.15(B)(2)(a)] and ampacity adjustment [310.15(B)(3)(a)]. ▶Figure 690–43

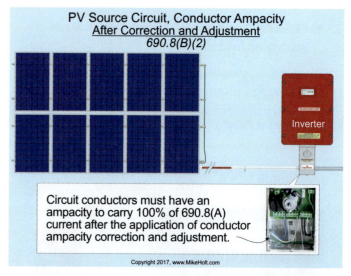

▶Figure 690–43

Author's Comment:

- When performing conductor ampacity correction and adjustment calculations, use the conductor ampacity listed in the 90°C column of Table 310.15(B)(16) for 90°C rated conductors.

- For ambient temperatures exceeding 30°C (86°F), conductor ampacities must be corrected in accordance with Table 690.31(A).

▶ **PV Source Circuit Ampacity After Correction and Adjustment, Example 1**

Example: What's the conductor ampacity after temperature correction for two current-carrying 14 USE-2 or PV conductors rated 90°C within a raceway or cable one in. above the roof, where the ambient temperature is 94°F in accordance with 310.15(B)(3)(c)? The supplying modules have a nameplate Isc rating of 8.90A. ▶Figure 690–44

Solution:

Conductor Ampacity = Table 310.15(B)(16) Ampacity at 90°C Column × Temperature Correction

Temperature Correction = 0.96, Table 310.15(B)(2)(a) based on 94°F ambient temperature.

14 AWG rated 25A at 90°C, Table 310.15(B)(16)]

Solar Photovoltaic (PV) Systems | 690.8

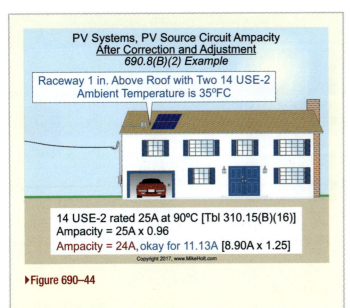

▶ Figure 690–44

Conductor Ampacity = 25A x 0.96

Conductor Ampacity = 24A, which has sufficient ampacity after correction and adjustment to supply the PV source circuit current of 11.13A (8.90A x 1.25) [690.8(A)(1)(1)].

Answer: The conductor ampacity = 24A.

▶ **PV Source Circuit Ampacity After Correction and Adjustment, Example 2**

Example: For an array with modules having a nameplate Isc rating of 8.90A for each circuit; what's the conductor ampacity after temperature correction and adjustment for four current-carrying 14 USE-2 conductors one in. above the roof, where the ambient temperature is 94°F? ▶ Figure 690–45

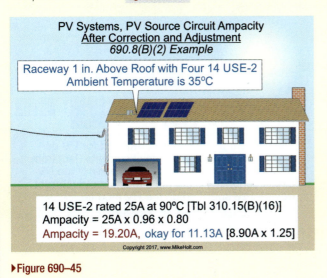

▶ Figure 690–45

Solution:

Conductor Ampacity = Table 310.15(B)(16) Ampacity at 90°C Column x Temperature Correction x Adjustment

Temperature Correction = 0.96, Table 310.15(B)(2)(a) based on 94°F ambient temperature.

Adjustment = 0.80, Table 310.15(B)(3)(a), based on four current-carrying conductors within a raceway or cable

14 AWG rated 25A at 90°C, Table 310.15(B)(16)]

Conductor Ampacity = 25A x 0.96 x 0.80

Conductor Ampacity = 19.20A, which has sufficient ampacity after correction and adjustment to supply the PV source circuit current of 11.13A [8.90A x 1.25, 690.8(A)(1)(1)].

Answer: The conductor ampacity = 19.20A.

▶ **Inverter ac Output Circuit Ampacity After Correction and Adjustment**

Example: What's the conductor ampacity after temperature correction for two current-carrying size 10 RHH/RHW-2/USE-2 or PV conductors rated 90°C supplying a 24A inverter output circuit and installed at a location where the ambient temperature is 94°F? ▶ Figure 690–46

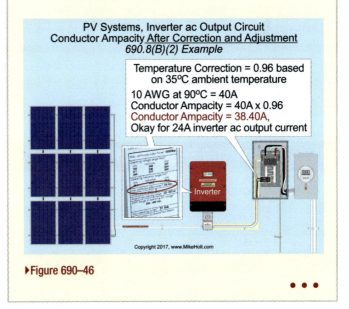

▶ Figure 690–46

Solution:

Conductor Ampacity = Ampacity at 90°C Column [Table 310.15(B)(16)] x Temperature Correction

Temperature Correction = 0.96, Table 310.15(B)(2)(a) based on 94°F ambient temperature

10 AWG rated 40A at 90°C, Table 310.15(B)(16)

Conductor Ampacity = 40A x 0.96 [Table 310.15(B)(2)(a)]
Conductor Ampacity = 38.40A, which has sufficient ampacity after correction to supply the inverter ac output circuit current of 24A [690.8(A)(3)].

Answer: The conductor ampacity = 38.40A.

(3) Adjustable Electronic Overcurrent Protective Device. PV source circuit conductors, PV output circuit conductors, and PV inverter output circuits must have an ampacity of not less than the rating or setting of an adjustable electronic overcurrent protective device installed in accordance with 240.6.

(C) Systems with Multiple Direct-Current Voltages. For a PV power source that has multiple output circuit voltages and employs a common-return conductor, the ampacity of the common-return conductor must not be less than the sum of the ampere ratings of the overcurrent protection devices of the individual output circuits.

(D) Sizing of Module Interconnection Conductors. Where a single overcurrent protection device is used to protect a set of two or more parallel-connected module circuits, the ampacity of each of the module interconnection conductors must not be less than the sum of the rating of the single overcurrent protection device plus 125 percent of the short-circuit current from the other parallel-connected modules.

690.9 Overcurrent Protection

(A) Circuits and Equipment. PV system dc circuit conductors, inverter output circuit conductors, and PV equipment must be protected against overcurrent in accordance with Article 240. ▶Figure 690–47

PV circuits connected to PV modules, dc-to-dc converters, or interactive inverter output circuits and parallel strings of modules or electric utility power, must be protected at the higher current source connection.

▶Figure 690–47

Ex: Overcurrent protection isn't required for PV modules, PV source circuit conductors, or dc-to-dc converters source circuit conductors where one of the following applies:

(1) There are no external sources such as parallel-connected source circuits, batteries, or backfeed from inverters.

(2) The short-circuit currents from all sources don't exceed the ampacity of the conductors and the maximum overcurrent protective device size rating specified for the PV module or dc-to-dc converter. ▶Figure 690–48

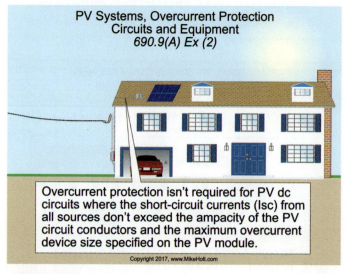

▶Figure 690–48

Note: PV system dc circuits are current limited circuits that need overcurrent protection only when connected in parallel to other dc circuits containing a higher current source. The overcurrent device is often installed on the circuit with the higher current source.

(B) Overcurrent Device Rating. Overcurrent protection devices used in PV system dc circuits must be listed for dc use in PV systems and must be rated in accordance with one of the following: ▶Figure 690–49

▶Figure 690–49

(1) Overcurrent protection for source circuits, output circuits, and inverter output circuits must be sized no less than 125 percent of the maximum circuit currents in accordance with 690.8(A).

> ▶ **PV Source Circuit Overcurrent Protection Device Size, Example 1**
>
> **Example:** Size the circuit overcurrent protection device (OCPD) for a string of modules having a nameplate short-circuit current (Isc) rating of 8.90A. ▶Figure 690–50
>
> **Solution:**
>
> OCPD = (Module Isc × 1.25)* × 1.25
>
> OCPD = (8.90A × 1.25)* × 1.25
> OCPD = (11.13A)* × 1.25
> OCPD = 13.91A
>
> **Answer:** The OCPD = 15A [240.6(A)].
> *690.8(A)(1)(1)

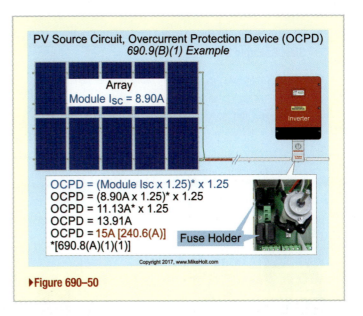

▶Figure 690–50

Author's Comment:

- The PV source circuit overcurrent protection device (OCPD) isn't permitted to exceed the maximum overcurrent rating marked on the PV module nameplate [110.3(B)]. ▶Figure 690–51

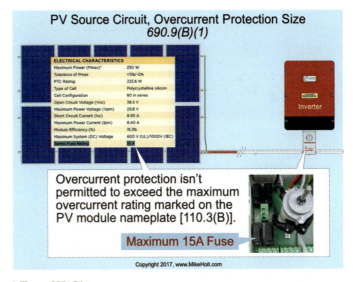

▶Figure 690–51

690.10 | Solar Photovoltaic (PV) Systems

▶ **PV Source Circuit Overcurrent Protection Device Size, Example 2**

Example: Size the circuit overcurrent protection device (OCPD) for two PV source circuits, each having a short-circuit current rating of 8.90A. ▶Figure 690–52

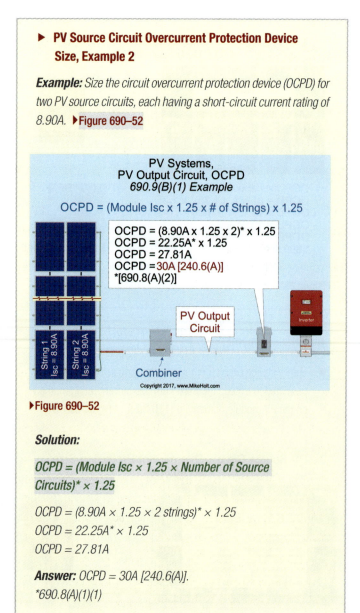

▶Figure 690–52

Solution:

OCPD = (Module Isc × 1.25 × Number of Source Circuits)* × 1.25

OCPD = (8.90A × 1.25 × 2 strings)* × 1.25
OCPD = 22.25A* × 1.25
OCPD = 27.81A

Answer: OCPD = 30A [240.6(A)].
*690.8(A)(1)(1)

▶ **Inverter Output Circuit Overcurrent Protection Device Size**

Example: Size the circuit overcurrent protection device (OCPD) for an inverter output circuit having a maximum inverter continuous ac output nameplate current rating of 24A. ▶Figure 690–53

Solution:

OCPD = Inverter ac Output Current Rating* × 1.25

OCPD = 24A* × 1.25
OCPD = 30A

Answer: Use a 30A circuit for the OCPD [240.6(A)].
*690.8(A)(1)(1)

▶Figure 690–53

(3) Adjustable electronic overcurrent protective devices must be rated or set in accordance with 240.6.

Note: Some electronic overcurrent protective devices prevent backfeed current.

(C) Photovoltaic Source and Output Circuits. A single overcurrent protection device can be used to protect the PV modules, source circuit conductors, or output circuit conductors. The overcurrent protection devices must be placed in the same polarity for all circuits within a PV system and must be accessible.

Author's Comment:

- This means that one polarity (typically positive) is required to have overcurrent protection.

Note: Due to improved ground-fault protection required in PV systems by 690.41(B), a single overcurrent protective device in either the positive or negative conductors of a PV system in combination with this ground-fault protection provides adequate overcurrent protection.

690.10 Stand-Alone Systems

The wiring system connected to a stand-alone system must be installed in accordance with 710.15.

690.11 Arc-Fault Circuit Protection (Direct Current)

PV systems operating at 80V dc or greater between any two conductors must be protected by a listed PV arc-fault circuit interrupter or other component listed to provide equivalent protection. The system must detect and interrupt arcing faults from a failure in the continuity of the conductor, connection, module, or other dc system component.

Note: Annex A includes the reference for the Photovoltaic DC Arc-Fault Circuit Protection product standard.

Ex: AFCI protection isn't required for PV systems not installed on or in buildings, PV output circuits and dc-to-dc converter output circuits that are direct buried, or if installed in metallic raceways. A detached structure whose sole purpose is to house PV system equipment isn't considered a building according to this exception.

690.12 Rapid Shutdown of PV Systems on Buildings

 Scan this QR code for a video of Mike explaining this topic; it's a sample from the DVDs that accompany this textbook.

PV dc circuits on or in a building must include a rapid shutdown function to reduce shock hazard for emergency responders in accordance with 690.12(A) through (D). ▶Figure 690–54

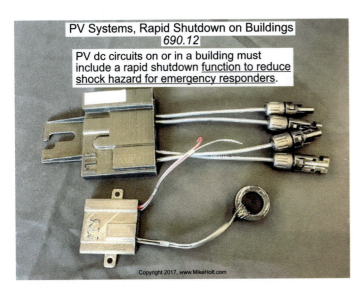

▶Figure 690–54

Ex: A rapid shutdown system isn't required for ground-mounted PV system circuits that enter buildings whose sole purpose is to house PV system equipment.

(A) Controlled Conductors. The rapid shutdown system requirements only apply to PV dc circuit conductors.

(B) Controlled Limits. The use of the term "array boundary" in this section is defined as 1 ft from the array in all directions. Controlled conductors outside the array boundary must comply with 690.12(B)(1) and those inside the array boundary must comply with 690.12(B)(2).

(1) Outside the Array Boundary. Effective January 1, 2017, PV dc circuit conductors located further than 1 ft from the array or more than 3 ft from the point of entry inside a building must have a rapid shutdown system that limits the PV dc circuits conductors to not more than 30V within 30 seconds of rapid shutdown initiation.

(2) Within the Array Boundary. Effective January 1, 2019, PV array conductors within 1 ft of the array must have a rapid shutdown system in accordance with one of the three following requirements:

(1) The PV array must be listed or field labeled as a rapid shutdown PV array.

Note: A listed or field labeled rapid shutdown PV array is evaluated as an assembly or system.

(2) PV dc circuit conductors located within 1 ft of the PV array or not more than 3 ft from the point of penetration of the surface of the building must be limited to not more than 80V within 30 seconds of rapid shutdown initiation.

(3) A rapid shutdown system isn't required for PV dc circuit conductors having no exposed wiring methods, no exposed grounded conductive parts, and installed more than 8 ft from exposed grounded conductive parts.

(C) Initiation Device. The rapid shutdown initiation device, when placed in the "off" position, will initiate rapid shutdown of the PV array. For one-family and two-family dwellings, the rapid shutdown initiation device must be located outside the building at a readily accessible location.

The rapid shutdown initiation device must be one or more of the following:

(1) The service disconnecting means

(2) The PV system disconnecting means (ac disconnect)

(3) A readily accessible switch that plainly indicates whether it's in the "off" or "on" position

690.13 | Solar Photovoltaic (PV) Systems

Where multiple PV systems are installed with rapid shutdown functions on a single service, the initiation device(s) must consist of not more than six switches or six sets of circuit breakers. The initiation device(s) must initiate the rapid shutdown of all PV systems with rapid shutdown functions on that service.

Where auxiliary initiation devices are installed, these auxiliary devices must control all PV systems with rapid shutdown functions on that service.

(D) Equipment. Equipment that performs the rapid shutdown functions, other than initiation devices, must be listed for providing rapid shutdown protection.

Note: Inverter input dc circuit conductors can remain energized for up to 5 minutes with inverters not listed for rapid shutdown.

Part III. Disconnecting Means

690.13 PV System Disconnecting Means

Means must be provided to disconnect the PV system from power systems, energy storage systems, utilization equipment, and associated premises wiring. ▶Figure 690–55

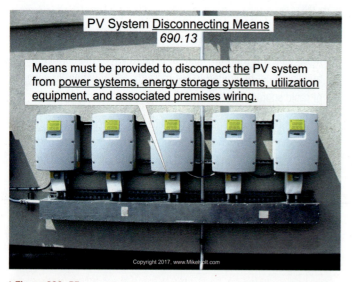

▶Figure 690–55

(A) Location. The PV system disconnect must be installed at a readily accessible location. ▶Figure 690–56

(B) Marking. Each PV system disconnect must plainly indicate whether in the open (off) or closed (on) position and be permanently marked "PV SYSTEM DISCONNECT" or equivalent. ▶Figure 690–57

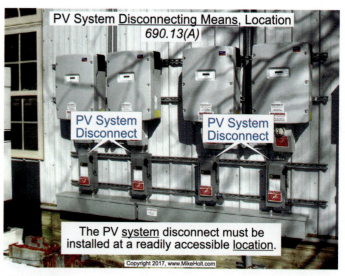

▶Figure 690–56

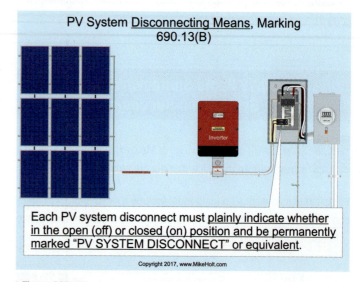

▶Figure 690–57

Where the PV system disconnect also opens the dc circuit conductors, the dc line and load terminals of the PV system disconnect may be energized in the open position. In this case, the PV system disconnect must be marked with a warning sign that's permanently affixed, having sufficient durability to withstand the environment involved [110.21(B)] with the following words or equivalent:

**WARNING: ELECTRIC SHOCK HAZARD
TERMINALS ON THE LINE AND LOAD SIDES
MAY BE ENERGIZED IN THE OPEN POSITION**

Solar Photovoltaic (PV) Systems | 690.15

(C) Suitable for Use. Where a PV system is connected to the supply side of the service disconnect, as permitted in 230.82(6) and 705.12(A), the PV system disconnect must be listed as suitable for use as service equipment.

(D) Maximum Number of Disconnects. Each PV system disconnecting means must consist of no more than six switches or six sets of circuit breakers, or a combination of no more than six switches and sets of circuit breakers, mounted in a single enclosure, or in a group of separate enclosures. A single PV system disconnecting means is permitted for the combined ac output of one or more inverters or ac modules in an interactive system. ▶Figure 690–58 and ▶Figure 690–59

Note: This requirement doesn't limit the number of PV systems connected to a service as permitted in 690.4(D). This requirement allows up to six disconnecting means to disconnect a single PV system. For PV systems where all power is converted through interactive inverters, a dedicated circuit breaker, in 705.12(B)(1), is an example of a single PV system disconnecting means.

(E) Current Rating. The PV system disconnect must have a short-circuit rating sufficient for the maximum available short-circuit current and voltage that's available at the terminals of the PV system disconnect.

(F) Type of Disconnect.

(1) Simultaneous Disconnection. The PV system disconnecting means must simultaneously disconnect the PV system conductors from other wiring system conductors.

The PV system disconnecting means must be an externally operable general-use switch, circuit breaker, or other approved means.

A dc PV system disconnecting means must be marked for use in PV systems or be suitable for backfeed operation.

(2) Devices Marked "Line" and "Load." Devices marked "line" and "load" aren't permitted for backfeed or reverse current, therefore they're not permitted to be used as the PV system disconnect.

(3) DC-Rated Enclosed Switches, Open-Type Switches, and Low-Voltage Power Circuit Breakers. DC-rated enclosed switches, open-type switches, and low-voltage power circuit breakers are permitted for backfeed operation, therefore they're permitted to be used as the PV system disconnect.

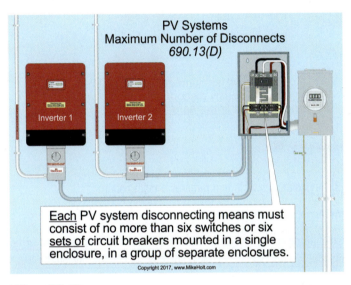

▶Figure 690–58

690.15 PV Equipment Isolating/Disconnecting

Isolating devices or disconnecting means are required to isolate PV modules, ac PV modules, fuses, dc-to-dc converters, inverters, and charge controllers from all conductors. ▶Figure 690–60

Where the current of a dc combiner output circuit, charge controller input circuit, or inverter is greater than 30A, an equipment disconnect is required for isolation, not an isolating device.

Where a charge controller or inverter has multiple input circuits, a single equipment disconnect can be used to isolate the equipment from the input circuits.

Note: The purpose of isolating equipment is to ensure the safe and convenient replacement or service of PV system equipment without exposing qualified persons to energized conductors.

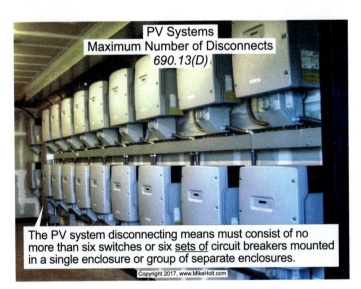

▶Figure 690–59

690.15 | Solar Photovoltaic (PV) Systems

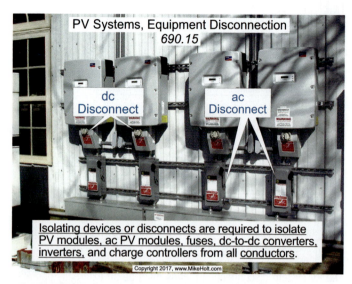

▶Figure 690–60

(A) Location. Isolating devices or equipment disconnecting means must be installed within the equipment or within sight and within 10 ft of the equipment, unless the equipment disconnect can be remotely operated from within 10 ft of the equipment. ▶Figure 690–61

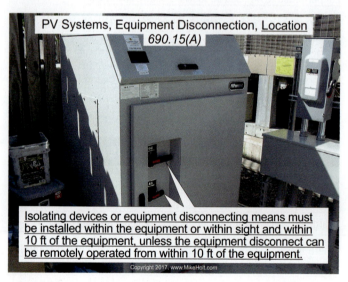

▶Figure 690–61

(B) Disconnect Interrupting Rating. An equipment disconnecting means must have an interrupting rating sufficient for the maximum short-circuit current and voltage that's available at the terminals of the equipment. An isolating device isn't required to have an interrupting rating.

(C) Isolating Device. Isolating devices aren't required to simultaneously disconnect circuit conductors and can be any one of the following:

(1) A connector meeting the requirements of 690.33 listed and identified for use with specific equipment.

(2) A finger safe fuse holder ▶Figure 690–62

▶Figure 690–62

(3) An isolating switch that requires a tool to open

(4) An isolating device listed for the intended application

Isolating devices must be rated to open the current under load or be marked "Do Not Disconnect Under Load" or "Not for Current Interrupting."

(D) Equipment Disconnect Requirements. The equipment disconnecting means must simultaneously disconnect all current-carrying conductors, be externally operable, indicate whether in the open (off) or closed (on) position, and be capable of being locked in the open position. The provisions for locking in the open position must remain in place with or without the lock installed [110.25]. ▶Figure 690–63

An equipment disconnecting means must be one of the following devices:

(1) A manually operable switch or circuit breaker

(2) A connector which must be rated to interrupt current without hazard to the operator [690.33(E)(1)]

(3) A load break fused pull out switch

(4) A remote-controlled circuit breaker that's operable locally and opens automatically when control power is interrupted

Where the line and load terminals can be energized in the open position, the equipment disconnect must be marked in accordance with the warning in 690.13(B).

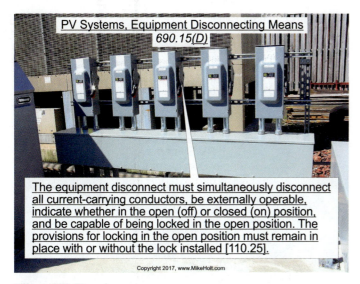

▶Figure 690–63

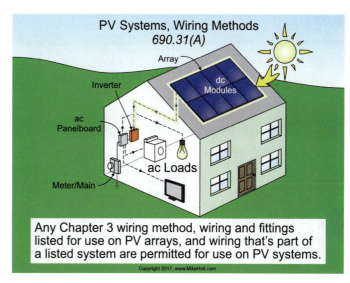

▶Figure 690–64

Author's Comment:

- Section 690.13(B) requires a warning sign that's permanently affixed, having sufficient durability to withstand the environment involved [110.21(B)], and with the following words or equivalent: WARNING: ELECTRIC SHOCK HAZARD TERMINALS ON THE LINE AND LOAD SIDES MAY BE ENERGIZED IN THE OPEN POSITION

Part IV. Wiring Methods

690.31 Wiring Methods

(A) Wiring Systems. Any Chapter 3 wiring method, wiring and fittings listed for use on PV arrays, and wiring that's part of a listed system are permitted for use on PV systems. ▶Figure 690–64

Author's Comment:

- Wiring that's part of a listed system includes the wiring harness of a micro- or mini-inverter.

PV dc circuit conductors operating at over 30V, must be guarded or installed within Type MC cable or a raceway, where readily accessible. ▶Figure 690–65

For ambient temperatures exceeding 30°C (86°F), conductor ampacities must be corrected in accordance with Table 690.31(A).

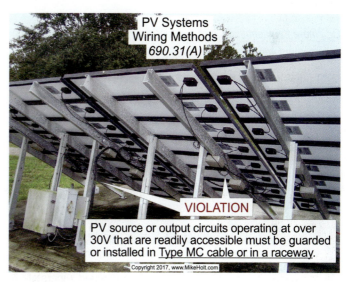

▶Figure 690–65

(B) Identification and Grouping. PV source and output circuits (dc) are permitted to be installed in the same raceways or enclosure with each other, but not with feeders, branch circuits, or inverter output circuits (ac), unless the dc and ac circuits are separated by a partition. ▶Figure 690–66

PV dc circuit conductors must be identified and grouped as follows:

(1) Identification. PV system circuit conductors must be identified at accessible points of termination, connection, and splices by the use of color coding, marking tape, tagging, or other approved means.

Only solidly grounded PV system circuit conductors, in accordance with 690.41(A)(5), are required to be marked with the color white or gray in accordance with 200.6.

690.31 | Solar Photovoltaic (PV) Systems

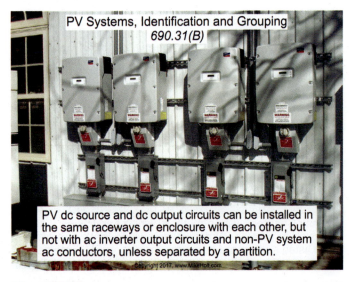

▶Figure 690–66

Ex: Where the identification of the conductors is evident by spacing or arrangement, identification isn't required.

(2) Grouping. Where the dc and ac conductors of more than one PV system occupy the same junction box or raceway with a removable cover(s), the ac and dc conductors of each system must be grouped separately by cable ties, and then grouped at intervals not to exceed 6 ft. ▶Figure 690–67

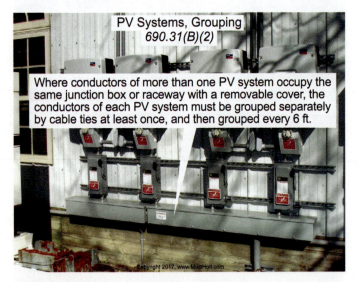

▶Figure 690–67

Ex: Grouping isn't required if the PV circuit enters from a cable or raceway unique to the circuit that makes the grouping obvious.

(C) Single-Conductor Cable.

(1) General. PV source circuit conductors consisting of Type USE-2 and single-conductor cable listed and identified as PV wire are permitted to be run exposed within the PV array where the conductors are guarded or they're not readily accessible [690.31(A)]. ▶Figure 690–68

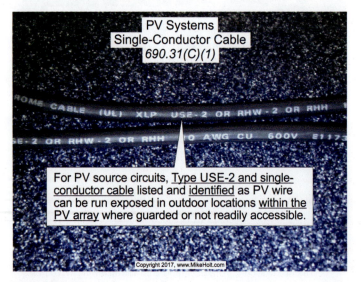

▶Figure 690–68

Note: Because PV wire and PV cable have a nonstandard outer diameter, conductor fill is based on the actual area of the conductor (see manufacturer's specifications) in conjunction with the allowable percent of cross-section raceway for conductor and cable fill contained in Table 1 of Chapter 9. ▶Figure 690–69

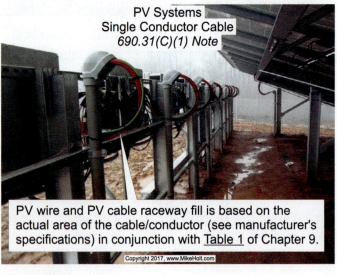

▶Figure 690–69

(D) Multiconductor Cable. Jacketed multiconductor cable assemblies listed and identified for the application are permitted to be installed outdoors. Jacketed cable assemblies must be secured at intervals not exceeding 6 ft.

(E) Flexible Cords and Flexible Cables Connected to Tracking PV Arrays. Flexible cords and flexible cables connected to moving parts of tracking PV arrays must be hard service cord or portable power cable suitable for extra-hard usage, and listed for outdoor use, water resistant, and sunlight resistant.

PV wire connected to moving parts of tracking PV arrays must have a minimum number of strands as specified in Table 690.31(E).

(F) Small-Conductor Cables. Single-conductor cables listed for outdoor use that are sunlight resistant and moisture resistant in sizes 16 AWG and 18 AWG are permitted for module interconnections where such cables meet the ampacity requirements of 400.5.

(G) Direct-Current Circuits in Buildings. PV system dc circuit conductors run inside a building must be installed in a metal raceway, Type MC cable, or a metal enclosure. The wiring methods must also comply with the following: ▶Figure 690–70

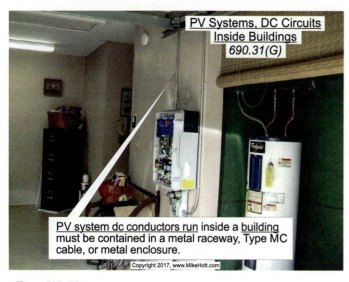

▶Figure 690–70

(1) Embedded in Building Surfaces. PV dc circuit conductors embedded in built-up, laminate, or membrane roofing materials in roof areas that aren't covered by a PV module and associated equipment, must have the location clearly marked in an approved manner using a marking protocol that's suitable for continuous exposure to sunlight and weather.

(2) Flexible Wiring Methods. Flexible metal conduit smaller than trade size ¾ or Type MC cable having a diameter smaller than 1 in. installed across ceilings or floor joists must be protected by substantial guard strips that are at least as high as the wiring method.

Flexible metal conduit smaller than trade size ¾ or Type MC cable having a diameter smaller than 1 in. run exposed further than 6 ft from their connection to equipment must closely follow the building surface or be protected from physical damage by an approved means.

(3) Marking and Labeling. The following wiring methods and enclosures containing PV system dc circuit conductors must be marked with the wording "WARNING: PHOTOVOLTAIC POWER SOURCE" by means of permanently affixed labels or other approved permanent marking: ▶Figure 690–71

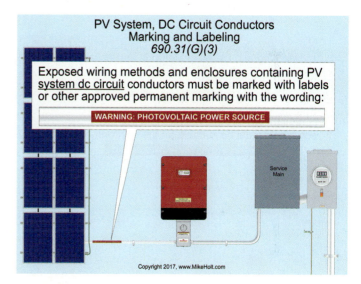

▶Figure 690–71

(1) Exposed raceways, cables, cords, and cable trays

(2) Covers or enclosures of pull and junction boxes

(4) Marking/Labeling Methods and Location. The PV system dc warning marking or labels required by 690.31(G)(3) must be visible after installation and appear on every section of the wiring system separated by enclosures, walls, partitions, ceilings, or floors.

The PV system dc circuit warning label(s) must be reflective, having white text in capital letters not smaller than ⅜ in. on a red background. Spacing between PV system dc warning labels must not exceed 10 ft, and the labels must be suitable for the environment in which they're installed. ▶Figure 690–72 and ▶Figure 690–73

690.31 | Solar Photovoltaic (PV) Systems

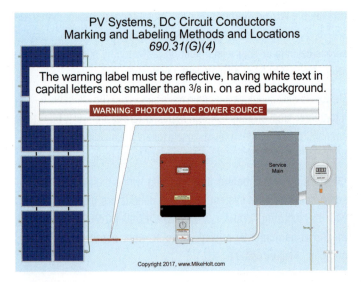

▶Figure 690–72

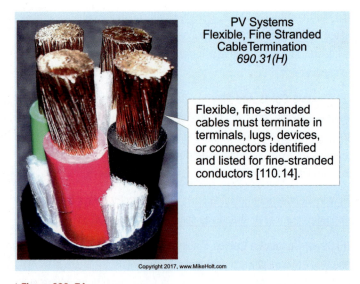

▶Figure 690–74

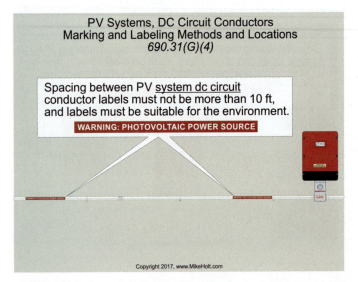

▶Figure 690–73

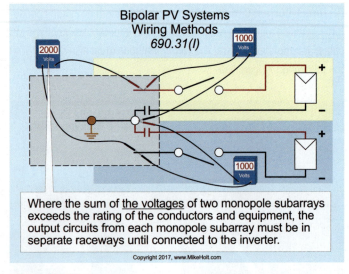

▶Figure 690–75

(H) Flexible, Fine-Stranded Conductors. Flexible, fine-stranded conductors must terminate in terminals, lugs, devices, or connectors identified and listed for fine-stranded conductors in accordance with 110.14. ▶Figure 690–74

(I) Bipolar Photovoltaic Systems. Where the sum of the PV system voltages of two monopole subarrays exceeds the rating of the conductors and equipment, monopole subarrays must be physically separated, and the electrical output circuits from each monopole subarray must be installed in separate raceways until connected to the inverter. ▶Figure 690–75

The disconnecting means and overcurrent protective devices for each monopole subarray output must be in separate enclosures.

Solidly grounded bipolar PV systems must be clearly marked with a permanent, legible warning notice indicating that the disconnection of the grounded conductor(s) may result in overvoltage on the equipment.

Ex: Listed switchgear for bipolar systems rated for the maximum voltage between circuits with a physical barrier separating the disconnecting means for each monopole subarray can be used instead of disconnecting means in separate enclosures.

690.32 Component Interconnections

Fittings and connectors that are intended to be concealed at the time of on-site assembly, where listed for such use, can be used for on-site interconnection of modules or other array components. Such fittings and connectors must be equal to the wiring method employed in insulation, temperature rise, and fault-current withstand, and be capable of resisting the effects of the environment in which they're used. ▶Figure 690–76

▶Figure 690–76

690.33 Connectors

Connectors, other than those covered in 690.32, must comply with the following requirements:

(A) Configuration. The connectors must be polarized.

(B) Guarding. The connectors must be constructed and installed so that they guard against inadvertent contact with live parts by persons.

(C) Type. The connectors must be of the latching or locking type. Where readily accessible and used in circuits operating at over 30V dc or 15V ac, the connector must require a tool for opening.

(D) Grounding Member. The grounding member must be the first to make and the last to break contact with the mating connector.

(E) Interruption of Circuit. Connectors must be one of the following: ▶Figure 690–77

▶Figure 690–77

(1) Rated to interrupt current without hazard to the operator, or

(2) Require a tool to open and be marked "Do Not Disconnect Under Load" or "Not for Current Interrupting."

690.34 Access to Boxes

Junction, pull, and outlet boxes are permitted to be located behind PV modules. ▶Figure 690–78

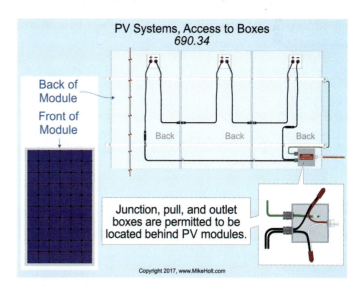

▶Figure 690–78

Part V. Grounding and Bonding

690.41 System Grounding

(A) PV System Grounding Configurations. PV systems must be grounded via one or more of the following grounding configurations:

(1) 2-wire PV arrays with one functional grounded conductor

(2) Bipolar PV arrays according to 690.7(C) with a functional ground reference (center tap)

(3) PV arrays not isolated from the grounded inverter output circuit

(4) Ungrounded PV arrays

(5) Solidly grounded PV arrays as permitted in 690.41(B) Ex

(6) PV systems that use other methods that accomplish equivalent system protection in accordance with 250.4(A) with equipment listed and identified for the use

(B) Ground-Fault Protection. To reduce fire hazards, dc PV arrays must be provided with dc ground-fault protection meeting the following requirements:

Ex: Ground-fault protection isn't required for solidly grounded PV arrays containing two or fewer PV source circuits and not installed on or in a building.

(1) Ground-Fault Detection. The ground-fault protective device or system must be listed for providing PV ground-fault protection.

(2) Isolating Faulted Circuits. The faulted circuits must be isolated by one of the following methods:

(1) The current-carrying conductors of the faulted circuit must automatically disconnected.

(2) The inverter or charge controller fed by the faulted circuit must automatically cease to supply power to output circuits and isolate the PV system dc circuits from the ground reference in a functional grounded system.

690.42 Point of Grounding Connection

Systems with ground-fault protection in accordance with 690.41(B) must have current-carrying conductor-to-ground connection made by the ground-fault protective device.

For solidly grounded PV systems, the dc circuit grounding connection must be made at any single point on the PV output circuit.

690.43 Equipment Grounding and Bonding

 Scan this QR code for a video of Mike explaining this topic; it's a sample from the DVDs that accompany this textbook.

Exposed noncurrent-carrying metal parts of PV module frames, electrical equipment, and conductor enclosures must be grounded in accordance with 250.134 or 250.136(A). ▶Figure 690–79

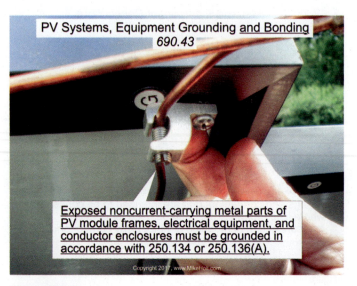

▶Figure 690–79

Equipment grounding conductors and devices must comply with the following:

(A) Photovoltaic Module Mounting Systems and Devices. Devices and systems used for mounting and bonding PV modules must be listed, labeled, and identified for bonding PV modules and are permitted to bond adjacent PV modules. ▶Figure 690–80, ▶Figure 690–81, and ▶Figure 690–82

(B) Equipment Secured to Grounded Metal Supports. Devices listed, labeled, and identified for bonding and grounding metal parts of PV systems can be used to bond the equipment to grounded metal supports.

Metallic support structures for PV modules must have identified bonding jumpers installed between separate metallic sections, or the metal support structure must be identified for equipment bonding and be connected to the equipment grounding conductor. ▶Figure 690–83

▶Figure 690–80

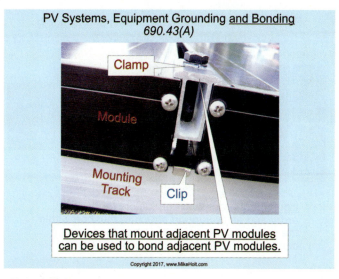
▶Figure 690–82

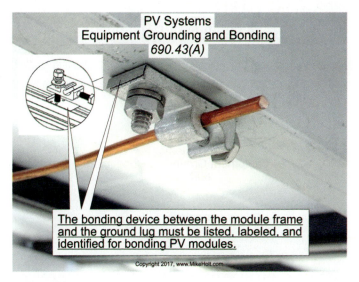
▶Figure 690–81

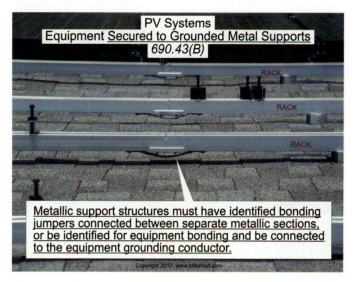
▶Figure 690–83

(C) With Circuit Conductors. Equipment grounding conductors for the PV array and array support structure must be within the same raceway or cable when those circuit conductors leave the vicinity of the PV array. ▶Figure 690–84

690.45 Size of Equipment Grounding Conductors

Equipment grounding conductors for PV source and PV output circuits must be sized in accordance with 250.122, based on the rating of the circuit overcurrent protection device. ▶Figure 690–85

Where no overcurrent protective device is provided for the PV source or PV output circuits, an assumed overcurrent protection device rated in accordance with 690.9(B) must be used when applying Table 250.122.

690.46 | Solar Photovoltaic (PV) Systems

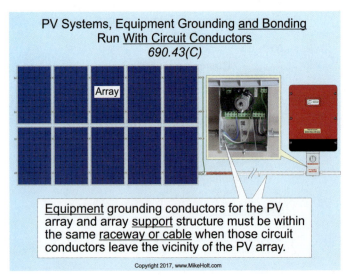

▶Figure 690–84

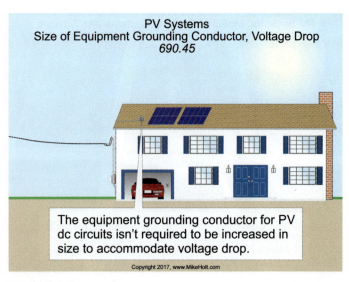

▶Figure 690–86

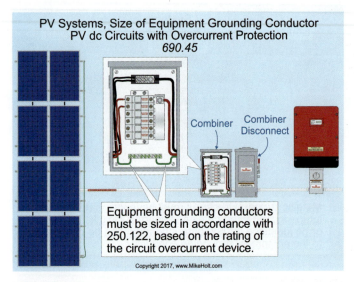

▶Figure 690–85

Author's Comment:

- Where the requirements of 690.9(B) are both applied, the resulting multiplication factor is 156 percent of the module-rated short-circuit current.

The equipment grounding conductor isn't required to be increased in size to address voltage-drop considerations. ▶Figure 690–86

690.46 Array Equipment Grounding Conductors

Exposed equipment grounding conductors, sized 8 AWG and smaller, that are subject to physical damage, must be installed within a raceway [250.120(C)]. ▶Figure 690–87

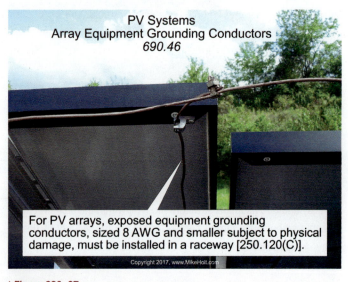

▶Figure 690–87

690.47 Grounding Electrode System.

 Scan this QR code for a video of Mike explaining this topic; it's a sample from the DVDs that accompany this textbook.

(A) Buildings or Structures Supporting a PV Array. A building or structure supporting a PV array must have a grounding electrode system installed at the building or structure that meets the requirements of Part III of Article 250. ▶Figure 690–88

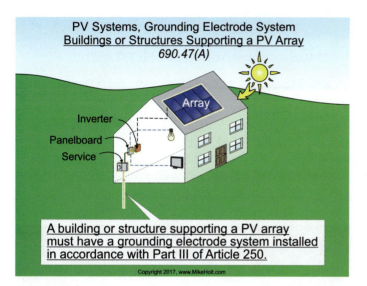

▶Figure 690–88

PV array equipment grounding conductors must be connected to the grounding electrode system of the building or structure supporting the PV array in accordance with Part VII of Article 250. This connection is in addition to any other equipment grounding conductor requirements in 690.43(C).

For functional grounded PV systems, the EGC for the inverter ac output circuit provides the ground connection for ground-fault protection and equipment grounding of the PV array. ▶Figure 690–89

For solidly grounded PV systems, as permitted in 690.41(A)(5), the grounded conductor must be connected to a grounding electrode system by means of a grounding electrode conductor sized in accordance with 250.166.

Note: Most PV systems are functional grounded systems; the ac equipment grounding conductor is the connection to ground for ground-fault protection and equipment grounding of the PV array.

(B) Auxiliary Electrode for Array Grounding. An auxiliary grounding electrode installed in accordance with 250.52 or 250.54 is permitted to be connected to the array frame(s) or structure.

The metal structure of a ground-mounted PV array can serve as a grounding electrode [250.52(A)(8)]. ▶Figure 690–90

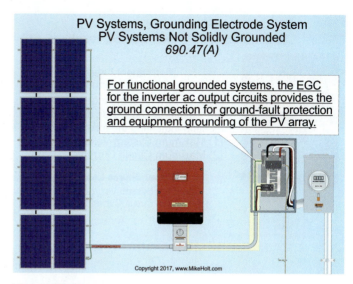

▶Figure 690–89

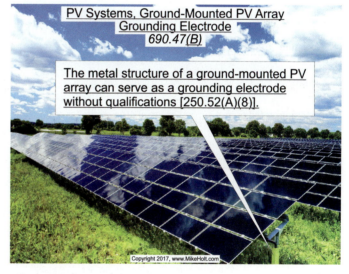

▶Figure 690–90

Roof-mounted PV arrays can use the metal frame of a building or structure if the metal in-ground support structure is in direct contact with the earth vertically for 10 ft or more [250.52(A)(2)].

Part VI. Marking

690.53 Power Source Label

A permanent label for the dc PV power source indicating the following must be installed at each PV system dc disconnecting means and each dc equipment disconnecting means required by 690.15. ▶Figure 690–91

(1) Maximum system voltage

690.54 | Solar Photovoltaic (PV) Systems

▶Figure 690–91

Note to (1): See 690.7 for maximum system voltage calculation.

(2) Maximum circuit current

Note to (2): See 690.8(A) for maximum circuit current calculation.

(3) Maximum rated output current of the charge controller or dc-to-dc converter (if installed)

Where a disconnecting means has more than one dc PV power source, the values in 690.53(1) through (3) must be specified for each source.

▶ PV dc Power Source Label

Example: Determine the maximum voltage and circuit current needed for the PV dc power source label of an array that consists of two source circuits (strings) of twelve 250W modules, each rated 8.40 Imp, 29.80 Vpm, 38.30 Voc (at -7°C), 8.90 Isc. The manufacturer's temperature coefficient is -0.36%/°C.

Solution:

(1) Maximum System Voltage (Voc); Information From Manufacturer

PV Voc = Rated Voc × {1 + [(Temp. °C - 25°C) × Module Coefficient %/°C]} × # Modules per Series String

Module Voc = 38.30 Voc × {1+ [(-7°C - 25°C) × -0.36%/°C]}
Module Voc = 38.30 Voc × {1 + [-32°C × -0.36%/°C]}
Module Voc = 38.30 Voc × {1 + 11.52%}
Module Voc = 38.30 Voc × 1.1152
Module Voc = 42.71V

PV Voltage = 42.71 x 12
PV Voltage = 513V

Imp = Module Rated Imp × Number of Strings in Parallel

Imp = 8.40A × 2
Imp = 16.80A

(2) Maximum Circuit Current (Isc x 1.25), 690.8(A)(1)(1)

Isc = Module Isc × 1.25 × Number of Strings in Parallel

Isc = (8.90A × 1.25) × 2
Isc = 11.13A × 2
Isc = 22.26A

Answer: PV Voltage = 513V, Isc = 22.26A

690.54 Interactive System Point of Interconnection

The point of interconnection of the PV system to other power systems must be marked, at the PV system disconnecting means, with the inverter rated ac output current and nominal ac voltage. ▶Figure 690–92

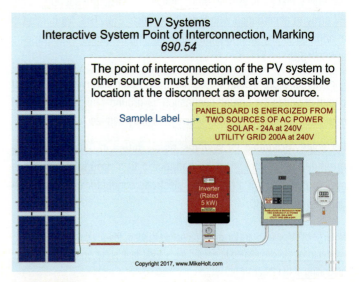

▶Figure 690–92

690.55 PV Systems Connected to Energy Storage Systems

Output circuit conductors connected to energy storage systems must be marked to indicate conductor polarity.

690.56 Identification of Power Sources

(A) Stand-Alone Systems. Any building or structure with a stand-alone PV system must have a permanent plaque or directory placed on the exterior of the building at a readily visible location. The plaque or directory must indicate the location of the stand-alone PV system disconnect and that the structure contains a stand-alone electrical power system. ▶Figure 690–93

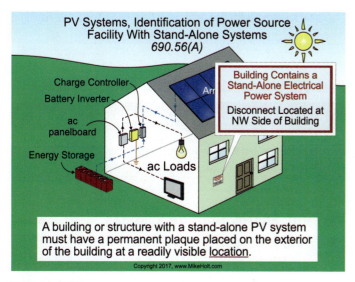

▶Figure 690–93

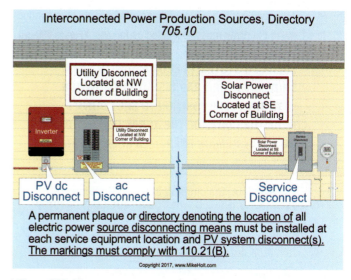

▶Figure 690–94

(B) Utility Power and PV Systems. Plaques or directories must be installed in accordance with 705.10.

Author's Comment:

- According to 705.10, a permanent plaque or directory denoting the location of all electric power source disconnecting means must be installed at service equipment and PV system disconnecting means. The plaque or directory must be permanently affixed and have sufficient durability to withstand the environment involved [110.21(B)] ▶Figure 690–94

(C) Buildings with Rapid Shutdown. Buildings with PV systems must have permanent labels as follows:

(1) Rapid Shutdown Type. Buildings with a PV system rapid shutdown must be labeled as follows:

(a) PV systems with rapid shutdown that shut down the array and conductors leaving the array must be labeled as follows: ▶Figure 690–95

SOLAR PV SYSTEM IS EQUIPPED WITH RAPID SHUTDOWN. TURN RAPID SHUTDOWN SWITCH TO THE "OFF" POSITION TO SHUT DOWN PV SYSTEM AND REDUCE SHOCK HAZARD IN ARRAY.

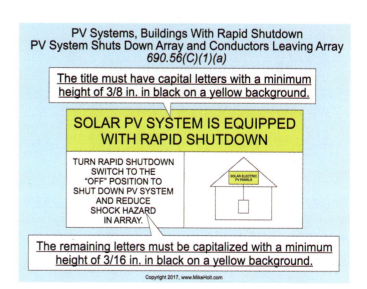

▶Figure 690–95

The title "SOLAR PV SYSTEM IS EQUIPPED WITH RAPID SHUTDOWN" must have capitalized characters with a minimum height of $3/8$ in. in black on a yellow background, and the remaining characters must be capitalized with a minimum height of $3/16$ in. in black on a white background.

(b) PV systems with rapid shutdown that shut down only the conductors leaving the array must be labeled as follows: ▶Figure 690–96

SOLAR PV SYSTEM IS EQUIPPED WITH RAPID SHUTDOWN TURN RAPID SHUTDOWN SWITCH TO THE "OFF" POSITION TO SHUT DOWN CONDUCTORS OUTSIDE THE ARRAY. CONDUCTORS IN ARRAY REMAIN ENERGIZED IN SUNLIGHT.

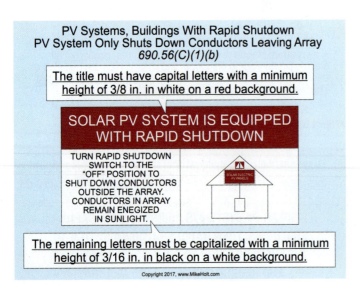

▶Figure 690–96

The title "SOLAR PV SYSTEM IS EQUIPPED WITH RAPID SHUTDOWN" must have capitalized characters with a minimum height of 3/8 in. in white on a red background, and the remaining characters must be capitalized with a minimum height of 3/16 in. in black on a white background.

The labels must include a diagram of a building with a roof and indicate in red the sections of the PV system that aren't shut down when the rapid shutdown switch is operated.

The rapid shutdown label must be located on or no more than 3 ft from the service disconnecting means to which the PV systems are connected and the label must indicate the location of all identified rapid shutdown switches if not at the same location.

(2) Buildings with More Than One Rapid Shutdown Type. Buildings that have PV systems with both rapid shutdown types or a PV system with a rapid shutdown type and a PV system with no rapid shutdown, a detailed plan view diagram of the roof must be provided showing each different PV system and a dotted line around areas that remain energized after the rapid shutdown switch is operated.

(3) Rapid Shutdown Switch. A rapid shutdown switch must have a label located on or no more than 3 ft from the switch that includes the following wording: RAPID SHUTDOWN SWITCH FOR SOLAR PV SYSTEM.

The label must be reflective, with all letters capitalized and having a minimum height of 3/8 in. in white on a red background.

Part VII. Connection to Other Power Sources

690.59 Connection to Other Power Sources

PV systems connected to other electrical power production systems must be installed in accordance with the provisions of Article 705.

Part VIII. Energy Storage Systems

690.71 Energy Storage, General

Energy storage systems must be installed in accordance with Article 706.

690.72 Self-Regulated PV Charge Control

The PV source circuit is considered to comply with the requirements of 706.23 if:

(1) The PV source circuit is matched to the voltage rating and charge current requirements of the interconnected battery cells and,

(2) The maximum charging current multiplied by 1 hour is less than 3 percent of the rated battery capacity expressed in ampere-hours or as recommended by the battery manufacturer.

ARTICLE 691 — LARGE-SCALE PHOTOVOLTAIC (PV) ELECTRIC POWER PRODUCTION FACILITY

Introduction to Article 691—Large-Scale Photovoltaic (PV) Electric Power Production Facility

The requirements for solar photovoltaic (PV) systems are covered by Article 690. That is, until such installations become large enough to be called large-scale PV systems. If they're not under exclusive utility control, they're also covered by Article 691. Article 691 is new with the 2017 *NEC*.

A PV system is considered large-scale when its production capacity is 500 kW or greater. When systems have this much energy available, they pose a much greater hazard than, for example, the small-scale systems you find in single-residence applications.

Because of the extra hazard, a documented review of the electrical portion of their engineered design by a licensed Professional Engineer is necessary to ensure their safe operation. And that review is part of what Article 691 requires beyond simply meeting the Article 690 requirements.

Article 691 specifies several items the documented review must include. Even the fence grounding details must be documented. Conformance to the Article 690 requirements is another of those items; but unlike Article 690, this new article requires the calculations to be documented.

691.1 Scope

This article covers the installation of large-scale PV electric power production facilities with a generating capacity of no less than 5,000 kW, and not under exclusive utility control. ▶Figure 691–1

Note 1: Facilities covered by this article have specific design and safety features unique to large-scale PV facilities and are operated for the sole purpose of providing electric supply to a system operated by a regulated utility for the transfer of electric energy.

▶Figure 691–1

691.2 Definitions

Electric Supply Stations. Locations containing the generating stations and substations, including their associated generator, storage battery, transformer, and switchgear areas.

691.4 | Large-Scale Photovoltaic (PV) Electric Power Production Facility

Generating Capacity. The sum of the parallel-connected inverter rated maximum continuous output power at 40°C in kilowatts (kW).

Generating Station. A plant wherein electric energy is produced by conversion from some other form of energy (for example, chemical, nuclear, solar, wind, mechanical, or hydraulic) by means of suitable apparatus.

691.4 Special Requirements for Large-Scale PV Electric Supply Stations

Large-scale PV electric supply stations must only be accessible to authorized personnel and comply with the following:

(1) Electrical circuits and equipment must only be maintained and operated by qualified personnel.

Note: Refer to NFPA 70E-2015, *Standard for Electrical Safety in the Workplace*, for electrical safety requirements.

(2) PV electric supply stations must be restricted by fencing or other means in accordance with 110.31 and have field-applied hazard markings in accordance with 110.21(B).

(3) The connection between the PV electric supply and the utility system must be through methods to safely and effectively interconnect the two systems.

(4) Loads within the PV electric supply station must only be used to power equipment for the generation of the PV power.

(5) Large-scale PV electric supply stations must not be installed on buildings.

691.5 Equipment Approval

All electrical equipment must be approved for installation by one of the following:

(1) Listing and labeling

(2) Field labeling

(3) Where products complying with 691.5(1) or (2) aren't available, by engineering review validating that the electrical equipment is tested to relevant standards or industry practice

691.6 Engineered Design

Documentation of the electric supply station must be stamped and provided upon request of the AHJ. Additional stamped independent engineering reports detailing compliance of the design with applicable electrical standards and industry practice must be provided upon request of the AHJ. The independent engineer must be a licensed professional electrical engineer retained by the system owner or installer. This documentation must include details of conformance of the design with Article 690, and any alternative methods to Article 690, or other articles of this *Code*.

691.7 Conformance of Construction to Engineered Design

Documentation that the construction of the electric supply station conforms to the electrical engineered design must be provided upon request of the AHJ. Additional stamped independent engineering reports detailing the construction conforms with this *Code*, applicable standards, and industry practice must be provided upon request of the AHJ. The independent engineer must be a licensed professional electrical engineer retained by the system owner or installer. This documentation, where requested, must be available prior to commercial operation of the station.

691.7 Direct-Current Operating Voltage

Large-scale PV electric supply station calculations must be included in the documentation required in 691.6.

691.9 Disconnection of Photovoltaic Equipment

Isolating devices are permitted to be more than 6 ft from the equipment where written safety procedures and conditions of maintenance and supervision ensure that only qualified persons service the equipment.

Note: For information on lockout/tagout procedures, see NFPA 70E, *Standard for Electrical Safety in the Workplace*. Buildings whose sole purpose is to house and protect supply station equipment aren't required to comply with 690.12. Written standard operating procedures must be available at the site detailing necessary shutdown procedures in the event of an emergency.

691.10 Arc-Fault Mitigation

PV systems that don't provide arc-fault protection as required by 690.11 must include details of fire mitigation plans to address dc arc faults in the documentation required in 691.6.

691.11 Fence Grounding

Fence grounding requirements and details must be included in the documentation required in 691.6

Notes

CHAPTER 6 PRACTICE QUESTIONS

Please use the 2017 *Code* book to answer the following questions.

Article 690. Solar Photovoltaic (PV) Systems

1. The provisions of Article 690 apply to solar _____ systems, including inverter(s), array circuit(s), and controller(s) for such systems.

   (a) photoconductive
   (b) PV
   (c) photogenic
   (d) photosynthesis

2. An alternating-current photovoltaic module is designed to generate ac power when exposed to _____.

   (a) electromagnetic induction
   (b) heat
   (c) sunlight
   (d) hysteresis

3. A mechanically integrated assembly of PV modules or panels with a support structure and foundation, tracker, and other components, as required, to form a dc or ac power-producing unit, is known as a(n) "_____."

   (a) pulse width modulator
   (b) array
   (c) capacitive supply bank
   (d) alternating-current photovoltaic module

4. A dc PV array that has two outputs, each having opposite polarity to a common reference point or center tap is known as a "_____."

   (a) bipolar photovoltaic array
   (b) polar photovoltaic array
   (c) a or b
   (d) none of these

5. For PV systems, equipment that regulates the charging process of a battery by diverting power from energy storage to direct-current or alternating-current loads or to an interconnected utility service is known as a(n) _____.

   (a) alternating charge controller
   (b) diversion charge controller
   (c) direct charge controller
   (d) alternating charge regulator

6. An electrical production and distribution network, such as a utility and connected load, is internal to and controlled by a photovoltaic power system.

   (a) True
   (b) False

7. A solar PV system that operates in parallel with and may deliver power to an electrical production and distribution network is known as a(n) "_____ system."

   (a) hybrid
   (b) inverted
   (c) interactive
   (d) internal

8. For PV systems, a(n) _____ is a device that changes direct-current input to an alternating-current output.

   (a) diode
   (b) rectifier
   (c) transistor
   (d) inverter

Chapter 6 | Practice Questions

9. The conductors connected to the direct-current input of an inverter for PV systems form the _____.
   (a) branch circuit
   (b) feeder
   (c) inverter input circuit
   (d) inverter output circuit

10. For PV systems, the conductors connected to the alternating-current output of an inverter form the _____.
    (a) bipolar photovoltaic array
    (b) monopole subarray
    (c) emergency standby power
    (d) inverter output circuit

11. In PV systems, a(n) _____ is a complete, environmentally protected unit consisting of solar cells, and other components, exclusive of tracker, designed to generate direct-current power when exposed to sunlight.
    (a) interface
    (b) battery
    (c) module
    (d) cell bank

12. A _____ subarray has two conductors in the output circuit, one positive (+) and one negative (-). Two of these subarrays are used to form a bipolar photovoltaic array.
    (a) bipolar
    (b) monopole
    (c) double-pole
    (d) module

13. For PV systems, a collection of modules mechanically fastened together, wired, and designed to provide a field-installable unit is called a(n) "_____."
    (a) panel
    (b) array
    (c) bank
    (d) gang

14. The circuit conductors between the inverter or direct-current utilization equipment and the PV source circuit(s) are part of the _____ circuit.
    (a) photovoltaic output
    (b) photovoltaic input
    (c) inverter input
    (d) inverter output

15. A single array or aggregate of arrays that generates direct-current power at system voltage and current is the photovoltaic _____.
    (a) output source
    (b) source circuit
    (c) power source
    (d) array source

16. For PV systems, the circuits between modules and from modules to the common connection point(s) of the direct-current system are known as the "photovoltaic _____ circuit."
    (a) source
    (b) array
    (c) input
    (d) output

17. The solar _____ is the basic PV device that generates electricity when exposed to light.
    (a) battery
    (b) cell
    (c) atom
    (d) ray

18. A _____ is an electrical subset of a photovoltaic array.
    (a) panel
    (b) module
    (c) circuit
    (d) subarray

19. PV systems are permitted to supply a building or other structure in addition to any other _____ supply system(s).
    (a) electrical
    (b) telephone
    (c) plumbing
    (d) none of these

20. All equipment intended for use in PV power systems shall be _____ for the PV application.

    (a) field labeled
    (b) listed
    (c) approved
    (d) a or b

21. Where multiple utility-interactive inverters are remotely located from each other, a directory in accordance with 705.10 shall be provided at each PV system disconnecting means.

    (a) True
    (b) False

22. Grounded dc PV arrays shall be provided with direct-current _____ meeting the requirements of 690.41(B)(1)(2) to reduce fire hazards.

    (a) arc-fault protection
    (b) rectifier protection
    (c) ground-fault monitors
    (d) ground-fault protection

23. A ground-fault protection device or system required for PV systems shall _____.

    (a) interrupt the flow of fault current
    (b) detect a ground-fault current
    (c) be listed for PV ground-fault protection
    (d) all of these

24. Faulted circuits required to have ground-fault protection in a photovoltaic system shall be isolated by automatically disconnecting the _____ conductors, or the inverter charge controller fed by the faulted circuits shall automatically stop supplying power to output circuits.

    (a) ungrounded
    (b) grounded
    (c) equipment grounding
    (d) all of these

25. Article 690 requirements pertaining to dc PV source circuits do not apply to ac PV modules. The PV source circuit, conductors, and inverters are considered as internal wiring of an ac module.

    (a) True
    (b) False

26. The output of an ac module is considered an _____ output circuit as defined in 690.2.

    (a) inverter
    (b) module
    (c) PV
    (d) subarray

27. The _____ of a dc PV source circuit or output circuit is used to calculate the sum of the rated open-circuit voltage of the series-connected PV modules multiplied by the correction factor provided in Table 690.7.

    (a) minimum allowable ampacity of conductors
    (b) maximum allowable ampacity of conductors
    (c) minimum photovoltaic system voltage
    (d) maximum photovoltaic system voltage

28. For PV systems, one source for lowest-expected ambient temperature is the "Extreme Annual Mean Minimum Design Dry Bulb Temperature" chapter found in the ASHRAE *Handbook-Fundamentals*, 2013.

    (a) True
    (b) False

29. For one- and two-family dwellings, the maximum voltage for PV system dc circuits is _____.

    (a) 24V
    (b) 48V
    (c) 250V
    (d) 600V

30. The PV maximum source circuit current is calculated by multiplying the sum of the parallel-connected PV module-rated short-circuit currents by 125 percent.

    (a) True
    (b) False

31. The PV maximum output circuit current is equal to the sum of parallel PV source circuit maximum currents as calculated in _____.

    (a) 690.8(A)(1)
    (b) 690.8(A)(2)
    (c) 690.8(A)(3)
    (d) none of these

Chapter 6 | Practice Questions

32. The maximum PV inverter output circuit current is equal to the _____ output current rating.

    (a) average
    (b) peak
    (c) continuous
    (d) intermittent

33. Currents of PV systems are to be considered _____.

    (a) safe
    (b) continuous
    (c) noncontiguous
    (d) inverted

34. Overcurrent devices for PV systems dc circuits shall be rated to carry not less than _____ percent of the maximum currents calculated in 690.8(A).

    (a) 80
    (b) 100
    (c) 125
    (d) 250

35. Fuses or circuit breakers for PV dc circuits shall be _____ for use in dc circuits and shall have the appropriate voltage, current, and interrupt ratings.

    (a) identified
    (b) approved
    (c) recognized
    (d) listed

36. Overcurrent devices for PV source circuits shall be readily accessible.

    (a) True
    (b) False

37. In grounded PV source circuits, one overcurrent protection device is not permitted to protect the PV modules and the interconnecting conductors.

    (a) True
    (b) False

38. For stand-alone PV systems, the ac current output from a stand-alone inverter(s) can be _____ the calculated load connected to the disconnect, but not less than the largest single utilization equipment connected to the system.

    (a) less than
    (b) equal to
    (c) greater than
    (d) any of these

39. A means is required to disconnect the PV system from all wiring systems including power systems, energy storage systems, and utilization equipment and its associated premises wiring.

    (a) True
    (b) False

40. The PV system disconnecting means shall be installed at a(n) _____ location.

    (a) guarded
    (b) accessible
    (c) protected
    (d) readily accessible

41. The PV system disconnecting means shall plainly indicate whether in the open (off) or closed (on) position and be _____ "PV SYSTEM DISCONNECT" or equivalent.

    (a) listed as a
    (b) approved as a
    (c) permanently marked
    (d) temporarily marked

42. For PV systems, means shall be provided to disconnect equipment, such as batteries, inverters, charge controllers, and the like, from all ungrounded conductors of all sources.

    (a) True
    (b) False

43. The PV disconnecting means shall be externally operable without exposing the operator to contact with live parts and shall indicate whether in the open or closed position.

    (a) True
    (b) False

44. For PV systems, where all terminals of a disconnecting means may be energized when the switch is in the open position, a warning sign shall be placed on or adjacent to the disconnecting means. The sign shall be similar to: WARNING ELECTRIC SHOCK HAZARD. TERMINALS ON THE LINE AND LOAD SIDES MAY BE ENERGIZED IN THE OPEN POSITION.

    (a) True
    (b) False

45. All raceway and cable wiring methods included in this *Code*, other wiring systems and fittings specifically listed for use on PV arrays, and wiring as part of a listed system shall be permitted.

    (a) True
    (b) False

46. Where PV source and output circuits operating at greater than ____ are installed in a(n) ____ location, the circuit conductors shall be guarded or installed in Type MC cable or in a raceway.

    (a) 30V, accessible
    (b) 30V, readily accessible
    (c) 60V, accessible
    (d) 60V, readily accessible

47. PV source circuits and PV output circuits are not permitted to be contained in the same raceway, cable tray, cable, outlet box, junction box, or similar fitting, with non-PV systems unless the two systems are separated by a partition.

    (a) True
    (b) False

48. PV system conductors shall be identified by separate color coding, marking tape, tagging, or other approved means.

    (a) True
    (b) False

49. PV source circuits shall be identified at all points of termination, connection, and splices.

    (a) True
    (b) False

50. The conductors of PV output circuits and inverter input and output circuits shall be identified at all points of termination, connection, and splices.

    (a) True
    (b) False

51. Where the conductors of more than one PV system occupy the same junction box, raceway, or equipment, the conductors of each system shall be identified at all termination, connection, and splice points.

    (a) True
    (b) False

52. Where the conductors of more than one PV system occupy the same junction box or raceway with removable cover(s), the ac and dc conductors of each system shall be grouped separately by cable ties or similar means at least once, and then shall be grouped at intervals not to exceed ____.

    (a) 6 in.
    (b) 12 in.
    (c) 36 in.
    (d) 6 ft

53. The requirement for grouping PV source and output circuits is not required if the circuit enters from a cable or raceway unique to the circuit that makes the grouping obvious.

    (a) True
    (b) False

54. Single-conductor Type USE-2 and single-conductor cable ____ as PV wire can be run exposed at outdoor locations for PV source circuits within the PV array.

    (a) approved
    (b) listed or labeled
    (c) listed and identified
    (d) none of these

55. Where the source circuit operates at over 30V, single-conductor Type USE-2 or listed and identified PV wires installed in a readily accessible location shall be installed in a raceway.

    (a) True
    (b) False

56. Where PV system dc circuits are run inside a building or structure, they shall be contained in _____.

    (a) metal raceways
    (b) Type MC cables
    (c) metal enclosures
    (d) any of these

57. The location of PV system dc circuits embedded in built-up, laminate, or membrane roofing materials in areas not covered by PV modules and associated equipment shall be clearly marked.

    (a) True
    (b) False

58. Which of the following wiring methods and enclosures that contain photovoltaic power source conductors shall be marked "WARNING PHOTOVOLTAIC POWER SOURCE" by means of permanently affixed labels or other approved permanent marking?

    (a) Exposed raceways, cable trays, and other wiring methods.
    (b) The covers or enclosures of pull boxes and junction boxes.
    (c) Conduit bodies in which any of the available conduit openings are unused.
    (d) all of these

59. Labels or markings of PV system raceways and enclosures shall be suitable for the environment and be placed with a maximum of _____ ft of spacing.

    (a) 5
    (b) 10
    (c) 20
    (d) 25

60. Photovoltaic wiring methods containing _____ shall be terminated only with terminals, lugs, devices, or connectors that are identified and listed for such use.

    (a) flexible, fine-stranded cables
    (b) solid conductors
    (c) flexible raceways
    (d) all of these

61. Monopole subarrays in a bipolar PV system shall be physically _____ where the sum of the PV system voltages, without consideration of polarity, of the two monopole subarrays exceeds the rating of the conductors and connected equipment.

    (a) separated
    (b) connected
    (c) joined
    (d) together

62. Listed fittings and connectors that are intended to be concealed at the time of on-site assembly are permitted for on-site interconnection of PV modules or other array components.

    (a) True
    (b) False

63. The connectors permitted by Article 690 shall _____.

    (a) be polarized
    (b) be constructed and installed so as to guard against inadvertent contact with live parts by persons
    (c) require a tool for opening if the circuit operates at over 30V nominal maximum dc or 15V ac
    (d) all of these

64. Junction, pull, and outlet boxes can be located behind PV modules that are secured by removable fasteners.

    (a) True
    (b) False

65. A grounded _____-wire PV system has one functional grounded conductor.

    (a) 2
    (b) 3
    (c) 4
    (d) 5

66. The direct-current system grounding connection shall be made at any _____ point(s) on the PV output circuit.

    (a) single
    (b) two
    (c) three
    (d) four

67. Devices and systems used for mounting PV modules that also provide grounding of the module frames shall be _____ for the purpose of grounding PV modules.

    (a) listed
    (b) labeled
    (c) identified
    (d) all of these

68. Devices _____ for grounding the metallic frames of PV modules and other equipment can be used to bond the exposed metal surfaces of the modules and equipment to the mounting structures.

    (a) identified
    (b) approved
    (c) listed
    (d) a and c

69. For PV systems, metallic support structures used for grounding purposes shall be _____ as equipment grounding conductors or have _____ bonding jumpers or devices connected between the separate metallic sections and be bonded to the grounding system.

    (a) listed, labeled
    (b) labeled, listed
    (c) identified, identified
    (d) listed, identified

70. Devices _____ for bonding the metallic frames of PV modules shall be permitted to bond the exposed metallic frames of PV modules to the metallic frames of adjacent PV modules.

    (a) listed
    (b) labeled
    (c) identified
    (d) all of these

71. All conductors of a circuit, including the equipment grounding conductor, shall be installed in the same raceway or cable, or otherwise run with the PV array circuit conductors when they leave the vicinity of the PV array.

    (a) True
    (b) False

72. Equipment grounding conductors for PV circuits having overcurrent protection shall be sized in accordance with _____.

    (a) 250.122
    (b) 250.66
    (c) Table 250.122
    (d) Table 250.66

73. Where no overcurrent protection is provided for the PV circuit, an assumed overcurrent device rated in accordance with 690.9(B) shall be used to size the equipment grounding conductor in accordance with _____.

    (a) 250.122
    (b) 250.66
    (c) Table 250.122
    (d) Table 250.66

74. Where exposed and subject to physical damage, PV array equipment grounding conductors smaller than 4 AWG shall be protected by a raceway or cable armor.

    (a) True
    (b) False

75. A permanent label shall be applied by the installer at the PV dc power source disconnect indicating the _____.

    (a) maximum voltage
    (b) maximum circuit current
    (c) maximum rated output current of the charge controller or dc-to-dc converter (if installed)
    (d) all of these

76. The point of interconnection of the PV system power source to other sources shall be marked at an accessible location at the _____ as a power source and with the rated ac output current and nominal operating ac voltage.

    (a) disconnecting means
    (b) array
    (c) inverter
    (d) none of these

77. Any building or structure with a stand-alone PV system (not connected to a utility service source) shall have a permanent _____ installed on the exterior of the building or structure at a readily visible location. The _____ shall indicate the location of the stand-alone PV system disconnecting means and that the structure contains a stand-alone electrical power system.

    (a) plaque
    (b) directory
    (c) a and b
    (d) a or b

78. Buildings/structures containing both utility service and a PV system shall have a _____ installed in accordance with 705.10.

    (a) plaque
    (b) directory
    (c) a and b
    (d) a or b

Article 691. Large-Scale Photovoltaic (PV) Electric Power Production Facility

79. Article 691 covers the installation of large-scale PV electric power production facilities with a generating capacity of no less than _____ kW, and not under exclusive utility control.

    (a) 1,000
    (b) 2,000
    (c) 5,000
    (d) 10,000

80. Large-scale PV electric power production facilities are for the sole purpose of providing electric supply to a system operated by a regulated utility for the transfer of electric energy.

    (a) True
    (b) False

81. Large-scale PV electric supply stations must only be accessible to authorized personnel and _____.

    (a) be maintained and operated by qualified personnel
    (b) be restricted by fencing or other means
    (c) the loads within the PV electric supply station must only power equipment for the generation of the PV power
    (d) all of these

82. Large-scale PV electric supply stations must only be accessible to authorized personnel and they are not permitted to be installed on buildings.

    (a) True
    (b) False

83. All electrical equipment for large-scale PV electric supply stations shall be approved for installation by _____.

    (a) listing and labeling
    (b) field labeling
    (c) where products complying with 691.5(1) or (2) are not available, by engineering review validating that the electrical equipment is tested to relevant standards or industry practice
    (d) any of these

84. Documentation of the electric supply station for large-scale PV electric supply stations must be stamped by a licensed professional electrical engineer and provided upon request of the _____. This documentation must include details of conformance of the design with Article 690, and any alternative methods to Article 690, or other articles of this *Code*.

    (a) AHJ
    (b) owner
    (c) building department
    (d) all of these

85. Documentation, by a licensed professional electrical engineer, that the construction of the electric supply station for large-scale PV electric supply stations conforms to the electrical engineered design must be provided upon request of the _____.

    (a) AHJ
    (b) owner
    (c) building department
    (d) all of these

86. Fence grounding for large-scale PV electric supply stations must be in accordance with Article 250.

    (a) True
    (b) False

CHAPTER 7
SPECIAL CONDITIONS

Introduction to Chapter 7—Special Conditions

Chapter 7, which covers special conditions, is the third of the *NEC* chapters that deal with special topics. Chapters 5 and 6 cover special occupancies, and special equipment, respectively. Remember, the first four chapters of the *Code* are sequential and form a foundation for each of the subsequent three chapters. Chapter 8 covers communications systems (twisted wire, antennas, and coaxial cable) and isn't subject to the requirements of Chapters 1 through 7 except where the requirements are specifically referenced there.

What exactly is a "Special Condition"? It's a situation that doesn't fall under the category of special occupancies or special equipment, but creates a need for additional measures to ensure the "safeguarding of people and property" mission of the *NEC*, as stated in 90.1(A).

- **Article 705—Interconnected Electric Power Production Sources.** Article 705 relates to power sources that operate in parallel with a primary source. Typically, a primary source is the utility supply, but it can be an on-site source instead. For instance, in addition to the requirements of Article 690, provisions of this one apply to solar photovoltaic systems that also use another source of energy, such as the electric utility.

- **Article 710—Stand-Alone Systems.** New with the 2017 *NEC*, this article covers electric power production sources operating in stand-alone mode. That is, they're independent of an electrical production and distribution network (such as a utility).

Notes

ARTICLE 705
INTERCONNECTED ELECTRIC POWER PRODUCTION SOURCES

Introduction to Article 705—Interconnected Electric Power Production Sources

Anytime there's more than one source of power production at the same building or structure, safety issues arise. In cases where a power production source such as a generator is used strictly for backup power, the *NEC* requires transfer switches and other safety considerations as covered in Articles 700, 701, or 702 depending on whether the backup power is an emergency system, a legally required system, or an optional standby system. When interactive electrical power production sources, such as wind powered generators, solar PV systems, or fuel cells are present, there usually isn't a transfer switch. In fact, it can be expected that there'll be multiple sources of electrical supply connected simultaneously. This requires careful planning to maintain a satisfactory level of safety when more than one electric power source is present.

Article 705 covers the connection of electric power sources that operate in parallel with a primary source. Typically, the primary source is the electric utility power source, but it can be an on-site source instead.

Part I. General

705.1 Scope

Article 705 covers the installation of interconnected generators, solar photovoltaic systems, and fuel cell systems that operate in parallel with a primary source of electricity. ▶Figure 705–1

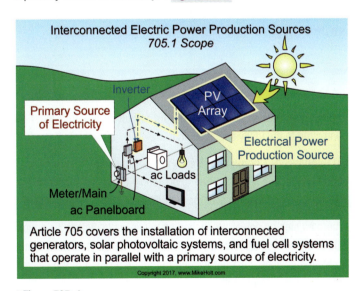

▶Figure 705–1

Note: Primary sources of electricity would be electric utility power or on-site power source(s).

705.2 Definitions

Interactive Inverter Output Circuit. The conductors between the PV interactive inverter and the service equipment or another electric power production source, such as a utility, for an electrical production and distribution network.

Multimode Inverter. Equipment having the capabilities of both the interactive inverter and the stand-alone inverter.

Power Production Equipment. The generating source, and all distribution equipment associated with it, that generates electricity from a source other than a utility supplied service. ▶Figure 705–2

Note: Examples of power production equipment include such items as generators, solar photovoltaic systems, and fuel cell systems.

705.6 | Interconnected Electric Power Production Sources

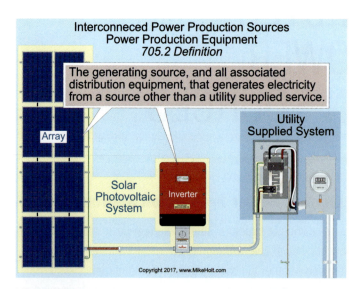

▶Figure 705–2

705.6 Equipment Approval

All equipment must be approved for the intended use. Interactive inverters, engine generators, and energy storage equipment that are to be connected in parallel with utility power must be listed or field labeled for the intended use of interconnection service.

705.8 System Installation

The installation of electrical power production sources operating in parallel with a primary power supply (utility interconnection) must be performed by qualified persons. ▶Figure 705–3

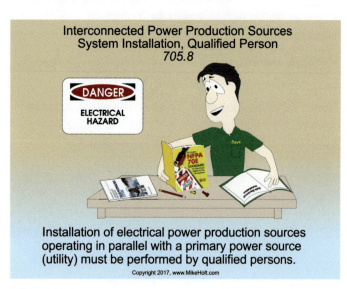

▶Figure 705–3

Note: A qualified person has the knowledge related to construction and operation of PV equipment and installations; along with safety training to recognize and avoid hazards to persons and property [Article 100].

705.10 Directory

A permanent plaque or directory denoting the location of all electric power source disconnecting means must be installed at service equipment and PV system disconnecting means. The plaque or directory must be permanently affixed and have sufficient durability to withstand the environment involved [110.21(B)]. ▶Figure 705–4

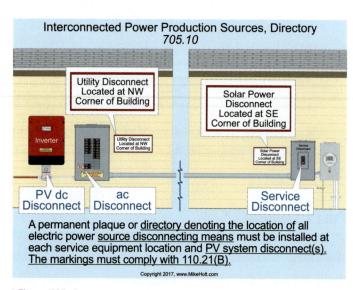

▶Figure 705–4

Exception: Installations with a large number of power production sources are permitted to be designated by groups.

705.12 Point of Connection

The system interactive inverter output circuit conductors must be connected to the utility supply as follows:

(A) Supply-Side Connection. The PV system interactive inverter output circuit conductors are permitted to be connected to the supply side of the service disconnect in accordance with 230.82(6). ▶Figure 705–5

Where an electric power production source is connected to the supply side of the service disconnect, the sum of the ratings of all overcurrent protection devices must not exceed the ampere rating of the electric utility service. ▶Figure 705–6

Interconnected Electric Power Production Sources | 705.12

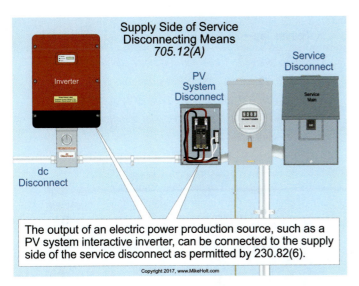

▶Figure 705–5

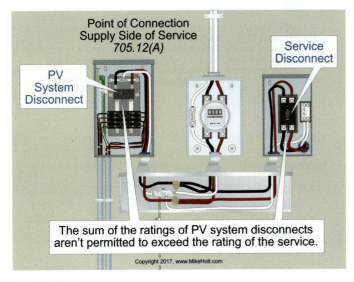

▶Figure 705–6

Author's Comment:

- When determining the number of disconnects per service in accordance with 230.71(A), the PV disconnect(s) connected on the supply side of service equipment isn't counted, since it's not a service disconnect as defined in Article 100.

(B) Load-Side Connection. PV systems terminate to the load side of the service disconnect must comply with the following requirements:

(1) Dedicated Overcurrent and Disconnect. PV system circuit conductors must terminate to a dedicated circuit breaker or fusible disconnecting means.

(2) Bus or Conductor Ampere Rating.

(1) Feeders.

Where the PV system connection is made to a feeder, that portion of the feeder on the load side of the power source output connection must be protected by one of the following methods:

a. The feeder must have an ampacity equal to or greater than the feeder protection device rating plus 125 percent of the PV system rated output circuit current. ▶Figure 705–7

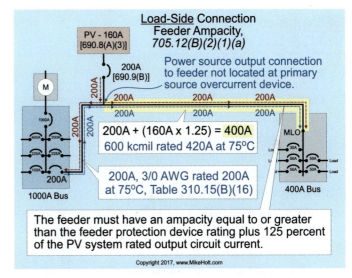

▶Figure 705–7

b. An overcurrent device on the load side of the PV system connection must not exceed the ampacity of the feeder. ▶Figure 705–8

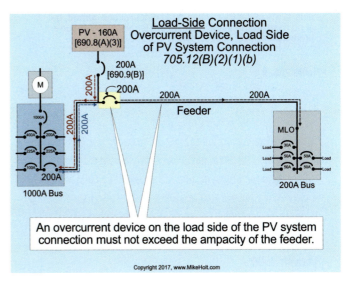

▶Figure 705–8

705.12 | Interconnected Electric Power Production Sources

(2) Feeder Tap Sizing.

10-Foot Tap. PV system taps not longer than 10 ft must have an ampacity not less than ten percent of the sum of the feeder protection device plus 125 percent of the PV system rated output circuit current, but in no case less than the rating of the terminating overcurrent protection device, in accordance with 240.21(B)(1).

25-Foot Tap. PV system taps not longer than 25 ft must have an ampacity not less than thirty-three percent of the sum of the feeder protection device plus 125 percent of the PV system rated output circuit current, but in no case less than the rating of the terminating overcurrent protection device, in accordance with 240.21(B)(1).

▶ **Feeder Tap—10-Foot Rule**

Example: What size feeder tap conductor (not longer than 10 ft) will be required for a tap to a 100A overcurrent protection device made between a feeder overcurrent protection device rated 200A and an inverter with ac output current rated 160A? ▶Figure 705–9

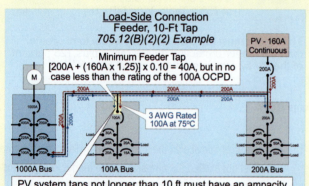

▶Figure 705–9

Solution:

Feeder tap conductors must have an ampacity not less than 1/10 the ampacity of the 200A feeder overcurrent protection device and 160A inverter ac output current rating. 200A + (160A x 1.25) = 400A x 0.10 = 40A [240.21(B)(2)(1)], and not less than the rating of the termination of the tap overcurrent protection device of 100A [240.21(B)(1)(4)].

Answer: 100A

▶ **Feeder Tap—25-Foot Rule**

Example: What size feeder tap conductor (longer than 10 ft but not over 25 ft) will be required for a tap to a 100A overcurrent protection device made between a feeder overcurrent protection device rated 200A and an inverter with ac output current rated 160A? ▶Figure 705–10

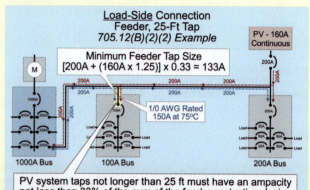

▶Figure 705–10

Solution:

Feeder tap conductors must have an ampacity no less than 1/3 the ampacity of the 200A feeder overcurrent protection device and 160A inverter ac output current rating, 200A + (160A x 1.25) = 400A x 0.3333 = 133A [240.21(B)(2)(1)], and not less than the rating of the termination of the tap overcurrent protection device of 100A [240.21(B)(2)(1)].

Answer: 133A

(3) Busbars Protection.

Busbars ratings must have an ampacity by one of the following methods.

(a) One-Hundred and Twenty-Five Percent Rule. The busbar must have an ampacity of no less than 125 percent of the PV system output circuit current rating, plus the rating of the overcurrent device protecting the busbar. ▶Figure 705–11

Interconnected Electric Power Production Sources | 705.12

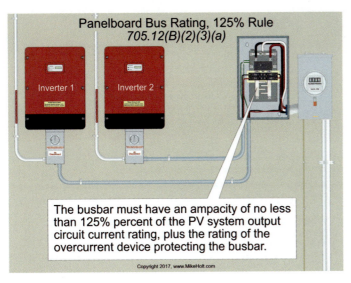

▶Figure 705–11

Solution:

Busbar Ampere Rating => Panelboard Overcurrent + (Inverter Output Current x 1.25)

Buss Rating => 200A + (24A x 1.25 x 2)
Buss Rating => 200A + 30A + 30A
Buss Rating => 260A

Answer: No, 260A required exceeds 200A bus rating.

(b) One-Hundred and Twenty Percent Rule. Where the PV system overcurrent protection device is located at the opposite end of the feeder conductor termination, the sum of 125 percent of the PV system output circuit current rating, plus the rating of the overcurrent device protecting the busbar isn't permitted to exceed 120 percent of the busbar ampacity.
▶Figure 705–13

▶ **Panelboard Busbar Ampere Rating—Not Opposite Feeder Termination, Example**

Example: Can a panelboard having a 200A rated busbar, protected by a 200A overcurrent protection device be supplied by two inverters each having an output ac current rating of 24A, located not opposite feeder termination? ▶Figure 705–12

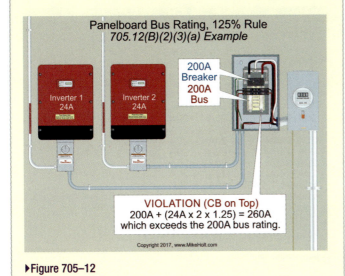

▶Figure 705–12

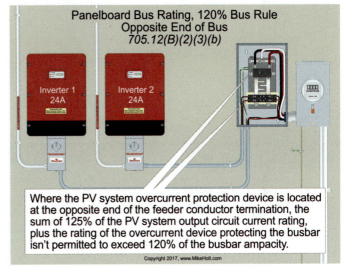

▶Figure 705–13

A permanent warning label, complying with 110.21(B), must be applied to the distribution equipment adjacent to the back-fed breaker:

**WARNING: POWER SOURCE OUTPUT CONNECTION—
DO NOT RELOCATE THIS OVERCURRENT DEVICE.**

705.12 | Interconnected Electric Power Production Sources

▶ **Panelboard Busbar Ampere Rating—Opposite Feeder Termination, Example**

Example: Can a panelboard having a 200A rated busbar, protected by a 175A overcurrent protection device be supplied by two inverters each having an output ac current rating of 24A located opposite the feeder termination? ▶Figure 705–14

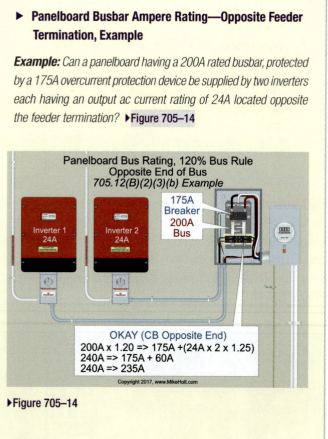

▶Figure 705–14

Solution:

Busbar Ampere Rating x 1.20 => Panelboard Overcurrent + (Inverter Output Current x 1.25)

200A x 1.20 => 175A + (24A x 1.25 x 2)

240A => 175A + 30A + 30A

240A => 235A

Answer: No

(c) One-Hundred Percent Rule. The sum of the ampere ratings of all overcurrent devices on the busbar does not exceed the ampacity of the busbar. ▶Figure 705–15

A permanent warning label, complying with 110.21(B), must be applied to the distribution equipment:

WARNING: THIS EQUIPMENT FED BY MULTIPLE SOURCES. TOTAL RATING OF ALL OVERCURRENT DEVICES EXCLUDING MAIN SUPPLY OVERCURRENT DEVICE SHALL NOT EXCEED AMPACITY OF BUSBAR.

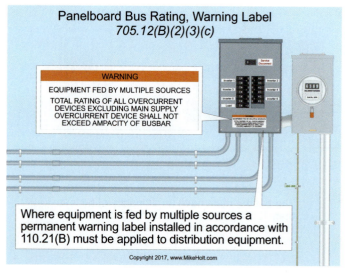

▶Figure 705–15

▶ **Panelboard Busbar Ampere Rating—Breakers Not to Exceed Busbar Ampere Rating, Example 1**

Example: What's the minimum busbar ampere rating for a panelboard containing two 30A, two-pole, 240V circuit breakers and six 20A, 240V, two-pole circuit breakers? ▶Figure 705–16

Answer: 180A

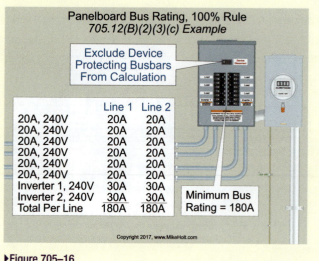

▶Figure 705–16

Interconnected Electric Power Production Sources | 705.12

▶ **Panelboard Busbar Ampere Rating—Breakers Not to Exceed Busbar Ampere Rating, Example 2**

Example: What's the minimum busbar ampere rating for a panelboard containing six 30A, two-pole, 240V circuit breakers and one 20A, 120V, one-pole circuit breaker? ▶Figure 705–17

Answer: (c) 200A

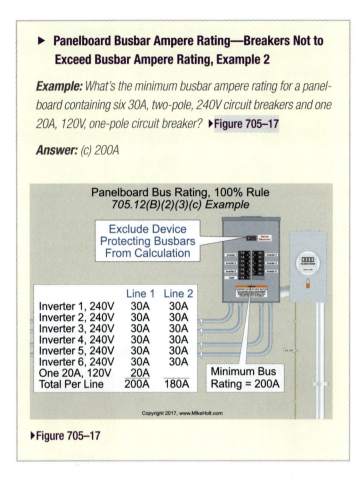

▶Figure 705–17

(3) Marking. Panelboards containing PV ac inverter circuit breakers must be field marked to indicate the presence of all sources of all power. ▶Figure 705–19

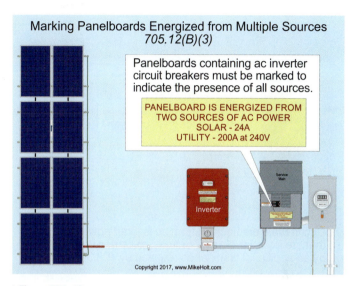

▶Figure 705–19

(4) Suitable for Backfeed. Circuit breakers that aren't marked "Line" and "Load" can be backfed. ▶Figure 705–20

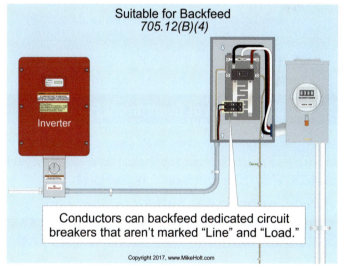

▶Figure 705–20

Note: Fused disconnects are suitable for backfeed applications, unless otherwise marked.

(d) Center-Fed Panelboard. The sum of 125 percent of the PV system output circuit current rating, plus the rating of the overcurrent device protecting the busbar isn't permitted to exceed 120 percent of the busbar ampacity. ▶Figure 705–18

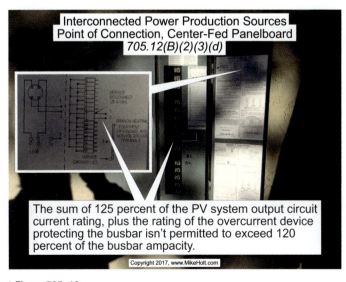

▶Figure 705–18

705.31 | Interconnected Electric Power Production Sources

(5) Fastening. Backfed circuit breakers for interactive inverter circuits aren't required to be secured in place by an additional fastener as required by 408.36(D). ▶Figure 705–21

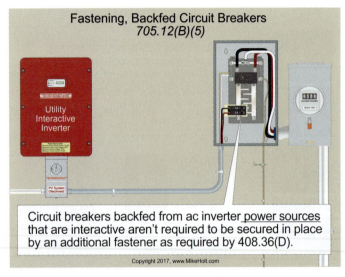

▶Figure 705–21

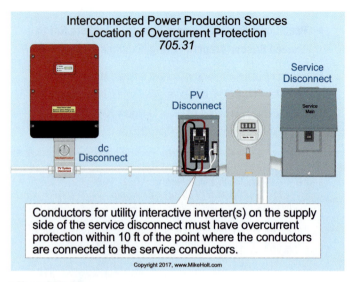

▶Figure 705–22

Author's Comment:

- PV ac inverter circuit breakers aren't required to be fastened in place because the PV interactive inverter automatically ceases to export ac current from the inverter when the breaker is removed.

705.31 Location of Overcurrent Protection

Supply-side conductor connections for PV systems must terminate in an overcurrent protection device that's located within 10 ft of the point of interconnection to the electric utility. ▶Figure 705–22

705.40 Loss of Utility Power

Upon loss of the electric utility power, the inverter ac output circuit must automatically disconnect from the electric utility power source and not reconnect until the electric utility power source has been restored.

Ex: A listed interactive inverter is permitted to automatically cease exporting power upon loss of electric utility power and resume exporting power once the electric utility power source has been restored. ▶Figure 705–23

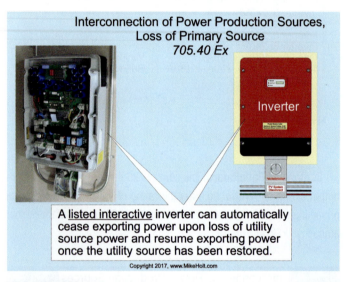

▶Figure 705–23

Part II. Interactive Inverters

705.100 Voltage Unbalanced (Imbalanced) Interconnections

(A) Single-phase. Single-phase inverters connected to a three-phase electric utility power source must not increase electric utility unbalanced system voltage at the service to more than three percent.

Note: See ANSI/C84.1, *Electric Power Systems and Equipment—Voltage Ratings (60 Hertz).*

Interconnected Electric Power Production Sources | 705.100

Author's Comment:

- An example of an unbalanced interconnection would be connecting two single-phase inverters to a three-phase system.

- ANSI C84.1 recommends that "electric supply systems should be designed to limit the maximum voltage unbalance to three percent when measured at the electric-utility revenue meter under no-load conditions." Improperly connecting single-phase inverters to a three-phase system can result in a significant increase in unbalanced system voltage. Three-phase motors will run hotter using unbalanced voltage because the unbalanced magnetic fields created by the windings work against each other. The formula to determine maximum unbalanced voltage is:

Maximum Unbalanced Voltage = 100 x Maximum Deviation from Average Voltage/Average Voltage.

▶ **Existing Installation**

Example: If we connect two single-phase PV systems to lines B – C and this causes the B – C voltage to increase from 200V to 202V because of a decrease in loading, the maximum unbalanced system voltage for the following line voltages: A – B 206V, B – C 201V, and A – C 204V will be _____ percent.

Solution:

Maximum Unbalanced Voltage = Maximum Deviation Volts from Average Voltage/Average Voltage x 100 (for Percent)

Average Voltage = (206V + 202V + 204V)/3 lines = 204V

Maximum Deviation from Average = 206V – 204 = 2V
Maximum Unbalanced Voltage = 2V/204V x 100 = 1%

Answer: 1 percent

▶ **Unbalanced System Voltage—Two Inverters, Example 1**

Example: If we connect two single-phase PV systems to lines B – C and this results in B – C voltage to rise from 200V to 201V because of a decrease in loading, the maximum unbalanced system voltage for the following line voltages: A – B 206V, B – C 201V, and A – C 204V will be _____ percent.

Solution:

Maximum Unbalanced Voltage = Maximum Deviation from Average Voltage/Average Voltage x 100 (for Percent)

Average Voltage = (206V + 201V + 204V)/3 lines = 203.66V

Maximum Deviation from Average = 206V – 203.66V = 2.34V
Maximum Unbalanced Voltage = 2.34V/203.66V x 100 = 1.15%

Answer: 1.15 percent

▶ **Unbalanced System Voltage—Two Inverters, Example 2**

Example: If we connect two single-phase PV systems to lines A – B and this causes the A – B voltage to increase from 206V to 208V because of a decrease in loading, the maximum unbalanced system voltage for the following line voltages: A – B 208V, B – C 200V, and A – C 204V will be _____ percent.

Solution:

Maximum Unbalanced Voltage = Maximum Deviation from Average Voltage/Average Voltage x 100 (for Percent)

Average Voltage = (208V + 200V + 204V)/3 lines = 204V

Maximum Deviation from Average = 208V – 204V = 4V
Maximum Unbalanced Voltage = 4V/204V x 100 = 1.96%

Answer: 1.96 percent

Notes

ARTICLE 710 — STAND-ALONE SYSTEMS

Introduction to Article 710—Stand-Alone Systems

The requirements for stand-alone power production sources are covered here in Article 710. Stand-alone sources are what the name implies; they aren't connected to the grid or any other power production/distribution network.

These sources must also comply with Chapters 1 through 4 of the *NEC*. Depending upon the purpose and design of a particular stand-alone source, it may also be covered by a Chapter 6 and/or another Chapter 7 article. For example, if it's a stand-alone fuel cell optional standby system, then it's also covered by Article 692 and Article 702.

Occupying about half a page, Article 710 is one of the shortest in the *Code*, but its brevity doesn't imply insignificance. In fact, this article will take on increasing significance as the growth in stand-alone system installations continues. Many of these are systems use wind, solar, and other "alternative energy" sources, but fossil fuel sources are also in the mix.

The main point of here is to relieve the designer from some of the constraints imposed upon interconnected systems. For example, you can size the source smaller than the total calculated load, but not smaller than the largest single connected utilization equipment. There are also restrictions; for example, you can't have backfed breakers. If you understand the requirements and what's permitted, you can design a safe system at a lower cost of construction/installation.

710.1 Scope

This article covers electric power production sources operating in stand-alone mode.

Author's Comment:

- The definition of a stand-alone system is contained in Article 100. ▶Figure 710–1

710.6 Equipment Approval

All equipment must be listed or field labeled for the intended use.

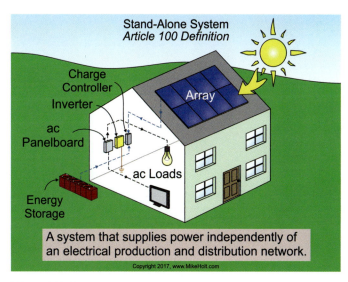

▶Figure 710–1

710.15 General

Premises wiring systems must be adequate to meet the requirements of this Code for similar installations supplied by a feeder or service. The wiring on the supply side of the building or structure disconnecting means must comply with the requirements of this Code, except as modified by 710.15(A) through (F).

(A) Supply Output. Power supply to premises wiring systems is permitted to have less capacity than the calculated load. The capacity of the stand-alone supply must be equal to or greater than the load posed by the largest single utilization equipment connected to the system.

(B) Sizing and Protection. The circuit conductors between a stand-alone source and a building or structure disconnecting means must be sized based on the sum of the output ratings of the stand-alone sources.

(C) Single 120V Supply. The sum of the ratings of the power sources isn't permitted to be greater than the neutral bus rating. This equipment must be marked with the following words or equivalent:

(D) Energy Storage or Backup Power System Requirements. Energy storage or backup power supplies aren't required.

(E) Back-Fed Circuit Breakers. Plug-in type back-fed circuit breakers connected to an interconnected supply must be secured in accordance with 408.36(D). Circuit breakers marked "line" and "load" must not be back-fed.

(F) Voltage and Frequency Control. The stand-alone supply must be controlled so that voltage and frequency remain within suitable limits for the connected loads.

CHAPTER 7

PRACTICE QUESTIONS

Please use the 2017 *Code* book to answer the following questions.

Article 705. Interconnected Electric Power Production Sources

1. Article _____ covers the installation of electric power production sources operating in parallel with a primary source(s) of electricity.

    (a) 700
    (b) 701
    (c) 702
    (d) 705

2. For interconnected electric power production sources, the circuit conductors from the inverter output terminals that supply ac power to the utility powered electric system is known as the "interactive inverter output circuit."

    (a) True
    (b) False

3. For interconnected electric power production sources, the generating source and all distribution equipment associated with it that generates electricity from a source other than a utility supplied service is called "_____."

    (a) a service drop
    (b) power production equipment
    (c) the service point
    (d) utilization equipment

4. For interconnected electric power production sources, interactive inverters shall be _____ for interconnection service.

    (a) listed
    (b) field labeled
    (c) identified
    (d) a and b

5. For interconnected electric power production sources, installation of one or more electrical power production sources operating in parallel with a primary source(s) of electricity shall be performed only by _____.

    (a) qualified persons
    (b) a utility company
    (c) the authority having jurisdiction
    (d) b or c

6. For interconnected electric power production sources, a permanent _____, denoting all electric power sources on or in the premises, shall be installed at each service equipment location and the system disconnect(s) for all interconnected electric power production sources.

    (a) label
    (b) plaque
    (c) directory
    (d) b or c

7. For interconnected electric power production sources, an electric power production source is permitted to be connected to the supply side of the service disconnecting means.

    (a) True
    (b) False

Chapter 7 | Practice Questions

8. For interconnected electric power production sources, the sum of the ratings of all overcurrent devices connected to power production sources are permitted to exceed the rating of the service.

   (a) True
   (b) False

9. For interconnected electric power production sources, the output can be connected to the load side of the service disconnecting means at any distribution equipment on the premises.

   (a) True
   (b) False

10. The source interconnection of one or more power sources installed in one system shall be made at a dedicated circuit breaker or fusible disconnecting means.

    (a) True
    (b) False

11. In accordance with Article 705, where two sources, one a utility and the other another power source, are located at opposite ends of a busbar that contains loads, a permanent warning label shall be applied to the distribution equipment adjacent to the back-fed breaker from the power source to warn others that the power source output connection circuit breaker shall not be relocated.

    (a) True
    (b) False

12. For interconnected electric power production sources, _____, unless otherwise marked, are suitable for backfeeding.

    (a) circuit breakers
    (b) PV system overcurrent devices
    (c) utility-interactive inverters
    (d) fused disconnects

13. For interconnected electric power production sources, dedicated ac inverter circuit breakers that are backfed shall be secured in place by an additional fastener as required by 408.36(D).

    (a) True
    (b) False

14. For interconnected electric power production sources, upon loss of utility source power, an electric power production source shall be manually disconnected from all ungrounded conductors of the utility source and shall not be reconnected until the utility source has been restored.

    (a) True
    (b) False

Article 710. Stand-Alone Systems

15. Article _____ covers electric power production sources operating in stand-alone mode.

    (a) 690
    (b) 691
    (c) 705
    (d) 710

16. All equipment used for electric power production sources operating in stand-alone mode must be _____ for the intended use.

    (a) listed
    (b) field labeled
    (c) marked
    (d) a or b

17. The power capacity of the stand-alone supply must be _____ the load posed by the largest single utilization equipment connected to the system.

    (a) equal to
    (b) greater than
    (c) not less than
    (d) a or b

18. The conductors between a stand-alone source and a building disconnecting means must be sized based on the sum of the output rating of the stand-alone source.

    (a) True
    (b) False

FINAL EXAM A

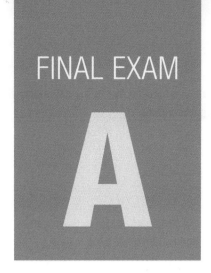

1. A permanent label shall be applied by the installer at the PV dc power source disconnect indicating the _____.
   (a) maximum voltage
   (b) maximum circuit current
   (c) maximum rated output current of the charge controller or dc-to-dc converter (if installed)
   (d) all of these

2. Where multiple utility-interactive inverters are remotely located from each other, a directory in accordance with 705.10 shall be provided at each PV system disconnecting means.
   (a) True
   (b) False

3. The source interconnection of one or more power sources installed in one system shall be made at a dedicated circuit breaker or fusible disconnecting means.
   (a) True
   (b) False

4. Devices and systems used for mounting PV modules that also provide grounding of the module frames shall be _____ for the purpose of grounding PV modules.
   (a) listed
   (b) labeled
   (c) identified
   (d) all of these

5. Where the source circuit operates at over 30V, single-conductor Type USE-2 or listed and identified PV wires installed in a readily accessible location shall be installed in a raceway.
   (a) True
   (b) False

6. The point of interconnection of the PV system power source to other sources shall be marked at an accessible location at the _____ as a power source and with the rated ac output current and nominal operating ac voltage.
   (a) disconnecting means
   (b) array
   (c) inverter
   (d) none of these

7. Plug-in type back-fed circuit breakers for a stand-alone or multimode inverter connected to a stand-alone PV system are not required to be secured in place by an additional fastener that requires other than a pull to release the breaker from the panelboard.
   (a) True
   (b) False

8. Which of the following wiring methods and enclosures that contain photovoltaic power source conductors shall be marked "WARNING PHOTOVOLTAIC POWER SOUCE" by means of permanently affixed labels or other approved permanent marking?
   (a) Exposed raceways, cable trays, and other wiring methods.
   (b) The covers or enclosures of pull boxes and junction boxes.
   (c) Conduit bodies in which any of the available conduit openings are unused.
   (d) all of these

9. For stand-alone PV systems, circuit breakers that are marked "Line" and "Load" can be back-fed.
   (a) True
   (b) False

Final Exam A

10. A solar PV system that operates in parallel with, and may deliver power to, an electrical production and distribution network is known as a(n) "____ system."
    (a) hybrid
    (b) inverted
    (c) interactive
    (d) internal

11. The PV maximum output circuit current is equal to the sum of parallel PV source circuit maximum currents as calculated in ____.
    (a) 690.8(A)(1)
    (b) 690.8(A)(2)
    (c) 690.8(A)(3)
    (d) none of these

12. A dc PV array that has two outputs, each having opposite polarity to a common reference point or center tap is known as a "____."
    (a) bipolar photovoltaic array
    (b) polar photovoltaic array
    (c) a or b
    (d) none of these

13. Single-conductor Type USE-2 and single-conductor cable ____ as PV wire can be run exposed at outdoor locations for PV source circuits within the PV array.
    (a) approved
    (b) listed or labeled
    (c) listed and identified
    (d) none of these

14. Where PV system dc circuits are run inside a building or structure, they shall be contained in ____.
    (a) metal raceways
    (b) Type MC cables
    (c) metal enclosures
    (d) any of these

15. For PV systems, one source for lowest-expected ambient temperature is the "Extreme Annual Mean Minimum Design Dry Bulb Temperature" chapter found in the ASHRAE *Handbook-Fundamentals*, 2013.
    (a) True
    (b) False

16. For PV systems, the conductors connected to the alternating-current output of an inverter form the ____.
    (a) bipolar photovoltaic array
    (b) monopole subarray
    (c) emergency standby power
    (d) inverter output circuit

17. A single array or aggregate of arrays that generates direct-current power at system voltage and current is the photovoltaic ____.
    (a) output source
    (b) source circuit
    (c) power source
    (d) array source

18. For PV systems, the circuits between modules and from modules to the common connection point(s) of the direct-current system are known as the "photovoltaic ____ circuit."
    (a) source
    (b) array
    (c) input
    (d) output

19. An alternating-current photovoltaic module is designed to generate ac power when exposed to ____.
    (a) electromagnetic induction
    (b) heat
    (c) sunlight
    (d) hysteresis

20. Overcurrent devices for PV systems dc circuits shall be rated to carry not less than ____ percent of the maximum currents calculated in 690.8(A).
    (a) 80
    (b) 100
    (c) 125
    (d) 250

21. A ____ subarray has two conductors in the output circuit, one positive (+) and one negative (-). Two of these subarrays are used to form a bipolar photovoltaic array.
    (a) bipolar
    (b) monopole
    (c) double-pole
    (d) module

22. Devices _____ for grounding the metallic frames of PV modules and other equipment can be used to bond the exposed metal surfaces of the modules and equipment to the mounting structures.

    (a) identified
    (b) approved
    (c) listed
    (d) a and c

23. The requirement for grouping PV source and output circuits is not required if the circuit enters from a cable or raceway unique to the circuit that makes the grouping obvious.

    (a) True
    (b) False

24. The _____ of a dc PV source circuit or output circuit is used to calculate the sum of the rated open-circuit voltage of the series-connected PV modules multiplied by the correction factor provided in Table 690.7.

    (a) minimum allowable ampacity of conductors
    (b) maximum allowable ampacity of conductors
    (c) minimum photovoltaic system voltage
    (d) maximum photovoltaic system voltage

25. An electrical production and distribution network, such as a utility and connected load, is internal to and controlled by a photovoltaic power system.

    (a) True
    (b) False

26. The provisions of Article 690 apply to solar _____ systems, including inverter(s), array circuit(s), and controller(s) for such systems.

    (a) photoconductive
    (b) PV
    (c) photogenic
    (d) photosynthesis

27. For PV systems, where all terminals of a disconnecting means may be energized when the switch is in the open position, a warning sign shall be placed on or adjacent to the disconnecting means. The sign shall be similar to: WARNING ELECTRIC SHOCK HAZARD. TERMINALS ON THE LINE AND LOAD SIDES MAY BE ENERGIZED IN THE OPEN POSITION.

    (a) True
    (b) False

28. For stand-alone PV systems, the ac current output from a stand-alone inverter(s) can be _____ the calculated load connected to the disconnect, but not less than the largest single utilization equipment connected to the system.

    (a) less than
    (b) equal to
    (c) greater than
    (d) any of these

29. Monopole subarrays in a bipolar PV system shall be physically _____ where the sum of the PV system voltages, without consideration of polarity, of the two monopole subarrays exceeds the rating of the conductors and connected equipment.

    (a) separated
    (b) connected
    (c) joined
    (d) together

30. For interconnected electric power production sources, the sum of the ratings of all overcurrent devices connected to power production sources are permitted to exceed the rating of the service.

    (a) True
    (b) False

31. In accordance with Article 705, where two sources, one a utility and the other another power source, are located at opposite ends of a busbar that contains loads, a permanent warning label shall be applied to the distribution equipment adjacent to the back-fed breaker from the power source to warn others that the power source output connection circuit breaker shall not be relocated.

    (a) True
    (b) False

32. For interconnected electric power production sources, dedicated ac inverter circuit breakers that are backfed shall be secured in place by an additional fastener as required by 408.36(D).

    (a) True
    (b) False

33. Photovoltaic wiring methods containing _____ shall be terminated only with terminals, lugs, devices, or connectors that are identified and listed for such use.

    (a) flexible, fine-stranded cables
    (b) solid conductors
    (c) flexible raceways
    (d) all of these

Final Exam A

34. The solar _____ is the basic PV device that generates electricity when exposed to light.

    (a) battery
    (b) cell
    (c) atom
    (d) ray

35. PV system conductors shall be identified by separate color coding, marking tape, tagging, or other approved means.

    (a) True
    (b) False

36. For interconnected electric power production sources, interactive inverters shall be _____ for interconnection service.

    (a) listed
    (b) field labeled
    (c) identified
    (d) a and b

37. Fuses or circuit breakers for PV dc circuits shall be _____ for use in dc circuits and shall have the appropriate voltage, current, and interrupt ratings.

    (a) identified
    (b) approved
    (c) recognized
    (d) listed

38. For stand-alone PV systems, energy storage or backup power supplies are required.

    (a) True
    (b) False

39. Junction, pull, and outlet boxes can be located behind PV modules that are secured by removable fasteners.

    (a) True
    (b) False

40. The connectors permitted by Article 690 shall _____.

    (a) be polarized
    (b) be constructed and installed so as to guard against inadvertent contact with live parts by persons
    (c) require a tool for opening if the circuit operates at over 30V nominal maximum dc or 15V ac
    (d) all of these

41. Faulted circuits required to have ground-fault protection in a photovoltaic system shall be isolated by automatically disconnecting the _____ conductors, or the inverter charge controller fed by the faulted circuits shall automatically stop supplying power to output circuits.

    (a) ungrounded
    (b) grounded
    (c) equipment grounding
    (d) all of these

42. Equipment grounding conductors for PV circuits having overcurrent protection shall be sized in accordance with _____.

    (a) 250.122
    (b) 250.66
    (c) Table 250.122
    (d) Table 250.66

43. For interconnected electric power production sources, _____, unless otherwise marked, are suitable for backfeeding.

    (a) circuit breakers
    (b) PV system overcurrent devices
    (c) utility-interactive inverters
    (d) fused disconnects

44. For one- and two-family dwellings, the maximum voltage for PV system dc circuits is _____.

    (a) 24V
    (b) 48V
    (c) 250V
    (d) 600V

45. The location of PV system dc circuits embedded in built-up, laminate, or membrane roofing materials in areas not covered by PV modules and associated equipment shall be clearly marked.

    (a) True
    (b) False

46. Grounded dc PV arrays shall be provided with direct-current _____ meeting the requirements of 690.41(B)(1)(2) to reduce fire hazards.

    (a) arc-fault protection
    (b) rectifier protection
    (c) ground-fault monitors
    (d) ground-fault protection

47. The direct-current system grounding connection shall be made at any _____ point(s) on the PV output circuit.
    (a) single
    (b) two
    (c) three
    (d) four

48. Overcurrent devices for PV source circuits shall be readily accessible.
    (a) True
    (b) False

49. Buildings/structures containing both utility service and a PV system shall have a _____ installed in accordance with 705.10.
    (a) plaque
    (b) directory
    (c) a and b
    (d) a or b

50. Where no overcurrent protection is provided for the PV circuit, an assumed overcurrent device rated in accordance with 690.9(B) shall be used to size the equipment grounding conductor in accordance with _____.
    (a) 250.122
    (b) 250.66
    (c) Table 250.122
    (d) Table 250.66

51. PV source circuits shall be identified at all points of termination, connection, and splices.
    (a) True
    (b) False

52. PV systems are permitted to supply a building or other structure in addition to any other _____ supply system(s).
    (a) electrical
    (b) telephone
    (c) plumbing
    (d) none of these

53. In PV systems, a(n) _____ is a complete, environmentally protected unit consisting of solar cells and other components, exclusive of tracker, designed to generate direct-current power when exposed to sunlight.
    (a) interface
    (b) battery
    (c) module
    (d) cell bank

54. For interconnected electric power production sources, a permanent _____, denoting all electric power sources on or in the premises, shall be installed at each service equipment location and the system disconnect(s) for all interconnected electric power production sources.
    (a) label
    (b) plaque
    (c) directory
    (d) b or c

55. The PV disconnecting means shall be externally operable without exposing the operator to contact with live parts and shall indicate whether in the open or closed position.
    (a) True
    (b) False

56. For PV systems, equipment that regulates the charging process of a battery by diverting power from energy storage to direct-current or alternating-current loads or to an interconnected utility service is known as a(n) _____.
    (a) alternating charge controller
    (b) diversion charge controller
    (c) direct charge controller
    (d) alternating charge regulator

57. Where exposed and subject to physical damage, PV array equipment grounding conductors smaller than 4 AWG shall be protected by a raceway or cable armor.
    (a) True
    (b) False

58. For interconnected electric power production sources, the output can be connected to the load side of the service disconnecting means at any distribution equipment on the premises.
    (a) True
    (b) False

59. For interconnected electric power production sources, installation of one or more electrical power production sources operating in parallel with a primary source(s) of electricity shall be performed only by _____.
    (a) qualified persons
    (b) a utility company
    (c) the authority having jurisdiction
    (d) b or c

60. The PV system disconnecting means shall plainly indicate whether in the open (off) or closed (on) position and be _____ "PV SYSTEM DISCONNECT" or equivalent.
    (a) listed as a
    (b) approved as a
    (c) permanently marked
    (d) temporarily marked

61. For PV systems, metallic support structures used for grounding purposes shall be _____ as equipment grounding conductors or have _____ bonding jumpers or devices connected between the separate metallic sections and be bonded to the grounding system.
    (a) listed, labeled
    (b) labeled, listed
    (c) identified, identified
    (d) listed, identified

62. Currents of PV systems are to be considered _____.
    (a) safe
    (b) continuous
    (c) noncontiguous
    (d) inverted

63. All equipment intended for use in PV power systems shall be _____ for the PV application.
    (a) field labeled
    (b) listed
    (c) approved
    (d) a or b

64. A means is required to disconnect the PV system from all wiring systems including power systems, energy storage systems, and utilization equipment and its associated premises wiring.
    (a) True
    (b) False

65. For PV systems, means shall be provided to disconnect equipment, such as batteries, inverters, charge controllers, and the like, from all ungrounded conductors of all sources.
    (a) True
    (b) False

66. Where the conductors of more than one PV system occupy the same junction box or raceway with removable cover(s), the ac and dc conductors of each system shall be grouped separately by cable ties or similar means at least once, and then shall be grouped at intervals not to exceed _____.
    (a) 6 in.
    (b) 12 in.
    (c) 36 in.
    (d) 6 ft

67. Article 690 requirements pertaining to dc PV source circuits do not apply to ac PV modules. The PV source circuit, conductors and inverters are considered as internal wiring of an ac module.
    (a) True
    (b) False

68. All conductors of a circuit, including the equipment grounding conductor, shall be installed in the same raceway or cable, or otherwise run with the PV array circuit conductors when they leave the vicinity of the PV array.
    (a) True
    (b) False

69. PV source circuits and PV output circuits are not permitted to be contained in the same raceway, cable tray, cable, outlet box, junction box, or similar fitting, with non-PV systems unless the two systems are separated by a partition.
    (a) True
    (b) False

70. The conductors connected to the direct-current input of an inverter for PV systems form the _____.
    (a) branch circuit
    (b) feeder
    (c) inverter input circuit
    (d) inverter output circuit

Final Exam A

71. The output of an ac module is considered an ____ output circuit as defined in 690.2.
    (a) inverter
    (b) module
    (c) PV
    (d) subarray

72. Article ____ covers the installation of electric power production sources operating in parallel with a primary source(s) of electricity.
    (a) 700
    (b) 701
    (c) 702
    (d) 705

73. Where the conductors of more than one PV system occupy the same junction box, raceway, or equipment, the conductors of each system shall be identified at all termination, connection, and splice points.
    (a) True
    (b) False

74. Listed fittings and connectors that are intended to be concealed at the time of on-site assembly are permitted for on-site interconnection of PV modules or other array components.
    (a) True
    (b) False

75. Where PV source and output circuits operating at greater than ____ are installed in a(n) ____ location, the circuit conductors shall be guarded or installed in Type MC cable or in a raceway.
    (a) 30V, accessible
    (b) 30V, readily accessible
    (c) 60V, accessible
    (d) 60V, readily accessible

76. The circuit conductors between the inverter or direct-current utilization equipment and the PV source circuit(s) are part of the ____ circuit.
    (a) photovoltaic output
    (b) photovoltaic input
    (c) inverter input
    (d) inverter output

77. In grounded PV source circuits, one overcurrent protection device is not permitted to protect the PV modules and the interconnecting conductors.
    (a) True
    (b) False

78. For interconnected electric power production sources, upon loss of utility source power, an electric power production source shall be manually disconnected from all ungrounded conductors of the utility source and shall not be reconnected until the utility source has been restored.
    (a) True
    (b) False

79. For PV systems, a collection of modules mechanically fastened together, wired, and designed to provide a field-installable unit is called a(n) "____."
    (a) panel
    (b) array
    (c) bank
    (d) gang

80. Devices ____ for bonding the metallic frames of PV modules shall be permitted to bond the exposed metallic frames of PV modules to the metallic frames of adjacent PV modules.
    (a) listed
    (b) labeled
    (c) identified
    (d) all of these

81. A ____ is an electrical subset of a photovoltaic array.
    (a) panel
    (b) module
    (c) circuit
    (d) subarray

82. The PV maximum source circuit current is calculated by multiplying the sum of the parallel-connected PV module-rated short-circuit currents by 125 percent.
    (a) True
    (b) False

Final Exam A

83. A grounded _____-wire PV system has one functional grounded conductor.
    (a) 2
    (b) 3
    (c) 4
    (d) 5

84. Any building or structure with a stand-alone PV system (not connected to a utility service source) shall have a permanent _____ installed on the exterior of the building or structure at a readily visible location. The _____ shall indicate the location of the stand-alone PV system disconnecting means and that the structure contains a stand-alone electrical power system.
    (a) plaque
    (b) directory
    (c) a and b
    (d) a or b

85. A mechanically integrated assembly of PV modules or panels with a support structure and foundation, tracker, and other components, as required, to form a dc or ac power-producing unit, is known as a(n) "_____."
    (a) pulse width modulator
    (b) array
    (c) capacitive supply bank
    (d) alternating-current photovoltaic module

86. A ground-fault protection device or system required for PV systems shall _____.
    (a) interrupt the flow of fault current
    (b) detect a ground-fault current
    (c) be listed for PV ground-fault protection
    (d) b and c

87. For interconnected electric power production sources, the circuit conductors from the inverter output terminals that supply ac power to the utility powered electric system is known as the interactive inverter output circuit.
    (a) True
    (b) False

88. Labels or markings of PV system raceways and enclosures shall be suitable for the environment and be placed with a maximum of _____ ft of spacing.
    (a) 5
    (b) 10
    (c) 20
    (d) 25

89. For interconnected electric power production sources, the generating source and all distribution equipment associated with it that generates electricity from a source other than a utility supplied service is called "_____."
    (a) a service drop
    (b) power production equipment
    (c) the service point
    (d) utilization equipment

90. The conductors of PV output circuits and inverter input and output circuits shall be identified at all points of termination, connection, and splices.
    (a) True
    (b) False

91. All raceway and cable wiring methods included in this *Code*, other wiring systems and fittings specifically listed for use on PV arrays, and wiring as part of a listed system shall be permitted.
    (a) True
    (b) False

92. The PV system disconnecting means shall be installed at a(n) _____ location.
    (a) guarded
    (b) accessible
    (c) protected
    (d) readily accessible

93. For PV systems, a(n) _____ is a device that changes direct-current input to an alternating-current output.
    (a) diode
    (b) rectifier
    (c) transistor
    (d) inverter

94. For interconnected electric power production sources, an electric power production source is permitted to be connected to the supply side of the service disconnecting means.

    (a) True
    (b) False

95. The maximum PV inverter output circuit current is equal to the _____ output current rating.

    (a) average
    (b) peak
    (c) continuous
    (d) intermittent

96. Article 691 covers the installation of large-scale PV electric power production facilities with a generating capacity of no less than _____ kW, and not under exclusive utility control.

    (a) 1,000
    (b) 2,000
    (c) 5,000
    (d) 10,000

97. The conductors between a stand-alone source and a building disconnecting means must be sized based on the sum of the output rating of the stand-alone source.

    (a) True
    (b) False

98. Fence grounding for large-scale PV electric supply stations must be in accordance with Article 250.

    (a) True
    (b) False

99. All equipment used for electric power production sources operating in stand-alone mode must be _____ for the intended use.

    (a) listed
    (b) field labeled
    (c) marked
    (d) a or b

100. Large-scale PV electric supply stations must only be accessible to authorized personnel and they are not permitted to be installed on buildings.

    (a) True
    (b) False

FINAL EXAM B

1. Power distribution blocks shall be permitted in pull and junction boxes over 100 cu in. when ____.
   (a) they are listed as a power distribution block
   (b) they are installed in a box not smaller than required by the installation instructions of the power distribution block
   (c) the junction box is sized so that the wire-bending space requirements of 312.6 can be met
   (d) all of these

2. For stand-alone PV systems, the ac current output from a stand-alone inverter(s) can be ____ the calculated load connected to the disconnect, but not less than the largest single utilization equipment connected to the system.
   (a) less than
   (b) equal to
   (c) greater than
   (d) any of these

3. Conductors other than service conductors shall not be installed in the same ____ in which the service conductors are installed.
   (a) service raceway
   (b) service cable
   (c) enclosure
   (d) a or b

4. Unused openings other than those intended for the operation of equipment, intended for mounting purposes, or permitted as part of the design for listed equipment shall be ____.
   (a) filled with cable clamps or connectors only
   (b) taped over with electrical tape
   (c) repaired only by welding or brazing in a metal slug
   (d) closed to afford protection substantially equivalent to the wall of the equipment

5. When LFNC is used, and equipment grounding is required, a separate ____ shall be installed in the conduit.
   (a) equipment grounding conductor
   (b) expansion fitting
   (c) flexible nonmetallic connector
   (d) none of these

6. Aluminum RMC shall be permitted to be installed where approved for the environment.
   (a) True
   (b) False

7. Monopole subarrays in a bipolar PV system shall be physically ____ where the sum of the PV system voltages, without consideration of polarity, of the two monopole subarrays exceeds the rating of the conductors and connected equipment.
   (a) separated
   (b) connected
   (c) joined
   (d) together

8. The power capacity of the stand-alone supply must be ____ the load posed by the largest single utilization equipment connected to the system.
   (a) equal to
   (b) greater than
   (c) not less than
   (d) a or b

9. When considering the ampacity of cables rated 2,000V or less in cable trays, refer to 110.14(C) for conductor temperature limitations due to termination provisions.
   (a) True
   (b) False

10. The conductors between a stand-alone source and a building disconnecting means must be sized based on the sum of the output rating of the stand-alone source.

    (a) True
    (b) False

11. For PV systems, a(n) _____ is a device that changes direct-current input to an alternating-current output.

    (a) diode
    (b) rectifier
    (c) transistor
    (d) inverter

12. A separate water piping bonding jumper shall be required if the metal frame of a building or structure is used as the grounding electrode for a separately derived system and is bonded to the metal water piping in the area served by the separately derived system.

    (a) True
    (b) False

13. LFNC shall be permitted for _____.

    (a) direct burial where listed and marked for the purpose
    (b) exposed work
    (c) outdoors where listed and marked for this purpose
    (d) all of these

14. Large-scale PV electric supply stations must only be accessible to authorized personnel and they are not permitted to be installed on buildings.

    (a) True
    (b) False

15. Listed fittings and connectors that are intended to be concealed at the time of on-site assembly are permitted for on-site interconnection of PV modules or other array components.

    (a) True
    (b) False

16. The solar _____ is the basic PV device that generates electricity when exposed to light.

    (a) battery
    (b) cell
    (c) atom
    (d) ray

17. For interconnected electric power production sources, the sum of the ratings of all overcurrent devices connected to power production sources are permitted to exceed the rating of the service.

    (a) True
    (b) False

18. Where the conductors of more than one PV system occupy the same junction box or raceway with removable cover(s), the ac and dc conductors of each system shall be grouped separately by cable ties or similar means at least once, and then shall be grouped at intervals not to exceed _____.

    (a) 6 in.
    (b) 12 in.
    (c) 36 in.
    (d) 6 ft

19. The provisions of Article 690 apply to solar _____ systems, including inverter(s), array circuit(s), and controller(s) for such systems.

    (a) photoconductive
    (b) PV
    (c) photogenic
    (d) photosynthesis

20. Buildings/structures containing both utility service and a PV system shall have a _____ installed in accordance with 705.10.

    (a) plaque
    (b) directory
    (c) a and b
    (d) a or b

21. The *NEC* does not apply to electric utility-owned wiring and equipment _____.

    (a) installed by an electrical contractor
    (b) installed on public property
    (c) consisting of service drops or service laterals
    (d) in a utility office building

22. Where fuses are used as the service overcurrent device, the disconnecting means shall be located ahead of the load side of the fuses in accordance with 230.91.

    (a) True
    (b) False

Final Exam B

23. Where the resistance-to-ground of 25 ohms or less is not achieved for a single rod electrode, _____.

    (a) other means besides electrodes shall be used in order to provide grounding
    (b) the single rod electrode shall be supplemented by one additional electrode
    (c) no additional electrodes are required
    (d) none of these

24. A building disconnecting means that supplies only limited loads of a single branch circuit shall have a rating of not less than _____.

    (a) 15A
    (b) 20A
    (c) 25A
    (d) 30A

25. The PV system disconnecting means shall plainly indicate whether in the open (off) or closed (on) position and be _____ "PV SYSTEM DISCONNECT" or equivalent.

    (a) listed as a
    (b) approved as a
    (c) permanently marked
    (d) temporarily marked

26. A switchboard or panelboard containing an ungrounded ac electrical system is required to be legibly and permanently field marked to caution that the system is ungrounded and include the _____.

    (a) contact information for the power supplier
    (b) contact information for emergency services
    (c) operating voltage between conductors
    (d) transformer impedance rating

27. For PV systems, means shall be provided to disconnect equipment, such as batteries, inverters, charge controllers, and the like, from all ungrounded conductors of all sources.

    (a) True
    (b) False

28. Two or more grounding electrodes bonded together are considered a single grounding electrode system.

    (a) True
    (b) False

29. Electrical installations in hollow spaces, vertical shafts, and ventilation or air-handling ducts shall be made so that the possible spread of fire or products of combustion is not _____.

    (a) substantially increased
    (b) allowed
    (c) inherent
    (d) possible

30. Where exposed and subject to physical damage, PV array equipment grounding conductors smaller than 4 AWG shall be protected by a raceway or cable armor.

    (a) True
    (b) False

31. Where correction or adjustment factors are required by 310.15(B)(2) or (3), for single-phase feeder conductors installed for _____ dwellings, they shall be permitted to be applied to the ampacity associated with the temperature rating of the conductor.

    (a) one-family
    (b) the individual dwelling units of two-family
    (c) the individual dwelling units of multifamily
    (d) all of these

32. Service raceways threaded into metal service equipment such as bosses (hubs) are considered to be effectively _____ to the service metal enclosure.

    (a) attached
    (b) bonded
    (c) grounded
    (d) none of these

33. The ampacity adjustment factors of 310.15(B)(3)(a) shall not apply to conductors installed in surface metal raceways where the _____.

    (a) cross-sectional area exceeds 4 sq in.
    (b) current-carrying conductors do not exceed 30 in number
    (c) total cross-sectional area of all conductors does not exceed 20 percent of the interior cross-sectional area of the raceway
    (d) all of these

34. A one-family dwelling unit and its accessory structure(s) shall be permitted to have one set of service-entrance conductors run to each structure from a single service drop, set of overhead service conductors, set of underground service conductors, or service lateral.

    (a) True
    (b) False

35. Grounding electrode conductors and grounding electrode bonding jumpers in contact with _____ shall not be required to comply with 300.5, but shall be buried or otherwise protected if subject to physical damage.

    (a) water
    (b) the earth
    (c) metal
    (d) all of these

36. An electrical production and distribution network, such as a utility and connected load, is internal to and controlled by a photovoltaic power system.

    (a) True
    (b) False

37. For indoor installations, piping, ducts, leak protection apparatus, or other equipment foreign to the electrical installation shall not be installed in the dedicated space above a panelboard or switchboard.

    (a) True
    (b) False

38. Type TC cable shall be permitted to be direct buried, where _____ for such use.

    (a) identified
    (b) approved
    (c) listed
    (d) labeled

39. For a single separately derived system, the grounding electrode conductor connects the grounded conductor of the derived system to the grounding electrode at the same point on the separately derived system where the _____ is connected.

    (a) metering equipment
    (b) transfer switch
    (c) system bonding jumper
    (d) largest circuit breaker

40. The receptacle grounding terminal of an isolated ground receptacle shall be connected to a(n) _____ equipment grounding conductor run with the circuit conductors.

    (a) insulated
    (b) covered
    (c) bare
    (d) solid

41. Outside wiring shall not be installed beneath openings through which materials may be moved, and shall not be installed where they will obstruct entrance to these buildings' openings.

    (a) True
    (b) False

42. For PV systems, equipment that regulates the charging process of a battery by diverting power from energy storage to direct-current or alternating-current loads or to an interconnected utility service is known as a(n) _____.

    (a) alternating charge controller
    (b) diversion charge controller
    (c) direct charge controller
    (d) alternating charge regulator

43. Underground service conductors shall be protected from damage in accordance with _____ including minimum cover requirements.

    (a) 240.6(A)
    (b) 300.5
    (c) 310.15(B)(16)
    (d) 430.52

44. Grounded dc PV arrays shall be provided with direct-current _____ meeting the requirements of 690.41(B)(1)(2) to reduce fire hazards.

    (a) arc-fault protection
    (b) rectifier protection
    (c) ground-fault monitors
    (d) ground-fault protection

45. Ground-fault protection of equipment shall be provided for solidly grounded wye electrical systems of more than 150 volts-to-ground, but not exceeding 1,000V phase-to-phase for each individual device used as a building or structure main disconnecting means rated _____ or more, unless specifically exempted.

    (a) 1,000A
    (b) 1,500A
    (c) 2,000A
    (d) 2,500A

46. The grounding electrode conductor shall be connected to the grounded service conductor at the _____.

    (a) load end of the service drop
    (b) load end of the service lateral
    (c) service disconnecting means
    (d) any of these

Final Exam B

47. A flexible cord conductor intended to be used as a(n) ____ conductor shall have a continuous identifying marker readily distinguishing it from the other conductor or conductors. One means of identification is a braid finished to show a continuous green color or a green color with one or more yellow stripes on one conductor.

    (a) ungrounded
    (b) equipment grounding
    (c) service
    (d) high-leg

48. Listed FMC can be used as the equipment grounding conductor if the conduit does not exceed trade size ____.

    (a) 1¼
    (b) 1½
    (c) 2
    (d) 2¼

49. The direct-current system grounding connection shall be made at any ____ point(s) on the PV output circuit.

    (a) single
    (b) two
    (c) three
    (d) four

50. Fuses shall be marked with their ____.

    (a) ampere and voltage rating
    (b) interrupting rating where other than 10,000A
    (c) name or trademark of the manufacturer
    (d) all of these

51. Conduits and raceways, including end fittings, shall not rise more than ____ in. above the bottom of a switchboard enclosure.

    (a) 3
    (b) 4
    (c) 5
    (d) 6

52. The maximum PV inverter output circuit current is equal to the ____ output current rating.

    (a) average
    (b) peak
    (c) continuous
    (d) intermittent

53. PV source circuits and PV output circuits are not permitted to be contained in the same raceway, cable tray, cable, outlet box, junction box, or similar fitting, with non-PV systems unless the two systems are separated by a partition.

    (a) True
    (b) False

54. Type NM cable and associated fittings shall be ____.

    (a) marked
    (b) approved
    (c) identified
    (d) listed

55. Article ____ covers electric power production sources operating in stand-alone mode.

    (a) 690
    (b) 691
    (c) 705
    (d) 710

56. For installations that supply only limited loads of a single branch circuit, the service disconnecting means shall have a rating not less than ____.

    (a) 15A
    (b) 20A
    (c) 25A
    (d) 30A

57. For interconnected electric power production sources, the circuit conductors from the inverter output terminals that supply ac power to the utility powered electric system is known as the interactive inverter output circuit.

    (a) True
    (b) False

58. In PV systems, a(n) ____ is a complete, environmentally protected unit consisting of solar cells, and other components, exclusive of tracker, designed to generate direct-current power when exposed to sunlight.

    (a) interface
    (b) battery
    (c) module
    (d) cell bank

59. For installations consisting of not more than two 2-wire branch circuits, the building disconnecting means shall have a rating of not less than ____.

    (a) 15A
    (b) 20A
    (c) 25A
    (d) 30A

60. PV systems are permitted to supply a building or other structure in addition to any other ____ supply system(s).

    (a) electrical
    (b) telephone
    (c) plumbing
    (d) none of these

61. The service disconnecting means rated 1,000V or less shall be marked to identify it as being suitable for use as service equipment and shall be ____.

    (a) weatherproof
    (b) listed or field labeled
    (c) approved
    (d) acceptable

62. For PV systems, metallic support structures used for grounding purposes shall be ____ as equipment grounding conductors or have ____ bonding jumpers or devices connected between the separate metallic sections and be bonded to the grounding system.

    (a) listed, labeled
    (b) labeled, listed
    (c) identified, identified
    (d) listed, identified

63. Any building or structure with a stand-alone PV system (not connected to a utility service source) shall have a permanent ____ installed on the exterior of the building or structure at a readily visible location. The ____ shall indicate the location of the stand-alone PV system disconnecting means and that the structure contains a stand-alone electrical power system.

    (a) plaque
    (b) directory
    (c) a and b
    (d) a or b

64. Fuses or circuit breakers for PV dc circuits shall be ____ for use in dc circuits and shall have the appropriate voltage, current, and interrupt ratings.

    (a) identified
    (b) approved
    (c) recognized
    (d) listed

65. The grounded conductor of an alternating-current system operating at 1,000V or less shall be routed with the ungrounded conductors and connected to each disconnecting means grounded conductor terminal or bus, which is then connected to the service disconnecting means enclosure via a(n) ____ that is installed between the service neutral conductor and the service disconnecting means enclosure.

    (a) equipment bonding conductor
    (b) main bonding jumper
    (c) grounding electrode
    (d) intersystem bonding terminal

66. The PV maximum source circuit current is calculated by multiplying the sum of the parallel-connected PV module-rated short-circuit currents by 125 percent.

    (a) True
    (b) False

67. Grounding electrodes of bare or electrically conductive coated iron or steel plates shall be at least ____ in. thick.

    (a) $1/8$
    (b) $1/4$
    (c) $1/2$
    (d) $3/4$

68. A single array or aggregate of arrays that generates direct-current power at system voltage and current is the photovoltaic ____.

    (a) output source
    (b) source circuit
    (c) power source
    (d) array source

69. For PV systems, the circuits between modules and from modules to the common connection point(s) of the direct-current system are known as the "photovoltaic _____ circuit."

    (a) source
    (b) array
    (c) input
    (d) output

70. The _____ of a dc PV source circuit or output circuit is used to calculate the sum of the rated open-circuit voltage of the series-connected PV modules multiplied by the correction factor provided in Table 690.7.

    (a) minimum allowable ampacity of conductors
    (b) maximum allowable ampacity of conductors
    (c) minimum photovoltaic system voltage
    (d) maximum photovoltaic system voltage

71. Large-scale PV electric power production facilities are for the sole purpose of providing electric supply to a system operated by a regulated utility for the transfer of electric energy.

    (a) True
    (b) False

72. Junction, pull, and outlet boxes can be located behind PV modules that are secured by removable fasteners.

    (a) True
    (b) False

73. Which of the following wiring methods and enclosures that contain photovoltaic power source conductors shall be marked "WARNING PHOTOVOLTAIC POWER SOUCE" by means of permanently affixed labels or other approved permanent marking?

    (a) Exposed raceways, cable trays, and other wiring methods.
    (b) The covers or enclosures of pull boxes and junction boxes.
    (c) Conduit bodies in which any of the available conduit openings are unused.
    (d) all of these

74. Where a service raceway enters a building or structure from a(n) _____, it shall be sealed in accordance with 300.5(G).

    (a) transformer vault
    (b) underground distribution system
    (c) cable tray
    (d) overhead rack

75. Single-conductor Type USE-2 and single-conductor cable _____ as PV wire can be run exposed at outdoor locations for PV source circuits within the PV array.

    (a) approved
    (b) listed or labeled
    (c) listed and identified
    (d) none of these

76. For interconnected electric power production sources, upon loss of utility source power, an electric power production source shall be manually disconnected from all ungrounded conductors of the utility source and shall not be reconnected until the utility source has been restored.

    (a) True
    (b) False

77. All electrical equipment for large-scale PV electric supply stations shall be approved for installation by _____.

    (a) listing and labeling
    (b) field labeling
    (c) where products complying with 691.5(1) or (2) are not available, by engineering review validating that the electrical equipment is tested to relevant standards or industry practice
    (d) any of these

78. ENT is composed of a material resistant to moisture and chemical atmospheres, and is _____.

    (a) flexible
    (b) flame retardant
    (c) fireproof
    (d) flammable

79. The point of interconnection of the PV system power source to other sources shall be marked at an accessible location at the _____ as a power source and with the rated ac output current and nominal operating ac voltage.

    (a) disconnecting means
    (b) array
    (c) inverter
    (d) none of these

80. A means external to enclosures for connecting intersystem _____ conductors shall be provided at the service equipment or metering equipment enclosure and disconnecting means of buildings or structures supplied by a feeder.

    (a) bonding
    (b) ungrounded
    (c) secondary
    (d) a and b

81. Where equipment operating at 1,000 volts, nominal, or less to ground and likely to require examination, adjustment, servicing, or maintenance while energized is required by installation instructions or function to be located in a space with limited access, and where equipment is installed above a lay-in ceiling, there shall be an opening not smaller than _____.

    (a) 6 in. x 6 in.
    (b) 12 in. x 12 in.
    (c) 22 in. x 22 in.
    (d) 22 in. x 30 in.

82. Separately installed pressure connectors shall be used with conductors at the _____ not exceeding the ampacity at the listed and identified temperature rating of the connector.

    (a) voltages
    (b) temperatures
    (c) listings
    (d) ampacities

83. Where PV source and output circuits operating at greater than _____ are installed in a(n) _____ location, the circuit conductors shall be guarded or installed in Type MC cable or in a raceway.

    (a) 30V, accessible
    (b) 30V, readily accessible
    (c) 60V, accessible
    (d) 60V, readily accessible

84. Where the source circuit operates at over 30V, single-conductor Type USE-2 or listed and identified PV wires installed in a readily accessible location shall be installed in a raceway.

    (a) True
    (b) False

85. A permanent label shall be applied by the installer at the PV dc power source disconnect indicating the _____.

    (a) maximum voltage
    (b) maximum circuit current
    (c) maximum rated output current of the charge controller or dc-to-dc converter (if installed)
    (d) all of these

86. The ampacity adjustment factors of Table 310.15(B)(3)(a) do not apply to Type AC or Type MC cable without an overall outer jacket, if which of the following condition(s) is(are) met?

    (a) Each cable has not more than three current-carrying conductors.
    (b) The conductors are 12 AWG copper.
    (c) No more than 20 current-carrying conductors are installed without maintaining spacing.
    (d) all of these

87. A listed expansion/deflection fitting or other approved means shall be used where a raceway crosses a _____ intended for expansion, contraction or deflection used in buildings, bridges, parking garages, or other structures.

    (a) junction box
    (b) structural joint
    (c) cable tray
    (d) unistrut hanger

88. For one- and two-family dwellings, the maximum voltage for PV system dc circuits is _____.

    (a) 24V
    (b) 48V
    (c) 250V
    (d) 600V

89. Direct-buried service conductors that are not encased in concrete and that are buried 18 in. or more below grade shall have their location identified by a warning ribbon placed in the trench at least _____ in. above the underground installation.

    (a) 6
    (b) 10
    (c) 12
    (d) 18

Final Exam B

90. A dc PV array that has two outputs, each having opposite polarity to a common reference point or center tap is known as a "____."

    (a) bipolar photovoltaic array
    (b) polar photovoltaic array
    (c) a or b
    (d) none of these

91. The conductors of PV output circuits and inverter input and output circuits shall be identified at all points of termination, connection, and splices.

    (a) True
    (b) False

92. Conductors installed in nonmetallic raceways run underground shall be permitted to be arranged as ____ installations. The raceways shall be installed in close proximity, and the conductors shall comply with the provisions of 300.20(B).

    (a) neutral
    (b) grounded conductor
    (c) isolated phase
    (d) all of these

93. All equipment used for electric power production sources operating in stand-alone mode must be ____ for the intended use.

    (a) listed
    (b) field labeled
    (c) marked
    (d) a or b

94. A ____ subarray has two conductors in the output circuit, one positive (+) and one negative (-). Two of these subarrays are used to form a bipolar photovoltaic array.

    (a) bipolar
    (b) monopole
    (c) double-pole
    (d) module

95. Equipment grounding conductors for PV circuits having overcurrent protection shall be sized in accordance with ____.

    (a) 250.122
    (b) 250.66
    (c) Table 250.122
    (d) Table 250.66

96. The required working space for access to live parts of equipment operating at 300 volts-to-ground, where there are exposed live parts on both sides of the workspace is ____ ft.

    (a) 3
    (b) 3½
    (c) 4
    (d) 4½

97. The connectors permitted by Article 690 shall ____.

    (a) be polarized
    (b) be constructed and installed so as to guard against inadvertent contact with live parts by persons
    (c) require a tool for opening if the circuit operates at over 30V nominal maximum dc or 15V ac
    (d) all of these

98. Type NM cable shall be protected from physical damage by ____.

    (a) EMT
    (b) Schedule 80 PVC conduit
    (c) RMC
    (d) any of these

99. The armor of Type AC cable is recognized by the *NEC* as an equipment grounding conductor.

    (a) True
    (b) False

100. All equipment intended for use in PV power systems shall be ____ for the PV application.

    (a) field labeled
    (b) listed
    (c) approved
    (d) a or b

APPENDIX A

ANALYSIS OF 2017 *NEC* CHANGES RELATING TO SOLAR PHOTOVOLATIC SYSTEMS

This appendix contains the summaries and analyses of of the changes to the 2017 *NEC* relating to solar photovolatic systems.

ARTICLE 690—SOLAR PHOTOVOLTAIC (PV) SYSTEMS

690.1 Scope

The scope of this article was changed to correlate with the new Article 691, and the existing diagrams in this section were replaced with new ones.

Analysis

 NEW The 2017 *NEC* added a new Article 691—Large-Scale PV Electric Power Production Facility; due to this, the scope of Article 690 needed to be revised to specifically accept those systems, as they have their own unique hazards and therefore their own unique provisions in Article 691.

The new diagrams included in 690.1 are intended to help the *Code* user identify and understand some of the various components in a PV installation related to Article 690. The new graphic helps us understand that the PV system ends at the PV system disconnect, which can be on the dc or ac side. These graphics are particularly useful to those who aren't familiar with PV systems. The hybrid system diagram in the 2014 *NEC* was removed and replaced by two new ones.

690.2 Definitions

Some definitions have been deleted, others added, and some clarified.

Analysis

 CLARIFIED **Array.** This definition was changed to clarify that an array can create either a dc or ac power-producing unit. The previous definition only included direct current, which left alternating-current modules in a sort of no man's land.

 EDITED **Bipolar Photovoltaic Array.** The change to this definition clarifies that a bipolar PV array is a dc system only.

 NEW **DC-to-DC Converter Output Circuit.** This new term was added to provide a definition in order to delineate some of the new requirements in Article 690.

 NEW **DC-to-DC Converter Source Circuit.** This new term was also added to provide a definition in order to delineate some of the new requirements in this article.

...

Functional Grounded PV System. This is a new term in the *Code*, but it's not new to the PV industry, and it really isn't a new concept either. This term is used internationally to describe a PV system that isn't solidly grounded, but is grounded through a fuse, circuit breaker, resistance device, non-isolated grounded ac circuit, or ground-fault protection system. These systems were employed long before this term was in the *NEC*, and they're discussed in Part V (Grounding and Bonding) of this article.

 Generating Capacity. This new term is pretty much what you would expect it to be. It's the amount of power that parallel-connected inverters can deliver. This new term is used in multiple locations in Article 690.

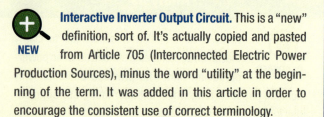 **Interactive System.** This definition was revised to change the term "solar" to "PV" in two locations was removed. The second sentence, which referred to energy storage, was removed as that concept is dealt with in the new Article 706—Energy Storage Systems.

 Interactive Inverter Output Circuit. This is a "new" definition, sort of. It's actually copied and pasted from Article 705 (Interconnected Electric Power Production Sources), minus the word "utility" at the beginning of the term. It was added in this article in order to encourage the consistent use of correct terminology.

 Inverter Input Circuit. This definition was simplified dramatically. The input circuit is just what it sounds like, so why did we need so many words before?

 Inverter Output Circuit. This definition was also simplified dramatically. The output circuit is just what it sounds like, so, once again, why did we need so many words before?

 Multimode Inverter. The definition of multimode inverter no longer uses the term "utility," since a utility isn't the only source of energy to which a multimode inverter can be connected.

 Photovoltaic System DC Circuit. This is a new definition for a circuit that was formerly called a "PV circuit" throughout this article. The term "PV circuit" is incredibly broad, so hopefully this new term will aid in understanding the requirements of this tricky article.

690.4 General Requirements

Changes to this section include an allowance for field labeled equipment, clarify the disconnect requirements for multiple PV systems, and prohibit disconnects in bathrooms.

Analysis

 Field Labeling. Section 690.4(B) was clarified to indicate that using listed products ensures the product will both operate and fail in a safe manner. Listed equipment has been evaluated by a qualified testing laboratory in ways the typical inspector simply can't duplicate. Product standards for equipment aren't free, and an inspector would need to own literally thousands of them if he or she wanted them all. That's one of the reasons we depend on product listing. When a product isn't listed, field evaluation by a qualified testing laboratory is another option. A representative of the laboratory can visit the site, examine the equipment for suitability, and ensure its safety. This isn't a new concept at all, and it's finally being specifically recognized in the *Code*.

 Multiple Systems. Section 690.4(D) was revised to use more accurate language and to fix some errors. The new language specifies that the "PV System Disconnect" can be either dc or ac. The title and text of this subsection were changed from discussing one system with multiple inverters to discussing multiple systems with multiple inverters.

Bathrooms. A new subsection (E) was added that prohibits PV equipment from being installed in a bathroom. The Code Making Panel submitted this input (proposal) with no technical substantiation whatsoever, but my guess is that it was added to correlate with the rule in 230.70(A)(2). Even though there was no technical substantiation, it's pretty tough to argue that PV equipment should be allowed in a bathroom.

Bipolar. What was 690.7(E) is now 690.7(C), which covers bipolar source and output circuits. This section was reduced from a paragraph, an exception, a three-item list, and a warning label, to two simple sentences.

REORGANIZED

690.7 Maximum Voltage

The rules regarding the maximum voltage of a PV system were extensively revised, language was added addressing dc-to-dc converters, wiring method requirements were removed from this section, and the rules for bipolar circuits were simplified and relocated.

690.8 Circuit Current and Circuit Sizing

Changes to this section include an optional method of calculation for systems of 100 kW or more, adding provisions for dc-to-dc converter source and output circuits, and addressing adjustable electronic overcurrent devices.

Analysis

Maximum Voltage. Most of the material in this section was relocated or removed. What was 690.7(C), which provided the maximum voltage allowed for a PV system, is now the opening statement to 690.7. This is, without question, a better location for it.

CLARIFIED

When you read the title of a section that says "maximum voltage" you expect to read what that maximum voltage is immediately, not in the third subsection. Dwellings are still permitted to have up to 600V PV systems, whereas other installations can go up to 1,000V. PV systems that operate up to 1,500V are permitted when not on or in a building.

The maximum voltage for PV systems of 100 kW or larger can now be calculated under engineering supervision [690.7(A)(3)], and a new Informational Note was added to alert *Code* users of a method that can be used for compliance.

DC-to-DC Converters. The new version of 690.7(B) provides guidance on how to calculate dc-to-dc converter source and output circuits for one or more converters.

NEW

Wiring Methods. The wiring methods that were formerly discussed in 690.7(D) were moved to 690.31, since there was no reason to be talking about wiring methods in the section dealing with maximum voltages.

REORGANIZED

Analysis

Large Systems. Calculating the current of 100 kW or larger systems is now clearly addressed in 690.8(A)(2). Like the change to 690.7, it includes an Informational Note that refers to a calculation model from Sandia National Laboratories.

NEW

DC-to-DC Converters. Added and revised text in 690.8(A)(5) and 690.8(A)(6) clarifies that both the source and output circuits of dc-to-dc converters are determined in the same way using the continuous output current rating.

CLARIFIED

Adjustable Overcurrent Devices. Section 690.8 has new (and better) titles for subsections (A) and (B) without changing any of the provisions therein, and a new subsection (C) was added to address adjustable overcurrent devices. This "new" material really isn't new at all, as it only points the *Code* user back to 240.6, which covers these devices.

In a nutshell, the rating of an adjustable overcurrent device is considered to be the highest possible setting [240.6(B)] unless it has restricted access as described in 240.6(C). Most devices meet at least one of the items in 240.6(C)(1), (2), or (3), allowing for the rating of the device to be considered whatever it's adjusted to.

690.9 Overcurrent Protection

Changes made to this section, which covers overcurrent protection, include editorial revisions, correlating changes, and changes to the allowances for a single overcurrent device.

Analysis

EDITED This section, along with much of this article, has seen a lot of changes over the last few *NEC* cycles. Due to this, some errors have been made that have been corrected in this edition. The 2014 version of 690.9(C) and 690.9(D) were deleted in this revision cycle, as they didn't contain any information that wasn't discussed elsewhere in this section. This removed some conflicts that could occur if one were willing to jump down the rabbit hole and find them.

EDITED Section 690.9(A) was simplified by giving a requirement that PV system dc circuits and inverter output circuits must have overcurrent protection, then stating that overcurrent protection isn't required for circuits that are sized to handle the highest available current.

EDITED The overcurrent device ratings in 690.9(B) were revised to mirror the requirements in 690.8 for conductor sizing. This concept works exceptionally well in 210.19 and 210.20 for branch circuits, as well as in 215.2 and 215.3 for feeder circuits. This will be a welcome change to experienced *Code* users, and even new ones will quickly appreciate the concept of the parallel requirements.

CLARIFIED **Single Overcurrent Device.** Section 690.9(C) was revised to allow for a single overcurrent device when overcurrent protection is needed to protect the modules and output or source circuits. Of particular interest is the fact that ungrounded systems no longer require overcurrent protection in each conductor.

690.10 Stand-Alone Systems

This section was more or less deleted due to the new Article 710—Stand-Alone Systems.

Analysis

NEW A new Article 710—Stand-Alone Systems has been created, therefore a simple reference to this Article was all that was needed.

690.11 Arc-Fault Circuit Protection (Direct Current)

A new exception for the dc AFCI requirement was added.

Analysis

REDUCED Not all PV installations have the same hazards. A PV system that has its output circuit(s) directly buried, installed in a metal raceway, or installed in an enclosed metallic cable tray is inherently safer as it relates to arcing faults. A PV installation that isn't on or in a building isn't necessarily safer, but it also isn't going to burn a building down should an arcing fault occur. A detached building that houses only PV equipment can certainly burn down as a result of an arcing fault, but, well…who cares I guess! This actually wasn't part of the original proposal (input) and was added by Code Making Panel 4 without any explanation.

690.12 Rapid Shutdown of PV Systems on Buildings

The requirements for rapid shutdown have been extensively revised.

Analysis

CLARIFIED

When you make a new rule as significant as the 2014 rapid shutdown requirement, you're probably going to be rewriting the entire thing to fix the mistakes nobody thought about. The people who submit input and comments, and the members of the Code Making Panels are all doing the best they can, but things get missed and mistakes are made and technologies change rapidly. A new rule like this usually takes at least three *Code* cycles (nine years) before it says what everyone wanted it to say in the first place. Most of the changes to this edition of 690.12 came from input provided by the International Association of Fire Fighters (IAFF) and the Solar Energy Industries Association (SEIA).

The first change is to the opening paragraph of this section, which clarifies that the intent of this rule is to protect emergency responders. Without coming right out and saying it, this rule is for fire fighters. PV systems create a major additional hazard to those who now must worry about the fire and being electrocuted by the PV system!

An exception was added for buildings that house only PV equipment. The concern in these instances isn't losing the building, it's ensuring that the surrounding environment isn't destroyed as well. Losing such a building is certainly painful, but containing and confining it to just that building and preventing a forest fire (for example) is much more important.

The areas/equipment to which 690.12 applies have been clarified and are now referred to as the "array boundary." Of particular interest is a change from 10 seconds to 30 seconds in the time required for the voltage reduction to occur. This change happened for two reasons. First, manufacturers simply couldn't do it in 10 seconds, and secondly, there's no reason to do it that quickly. The TIA for this change from June of 2016 actually indicates the reason to go to 30 seconds stemmed from the utilities desire to "ride through grid disturbances for up to 20 seconds." "...to help distinguish between a full shutdown of ac supply for safety and intermittent problems with the utility supply." http://www.nfpa.org/assets/files/AboutTheCodes/70/ProposedTIA%201223_NFPA_70.pdf].

The fire fighter groups who provided input to this rule were fine with 30 seconds. Since this rule is for them, why not let them dictate the time? An effective date of January 1, 2019 was put into the *NEC* in order for the product standard to be completed.

The location of the rapid shutdown device is now discussed [690.12(C)], as is the type of device used [690.12(C)(1) and (2)]. The device must be installed at a readily accessible location outside of the building for one- and two-family dwellings. The device can be the service disconnect, the PV disconnect, or another device that plainly indicates "on" and "off."

Revised text discusses voltage thresholds and proximity (i.e. 80V or less within 30 seconds inside the array and within 1 meter (3 ft) of the outer edge of the array within 30 seconds after initiation, effective January 1, 2019).

690.13 PV System Disconnecting Means

The section dealing with PV disconnects was reorganized, language about disconnects on the supply side of the service was added, and a new subsection was relocated from 690.17 to indicate the types and ratings of disconnects permitted.

Analysis

REORGANIZED

Due to the amount of input to change Article 690 over the last several years, many sections receive complete makeovers every *Code* cycle; in 2017, it's Section 690.13.

Some of the language in 690.15 was moved to 690.13, as it's more applicable. Portions of the grouping subsection 690.13(E) were moved into the opening paragraph of the rule, as the statement "a PV disconnecting means shall not

•••

be required at the PV module or array location" had nothing to do with grouping. Changes like this may not be technical, but they really do make the *NEC* easier to use and understand, and therefore better.

Supply-Side Rating. Subsection (C) was revised in 2014 to state that a PV disconnect doesn't need to be listed as "Suitable for Use as Service Equipment (SUSE)." This makes sense if the PV disconnect is downstream of the service disconnect, but if it's installed ahead of the service disconnect the SUSE listing is required. Because equipment that carries the SUSE listing can be connected neutral-to-frame, this change addresses a hole that was in the 2014 *Code*.

Disconnect Types. The types of disconnects permitted have been relocated from 690.17 to this section, as have the rating requirements. Reminder there can be a maximum of six disconnecting means for each PV system [690.13(D)].

690.15 PV Equipment Disconnect

Changes to this section have been made mainly to clarify that a PV equipment disconnect is an isolating device.

Analysis

There are a number of different disconnecting means discussed in Article 690. PV disconnects, ac disconnects, equipment disconnects, isolating devices. The purpose of the disconnect discussed in this rule is to allow a technician to service or replace individual components, such as a charge controller, without being exposed to energized conductors. The 30A language in the rule is intended to allow ac modules and micro inverters to use connectors for isolation.

690.31 Wiring Methods

Type MC cable is now permitted for protecting readily accessible conductors, the table for temperature correction was relocated, the grouping requirements were editorially revised, and the old language about module connection arrangement was removed.

Analysis

Type MC Cable. Obviously conductors that are readily accessible need to be protected for the sake of electrical safety. This can certainly be done by installing them in a raceway, and this has been the recognized method of protection for some time now. Type MC cable that's suitable for the location, such as PVC jacketed MC cable, allows an adequate amount of protection as well, and is now recognized as an option when protection is required.

As with much of Article 690, this section received a fair amount of editing, including moving the temperature correction factor to subsection (A) and clarifying the grouping and identification provisions. These changes weren't technical, but do make for a more easily understood requirement.

690.33 Connectors

Changes to this rule clarify the connectors to which it applies.

Analysis

There are connectors that are used as part of building-integrated PV products (such as roofing materials). These connectors are listed to be field installed and then rendered inaccessible. It's not feasible, or even reasonable, to require them to meet the requirements of 690.33, particularly the rules relating to locking mechanisms and labeling.

690.41 System Grounding

The system grounding requirements for PV systems have been clarified, a new phrase "functional ground" is now used, and the ground-fault protection rules from 690.5 were relocated here.

Analysis

NEW

The *NEC* now addresses six different system grounding options instead of the four discussed in 2014. The revisions cover new options for PV arrays with up to two source circuits where none of the dc circuits are on or in buildings (option 5). These systems can be installed solidly grounded without ground-fault protection [690.41(B) Ex]. The other new option is non-isolated PV systems, which is item (3) in the list.

NEW

Functional Ground. There's a lot of debate about what to call the grounding configuration of a PV system. Most PV systems are grounded, but they aren't solidly grounded since they're grounded through a fuse or circuit breaker. They also aren't impedance grounded, since impedance is an alternating-current concept, not a direct-current concept. The originally accepted language for the 2017 *Code* was going to be "reference grounded," but it conflicted with term "reference grounding point" used in Article 517. "Functional ground" was chosen because it's similar to the term used in Europe.

The ground-fault protection rules formerly found in 690.5 were relocated here, which does seem to be a better location.

690.42 Point of Grounding Connection

The exception is now part of the rule, and the Informational Note was removed.

Analysis

CLARIFIED

DC Grounding Location. The previous edition of the *NEC* stated that the dc grounding connection could be located anywhere on the PV output circuit. The exception stated that systems with ground-fault protection built in (which most systems have) could use the built in protection to satisfy this requirement. That means that most installations required no action at all by the installer. Since this is the much more frequent type of installation, the exception covering it was changed into positive text within the rule itself.

EDITED

Informational Note. The Informational Note that was here stated that grounding the system as close to the source as possible was preferred. Although Informational Notes aren't mandatory [90.5(A)], inspectors were reading this and requiring that the connection be made at the array. This isn't, and wasn't, the intent of the rule; so in order to remove confusion the note was deleted altogether.

690.43 Equipment Grounding (Bonding)

This section, which deals with equipment grounding and bonding, was editorially revised.

Analysis

EDITED

Changes to this section simply consolidate five paragraphs of information into three. No technical changes were made.

690.47 Grounding Electrode System

The requirements for a grounding electrode system have been simplified.

Analysis

CLARIFIED The requirements for earth grounding a PV system are now handled by following the rules of Article 250. Additional electrodes are now allowed to be installed, but their installation isn't required.

690.56 Identification of Power Sources

The signage requirements for systems with rapid shutdown have been substantially increased.

Analysis

EXPANDED Fighting a fire on a building with a PV system is no joke. Fire fighters need to have as much information as possible, and the signage telling them how to shut down the system needs to be as plain and as easy to understand as possible. The new identification requirements are the result of a task group of over twenty individuals from Code Making Panel 4, testing laboratories, the solar industry, insurance industry, and fire service.

690.59 Connection to Other Sources

The requirements in this section for PV systems connected to other sources (like a utility) have been simplified.

Analysis

EDITED If you have a PV system that's connected to other systems too, you need to comply with Article 705. That's it. Part VII of this article has been relegated to a single sentence that contains no real information. Code Making Panel 4 has been taking the old editing advice of "omit needless words" to heart!

690.71 General

The title of Part VIII and its provisions from the 2014 *NEC* are now contained in a new Article 706 which covers energy storage systems.

Analysis

NEW The relocating of energy storage requirements to a new Article 706, made sense, since energy storage has nothing to do with solar PV systems.

ARTICLE 691—LARGE-SCALE PV ELECTRIC POWER PRODUCTION FACILITY

Article 691—Large-Scale PV Electric Power Production Facility

A new Article 691 was added, which covers large-scale PV electric power production facilities.

Analysis

NEW If you thought PV installations were a passing fad you might not have been alone, but you were wrong nonetheless. As the technology grows we're seeing more and more of these systems installed; and they're becoming bigger, better, and more advanced. This new article applies to PV systems over 5,000 kW, and it identifies provisions for systems operating over 1,000V.

It's important to remember, and there's an Informational Note right in the scope to tell us, that utility generation PV systems aren't covered by the *Code*. That alone will leave many of these installations beyond the reach of the *NEC*, but there certainly are, and will continue to be, installations of this magnitude that aren't owned by a utility.

INDEX

Description	Rule	Page
A		
Armored Cable (Type AC)		
Bends	320.24	345
Boxes and Fittings	320.40	346
Conductor Ampacity	320.80	347
Construction	320.100	347
Definition	320.2	343
Equipment Grounding Conductor	320.108	348
Exposed Work	320.15	344
In Accessible Attics or Roof Spaces	320.23	345
Listing Requirements	320.6	344
Securing and Supporting	320.30	345
Through or Parallel to Framing Members	320.17	344
Uses Not Permitted	320.12	344
Uses Permitted	320.10	344
B		
Branch Circuits		
Branch Circuits in Buildings with Multiple Occupancies	210.25	101
Conductor Sizing	210.19	95
Identification for Branch Circuits	210.5	93
Multiple Branch Circuits	210.7	94
Multiwire Branch Circuits	210.4	90
Other Articles	210.3	90
Overcurrent Protection	210.20	98
Permissible Loads, Individual Branch Circuits	210.22	99
Permissible Loads, Multiple-Outlet Branch Circuits	210.23	100
Receptacle Rating	210.21	99

Description	Rule	Page
C		
Cabinets		
Damp or Wet Locations	312.2	315
Deflection of Conductors	312.6	318
Enclosures	312.5	316
Installed in Walls	312.3	316
Overcurrent Protection Device Enclosures	312.8	318
Repairing Gaps	312.4	316
Cable Trays		
Bushed Raceway	392.46	430
Cable and Conductor Installation	392.20	430
Cable Splices	392.56	430
Cable Tray Installations	392.18	429
Definition	392.2	427
Equipment Grounding Conductor	392.60	431
Number of Conductors or Cables	392.22	430
Securing and Supporting	392.30	430
Uses Not Permitted	392.12	429
Uses Permitted	392.10	428
Cartridge Fuses and Fuseholders		
Classification	240.61	161
General	240.60	160
Circuit Breakers		
Applications	240.85	162
Arc Energy Reduction	240.87	163
Indicating	240.81	161
Markings	240.83	161
Method of Operation	240.80	161
Nontamperable	240.82	161

Index

Description	Rule	Page
C *(continued)*		
Conductors		
Conductor Ampacity	310.15	303
Conductor Construction and Application	310.104	312
Conductor Identification	310.110	313
Conductors	310.106	312
Uses Permitted	310.10	299
D		
Definitions	100	21
E		
Electrical Metallic Tubing (Type EMT)		
Bends	358.24	413
Couplings and Connectors	358.42	414
Definition	358.2	411
Grounding	358.60	415
Listing Requirements	358.6	411
Number of Bends (360°)	358.26	413
Number of Conductors	358.22	412
Reaming and Threading	358.28	413
Securing and Supporting	358.30	414
Trade Size	358.20	412
Uses Not Permitted	358.12	412
Uses Permitted	358.10	411
Electrical Nonmetallic Tubing (Type ENT)		
Bends	362.24	420
Bushings	362.46	421
Definition	362.2	417
Equipment Grounding Conductor	362.60	422
Joints	362.48	421
Number of Bends (360°)	362.26	420
Number of Conductors	362.22	420
Securing and Supporting	362.30	420
Trade Sizes	362.20	420
Trimming	362.28	420
Uses Not Permitted	362.12	419
Uses Permitted	362.10	418
Enclosures		
Conductors That Enter Boxes or Conduit Bodies	314.17	328
Covers and Canopies	314.25	333
Damp or Wet Locations	314.15	322
Flush-Mounted Box Installations	314.20	329
Handhole Enclosures	314.30	340
Metal Boxes	314.4	322
Nonmetallic Boxes	314.3	321
Number of Conductors in Boxes and Conduit Bodies	314.16	323
Outlet Box	314.27	334
Repairing Noncombustible Surfaces	314.21	330
Sizing Conductors 4 AWG and Larger	314.28	336
Support of Boxes and Conduit Bodies	314.23	330
Surface Extensions	314.22	330
Wiring to be Accessible	314.29	339
F		
Feeders		
Conductor Identification	215.12	108
Equipment Grounding Conductor	215.6	107
Feeders with Common Neutral Conductor	215.4	107
Ground-Fault Protection of Equipment	215.10	108
Minimum Rating	215.2	104
Overcurrent Protection Sizing	215.3	107
Flexible Cords		
Ampacity of Flexible Cords and Flexible Cables	400.5	442
Equipment Grounding Conductor Identification	400.23	445
Protection from Damage	400.17	445
Pull at Joints and Terminals	400.14	445
Suitability	400.3	441
Types of Flexible Cords and Flexible Cables	400.4	442
Uses Not Permitted	400.12	443
Uses Permitted	400.10	442
Flexible Metal Conduit (Type FMC)		
Bends	348.24	389
Definition	348.2	387
Fittings	348.42	390
Grounding and Bonding	348.60	390
Listing Requirements	348.6	387
Number of Bends (360°)	348.26	389
Number of Conductors	348.22	388
Securing and Supporting	348.30	389
Trade Size	348.20	388
Trimming	348.28	389
Uses Not Permitted	348.12	388
Uses Permitted	348.10	387

Index

Description	Rule	Page
Fuses Edison-Base		
Edison-Base Fuseholders	240.52	159
Edison-Base Fuses	240.51	159
General	240.50	159
Type S Fuses	240.53	159
Type S Fuses, Adapters, and Fuseholders	240.54	159

G

Description	Rule	Page
General		
Approval of Conductors and Equipment	110.2	47
Arc-Flash Hazard Warning	110.16	60
Available Fault Current	110.24	62
Boxes or Conduit Bodies	300.15	285
Code Arrangement	90.3	11
Conductor Material	110.5	48
Conductor Sizes	110.6	49
Conductor Termination and Splicing	110.14	54
Conductors	300.3	266
Deteriorating Agents	110.11	51
Electrical Continuity	300.10	280
Enclosure Types	110.28	72
Enforcement	90.4	12
Equipment Short-Circuit Current Rating	110.10	51
Examination of Equipment for Product Safety	90.7	14
Examination, Identification, Installation, Use, and Product Listing	110.3	48
Formal Interpretations	90.6	14
Guarding	110.27	71
High-Leg Conductor Identification	110.15	59
Identification of Disconnecting Means	110.22	62
Induced Currents in Ferrous Metal Enclosures and Raceways	300.20	291
Inserting Conductors in Raceways	300.18	290
Interrupting Overcurrent Protection Rating	110.9	50
Length of Free Conductors	300.14	285
Lockable Disconnecting Means	110.25	63
Mandatory Requirements and Explanatory Material	90.5	14
Markings	110.21	61
Mechanical Continuity	300.12	283
Mechanical Execution of Work	110.12	53
Mounting and Cooling of Equipment	110.13	54
Not Permitted in Raceways	300.8	280
Panels Designed to Allow Access	300.23	297
Protection Against Corrosion and Deterioration	300.6	278
Protection Against Physical Damage	300.4	269
Purpose of the *NEC*	90.1	7
Raceway or Cable to Open or Concealed Wiring	300.16	288
Raceway Sizing	300.17	288
Raceways Exposed to Different Temperatures	300.7	279
Raceways in Wet Locations Above Grade	300.9	280
Scope of the *NEC*	90.2	9
Securing and Supporting	300.11	281
Spaces About Electrical Equipment	110.26	63
Splices and Pigtails	300.13	283
Spread of Fire or Products of Combustion	300.21	292
Suitable Wiring Methods	110.8	49
Supporting Conductors in Vertical Raceways	300.19	290
Underground Installations	300.5	272
Units of Measurement	90.9	15
Voltages	110.4	48
Wiring in Ducts and Plenum Spaces	300.22	293
Wiring Integrity	110.7	49
Generators		
Ampacity of Conductors	445.13	468
Disconnecting Means and Shutdown of Prime Mover	445.18	468
Overcurrent Protection	445.12	467
Grounded Conductor		
General	200.2	82
Identification of Terminals	200.10	86
Neutral Conductor	200.4	82
Neutral Conductor Identification	200.6	83
Terminal Identification	200.9	86
Use of White or Gray Color	200.7	85
Grounding and Bonding		
Bonding		
Bonding Communications Systems	250.94	220
Bonding Equipment for Services	250.92	217
Bonding Loosely Jointed Metal Raceways	250.98	223
Bonding Metal Parts Containing 277V and 480V Circuits	250.97	222
Bonding of Piping Systems and Exposed Structural Metal	250.104	225
Bonding Other Enclosures	250.96	221
General	250.90	216
Grounded Conductor, Bonding Conductors, and Jumpers	250.102	223
Lightning Protection System	250.106	229

Index

Description	Rule	Page
G (continued)		
Enclosures and Raceways		
Other Enclosures	250.86	216
Service Raceways and Enclosures	250.80	216
Equipment Grounding and Equipment Grounding Conductors		
Connecting Receptacle Grounding Terminal to Metal Enclosure	250.146	244
Continuity and Attachment of Equipment Grounding Conductors in Metal Boxes	250.148	247
Cord-and-Plug-Connected	250.138	242
Cord-and-Plug-Connected Equipment	250.114	230
Equipment Connected by Permanent Wiring Methods	250.134	241
Equipment Considered Grounded	250.136	242
Equipment Grounding Conductor Connections	250.130	241
Equipment Grounding Conductor Installation	250.120	236
Fixed Equipment Connected by Permanent Wiring Methods-General	250.110	230
Identification of Equipment Grounding Conductors	250.119	235
Ranges, Ovens, and Clothes Dryers	250.140	242
Sizing Equipment Grounding Conductor	250.122	237
Specific Equipment Fastened in Place	250.112	230
Types of Equipment Grounding Conductors	250.118	231
Use of Equipment Grounding Conductors	250.121	237
Use of Neutral Conductor for Equipment Grounding (Bonding)	250.142	243
General		
Clean Surfaces	250.12	177
Definition	250.2	165
Objectionable Current	250.6	172
Performance Requirements for Grounding and Bonding	250.4	166
Protection of Fittings	250.10	177
Termination of Grounding and Bonding Conductors	250.8	176
Grounding Electrode System and Grounding Electrode Conductor		
Auxiliary Grounding Electrodes	250.54	205
Common Grounding Electrode	250.58	206
Grounding Electrode Conductor	250.62	207
Grounding Electrode Conductor Installation	250.64	208
Grounding Electrode Conductor Termination Fittings	250.70	215
Grounding Electrode Installation Requirements	250.53	200
Grounding Electrode System	250.50	196
Grounding Electrode Types	250.52	197
Lightning Protection Electrode	250.60	206
Sizing Grounding Electrode Conductor	250.66	212
Termination to the Grounding Electrode	250.68	213
System Grounding and Bonding		
Buildings Supplied by a Feeder	250.32	193
Generators-Portable and Vehicle-Mounted	250.34	195
High-Impedance Grounded Systems	250.36	196
Main Bonding Jumper and System Bonding Jumper	250.28	183
Permanently Installed Generators	250.35	195
Separately Derived Systems-Grounding and Bonding	250.30	184
Service Equipment-Grounding and Bonding	250.24	179
Systems Required to be Grounded	250.20	177
Ungrounded Systems	250.21	178
I		
Interconnected Electric Power Production Sources		
Definitions	705.2	537
Directory	705.10	538
Equipment Approval	705.6	538
Location of Overcurrent Protection	705.31	544
Loss of Utility Power	705.40	544
Point of Connection	705.12	538
System Installation	705.8	538
Voltage Unbalanced (Imbalanced) Interconnections	705.100	544
Intermediate Metal Conduit (Type IMC)		
Bends	342.24	377
Bushings	342.46	379
Couplings and Connectors	342.42	379
Definition	342.2	375
Dissimilar Metals	342.14	376
Listing Requirements	342.6	376
Number of Bends (360°)	342.26	377
Number of Conductors	342.22	376
Reaming	342.28	377
Securing and Supporting	342.30	377
Trade Size	342.20	376
Uses Permitted	342.10	376

Index

Description	Rule	Page

L

Large-Scale Photovoltaic (PV) Electric Power Production Facility

Arc-Fault Mitigation	691.10	525
Conformance of Construction to Engineered Design	691.7	524
Definitions	691.2	523
Direct-Current Operating Voltage	691.7	524
Disconnection of Photovoltaic Equipment	691.9	524
Engineered Design	691.6	524
Equipment Approval	691.5	524
Fence Grounding	691.11	525
Special Requirements for Large-Scale PV Electric Supply Stations	691.4	524

Liquidtight Flexible Metal Conduit (Type LFMC)

Bends	350.24	395
Definition	350.2	393
Fittings	350.42	396
Grounding and Bonding	350.60	396
Listing Requirements	350.6	394
Number of Bends (360°)	350.26	395
Number of Conductors	350.22	395
Securing and Supporting	350.30	395
Trade Size	350.20	394
Trimming	350.28	395
Uses Not Permitted	350.12	394
Uses Permitted	350.10	394

Liquidtight Flexible Nonmetallic Conduit (Type LFNC)

Bends	356.24	409
Definition	356.2	407
Equipment Grounding Conductor	356.60	410
Fittings	356.42	410
Listing Requirements	356.6	407
Number of Bends (360°)	356.26	409
Number of Conductors	356.22	408
Securing and Supporting	356.30	409
Trade Size	356.20	408
Uses Not Permitted	356.12	408
Uses Permitted	356.10	408

M

Metal Wireways

Conductors Connected in Parallel	376.20	424
Conductors-Maximum Size	376.21	424
Construction	376.100	426
Definition	376.2	423
Number of Conductors and Ampacity	376.22	424
Splices, Taps, and Power Distribution Blocks	376.56	425
Supports	376.30	425
Uses Not Permitted	376.12	424
Uses Permitted	376.10	424
Wireway Sizing	376.23	425

Metal-Clad Cable (Type MC)

Bends	330.24	352
Conductor Ampacities	330.80	354
Definition	330.2	349
Equipment Grounding Conductor	330.108	354
Exposed Work	330.15	351
In Accessible Attics or Roof Spaces	330.23	352
Listing Requirements	330.6	349
Securing and Supporting	330.30	352
Through or Parallel to Framing Members	330.17	351
Uses Not Permitted	330.12	351
Uses Permitted	330.10	350

N

Nonmetallic-Sheathed Cable (Types NM and NMC)

Attics and Roof Spaces	334.23	362
Bends	334.24	362
Boxes and Fittings	334.40	363
Conductor Ampacity	334.80	364
Conductors	334.104	365
Construction	334.100	365
Definition	334.2	357
Equipment Grounding Conductor	334.108	365
Exposed Work	334.15	360
Insulation	334.112	365
Listing Requirements	334.6	358
Securing and Supporting	334.30	362
Through or Parallel to Framing Members	334.17	361
Uses Not Permitted	334.12	359
Uses Permitted	334.10	358

Index

Description	Rule	Page

O

Outside Branch Circuits and Feeders

Access to Occupants	225.35	119
Attachment	225.16	113
Clearance for Overhead Conductors	225.18	114
Clearances from Buildings	225.19	115
Disconnect Construction	225.38	120
Disconnect Location	225.32	117
Disconnecting Means	225.31	117
Grouping of Disconnects	225.34	119
Identification of Multiple Feeders	225.37	120
Luminaires Installed Outdoors	225.7	112
Masts as Supports	225.17	113
Maximum Number of Disconnects	225.33	119
Minimum Size of Conductors	225.6	112
Number of Feeder Supplies	225.30	117
Open-Conductor Supports	225.12	113
Other Articles	225.2	112
Raceway Seals	225.27	117
Raceways on Exterior Surfaces	225.22	116
Rating of Disconnecting Means	225.39	120
Supports Over Buildings	225.15	113
Trees for Conductor Support	225.26	116
Type of Disconnecting Means	225.36	119

Overcurrent Protection—General

Definitions	240.2	144
Damp or Wet Locations	240.32	158
Ground-Fault Protection of Equipment	240.13	150
Location of Overcurrent Protection Devices	240.24	156
Overcurrent Protection Location in Circuit	240.21	151
Overcurrent Protection of Conductors	240.4	145
Overcurrent Protection of Equipment	240.3	145
Overcurrent Protection of Flexible Cords and Fixture Wires	240.5	148
Standard Ampere Ratings	240.6	149
Supplementary Overcurrent Protection	240.10	149
Ungrounded Conductors	240.15	150
Vertical Position	240.33	158

P

Power and Control Tray Cable (Type TC)

Ampacity	336.80	368
Bending Radius	336.24	368
Definition	336.2	367
Listing Requirements	336.6	367
Uses Not Permitted	336.12	368
Uses Permitted	336.10	367

R

Rigid Metal Conduit (Type RMC)

Bends	344.24	383
Bushings	344.46	386
Couplings and Connectors	344.42	385
Definition	344.2	381
Dissimilar Metals	344.14	382
Listing Requirements	344.6	382
Number of Bends (360°)	344.26	383
Number of Conductors	344.22	383
Reaming	344.28	383
Securing and Supporting	344.30	384
Trade Size	344.20	382
Uses Permitted	344.10	382

Rigid Polyvinyl Chloride Conduit (Type PVC)

Bends	352.24	402
Bushings	352.46	404
Definition	352.2	399
Equipment Grounding Conductor	352.60	405
Expansion Fittings	352.44	403
Joints	352.48	405
Number of Bends (360°)	352.26	402
Number of Conductors	352.22	401
Securing and Supporting	352.30	402
Trade Size	352.20	401
Trimming	352.28	402
Uses Not Permitted	352.12	401
Uses Permitted	352.10	400

S

Service-Entrance Cable (Types SE and USE)

Bends	338.24	371
Definitions	338.2	369
Listing Requirements	338.6	370
Uses Not Permitted	338.12	371
Uses Permitted	338.10	370

Index

Description	Rule	Page
Services		
Cable Supports	230.51	134
Clearance from Building Openings	230.9	125
Conductors Considered Outside a Building	230.6	123
Connected on Supply Side of the Service Disconnect	230.82	139
Connection to Terminals on Disconnect	230.81	139
Ground-Fault Protection of Equipment	230.95	142
Grouping of Disconnects	230.72	138
High-Leg Identification	230.56	134
Indicating of Disconnect	230.77	138
Location of Overload Protection	230.91	142
Manual or Power Operated Disconnect	230.76	138
Marking for Service Equipment	230.66	135
Means of Attachment	230.27	128
Not to Pass Through a Building	230.3	123
Number of Disconnects	230.71	137
Number of Service-Entrance Conductor Sets	230.40	130
Number of Services	230.2	122
Overhead Service Conductor Size and Rating	230.23	126
Overhead Service Locations	230.54	134
Overload Protection	230.90	141
Point of Attachment	230.26	128
Protection Against Damage	230.32	130
Protection Against Physical Damage	230.50	133
Raceway Seals	230.8	125
Raceways to Drain	230.53	134
Rating of Disconnect	230.79	139
Service Conductors Separate from Other Conductors	230.7	124
Service Disconnect Requirements	230.70	136
Service Masts Used as Supports	230.28	128
Size and Rating	230.42	131
Spliced Conductors	230.46	132
Supports over Buildings	230.29	129
Underground Service Conductor Size and Rating	230.31	129
Vegetation as Support	230.10	125
Vertical Clearance for Overhead Service Conductors	230.24	127
Wiring Methods	230.43	132
Solar Photovoltaic (PV) Systems		
Access to Boxes	690.34	515
Alternating-Current Modules	690.6	494
Arc-Fault Circuit Protection (Direct Current)	690.11	507
Circuit Current and Conductor Sizing	690.8	498
Component Interconnections	690.32	515
Connection to Other Power Sources	690.59	522
Connectors	690.33	515
Definitions	690.2	488
Energy Storage, General	690.71	522
General Requirements	690.4	493
Grounding—Array Equipment Grounding Conductors	690.46	518
Grounding—Equipment Grounding and Bonding	690.43	516
Grounding—Grounding Electrode System.	690.47	518
Grounding—Point of Grounding Connection	690.42	516
Grounding—Size of Equipment Grounding Conductors	690.45	517
Grounding—System Grounding	690.41	516
Identification of Power Sources	690.56	521
Interactive System Point of Interconnection	690.54	520
Maximum Voltage	690.7	494
Overcurrent Protection	690.9	504
Power Source Label	690.53	519
PV Equipment Isolating/Disconnecting	690.15	509
PV System Disconnecting Means	690.13	508
PV Systems Connected to Energy Storage Systems	690.55	520
Rapid Shutdown of PV Systems on Buildings	690.12	507
Self-Regulated PV Charge Control	690.72	522
Stand-Alone Systems	690.10	506
Wiring Methods	690.31	511
Stand-Alone Systems		
Equipment Approval	710.6	547
General	710.15	548
Storage Batteries		
Battery and Cell Terminations	480.4	476
Battery Disconnect	480.7	477
Battery Support Systems	480.9	477
Definitions	480.2	475
Listing Requirement	480.3	476
Wiring and Equipment Supplied from Batteries	480.5	476
Surge Protective Devices (SPDs)		
Listing	285.6	250
Location	285.11	251
Number Required	285.4	250
Routing of Conductors	285.12	251

Index

Description	Rule	Page
U		
Underground Feeder and Branch-Circuit Cable (Type UF)		
Ampacity	340.80	374
Bends	340.24	374
Definition	340.2	373
Insulation	340.112	374
Uses Not Permitted	340.12	374
Uses Permitted	340.10	374

ABOUT THE AUTHOR

Mike Holt—Author

Founder and President
Mike Holt Enterprises
Groveland, Florida

Mike Holt's electrical career has spanned all aspects of the trade, from being an apprentice to becoming a contractor and inspector. His teaching career began in 1974 when he became an exam preparation instructor at a local community school. He was so effective that his students encouraged him to open his own training school, dedicated to helping the electrical industry. In 1975, while also running a full-service electrical contracting firm, Mike opened his school. It became so successful that by 1980 he stopped electrical contracting to completely devote his time to electrical training at a national level. Today, Mike Holt Enterprises is a leading training and publishing company for the industry, specializing in helping electrical professionals take their careers to the next level.

Mike's own educational journey impacts the way he designs training programs. As a young man he was unable to complete the requirements for his high school diploma due to life circumstances. Realizing that success depends on one's education, he immediately attained his GED. Then ten years later, he attended the University of Miami's Graduate School for a Master's degree in Business Administration. He understands the needs of his students, and because of his own experience, strongly encourages and motivates them to continue their own education. He's never lost sight of how hard it can be for students who are intimidated by the complexity of the *NEC*, by school, or by their own feelings about learning. His ultimate goal has always been about increasing electrical safety and improving lives—this commitment and vision continue to guide him to this day.

Mike has written hundreds of books, and created DVDs, online programs, MP3s, and other training materials that have made a huge impact on the industry. He's mastered the art of explaining complicated concepts in a simple but direct style. His ability to simplify technical concepts, and his one-of-a-kind presentation style, explain his unique position as one of the premier educators and *Code* experts in the United States. In addition to the materials he's produced, and the extensive list of companies around the world for whom he's provided training, Mike has written articles that have been seen in numerous industry magazines including, *Electrical Construction & Maintenance* (EC&M), *CEE News, Electrical Design and Installation* (EDI), *Electrical Contractor* (EC), *International Association of Electrical Inspectors* (IAEI News), *The Electrical Distributor* (TED), *Power Quality* (PQ) *Magazine,* and *Solar Pro Magazine.*

Mike resides in Central Florida, is the father of seven children, has five grandchildren, and enjoys many outside interests and activities. His commitment to pushing boundaries and setting high standards has also extended into his personal life. He's an 8-time National Barefoot Waterskiing Champion, has set many world records in that sport, and has competed in three World Barefoot Waterskiing Tournaments. In 2015, he started a new career in competitive mountain bike racing and continues to find ways to motivate himself mentally and physically.

What distinguishes Mike is his commitment to living a balanced lifestyle; placing God first, family, career, and self.

Special Acknowledgments

My Family. First, I want to thank God for my godly wife who's always by my side and my children, Belynda, Melissa, Autumn, Steven, Michael, Meghan, and Brittney.

My Staff. A personal thank you goes to my team at Mike Holt Enterprises for all the work they do to help me with my mission of changing people's lives through education. In particular my daughter Belynda, who works tirelessly to ensure that in addition to our products meeting and exceeding the educational needs of our customers, we stay committed to building life-long relationships with them throughout their electrical careers.

The National Fire Protection Association. A special thank you must be given to the staff at the National Fire Protection Association (NFPA), publishers of the *NEC*—in particular, Jeff Sargent for his assistance in answering my many *Code* questions over the years. Jeff, you're a "first class" guy, and I admire your dedication and commitment to helping others understand the *NEC*. Other former NFPA staff members I would like to thank include John Calogero, Joe Ross, and Dick Murray for their help in the past.

ABOUT THE ILLUSTRATOR

Mike Culbreath—Illustrator

Mike Culbreath
Graphic Illustrator
Alden, MI

Mike Culbreath devoted his career to the electrical industry and worked his way up from apprentice to master electrician. He started in the electrical field doing residential and light commercial construction, and later did service work and custom electrical installations. While working as a journeyman electrician, he suffered a serious on-the-job knee injury. As part of his rehabilitation, Mike completed courses at Mike Holt Enterprises, and then passed the exam to receive his Master Electrician's license. In 1986, with a keen interest in continuing education for electricians, he joined the staff to update material and began illustrating Mike Holt's textbooks and magazine articles.

Mike started with simple hand-drawn diagrams and cut-and-paste graphics. When frustrated by the limitations of that style of illustrating, he took a company computer home to learn how to operate some basic computer graphic software. Upon realizing that computer graphics offered increased flexibility for creating illustrations, Mike took every computer graphics class and seminar he could to help develop his computer graphic skills. He's now worked as an illustrator and editor with the company for over 30 years and, as Mike Holt has proudly acknowledged, has helped to transform his words and visions into lifelike graphics.

Originally from South Florida, Mike now lives in northern lower Michigan where he enjoys hiking, kayaking, photography, gardening, and cooking; but his real passion is his horses. Mike loves spending time with his children (Dawn and Mac) and his grandchildren Jonah, Kieley, and Scarlet.

Special Acknowledgments—I would like to thank Eric Stromberg, an electrical engineer and super geek (and I mean that in the most complimentary manner because I think this guy is brilliant), for helping me keep our graphics as technically correct as possible. I would also like to thank all of our students for the wonderful feedback they provide that helps us improve our graphics.

I also want to give a special thank you to Cathleen Kwas for making me look good with her outstanding layout design and typesetting skills; to Toni Culbreath who proofreads all of my material; and to Dawn Babbitt who assists me in the production and editing of our graphics. I would also like to acknowledge Belynda Holt Pinto, our Director of Operations, Brian House for his input (another really brilliant guy), and the rest of the outstanding staff at Mike Holt Enterprises, for all the hard work they do to help produce and distribute these outstanding products.

And last but not least, I need to give a special thank you to Mike Holt for not firing me over 30 years ago when I "borrowed" one of his computers and took it home to begin the process of learning how to do computer illustrations. He gave me the opportunity and time needed to develop my computer graphic skills. He's been an amazing friend and mentor ever since I met him as a student many years ago. Thanks for believing in me and allowing me to be part of the Mike Holt Enterprises family.

ABOUT THE MIKE HOLT TEAM

Technical Writing

There are many people who played a role in the production of this textbook. Their efforts are reflected in the quality and organization of the information contained in this textbook, and in its technical accuracy, completeness, and usability.

Daniel Brian House

Brian House is a licensed unlimited electrical contractor who worked throughout the southeast United States, starting in the early 1990s. In 2000 he began teaching seminars and apprenticeship classes. Since 2010 he's been participating as a member of the Mike Holt video teams, and in 2014 he joined the Mike Holt Enterprises staff as technical director. Brian is a permanent addition to the technical writing team at Mike Holt Enterprises. He played a key role by assisting in the re-writing and editing of the textbooks for the 2017 NEC series, coordinating the content and the illustrations, and assuring the technical accuracy and flow of the information presented. He continues to teach seminars and is actively involved in developing apprenticeship curriculum.

Brian and his wife Carissa have shared the joy of four children and many foster children during 19 years of marriage. When not mentoring youth at work or church, he can be found racing mountain bikes with his kids or fly fishing on Florida's Intracoastal Waterway.

Ryan Jackson

Ryan Jackson created the first draft text for the introduction and analysis of the *Code* changes covered in the Appendix of this textbook.

Editorial and Production

A special thanks goes to **Toni Culbreath** for her outstanding contribution to this project. She worked tirelessly to proofread and edit this publication. Her attention to detail and her dedication is irreplaceable.

Many thanks to **Cathleen Kwas** who did the design, layout, and production of this textbook. Her desire to create the best possible product for our customers is greatly appreciated.

Also, thanks to **Paula Birchfield** who was the Production Coordinator for this product. She helped keep everything flowing and tied up all the loose ends. She and **Jeff Crandall** did a great job proofing the final files prior to printing.

Thanks to **Bruce Marcho** for doing such an excellent job recording, editing, and producing our DVDs. Bruce has played a vital role in the production of our products for over 25 years.

About the Mike Holt Team

DVD Team

The following special people provided technical advice in the development of this textbook as they served on the video team along with author **Mike Holt** and graphic illustrator **Mike Culbreath**.

Bill Brooks
Principal Engineer
Vacaville, California

Bill Brooks has over 25 years of experience designing, installing, and evaluating grid-connected PV systems. He holds B.S. and M.S. degrees in Mechanical Engineering from North Carolina State University, and is a registered Professional Mechanical and Electrical Engineer. More than 12,000 installers and inspectors have attended his courses throughout the U.S. and abroad. His field troubleshooting skills have been valuable in determining where problems occur, to focus training on those issues of greatest need. He's written several important technical manuals for the industry that are now widely used throughout the United States and beyond. His recent publications include the *Expedited Permit Process for PV Systems*, the *Field Inspection Guidelines for PV Systems*, and *Understanding the CalFire Solar PV Installation Guidelines*, as well as articles in *Photon* and *SolarPro* magazines.

Bill is actively involved in the development of PV codes and standards including IEEE-929 and IEEE1547 (PV Utility Interconnection), the *National Electrical Code* Article 690 (Solar Photovoltaic Systems), and IEC TC82 (International PV Standards). He's an active participant on many codes and standards panels including Code Making Panel 4 of the *NEC*, UL1703 and UL1741 Standards Technical Panels, and IEC TC82 Working Group 3 and 6. He was a member of the California Office of the State Fire Marshal's (Cal Fire) PV Task force that developed the Solar Photovoltaic Installation Guideline, which became the model for national fire regulation. In addition, he chaired the NFPA Large-Scale PV Electric Supply Station task group, the NFPA Firefighter Safety and PV systems task group, and the Article 690 and 691 task groups for Code Making Panel 4 for the 2017 *NEC*.

Bill enjoys helping people make progress toward reaching their God-given potential. His interests include sailing, motorcycle riding, performance automobiles, home theater, and all types of music.

Dave Click
VP of Engineering, ESA Renewables, LLC
Sanford, Florida

Dave Click, PE has worked in solar energy since the University of Virginia's 2002 Solar Decathlon. After learning a lot from his time with Solar Design Associates and then the Florida Solar Energy Center, he joined ESA Renewables in 2015. With ESA, Dave leads the engineering team in design, interconnection, grid integration, project management, commissioning, and operations and maintenance. He's worked on 200MW of utility-scale projects on the east coast of the U.S., and over 200 residential and commercial PV projects.

Dave is a licensed Professional Engineer in seven states, a Florida-licensed Electrical Contractor and Solar Contractor, and a NABCEP-certified PV Installation Professional.

Dave and his family live under their 11 kW PV system in Orlando, Florida where they're in their eighth year of not paying an electric bill!

Rebekah Hren
Electrical Contractor/PV Instructor
Winston-Salem, North Carolina

Rebekah Hren is a licensed electrical contractor, NABCEP-certified PV Installation Professional, and a member of the NABCEP board and PV Installation Professional Exam Committee. She has over a decade of experience working in the PV industry as a system designer and installer. Since 2007 she's enjoyed teaching PV system design and inspection classes to thousands of students and code officials throughout the United States, both online and in person. Rebekah frequently authors technical articles for PV trade magazines, has co-authored two books on renewable energy, and has presented workshops at solar industry conferences around the world, including Solar Power International and Intersolar North America, India, and Middle East.

Rebekah has worked as a system designer, consultant, and field-service provider for large-scale ground-mounted PV farms since 2009. Prior to that she focused on installing residential PV systems in North Carolina. Her primary goal is ensuring that the design and construction of every project with which she's involved meets and exceeds *National Electrical Code* requirements and other applicable codes and standards, as safety and reliability are her greatest concerns.

When she's not traveling, Rebekah lives in the solar-powered off-grid house she built in 2003 in Winston-Salem, North Carolina.

About the Mike Holt Team

Ryan Mayfield
President, Renewable Energy Associates
Corvallis, Oregon

Ryan Mayfield has been working in the renewable energy field since 1999 and currently focuses on commercial photovoltaic (PV) system design and education. As the President at Renewable Energy Associates, he provides design, support, and educational services for contractors, architectural and engineering firms, manufacturers, and government agencies. Typical projects include commercial and residential PV system designs and training for PV system designers and installers. He also works directly with manufacturers of PV-specific products, to help gain market acceptance and develop products that directly aid in the implementation and use of their products.

Ryan serves as Photovoltaic Systems Technical Editor for *SolarPro* magazine, and regularly writes feature articles in *SolarPro* and *Home Power* magazines. He's also the author of *PV Design and Installation for Dummies*, published in 2010. In addition, Ryan teaches various PV courses across the country for electricians, existing solar professionals, code officials, inspectors, and individuals seeking to join the solar industry. He holds a Limited Renewable Energy Technician (LRT) license in Oregon.

Ryan lives in Corvallis, Oregon with his wife, Amy, and three children, A.J., Lauren and Kai. They enjoy being outdoors as much as possible, especially when they have the opportunity to spend a few days in the canoe.

Richard Stoval
CEO, SolPowerPeople, Inc.
Austin, Texas

Richard Stovall has been actively involved in the Solar Industry since 2008, and is motivated by his belief that solar technology will be an engine for economic growth for at least the next century. He's worked in two different accredited and industry-recognized solar training organizations. Richard has been involved in developing state-of-the-art hands-on training labs for on-site and mobile education, developing curriculum, and training thousands of electricians, firefighters, solar installers, and utility workers.

His company, SolPowerPeople, is known for the SolarMOOC Academy, which features free live lectures by industry experts (Mike Holt being the very first) that have been viewed by over 50,000 people globally. Since 2014 Richard and SolPowerPeople's focus has been on residential PV quality control and inspection, with over 7,000 residential PV inspections (company-wide), in addition to developing a fully integrated mobile platform (app, web portal, and hardware) for onsite solar inspection and shade analysis.

His professional experience includes: CEO and owner of SolPowerPeople, Inc. (since 2011); Director of Operations and Lead Instructor for a leading solar training organization (2009 to 2011); IREC Certified Master Trainer in Photovoltaics; Certified NABCEP PV Installation Professional; LEED AP (Legacy); NABCEP's technical committees for Solar PV Installation Professional and Solar PV Inspector Credential; IAFF National Trainer for Firefighter PV Safety Training; and assisting other organizations in developing interactive online content, including IREC's Online Fire Safety Program.

Richard lives with his wife, Leanne, and two children, Piper and Levi, on a ranch just outside Austin, Texas.

Save 25% On These Best-Selling Libraries

Understanding the NEC® Complete Training Library

This library makes it easy to learn the Code. Your library includes the following best-selling textbooks and DVDs:

Understanding the National Electrical Code® Volume 1 Textbook
Understanding the National Electrical Code® Volume 2 Textbook
NEC® Exam Practice Questions Workbook
General Requirements DVD
Wiring and Protection DVD
Bonding and Grounding DVDs (3)
Wiring Methods and Materials DVDs (2)
Equipment for General Use DVD
Special Occupancies and Special Equipment DVDs (3)
Limited Energy & Communications Systems DVD

Product Code: 17DECODVD   List Price: $599.00   Now only $449.25*

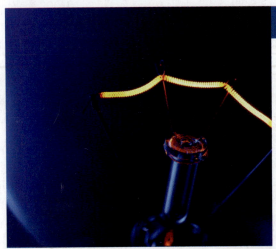

Electrical Theory DVD Training Program

Understanding electrical theory is critical for everyone who works with electricity. The topics in this textbook will help you understand what electricity is, how it's produced, and how it's used. You'll learn everything from a brief study of matter, to how to perform basic electrical calculations critical for everyday use.

Package includes:

Electrical Theory Textbook
Electrical Fundamentals and Basic Electricity DVD
Electrical Circuits, Systems, and Protection DVD
Alternating Current, Motors, Generators, and Transformers DVD

Product Code: ETLIBD   List Price: $299.00   Now only $224.25*

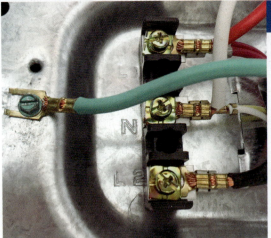

Bonding and Grounding DVD Training Program

Grounding and Bonding is the least understood and most important article in the NEC®. This program focuses on Article 250 but also addresses grounding rules found throughout the Code Book. The textbook and DVDs are informative and practical, and include in one single place, all articles that relate to bonding and grounding. The full-color illustrations help break down the concepts and make them easier to understand. This topic is at the core of most power quality and safety issues, making this program a must-have for everyone in the industry. Order your copy today.

Library includes:

Bonding and Grounding Textbook
Bonding and Grounding DVDs (3)

Product Code: 17NCDVD2   List Price: $299.00   Now only $224.25*

* Prices subject to change. Discount applies to price at time of order.

Call Now 888.NEC.CODE (632.2633)
& mention discount code: B17SOLB25

Mike Holt Enterprises